# Minority Influence and Innovation

Social groups form an important part of our daily lives. Within these groups pressures exist which encourage the individual to comply with the group's viewpoint. This influence, which creates social conformity, is known as 'majority influence' and is the dominant process of social control. However, there also exists a 'minority influence', which emerges from a small subsection of the group and is a dynamic force for social change.

*Minority Influence and Innovation* seeks to identify the conditions under which minority influence can prevail, to change established norms, stimulate original thinking and help us to see the world in new ways.

With chapters written by a range of expert contributors, areas of discussion include:

- processes and theoretical issues
- the factors which affect majority and minority influence
- interactions between majority and minority group members.

This book offers a thorough evaluation of the most important current developments within this field and presents consideration of the issues that will be at the forefront of future research. As such it will be of interest to theorists and practitioners working in social psychology.

**Robin Martin** is Professor of Social and Organizational Psychology at Aston University.

**Miles Hewstone** is Professor of Social Psychology and Fellow of New College, Oxford University.

You would be delighted to hear Galileo argue, as he often does in the midst of some fifteen or twenty persons who attack him vigorously, now in one house, now in another. But he is so well buttressed that he laughs them off; and although the novelty of his opinion leaves people unpersuaded, yet he shows that most of the arguments, with which his opponents try to overthrow him, are spurious.

(Letter from Monsignor Querengo to his superior Cardinal Alessandro d'Este, during a visit by Galileo to Rome; quoted in *Galileo Antichrist*, Michael White, 2007, Weidenfeld & Nicolson: London, pp. 151–152)

I have also to set down some points in writing, and to arrange that they should come privately into the hands of those I want to read them, for I find in many quarters that people are more ready to yield to dead writing than to live speech, for the former allows them to agree or dissent without blushing and, finally, to yield to the arguments since in such discussions we have no witnesses but ourselves. This is not done so easily when we have to change our mind in public.

(Letter from Galileo to a friend, Curzio Picchena, quoted in *Galileo Antichrist*, Michael White, 2007, Weidenfeld & Nicolson: London, pp. 151–152)

# Minority Influence and Innovation

## Antecedents, Processes and Consequences

### Edited by Robin Martin and Miles Hewstone

Psychology Press
Taylor & Francis Group

HOVE AND NEW YORK

Published in 2010
by Psychology Press
27 Church Road, Hove, East Sussex BN3 2FA

Simultaneously published in the USA and Canada
by Psychology Press
711 Third Avenue, New York, NY 10017

*Psychology Press is an imprint of the Taylor & Francis Group, an Informa business*

First issued in paperback 2012

Typeset in Times by Garfield Morgan, Swansea, West Glamorgan

Cover design by Andy Ward
Front cover photographs
*Galileo On Trial* circa 1847: Galileo (centre) (1564–1642), Italian physicist and astronomer. Galileo Before The Papal Tribunal, by Robert Henry. (Photo by Hulton Archive/Getty Images).
*Civil Rights Leader* circa 1964: American civil rights leader Martin Luther King Jr. (1929–1968). (Photo by American Stock/Getty Images).
*Woman Restrained* A woman being restrained by three policemen during the suffragette disturbances outside Buckingham Palace, London. (Photo by Hulton Archive/Getty Images).

*British Library Cataloguing in Publication Data*
A catalogue record for this book is available from the British Library

*Library of Congress Cataloging-in-Publication Data*
Minority influence and innovation : antecedents, processes and consequences / edited by Robin Martin and Miles Hewstone.
     p. cm.
  Includes bibliographical references and index.
  ISBN: 978-1-84169-594-5 (hb)
1. Social influence. 2. Conformity. 2. Influence (Psychology).
4. Small groups–Psychological aspects. 5. Social groups–Pschological aspects. 6. Minorities. 7. Majorities. I. Martin, Robin, 1960–.
II. Hewstone, Miles.
  HM1176 M56 2010
  303.3'2–dc22
                                                    2009020085

ISBN 13: 978-0-415-65017-5 (pbk)
ISBN 13: 978-1-84169-594-5 (hbk)

To Serge Moscovici
*Maître à penser*

# Contents

# Figures

# Tables

# Contributors

**Federico Aime**, Oklahoma State University, USA

**Gerd Bohner**, University of Bielefeld, Germany

**Fabrizio Butera**, University of Lausanne, Switzerland

**Hoon-Seok Choi**, Sungkyunkwan University in Seoul, Korea

**William D. Crano**, Claremont Graduate University, USA

**Victoria L. DeSensi**, Indiana University, USA

**Hans-Peter Erb**, Helmut Schmidt-University, Germany

**Juan Manuel Falomir-Pichastor**, University of Geneva, Switzerland

**Antonis Gardikiotis**, Aristotle University of Thessaloniki, Greece

**Miles Hewstone**, University of Oxford, UK

**John M. Levine**, University of Pittsburgh, USA

**Pearl Y. Martin**, Aston University, UK

**Robin Martin**, Aston University, UK

**Angelica Mucchi-Faina**, University of Perugia, Italy

**Gabriel Mugny**, University of Geneva, Switzerland

**Richard E. Petty**, Ohio State University, USA

**Radmila Prislin**, San Diego State University, USA

**Alain Quiamzade**, University of Geneva and University of Fribourg, Distance Learning University Switzerland

**Andreas W. Richter**, Instituto de Empresa Business School, Madrid, Spain

**Claudia A. Sacramento**, Aston University, UK

**Christine M. Smith**, Grand Valley State University, USA

**Wolfgang Stroebe**, Utrecht University, Netherlands

**R. Scott Tindale**, Loyola University, USA

**Zakary L. Tormala**, Stanford University, USA

**Linn Van Dyne**, Michigan State University, USA

**Michael A. West**, Aston University, UK

# Preface

What do the following people have in common: Galileo Galilei, Sigmund Freud, Dr John Snow, Dame Cicely Saunders, Martin Luther King, Peter Roberts, Bob Geldof, and Aung San Suu Kyi? All are, or were, minorities, whose views ultimately succeeded in influencing many people, often against great odds.

In 1633 Galileo was forced by the Roman Inquisition to retract his heretical teaching that the earth revolved around the sun (in 1980 the Pontifical Academy of Science reviewed his case, taking 12 years to concede that he was right). Sigmund Freud was the founding father of psycho-analysis, and a major figure in the history of psychology. In nineteenth-century London English physician Dr John Snow attempted to persuade majority opinion that the epidemic disease it faced was carried in the capital's water supply, and not due to atmospheric 'miasmas'. Dame Cicely Saunders is credited with founding the modern hospice movement in 1967, and successfully campaigning to establish hospices around the world. Martin Luther King Jr. was a leading figure in the human rights movement in the United States, who successfully forced progressive change in the American South through non-violent protest, and was awarded the 1964 Nobel Peace Prize. Peter Roberts founded Compassion in World Farming in 1967, and effected a transformation in more humane practices of animal welfare. Bob Geldof awakened compassion and raised astronomical sums of money for the starving of Africa, with 'Live Aid' in 1985 and 'Band Aid' in 2004. Aung San Suu Kyi was awarded the 1991 Nobel Peace Prize for her courageous, committed, but thus far unsuccessful opposition to the military regime in Burma.

Minorities are, however, by no means always lone individuals. Indeed, solo minorities are handicapped from the outset, their views likely to be attributed to idiosyncrasies and thus denied credibility or detailed scrutiny. Prevailing attitudes are more likely to be overturned, and social movements galvanized, by a minority in the shape of a small *group*, such as the twelve men who met in a printing shop above a London pub and began the process that would end just over 200 years ago in the abolition of the slave trade in the British Empire. As anthropologist Margaret Mead (1901–1978) wrote, 'Never doubt that a small group of thoughtful, committed citizens can change the world. Indeed, it is the only thing that ever has'. In fiction, just as in fact, minorities make for compelling reading and viewing, the classic example being Sidney Lumet's film *Twelve Angry Men*, a gripping courtroom, actually jury-chamber, drama starring the young Henry Fonda, who starts out as a sole individual questioning the guilt of the defendant, and ends up convincing all eleven other jurors of the veracity of his verdict. More contemporary examples of active minorities, in fact rather than fiction, include the anti-smoking group ASH ('Action on Smoking and Health'), its direct opponent FOREST ('Freedom Organisation for the Right to Enjoy Smoking Tobacco'), numerous pro-life organizations (e.g., 'Pro-Life Alliance'), and groups campaigning for the right to voluntary euthanasia (e.g., 'Dignity in Dying').

Although it is evident that minority influence has a long and distinguished history, the study of when and how minorities can influence majorities was only belatedly introduced into social psychology by the pioneering theorizing and research of the distinguished French social psychologist, Serge Moscovici. He challenged the discipline's exclusive focus on majority influence, and developed a field of scholarly research that is now recognized as one of Europe's two major contributions to the field of social psychology (the other being the study of intergroup relations). We dedicate this volume to Serge Moscovici in honour of this major contribution to our discipline. Serge merits the honorific that the French reserve exclusively for their leading intellectuals, *maître à penser* (literally a 'master for thinking'). This term denotes a teacher from whom one learns not simply a set of facts or even a point of view, but rather a *way* of thinking, which is particularly apposite given the empirical evidence that minorities can change not just what we think, but *how we think*.

This volume reveals the enduring ferment in the field, whose far-flung scholars continue to develop the field theoretically, enrich it empirically, and apply its ideas widely. The picture that emerges is of a field still enjoying the healthy confrontation of competing theories, of empirical as well as theoretical innovation, and of links increasingly being made between the field of social influence and other areas, particularly the fields of attitude change, group processes, and decision making. The chapters in this volume reveal a number of underlying themes, which confirm the contributions of contemporary research on minority, as well as majority, influence and that will help to map out an equally constructive future: adopting a more sophisticated concept of attitudes in this domain of research; exploiting the potential of dual-process models of persuasion; documenting the indirect, as well as direct, nature of influence; exploring influence using a variety of tasks; returning minority influence to its roots in dynamic, intragroup contexts; highlighting the lessons of minority influence for organizational psychology; and emphasizing the many types of minority that can serve as sources of influence.

Finally, we gratefully acknowledge some organizations and individuals who helped to bring this volume to fruition. The idea for this book grew out of a small-group meeting held at New College, Oxford, on 'Minority Influence Processes' sponsored by the European Association of Social Psychology (EASP) in 2003; this was the fifth such meeting, reflecting the EASP's longstanding interest in and commitment to this research area. We reciprocate by gratefully donating all royalties from this volume to the association. We also thank Michael Forster, Managing Director of Psychology Press, for his long-term support for social psychology, and Tara Stebnicky for her encouragement, professionalism and, of course, patience in seeing this volume through to publication.

Robin Martin, *Birmingham*
Miles Hewstone, *Oxford*

# Part I

# Introduction

# 1 Introduction: Theory and research on minority influence

*Robin Martin*
Aston University, UK

*Miles Hewstone*
University of Oxford, UK

Picture a time in history when books on etiquette were the best sellers of the day, when the subject of morality was not discussed in refined society, and when the family was sacrosanct. Picture a time when the preservation of the family in all its purity and sanctity was of supreme importance, when women were revered for their virginity and simplicity, when the marriage chamber was invested with a taboo of absolute secrecy, and when sexual instincts were not allowed expression except in marriage. This was the Victorian era. Picture then a lone scientist, in that day and age, proposing a theory of infantile sexuality, a man stating that children have both hostile and erotic relations with their parents, that a son desires his mother. This was Sigmund Freud. The outcry, the criticism that you are undoubtedly imagining, is in fact what happened.

(Moscovici & Nemeth, 1974, p. 217)

Freud was clearly a minority in the sense that his ideas were very different from the conventions of the time and what was accepted by the majority of people in society. Reaction to Freud was typical of that experienced by minorities. His work was initially not allowed to be printed, and, when it was, it was boycotted by the main scientific community, and both he and his supporters were labelled 'perverts'. But as history tells us, despite the outrage and resistance that initially met Freud, his ideas became accepted and developed into the enduring, if still disputed, approach of psychoanalysis. This story is not a one-off. We could replace Freud with a range of historical figures including Copernicus, Galileo, and Jesus, or indeed their modern counterparts. The underlying theme is similar—a lone person who initially had very different opinions from those of society in general, who was chastised for holding those beliefs, but who subsequently had a profound and lasting impact upon the same people who had initially vilified them.

We can draw many insights from these case studies of people who have successfully influenced society; we will limit ourselves here to just two. First, societies have a tendency to resist change and will invest an enormous amount of effort to maintain the status quo. Society does not take kindly to those people who wish to oppose popular opinion or wish to go against the *Zeitgeist*. Second, whoever wants to change societal opinions is taking on a very big task—by advocating a new way of thinking or an original perspective they have to overcome resistance in the form of the *status quo ante*. As indicated above, such people often suffer for their beliefs through psychological, and even physical, abuse. The way in which people with minority opinions subsequently influence members of the majority to adopt their views is the subject matter of this book. We refer to this as 'minority influence' because it describes situations where a person or subgroup of people, who hold a position that is different from the majority of people in their society, attempt to change the majority towards their position. More specifically the book examines the factors that can increase minority influence (antecedents), the strategies and techniques employed by successful minorities (processes) and the effects of minority influence on people's attitudes and opinions (consequences). This progression is reflected in the title of the volume, *Minority influence and innovation: Antecedents, processes and consequences.*

The remainder of this chapter is divided into three sections, which set the scene for the following 14 chapters. In the first section we define the terms 'majority' and 'minority' more clearly. We then give a brief historical review of the development of research in this area, highlighting the main research questions and theoretical milestones. Finally, we describe the structure of the book and give a brief outline of each chapter.


## Majority and minority influence

There are many attempts to influence our opinions every day. These attempts can come from a multitude of directions—reading a newspaper, watching the television, listening to the radio, or hearing a debate are all situations in which one person or group is trying to change the attitudes and opinions of another person or group. Often people try to support (or even denigrate) a particular position by claiming that many people, *the majority*, or relatively few people, *the minority*, support that position. A good example is provided by newspapers, where often the headline of the article suggests that either a majority (e.g., 'Exclusive poll reveals 68% of English voters want own parliament'; *Daily Telegraph*, 26 November 2006) or a minority (e.g., 'Only 34% back being in the EU'; *Daily Mail*, 12 December 2006) support a particular position (see Gardikiotis, Martin, & Hewstone, 2004). The proportion of people who support a position is known as the level of consensus and this can be represented in a number of ways (such as '80%', '8 out of 10', 'the majority', or '20%', '2 out of 10', 'the minority'). It is this potential source of attitude change that is the subject of this book and, in particular, what the situations are in which people will pay attention to and be influenced by either a majority or a minority.

At the outset we need to give some working definitions for our key terms—'majority' and 'minority'. One can identify at least three ways to define these terms. First, we might simply refer to *consensus information* concerning the number of people in the group, whether majority or minority. By definition the majority has to be numerically larger than the minority but it does not necessarily have to be above 50% of the population. In many political elections the winning party does not have the majority of the votes (the majority of votes being distributed over a number of parties). Representing majority and minority positions in terms of percentages is a common format, but not the only one. Saying that '9 out of 11' or '2 out of 11' hold different positions is similar to saying '82% (majority)' or '18% (minority)', respectively—what varies is the size of the underlying population upon which this is based (in the first case it is 11 people, in the second it is unknown).

Second, we can define these terms with reference to *normative positions* (that is, the opinions and beliefs that reflect 'accepted' standards in society). For example, most people in society believe that smoking is bad for your health and therefore people who are against smoking would be taking a pro-normative position while people who are in favour of smoking would be holding an anti-normative position. In this sense, the majority typically holds the normative position (against smoking) and the minority the anti-normative or deviant position (in favour of smoking). This distinction is fairly obvious with a topic such as smoking because it is now widely accepted, even among most smokers, that smoking is bad for your health. The situation becomes more complex with other attitudes. Consider, for example, abortion, where in some parts of the world a pro-abortion position would be a normative position held by the majority while in other countries it might be an anti-normative position held by the minority. What is important is that majority and minority positions are defined by the normative context that applies to the population with whom the potential recipient of influence identifies.

Finally, we can refer to the *power relationship* between the source and recipient of influence; that is, the ability of the source to exert influence over the recipient. In this sense, power refers to the ability to control important resources (such as praise, support, cooperation, etc.) with respect to another person. Majorities are numerically large and sometimes also have high status and therefore power over other people because they can control important resources. By contrast, minorities are neither numerically large nor typically high in status and are consequently low in power, and because of this they are often discriminated against and marginalized in society.

As we can see, there are many ways to define majority and minority status. Across these dimensions, one might define a 'majority' as the numerically larger group that holds the normative position and has power over others. In contrast, minorities tend to be numerically small, hold anti-normative positions, and lack power over others. We should stress that this is a generalized definition and there are exceptions; e.g., blacks in South Africa during the period of apartheid were the numerically larger group in the population but lacked power. In addition, it should be noted that in terms of the research described in this book, the general conception of majority and minority status has been based upon normative criteria—the majority and minority holding the pro- and anti-normative positions, respectively.

## Brief overview of the development of research

Research in the area of majority and minority influence has gone through five distinct chronological phases and it is this historical development which forms the background of this brief review (see Martin & Hewstone, 2003; Martin, Hewstone, Martin, & Gardikiotis, 2008, for more detailed reviews).

The first phase of research, what we term *early research on majority influence (pre-1970)* examined how the majority was able to cause individuals to conform to or comply with its position (e.g., Asch, 1951; Crutchfield, 1955). These studies typically involved objective judgement tasks (such as judging the length of lines), and exposed participants to the erroneous responses of a numerical majority. The research question was, would naive participants agree with a majority of people who gave the obviously wrong judgement? Research has consistently shown that they do. Across a variety of different situations and topics, studies show that people will often agree with a majority of other people, even if they believe that the majority's judgement is, in fact, incorrect (see meta-analysis of Asch studies by Bond & Smith, 1996).

The theoretical framework for explanations of conformity was based on the functionalist perspective of small-group behaviour derived from work by Festinger (1950). According to Festinger, there are pressures for uniformity within groups to reach consensus, particularly when there is an explicit group goal. These pressures create a psychological dependency of the individual on the group. Festinger argued that individuals are dependent on others for social approval and verification of opinions and beliefs. In this sense, the majority is able to satisfy both these needs: first, because people generally wish to belong to majority groups, and, second, because people accept as true, opinions that are widely shared (Jones & Gerard, 1967). Building on these ideas, Deutsch and Gerard (1955) drew an important distinction between two social influence processes underlying conformity: *normative social influence* ('an influence to conform with the positive expectations of others', p. 629) and *informational social influence* ('an influence to accept information obtained from another as evidence about reality', p. 629) (see assessment of this approach by Prislin & Wood, 2005; Turner, 1991).

The focus of this first phase of research was how the majority influenced the individual, and this neglected the possibility that the individual (or minority) could influence the majority. According to the dependency account of conformity, minorities lack the resources to make majority members dependent on them (such as, power, status, size) and therefore do not have the means to enforce normative or informational influence. Therefore, according to the conformity approach, social influence can only flow from those who have the power to create psychological dependency (such as a majority) to those who do not (such as a minority). Deviancy, within the functionalist approach, was seen as dysfunctional and a threat to group harmony; consequently, deviants either conform to the group or face rejection.

The second phase of research, which we term *early research on minority influence (late 1960s–1980)*, reversed the research question from the first phase and focused on the conditions under which a minority can influence the attitudes of the majority. While nearly all the research in the first phase (until the late 1960s) had focused on how the majority can make individuals conform to their position, it is clear that there are many examples of individuals and minorities who have had a tremendous impact on the majority in society (from the 'ancients', such as Galileo, Freud, and Copernicus; to the 'moderns', Bob Geldof, Noam Chomsky, and Aung San Suu Kyi). It was this observation by the French social psychologist Serge Moscovici that led to a theoretical reshaping of the area and is considered the starting point for research into minority influence. Moscovici argued that if social influence only relied on conformity to the majority, then it would be difficult to see how groups changed, new ideas developed, and innovation might occur (Moscovici & Faucheux, 1972; Moscovici, Lage, & Naffrechoux, 1969). In fact, we would not conceive of, let alone account for, social change. Moscovici challenged the unilateral or asymmetrical perspective on social influence that views influence as flowing only *from* the majority *to* the minority, which, he pointed out, ran counter to the numerous real-life examples of successful minorities.

Moscovici (1976) argued that all attempts at social influence create conflict between the source and the recipient of influence. Minorities can, and often do, create conflict because they challenge the dominant majority view and, in so doing, offer a new and different perspective. Because people wish to avoid conflict, they will typically dismiss the minority position— often attributing its deviancy to an underlying, undesirable psychological dimension (Papastamou, 1986) such as seeing the minority as 'crazy', 'provocative' or 'unstable'. In order for the minority to avoid these negative attributions it must demonstrate that it is certain and committed to its position, that it will not compromise, and that its members believe that the majority should change to its position. Research focused especially on the style of the minority's behaviour (Moscovici, 1976; Mugny, 1975)—in particular whether it was seen as consistent and committed to its position, showing that it was 'standing up' to the majority.

Some of the first studies of minority influence employed a colour perception task and showed that a minority that consistently called a blue slide 'green' led some majority members to also call the same slide 'green' (e.g., Moscovici et al., 1969; Nemeth, Swedlund, & Kanki, 1974). Mugny (1975, see 1982, for a review) extended this research and showed that minorities can influence the majority on a range of social attitudes that were topical within the participants' population (in Swiss society, for example, topics included pollution, acceptance of foreign workers, and military service).

The theoretical explanation for minority influence was based, in part, on attribution theory (Kelley, 1967). By consistently adopting its position, the minority is 'visible' within the group and attracts attention (Schachter, 1951), and its consistency leads to attributions of certainty and confidence, especially when the minority is seen to reject publicly the majority position (see Buschini, 1998, for more recent work on behavioural style). One consequence of minority influence, however, is that people do not wish to agree publicly with the minority for fear of being seen as part of the minority, and so influence is sometimes indirect or private (what Maass & Clark, 1984, refer to as the 'hidden impact of minorities').

The third phase of research focused on *comparing majority and minority influence (1980–early 1990s)* and examined both majority and minority influence within the same paradigm. The main research question focused on the psychological processes underlying majority and minority influence and what impact they had on attitude change. It was during this phase that some of the major theoretical positions were developed. Some of these theories proposed that majorities and minorities exerted their influence, or impact, by the same means, albeit to different extents. Thus *social impact theory* (Latané & Wolf, 1981) views influence as a unitary process regardless of its source; social influence, or social impact, is a multiplicative function of the strength (power, expertise), immediacy (proximity in space and time) and size (number) of the influence source, whether majority or minority.

Other theories advocated that majority and minority influence are each associated with distinct processes that lead to specific patterns of influence on public/direct and private/indirect levels. For example *conversion theory* (Moscovici, 1980) proposes that majorities induce a comparison process where people focus on the characteristics of the majority and comply with them without changing their underlying attitudes; while minorities induce a validation process that involves an evaluation of the minorities' arguments and this can lead to conversion to the minority position. *Convergent–divergent theory* (Nemeth, 1986) proposes that majority and minority influence lead to different thinking styles, with majorities leading to a focus mainly on their arguments while minorities lead to a focus on both the arguments *and* a wider range of issues related to the topic of influence, and this can lead to greater creativity and enhanced performance. Finally, the *objective consensus approach* (Mackie, 1987) proposes that people are guided by consensus beliefs to feel that they share similar opinions to those in the majority and have different opinions from those in the minority. Therefore, a counter-attitudinal majority is counter-intuitive and people examine the majority arguments in detail to understand the reason for the difference in opinion, which can lead to change to the majority position, whilst a counter-attitudinal minority is expected and thus there is no need to examine their arguments in detail, resulting in little if any attitude change.

Research during this phase of research showed that both majorities and minorities can have influence on public and private levels in different circumstances. Therefore, research in this phase began to examine the moderating factors determining when this would occur (what are referred to as the 'contingency approaches'). Some notable contingency theories developed during this time were the *conflict elaboration theory* (Mugny, Butera, Sanchez-Mazas, & Pérez, 1995) and the *dual role model* (De Vries, De Dreu, Gordijn, & Schuurman, 1996). Each of these perspectives proposed that the processes underlying majority and minority influence, and their subsequent impact on attitude change, were determined by a range of contingency factors.

The fourth phase of research focuses on the *role of cognitive responses (1990s–present)*. This is a continuation of the third phase where the examination of majority and minority influence is undertaken through the application of methodologies and theories derived from social cognition research generally and, in particular, from cognitive theories of persuasion. The emphasis in this research has been to examine the different information-processing strategies employed by recipients of either a majority or a minority persuasive message, the consequences of these for thought elaborations and attitude change, and to detail the contingency factors that determine when they will be utilized. This approach has led to the development of new contingency theories of majority and minority influence such as *source–position congruity* (Baker & Petty, 1994), the *context/comparison model* (Crano & Alvaro, 1998), and the *source–context elaboration model* (Martin & Hewstone, 2008).

The underlying framework is based on an information-processing analysis examining people's cognitions (notably their thoughts while exposed to a persuasive message) and how this affects the acceptance (or rejection) of majority and minority positions. The extent to which a majority or minority encourages people to generate thoughts that are consistent with their message determines whether they will be influenced by it. The application of methodologies developed within the cognitive-response approach has offered new ways to examine the processes involved in majority and minority influence. The most notable development has been the application of a thought-listing methodology to examine people's cognitions as they heard or read a message. This approach is now widely used in the majority and minority influence literature to assess cognitive activity during the persuasive process, and an index of thought-listing is then used as a mediating variable between source status and influence.

The fifth and final phase of research focuses on *applied research and situational awareness (mid 1990s–present)* of the effects of majority and minority influence. There has been a noticeable increase in the amount of research applying the findings of basic majority/minority influence research to real-life issues and/or in more ecologically valid situations. These include studies of the interaction between majority and minority in interacting groups (e.g., Prislin & Christensen, 2005; Smith, Tindale, & Anderson, 2001), examining real-life minority movements and political groups (e.g., Smith & Diven, 2002), the effects of minority opinions on group decision making (e.g., Schulz-Hardt, Brodbeck, Mojzisch, Kerschreiter, & Frey, 2006; Velden, Beersma, & De Dreu, 2007), the ability of minorities to change people's behaviour (e.g., Falomir-Picastor, Butera, & Mugny, 2002; Martin, Martin, Smith, & Hewstone, 2007), and in understanding innovation in organizations (e.g., De Dreu & Beersma, 2001; De Dreu & West, 2001). Our expectation is that future research will continue to focus on the application of theoretical knowledge to the understanding of the role of minorities in contemporary society.

## Overview of the book

The remainder of this book consists of 14 chapters that are organized into four parts. Each of these parts reflects an area of significant contemporary research activity.

Part II focuses on *Processes and Theoretical Issues* and contains four chapters (Chapters 2 to 5).

Chapter 2, by Alain Quiamzade, Gabriel Mugny, Juan Manuel Falomir-Picaster and Fabrizio Butera, is based upon a considerable research programme conducted by the Geneva-Lausanne group leading to their *conflict elaboration theory*. This theory provides a framework for understanding a variety of social influence phenomena, including majority and minority influence. The basic concept concerns 'conflict elaboration', which occurs when people give meaning to the difference between themselves and a source of influence. These authors contend that many contradictory findings in majority and minority influence can be explained with reference to the different types of task that they employ. In particular they describe the difference between a 'representation of unity' (the belief that there is only one possible answer to a task) and 'plurality' (the belief that many positions are possible). The chapter then describes part of their research programme into two particular types of tasks: objective non-ambiguous tasks (where there is clearly a correct judgement) and aptitude tasks (where there may be several correct judgements). Through the use of a variety of paradigms they show that majority and minority influence can be affected by the way people perceive the task as being represented in terms of unity versus plurality of opinion.

Chapter 3, by William Crano, presents the *leniency contract theory* of majority and minority influence. The chapter makes a useful distinction between theoretical approaches examining attitude formation versus attitude change and argues that source status will have different effects in each of these contexts. Crano's theory identifies a number of contingency variables that affect majority and minority influence, including whether the task leads to a response that is subjective or objective, the source of influence is part of the in-group or out-group with respect to the recipients of influence, and whether the source is perceived as legitimate. Classification in terms of these contingency variables determines whether the source is derogated or it leads to message elaboration. Both majorities and minorities can lead to message elaboration and direct/indirect influence under different combinations of these contingency variables.

Chapter 4, by Hans-Peter Erb and Gerd Bohner, focuses on the role of consensus in social influence. The authors argue that consensus information is the key construct in examining majority and minority influence, and to examine this they have developed the 'mere consensus paradigm'. This is an experimental paradigm that deliberately avoids many of the contingency variables known to be related to social influence, and examines in isolation the effects of mere consensus information on thought elaborations and attitudes. These authors then describe some of their own research that employs the mere consensus paradigm, and they report some of the variables that determine when people will process a majority or minority source. Some of these studies focus on examining the difference between people's prior attitude and that of the source of influence (large vs. moderate) and whether consensus information is inferred or explicit. The theoretical underpinning of this research programme is the use of concepts and methodologies derived from the heuristic-systematic model of persuasion.

Chapter 5, by Zak Tormala, Rich Petty and Victoria DeSensi, develops a meta-cognitive framework for understanding majority and minority influence based on the elaboration likelihood model of persuasion. These authors argue that when people resist persuasion they seek reasons for doing this. Depending on whether the reason for resisting persuasion is believed to be either legitimate or illegitimate, people become more or less certain of their attitudes, respectively. In the context of minority influence Tormala et al. postulate that if people believe that they resisted minority influence on their public attitudes due to some illegitimate reason (e.g., because it is a deviant group), they may become less certain of their attitudes. On the other hand, if they believe the reason they resisted the minority is due to legitimate reasons (its position is not worthy), then there should be no corresponding reduction in attitude certainty. The authors report a number of experiments to support this basic premise and employ this metacognitive framework to help to understand delayed and indirect attitude change.

Part III focuses on *Factors Affecting Majority and Minority Influence* and it consists of four chapters (Chapters 6 to 9). Chapter 6, by Angelica

Mucchi-Faina, examines the role of attitude ambivalence on majority and minority influence. Attitude ambivalence refers to situations where people simultaneously hold both positive and negative beliefs about the same attitude object. Mucchi-Faina argues that attitude ambivalence might act as a moderator of majority and minority influence. Based on a theoretical analysis and her own experimental research, she shows that people high in attitude ambivalence will be more likely to conform to a majority compared to people low in attitude ambivalence. In the case of minority influence the relationship between attitude ambivalence and attitude change is more complex. This is because minorities themselves might increase ambivalence towards attitude issues (because they offer a different view from the majority) and so this factor might act as a mediator in determining attitude change. It appears that what is important in this context is whether the ambivalence derives from exposure to a minority source or from the issue of influence.

Chapter 7, by Antonis Gardikiotis, Robin Martin and Miles Hewstone, examines the effect of different levels of consensus information on majority and minority influence. These authors point out that consensus information can be conveyed in many ways including the percentage of people supporting a position (e.g., 82% vs. 18%) and via verbal labels (e.g., 'small' vs. 'large' group). The authors present results from a series of experiments that varied consensus information (in the form of percentages) together with a content analysis of the use of 'majority' and minority' terms in newspaper headlines. They conclude that consensus information has different meanings according to the source of influence. For a majority the level of the consensus (as long as it is above 50%) does not have a large impact in terms of the ability of the majority to induce compliance. For the minority, however, there are some advantages of being seen as small (either numerically or termed 'small') in terms of whether people will process their arguments, and this will affect their attitudes.

Chapter 8, by Robin Martin, Miles Hewstone and Pearl Martin, focuses on the consequences for attitudes that are formed following majority and minority influence. The authors argue that most studies examine the impact of source status on attitudes and do not consider the nature of these attitudes in terms of their being strong or weak. Based on their source–context elaboration model, these authors argue that majority and minority sources typically lead to non-elaborative and elaborative message processing, respectively, and this affects the strength of the attitudes that are formed. If attitudes formed by minority influence are based on elaborative processing then these attitudes should be strong and therefore more likely to resist counter-persuasion, persist over time and be predictive of behaviour compared to attitudes formed via majority influence that are based upon non-elaborative processing and are therefore weak in nature. The authors present the results from several studies that test and confirm these hypotheses. In short, attitudes formed following minority influence were better able to resist a future counter-persuasive message, and more likely to persist over time and to predict attitude-consistent behaviours than attitudes that were formed following majority influence.

Chapter 9, by Wolfgang Stroebe, considers a range of methodological issues associated with research in this area. The chapter focuses on potential methodological problems in experiments examining which source (majority vs. minority) is associated with most message processing. The chapter reviews a range of potential moderators of when majorities and minorities lead to processing of their arguments, such as personal relevance, source–position incongruity and prior attitude. This chapter concludes that it is difficult to draw firm conclusions in this research about which source is associated with most message processing because research has tended to omit important control conditions. Stroebe identifies three types of control conditions that are needed to rule out rival hypotheses: no message control (to assess the impact of consensus information); no consensus information (to assess the impact of the message); and neither source/message control (to assess impact of majority and minority influence).

Part IV focuses on the *Dynamic Interplay Between Majority and Minority Factions* and contains five chapters (Chapters 10 to 14) that examine interactions between majority and minority group members. The previous chapters in this book have compared the effects of influence from either the majority or the minority separately, while chapters in this part describe research that explicitly examines the interaction between these groups. This approach offers an important extension of previous research and also examines majority and minority influence processes in real-life contexts.

Chapter 10, by John Levine and Hoon-Seok Choi, focuses on newcomers to a group as potential change agents and innovators. They start with the observation that newcomers to the group are invariably minorities and that such individuals might be in a position to create innovation within the group. This provides a novel situation in which to examine the dynamics between newcomers (minorities) and the majority of the group (who the authors refer to as 'oldtimers'). The analysis centres on the social dynamics between newcomers and oldtimers, and this approach contrasts with the majority of research that focuses on the role of cognitive processes. The framework for this research is decision-making teams and specifically on what newcomers need to do in order to influence the group. The authors report some of their research that examines the role of newcomer influence in teams that carry out complex decision-making tasks. These studies show three key factors that affect newcomers' ability to affect group functioning: newcomers' expertise, status and shared social identity with oldtimers.

Chapter 11, by Christine Smith and Scott Tindale, examines majority and minority influence in freely interacting groups. The focus is on how majorities and minorities interact in groups and how this leads to direct and indirect influence. Their approach draws on the small-groups literature in two domains of social psychology, research on small groups or group dynamics (especially on the role of decision-making rules) and theories of minority influence (especially Nemeth's, 1986, concept of divergent thinking). The authors describe a number of their studies wherein typically, minority members argue counter-attitudinal positions within a group context and then examine the impact of the minority on majority group members' attitudes and measures of group creativity. A particularly interesting finding from these studies is the ability of the minority to block majority-supported change and to make the group less polarized in the majority-endorsed direction. The examination of minority influence within the context of interacting groups opens up new ways to examine the impact of minorities.

Chapter 12, by Radmila Prislin, examines some of the consequences that occur when people change between majority and minority group membership. The analysis focuses on the consequences of changing from a majority to a minority position and vice versa. Prislin argues that minority members who join the majority should experience some type of psychological 'gain' while majority members who become members of the minority should experience psychological 'loss' (in terms of approval of the group, identification, and so on). These hypotheses are tested in a series of cleverly designed studies where a lone participant is in a group of several confederates. Via a number of different manipulations, situations were created in which confederates either shared the view of or opposed the naive participant on a range of group tasks, but at a later stage in the study these confederates began to oppose the naive participant. These manipulations created situations in which the naive participant experienced change from one source group to another. The results not only supported the hypotheses above but also showed some additional interesting findings. For example, 'successful' minority influence can, somewhat paradoxically, lead to some negative group reactions (e.g., lowering of group identity) and to psychological feelings of 'loss' experienced by new minority members giving up majority group membership.

The final two chapters in this part focus on the role of majority and minority influence in work situations. Chapter 13, by Federico Aime and Linn Van Dyne, applies a social network analysis to understand why certain people in groups can be initiators of social influence and change. This analysis focuses on the strength of the proximal and distal ties that exist between group members, and how this interacts with majority and minority positions. This analysis is applied to workgroups because, Aime and Van Dyne argue, these are situations where there is invariably interdependence between group members and this is reflected in their social ties. The analysis of the social network relationship between group members can provide insights into how majorities and minorities bring about influence within a group. This analysis leads to the development of a typology of workgroup networks that incorporates two dimensions: the types of ties between group members (distal vs. proximal) and the strength of these ties (weak vs. strong). The implications of the resulting four quadrants for majority and minority influence are then discussed.

Chapter 14, by Andreas Richter, Claudia Sacramento and Michael West, examines the role of minority dissent in organizations. The authors draw parallels between research on minority influence theory and the study of innovation in organizations. They argue that minorities can be powerful agents of change in organizations, and indeed are vital to ensure that innovation occurs. They review research that shows that the more individual group members offer new perspectives (i.e., dissent from the group norm) on workgroup procedures, the greater is the level of workgroup innovation—especially when the group is one that favours participation by its members. The authors then expand their analysis from individual dissent to the group level to consider how groups can influence organizational processes (such as organizational identity and culture). The analysis of the organizational level helps us to understand how minorities can bring about change not only to their own group but to others within their environment and, ultimately, to the organization as a whole.

Finally, Part V contains one chapter that provides an 'Epilogue'. Chapter 15, by Miles Hewstone and Robin Martin, identifies seven themes that emerge in the course of the book: the need to take a more sophisticated conception of attitudes; the interplay between minority influence and dual process models of persuasion; the importance of indirect, as well as direct, influence; the variety of tasks used in minority influence studies; minority influence in dynamic, intra-group contexts; minority influence in organizational contexts; and the diversity of minority sources of social influence. This chapter also points to issues for future research, and assesses the state of theory and research in this classic area of social psychology after its first 50 or so years.

## References

Asch, S. E. (1951). Effects of group pressure upon the modification and distortion of judgments. In H. Guetzkow (Ed.), *Groups, leadership, and men* (pp. 177–190). Pittsburgh, PA: Carnegie Press.

Baker, S. M., & Petty, R. E. (1994). Majority and minority influence: Source–position imbalance as a determinant of message scrutiny. *Journal of Personality and Social Psychology, 67*, 5–19.

Bond, R., & Smith, P. B. (1996). Culture and conformity: A meta-analysis of studies using Asch's (1952b, 1956) line judgment task. *Psychological Bulletin, 119*, 111–137.

Buschini, F. (1998). L'impact de messages aux styles d'expression positif ou negatif en fonction du statut minoritaire ou majoritaire de la source d'influence. *Cahiers Internationaux de Psychologie Sociale, 39*, 9–22.

Crano, W. D., & Alvaro, E. M. (1998). The context/comparison model of social influence: Mechanisms, structure, and linkages that underlie indirect attitude change. In W. Stroebe & M. Hewstone (Eds.), *European review of social psychology* (Vol. 8, pp. 175–202). Chichester, UK: Wiley.

Crutchfield, R. S. (1955). Conformity and character. *American Psychologist, 10,* 191–198.

De Dreu, C. K. W., & Beersma, B. (2001). Minority influence in organizations: Its origins and implications for learning and group performance. In C. K. W. De Dreu & N. K. De Vries (Eds.), *Group consensus and innovation* (pp. 258–283). Oxford, UK: Blackwell.

De Dreu, C. K. W., & West, M. A. (2001). Minority dissent and team innovation: The importance of participation in decision making. *Journal of Applied Psychology, 86,* 1191–1201.

De Vries, N. K., De Dreu, C. K. W., Gordijn, E., & Schuurman, M. (1996). Majority and minority influence: A dual interpretation. In W. Stroebe & M. Hewstone (Eds.), *European review of social psychology* (Vol. 7, pp. 145–172). Chichester, UK: Wiley.

Deutsch, M., & Gerard, H. G. (1955). A study of normative and informational social influence upon individual judgment. *Journal of Abnormal and Social Psychology, 51,* 629–636.

Falomir-Picastor, J. M., Butera, F., & Mugny, G. (2002). Persuasive constraint and expert versus non-expert influence in intention to quit smoking. *European Journal of Social Psychology, 32,* 209–222.

Festinger, L. (1950). Informal social communication. *Psychological Review, 57,* 271–282.

Gardikiotis, A., Martin, R., & Hewstone, M. (2004). The representation of majorities and minorities in the British press: A content analytic approach. *European Journal of Social Psychology, 34,* 637–646.

Jones, E. E., & Gerard, H. B. (1967). *Foundations of social psychology.* New York: Wiley.

Kelley, H. H. (1967). Attribution theory in social psychology. In D. Levine (Ed.), *Nebraska symposium on motivation* (pp. 192–241). Lincoln: University of Nebraska Press.

Latané, B., & Wolf, S. (1981). The social impact of majorities and minorities. *Psychological Review, 88,* 438–453.

Maass, A., & Clark, R. D., III (1984). Hidden impact of minorities: Fifteen years of minority influence research. *Psychological Bulletin, 95,* 428–450.

Mackie, D. M. (1987). Systematic and nonsystematic processing of majority and minority persuasive communications. *Journal of Personality and Social Psychology, 53,* 41–52.

Martin, R., & Hewstone, M. (2003). Social influence processes of control and change: Conformity, obedience to authority, and innovation. In M. A. Hogg & J. Cooper (Eds.), *Sage handbook of social psychology* (pp. 347–366). London: Sage.

Martin, R., & Hewstone, M. (2008). Majority versus minority influence, message processing and attitude change: The source–context-elaboration model. In M. Zanna (Ed.), *Advances in experimental social psychology* (Vol. 40, pp. 237–326). San Diego, CA: Academic Press.

Martin, R., Hewstone, M., Martin, P. Y., & Gardikiotis, A. (2008). Persuasion from majority and minority groups. In W. Crano & R. Prislin (Eds.), *Attitudes and attitude change* (pp. 361–384). New York: Psychology Press.

Martin, R., Martin, P. Y., Smith, J., & Hewstone, M. (2007). Majority and minority influence and prediction of behavioral intentions and behavior. *Journal of Experimental Social Psychology*, *43*, 763–771.

Moscovici, S. (1976). *Social influence and social change*. London: Academic Press.

Moscovici, S. (1980). Toward a theory of conversion behavior. In L. Berkowitz (Ed.), *Advances in experimental social psychology* (Vol. 13, pp. 209–239). New York: Academic Press.

Moscovici, S., & Faucheux, C. (1972). Social influence, conformity bias and the study of active minorities. In L. Berkowitz (Ed.), *Advances in experimental social psychology* (Vol. 6, pp. 149–202). New York: Academic Press.

Moscovici, S., Lage, E., & Naffrechoux, M. (1969). Influence of a consistent minority on the responses of a majority in a color perception task. *Sociometry*, *32*, 365–380.

Moscovici, S., & Nemeth, C. (1974). Social influence II: Minority influence. In C. Nemeth (Ed.), *Social psychology: Classic and contemporary integrations* (pp. 217–249). Chicago: Rand McNally.

Mugny, G. (1975). Negotiations, image of the other and the process of minority influence. *European Journal of Social Psychology*, *5*, 209–228.

Mugny, G. (1982). *The power of minorities*. London: Academic Press.

Mugny, G., Butera, F., Sanchez-Mazas, M., & Pérez, J. A. (1995). Judgements in conflict: The conflict elaboration theory of social influence. In B. Boothe, R. Hirsig, A. Helminger, B. Meier, & R. Volkart (Eds.), *Perception–evaluation–interpretation* (pp. 160–168). Göttingen, Germany: Hogrefe and Huber.

Nemeth, C. (1986). Differential contributions of majority and minority influence. *Psychological Review*, *93*, 23–32.

Nemeth, C., Swedlund, M., & Kanki, B. (1974). Patterning of the minority's response and their influence on the majority. *European Journal of Social Psychology*, *4*, 53–64.

Papastamou, S. (1986). Psychologization and processes of minority and majority influence. *European Journal of Social Psychology*, *16*, 165–180.

Prislin, R., & Christensen, P. N. (2005). Social change in the aftermath of successful minority influence. In W. Stroebe & M. Hewstone (Eds.), *European review of social psychology* (Vol. 16, pp. 43–73). Hove, UK: Psychology Press (Taylor & Francis).

Prislin, R., & Wood, W. (2005). Social influence in attitudes and attitude change. In D. Albarracín, B. T. Johnson, & M. P. Zanna (Eds.), *The handbook of attitudes* (pp. 671–706). Mahwah, NJ: Lawrence Erlbaum Associates, Inc.

Schachter, S. (1951). Deviation, rejection, and communication. *Journal of Abnormal and Social Psychology*, *46*, 190–207.

Schulz-Hardt, S., Brodbeck, F. C., Mojzisch, A., Kerschreiter, R., & Frey, D. (2006). Group decision making in hidden profile situations: Dissent as a facilitator for decision quality. *Journal of Personality and Social Psychology*, *91*, 1080–1093.

Smith, C. M., & Diven, P. J. (2002). Minority influence and political interest groups. In V. C. Ottati & R. S. Tindale (Eds.), *The social psychology of politics: Social psychological applications to social issues* (pp. 175–192). New York: Kluwer Academic.

Smith, C. M., Tindale, R. S., & Anderson, E. M. (2001). The impact of shared representations on minority influence in freely interacting groups. In C. K. W. De

Dreu & N. K. De Vries (Eds.), *Group consensus and innovation* (pp. 183–200). Oxford, UK: Blackwell.

Turner, J. C. (1991). *Social influence*. Milton Keynes, UK: Open University Press.

Velden, F. S., Beersma, B., & De Dreu, C. K. W. (2007). Majority and minority influence in group negotiation: The moderating effects of social motivation and decision rules. *Journal of Applied Psychology, 92*, 259–268.

# PART II
# Processes and theoretical issues

# 2 The complexity of majority and minority influence processes

*Alain Quiamzade*
University of Geneva and University of Fribourg, Distance
Learning University Switzerland

*Gabriel Mugny and Juan Manuel
Falomir-Pichastor*
University of Geneva, Switzerland

*Fabrizio Butera*
University of Lausanne, Switzerland

## Straightforward theories and complex results

Since Moscovici's seminal work on minority influence (cf. Moscovici, 1976, 1985a, 1985b; Moscovici & Faucheux, 1972), a number of studies confirmed that both majorities and minorities can induce a certain amount of influence (see Chaiken & Stangor, 1987; De Dreu & De Vries, 2001; Maass & Clark, 1984; Moscovici, Mucchi-Faina, & Maass, 1994; Moscovici, Mugny, & Van Avermaet, 1985; Pérez & Mugny, 1993; Wood, Lundgren, Ouellette, Busceme, & Blackstone, 1994, for reviews). According to Moscovici (1980), when confronted with majority positions, targets focus on discrepancies between the majority's position and their own, and the influence results from their motivation to reduce such discrepancies (a *comparison process*). Conversely, when confronted with minorities, targets' attention is focused on the minority's position, and influence results from the careful processing of the situation and the relevant information (a *validation process*). These distinct processes result in differences in the nature of influence: Majorities obtain more manifest influence (i.e., on immediate, focal or public measures) than latent influence (i.e., on delayed, indirect or private measures) in the form of compliance, while minorities obtain more latent than manifest influence (i.e., conversion). This is a crucial point because the distinction between levels of influence has received little attention in recent influence approaches based on information processing.

In line with the dual approach of social influence, Nemeth's research supports qualitatively different processes for each source. Nemeth (1986) initially proposed that majorities elicit *convergent thinking*: Targets mainly take into account the information proposed by the source without considering alternative points of view. Conversely, minorities stimulate *divergent thinking*: Targets attend to more aspects of the situation and consider other alternatives to the minority's position. Nemeth and colleagues' research showed that individuals generate more creative and novel solutions to different problems or better performance when confronted with solutions proposed by a minority, as compared to a majority (e.g., Nemeth & Kwan, 1985, 1987; Nemeth, Mayseless, Sherman, & Brown, 1990; Nemeth & Wachtler, 1983).

Overall, there has been some apparent agreement that validation is generally related to a more extensive information processing than social comparison, and that minority influence should then be related to a more extensive message processing than majority influence (e.g., Chaiken & Stangor, 1987; Maass & Clark, 1983, 1984; Moscovici, 1980; Moskowitz & Chaiken, 2001). The same seems true for divergent and convergent thinking. However, recent findings suggest a more complex picture for majority and minority processes.

Indeed, research has specified a complex set of conditions favouring minority influence. For instance, minority influence is greater when minority attributes are positive (e.g., objectivity, credibility, consistency, low self-interest, distinctiveness; cf. Bohner, Erb, Reinhard, & Frank, 1996; Bohner, Frank, & Erb, 1998; Clark & Maass, 1988; Maass, Clark, & Haberkorn, 1982; Moscowitz, 1996; Mugny, 1982; Papastamou & Mugny, 1990). It has also been observed that minority advocacy leads to more positive message elaboration (e.g., Martin, Gardikiotis, & Hewstone, 2002; Mucchi-Faina, 2000) and greater resistance to a counter-message (Martin, Hewstone, & Martin, 2003; see also Nemeth & Chiles, 1988), and that greater processing appears mainly when the targets' personal relevance is low (e.g., Alvaro & Crano, 1997; Crano & Alvaro, 1998; Crano & Chen, 1998; Kerr, 2002; Maass & Clark, 1983, 1984; Martin & Hewstone, 2003; Mucchi-Faina & Cicoletti, 2006; Trost & Kenrick, 1994; Trost, Maass, & Kenrick, 1992). Regarding Moscovici's perspective, it is interesting to note that other research showed that minority influence appears when conflict cannot be neglected by targets (cf. Baron & Bellman, 2007; De Vries, De Dreu, Gordijn, & Schuurman, 1996; Kruglanski & Mackie, 1990; Sanchez-Mazas, Mugny, & Falomir, 1997; Wolf, 1979). In this way, more influence is observed among participants who initially disagree with the minority positions (Papastamou & Mugny, 1990), and when participants pay more attention to the advocacy's content even though they intend to deny the message's credibility (Falomir, Mugny, & Pérez, 1996; Moscovici, Mugny, & Pérez, 1984–1985; Pérez, Moscovici, & Mugny, 1991; Pérez, Mugny, & Moscovici, 1986).

Research also revealed that there are conditions for majority influence as well. For instance, Mackie (1987) suggested an explanation in terms of expectancy violation: People consider that majorities are right, and expect to be in agreement with majorities and in disagreement with minorities. Violations of this expectancy elicit more careful examination of persuasive arguments. Accordingly, but in opposition to Moscovici's hypothesis, Mackie (1987) observed that message processing and attitude change (both direct and indirect) was greater when supported by a majority rather than a minority. In the same vein, it has been observed that majorities can elicit greater systematic processing than minorities (e.g., Erb, Bohner, Schmälzle, & Rank, 1998), when the personal involvement is high (e.g., Crano & Chen, 1998; Trost & Kenrik, 1994), or when the message argues for a negative personal outcome for the target (e.g., Martin & Hewstone, 2003). In line with Moscovici's hypotheses, Erb, Bohner, Rank, and Einwiller (2002) showed that minorities elicit more cognitive processing when there is high discrepancy, i.e., conflict, whereas majorities elicit more cognitive processing, as Mackie (1987) predicts, when there is low discrepancy. However, effects considering message direction and/or discrepancy are to be considered very carefully because they are not always consistent (Baker and Petty; 1994; Erb et al., 2002; Martin & Hewstone, 2003; Martin, Hewstone, & Martin, 2003).

With regards to Nemeth's theory (1986), minorities do not always stimulate greater originality or better performance than majorities. For example, divergent thinking seems more likely when the minority is original and the majority is not (Mucchi-Faina, Maass, & Volpato, 1991), and when personal relevance is high (Mucchi-Faina & Cicoletti, 2006). Nemeth herself has shown that confrontation with majorities is not necessarily associated with poor performance. Indeed, when convergent thinking is more appropriate than divergent thinking to solve the task, confrontation with majorities elicits better performance than confrontation with minorities (Nemeth, Mosier, & Chiles, 1992; see also Peterson & Nemeth, 1996). Moreover, in an attempt to integrate Nemeth's theory and information processing approaches to social influence (Eagly & Chaiken, 1993; Petty & Cacioppo, 1986), De Vries et al. (1996) acknowledged that majority versus minority influence can be mediated by either heuristic or systematic processing, but that the nature of systematic processing is different according to the status of the source: Arguments receiving majority support elicit a convergent systematic processing, while arguments receiving minority support that cannot be neglected or discredited by heuristics elicit a divergent or constructive systematic processing. In the same vein, Erb et al. (1998) observed that majority support for an advocacy elicited fewer unfavourable thoughts and more positive evaluations than minority support, but that a minority support elicited more novel thoughts than majority support.

To sum up, there is not one specific level of influence, nor one specific process, inherently and exclusively associated with either majority or minority influence (see Martin & Hewstone, 2001a, for a similar idea about systematic-heuristic processing). Thus, a conclusion could be that Moscovici's and Nemeth's theories appear today to be too straightforward, or at least too simple, to account for the complexity of the above results and are strongly challenged by this abundant and diverse body of research.

## The origin of complexity: Conflict elaboration theory

Conflict elaboration theory (CET; Pérez & Mugny, 1993) is an attempt to organize such complex patterns of influences and contradictions on the basis of some basic principles.[1] One of them is that the complexity of social influence dynamics has led to the recognition that in order to predict influence, one needs to take into account the specific context in which influence is attempted, in particular the type of task involved. Based on this principle, a simple hypothesis can be that the apparent contradictions between Moscovici, Nemeth and subsequent findings could rest on one simple fact: They are not concerned with the same type of tasks.

To show this, let us start with the principles of CET that allow us to differentiate the relevant types of tasks. First of all, CET argues that in spite of the multiple types of tasks, sources, levels of influence and processes through which social influence operates, social influence can be understood from a common basic explanatory notion: *conflict elaboration*. Given that any influence process is a consequence of a divergence with some relevant others (namely, the source of influence), the notion of conflict elaboration refers to the way people manage the opposition of judgement a meaning to this divergence. It is noteworthy that in this theory, conflict is not intended in the classic, conflict-of-interests sense (e.g., Deutsch, 1973), but rather as the way people give meaning to the divergence with the source. The core of the theory is that the specific representation targets have of a task induces them to attribute a particular meaning to the divergence (i.e., conflict elaboration), thereby leading to different possible patterns of manifest and latent influence. One key dimension that determines people's representation of the task is what has been called a *representation of unity* as opposed to a *representation of plurality* (Brandstätter et al., 1991). By 'representation' we mean lay-people's knowledge or beliefs about the tasks that determines specific expectations and guides people's behaviour when the contextual elements and the confrontation with a source match or do not match, these expectations. Representation of unity corresponds to the belief that there is only one way to see the object and that there is one possible answer to the task. A strong need for consensus ensues from this representation. By contrast, representation of plurality refers to the belief that some diversity of positions is plausible, even expected, and that different points of view about the object can exist simultaneously (cf. Butera, Huguet, Mugny, & Pérez, 1994). These two types of representations are differentially activated depending on the nature of the task and on the source of influence. The main notion is that the activated representation guides the influence targets' behaviours and thus determines influence processes.

The theory distinguishes four main types of tasks. (1) In *objective non-ambiguous tasks*, objectivity judgements are at stake. The prototype of studies using this type of task is the conformity paradigm used by Asch

(1956). Participants know that only one answer is valid, and they know which one it is. As a consequence, consensus expectation is high, even absolute. It means that the representation of unity clearly dominates, because the task is evident, with the consequence that everybody is expected to give the same answer. Conflict elaboration is thus oriented by two questions that ask why unanimity is not achieved, and why the source is wrong. In other words, what matters is the existence or absence of unanimity. Due to the absolute unanimity expectation, anyone who breaks it will always introduce a conflict.

(2) In *aptitude tasks*, competence is at stake. In these tasks—for instance problem-solving or learning tasks—participants believe that one (or some) answer(s) must be correct or more valid than others, but they initially do not know which one(s) (i.e., it is not immediately perceptible, in contrast with objective non-ambiguous tasks). Conflict elaboration is thus shaped by people's concern to increase the correctness of their judgements and/or to give the best self-image in terms of their own abilities. As a consequence, in these tasks the source's competence or expertise will be of utmost importance. As we will see, in this kind of task both unity and plurality can be activated: Consensus introduced by majority or competent sources activates unity, whereas minorities or low-competence sources leads to plurality.

(3) In *opinion tasks*, dimensions such as social identity and categorization are the most relevant. They refer to attitude judgements, i.e., they are tasks in which there is no objective way to determine who is right or wrong. In these types of tasks, a direct correspondence is expected between different opinions and relevant social differentiations. Conflict elaboration is thus shaped by categorical differentiation (Doise, 1978; Tajfel, 1978). In other words, conflict depends on whether or not the source belongs to the same group or social category as the targets, and whether or not this introduces a threat to their identity. As for aptitude tasks, the frame of influence can be unity as well as plurality, even if the elements activating them are radically different. For example, unity could be activated when an in-group is the frame of reference, since pressure towards uniformity makes consensus expectation salient, whereas plurality could be more present when the context is an inter-group one, since differences between groups are expected.

(4) In *non-implicating tasks*, there is nothing in particular at stake, and participants simply express personal preferences among a plurality of viewpoints. They refer to issues that are new or relatively novel, or of very low social relevance. Thus, people would have no special expectation of reaching a consensus or not. Since everyone is entitled to express a preference on these matters, plurality is the norm in this kind of task. Differing views from other people are not considered to be in conflict, and any source characteristic may lead to influence if it is a socially shared heuristic (Chaiken, 1987), like credibility or likeability heuristics.

An important implication of distinguishing different types of tasks is that a specific source will not always induce the same pattern of influences.

Changes in crucial parameters determining the representation of the task should lead to major modifications in the pattern of influences. The main argument is that CET is also a heuristic device that may be useful to account for the conceptual diversity of the existing theories, as each one has been associated with experimental paradigms using a particular type of task, which is clearly the case for Moscovici's and Nemeth's conceptualizations. To illustrate this claim, we will focus on the two kinds of tasks these authors have used to provide support for their theory, and more precisely on the expectations these tasks make salient.

Moscovici's and Nemeth's theories of majority–minority influence both offer a high internal coherence, but propose different mechanisms accounting for apparently similar influence effects. Referring to these two theories, Maass and Volpato (1994, p. 136) note that Nemeth's theory as well as Moscovici's 'make valid predictions under specific circumstances', even if 'it remains unclear what these circumstances are'. We contend that the differences between the two theories are linked to the particular tasks used in the experiments designed to provide support for each theory.[2] Indeed, Moscovici's blue/green paradigm is clearly based on an objective non-ambiguous task where there is only one evident correct response, as participants have no doubt about the colour of the slides, whereas most of Nemeth's problem-solving tasks are examples of aptitude tasks in which people try to find or discover a correct response among a multitude of possible responses.

Curiously, the great majority of the theoretical and experimental work carried out on majority/minority influence in the last twenty years, mainly within persuasion-based paradigms, is grounded on opinion tasks, whereas Moscovici's (1980) conversion theory and Nemeth's (1986) theory of convergent and divergent thinking seldom employed such tasks. In fact, very few researchers have recognized the importance of considering the nature of the task as a central element in majority–minority influence processes (cf. Maass & Volpato, 1996). As an often-cited example, Mackie's (1987) results seem to be inconsistent with Moscovici's propositions. However, as noticed by Erb et al. (2002), the issues used in Mackie's experiments were not related to participant's strong convictions and could have elicited lesser, or perhaps different, conflicts than Moscovici's blue/green experiments. This suggests that Mackie's experimental results could be more typical of non-implicating tasks (or of some opinion tasks) rather than of objective non-ambiguous tasks. As a consequence, her results do not necessarily challenge Moscovici's propositions, which are based on tasks fundamentally different in nature. Misunderstandings or contradictions could arise as consequences of some researchers trying to test, within the same paradigm, propositions which are, in reality, relevant for different kinds of tasks and for different processes of conflict elaboration. As we will see, the point is that Moscovici's approach seems to correspond more to situations in which a representation of unity pre-exists and that Nemeth's approach could be more appropriate for tasks in which plurality (as unity) is a possible representation. In other words, the former could be most appropriate to account for influence dynamics observed in objective non-ambiguous tasks where there is only one evident correct response, whereas the latter would fit more with aptitude tasks where people try to find or discover the correct (or at least the best) response(s) among two or more possible responses. The remainder of the present chapter will discuss majority and minority influence processes in these two kinds of tasks, as they seem to be neglected in recent research (see, however, Crano, 2000, who takes into consideration the nature of the task, which he specifies as the issue under consideration, and its self-relevance). This discussion will allow us to pinpoint the areas of relevance and the limits of Moscovici's and Nemeth's theories.

### Majority–minority influence in objective non-ambiguous tasks

In Moscovici's work, it is necessary to distinguish, on the one hand, his general theory of minority influence that accounts for social change and that encompasses a wide variety of conflict-based influence dynamics most often related to opinions, values and ideologies (see Moscovici, 1976), and, on the other hand, the blue/green paradigm (Moscovici & Lage, 1976, 1978; Moscovici, Lage, & Naffrechoux, 1969; Moscovici & Personnaz, 1980), which is similar to the one developed by Binet (1900) in his pioneer work on suggestion. In fact, the mechanisms brought to light by this paradigm are not likely to simulate the social changes described in the general theory of social change, because the conflicts intervening in this particular task are induced by this task's specific expectations, i.e., total consensus. It is important to say at this stage that our claim specifically concerns Moscovici's blue/green paradigm and the theory he developed on the basis of this paradigm in 1980 (in fact the most frequently cited paper referring to Moscovici's theory), because both paradigm and theory are about objective non-ambiguous tasks. Our propositions are thus not valid for his larger theory (Moscovici, 1976), which more appropriately fits opinion tasks.

Let us look at his specific theory. He came to the conclusion that when faced with a majority source, the exclusive focus on social comparison accounts for the dominant pattern of majority influence: mere compliance, i.e., manifest influence only. When the source is a majority, or when there is a dominant norm, its response is generally considered as being legitimate and consensual, therefore leaving the target in a deviant position. The target then focuses its attention on its relationship with the source, engaging in a social comparison process resulting in a manifest change without actually processing the information relative to the stimulus. Minorities, on the contrary, lead to a completely opposite influence pattern. Manifest influence is weak or null, because in this case it is the source's answer that may be considered deviant or even ridiculous, and because the source is not legitimated to foster any social uniformity. However, if the minority source is consistent (Moscovici & Lage, 1976), the judgement emitted by the minority arouses a conflict that leads targets to look more carefully at the stimulus. In this case, the target is brought to a more complex processing of the object under influence, consisting of examining the link between the object properties and the information provided by the source. This is what has been called the validation process. This process leads to a latent change of the very perception of the object, sometimes without any manifest change, which has been called the conversion phenomenon.

In the terms of CET, these dynamics are typical of an objective non-ambiguous task similar to that of Asch. Because individuals know the correct answer, they are very confident. Social reality and physical reality (see Festinger, 1950) are not just similar but substitutable. In other words, people activate a representation of unity, which means that total consensus is the core of the individual's expectations: The answer being evident, people expect unanimity (Asch, 1956). Conformity is not so much the result of a normative dependence as an attempt to restore consensus with the majority, which the object appeals for. In this way, it is the failure of consensus in itself that leads to the presence or absence of influence dynamics, rather than the amount of social support provided through the similarity/difference of judgements (Allen & Levine, 1968). Opposing an incorrect majority, people are in a paradoxical situation in which the expected consensus is broken, and astonishingly by their own answer. Participants thus experience an 'epistemological nightmare' (Brown, 1965): They do not know whether they should trust the unanimous experimental majority whose numerical power legitimates it to give an answer that should be considered consensual, or if they should trust the perceptual evidence based on their own past experience that clear physical evidence always leads to absolute consensus.

Faced with a majority, however, targets are not regulating the conflict by being primarily interested in determining the truth about what the object is, but rather by trying urgently to reduce the divergence with the source. The regulation of the conflict is here of an eminently relational nature (Moscovici & Personnaz, 1980): The target is in a deviant position, fears appearing ridiculous, and solves the conflict by adopting a solution that restores the broken consensus, i.e., conformity at a manifest level. As Moscovici (1980, p. 214) wrote, the target's preoccupation is: 'Why do I not see or think like them?' In fact, in this kind of task we shall call this conformity behaviour *yielding*, because yielding to the source here is not so much a way to conform to a source's norm but is simply the easier way to restore consensus.

When facing a minority, restoration of consensus takes another path. Because there is no relational problem, targets regulate the conflict in a more socio-cognitive way. Indeed, as a minority has neither power nor legitimacy to induce compliance, the relational problem is solved by keeping one's own evident judgement at the manifest level. However, this does not allow us to answer the question as to why consensus is not reached in a self-evident task. By looking at the source and trying to determine 'how can it see what it sees, think what it thinks?' (Moscovici, 1980, p. 215), targets restore consensus by examining the object and rebuilding its properties through an involuntary integration of the minority's position at a latent level. The interpretation proposed by Moscovici appears the most appropriate in this type of task, and indeed relies on the unanimity expectations that characterize them.

In sum, CET proposes that Moscovici's (1980) analysis of majority/minority influence is driven by the use of the blue/green paradigm (whereas his theory in the 1976 book mostly concerns opinions). Indeed, majority influence has been described as limited to the manifest level because in objective non-ambiguous tasks—such as in the blue/green paradigm—the need for unanimity forces participants to solve the problem at the manifest level, in the form of mere compliance (cf. Bond & Smith, 1996). As a consequence, and this is a specific prediction of CET, majorities are not condemned to obtain influence situated exclusively at this level: If the representation of the task or of the relationship with the majority could be modified in such a way that the pressure to mere yielding is reduced, conflict should be reported at a latent level, and majorities would produce latent influence.

Indeed, even if the target resists the majority source at a manifest level, the objective non-ambiguous task still calls for high levels of consensus, as only one definition of the object is possible. Thus, targets will be led to restore consensus at a latent level by re-examining the object and rebuilding its properties on the basis of the source's judgement, in such a way as to symbolically re-obtain a single definition of the object. It is interesting to note that researchers who found majority latent influence in contradiction with Moscovici's results[3] suggested that such latent influence could be due to the fact that for some reason, participants pay more attention to the stimulus (Doms & Van Avermaet, 1980), as could be the case for suspicious participants in particular (Sorrentino, King, & Leo, 1980).

To determine whether individuals change in order to re-establish consensus and not just because of normative dependence, it was necessary to confront them with a majority stripped of its normative power. Indeed, suppressing the normative power of the majority should not reduce the consensus expectation inherent to the task. Thus, targets will not necessarily accept the source's responses at a manifest level, but will change at a latent level. Several studies on majority influence found a set of manifest and/or latent dynamics supporting the above analysis in terms of consensus expectations.

The first study providing support for the above hypothesis employed an Asch-like paradigm (Mugny, 1984). Two independent variables were manipulated: the nature of the source and the representation of the task. According to the first manipulation, participants were confronted with incorrect answers allegedly coming from a majority versus a minority. A control group without any source was also run. In the second experimental manipulation half of the participants were told that perceptual illusions are commonplace when performing this task, and were given examples of an inverted T (a 'T' shape with horizontal and vertical bars of equal length that are perceived as having unequal lengths) and the Müller–Lyer illusions (two horizontal bars of equal length marked out by concave or convex limits that are perceived as having unequal lengths). This procedure legitimates apparent differences in answers, thereby reducing normative pressure, and the necessity for compliance. The other half received no information about the illusions. Then they underwent the influence phase. Asch's usual influence procedure was modified for all participants by introducing a systematic underestimation in the source's answers (the source always chose a longer comparison line) indicating an organizing principle of the answers. The manifest influence measure was similar to Asch's one and the latent measure consisted of a length-estimation task where latent influence was indicated by a general underestimation of the length which corresponded to the source's organizing principle.

Results showed that in the usual situation in which no illusions were introduced, Moscovici's pattern of results was replicated: the majority obtained more manifest influence, whereas the minority obtained more latent influence, as compared to the control condition. However, when illusions were introduced, results were quite different. First, the minority source lost its latent influence and had no influence at all. This is probably due to the fact that it is possible to attribute the minority's incorrect answer to illusions, in a sort of 'psychologization' process that is known to block minority influence (cf. Mugny & Papastamou, 1980; Papastamou, 1983, 1986; Papastamou & Mugny, 1990; Papastamou, Mugny, & Kaiser, 1980; Papastamou, Mugny, & Pérez, 1991–1992). Second, as expected, the majority obtained latent influence, more than in the control condition and more than in the majority/no illusion condition. However, and surprisingly, manifest conformity to the majority was not suppressed. In sum, majority latent influence is indeed possible, as long as conflict is displaced at the latent level.

Using an angle estimation task, Brandstätter et al. (1991) reasoned that it was possible that in the previous experiment, the persistence of the majority's manifest influence could have been due to the fact that illusions increase uncertainty and raise some doubt in the targets' minds about their own answer, rather than only about the source's answer. In other words, the decrease in normative dependence could have been replaced by an increase in informational dependence (cf. Deutsch & Gerard, 1955). In Brandstätter et al.'s (1991) study, the source was then explicitly denied, i.e., targets were informed that the source was a victim of an illusion in the task and that their judgements were incorrect. If influence depends on the need to re-establish consensus, removing informational dependence should lead to a disappearance of manifest influence but a continued presence of latent influence.

If influence does not depend on re-establishing consensus, both manifest and latent influence should disappear. However, this should be true only if the task is an objective non-ambiguous task. Two variables were then manipulated in this study. The first one was about the nature of source, either a majority or a minority. The second one was about the size of the angles to be judged during the influence phase. In one condition, participants had to estimate 90° angles, i.e., angles calling for one single, evident answer, which corresponded to an objective non-ambiguous task, as in the Asch paradigm. In the other condition, participants were confronted with 85° angles, i.e., angles leaving some uncertainty as to their estimation. The alleged majority versus minority judgement stated that angles measured 50°. Manifest influence was based on direct angle estimates, and latent influence was assessed by asking participants to estimate the weight of a slice of cheese delimited by an angle: The lower the weight indicated by participants, the higher the integration of the source's underestimation of angles. With the non-ambiguous angles, i.e., 90° angles, results replicated those of the previous experiment with one difference: If the minority obtained the same pattern as before, the manifest influence of the majority was suppressed, but, as expected, gave way to latent influence. Conversely, 85° angles introduced strong informational dependence. In this case, the minority obtained some latent influence even when contradicted, whereas the majority achieved only manifest influence. In sum, in objective non-ambiguous tasks, it was shown that a majority source can induce a conversion pattern (latent influence without manifest influence). This was possible in the condition, as predicted by CET, where the reduction of normative dependence (as informational dependence) allowed for a displacement of conflict from the manifest to the latent level.

Pérez, Mugny, Butera, Kaiser, and Roux (1994) tested even more directly the role of consensus expectations within the same paradigm (using here only 90° angles), by manipulating two variables concerning the representation of the task: Its unity versus plurality and normative pressure. Half of the participants were told that, in spite of the perceptual evidence, differences in responses could be expected allegedly because of interindividual differences related to the physiology of the visual apparatus. The other half were told the opposite, i.e., that all human beings have the same visual system. This allowed for a modification of the representation of the task, from a situation where consensus is needed (what is typical of objective non-ambiguous tasks), to a situation where it is no more the case. Normative pressure was manipulated through categorical membership: when the source represents the majority, an in-group should generate more pressure to conform than an out-group (cf. Turner, 1991). Thus, participants were confronted with an in-group versus an out-group majority.

The same dependent variables were used to assess influence using direct angle estimates for manifest influence, and asking participants to estimate the weight of a slice of cheese delimited by angles for latent influence.

Results showed that when the induced representation was the typical feature of objective non-ambiguous tasks, in-group and out-group majorities induced influence, but at different levels. Indeed, under induction of the belief of similarity, the in-group majority appeared to be more influential than the out-group majority at the manifest level. Clearly, the out-group nature of the majority reduced the normative pressure to conform. But resisting at the manifest level does not explain why consensus, i.e., similarity in perception, is not achieved in a task where it is needed. Conflict with the out-group majority is then reported at the latent level. Indeed, on the latent measure participants showed greater influence when confronted with the out-group majority than when opposed to the in-group majority. These results, an advantage of the in-group over the out-group majority at the manifest level and an advantage of the out-group over the in-group majority at the latent level, appeared to be directly dependent on similarity expectations. No such differences in restoring consensus among conditions appeared under a context of perceptual dissimilarity (but see Butera et al., 1994).

As a conclusion, these studies demonstrate that the representation of unity is one of the key features that accounts for the differences in majority and minority influence in objective non-ambiguous tasks. Indeed, it appeared that the yielding typically induced by the majority cannot be described merely in terms of a dependence relationship. This yielding is determined by the obligation to re-establish a broken consensus on an object (here a 90° angle) implicated by the representation of unity. When normative dependence is high, the consensus is re-established at the manifest level. However, when normative dependence is reduced—either because the source is a minority or because the majority is an out-group—yielding is psychologically not possible, but the task still calls for the unity of response typical of objective non-ambiguous tasks. This need for unity is the force that drives latent influence whenever normative dependence is reduced in objective non-ambiguous tasks.

### Majority–minority influence in aptitude tasks

Let us consider now the theory of convergent and divergent thinking, which, in its scope of going 'beyond conversion', explicitly differentiated itself from conversion theory. In Nemeth's theory, as compared to conversion theory, the nature of the source determines the modes of thinking, and not the levels of influence. Nemeth (1986) proposed that, confronted with a majority, people develop a convergent form of thinking. Deviating from a majority induces great stress, leading people to narrow their attentional focus on the majority's positions. This implies that the majority's judgements will be used as a frame of reference in place of other elements of the task, and to the detriment of any other alternative perspective. Conversely, minority influence favours a divergent type of thinking. Minority dissent induces less stress, in fact optimal stress, and leads people to broaden their attentional focus and to consider multiple aspects of the situation and of the task. Targets take into account multiple perspectives, which lead to the discovery of novel solutions.

As noted by Maass and Volpato (1994), Nemeth's research tested hypotheses in the domain of cognition and problem solving, and mainly studied the individual mechanisms of information processing arising in majority and minority influence situations. In terms of the CET, these mechanisms are typical of aptitude tasks, i.e., creativity, reasoning and problem-solving tasks, in which individuals do not know the answer because it is not obvious. Therefore, they are highly uncertain about their answers and search for comparisons with others in order to evaluate themselves (Festinger, 1954). The reason for this is because their ability and competence are at stake: Their level of (in)competence is reflected by the (in)correctness of their judgements. Different judgements then turn out to be a significant source of information when they help reduce uncertainty and reveal the most probable correct answer. Although individuals may feel the need for consensus, especially with the majority, it is not at all surprising that people have different answers in such a task. It is indeed plausible that different people with different levels of competence may come up with different solutions.

One basic assumption of Nemeth's theory is that convergent and divergent thinking have their origin in the inferences people make concerning the degree of competence of majorities and minorities: People are motivated to assume that majorities are correct and minorities are incorrect (Nemeth et al., 1990). In our meaning, if the majority induces cognitive functioning of a convergent type, it is because it is supposed to be competent, especially compared to a minority. The force of the majority's answer does not originate in a collective norm representing a group, but simply in the inference that different individuals arriving independently at an identical answer are probably more correct and therefore more credible (cf. Wilder, 1977). Thus, it is not surprising that individuals search for social comparison with dissimilar rather than similar others in aptitude tasks (Gorenflo & Crano, 1989; Mayseless & Kruglanski, 1987) in order to reduce uncertainty (cf. Mettee & Smith, 1977). If a similar answer is given by a dissimilar other, one will be more certain of the correctness of one's own answer. Following common sense, it is highly unlikely that everyone arrives at the same wrong answer at the same time. Consequently, people assume that a majority's answer is probably correct. Even if it is possible that some normative dependence is induced by the majority's status, informational dependence is the guiding mechanism that leads people to adopt the majority's position. Diverging from the majority informs individuals that they are certainly wrong, thereby threatening their own competence. Therefore, imitation of the majority is a way to avoid incompetence: Proposing the same answer as the majority is the easiest way to be correct.

Minorities, in contrast, are considered incompetent. Targets simply cannot reproduce the source's answer, as it is probably wrong. However, aptitude tasks are generally difficult tasks, and targets remain uncertain since differentiating from the minority does not guarantee that their own answer is right. In this sense, it is not surprising that minority influence is greater when participants are uncertain about their own position (Maass & Volpato, 1996). In other words, under minority influence, fear of invalidation becomes salient since the target is uncertain and the source is not reliable. This leads targets to process the different elements of the task in such a way as to obtain more information (Nemeth & Rogers, 1996): fear of invalidation can become constructive because it allows one to go beyond the dual choice between one's own answer and that of the minority. It follows that minority influence does not involve espousing the minority position (even if at a latent level, contrarily to non-ambiguous tasks), but rather it involves a deeper processing of the task, as well as the integration of several dimensions of the problem (Nemeth & Kwan, 1987) and the formulation of new, potentially original or creative, responses (Nemeth & Kwan, 1985; Volpato, Maass, Mucchi-Faina, & Vitti, 1990).

Nemeth's theory therefore seems more appropriate to explain minority–majority influence processes in aptitude tasks. However, at this point, two questions arise. First, is the representation that the source activates (unity or plurality) a key element that determines convergent or divergent thinking, and, more generally, the reasoning and processing of the task? Second, is numerical support—understanding influence in terms of majority–minority processes—the most appropriate dimension to account for social influence when aptitude tasks are involved? Indeed, as pointed out above, people performing aptitude tasks are concerned with the likelihood of reaching the correct answer, and are interested in the specific feature of the influence source that is informative with regards to this likelihood: Its level of competence. Below we present a research programme intended (1) to explain Nemeth's convergent and divergent thinking in terms of the way targets reason under representations of unity versus plurality, and (2) to show that competence is the key feature that organizes social influence dynamics in aptitude tasks.

As much as conformity preserves social consensus, confirmation preserves consensus about knowledge (cf. Gorman & Carlson, 1989). To protect a theory, studies should be carried out to validate rather than contest it. In other words, it is not uncommon to undergo a confirming rather than a disconfirming process even if it can be an erroneous strategy (see Popper, 1955, for the importance of disconfirmation in scientific thinking). Disconfirmation originates from the capacity to consider alternatives, which is not possible when the fundamental goal is the maintenance of the paradigm. In the same vein, divergent thinking consists of considering more parameters as alternative standpoints, whereas convergent thinking consists of focusing on a unique perspective: that of the majority. One may hypothesize that confirmation refers to the maintenance of the established majority answer because it would be problematic to abandon and substitute this answer. Reasoning strategies aimed at verifying the predominant majority's hypothesis would then correspond to a representation of unity and thus introduce social consensus seeking. On the other hand, one could suppose that disconfirmation would be a strategy requiring decentring (cf. Butera et al., 1994) from one's own unique standpoint, and consideration of alternatives that the minority standpoint renders salient, i.e., consideration of plurality. Thus, a social structure in which alternatives are introduced should induce plurality and strategies that consider existing alternatives and foresee falsification of one's own hypothesis in particular. To summarize, conformity and confirmation might express the same larger socio-cognitive process of conservation and protection of an answer, which is predominant because it stems from a representation of the task in terms of unity. On the contrary, innovation and invalidation might express a larger process of reappraising and falsification because it stems from a representation of the task in terms of plurality.

To test these ideas, some of us carried out a set of experiments using Wason's (1960) '2–4–6' task. It is an inductive reasoning task requiring participants to discover the rule underlying the triad of numbers 2–4–6 and to propose new triads in order to test their hypothesis. Cognitive psychology research has pointed out a peculiarity of this task involving a systematic bias in hypothesis testing: People tend to test their hypotheses using a confirmatory strategy (Butera, Legrenzi, & Mugny, 1993; Legrenzi, 1983). In this task, disconfirmation is actually more diagnostic because it allows one to rule out specific non-sufficient hypotheses. Confirmation is a testing strategy that indicates focused thinking mechanisms, such as convergent thinking, whereas disconfirmation necessitates decentring from a single hypothesis and the consideration of alternative hypotheses, since it would be absurd to disconfirm the only hypothesis at hand (Butera & Buchs, 2005).

In the first experiment (Legrenzi, Butera, Mugny, & Pérez, 1991), participants confronted with the '2–4–6' problem were told the hypothesis and the triad proposed by a majority versus a minority source. Moreover, a second independent variable was manipulated: the source's triad was either confirmatory (e.g., 8–10–12), or disconfirmatory (e.g., 12–10–8) with respect to the source's hypothesis. The dependent variables comprised the hypothesis that participants proposed and the strategy they used (i.e., the triads they produced, confirmatory or disconfirmatory). Concerning the hypothesis, the results showed that more participants used the source's hypothesis in the majority conditions, and that more participants formulated new hypotheses when the minority used a confirmatory strategy. For the second dependent variable, although the participants' main strategy in all conditions was confirmation, more participants used disconfirmation when this strategy was used in the initial triad proposed by the source, which corroborates the results of Gorman and Gorman (1984). More importantly, when the source used confirmation for testing the hypothesis, the participants' strategy depended on whether the source was the majority or the minority. Faced with the minority, participants used more disconfirmation, regardless of whether or not the minority itself used disconfirmation. However, faced with the majority, participants merely conformed to the majority's strategy by simply reproducing it. Indeed, when the majority used disconfirmation, participants displayed disconfirmation, whereas when the majority used confirmation, the participants almost never used disconfirmation but confirmation. This suggests that when faced with the majority, the disconfirmation exhibited by the participants resembles mere imitation more than true disconfirmation.

In sum, a minority is expected to elicit disconfirmation, while a majority is expected to elicit a reproduction of its strategy. In the next step, we tested whether a majority source induces more confirmation because it is associated with a representation of unity, and whether a minority source elicits alternative hypotheses and disconfirmation because it activates a context of plurality (Butera, Mugny, Legrenzi, & Pérez, 1996). Two independent variables were manipulated. The first one was the nature of the source, either a majority or a minority. The second variable concerned the representation of the task. Participants were told either that the task allowed one single correct answer (the unity condition) or that several answers were possible (the plurality condition). The results showed that the nature of the source induced different dynamics, as did the representation of the task. Moreover, the interaction effect showed that participants given the majority view most strongly accepted the source's hypothesis and used confirmation when the task was represented as having a single solution. Conversely, participants given a minority view most strongly considered alternative hypotheses (i.e., different from those of the source) and used disconfirmation when the task was represented as allowing several solutions.

Another important question is whether numerical support is an important source feature in aptitude tasks. This question arises from the observation that, often, we simply associate correctness with the majority nature of the source, although these two dimensions do not necessarily coincide (see Nemeth & Wachtler, 1983). An experiment employing the same paradigm (Butera & Mugny, 1992) independently manipulated the numerical support (majority vs. minority) and its correctness (a bogus feedback stated that the source's answer was either correct or incorrect). To simplify, we report here only the results concerning the imitation of the source's hypothesis. These results showed that when both numerical support and correctness were manipulated together, only correctness produced an effect: participants imitated the source's hypothesis more when it was declared correct than when it was declared incorrect, regardless of numerical support (see Aronson & Golden, 1962, for similar results with credible in-group and out-group sources). As a result, for manifest influence, the majority (minority) nature of the source is not essential. When information on the correctness of the source is directly available on aptitude tasks, numerical support does not produce any supplementary effect. Thus, it could be proposed that numerical support is an element that enables inferences on the competence of the source (on a 'consensus implies correctness' basis; Moscovici & Personnaz, 1991) when no direct information on correctness or competence level is available.

Results like this last one have an essential, although non-obvious, implication. If in objective non-ambiguous tasks the majority or minority status of the source is essential to determine the type of influence, it is no longer the most relevant dimension in the case of aptitude tasks (Mugny & Butera, 1995). According to CET, because in aptitude tasks confrontation with a source engages the individual's skills, it is competence that constitutes the fundamental dimension of influence processes. However, in spite of the general consensus about the importance of competence in majority versus minority influence (cf. Chaiken & Stangor, 1987; De Vries & De Dreu, 2001; De Vries et al., 1996; Levine & Russo, 1987; Moscovici, 1980; Nemeth, 1986), it was understood that competence was a necessary but not sufficient dimension to account for majority or minority influence. Moscovici (1980) himself mentioned early on that competence or credibility would account for majority or minority influence. In an elegant analogy, the reasoning he applied to sources of high versus low credibility for explaining majority versus minority influence was *mutatis mutandis*. In aptitude tasks, this position would need to be reversed. The numerous studies on majority and minority sources help us understand the influence mechanisms related to the competence of the source, which constitute the central dimension for influence in this type of task. To return to Moscovici's analogy, *mutatis mutandis*, it would be more judicious from now on to contemplate competent and incompetent sources, and no longer majority versus minority sources, when discussing influence in relation to aptitude tasks.

To support this idea, the first step was to demonstrate that it was possible to replicate the results obtained with majorities and minorities when using high and low competence sources. Thus, in the inductive reasoning paradigm (see above), a high-competence source should lead to an imitation of the source's hypothesis and to a confirmatory testing strategy, whereas a low-competence source should induce more alternative hypotheses and lead to a disconfirmatory strategy. Butera, Mugny, and Tomei (2000, Experiment 1; see Butera & Mugny, 2001, for an account in English) indeed showed that under uncertainty, high competence increased imitation of the source's hypothesis, compared to a no-source control condition, whereas low competence decreased imitation. Conversely, the high-competence source induced more confirmation than the control condition, while the low-competence source induced more disconfirmation (see also Butera, Caverni, & Rossi, 2005).

Beyond the similarity of influence patterns between the majority–minority studies and the high–low competence ones, it is crucial at this point to address the role of competence in influence dynamics, i.e., how competence gives meaning to the divergence between the source and target in aptitude tasks. First of all, as widely recognized in the persuasion literature (e.g., McGuire, 1985), the characteristics of the targets also play an important role in determining influence processes. When confronted with a majority, targets can automatically infer that they are holding a minority position. Therefore, if the majority is supposed to be correct (and competent), targets will probably perceive themselves as being incorrect (and incompetent). However, the opposite is not true for minority sources. Indeed, being opposed to a probably incorrect minority maintains the targets in a state of uncertainty, since the minority's incorrectness does not guarantee that one's own answer is right. It just makes salient that one's own answer could also be wrong. In other words, whatever the source (majority or minority), influence ensues from the fact that targets are implicitly of low competence. Consequently, we can hypothesize that competent and incompetent sources should produce similar influence patterns to the majority and minority source, but only when the targets' competence is low, and not when the targets believe that they are highly competent.

Maggi, Butera, and Mugny's (1996) study on the representation of the centimetre supported the validity of this prediction. The supposed competence of both the source and the targets was manipulated: the source and the targets were declared to be of high versus low competence with regards to their alleged result obtained after completing a bogus task. Manifest influence was measured through length estimates of lines, which the source consistently underestimated. Several lines of different sizes were shown to the participants. Their task was to estimate their length. For each line, they were provided the source's answer, which systematically underestimated the lines' actual lengths. Latent influence was measured after the influence phase. Participants were asked to draw a line of 8 centimetres. The reasoning behind this latent measure was that if the source underestimated a line's length in the influence phase, it implies that the source had a longer representation of the centimetre (cf. Pérez, Dasi, & Lucas, 1997): If one estimates, for example, that there are only 10 centimetres in a line with an actual length of 20 centimetres, it means that one's subjective evaluation of the centimetre is two times longer than it should be. Thus, if latent influence occurs (if participants integrate the source's representation of the centimetre), participants should draw longer lines (see Mugny, 1984, for similar reasoning). Results showed that the high-competence source generated influence at a manifest level but not at a latent level, and the low-competence source obtained the opposite pattern of influence. However, this was true only for participants declared to be of low competence. For the participants declared high in competence, there was no influence, neither manifest, nor latent.

An easy but risky conclusion that one could be tempted to draw would be that influence situations in which low-competence targets are confronted with high-competence sources will lead to manifest influence at best, and that only low-competence sources obtain latent influence. Recent developments of CET allow us to make less Manichean predictions. In social influence situations concerning aptitude tasks, conflict elaboration is determined not only by the competence (high or low) attributed both to the source and to the target, but also by the threat (high or low) introduced by the social comparison of competencies between the source and the target (Mugny, Butera, & Falomir, 2001; Mugny, Butera, Quiamzade, Dragulescu, & Tomei, 2003; Quiamzade, Falomir, Mugny, & Butera, 1999; Quiamzade & Mugny, 2001). Thus, influence processes are not determined solely by the relative competence of source and target, but also by a social comparison process that may (or may not) threaten the target's competence and self-esteem. A general idea is that when there is a threat to the target, the resolution of the conflict is mainly relational and that influence, if any, is situated at a manifest level at best. When the target feels no threat, the resolution of the conflict proceeds in a more socio-cognitive way, which allows influence to be expressed at both levels, i.e., at a manifest level and/or at a deeper one. Below we will limit our presentation to the cases in which the target is of low competence.[4]

Let us start with the case of a low-competence target confronted with a high-competence source (see Quiamzade & Mugny, 2004, for more details). The dynamic of *informational constraint* occurs when the competence of the source is perceived as a threat by the low-competence targets. A salient differential in competence that is more favourable to the source than the target is, by default, ego deflating and costly to self-appraisal. This difference threatens the targets' self-esteem (Morse & Gergen, 1970), because it lowers their relative competence. This would focus the influence relationship on identity rather than on task resolution, which may prevent any influence at a deep level. Imitation appears as an easy solution to re-establish lost self-esteem: By reducing the perceived difference between the self and superior others, imitation reduces the threat to self-esteem. From this point onwards, no further elaboration of the task is necessary, and targets would disengage from the task.

*Informational dependence* can occur when social comparison is not threatening. In this case, the high competence of the source is perceived as a means to learn more about the task, and not as a challenge to self-esteem (cf. Collins, 1996; Taylor & Lobel, 1989; Tesser, 1988). Moreover, comparison with the high-competence source allows people to determine their level of competence (Goethals & Darley, 1977) and their ability to solve the task (Wheeler, Martin, & Suls, 1997). Accordingly, imitation of the source is not just a means of restoring self-esteem but provides a real possibility of performing the task more effectively. Imitation is the result of a socio-cognitive resolution of the conflict rather than a relational one. So, imitation is completed by genuine information processing that allows transfer and generalization of learned information to the targets' response systems. This learning relates to the acquisition of knowledge or the improvement of cognitive skills for processing the task.

A research paradigm tested these hypotheses (cf. Mugny, Quiamzade, & Tafani, 2001; Tafani, Falomir, & Mugny, 2000). In a series of experiments, participants were confronted with a bogus study carried out by a bogus researcher, challenging the widespread belief that group satisfaction in friendship groups is negatively linked to the presence of a leader in the group. In one experiment (Mugny, Tafani, Falomir, & Layat, 2000), participants were confronted with a low- versus high-competence source, and had to compare themselves with the source in a threatening versus non-threatening social comparison. Indeed, half of the participants had to estimate self-competence and the source's competence in a negatively interdependent manner, i.e., by distributing 100 competence points between the source and themselves (i.e., what is given to the source is lost for the participant). For the other half of the participants, the comparison was independent, i.e., they could distribute up to 100 competence points for themselves and up to 100 separate points for the source. Two measures were used. Manifest influence was measured through direct attitude towards the researcher's study. Deep influence was collected by asking the participants to what extent a group of friends with a leader was an ideal group of friends (cf. Moliner, 1988; Quiamzade, 2003). Results showed, first, that participants allocated more competence points to the high-competence source regardless of the modality of social comparison. Second, participants expressed more manifest influence when the source was of high competence than when the source was of low competence. However, the high-competence source obtained more deep change when the social comparison was independent and thus not threatening (the same result was obtained in a study where social comparison was not made salient; Tafani, Mugny, & Bellon, 1999) than when it was negatively interdependent and thus threatening (see Mugny, Tafani, Butera, & Pigière, 1998, for a similar dynamic). Thus, whether or not a source has a deep impact on a low-competence target depends not only on the source's competence, but also on the threat introduced by the social comparison context in which the influence relationship occurs (see Quiamzade, Tomei, & Butera, 2000, for similar results in an anagram task).

When both source and target have low levels of competence, the conflict generated is a *conflict of incompetence* (see Quiamzade, Mugny, & Darnon, 2002). Given the source's low competence, people assume that the source's answers are incorrect. For this reason, it is not acceptable for targets to imitate the source. As a first step, targets seek to distance themselves from the source. But an incorrect answer from the source does not guarantee the correctness of the targets' own answers. It is not because the source is wrong that targets are right. On the contrary, the low competence of targets (aptitude tasks are generally difficult) imply that their answer may also be wrong. This places targets in a situation of high uncertainty. As the main objective in aptitude tasks is to affirm self-competence through the discovery of correct solutions, targets are motivated by the fear of invalidation to examine and process the task more deeply. However, this specific conflict elaboration appears because sources of low competence are, most of the time, non-threatening for the targets' competence. Targets are not focused on identity aspects of the relationship and their behaviour is not motivated by self-enhancement (Brown, 1986).

Indeed, if social comparison is rendered threatening (e.g., by introducing some sort of competition), self-enhancement becomes the main motivation, to the detriment of task processing. This idea was tested by Butera and Mugny (1995). Participants were confronted with a low-competence source, either in a negatively interdependent or in an independent modality of social comparison, and had to solve a task similar to the 2–4–6 problem (see above). Two dependent variables were measured: the confirmation or disconfirmation strategy used in the task and the estimations of competencies (distribution of competence points) for determining social comparison. As in Butera et al.'s study (2000), results revealed that, when social comparison was non-threatening (independent), a low-competence source produced high rates of disconfirmatory hypothesis testing. Thus, the conflict of incompetence did lead participants to a deeper processing of the task. However, when the source's competence was evaluated within a competitive, threatening relationship (negative interdependence), all benefits were lost, and participants turned to an active *downward comparison* (Wills, 1981, 1991), i.e., a form of conflict elaboration that aims more at self-enhancement than at self-improvement. Indeed, participants evaluated their competence as being much higher than the source's through the distribution of competence points, but they mainly used confirmatory testing strategies in that situation.

In sum, when explaining social influence dynamics in aptitude tasks, it is important to take into account the source's and the target's competence, but also the threat introduced by the social comparison of competences. A competent source (as a majority) may be problematic for individuals of low competence, since an apparent unity of judgements calls for conformity and for confirmation as a sort of self-protection: a difference in judgements implies self-incompetence, whereas confirmation and mere imitation asserts self-competence. This pattern of results would be obtained because most of the time, the source's high competence is perceived as a threat. This is an important contribution, as it allows us to conceive that competent sources (as majorities) are not condemned to obtain only manifest influence, and that, by reducing the threat, competent sources (as majorities) can obtain influence at a deeper level.[5] Conversely, an incompetent source (as a minority) allows disconfirmation, i.e., decentring as a way to deeply process other elements of the task, because these sources are generally viewed as non-threatening. However, it was shown that as soon as threat is introduced in the social comparison with a low-competence source, the benefits in terms of deep processing are lost. This contribution also provides a theoretical framework for predicting the various complex influence patterns observed in the literature.

# Conclusions

Moscovici's conversion theory and Nemeth's convergent–divergent thinking theory have contributed to the systematic study of majority and minority influence and have provided theoretical foundations for many domains of research. As is often the case in classical theories, the effects observed in the hundreds of subsequent studies carried out to test these theories are so diverse that, today, neither of the two theories adequately accounts for the totality of research findings. Besides, it would be an overgeneralization to apply these two theories to influence dynamics occurring in opinion tasks. Both theories were developed with tasks lacking the social component typical of opinion tasks that involve topics of social debate, such as xenophobia, gay rights, abortion or contraception (see Maass & Volpato, 1994).

Other theories seem more relevant to predict influence dynamics in opinion tasks, as they have been directly developed on the basis of studies using opinion tasks, including the self-categorization approach (Turner, 1991) and dissociation theory (Falomir, Mugny, & Pérez, 2000; Pérez & Mugny, 1990, 1998; see also Quiamzade, Pérez, Mugny, & Alonso, 2003). However, their consideration is beyond the scope of the present chapter.

On the one hand, Moscovici's theory predicts a conversion effect that consists of the adoption of the minority's proposals at a latent level. It does not make predictions regarding a specific form of thinking, therefore implying the integration of new parameters (i.e., not evoked by the minority or by the majority). Moreover, the effect of majority sources is confined to the production of compliance, and Moscovici's theory does not account for the possibility of latent majority effects. On the other hand, the mechanisms proposed by Nemeth do not allow predictions for the way in which minority ideas are integrated at a latent level. In addition, this theory does not envisage the possibility that a majority can achieve latent influence. In the present chapter we have tried to show how each theory is highly relevant to explain influence dynamics in the tasks that have been used to provide them support, namely objective non-ambiguous tasks for Moscovici's theory and aptitude tasks for Nemeth's theory. However, even if both theories are considered within the framework of the tasks they involve, it appears that the diversity of the effects observed in the literature is greater than the predictive power of each theory.

In sum, the present chapter has argued that straightforward theories are elegant and stimulating, but that they do not account for the complexity of social influence dynamics. (Indeed, this conclusion applies to most conceptualizations of majority/minority influence processes, including those presented in this volume). We have proposed that this complexity is best explained by studying conflict elaboration in the specific tasks according to their subjective properties. Conflict elaboration is a heuristic concept because it depends on the representation of the task, i.e., the specific expectations that targets develop regarding the possible definitions of a given object. The consequence is that cognitive processing is not limited to the message content, but extends to the overall meaning of divergence.

## Notes

1  We do not describe the theory here, but use some of its principles for our purpose. Interested readers will find a brief English-language account of CET in Mugny, Butera, Sanchez-Mazas, & Pérez, 1995, or in Pérez & Mugny, 1996.
2  We do not assert that all of Moscovici's and Nemeth's experiments are based on such tasks, however these tasks constitute the core paradigm used by Moscovici to validate conversion and most of Nemeth's tasks. Indeed, some of the experiments they have conducted do not fit these tasks categories, but they are not often cited in the literature and thus are not considered the most determinant for testing their theories.
3  Results obtained within this specific paradigm are subject to controversy (Martin, 1995, 1998; cf. Martin & Hewstone, 2001b) when they are not considered as magical, or even mystical (cf. Wood et al., 1994).
4  Other studies have considered the case in which the targets are high in competence, and, in particular, when they are confronted with the divergent judgement of a source that is of equal (high) competence. This situation induces dynamics of conflict of competence (Butera & Mugny, 2001; Quiamzade, 2007; Quiamzade & Mugny, 2009; Selimbegovic, Quiamzade, Chatard, Mugny, & Fluri, 2007).
5  This idea has recently been extended to propose that a highly competent source's influence is facilitated whenever targets are faced with a correspondence between the representation or beliefs of the targets and the type of relationship they have with the source (Mugny, Chatard, & Quiamzade, 2006; Mugny, Quiamzade, Falomir, & Tafani, 2006; Mugny, Quiamzade, Pigière, Dragulescu, & Buchs, 2002; Mugny, Quiamzade, & Trandafir, 2006; Quiamzade, Mugny, & Buchs, 2005; Quiamzade, Mugny, Dragulescu, & Buchs, 2003; see Quiamzade et al., 2004, for a description of the core of the theory).

## References

Allen, V. L., & Levine, J. M. (1968). Social support, dissent and conformity. *Sociometry, 31*, 138–149.

Alvaro, E. M., & Crano, W. D. (1997). Indirect minority influence: Evidence for leniency in source evaluation and counterargumentation. *Journal of Personality and Social Psychology, 72*, 949–964.

Aronson, E., & Golden, B. W. (1962). The effect of relevant and irrelevant aspects of communicator credibility on opinion change. *Journal of Personality, 30*, 135–146.

Asch, S. E. (1956). Studies on independence and conformity: A minority of one against an unanimous majority. *Psychological Monographs, 70* (No. 416).

Baker, S. M., & Petty, R. E. (1994). Majority and minority influence: Source–position imbalance as a determinant of message scrutiny. *Journal of Personality and Social Psychology, 67*, 5–19.

Baron, R. S., & Bellman, S. B. (2007). No guts, no glory: Courage, harassment and minority influence. *European Journal of Social Psychology, 37*, 101–124.

Binet, A. (1900). Attention et adaptation [Attention and adaptation]. *L'Année Psychologique, 6*, 248–404.

Bohner, G., Erb, H. P., Reinhard, M. A., & Frank, E. (1996). Distinctiveness across topics in minority and majority influence: An attributional analysis and preliminary data. *British Journal of Social Psychology, 35,* 27–46.

Bohner, G., Frank, E., & Erb, H. P. (1998). Heuristic processing of distinctiveness information in minority and majority influence. *European Journal of Social Psychology, 28,* 855–860.

Bond, M. H., & Smith, P. B. (1996). Culture and conformity: A meta-analysis of the Asch line judgment task. *Psychological Bulletin, 119,* 111–137.

Brandstätter, V., Ellemers, N., Gaviria, E., Giosue, F., Huguet, P., Kroon, M., et al. (1991). Indirect majority and minority influence: An exploratory study. *European Journal of Social Psychology, 21,* 199–211.

Brown, J. D. (1986). Evaluations of self and others: Self-enhancement biases in social judgment. *Social Cognition, 4,* 353–376.

Brown, R. (1965). *Social psychology.* New York, London: The Free Press, Collier–Macmillan.

Butera, F., & Buchs, C. (2005). Reasoning together: From focusing to decentring. In V. Girotto & P. N. Johnson-Laird (Eds.), *The shape of reason* (pp. 193–203). Hove, UK: Psychology Press.

Butera, F., Caverni, J. P., & Rossi, S. (2005). Interaction with a high- versus low-competence influence source in inductive reasoning. *The Journal of Social Psychology, 145,* 173–190.

Butera, F., Huguet, P., Mugny, G., & Pérez, J. A. (1994). Socio-epistemic conflict and constructivism. *Swiss Journal of Psychology, 53,* 229–239.

Butera, F., Legrenzi, P., & Mugny, G. (1993). De l'imitation à la validation: études sur le raisonnement [From imitation to validation: Studies on reasoning]. In J. A. Pérez & G. Mugny (Eds.), *La théorie de l'élaboration du conflit* (pp. 99–120). Neuchâtel, Switzerland: Delachaux et Niestlé.

Butera, F., & Mugny, G. (1992). Influence minoritaire et falsification. A propos de "quelques réflexions psycho-sociologiques sur une controverse" de B. Matalon [Minority influence and falsification. A rejoinder to B. Matalon on "some psycho-sociological conjectures on a controversy"]. *Revue Internationale de Psychologie Sociale, 5,* 115–132.

Butera, F., & Mugny, G. (1995). Conflict between incompetences and influence of a low-expertise source in hypothesis testing. *European Journal of Social Psychology, 25,* 457–462.

Butera, F., & Mugny, G. (2001). Conflict and social influences in hypothesis testing. In C. K. W. De Dreu & N. K. De Vries (Eds.), *Group consensus and minority influence implications for innovation.* Oxford, UK: Blackwell.

Butera, F., Mugny, G., Legrenzi, P., & Pérez, J. A. (1996). Majority and minority influence, task representation, and inductive reasoning. *British Journal of Social Psychology, 35,* 123–136.

Butera, F., Mugny, G., & Tomei, A. (2000). Incertitude et enjeux identitaires dans l'influence sociale [Uncertainty and identity in social influence]. In J. L. Beauvois, R. V. Joule, & J. M. Monteil (Eds.), *Perspectives cognitives et conduites sociale* (Vol. 7, pp. 205–229). Rennes, France: Presses Universitaires de Rennes.

Chaiken, S. (1987). The heuristic model of persuasion. In M. P. Zanna, J. M. Olson, & C. P. Herman (Eds.), *Social influence: The Ontario symposium* (Vol. 5, pp. 3–39). Hillsdale, NJ: Lawrence Erlbaum Associates, Inc.

Chaiken, S., & Stangor, C. (1987). Attitudes and attitude change. *Annual Review of Psychology, 38,* 575–630.

Clark, R. D., III, & Maass, A. (1988). Social categorization in minority influence: The case of homosexuality. *European Journal of Social Psychology, 18,* 347–364.

Collins, R. L. (1996). For better or worse: The impact of upward social comparison on self-evaluation. *Psychological Bulletin, 1,* 51–69.

Crano, W. D. (2000). Social influence: Effects of leniency on majority- and minority-induced focal and indirect attitude change. *Revue Internationale de Psychologie Sociale, 13,* 89–121.

Crano, W. D., & Alvaro, E. M. (1998). Indirect minority influence: The leniency contract revisited. *Group Processes and Intergroup Relations, 1,* 99–115.

Crano, W. D., & Chen, X. (1998). The leniency contract and persistence of majority and minority influence. *Journal of Personality and Social Psychology, 74,* 1437–1450.

De Dreu, C. K. W., & De Vries, N. K. (Eds.). (2001). *Group consensus and minority influence: Implications for innovation.* Oxford, UK: Blackwell.

De Vries, N. K., & De Dreu, C. K. W. (2001). Group consensus and minority influence: Introduction and overview. In C. K. W. De Dreu & N. K. De Vries (Eds.), *Group consensus and minority influence: Implications for innovation* (pp. 1–14). Oxford, UK: Blackwell.

De Vries, N. K., De Dreu, C. K. W., Gordijn, E., & Schuurman, M. (1996). Majority and minority influence: A dual role interpretation. In W. Stroebe & M. Hewstone (Eds.), *European review of social psychology* (Vol. 7, pp. 145–172). Chichester, UK: Wiley.

Deutsch, M. (1973). *The resolution of conflict. Constructive and destructive processes.* New Haven, CT: Yale University Press.

Deutsch, M., & Gerard, H. B. (1955). A study of normative and informational social influence upon individual judgment. *Journal of Abnormal and Social Psychology, 51,* 629–636.

Doise, W. (1978). Images, représentations, idéologies, et expérimentations psychosociologique [Images, representations, ideologies and psycho-sociological experiments]. *Social Science Information, 17,* 41–69.

Doms, M., & Van Avermaet, E. (1980). Majority influence, minority influence and conversion behaviour: A replication. *Journal of Experimental Social Psychology, 16,* 283–292.

Eagly, A. H., & Chaiken, S. (1993). *The psychology of attitudes.* Fort Worth, TX: Harcourt Brace College Publishers.

Erb, H. P., Bohner, G., Rank, S., & Einwiller, S. (2002). Processing minority and majority communications: The role of conflict with prior attitudes. *Personality and Social Psychology Bulletin, 28*(9), 1172–1182.

Erb, H. P., Bohner, G., Schmälzle, K., & Rank, S. (1998). Beyond conflict and discrepancy: Cognitive bias in minority and majority influence. *Personality and Social Psychology Bulletin, 24,* 620–633.

Falomir, J. M., Mugny, G., & Pérez, J. A. (1996). Le paradoxe du déni [The paradox of denial]. In J. C. Deschamps & J. L. Beauvois (Eds.), *La psychologie sociale* (Vol. 2, pp 91–97). Grenoble, France: Presses Universitaires de Grenoble.

Falomir, J. M., Mugny, G., & Pérez, J. A. (2000). Social influence and identity conflict. In D. Terry & M. Hogg (Eds.), *Attitudes, behavior, and social context: The role of norms and group membership* (pp. 245–264). Mahwah, NJ: Lawrence Erlbaum Associates, Inc.

Festinger, L. (1950). Informal social communication. *Psychological Review, 57*, 271–282.

Festinger, L. (1954). A theory of social comparison processes. *Human Relations, 7*, 117–140.

Goethals, G. R., & Darley, J. M. (1977). Social comparison theory: An attributional approach. In J. M. Suls & R. L. Miller (Eds.), *Social comparison processes: Theoretical and empirical perspectives* (pp. 259–278). New York: Hemisphere.

Gorenflo, D. W., & Crano, W. D. (1989). Judgmental subjectivity/objectivity and locus of choice in social comparison. *Journal of Personality and Social Psychology, 57*, 605–614.

Gorman, M. E., & Carlson, B. (1989). Can experiments be used to study science? *Social Epistemology, 3*, 89–106.

Gorman, M. E., & Gorman, M. E. (1984). A comparison of disconfirmatory, confirmatory and control strategies on Wason's 2–4–6 task. *Quarterly Journal of Experimental Psychology: Human Experimental Psychology, 36A*(4), 629–648.

Kerr, N. L. (2002). When is a minority a minority? Active versus passive minority advocacy and social influence. *European Journal of Social Psychology, 32*(4), 471–483.

Kruglanski, A., & Mackie, D. M. (1990). *Majority and minority influence: A judgmental process analysis.* In W. Stroebe & M. Hewstone (Eds.), *European review of social psychology* (Vol. 1, pp. 229–261). Chichester, UK: Wiley.

Legrenzi, P. (1983). Il ragionamento [Reasoning]. *Giornale Italiano di Psicologia, 10*, 251–267.

Legrenzi, P., Butera, F., Mugny, G., & Pérez, J. A. (1991). Majority and minority influence in inductive reasoning: A preliminary study. *European Journal of Social Psychology, 21*, 359–363.

Levine, J. M., & Russo, E. M. (1987). Majority and minority influence. In C. Hendrick (Ed.), *Group processes* (pp. 13–54). Newbury Park, CA: Sage.

Maass, A., & Clark, R. D., III (1983). Internalization versus compliance: Differential processes underlying minority influence and conformity. *European Journal of Social Psychology, 13*, 45–55.

Maass, A., & Clark, R. D., III (1984). The hidden impact of minorities: Fourteen years of minority influence research. *Psychological Bulletin, 95*, 428–450.

Maass, A., Clark, R. D., III, & Haberkorn, G. (1982). The effect of differential ascribed category membership and norms on minority influence. *European Journal of Social Psychology, 12*, 89–104.

Maass, A., & Volpato, C. (1994). Theoretical perspectives on minority influence: Conversion versus divergence? In S. Moscovici, A. Mucchi-Faina, & A. Maass (Eds.), *Minority influence* (pp. 135–147). Chicago: Nelson-Hall.

Maass, A., & Volpato, C. (1996). Social influence and the verifiability of the issue under discussion: Attitudinal versus objective items. *British Journal of Social Psychology, 35*, 15–26.

Mackie, D. M. (1987). Systematic and nonsystematic processing of majority and minority persuasive communications. *Journal of Personality and Social Psychology, 53*, 41–52.

Maggi, J., Butera, F., & Mugny, G. (1996). The conflict of incompetences: Direct and indirect influences on the representation of the centimeter. *International Review of Social Psychology, 9*, 91–105.

Martin, R. (1995). Majority and minority influence using the afterimage paradigm:

A replication with an unambiguous blue slide. *European Journal of Social Psychology, 25,* 373–381.

Martin, R. (1998). Majority and minority influence using the afterimage paradigm: A series of attempted replications. *Journal of Experimental Social Psychology, 34,* 1–26.

Martin, R., Gardikiotis, A., & Hewstone, M. (2002). Levels of consensus and majority and minority influence. *European Journal of Social Psychology, 32,* 645–665.

Martin, B., & Hewstone, M. (2001a). Determinants and consequences of cognitive processes in majority and minority influence. In J. P. Forgas & K. D. Williams (Eds.), *Social influence: Direct and indirect processes* (pp. 315–330). Philadelphia: Psychology Press.

Martin, R., & Hewstone, M. (2001b). Afterthought on afterimages: A review of the afterimage paradigm in majority and minority influence research. In C. K. W. De Dreu & N. K. De Vries (Eds.), *Group consensus and minority influence: Implications for innovation* (pp. 15–39). Oxford, UK: Blackwell.

Martin, R., & Hewstone, M. (2003). Majority versus minority influence: When, not whether, source status instigates heuristic or systematic processing. *European Journal of Social Psychology, 33,* 313–330.

Martin, R., Hewstone, M., & Martin, P. Y. (2003). Resistance to persuasive messages as a function of majority and minority source status. *Journal of Experimental Social Psychology, 39,* 585–593.

Mayseless, O., & Kruglanski, A. W. (1987). What makes you so sure? Effects of epistemic motivations on judgmental confidence. *Organizational Behaviour and Human Decision Processes, 39,* 162–183.

McGuire, W. J. (1985). Attitudes and attitude change. In G. Lindzey & E. Aronson (Eds.), *The handbook of social psychology* (Vol. II, pp. 233–346). New York: Lawrence Erlbaum Associates, Inc.

Mettee, D. R., & Smith, G. (1977). Social comparison and interpersonal attraction: The case for dissimilarity. In J. M. Suls & R. L. Miller (Eds.), *Social comparison processes: Theoretical and empirical perspectives* (pp. 69–101). New York: Hemisphere.

Moliner, P. (1988). Validation expérimentale de l'hypothèse du noyau central des représentations sociales. *Bulletin de Psychologie, 42,* 759–762.

Morse, S., & Gergen, K. J. (1970). Social comparison, self-consistency, and the concept of self. *Journal of Personality and Social Psychology, 16,* 148–156.

Moscovici, S. (1976). *Social influence and social change.* London: Academic Press.

Moscovici, S. (1980). Toward a theory of conversion behavior. In L. Berkowitz (Ed.), *Advances in experimental social psychology* (Vol. 13, pp. 209–239). New York: Academic Press.

Moscovici, S. (1985a). Social influence and conformity. In G. Lindzey & E. Aronson (Eds.), *The handbook of social psychology* (Vol. II, pp. 347–412). New York: Lawrence Erlbaum Associates, Inc.

Moscovici, S. (1985b). Préface de l'ouvrage de G. Paicheler [Preface to G. Paicheler's book]. *Psychologie des influences sociales.* Neuchâtel, Switzerland: Delachaux et Niestlé.

Moscovici, S., & Faucheux, C. (1972). Social influence, conformity bias and the study of active minorities. In L. Berkowitz (Ed.), *Advances in social psychology* (Vol. 6, pp. 150–202). New York: Academic Press.

Moscovici, S., & Lage, E. (1976). Studies in social influence III: Majority versus minority influence in a group. *European Journal of Social Psychology, 6,* 149–174.

Moscovici, S., & Lage, E. (1978). Studies in social influence IV: Minority influence in a context of original judgments. *European Journal of Social Psychology, 8,* 349–365.

Moscovici, S., Lage, E., & Naffrechoux, M. (1969). Influence of a consistent minority on the responses of a majority in a color perception task. *Sociometry, 32,* 365–380.

Moscovici, S., Mucchi-Faina, A., & Maass, A. (Eds.). (1994). *Minority influence.* Chicago: Nelson-Hall.

Moscovici, S., Mugny, G., & Pérez, J. A. (1984–1985). Les effets pervers du déni (par la majorité) des opinions d'une minorité [Paradoxical effects of denial of minority opinions (by the majority)]. *Bulletin de Psychologie, 38,* 365–380.

Moscovici, S., Mugny, G., & Van Avermaet, E. (Eds.). (1985). *Perspectives on minority influence.* Cambridge, UK: Cambridge University Press. Paris: Editions de la Maison des Sciences de l'Homme.

Moscovici, S., & Personnaz, B. (1980). Studies in social influence V. Minority influence and conversion behaviour in a perceptual task. *Journal of Experimental Social Psychology, 16,* 270–282.

Moscovici, S., & Personnaz, B. (1991). Studies in social influence VI: Is Lenin orange or red? Imagery and social influence. *European Journal of Social Psychology, 21,* 101–118.

Moskowitz, G. B. (1996). The mediational effects of attributions and information processing in minority social influence. *British Journal of Social Psychology, 35,* 47–66.

Moskowitz, G. B., & Chaiken, S. (2001). Mediators of minority social influence: Cognitive processing mechanisms revealed through a persuasion paradigm. In C. K. W. De Dreu & N. K. De Vries (Eds.), *Group consensus and minority influence: Implications for innovation* (pp. 60–90). Oxford, UK: Blackwell.

Mucchi-Faina, A. (2000). Minority influence and ambivalence. *Revue Internationale de Psychologie Sociale, 13*(3), 65–87.

Mucchi-Faina, A., & Cicoletti, G. (2006). Divergence vs. ambivalence: Effects of personal relevance on minority influence. *European Journal of Social Psychology, 36,* 91–104.

Mucchi-Faina, A., Maass, A., & Volpato, C. (1991). Social influence: The role of originality. *European Journal of Social Psychology, 21*(3), 183–197.

Mugny, G. (1982). *The power of minorities.* London: Academic Press.

Mugny, G. (1984). Compliance, conversion and the Asch paradigm. *European Journal of Social Psychology, 14,* 353–368.

Mugny, G., & Butera, F. (1995). Influence majoritaire et minoritaire: vers une intégration [Majority and minority influence: Toward an integration]. *Psychologie Française, 40,* 339–346.

Mugny, G., Butera, F., & Falomir, J. M. (2001). Social influence and threat in social comparison between self and source's competence: Relational factors affecting the transmission of knowledge. In F. Butera & G. Mugny (Eds.), *Social influence in social reality: Promoting individual and social change* (pp. 225–247). Seattle, WA: Hogrefe & Huber.

Mugny, G., Butera, F., Quiamzade, A., Dragulescu, A., & Tomei, A. (2003). Comparaisons sociales des compétences et influence sociale [Social comparison of competences and social influence]. *L'Année Psychologique, 103,* 469–496.

Mugny, G., Butera, F., Sanchez-Mazas, M., & Pérez, J. A. (1995). Judgements in conflict: The conflict elaboration theory of social influence. In B. Boothe, R. Hirsig, A. Helminger, B. Meier, & R. Volkart (Eds.), *Perception–Evaluation– Interpretation. Swiss monographs in psychology* (Vol. 3, pp.160–168). Bern, Switzerland: Huber.

Mugny, G., Chatard, A., & Quiamzade, A. (2006). The social transmission of knowledge at the university: Teaching style and epistemic dependence. *European Journal of Psychology of Education, 21,* 413–427.

Mugny, G., & Papastamou, S. (1980). When rigidity does not fail: Individualization and psychologization as resistance to the diffusion of minority innovations. *European Journal of Social Psychology, 10,* 43–61.

Mugny, G., Quiamzade, A., Falomir, J. M., & Tafani, E. (2006). Diagnosticité de la tâche dans l'évaluation des compétences et dépendance informationnelle [Task diagnosticity in competence evaluation and informational dependence]. *Revue Internationale de Psychologie Sociale, 19,* 5–26.

Mugny, G., Quiamzade, A., Pigière, D., Dragulescu, A., & Buchs, C. (2002). Self-competence, interaction style and expert social influence: Toward a corre-spondence hypothesis. *Swiss Journal of Psychology, 61,* 153–166.

Mugny, G., Quiamzade, A., & Tafani, E. (2001). Dynamique représentationnelle et influence sociale [Representational dynamics and social influence]. In P. Moliner (Ed.), *La dynamique des représentations sociales* (pp. 123–161). Grenoble, France: Presses Universitaires de Grenoble.

Mugny, G., Quiamzade, A., & Trandafir, A. (2006). Dépendance informationnelle et styles de comportement dans l'influence sociale [Informational dependence and behavioural styles in social influence]. *Psihologie Sociala, 17,* 43–56.

Mugny, G., Tafani, E., Butera, F., & Pigière, D. (1998). Contrainte et dépendance informationnelles: influence sociale sur la représentation du groupe d'amis idéal [Informational dependence and informational constraint: Social influence of the representation of an ideal group of friends]. *Connexions, 72,* 55–72.

Mugny, G., Tafani, E., Falomir, J. M., & Layat, C. (2000). Source credibility, social comparison and social influence. *International Review of Social Psychology, 13,* 151–175.

Nemeth, C. J. (1986). Differential contributions of majority and minority influence. *Psychological Review, 93,* 1–10.

Nemeth, C. J., & Chiles, C. (1988). Modelling courage: The role of dissent in fostering independence. *European Journal of Social Psychology, 18,* 275–280.

Nemeth, C. J., & Kwan, J. (1985). Originality of word associations as a function of majority vs. minority influence. *Social Psychology Quarterly, 48,* 277–282.

Nemeth, C. J., & Kwan, J. (1987). Minority influence, divergent thinking and detection of correct solutions. *Journal of Applied Social Psychology, 17,* 786–797.

Nemeth, C. J., Mayseless, O., Sherman, J., & Brown, Y. (1990). Exposure to dissent and recall of information. *Journal of Personality and Social Psychology, 58,* 429–437.

Nemeth, C. J., Mosier, K., & Chiles, C. (1992). When convergent thought improves performance: Majority versus minority influence. *Personality and Social Psychology Bulletin, 18,* 139–144.

Nemeth, C. J., & Rogers, J. (1996). Dissent and the search for information. *British Journal of Social Psychology, 35,* 67–76.

Nemeth, C. J., & Wachtler, J. (1983). Creative problem solving as a result of majority vs. minority influence. *European Journal of Social Psychology, 13,* 45–55.

Papastamou, S. (1983). Strategies of minority and majority influences. In W. Doise & S. Moscovici (Eds.), *Current issues in European social psychology* (Vol. 1, pp. 33–83). Cambridge, UK: Cambridge University Press.

Papastamou, S. (1986). Psychologization and processes of minority and majority influence. *European Journal of Social Psychology, 16*, 165–180.

Papastamou, S., & Mugny, G. (1990). Synchronic consistency and psychologization in minority influence. *European Journal of Social Psychology, 20*(2), 85–98.

Papastamou, S., Mugny, G., & Kaiser, S. (1980). Echec à l'influence minoritaire: la psychologisation [The failure of minority influence: Psychologization]. *Recherches de Psychologie Sociale, 2*, 41–56.

Papastamou, S., Mugny, G., & Pérez, J. A. (1991–1992). La valeur stratégique de la psychologisation dans l'influence sociale [Strategic value of psychologization in social influence]. *Bulletin de Psychologie, 45*, 164–172.

Pérez, J. A., Dasi, F., & Lucas, A. (1997). Length overestimation bias as a product of normative pressure arising from anthropocentric vs. geocentric representations of length. *Swiss Journal of Psychology, 56*, 243–255.

Pérez, J. A., Moscovici, S., & Mugny, G. (1991). Effets de résistance à une source experte ou minoritaire, et changement d'attitude [Resistance to an expert versus minority source and attitude change]. *Revue Suisse de Psychologie, 50*, 260–267.

Pérez, J. A., & Mugny, G. (1990). Minority influence: Manifest discrimination and latent influence. In D. Abrams & M. Hogg (Eds.), *Social identity theory: Constructive and critical advances* (pp. 152–168). Hemel Hempstead, UK: Harvester-Wheatsheaf.

Pérez, J. A., & Mugny, G. (1993). *La théorie de l'élaboration du conflit [The conflict elaboration theory]*. Neuchâtel, Switzerland: Delachaux et Niestlé.

Pérez, J. A., & Mugny, G. (1996). The conflict elaboration theory of social influence. In E. Witte & J. Davis (Eds.), *Understanding group behaviour: Small group processes and interpersonal relations* (Vol. 2, pp. 191–210). Hillsdale, NJ: Lawrence Erlbaum Associates, Inc.

Pérez, J. A., & Mugny, G. (1998). Categorization and social influence. In S. Worchel, J. F. Morales, D. Paez, & J. Deschamps (Eds.), *Social identity: International perspectives* (pp. 142–153). Thousand Oaks, CA: Sage.

Pérez, J. A., Mugny, G., Butera, F., Kaiser, C., & Roux, P. (1994). Integrating minority and majority influence: Conversion, consensus and uniformity. In S. Moscovici, A. Mucchi-Faina, & A. Maass (Eds.), *Minority influence* (pp. 185–208). Chicago: Nelson-Hall.

Pérez, J. A., Mugny, G., & Moscovici, S. (1986). Les effets paradoxaux du déni dans l'influence sociale [Paradoxical effects of denial in social influence]. *Cahiers de Psychologie Sociale, 32*, 1–14.

Peterson, R., & Nemeth, C. J. (1996). Focus versus flexibility: Majority and minority influence can both improve performance. *Personality and Social Psychology Bulletin, 22*, 14–23.

Petty, R. E., & Cacioppo, J. T. (1986). *Communication and persuasion*. New York: Springer Verlag.

Popper, K. R. (1955). *The logic of scientific discovery*. New York: Harper & Row.

Quiamzade, A. (2002). *Influence sociale et élaboration du conflit dans les tâches d'aptitudes: le conflit d'incompétences* [Social influence and conflict elaboration in aptitude tasks: The conflict of incompetencies]. Doctoral thesis. University of Geneva & University of Grenoble.

Quiamzade, A. (2003). Mesure de la réorganisation du noyau central d'une représentation sociale: mise en cause de Moliner (1988) [Measuring the reorganization of the central core of a social representation (Moliner, 1988): A potential flaw]. *International Review of Social Psychology, 16*, 25–46.

Quiamzade, A. (2007). Imitation and performance in confrontations between competent peers: The role of the representation of the task. *European Journal of Psychology of Education, 22*, 243–258.

Quiamzade, A., Falomir, J. M., Mugny, G., & Butera, F. (1999). Gestion identitaire vs épistémique des compétences [Identity versus epistemic competence management]. In H. Hansen, B. Sigrist, H. Goorhuis, & H. Landolt (Eds.), *Formation et travail. La fin d'une distinction?* (pp. 267–276). Aarau, Germany: Sauerländer.

Quiamzade, A., & Mugny, G. (2001). Social influence dynamics in aptitude tasks. *Social Psychology of Education, 4*, 311–334.

Quiamzade, A., & Mugny, G. (2004). Les niveaux d'analyse: le cas de l'influence des sources compétentes [Levels of analysis: The case of competent sources]. *Nouvelle Revue de Psychologie Sociale, 3*(1–2), 65–72.

Quiamzade, A., & Mugny, G. (2009). Social influence and threat in confrontations between competent peers. *Journal of Personality and Social Psychology, 97*, 652–666.

Quiamzade, A., Mugny, G., & Buchs, C. (2005). Correspondance entre rapport social et auto-compétence dans la transmission de savoir par une autorité épistémique: une extension [Correspondence between social relationships and self-competence in knowledge transmission by an epistemic source. An extension]. *L'Année Psychologique, 105*, 423–449.

Quiamzade, A., Mugny, G., & Darnon, C. (2009). The coordination of problem solving strategies: When low competence sources exert more influence on task processing than high competence ones. *British Journal of Social Psychology, 48*, 159–182.

Quiamzade, A., Mugny, G., Dragulescu, A., & Buchs, C. (2003). Interaction styles and expert social influence. *European Journal of Psychology of Education, 18*(4), 389–404.

Quiamzade, A., Mugny, G., Falomir, J. M., Invernizzi, F., Buchs, C., & Dragulescu, A. (2004). Correspondance entre style d'influence et significations des positions initiales de la cible: le cas des sources experts [Correspondence between influence style and target's initial positions: The case of expert sources]. In J. L. Beauvois, R. V. Joule, & J. M. Monteil (Eds.), *Perspectives cognitives et conduites sociales* (Vol. 9, pp. 341–363). Rennes, France: Presses Universitaires de Rennes.

Quiamzade, A., Pérez, J. A., Mugny, G., & Alonso, R. (2003). Le patron de la conversion minoritaire, vers une articulation des théories de la dissociation et de l'auto-catégorisation: les multiples catégorisations simultanées [Minority conversion integrates dissociation theory and self-categorization theory: The multiple simultaneous categorizations]. *International Review of Social Psychology, 16*, 87–123.

Quiamzade, A., Tomei, A., & Butera, F. (2000). Informational dependence and informational constraint: Social comparison and social influences in anagram resolution. *International Review of Social Psychology, 13*, 123–150.

Sanchez-Mazas, M., Mugny, G., & Falomir, J. M. (1997). Minority influence and intergroup relations: Social comparison and validation processes in the context of xenophobia in Switzerland. *Swiss Journal of Psychology, 56*(3), 182–192.

Selimbegovic, L., Quiamzade, A., Chatard, A., Mugny, G., & Fluri, D. (2007). Competence Conflict, Counterfactual thinking and Performance. *Swiss Journal of Psychology, 66*, 153–161.

Sorrentino, R. M., King, G., & Leo, G. (1980). The influence of the minority on perception: A note on a possible alternative explanation. *Journal of Experimental Social Psychology, 16*, 293–301.

Tafani, E., Falomir, J. M., & Mugny, G. (2000). Influence sociale et représentations sociales: études expérimentales sur le groupe d'amis idéal [Social influence and social representation: Experimental studies on the ideal group of friends]. In J. L. Beauvois, R. V. Joule, & J. M. Monteil (Eds.), *Perspectives cognitives et conduites sociales* (Vol. 7, pp. 95–124). Rennes, France: Presses Universitaires de Rennes.

Tafani, E., Mugny, G., & Bellon, S. (1999). Irréversibilité du changement et enjeux identitaires dans l'influence sociale sur une représentation sociale [Irreversibility of change and identity stakes in social influence over a social representation]. *Psychologie et Société, 1*, 73–104.

Tajfel, H. (1978). *Differentiation between social groups: Studies in the social psychology of intergroup relations.* London: Academic Press.

Taylor, S., & Lobel, M. (1989). Social comparison activity under threat: Downward evaluation and upward contacts. *Psychological Review, 96*, 569–575.

Tesser, A. (1988). Toward a self-evaluation maintenance model of social behaviour. In L. Berkowitz (Ed.), *Advances in experimental social psychology* (Vol. 21, pp. 181–227). New York: Academic Press.

Trost, M. R., & Kenrick, D. T. (1994). Ego involvement in the minority influence paradigm: The double-edged sword of minority advocacy. In S. Moscovici, A. Mucchi-Faina, & A. Maass (Eds.), *Minority influence* (pp. 149–161). Chicago: Nelson-Hall.

Trost, M., Maass, A., & Kenrick, D. T. (1992). Minority influence: Personal relevance biases cognitive processes and reverses private acceptance. *Journal of Experimental Social Psychology, 28*(3), 234–254.

Turner, J. C. (1991). *Social influence.* Buckingham, UK: Open University Press.

Volpato, C., Maass, A., Mucchi-Faina, A., & Vitti, E. (1990). Minority influence and social categorization. *European Journal of Social Psychology, 20*(2), 119–132.

Wason, P. C. (1960). On the failure to eliminate hypotheses in a conceptual task. *The Quarterly Journal of Experimental Psychology, 12*, 129–140.

Wheeler, L., Martin, R., & Suls, J. (1997). The proxy model of social comparison for self-assessment of ability. *Personality and Social Psychology Review, 1*, 54–61.

Wilder, D. A. (1977). Perception of groups size of opposition, and social influence. *Journal of Experimental Social Psychology, 13*, 253–268.

Wills, T. A. (1981). Downward comparison principles in social psychology. *Psychological Bulletin, 90*, 245–271.

Wills, T. A. (1991). Similarity and self-esteem in downward comparison. In J. Suls & T. A. Wills (Eds.), *Social comparison: Contemporary theory and research* (pp. 51–78). Hillsdale, NJ: Lawrence Erlbaum Associates, Inc.

Wolf, S. (1979). Behavioral style and group cohesiveness as sources of minority influence. *European Journal of Social Psychology, 9*, 381–395.

Wood, W., Lundgren, S., Ouellette, J. A., Busceme, M. S., & Blackstone, T. (1994). Minority influence: A meta-analytical review of social influence processes. *Psychological Bulletin, 115*, 323–345.

# 3 Majority and minority influence in attitude formation and attitude change: Context/categorization – leniency contract theory

*William D. Crano*
Claremont Graduate University, USA

That minority groups can have a powerful influence on the thoughts and behaviours of members of the majority is no longer at issue in social psychology. Compelling evidence of minority influence is readily available, and has been so for nearly four decades, beginning with Moscovici's seminal contributions to the literature of social influence (Moscovici & Lage, 1976; Moscovici, Lage, & Naffrechoux, 1969). The pace of experimentation, theory building, and application of insights into minority influence has quickened over the years (see Butera & Mugny, 2001a, 2001b; Crano & Prislin, 2006; De Dreu & De Vries, 2001; Prislin & Wood, 2005; Wood & Quinn, 2003), and has provided psychology with a model of progress. Indeed, it is arguable that Moscovici's dogged persistence in the face, initially, of disregard or outright rejection, his contention that an asymmetrical understanding of social influence that focused on majority but not minority influence was myopic if not illogical, and his consequent insistence on the necessity to focus on minority *as well as* majority influence, revitalized a critical facet of social psychology—attitude change and social influence—that had lost intellectual direction and velocity (Crano, 2000a).

Moscovici's (1980, 1985b) conversion theory, the model he developed to explain the effects of the minority on majority group members' reported perceptions, attitudes, and actions has remained relatively static (Martin, Hewstone, & Martin, 2003). Conversion theory has stimulated considerable research, but it clearly did not—indeed, perhaps could not—anticipate many of the results that have been unearthed as the inexorable pace of research quickened over the years. For example, today we are concerned with many factors that powerfully affect the minority's capacity to influence, but that were not even considered in the original model. Including these elements in our theories and designs has enhanced the predictive validity of the models of minority influence that now are available, and has extended our understanding of majority influence processes as well. This theoretical evolution is necessary given the body of findings that has evolved since Moscovici's early studies. For example, for any model of minority influence to map the difficult topography of the data that have been produced, it must:

- predict the conditions under which in-group and out-group minorities prevail;
- explain when the majority will have an immediate short-term effect, an immediate lasting effect, or no effect at all;
- elucidate the conditions under which the minority group will have an immediate effect, if and when its persuasive effects will be delayed, and when it might be expected to have no persuasive effect on the majority; and
- contrast the conditions under which a change on the focal (i.e., the targeted) belief will ensue as a result of the minority group's message, and when change on an indirect attitude (a belief associated with the focal attitude, but not identical to it) will occur.

Moscovici's original model did not anticipate many of these questions, but today's theories must confront them. Consequently, a host of additions and modifications to conversion theory have been proposed. These modifications include, among others, the elaboration likelihood-based (Petty & Wegener, 1999) model of Martin et al. (2003); social consensus-based treatments by Mackie (1987) and Erb and Bohner (2001); the conflict-based models of Mugny and colleagues (Butera & Mugny, 2001a, 2001b; Mugny, 1982); Nemeth's (1995) convergent and divergent thought approach (see also Antonio et al., 2004; De Dreu & West, 2001); the self-categorization-based interpretation (David & Turner, 1999, 2001a, 2001b; Turner, 1991); dynamic change theory developed by Prislin and colleagues (Prislin, Brewer, & Wilson, 2002; Prislin & Christensen, 2002, 2005; Prislin, Limbert, & Bauer, 2000); and the context/categorization – leniency contract model (Alvaro & Crano, 1997; Crano, 2000b; Crano & Alvaro, 1998b; Crano & Chen, 1998), whose development and application will receive the lion's share of attention in this chapter.

## Conversion theory essentials

The fundamental tenets of conversion theory are relatively well known, and thus will not be treated extensively here. In brief, Moscovici's (1980, 1985a, 1985b) model holds that majorities effect compliance by virtue of their control of resources—rewards, information, the power to ostracize, and so on (Williams, 2001). Being out of synchrony with the majority can incur costs and is to be avoided. Minorities, conversely, appear to persuade by stimulating curiosity. The minority raises questions in the minds of their message recipients regarding the how and why of their perceptions or opinions. Mulling over the minority's apparently counter-normative perceptions can produce change. Theoretically, this consideration of the minority's message takes time, and thus minority influence, should it occur, is expected to be delayed rather than immediate.

The delayed minority change hypothesis is an interesting proposition, and there are many compatible findings in the near and ancient history of social influence that anticipate this prediction. In Hovland, Janis, and Kelley's (1953) classic message-learning theory of persuasion, for example, the postulate of delayed minority influence is not surprising. For example, the early sleeper effect research (Hovland, Lumsdaine, & Sheffield, 1949; see Kumkale & Albarracín, 2004; Priester, Wegener, Petty, & Fabrigar, 1999, for reviews) anticipated and found a delayed change in response to sources of high or low credibility. Attributing a persuasive message to a highly credible source enhances immediate attitude change; dissociating source from message, an apparently inexorable process as time passes, attenuates change. Conversely, attributing a persuasive message to a non-credible source diminishes attitude change; however, dissociating source from message in such instances results in a persuasive gain, if the original persuasive message was of high quality. If an out-group or a minority group is the source of a counter-attitudinal message, the early sleeper effect literature fosters the expectation of no immediate change, but a message effect as time passes, if source and message are dissociated. Research by Moscovici, Mugny, and Papastamou (1981) built on the sleeper literature and found precisely this—a delayed minority influence effect, as expected. The logic of this research is straightforward. If an out-group (the term out-group and minority were used interchangeably in Moscovici's theoretical treatments of minority influence) were associated with a particular message, it would have relatively little impact. However, the negative association of source and message could be expected to dissolve with time, and, thus, the out-group's message, unfettered by an unflattering source association, would come to have an effect. Extrapolating from the elaboration likelihood model (ELM), we would expect the sleeper to be especially powerful if the minority's message were strong; the target's ability and motivation to elaborate the message were unimpeded; information regarding the minority status of the source was delivered *after* its message was elaborated; and the source–message dissociation was complete. Findings of Gruder and his colleagues (1978) are consistent with these expectations.

This set of qualifications suggests a series of possible additions to conversion theory that may enhance its predictive validity. In fact, all of these additions have been put forward in one theoretical refinement or another, and all have played roles in the continued growth of our understanding of minority (and majority) influence. All of these modifications, many of which were alluded to earlier, owe a debt to the original model of Moscovici, and all of them, in one way or another, add variables to the predictive mix that inevitably complicate matters, but that ultimately enhance predictive validity. Let us consider one such theoretical modification, Crano and associates' context/categorization theory (Crano, 1993; Crano & Alvaro, 1998a; Crano

& Hannula-Bral, 1994), a predictive device that subsumes the leniency model (Crano & Chen, 1998), and which was designed to explain the conditions that foster majority *and* minority influence, immediate *and* delayed change, focal *and* indirect attitude adjustments, and to explicate the psychological processes that underlie these variations.

## Context/categorization considerations: Attitude formation vs. attitude change

A rather glaring complication with conversion theory's prediction that the minority will have only a delayed influence is that many studies in minority influence have produced findings that involve an immediate minority-induced effect on reported perceptions or beliefs (Crano & Hannula-Bral, 1994; Martin, Gardikiotis, & Hewstone, 2002; Martin et al., 2003). There is no convenient way in which the standard (conversion) model can be made to account for this result if, as the theory holds, minority effects are mediated by contemplation of the minority's counter-attitudinal position. Incidentally, immediate change in response to the minority was not all that rare even in early research on minority influence conducted in the home of conversion theory, Moscovici's lab in Paris (e.g., Moscovici & Lage, 1976; Moscovici et al., 1969), so how can we integrate these findings with the original theory?

A possible route to a solution to the problem of immediate minority influence may be found in an interesting review of the attitude and persuasion literature by Chaiken, Wood, and Eagly (1996), in which the authors argued for the distinction between attitude formation and attitude change, a call that had been made previously (Johnson & Eagly, 1990) and has been made since (Crano & Prislin, 2008; Wood, 2000). The relevance of this distinction for minority influence bears examination. In an attitude-formation context, the strength of the focal attitude, by definition, cannot be great. Indeed, in some contexts, the attitude cannot reasonably be thought even to exist.

In attitude-change contexts, however, the attitude does indeed exist, and it may be held with some conviction; that is, attitude strength in attitude-change contexts, almost by definition, is considerably greater than negligible, and certainly greater than that found in settings involving attitude formation. The presence of a strongly held belief has clear implications for resistance (Knowles & Linn, 2004). In the case of a minority attack on an established belief, we would expect that some form of belief defence would be mounted, be it strong counter-argumentation, source derogation, biased processing, or distortion. Logically, defensive responses to a counter-attitudinal or counter-normative message would be exacerbated when the source of the contrary message occupied a minority status.

Consideration of variations in response to a counter-attitudinal message in attitude-formation versus attitude-change contexts gives rise to a set of intriguing possibilities. For example, in an attitude-formation context, it is unlikely that strong resistance would arise in response to a counter-attitudinal message. In the absence of a strongly held belief or norm, the recipient of the counter-message would have little to defend. As such, cognitive defences would not be invoked, or if invoked, would not be extreme. In circumstances such as these, we might postulate an initially counter-intuitive postulate, namely that the minority might be *more* influential than the majority. In addition, the influence that would transpire in attitude- or norm-formation contexts would be immediate rather than delayed. Both of these propositions deserve consideration, as in combination they have the potential to regularize much of the uneven literature we encounter in our study of minority influence.

### Role of minorities in attention capture

Why would the minority be a more powerful influence source than the majority in attitude- or norm-formation contexts? The answer to this question may be anticipated from two independent lines of research. The first of these is drawn from the psychophysiological literature concerned with stimulus salience and the orienting response (e.g., Folk & Gibson, 2001). This literature is relevant for present purposes because researchers consistently have found that novel or salient stimuli capture attention (Gati, Ben-Shakhar, & Avni-Liberty, 1996; O'Gorman, 1979; Wright, 2005). A member of a minority group, whether minority is defined in terms of observable physical features or opinion deviance, is salient because the member is, relatively speaking, rare, unusual, or atypical. At a minimum, therefore, the minority will attract attention to its position. In some contexts, this attention will result in rapid refutation. But in other circumstances, the attentional advantage afforded a minority may work in its favour. One such facilitative circumstance involves attitude or norm formation. In contexts in which no strong belief or response norm is already in place, the minority may be an advantaged influence source. In these situations, the ancillary salience of the minority affords a persuasive advantage. Because of its salience the minority draws attention to its position. In attitude-formation situations, the enhanced attention afforded the minority's position would not be met with strong counter-argumentation, as there is, by definition, nothing to defend. Accordingly, we might expect that immediate focal minority influence (on a belief or norm) would occur in circumstances that involve attitude or norm formation—that is, in contexts in which no strong beliefs or established response norms exist. A review of the literature on minority influence suggests that this is precisely the circumstance in which immediate focal minority effects do occur. Typically, such outcomes are found when the attitude object is not strongly held, or the response norm is not well established (i.e., in unusual or novel judgement situations, or on issues on which the target has an ill-formed belief).

### Minorities as dissimilar comparators

A second line of research that suggests circumstances in which a minority might actually be favoured as an information source is found in the literature concerned with social comparison. In his model of social comparison processes, Festinger (1954) theorized that in the absence of objective guidelines, we use other people as sources of information regarding the propriety of our beliefs or the relative level of our abilities. An interesting feature of the theory is that not all comparison partners were postulated as equally desirable. In developing this theory, Festinger anticipated that comparators who were similar to the individual making the comparison would be preferred. This feature of the theory has not received consistent support (Suls, Martin, & Wheeler, 2003; Suls & Wills, 1991). However, there is some indication that the nature of the task on which the comparison is undertaken may influence comparator choice. Goethals and colleagues (Goethals & Darley, 1977; Goethals & Nelson, 1973), perhaps following the lead of the philosopher Ayer (1952), suggested that dissimilar others would be sought out more avidly than similar comparators when the task about which the comparison revolved admitted to an objective or consensually agreed-upon solution (Olson, Ellis, & Zanna, 1983). Thus, in solving a tough problem in mathematics, we might prefer to confer with a person whose training and orientation were quite different from ours, in hopes that the preferred partner would share strengths and weaknesses different from our own. In this way, we would be more likely to triangulate on the proper solution. We would not share common sources of bias, which could doom us to a consensually agreeable mistake. Research by Laughlin (1980, 1988) on collective induction, and intellective versus judgemental tasks, is consistent with the findings of Goethals and his colleagues.

A different rubric would obtain when seeking a comparison partner to bolster a subjective judgement. In that case, with Ayer (1952), it is reasonable to expect that individuals would prefer comparators similar to themselves. In circumstances involving subjective choices, it makes sense that we would want someone who shared our beliefs and values, as the grounds for subjective comparisons with very dissimilar others are not readily obvious. Gorenflo and Crano (1989) formally tested the implications of these arguments in a research series in which participants were asked to make judgements that were characterized as being either subjective or objective. In their first study, participants played the role of admissions officers of a university. The participant's job was to consider the credentials of an applicant, decide upon his admission, and write a brief defence of the decision that he or she had made. One group of participants was told that the information that had been made available to them was not sufficient to allow an objective judgement, and thus they were to fall back upon prior attitudes, values, and preferences in forming their decisions. The remaining participants were told that the information given was sufficient to allow for an objective judgement, and they were to base their decisions solely on the given data. In fact, all received identical information.

After making their judgements, participants were told that standard practice in universities involved admissions officers conferring with their peers after having formed an initial impression of a candidate, and they were to be given this same opportunity. Participants could confer with another admissions officer of their choice. A minimal-groups procedure had been conducted at the beginning of the study, and thus, participants knew whether they were 'similar' or 'different' from the available comparators. In the minimal-groups procedure, participants make a trivial choice, and are assigned arbitrarily to one or another (in-)group on the basis of this choice. Such assignment has been shown to have powerful effects on participants' identification with, and evaluation of, the groups to which they were (or were not) assigned, with more positive evaluations being accorded the in-group (see Dobbs & Crano, 2001, for a review). Both in-group and out-group comparison partners were made available. The central issue was the effect of the task description (as objective or subjective) on participants' choice of comparator.

The results of the study confirmed expectations. Participants who believed they were making a subjective judgement strongly preferred to confer with judges who were similar to themselves (similarity was inferred on the basis of the minimal-groups classification). The opposite was found among the judges who believed they were making an objective judgement. In this case, judges evidenced a strong preference for out-group over in-group judges.

A second experiment, conceptually similar in design to the first, had participants play the role of jurors in a mock murder trial. As before, the central manipulation concerned the objective or subjective nature of the judgement they were to make. After reading the essential facts of the case, jurors made individual judgements and then were given the opportunity to confer with one of their peers. The central measure of the study was concerned with their choice of partner. As before, partner similarity–dissimilarity was manipulated via a minimal-groups procedure that had been conducted at the beginning of the experimental session. The results were striking. Of the participants who had been told that they were to rely on subjective preferences when making their judgement, 32 of 44 (73%) sought to confer and compare with a similar other. Among those who believed that theirs was an objective judgement, 35 of 43 (81%) chose a dissimilar comparator with whom to discuss their judgements.

These strong preference reversals suggest that the perceived subjective or objective nature of the issue under consideration may powerfully affect a target's openness to similar or dissimilar information (or influence) sources. Extrapolating from the social-comparison literature, it may be argued that a 'different' other would be advantaged when pressing a position on an issue that appears to admit to an objective judgement. Conversely, on subjective issues, a similar (i.e., in-group) other might be advantaged.

The words similar and different emphasize the importance of considering the social identity of the target. Influence recipients of majority status would be more susceptible to majority influence on issues perceived as involving subjective judgements (e.g., attitudes, beliefs, preferences). Minority targets would be more susceptible to fellow minority-group members in such circumstances. However, by this logic, in circumstances involving objective judgements, outsiders would enjoy a natural advantage. That is, in such contexts, a member of the majority would be more influenced by a minority-group member than a fellow majority-group member; the opposite would be the case for the minority-influence target. However, salience differences, discussed earlier, force a slight modification of these main effect predictions. As argued, the minority enjoys the advantage of relative uniqueness. Coupled with this advantage is the persuasive advantage assigned to dissimilar comparators in objective-judgement contexts. The most powerful minority-influence effects would be seen in this circumstance. In subjective contexts, in which the persuasive advantage is accorded the in-group, the minority salience advantage may still hold. This suggests that a minority-influence source may be more successful with fellow minority members than the majority-influence source is with fellow majority members. All of this assumes, of course, that the issue on which the influence is levied is not highly vested or strongly established.

Crano and Hannula-Bral (1994) tested these possibilities in a study that involved the formation of a novel response norm. In their experiment, participants first completed a minimal-groups task, and were informed that the group to which they belonged was composed of a majority or a minority of their fellow students. They then answered a series of obscure factual questions that were presented on individual computer screens. The questions were drawn from Pettigrew's (1958) Category Width scale, and were exceptionally difficult, as the following examples illustrate:

An average of 50 ships entered or left New York harbour daily during the period from 1950 through 1955. What do you think was the largest number of ships to enter or leave New York in a single day during this period?

| 1 | 2 | 3 | 4 | 5 | 6 | 7 | 8 | 9 |

76 ships                         115 ships                         153 ships

and

Weather officials report that during this century Washington, DC, has received an average rainfall of 41.1 inches annually. What do you think is the largest amount of rain that Washington has received in a single year during this century?

| 1 | 2 | 3 | 4 | 5 | 6 | 7 | 8 | 9 |
|---|---|---|---|---|---|---|---|---|

51.2 inches               66.8 inches             82.4 inches

The introduction to this task was designed to influence participants' perceptions of the objective or subjective nature of the judgements they were asked to make. Both the subjective and the objective scripts allowed that the participant might not have thought much about the topics addressed in the questionnaire, and as such they were to be privy to the answers of one of their peers, whose answers, along with the peer's in-group/out-group majority/minority status, was transmitted on the computer screen.

In the subjective condition, participants were told that the task was so difficult that they would have to rely on their best intuitions in answering each item. In the objective task condition, participants were told that there was an objective, correct answer to all of the questions, and that they should be as accurate as possible.

In sum, in the judgement phase of the study, participants were paired ostensibly with a partner who was either in-group or out-group, and of minority or majority status. These factors were crossed across all other conditions of Crano and Hannula-Bral's mixed factorial experimental design. The partner actually was a computer program designed to respond, on average, two scale units higher than the participant had, on each of 15 judgement trials. If the participant were influenced by the consistent upward pressure, then his or her responses over the course of the judgement trials would be consistently greater than those of individuals who resisted their partner's influence. A final block of 5 'private' trials also was administered. On these judgements, no information from the programmed confederate was transmitted to participants.

Responses on the 15 public trials were analysed first. The analysis revealed a series of results consistent with expectations. First, immediate minority influence occurred, as predicted. Analysis of the effect of the programmed confederate revealed that sources identified as being of minority-group status had a stronger effect on judgements than did those ostensibly emanating from a source of majority status. A close consideration of the results, however, revealed that this general (main effect) observation needed to be modified. Consistent with expectations based on the findings of Gorenflo and Crano (1989), we found that when majority-group participants perceived the task as involving objective judgements, they were especially susceptible to their partner if the partner was from the minority. This interaction effect was anticipated; the majority target was predicted to be more sensitive to out-group (i.e., minority-based) communications when the task involved objective judgements. Furthermore, this (minority influence) effect was expected to be intensified because of the minority's enhanced salience, which has been shown to capture attention. Minority group participants, conversely, were expected to be more susceptible to majority sources when making an objective judgement, and they were; however, this effect was not as great, as the majority source was not expected to capture attention as powerfully as the minority.

On subjective judgements a different pattern emerged. In this case participants cast in the minority status through the minimal groups procedure proved substantially more influenced by an in-group (i.e., minority) source. However, among participants who had been placed in the majority status, no reliable difference emerged in susceptibility to the information attributed to a response partner of majority or minority status. As before, this pattern is consistent with salience-based expectations. In circumstances involving a subjective judgement, majority-group participants were predicted to be more susceptible to in-group (i.e., majority) information sources. However, this tendency was offset by the salience of the minority source. In this case, the two influences worked in opposition and cancelled any difference that might have emerged between majority participants exposed to in-group or out-group influence sources.

In summary, in contexts involving attitude formation or norm formation, in which, by definition, no strong initial position exists, the minority source enjoys the advantage owing to its salience. This advantage is intensified when the judgement task is cast as involving an objective choice. Insofar as participants in Crano and Hannula-Bral's study plausibly could not have had a strong position on the judgements tapped in Pettigrew's scale, it would seem that this research is properly classified as a study of response norm formation. The results of this study clearly point to at least one circumstance in which the minority may have an immediate rather than a delayed impact, and this circumstance may prove useful in explicating findings in the literature that are contrary to expectations of standard conversion theory. When the issue under consideration is novel, or when the strength of the attitude under attack is weak (Petty & Krosnick, 1995), the minority holds a persuasive advantage owing to its salience. In circumstances such as these, influence targets generally will not be strongly motivated to counter-argue, and the relative advantage owned by the minority by virtue of its rarity (and hence salience) results in its greater influence power.

Whether or not the minority need be in-group was not definitively answered in Crano and Hannula-Bral's research. The minimal-groups procedure was engaged to create in-group and out-group allegiances. However, the minimal-groups differentiation, which was based on similarity/ dissimilarity of judgements on a dot-estimation task, might not have been sufficient to overcome students' common and well-established social identification as members of the same university, a university that students have traditionally employed as a strong source of social identity (Pool, Wood, & Leck, 1998; Wood, Pool, Leck, & Purvis, 1996). Nonetheless, despite this uncertainty, the research highlighted the importance of the subjective or objective nature of the task, along with the status of the influence source and the source's in-group or out-group identity in contexts involving attitude or norm formation.

## Minority/majority effects in attitude change

### *Subjective issues*

The discussion to this point has been concerned with attitude or norm formation. What is expected in situations in which a strong or established belief is attacked by a minority or the majority group? As in our consideration of the consequences of majority and minority pressure on attitude/norm formation, we must judge the main effects orientation of this question to be oversimplified. The factors that affected majority and minority influence in attitude-formation contexts must be considered in attitude-change contexts as well. These factors include, among others, the subjective or objective nature of the task, the in-group or out-group nature of the influence source, especially in the case of minority influence, and the strength of the minority (or majority) source's message. Failure to consider these features of the influence setting, at minimum, results in an impoverished understanding of the complex interplay of forces that determine the outcome of a persuasion experience.

On purely subjective judgements, the discussion to this point would strongly suggest that the in-group will enjoy an initial advantage. Thus, members of the majority group would be more susceptible to majority-group influence in subjective contexts, and minority-group members would be more susceptible to members of the minority. This initial advantage is shown in Figure 3.1. In these circumstances, this advantage would be immediate.

The question of persistence then arises. On the basis of considerable evidence gathered in research on dual-process models (Chaiken & Trope, 1999), it is reasonable to predict that persistence would depend on the motivation of the target to elaborate the source's information, and the quality of that information. If the target were not particularly exorcized by the issue at hand, it is unlikely that the source's message would be scrutinized closely. In that instance, the initial advantage of the in-group source would hold, and the quality of the message would not matter much, insofar as it would not be scrutinized closely. The change that occurs in this

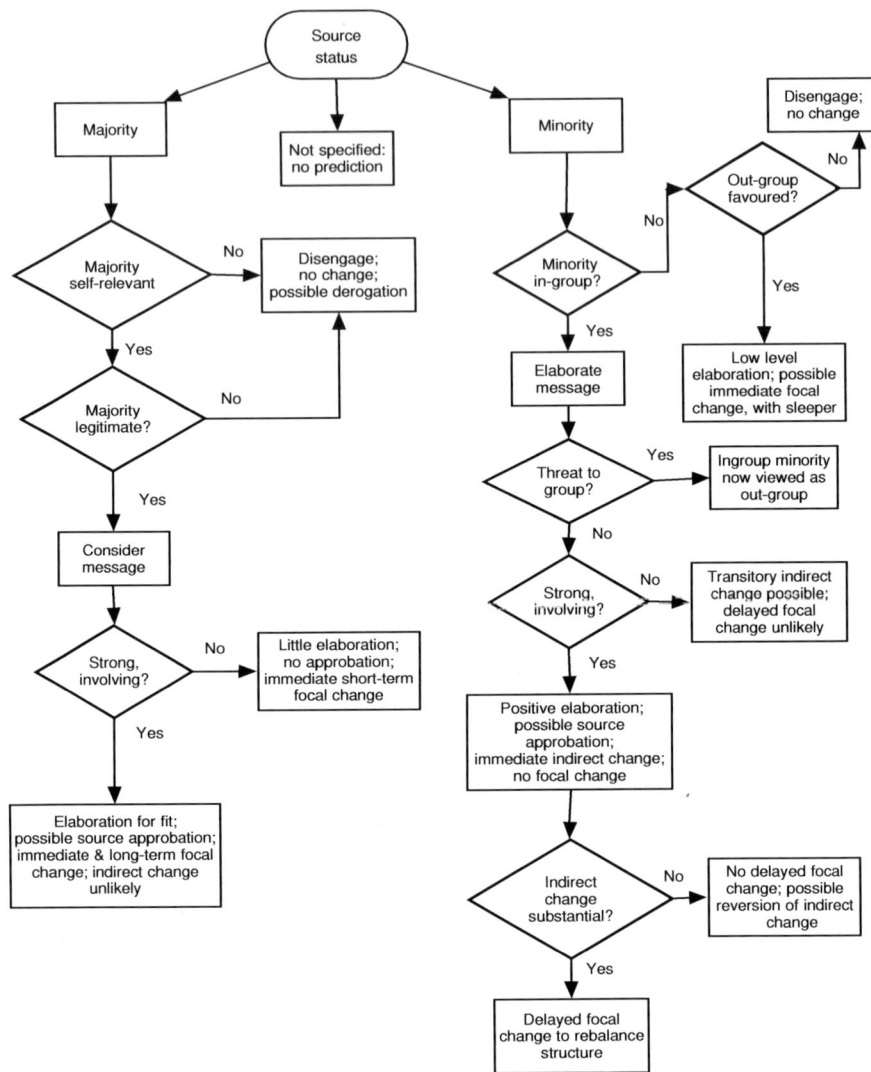

*Figure 3.1* Minority and majority influence expectations: Subjective judgements.

circumstance is the result of heuristic processing, and it would be manifest in initial differences favouring the in-group position. However, the resultant attitudes would be weak. Weak attitudes, as we know from considerable work in persuasion, are not persistent, they are easy to change, and they are unlikely to impel action (Petty & Krosnick, 1995).

A different outcome may be anticipated in circumstances in which the issue under attack is vested or highly relevant (Crano, 1995, 1997; Crano & Burgoon, 2001). In this case, the target would be expected to attend closely to the source's message. As before, the in-group would be favoured; however, in the case of a strong message, the resultant attitude would be expected to be strong. It would persist, be resistant to counter- persuasion, and impel action. Accordingly, a strong message emanating from the favoured source (majority source for majority targets, a minority source for minority targets), under conditions of high elaboration, would be expected to result in both immediate *and* persistent change.

## Importance of the subjective/objective distinction

The predictions developed here would seem contrary to a host of studies that are well known and readily available in the literature on minority influence. However, it is important to understand the very particularistic nature of the issues to which these predictions apply. The predictions outlined thus far are expected to hold only for issues that are experienced as involving subjective choices, and the word subjective is to be understood very precisely. Subjective choices involve issues that are perceived clearly as matters of preference or palate. These issues concern choices that the individual sees as involving personal preferences, not verifiable, right or wrong judgements—which is the better flavour of ice cream, chocolate or vanilla, the better colour of automobile, red or yellow, the tastier pizza. Issues perceived as corrigible, as capable of correction, do not fall into the category labelled subjective. One cannot set right another's preference for Coke over Pepsi. One cannot ask whether or not the preference is correct— the question itself is a *non sequitur*. The probative value of the preference is fundamentally immaterial. Defined in this way, subjective issues typically are not viewed by the perceiver as involving life-or-death decisions, and, as such, they generally do not generate feelings of high vested interest, nor are they likely to stimulate much emotion (Lehman & Crano, 2002). There are exceptions to this rule, but these exceptions are rare. On issues of low importance or vested interest, social influence, should it occur, generally would not induce strong allegiance to the induced position (Crano, 1995).

## Majority/minority effects in attitude change

### Objective issues

A different set of predictions are made for issues under persuasive attack that are *perceived* as involving an objective truth. In these cases, the dynamics of minority- or majority-induced attitude change are considerably more complex, as shown in the predictive model of Figure 3.2. The perception that there is a right or wrong position on an issue renders the issue objective. Thus, an individual who is completely convinced that capital punishment is wrong, that it must be abolished worldwide, and that there are compelling reasons for this position, would be seen as holding a view

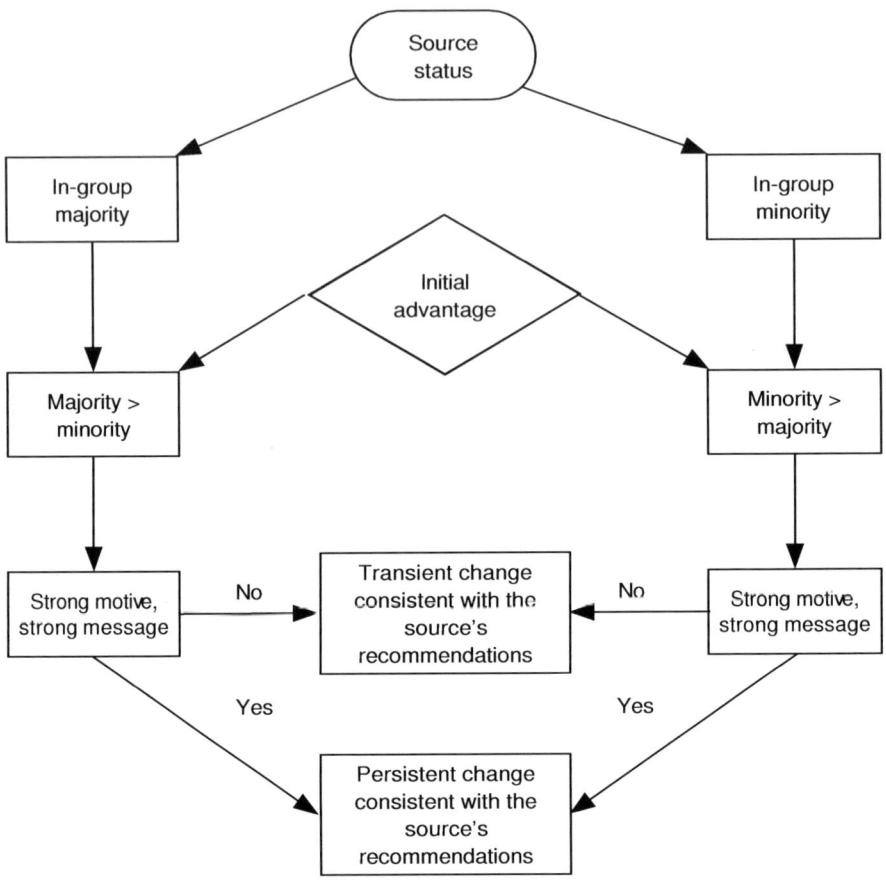

*Figure 3.2* Minority and majority influence expectations: Objective judgements (context/categorization model with leniency contract).

that is (self-)defined as objective. Unlike subjective judgements, as defined here, objective judgements are more likely to be vested and held with some degree of conviction or passion. In this sense, therefore, at least some classes of beliefs perceived to be objective are likely to be held more strongly. As such, these judgements may prove more difficult to change; however, once changed, the changes are more likely to persist, and to motivate attitude-consistent action.

In classical conversion theory, the majority is thought to impart influence by threat of ridicule or ostracism. Its effects are predicted to persist so long as the majority can maintain surveillance. This is a reasonable position that has received good support (see Moscovici, 1985b, for a review). However, this theoretical position begs a number of questions. For example, why should a target of majority pressure change if the pressure is delivered via persuasive communication, which simply states the fact that, say, 88% of a particular group feels a particular way about a position, or judges a particular slide to be green? In this instance, there is no direct threat, and even less implied threat; further, there is little chance that the majority group is watching the hapless judge. If majority influence truly depends on pressure and surveillance, it would seem that mass-mediated majority influence would not stand much chance of success. Yet, there is plenty of evidence throughout the history of persuasion research that such messages sometimes have a profound impact. A second problem with the classic theory vis-à-vis the data at hand is that it does not allow for persistent change when majority surveillance is relaxed, nor does it explain why the majority sometimes fails to exert any influence whatsoever despite its best efforts. The context/categorization model was developed to address these theoretical shortcomings. This model depicts the theoretical decision points that must be traversed on the route to resistance or change. It is presented from the perspective of the target. For ease of presentation, it is assumed that the target is a member of the majority. Predicting minority-group members' responses to social influence also is in the purview of the model, but this explication would carry us beyond the limits of this chapter.

### Majority influence

The model begins with the assumption that on objective judgements, attributing a communication to a source of either majority or minority status initiates a series of regular, systematic, and predictable cognitive responses. Mentioning the majority or minority status of an influence source fundamentally changes the persuasion context from one of cold elaboration to one involving interpersonal issues of self-identity and group belongingness. This modification has important implications for message processing. The usual ELM expectation, for example, is that source characteristics are most relevant in peripheral processing. Thus, targets with low motivation might use source status to infer the correctness of a position. However, mentioning the minority or majority status of a source raises the issue of social identity. A person's responses to a persuasive message delivered under conditions that trigger identity concerns are motivated by the target's need to belong to the social group that provides some aspects of his or her social identity. Involving the self-concept in the persuasion setting changes the context from one of mere information processing to valenced and motivated elaboration, because succumbing to, or resisting, an influence source may have implications for membership in a group that at least in part contributes to one's self-definition.

To understand the approach taken, let us begin with considerations of individuals' responses to influence levied by the majority, on issues deemed objective by the influence target. The left side of the model presented in Figure 3.2 outlines a series of decision points that allow prediction of transient, lasting, or no compliance to majority influence. The model suggests that when individuals are confronted with pronouncements attributed to the majority, they first decide whether the majority group is self-relevant. That is, does membership in the majority play a role in the individual's social identity? If the majority does not serve as an important feature of the individual's self-definition, then majority pressure to adopt a counter-attitudinal position will fail. As diagrammed, no majority-influence effect is expected in this circumstance. However, suppose that the group is important to the target's social identity. The next decision point concerns the legitimacy of majority-generated pressure. Is the majority a legitimate source of influence on the topic at hand? A member of a club soccer team, for example, might well be influenced by the group's consensual decision to use Nike shoes, even though the individual might favour Adidas. In this instance, majority pressure might be judged legitimate, thus opening the door to elaborating the group's reasons. However, suppose the majority of that same soccer club were to argue that it was the duty of all members to vote for a particular political party in a coming election. In that case, the target might reason that politics and soccer are not mutually relevant, and that the pressure exerted by the club is illegitimate. In that instance, the attempt would fail. The target would disengage from the group, psychologically if not physically, and no change would occur. Indeed, research by Tormala and Petty (Tormala, 2004; Tormala & Petty, 2002, 2004a, 2004b, 2004c) on the ramifications of successful resistance suggests that in some circumstances, the majority source might lose value in the eyes of the unmoved influence target, and might find its subsequent persuasion attempts met with strong counter-argument.

Suppose, however, that the majority group's counter-attitudinal message is judged both self-relevant and legitimate. Under these conditions, the target will consider the message carefully. At this stage, message strength becomes an important issue. Elaboration of a weak message will result in a relatively weak response. The targeted individual will change in response to the message, given its judged self-relevance (for group membership) and legitimacy. However, this change is not expected to persist. If the message is strong, however, elaboration will produce both immediate and persistent change on the focal issue. Such change is not expected to spread to related beliefs, however, because the elaboration that occurs in this circumstance is an *elaboration for fit*, rather than an elaboration for gist; the purpose of elaboration in this circumstance is not to absorb the essence of the message, but rather to determine how best to act in light of the position so as to bolster (or not to endanger) one's membership in the group. Prislin's work (Prislin et al., 2000, 2002) demonstrates the strong pull of majority-group membership. The motive for elaboration in this case is to learn how best to present oneself to ensure continued group approval. For this reason, even if the majority's message is adopted, it will not have much influence on related beliefs, because its adoption is motivated by concerns for self-presentation rather than validity. As such, it is not likely to cause serious cognitive imbalance via its lack of congruity with other, related, beliefs. An interesting feature of this model is the possibility that an individual who adopts the majority's position may come to accept it if the induced behaviour is emitted over an extended time period. One whose behaviour is monitored for a sufficient period may come to accept the behaviour as legitimate, even though it was induced initially by majority pressure. This possibility awaits future confirmation.

### Minority influence

The motivational structure of the target is considerably different when the counter-attitudinal message is attributed to a minority group. In this case, the pressure to comply is minimal. This is not to say that the minority cannot persuade, however. In the case of minority influence, the target's first reaction is to determine the status of the minority. Is the minority in-group? If not, as indicated in Figure 3.2, a series of decisions ensue. The first is concerned with a refinement of the minority categorization. Is the out-group minority favoured? If not, its message is readily dismissed without elaboration. The message has little effect, and the out-group is dismissed from further consideration. The impact of the message usually is so slight that its rejection is not translated into further rejection of the out-group. If the out-group is favoured, however, its position is considered, and may well have an immediate effect. The effect will fade over time as it is not based on strong elaboration. Favoured out-groups are groups of high status or of high regard, but who do not play a role in the target's social identity. The types of sources used by Hovland in his study of high source credibility fit the description of favoured (e.g., J. Robert Oppenheimer speaking on the feasibility of nuclear submarines in the 1950s represented a favoured out-group—at least to those who were not famous physicists; Hovland et al., 1953).

If the minority is in-group, however, a different process is evoked. The presentation of a counter-attitudinal message by a member of one's in-group is surprising precisely because it is non-normative. As such, the receiver is motivated to understand why the message was delivered and what it entails—in short, to elaborate it. The first stage of the elaboration is concerned with the continued existence of the group in light of the in-group minority's counter-normative communication. If the group serves a social identity function, it is important to the target that it remains viable. Thus, a central concern is whether or not the message is a threat to the group's existence. If it is, and the minority cannot be dissuaded, the message will be rejected and the in-group minority will be seen as out-group (Kerr, 2002; Kerr & Tindale, 2004). The response to turncoats is often extreme. Such members are rejected and ostracized.

These extreme responses are rare, probably because in-group minorities rarely propose positions that threaten to destroy the groups from which they derive some part of their identities. In the more common case, in which the minority's message is not seen as a threat to the group's viability, the next decision point concerns the strength of the message itself. With Petty and Cacioppo (1986a, 1986b), the leniency model holds that message strength plays a major role in determining the course of persuasion. Elaborating a weak message at this point in the model will have relatively little obvious effect. The focal attitude will not be affected. It is possible that related issues might be swayed in the direction of the gist of the message, but these changes will be transitory.

However, suppose the message is strong and persuasive. In this case, although focal change will not transpire, attitudes associated with the issue under attack will be affected. The reasons for this prediction give the leniency contract its name. The model holds that the in-group minority will stimulate relatively open-minded elaboration of its message, by virtue of its group membership. For this same reason, it is not likely that this message source will be derogated. After all, the minority is in-group, part and parcel of one's own identity. To derogate the minority would be to derogate oneself.

Under these conditions—open-minded elaboration without derogation—we might expect that immediate focal change would be readily evident. It is not. The model predicts a lack of apparent effect, the result of an implicit contract between the in-group minority and the majority receivers. This leniency contract stipulates a reasonable and courteous hearing of the minority's position, as described. In this way, the viability and civility of the group is maintained, much as politeness theory suggests strategies inter-actants use to facilitate social interchange (Brown, 1990). However, in recompense (this is, after all, a contract), the majority and minority implicitly understand that change is unlikely. In this way, the minority is accommodated, in that it is given a hearing, without derogation, and the majority helps ensure the viability of the group by placating the minority while simultaneously maintaining its position on important issues. This leniency contract need not be explicit or even conscious. It is a convention that is part and parcel of group maintenance. The leniency contract allows considerable in-group variation on all non-vital issues, because in-group deviance is not viewed as a threat. Theoretically, more cohesive groups would allow the greatest levels of in-group opinion deviance (Brewer & Brown, 1998; Capozza & Brown, 2000).

## Indirect attitude change

This is not to imply that the minority is impotent as a change agent. The open-minded elaboration of a counter-attitudinal message with little counter-argumentation and no source derogation can create considerable pressure for change. Although focal change is contractually precluded, the reality of the pressure cannot be denied. The leniency model holds that this change pressure will spread to other, related, attitudes. Indirect attitude change, a common feature of minority-influence research, is a result of this spread of effect. This proposition is consistent with considerable research on cognitive structure (e.g., Anderson, 1983; Judd, Drake, Downing, & Krosnick, 1991; McGuire & McGuire, 1991), and its plausibility rests on a few easily accepted postulates. The first of these is that attitudes are not held in isolation; that is, attitudes are linked in the cognitive system. The second assumption is that changing one attitude might have implications for other beliefs, especially those with which the focal attitude is linked most strongly. These propositions would prove readily acceptable to most social psychologists. Let's take the logic one step farther. In light of these two postulates, it seems reasonable to assume that applying change pressure to one attitude might have implications for linked or proximal beliefs. Even if the targeted attitude cannot or does not change, those beliefs that are related to it might. This change could be both profound and insidious, insofar as one would not raise defences to bolster an attitude that was not, apparently, under attack.

## Delayed focal change

If we follow this argument, then the model also provides an explication of delayed focal change. The leniency model, which assumes a structural interrelation among beliefs within the cognitive system, presupposes that massive change in one aspect of the structure will have implications for change in related facets of the structure. A major change in one belief will affect the structural integrity of the system, in effect, throwing the system out of equilibrium. How is the system to right itself in the case of such change? Two means readily suggest themselves. The changed feature may regress to its original position. In cases of minor change, this seems a likely prospect. The inertia of the total system would prove difficult to offset, and the changed member would return to its original position to re-establish balance.

However, when indirect change is profound, such an easy expedient probably is not available. In this second instance, the structure would adjust. Theoretically, the attitudes most closely linked to the changed belief would move toward it (i.e., become more congruous with it), thereby re-establishing cognitive equilibrium. A process like this one could be expected to result in the delayed focal change that is commonly observed in the minority-influence arena, and this is precisely what Crano and Chen (1998) found in their study—those participants who showed the greatest indirect minority-induced attitude change exhibited delayed focal change. Delayed focal change, however, is not inevitable. It was absent in those who were only modestly moved by the in-group minority. This result pattern helps explain why some studies on delayed focal change produce positive results, whereas others fail to find the effect.

## Closing remarks

The study of social influence and persuasion is the defining feature of social psychological inquiry. Almost all that is considered worthy of study in this wildly intellectually imperialistic field is linked in one way or another to questions of influence. Moscovici's emphasis on the importance of the minority in the persuasion equation helped energize the field when it had begun to lose steam. If nothing else, his insights opened a wealth of possibilities that remain to be explored. The context/categorization approach, and its allied leniency contract, is offered in hopes of furthering that exploration. The context/categorization model draws attention to variables that have been largely neglected in systematic study, but that arguably may have massive effects on the persuasion process. Consideration of the perceived subjective or objective nature of the task at hand, the social-identity concerns of targets, the in-group or out-group nature of the influence source, the source's majority or minority status, and so on, all play important roles in determining the outcome of a persuasion attempt. In the case of majority influence, the model outlined on these pages provides clear and testable predictions regarding the likely outcomes of persuasion attempts, and details the conditions under which transitory, lasting, or no change may be expected. Further, it details the circumstances in which minority influence will occur, and provides a plausible explication of the social psychological underpinnings responsible for the predicted effects. It is not sufficient to predict, but to explain why. The context/categorization model is built to predict and to explain—the what and the how. It is my hope that this exposition will stimulate other researchers to examine the model rigorously, to expose its shortcomings, to modify and improve it in the search for a more complete understanding of the processes that cause us to change, for it is in this realm that social psychology is uniquely positioned to make its true contribution.

## References

Alvaro, E. M., & Crano, W. D. (1997). Indirect minority influence: Evidence for leniency in source evaluation and counter-argumentation. *Journal of Personality and Social Psychology, 72,* 949–965.

Anderson, J. E. (1983). *The architecture of cognition.* Cambridge, MA: Harvard University Press.

Antonio, A. L., Change, J. J., Hakuta, K., Kenny, D. A., Levin, S., & Milem, J. F. (2004). Effects of racial diversity on complex thinking in college students. *Psychological Science, 15,* 507–510.

Ayer, A. J. (1952). *Language, truth, and logic.* New York: Dover.

Brewer, M. B., & Brown, R. J. (1998). Intergroup relations. In D. T. Gilbert, S. T. Fiske, & G. Lindsey (Eds.), *The handbook of social psychology* (4th ed., Vol. 2, pp. 554–594). Boston: McGraw-Hill.

Brown, R. (1990). Politeness theory: Exemplar and exemplary. In I. Rock (Ed.), *The legacy of Solomon Asch: Essays in cognition and social psychology* (pp. 23–38). Hillsdale, NJ: Lawrence Erlbaum Associates, Inc.

Butera, F., & Mugny, G. (2001a). Conflicts and social influences in hypothesis testing. In C. K. W. De Dreu & N. K. De Vries (Eds.), *Group consensus and minority influence: Implications for innovation* (pp. 160–182). Malden, MA: Blackwell.

Butera, F., & Mugny, G. (2001b). *Social influence in social reality: Promoting individual and social change.* Ashland, OH: Hogrefe & Huber.

Capozza, D., & Brown, R. J. (2000). *Social identity processes.* Thousand Oaks, CA: Sage.

Chaiken, S., & Trope, Y. (Eds.). (1999). *Dual process theories in social psychology.* New York: Guilford Press.

Chaiken, S., Wood, W., & Eagly, A. H. (1996). Principles of persuasion. In E. T. Higgins & A. W. Kruglanski (Eds.), *Social psychology: Handbook of basic principles* (pp. 702–742). New York: Guilford Press.

Crano, W. D. (1993). Context, categorization, and change: Consequences of cultural contrasts on compliance and conversion. In M.-F. Pichevin, M.-C. Hurtig, & M. Piolat (Eds.), *Studies on the self and social cognition* (pp. 248–257). Singapore: World Scientific.

Crano, W. D. (1995). Attitude strength and vested interest. In R. Petty & J. Krosnick (Eds.), *Attitude strength: Antecedents and consequences* (pp. 131–157). Hillsdale, NJ: Lawrence Erlbaum Associates, Inc.

Crano, W. D. (1997). Vested interest, symbolic politics, and attitude–behavior consistency. *Journal of Personality and Social Psychology, 72,* 485–491.

Crano, W. D. (2000a). Milestones in the psychological analysis of social influence. *Group Dynamics: Theory, Research, and Practice, 4,* 68–80.

Crano, W. D. (2000b). Social influence: Effects of leniency on majority- and minority-induced focal and indirect attitude change. *Revue Internationale de Psychologie Sociale, 15,* 89–121.

Crano, W. D., & Alvaro, E. M. (1998a). The context/comparison model of social influence: Mechanisms, structure, and linkages that underlie indirect attitude change. In W. Stroebe & M. Hewstone (Eds.), *European review of social psychology* (pp. 175–202). Chichester, UK: Wiley.

Crano, W. D., & Alvaro, E. M. (1998b). Indirect minority influence: The leniency contract revisited. *Group Process and Intergroup Relations, 1,* 99–115.

Crano, W. D., & Burgoon, M. (2001). Vested interest theory and AIDS: Self-interest, social influence, and disease prevention. In F. Butera & G. Mugny (Eds.), *Social influence in social reality: Promoting individual and social change* (pp. 277–289). Seattle, WA: Hogrefe & Huber.

Crano, W. D., & Chen, X. (1998). The leniency contract and persistence of majority and minority influence. *Journal of Personality and Social Psychology, 74,* 1437–1450.

Crano, W. D., & Hannula-Bral, K. A. (1994). Context/categorization model of social influence: Minority and majority influence in the formation of a novel response norm. *Journal of Experimental Social Psychology, 30,* 247–276.

Crano, W. D., & Prislin, R. (2006). Attitudes and persuasion. *Annual Review of Psychology, 57,* 345–374.

Crano, W. D., & Prislin, R. (2008). *Attitude and attitude change.* New York: Psychology Press.

David, B., & Turner, J. C. (1999). Studies in self-categorization and minority conversion: The in-group minority in intragroup and intergroup contexts. *British Journal of Social Psychology, 38,* 115–134.

David, B., & Turner, J. C. (2001a). Majority and minority influence: A single process self-categorization analysis. In C. K. W. De Dreu & N. K. De Vries (Eds.), *Group consensus and minority influence: Implications for innovation* (pp. 91–121). Malden, MA: Blackwell.

David, B., & Turner, J. C. (2001b). Self-categorization principles underlying majority and minority influence. In J. P. Forgas & K. D. Williams (Eds.), *Social influence: Direct and indirect processes* (pp. 293–313). New York: Psychology Press.

De Dreu, C. K. W., & De Vries, N. K. (Eds.). (2001). *Group consensus and minority influence: Implications for innovation.* Oxford, UK: Blackwell.

De Dreu, C. K. W., & West, M. (2001). Minority dissent and team innovation: The importance of participation in decision making. *Journal of Applied Psychology, 86,* 1191–1201.

Dobbs, M., & Crano, W. D. (2001). Outgroup accountability in the minimal group paradigm: Implications for aversive discrimination and social identity theory. *Personality and Social Psychology Bulletin, 27,* 355–364.

Erb, H.-P., & Bohner, G. (2001). Mere consensus effects in minority and majority influence. In C. K. W. De Dreu & N. K. De Vries (Eds.), *Group consensus and minority influence: Implications for innovation* (pp. 40–59). Malden, MA: Blackwell.

Festinger, L. (1954). A theory of social comparison processes. *Human Relations, 7,* 117–140.

Folk, C. L., & Gibson, B. S. (Eds.). (2001). *Attraction, distraction and action: Multiple perspectives on attentional capture.* New York: Elsevier Science.

Gati, I., Ben-Shakhar, G., & Avni-Liberty, S. (1996). Stimulus novelty and significance in electrodermal orienting responses: The effects of adding versus deleting stimulus components. *Psychophysiology, 33,* 637–643.

Goethals, G. R., & Darley, J. M. (1977). Social comparison theory: An attributional approach. In J. M. Suls & R. L. Miller (Eds.), *Social comparison processes: Theoretical and empirical perspectives* (pp. 259–278). Washington, DC: Hemisphere.

Goethals, G. R., & Nelson, R. E. (1973). Similarity in the influence process: The belief–value distinction. *Journal of Personality and Social Psychology, 25,* 117–122.

Gorenflo, D. W., & Crano, W. D. (1989). Judgmental subjectivity/objectivity and locus of choice in social comparison. *Journal of Personality and Social Psychology, 57,* 605–614.

Gruder, C. L., Cook, T. D., Hennigan, K. M., Flay, B. R., Alessi, C., & Halamaj, J. (1978). Empirical tests of the absolute sleeper effect predicted from the discounting cue hypothesis. *Journal of Personality and Social Psychology, 36,* 1061–1074.

Hovland, C. I., Janis, I. L., & Kelley, H. H. (1953). *Communication and persuasion: Psychological studies of opinion change.* New Haven, CT: Yale University Press.

Hovland, C. I., Lumsdaine, A., & Sheffield, F. (1949). *Experiments on mass communications* (Vol. 3). Princeton, NJ: Princeton University Press.

Johnson, B. T., & Eagly, A. H. (1990). Involvement and persuasion: Types, traditions, and the evidence. *Psychological Bulletin, 107,* 375–384.

Judd, C. M., Drake, R. A., Downing, J. W., & Krosnick, J. A. (1991). Some dynamic properties of attitude structures: Context-induced response facilitation and polarization. *Journal of Personality and Social Psychology, 60,* 193–202.

Kerr, N. (2002). When is a minority a minority? Active versus passive minority advocacy and minority influence. *European Journal of Social Psychology, 32,* 471–483.

Kerr, N. L., & Tindale, R. S. (2004). Group performance and decision making. *Annual Review of Psychology, 55,* 623–655.

Knowles, E. S., & Linn, J. A. (2004). *Resistance and persuasion.* Mahwah, NJ: Lawrence Erlbaum Associates, Inc.

Kumkale, G. T., & Albarracín, D. (2004). The sleeper effect in persuasion: A meta-analytic review. *Psychological Bulletin, 130,* 143–172.

Laughlin, P. R. (1980). Social combination processes of cooperative problem-solving groups on verbal intellective tasks. In M. Fishbein (Ed.), *Progress in social psychology* (pp. 127–155). Hillsdale, NJ: Lawrence Erlbaum Associates, Inc.

Laughlin, P. R. (1988). Collective induction: Group performance, social combination processes and mutual majority and majority influence. *Journal of Personality and Social Psychology, 54,* 254–267.

Lehman, B., & Crano, W. D. (2002). The pervasive effects of vested interest on attitude–criterion consistency in political judgment. *Journal of Experimental Social Psychology, 38,* 101–112.

Mackie, D. M. (1987). Systematic and nonsystematic processing of majority and minority persuasive communications. *Journal of Personality and Social Psychology, 43,* 41–52.

Martin, R., Gardikiotis, A., & Hewstone, M. (2002). Levels of consensus and majority and minority influence. *European Journal of Social Psychology, 32,* 645–665.

Martin, R., Hewstone, M., & Martin, P. Y. (2003). Resistance to persuasive messages as a function of majority and minority source status. *Journal of Experimental Social Psychology, 39,* 585–593.

McGuire, W. J., & McGuire, C. V. (1991). The content, structure, and operation of thought systems. In R. S. Wyer & T. Srull (Eds.), *Advances in social cognition* (Vol. 4, pp. 1–78). Hillsdale, NJ: Lawrence Erlbaum Associates, Inc.

Moscovici, S. (1980). Toward a theory of conversion behavior. In L. Berkowitz (Ed.), *Advances in experimental social psychology* (Vol. 13, pp. 209–239). New York: Academic Press.

Moscovici, S. (1985a). Innovation and minority influence. In S. Moscovici, G. Mugny, & E. Van Avermaet (Eds.), *Perspectives on minority influence* (pp. 9–52). Cambridge, UK: Cambridge University Press.

Moscovici, S. (1985b). Social influence and conformity. In G. Lindsey & E. Aronson (Eds.), *The handbook of social psychology* (3rd ed., Vol. 2, pp. 347–412). New York: Random House.

Moscovici, S., & Lage, E. (1976). Studies in social influence III: Majority versus minority influence in a group. *European Journal of Social Psychology, 8,* 349–365.

Moscovici, S., Lage, E., & Naffrechoux, M. (1969). Influence of a consistent minority on the responses of a majority in a color perception task. *Sociometry, 32,* 365–380.

Moscovici, S., Mugny, G., & Papastamou, S. (1981). 'Sleeper effect' et/ou effet minoritaire? Etude theorique et experimentale de l'influence sociale a retardement. *Cahiers de Psychologie Cognitive, 1,* 199–221.

Mugny, G. (1982). *The power of minorities.* London: Academic Press.

Nemeth, C. J. (1995). Dissent as driving cognitions, attitudes, and judgments. *Social Cognition, 13,* 273–291.

O'Gorman, J. G. (1979). The orienting reflex: Novelty or significance detector? *Psychophysiology, 16,* 253–262.

Olson, J. M., Ellis, R. J., & Zanna, M. P. (1983). Validating objective versus subjective judgments: Interest in social comparison and consistency information. *Personality and Social Psychology Bulletin, 9,* 427–436.

Pettigrew, T. F. (1958). The measurement and correlates of category width as a cognitive variable. *Journal of Personality, 26,* 532–544.

Petty, R., & Cacioppo, J. T. (1986a). *Communication and persuasion: Central and peripheral routes to attitude change.* New York: Springer-Verlag.

Petty, R., & Cacioppo, J. T. (1986b). The elaboration likelihood model of persuasion. In L. Berkowitz (Ed.), *Advances in experimental social psychology* (Vol. 19, pp. 123–205). New York: Academic Press.

Petty, R., & Krosnick, J. (Eds.). (1995). *Attitude strength: Antecedents and consequences.* Hillsdale, NJ: Lawrence Erlbaum Associates, Inc.

Petty, R. E., & Wegener, D. T. (1999). The elaboration likelihood model: Current status and controversies. In S. Chaiken & Y. Trope (Eds.), *Dual-process theories in social psychology* (pp. 37–72). New York: Guilford Press.

Pool, G. J., Wood, W., & Leck, K. (1998). The self-esteem motive in social influence: Agreement with valued majorities and disagreement with derogated minorities. *Journal of Personality and Social Psychology, 75,* 967–975.

Priester, J., Wegener, D., Petty, R., & Fabrigar, L. (1999). Examining the psychological process underlying the sleeper effect: The elaboration likelihood model explanation. *Media Psychology, 1,* 27–48.

Prislin, R., Brewer, M. B., & Wilson, D. J. (2002). Changing majority and minority positions within a group versus an aggregate. *Personality and Social Psychology Bulletin, 28,* 504–511.

Prislin, R., & Christensen, P. N. (2002). Group conversion versus group expansion as modes of change in majority and minority positions: All losses hurt but only some gains gratify. *Journal of Personality and Social Psychology, 83,* 1095–1102.

Prislin, R., & Christensen, P. N. (2005). The effects of social change within a group on membership preferences: To leave or not to leave? *Personality and Social Psychology Bulletin, 31,* 595–609.

Prislin, R., Limbert, W., & Bauer, E. (2000). From majority to minority and vice versa: The asymmetrical effects of gaining and losing majority position within a group. *Journal of Personality and Social Psychology, 79,* 385–395.

Prislin, R., & Wood, W. (2005). Social influence: The role of social consensus in attitude and attitude change. In D. Albarracin, B. T. Johnson, & M. P. Zanna

(Eds.), *The handbook of attitudes* (pp. 671–706). Hillsdale, NJ: Lawrence Erlbaum Associates, Inc.

Suls, J., Martin, R., & Wheeler, L. (2003). The importance of the question in the judgment of abilities and opinions via social comparison. In J. P. Forgas, K. D. Williams, & W. von Hippel (Eds.), *Social judgments: Implicit and explicit processes* (pp. 273–289). New York: Cambridge University Press.

Suls, J., & Wills, T. A. (Eds.). (1991). *Social comparison: Contemporary theory and research*. Hillsdale, NJ: Lawrence Erlbaum Associates, Inc.

Tormala, Z. L. (2004). A new framework for resistance to persuasion: The resistance appraisals hypothesis. In W. D. Crano & R. Prislin (Eds.), *Attitudes and attitude change* (pp. 213–234). New York: Psychology Press.

Tormala, Z. L., & Petty, R. (2002). What does not kill me makes me stronger: The effects of resisting persuasion on attitude certainty. *Journal of Personality and Social Psychology, 83*, 1298–1313.

Tormala, Z. L., & Petty, R. (2004a). Resistance to persuasion and attitude certainty: The moderating role of elaboration. *Personality and Social Psychology Bulletin, 30*, 1446–1457.

Tormala, Z. L., & Petty, R. (2004b). Source credibility and attitude certainty: A metacognitive analysis of resistance to persuasion. *Journal of Consumer Psychology, 14*, 427–442.

Tormala, Z. L., & Petty, R. E. (2004c). Resistance to persuasion and attitude certainty: The moderating role of elaboration. *Personality and Social Psychology Bulletin, 30*, 1446–1457.

Turner, J. C. (1991). *Social influence*. Milton Keynes, UK: Open University Press.

Williams, K. D. (2001). *Ostracism: The power of silence*. New York: Guilford Press.

Wood, W. (2000). Attitude change: Persuasion and social influence. *Annual Review of Psychology, 51*, 539–570.

Wood, W., Pool, G. J., Leck, K., & Purvis, D. (1996). Self-definition, defensive processing, and influence: The normative impact of majority and minority groups. *Journal of Personality and Social Psychology, 71*, 1181–1193.

Wood, W., & Quinn, J. M. (2003). Forewarned and forearmed? Two meta-analysis syntheses of forewarnings of influence appeals. *Psychological Bulletin, 129*, 119–138.

Wright, M. J. (2005). Saliency predicts change detection in pictures of natural scenes. *Spatial Vision, 18*, 413–430.

# 4 Consensus as the key: Towards parsimony in explaining majority and minority influence

*Hans-Peter Erb*
Helmut Schmidt University, Germany

*Gerd Bohner*
University of Bielefeld, Germany

## Introduction

It is literally impossible to go through life without being influenced by other people. Social influence, in particular, is closely related to the number of those other people who express or advocate a particular view or position. Research has long been concerned with conformity as the psychological process to explain the influence by a large number or majority of others (see Cialdini & Trost, 1998). Since Moscovici's work (e.g., Moscovici, Lage, & Naffrechoux, 1969) it has also been known that minorities who hold positions shared by only a few others can exert considerable influence. The number of studies on majority and minority influence is large, and they often provide conflicting findings. Moreover, comparisons between studies are difficult because the effects of majorities and minorities have been studied with multiple operationalizations (see Wood, Lundgren, Ouellette, Busceme, & Blackstone, 1994).

Recently, we have made attempts at integration to explain social influence with the most basic variable that was found to necessarily covary with majority or minority status, namely *consensus*. In this sense, consensus provides nothing more than information about the amount of socially shared agreement. Kruglanski and Mackie (1990) discussed the effects of a number of variables previously examined in research on social influence. These authors concluded that consensus is the only variable that defines majorities and minorities in any context: A majority necessarily reflects higher consensus than a minority.

Consensus, then, seems to be the key variable in any attempt to explain social influence by majorities and minorities (Erb & Bohner, 2001). Our 'mere-consensus approach', to be described in this chapter, builds on this assumption. We first introduce the notion of 'mere consensus' and then review empirical evidence in favour of the consensus approach to explain social influence by majorities. Next, we discuss research demonstrating that consensus can influence attitude judgements even if it was not explicitly provided. We then turn to minority influence and report conditions that promote influence under low consensus. We conclude with a discussion of how future research may potentially profit from a consensus-based perspective.

## The notion of mere consensus

Majority and minority influence have been connected to an immense number of variables supposed to produce, alter, mediate or moderate their impact. We cannot review here all those variables such as the *Zeitgeist* (e.g., Maass & Clark, 1984), the in-group versus out-group distinction (e.g., Crano, 2001; Turner, 1991), social power (e.g., Mugny, 1982), social conflict (e.g., Moscovici, 1980), double minorities (Maass, Clark, & Haberkorn, 1982), normative contexts (e.g., Paicheler, 1977), opinion discrepancy (e.g., Nemeth, 1986), source–position imbalance (Baker & Petty, 1994), and so forth. However, we propose that many of these variables may not be *necessary* explanatory constructs. Following this reasoning, we propose that studying majority and minority influence detached from such variables may provide new insights into influence phenomena. That is not to say, however, that variables other than consensus should not be studied, and we will present examples on how such variables can moderate the impact of consensus on attitude judgements.

In fact, in our empirical work we varied consensus in the absence of almost any information about the influence group as a socially defined category, deliberately chose minorities and majorities that were socially irrelevant to the recipients, and issues that were fictitious, in order to minimize any effect of *Zeitgeist*, opinion discrepancy and conflict, normative context, and so on. We hypothesized that even in such seemingly 'impoverished' situations, consensus would have an impact on recipients' information processing and judgement formation (Erb, Bohner, Schmälzle, & Rank, 1998). In a most simple test of this hypothesis, participants at the University of Mannheim, Germany, were exposed to a persuasive message that argued in favour of a fictitious large-scale building project planned in the harbour of Rotterdam, a big city in the Netherlands. Depending on the condition, the participants learned that the message was supported by either a majority (high consensus) or a minority (low consensus) of Rotterdam citizens who had attended a public discussion meeting. In a control condition they received no consensus information. The use of a fictitious issue prevented any conflict arising between the position forwarded by the influence group and prior attitudes held by the recipients. The use of Rotterdam citizens as the influence group ensured that any tendency to identify with the influence group could not interfere with a mere effect of consensus on processing the message and forming the final attitude judgements. After reading the message, participants were asked to list any thoughts that they had had while reading the text and to indicate their own attitudes toward

*Table 4.1* Thought listing measures and attitude index as a function of consensus

|  | | Consensus | | |
|---|---|---|---|---|
|  | | *Low* | *High* | *None* |
| (a) | Valence of thoughts | −0.21 | +0.08 | −0.09 |
| (b) | Novelty of thoughts | 6.51 | 4.08 | 5.80 |
| (c) | Attitudes | 5.39 | 6.41 | 5.86 |

*Note*: Higher numbers indicate (a) higher favourability, range from −1 *unfavourable* to +1 *favourable*; (b) higher novelty, range from 1 *old idea* to 9 *new idea*; and (c) higher favourability, range from 1 *unfavourable* to 9 *favourable*.

*Source*: Erb et al. (1998).

the project on several attitude items that were later combined to form an index of general agreement.

Results (Table 4.1) showed that consensus information biased the processing of issue-related information so that the cognitive responses to the message were more favourable under high consensus and were less favourable under low consensus, when compared to control conditions where no consensus information was provided. Moreover, mere consensus influenced cognitive responding on the divergence–convergence dimension introduced by Nemeth (1986). Under low consensus, thinking diverged from the information provided and respondents came up with new and original ideas about the issue. Under high consensus, processing focused more narrowly on the information already given in the influence setting. In contrast to Nemeth's (1986) theorizing where discrepancy between the recipients' attitudes and the influence group's position was assigned major explanatory relevance for the effects on the divergence–convergence dimension, in our study consensus that was completely detached from prior attitudes proved to be sufficient to produce such effects. Obviously, effects on the divergence–convergence dimension are related to a more general aspect of minority and majority influence, namely consensus. Finally, attitude judgements varied as a function of consensus: high consensus produced more favourable attitudes, low consensus less favourable attitudes when compared to the control condition (see Erb et al., 1998, Experiment 1, for details).

In sum, this research demonstrated that consensus itself—detached from other variables formerly proposed to shape majority and minority influence—produces evaluative and cognitive consequences. As such, mere consensus provides a more parsimonious explanation for majority influence than do competing models. Moreover, mere consensus effects can be used as a starting point to analyse the impact of other variables previously studied in the realm of majority and minority influence. From our perspective, a candidate variable to explain majority or minority influence would have to produce an interaction effect with consensus, that is, operate differently under majority influence than under minority influence.

## Interaction of consensus with prior attitudes

One example of an interaction effect with consensus refers to the conditions determining whether minorities or majorities instigate more processing effort on the part of the recipient. According to Mackie's (1987) objective-consensus approach, the majority position 'is accepted as reflecting objective reality' (Mackie, 1987, p. 42). In turn, a recipient's attention will be directed to the majority message, which results in extensive processing. A minority, on the other hand, lacks objective consensus; hence minority messages will be processed less extensively. This prediction was supported in a series of studies (Mackie, 1987).

Seemingly, Mackie's objective consensus approach is difficult to reconcile with Moscovici's earlier conversion theory. Moscovici (1980) proposed that under majority influence, recipients engage in a comparison process whereby they compare their own attitude with the conflicting attitude proposed by the majority. This process is one of social comparison. As far as the social conflict between the majority and the recipient's own deviant position is the focus of concern, message content will be of low importance and processed rather superficially. On the other hand, informational conflict with a minority leads to an active validation process in which issue-relevant information processing prevails. Hence, the minority message will be scrutinized extensively. It is this extensive processing that leads to conversion. Thus, in conversion theory, conflict between recipients' prior attitudes and the position proposed by the influence group plays a decisive role.

Empirical tests confirmed that information attributed to a minority was processed more extensively than information attributed to a majority (e.g., Moscovici, 1980). These effects were studied under conditions of strong discrepancies between recipients' prior attitudes and the position proposed by the influence group. Such discrepancies arose from conflicting judgements in a colour-perception task where a minority insisted on calling blue-coloured slides green (e.g., Moscovici et al., 1969; but see Martin, 1998) or from persuasive messages that clashed with important values, for example European students' views regarding environmental protection in the late 1970s (Moscovici, 1980).

The contradiction between Mackie's and Moscovici's findings points to the possibility that moderating factors have to be taken into account (Wood et al., 1994, p. 337). In order to explain the effect of more scrutiny for the majority message in Mackie's studies and its divergence from Moscovici's findings, we (Erb, Bohner, Rank, & Einwiller, 2002b) speculated that the attitudes used in Mackie's experiments were likely not related to strong convictions on part of the recipients. The issues (e.g., 'the US should act to ensure a military balance in the Western hemisphere') were relatively

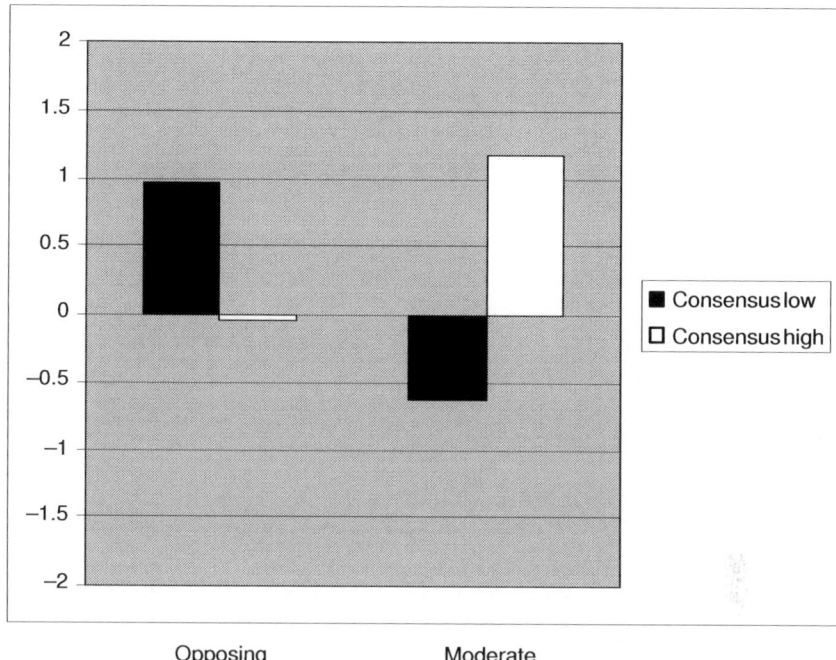

*Figure 4.1* Attitude difference (strong minus weak) as a function of consensus (low vs. high) and prior attitude (opposing vs. moderate). Data from Erb et al. (2002b).

unfamiliar to Mackie's participants. Therefore, the situation was not likely to induce strong conflict when compared to situations where one's own colour-perception ability or deep concern with environmental issues were challenged. Accordingly, we predicted consensus to interact with recipients' prior attitudes in its effect on the level of message processing.

In one test of this prediction, we (Erb et al., 2002b) measured prior attitudes toward the fluoridation of drinking water in Germany. This issue was chosen because pilot testing had shown that attitudes were distributed in a bi-modal shape, that is, our participants were either strongly opposed or rather moderate. A total of 110 students at the University of Heidelberg, Germany, read a message containing either weak or strong arguments, ostensibly favoured by either a majority or a minority. Argument quality was varied to assess the amount of information processing dedicated to the message: high processing effort would result in higher agreement with the strong rather than with the weak arguments, whereas low processing effort would not result in such a differentiation.

Results (Figure 4.1) confirmed that recipients who held an attitude that was in conflict with the forwarded position (opposing prior attitude) dedicated more processing effort to the minority than to the majority message.

Conversely, participants whose attitudes were not in strong conflict with the influence source's position (moderate prior attitude) processed the majority message more extensively than the minority message.

In another study on the Mackie versus Moscovici controversy, we (Bohner, Dykema-Engblade, Tindale, & Meisenhelder, 2008) also showed that the framing of consensus information can determine how majority and minority messages are processed. Specifically, we proposed that consensus information would create expectancies of message validity if the source was framed as knowledgeable, which would activate concerns about accuracy (cf. Mackie's objective-consensus approach). We further proposed, however, that consensus information would activate social-relational concerns if the source was framed as similar to the participants (cf. Moscovici's conversion theory). These ideas were tested in a study with undergraduates at Loyola University Chicago, USA, who read strong, ambiguous, or weak arguments on a construction project said to be planned in Rotterdam. The influence source, a group of Rotterdam students, was introduced either as well-informed on the issue (accuracy concern), or as similar to Loyola students (social-relational concern); consensus was said to be either low (minority of 15%) or high (majority of 85%). The main dependent variables were the favourability of cognitive responses and post-message attitudes.

As predicted, the knowledge framing caused consensus-based assimilation of cognitive responses for ambiguous arguments, and contrast for both strong and weak arguments. That is, when the arguments were sufficiently ambiguous to allow consensus to bias their processing, cognitive responses were more favourable under high than under low consensus (replicating earlier findings; Erb et al., 1998). When the arguments were unambiguously weak, high consensus (implying correctness) produced more negative reactions than did low consensus. When the arguments were unambiguously strong, low consensus (implying incorrectness) produced more positive reactions than did high consensus. This pattern of results closely replicated the effects of a direct manipulation of source expertise in a different study (Bohner, Ruder, & Erb, 2002). Also as predicted, the similarity framing caused more extensive processing of the minority arguments but uncritical acceptance of majority arguments. This pattern would be congenial to conversion theory. It should be noted, however, that it was obtained in the absence of any realistic social relationship between source and recipients. The patterns of means for valenced cognitive responses are displayed in Figure 4.2. Similar, but less pronounced patterns resulted for post-message attitudes (see Bohner et al., 2008).

By studying the effects of prior attitudes and social identity versus accuracy concerns in interaction with consensus on information processing and judgement formation, we were able to reconcile seemingly contradictory findings in the literature by Moscovici (1980) and Mackie (1987). The components of the objective-consensus approach and conversion theory that deal with majority and minority source effects on information

A: Knowledge framing conditions

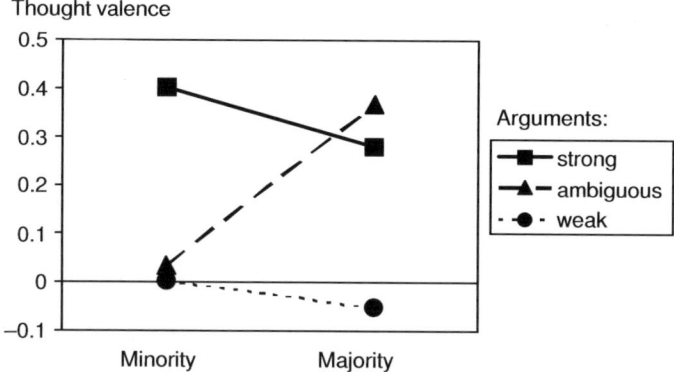

B: Similarity framing conditions

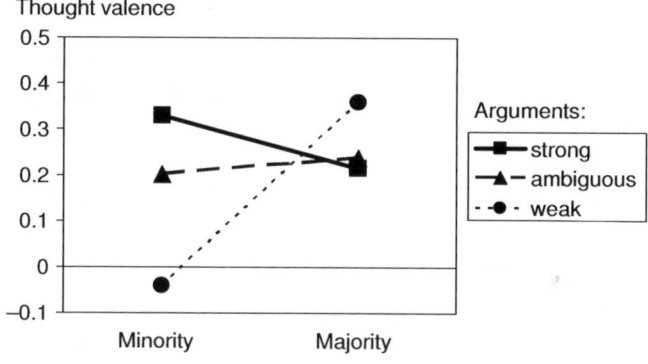

*Figure 4.2* Valenced cognitive responses as a function of consensus (minority vs. majority) and argument quality (strong vs. ambiguous vs. weak) under knowledge framing (Panel A) and similarity framing (Panel B). Adapted from Bohner et al. (2008).

processing are applicable only to specific conditions. The effect that majorities instigate more processing effort than minorities may operate under conditions where recipients are relatively open minded, concerned with the accuracy of the proposed position, and not strongly committed to an attitude that has already been formed prior to the influence attempt. On the other hand, when conflict between the influence source's position and the recipient's own deviant attitude is of major concern, it is likely that the minority message will receive more attention. In sum, these findings point to the usefulness of a consensus approach for studying social influence and encourage the search for other variables that interact with consensus in their effects on information processing and attitude judgements.

## Inferred and explicit consensus

From the mere consensus perspective, examples of minority or majority influence when numerical consensus information is not explicitly provided represent an interesting phenomenon that requires explanation. A recipient who only knows that 'a majority' or 'a minority' of others agrees may reach a favourable or unfavourable conclusion even though the exact numerical consensus is unknown. Such an effect can be explained in terms of the operation of *inferred* consensus information. That is, when a recipient in a social-influence situation learns that a majority or a minority agrees, he or she generates a representation of the numerical strength of the respective group. It can readily be assumed that such inferred consensus is higher for majority than for minority sources. Inferred consensus, in turn, can be used as a basis for subsequent attitude judgements, resulting in (un)favourable judgements in response to majority (minority) source information.

Inferred consensus refers to a subjective representation of how most others will behave, think, or judge in a particular situation. For example, Baker and Petty (1994) studied effects of the unexpectedness of certain source/position combinations. In their studies, if a majority of students were perceived as favouring (or only a minority as disapproving of) a mandatory programme committing students to a 2-year community service or a rise in tuition fees, this obvious source–position imbalance fostered message scrutiny. Obviously, recipients in these studies expected high consensus on disapproval for a proposal that ran counter to the influence group's own interest.

In our own studies, we have repeatedly found that consensus estimates in control conditions, where neither minority/majority source information nor explicit consensus had been provided, were similar to those in the majority conditions and significantly different from those in the minority conditions (e.g., Erb et al., 1998). Participants may thus generally expect the experimenter to provide information about which there is high agreement (see Grice's, 1977, 'maxim of quality'). The simple fact that the participant learns about one side of the issue and not the other side may contribute to the representation of high consensus even when no such information is provided.

In addition to these sources of (inferred) consensus, we propose that exposure to minority or majority source information leads to the generation of consensus (cf. an inference with regard to the numerical strength of the influence group). Furthermore, a recipient may expect an influence group to represent a certain amount of numerical consensus, but may learn that explicit consensus deviates from assumptions derived from minority or majority source information. Such a condition of discrepancy between inferred and explicit consensus provides a critical test for the hypothesis that source status implies a certain amount of consensus. Consensus inferred from majority or minority source information may contradict explicit consensus.

Under conditions of such discrepancy, we expected that inferred and explicit consensus would combine interactively to determine attitude judgements. Whenever explicit consensus exceeds (falls short of) inferred consensus, social influence should increase (decrease). A minority that represents higher explicit consensus (e.g., 48%) than inferred (e.g., 20%) should be more influential than a minority whose actual numerical strength is unknown or fits inferred consensus (e.g., 18%). Conversely, a majority that represents lower explicit consensus (e.g., 52%) than inferred (e.g., 80%) should be less influential than a majority whose numerical strength is unknown or fits expectations.

A series of experiments confirmed this hypothesis (Erb, Bohner, Werth, Hewstone, & Reinhard, 2006). In one study, we varied explicit consensus and minority/majority source information in a 2 (minority vs. majority influence) × 2 (explicit consensus 48%/52% vs. 14%/86%) design. A total of 60 students at the University of Maryland, College Park, USA, learned that they participated in a study on 'text comprehension'. The influence group was said to be a minority or majority of students at another university who had attended a meeting where the vacation spot 'Curutao Lake' had been promoted. Participants read a persuasive message promoting a fictitious holiday resort area in Brazil named 'Curutao Lake'. It was further said that 'at the conclusion of the meeting an informal poll showed that . . .', depending on condition, '. . . a majority of 52% (86%)' or '. . . a minority of 48% (14%) of attending students agreed that Curutao Lake was a rewarding vacation spot, while a minority of 48% (14%)' or '. . . a majority of 52% (86%) disagreed'. After reading the message, respondents indicated their agreement with five attitude statements that were later combined to form an attitude index.

As predicted, we found that the relatively large minority of 48% was even more influential than a relatively small majority of 52%, even though consensus was still lower for the minority than for the majority (Figure 4.3). The interactive effect of inferred and explicit consensus demonstrates that recipients of majority and minority source information generate a specific representation of consensus. Such inferred consensus can be used as a basis for subsequent judgements.

In a more recent experiment (Erb, 2006) within the same experimental paradigm, it was found that experimentally introducing an expectation of narrow consensus relations ('a narrow result was to be expected') cancelled out the interactive effect of inferred and explicit consensus on attitudes and resulted in generally higher influence of the majority independent of its numerical strength. Accordingly, the interactive effect of inferred and explicit consensus on attitudes depends on the context. For example, in

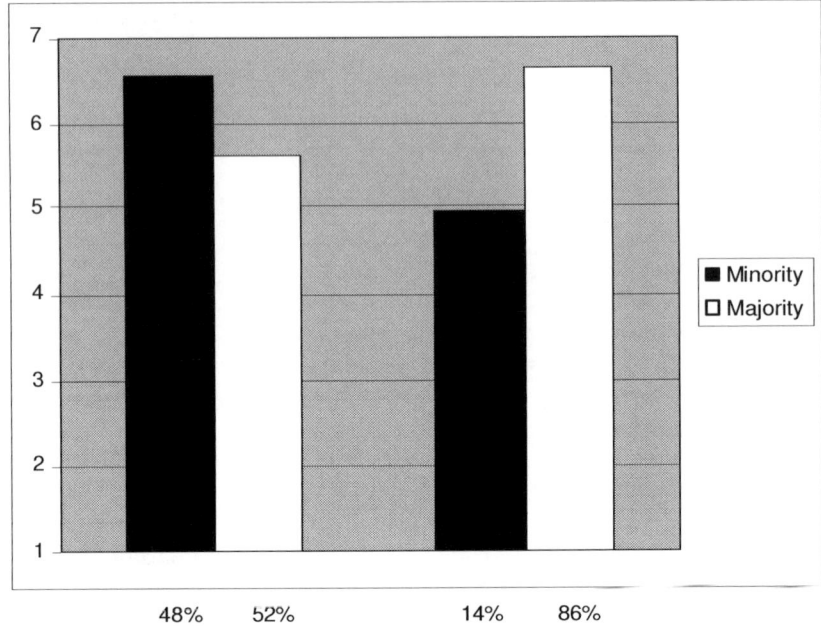

*Figure 4.3* Attitudes as a function of source information (minority vs. majority) and explicit consensus (48/52% vs. 14/86%). Data from Erb et al. (2006).

political contexts consensus relations are often so narrow that people speak of an 'absolute majority' whenever it exceeds the 50% benchmark. In such contexts consensus of 52% (48%) may not be regarded as a small majority (large minority).

Only this latter finding parallels results by Mackie (1987), Martin, Gardikiotis, and Hewstone (2002), and Gardikiotis, Martin, and Hewstone (2005), who found that the absolute amount of explicit consensus had no effect on attitude judgements in their studies. Mackie (1987, p. 47) speculated, that the '. . . gulf between a majority of 52% and a minority of 48% is wider than the numbers alone suggest . . .', and individuals '. . . who found themselves in disagreement with a substantial majority seemed to be more concerned by the fact that they were in conflict with a majority than by the relative size of that majority . . .'. Obviously, majority influence studied by Mackie (1987), Martin and colleagues (2002), and Gardikiotis and colleagues (2005) was based on the social motive not to appear deviant from a highly valued in-group majority and to identify with this in-group.

In our studies, however, care was taken to prevent the occurrence of any effects of conflict with a socially valued influence source. We did so under the premises that (a) conflict is not necessarily involved in an influence situation (see Erb et al., 2002b) and (b) being socially valued is not necessarily combined with minority and majority status (Kruglanski & Mackie,

1990). We agree with Mackie's analysis that social motives may well obscure the operation of consensus. Whenever social or other motives play a prominent role, the use of consensus may be offset because motivational concerns provide a more accessible and subjectively more important basis for attitude judgements.

## Mere consensus in minority influence

Minorities who advocate positions of low consensus carry the potential for innovation and progress within groups and societies. Since Moscovici's seminal work, numerous models have been proposed to identify conditions of minority influence (see Maass & Clark, 1984; Wood et al., 1994, for reviews). Often, the term 'minority' refers to socially defined groups or subgroups that are ascribed negative attributes. Sometimes a minority is perceived as an oppressed, underprivileged, or powerless group of defectors or underdogs ('communists', 'rebellious youth', etc.). Such negative characteristics cannot be attributed to every minority—counter-examples are the White population in some African countries, members of 'The Club of Rome', and so forth (e.g., Kruglanski & Mackie, 1990). In social-influence settings, however, even such privileged minorities experience the drawback that is common to all minority groups: By definition, their position is held by relatively few people and therefore represents a position of *low consensus*.

Low consensus has repeatedly been shown to have negative evaluative consequences. For example, low consensus cannot provide group members with social support for, and validation of, their views (Festinger, 1954), and group members react negatively to minorities who impede consensus (e.g., Levine, 1989). Responses to influence attempts are usually more positive for majorities than for minorities (e.g., Erb et al., 1998; Mackie, 1987; Moscovici & Lage, 1976; Mugny, 1982; Wood et al., 1994). A minority source can serve as a discounting cue in persuasion by calling to mind negatively valenced heuristic inferences (cf. 'low consensus implies incorrectness'; e.g., Axsom, Yates, & Chaiken, 1987; Darke et al., 1998) that guide information processing and subsequent judgement formation (e.g., Bohner et al., 2008; Erb et al., 1998; Mackie, 1987). In sum, there are numerous findings that attest to the negative implications of low consensus in influence settings. As Moscovici (1980, p. 210) put it, 'What the minority does is bad, because there are few who do it'.

Against this background, researchers sought (and found) conditions that promote minority influence *despite* the drawback that their position is one of low consensus. A full discussion of all pertinent models is far beyond the present chapter, but some examples may illustrate how theorizing on minority influence was concerned with the identification of conditions that would help to compensate for seemingly inevitable disadvantages inherent in minority status.

According to Moscovici's *conversion theory*, the key to minority influence lies in the consistent behavioural style and the positive attributions such behaviour elicits. Inconsistent minorities, on the other hand, would not be influential. In the framework of *self-categorization theory* (e.g., David & Turner, 2001; Turner, 1991), minority influence rests on the fact that minorities are (still) part of the in-group, thus taking advantage of the majority members' interest in maintaining group coherence and an overall positive group evaluation. In a similar vein, the *leniency-contract model* (e.g., Crano, 2001) holds that minority influence hinges on the majority's leniency toward the deviant minority members of their in-group.

Drawing on the *heuristic-systematic model* of persuasion (e.g., Chaiken, Liberman, & Eagly, 1989), Moskowitz (1996) proposed that positive attributions toward the minority or other conditions such as surprise (see also Baker & Petty, 1994) motivate recipients to systematically process the minority's (convincing) arguments (see also Bohner, Moskowitz, & Chaiken, 1995, for an extensive discussion of minority influence within the heuristic-systematic model). Similarly, De Vries and colleagues (De Vries, De Dreu, Gordijn, & Schuurman, 1996) argued that minorities can only be influential when some external factors motivate recipients to engage in effortful and divergent processing (see Nemeth, 1986) of their arguments. In Latané's *social impact theory* (Latané & Wolf, 1981; Nowak, Szamrej, & Latané, 1990), the minority can surmount the disadvantage of being small in number by the immediacy (e.g., physical closeness) and the strength (e.g., social power) of their appeal. In sum, these examples (and many others not mentioned) demonstrate that research has mainly been concerned with the discovery of conditions where minorities are influential *in spite of* the fact that their position receives only little social support. Moreover, much of the minority influence studied referred to the 'hidden impact' of minorities (Maass & Clark, 1984), that is, delayed influence on issues related to but not identical with the focal issue of the influence attempt (see Tanford & Penrod, 1984; Wood et al., 1994).

Presently, we propose to view minority influence from a consensus per-spective. Instead of asking the question under what conditions a minority may overcome the obstacle of being small in number, we examine condi-tions that make the minority's low consensus appear attractive to the recipient. Under such conditions a minority is expected to exert greater influence than a majority, even on the focal issue of influence.

What might such conditions be? There is a considerable amount of research suggesting that events, characteristics, and objects are evaluated more *extremely* the lower their perceived prevalence. For example, attri-butional logic states that success will have more positive consequences and failure more negative consequences when consensus among actors is low, whereas evaluations will be less extreme when consensus is high (e.g., Kelley, 1967). Research on the 'scarcity principle' has shown that identical characteristics were evaluated more extremely the lower their perceived prevalence (e.g., Ditto & Jemmott, 1989). Research on commodity theory (e.g., Brock & Brannon, 1992) and self-categorization (e.g., Simon & Hamilton, 1994) also attests to the idea that evaluative judgements are more extreme when an object or characteristic is scarce.

As minorities hold positions of low consensus, it is only a small step to assume that minority positions represent an object of evaluative extremity: If a certain position is correct, it appears more positive to share it with a minority, but less so with a majority. On the other hand, sharing a position with a majority of others is of less evaluative extremity. We propose that this asymmetry in valence has an important consequence.

Evaluative extremity renders the minority position a risk-inclined option in the sense that consequences are either very positive or very negative (i.e., you appear foolish if you are wrong, but brilliant if you are right), whereas it is safe to yield to majority influence, because any consequence is less extreme when you share it with many others (i.e., it doesn't hurt much to be wrong if most others are wrong as well, but neither is it very rewarding to be right if that is true of most others as well). Accordingly, targets of influence will tend toward the minority position if they are inclined to take a risky decision.

A literature search for publications where minority/majority influence and risk taking were studied in combination yielded only a few studies. Clark (1988) tested the hypothesis that minorities who argue in favour of a dominant value within a group should exert greater influence than minorities who argue against the dominant value. He used the choice-dilemma scenarios developed by Kogan and Wallach (1964), which are known to elicit the value of either risk taking or caution to manipulate the dominant value. His hypothesis was that the minority group would only be influential when it argued in favour of risk, regarding those scenarios that normally elicit risky judgements, or when it argued for caution, regarding those scenarios that normally elicit caution. As predicted, a risky minority exerted considerable influence on risky items, but contrary to predictions the cautious minority was not particularly influential on cautious items. To explain the latter finding, Clark (1988, p. 523) speculated that '. . . the value that Western individuals place on risk is in some general way more dominant and powerful than the value they place on caution'. In light of the present view, however, the results may be explained differently: If minority positions represent risky options, any context that fosters risky decisions (like the risky scenarios) will promote minority influence, whereas contexts that foster cautious decisions will inhibit minority influence.

Tindale, Sheffey, and Scott (1993) also demonstrated that small-group decision making involving risk can produce minority influence. These authors used Kahneman and Tversky's (1979) 'Asian Disease' problem in a group discussion situation. This decision problem can be framed in terms of either gains or losses. The loss version favours tendencies toward risky decisions, whereas the gain version consistently yields risk-aversive reactions (e.g., Kahneman & Tversky, 1979). Tindale and colleagues (1993) found minority influence specifically in the loss condition, but not in the gain condition. They discussed their results in terms of issue-specific *Zeitgeist* effects (similar to Clark, 1988). However, the findings are also in line with the implications of the present analysis: The loss version of the 'Asian Disease' problem promotes tendencies towards risky decisions which in turn renders minority influence more likely; the gain version, conversely, promotes risk aversion, thus impeding minority influence.

In our own research (Erb, Hilton, Bohner, & Krings, 2009) we tested the hypothesis that the minority position would be judged as more risk inclined than the majority position. In one study, students at the University of Jena, Germany, were exposed to a description of a TV game show where players competed to gain money. It was explained that a player could succeed by correctly answering knowledge questions with either 'yes' or 'no'. To answer a question a player would have to place her- or himself on one of two squares on the stage, one representing the 'yes' answer and the other representing the 'no' answer. It was further said that 13 players were on stage at a time. Then, participants learned about a certain 'Mrs G.' who was one of the 13 players but had absolutely no idea what the correct answer to the question was. After observing that, depending on the condition, 2 (vs. 10) other players had chosen the 'yes' square and 10 (vs. 2) others had chosen the 'no' square, she decided for 'yes'. Thus, consensus for Mrs G's decision was either low or high.

Results strongly confirmed that the minority decision was judged as more risk inclined than the majority decision on a number of risk-related items (Table 4.2). But would recipients of consensus information yield to minority influence under preference for risk, when their own decisions and attitudes were at stake?

We explored this possibility in three studies. To induce preference for risk-inclined versus cautious judgements we used a priming procedure

*Table 4.2* Perception of risk as a function of consensus (low, high) on risk-related items

| Item | Consensus | | Significance test | |
| --- | --- | --- | --- | --- |
| | Low | High | $F(1, 44)$ | $p <$ |
| Rash | 4.04 | 2.74 | 6.36 | .02 |
| Risk-inclined | 7.07 | 2.78 | 75.96 | .001 |
| Security-oriented | 2.00 | 7.39 | 98.39 | .001 |
| Risky | 7.26 | 3.70 | 31.95 | .001 |
| Adventurous | 7.00 | 2.88 | 42.19 | .001 |
| Over-anxious | 1.70 | 5.39 | 42.05 | .001 |

*Note*: Higher numbers indicate a higher extent of agreement with the respective item on 9-point rating scales.

*Source*: Erb et al. (2009).

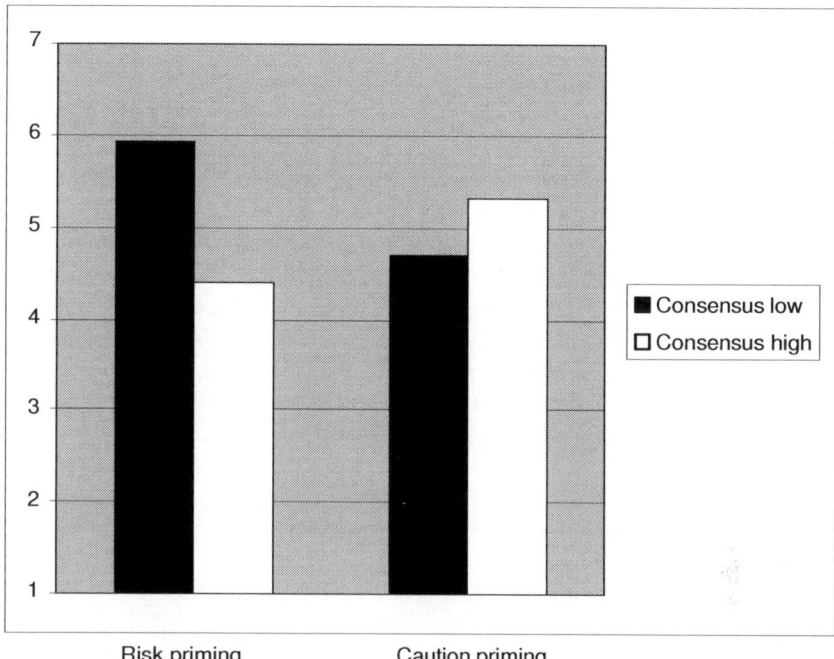

*Figure 4.4* Attitudes as a function of consensus (low vs. high) and risk priming (risk vs. caution). Data from Erb et al. (2009).

introduced by Erb, Bioy, and Hilton (2002a). Specifically, participants were asked to rank order the frequency of occurrence in ordinary speech of fifteen words in their native language. In the risk-seeking set, the words included four adjectives with positive connotations for risk seeking (e.g., 'enterprising') as well as four adjectives with negative connotations for risk avoidance (e.g., 'over anxious'), plus seven distractor adjectives (e.g., 'polite'). In the risk-avoidance set, the same distractor words were used, but adjectives with negative connotations for risk seeking (e.g., 'rash') and positive connotations for risk avoidance (e.g., 'conscientious') replaced the primes of the first set (see Erb et al., 2002a, for more details and a thorough discussion of this method).

In one of these studies (Erb et al., 2009), after the risk-priming procedure students at the University of Bonn, Germany, received a message that argued in favour of the introduction of a small lending fee in public libraries. The message was said to be supported by either a minority or a majority of students at a different university. As predicted attitude judgements varied as a function of risk priming and consensus (Figure 4.4). Recipients in the risk-seeking conditions were more influenced by the minority than by the majority, whereas recipients in the risk-avoiding conditions showed an opposite pattern. Other studies confirmed that this effect was independent of whether the influence group represented an in-group or an out-group.

The effect disappeared, however, when the influence group was portrayed as representing experts on the topic under consideration. Obviously 'competing' inferences drawn from the expertise of the influence group cancelled out the effect of the consensus information. This latter result speaks to the idea that accuracy concerns are driving the observed effects. If an individual follows the minority, he or she will appear to be foolish if the minority position turns out to be wrong but brilliant if this position turns out to be correct. To share a position with a majority of others would be safe, however, because there are many who are wrong or right. When the influence group represents experts themselves, which directly points to the correctness of the proposed position, considerations based on consensus do not play a major role any more. So far the research on risk preference provides a unique example of a condition under which the minority position appears more attractive to the recipient than does the majority position. Minority influence exceeded majority influence on the focal issue under consideration.

Most recently, we (Imhoff & Erb, 2009) started researching another factor that may render low consensus attractive to targets of influence, namely *deindividuation*. As Maslach (1974, p. 411) put it, 'People try to make themselves different and to stand out from others but they also try to minimize their differences and to be just like everyone else'. Deindividuation is a state in which an individual feels indistinguishable from other individuals (Ziller, 1964; Zimbardo, 1969). Findings in the literature suggest that individuals at times strive to avoid deindividuation (e.g., Snyder & Fromkin, 1980) and seek 'optimal distinctiveness' (e.g., Brewer, 1991). Accordingly, a minority position would be more attractive than a majority position for recipients who feel deindividuated, because sharing a high-consensus position would magnify the feeling of being a non-distinct member of a 'silent majority'. On the other hand, a low-consensus position represents something 'special', something of particular distinction, and thus allows one to regain individuation.

In a first study linking deindividuation and minority influence, we used the 'test-feedback method' introduced by Snyder and Fromkin (1980) to induce deindividuation. Specifically, students at the University of Bonn, Germany, responded to a fictitious 'Personality Inventory' and then, depending on the condition, received bogus feedback that their personality was either 'average' or 'specific' (control condition). We expected that participants in the 'average' condition would experience a feeling of deindividuation (Snyder & Fromkin, 1980). In an ostensibly unrelated 'second' experiment, participants were later exposed to a persuasive message about a fictitious holiday resort area promoted by either a minority or a majority of others. Attitude judgements in the deindividuation condition were more favourable under minority influence than under majority influence, whereas

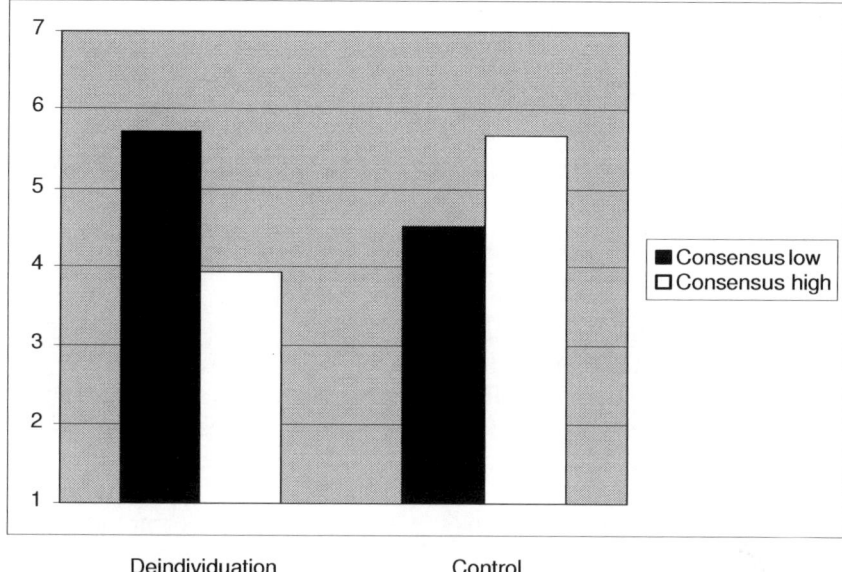

*Figure 4.5* Attitudes as a function of consensus (low vs. high) and deindividuation. Data from Imhoff and Erb (2009).

in the control condition we found the opposite pattern (Figure 4.5). These results supported our hypothesis.

In a second experiment (Imhoff & Erb, 2009), an additional condition involved providing an alternative means to regain individuation to participants before exposure to minority influence. These recipients were asked to list a number of attributes that would describe them as unique individuals. We hypothesized that an individual who can thus regain individuation and satisfy the motive of optimal distinctiveness would subsequently not prefer the low-consensus position. This is what was found empirically, and our hypothesis was strongly confirmed. As such, with the state of deindividuation we identified a motivational factor to promote the attractiveness of a low-consensus position and thus foster minority influence.

Research on minority influence under risk preference and deindividuation goes well beyond previous work on minority influence, because in our approach minority status is not regarded as a negative feature of the influence group to begin with (see discussion above). Other models of minority influence discuss conditions that encourage minority influence despite the drawback that minorities represent positions of low consensus. If minority status is regarded as negative by default it makes little sense to inquire into conditions where minority status appears attractive to recipients. We suspected the notion that minority status inevitably denotes a negative feature, chose a different approach, and asked whether there exist conditions that render the minority's low consensus appealing. In fact, there do exist conditions that render minorities influential because they represent sources of low consensus. Such conditions will prove to affect judgements on the focal issue (and not only on related issues) and, at the same time, will reduce influence from high-consensus sources, thus producing an interaction effect of consensus information with variations of these conditions.

## Some conclusions

Our research is based on the idea that consensus is the key variable to explain majority and minority influence: Consensus is the only variable that necessarily covaries with majority and minority status. In a first series of studies we found that mere consensus, that is consensus deprived of other variables that competing models introduced as explanatory constructs, can have evaluative consequences in that high consensus led to more influence than low consensus. Moreover, mere consensus influenced cognitive responding on the divergence–convergence dimension. This calls into question Nemeth's (1986) explanation for these effects, which emphasizes discrepancy between recipients' prior attitudes and the position forwarded by the influence group as the crucial explanatory variable.

The mere-consensus paradigm may be criticized for creating research conditions that in the real social world do not exist, and thus our findings may be of little relevance. In response to such a critique we would like to draw the reader's attention to two aspects. First, there may well exist conditions in the real world that at least come close to our operationalizations. For example, consensus information is increasingly conveyed via the results of opinion polls in modern mass media, and survey results are typically perceived to provide a reliable source of information about consensus in the surveyed population (e.g., Darke et al., 1998; Traugott & Kang, 2000). From our perspective, attributional factors, the motive to identify, social conflict, and so forth are unlikely to obscure the operation of consensus in such situations.

It seems likely, however, that consensus information provided by opinion-poll results in the media will influence the attitudes of its receivers. In a series of preliminary studies, we (Erb & Thoben, 2009) presented opinion-poll results to recipients under the cover story that we were researching the effects of different lay-out formats. Consensus was varied in between-subjects designs, and we found considerable influence of high consensus on judgements with regard to two attitude objects (Figure 4.6). Thus, mere consensus may well have effects in real-world settings.

Second, we believe that the usefulness of an experimental paradigm should not be evaluated on whether it represents real-world or artificial situations. Take as an example Tajfel and colleagues' (Tajfel, Billig, Bundy, & Flament, 1971) minimal-group paradigm, which inspired a tremendous

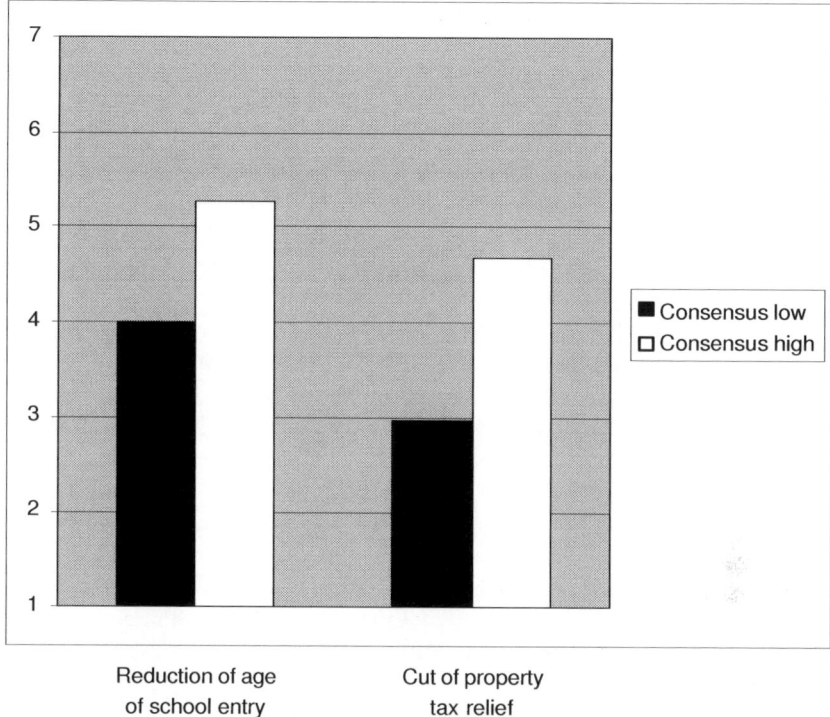

*Figure 4.6* Attitudes toward 'reduction of age of school entry' and 'cut of property tax relief' as a function of consensus (low vs. high) provided in opinion poll results. Data from Erb and Thoben (2009).

amount of research into inter-group relations, although minimal groups can hardly be found in real-world settings (cf. the concepts of 'mundane' vs. 'experimental realism'; Aronson, Ellsworth, Carlsmith, & Gonzalez, 1990). We see the benefits of the mere-consensus approach where it offers more parsimonious explanations than alternatives (Erb et al., 1998), enables us to re-examine contradictory findings in the literature (Erb et al., 2002b), and guides research into conditions of minority influence that are uniquely tied to the low consensus minorities necessarily represent (Erb et al., 2009; Imhoff & Erb, 2009).

Moreover, the mere-consensus approach sheds new light on findings of previous research. In this regard three major aspects seem to be of parti-cular importance. First, there is no variable that is inevitably connected with low or high consensus. When conversion theory (Moscovici, 1980) treats social versus informational conflict as one such variable, it neglects the possibility that conflict may vary along a continuum up to a point where there is no conflict at all. At times, recipients do not hold an attitude opposing the proposed position, be it because they are confronted with an attitude object that is new and unfamiliar to them, or because they encounter an attitude object about which they have not yet made up their mind (e.g., Hastie & Park, 1986). Similarly, when Mackie (1987) speaks of socially valued influence groups, this notion does not cover cases in which the influence group is socially irrelevant to recipients. As shown in our own work (Erb et al., 2006), reactions to the absolute size of the influence group may be quite different depending on whether conflict with a valued influence group is at stake or not. Last, but not least, it does not seem to hold true that majorities are generally and without exception valued more positively than minorities. Although this assumption seems to be at least implicitly made in all previous theorizing on minority influence, our studies on the effects of risk-preference (Erb et al., 2009) and deindividuation (Imhoff & Erb, 2009) suggest otherwise.

Second, at times 'competing inferences' offset the effect of consensus information on information processing and judgement formation. For example, in Mackie's (1987), Martin and colleagues' (2002), and Gardikiotis and colleagues' (2005) studies the actual size of the influence group was not the crucial variable. It seems that concern with the possibility of appearing deviant from a highly valued influence group cancelled out the effect of consensus in these cases. Similarly, accuracy concerns that produce minority influence under risk preference (Erb et al., 2009) can override the effect of consensus, for example when the influence group is presented as a group of experts who are likely to promote the correct position.

Other research can also be reinterpreted in terms of this analysis. Take as only one example work by Moskowitz (1996). In this research minorities were influential when factors such as positive attributions or surprise encouraged the effortful processing of the minority's convincing arguments. In this case, it may be that the persuasive arguments provided 'competing inferences' to offset the use of the low-consensus information and to finally agree with the influence source, regardless of whether it was a minority or majority. There is already evidence indicating that majorities are also more influential if they provide convincing arguments that the recipient opts to process with sufficient effort (Bohner, Frank, & Erb, 1998; see also Maheswaran & Chaiken, 1991). Convincing arguments should thus not be regarded as a variable to explain minority influence, because they foster the influence of majorities as well, and likely foster the influence of any source (a friend, an expert, one's spouse, etc., will be more influential when presenting strong arguments), given that recipients are sufficiently motivated and able to process the contents of these arguments. The bottom line is that providing recipients with consensus information does not come with the guarantee that they use consensus to form their judgements.

Third, and related to the second point, recipients sometimes use consensus plus some other variable to form their judgements. For example, behavioural consistency was ascribed major explanatory relevance in Moscovici's (1980) conversion theory to explain minority influence. However, consistency also played a major role in Asch's (1956) experiments on majority influence, as majority influence decreased considerably as soon as one confederate deviated from the majority. Similarly, in work by Bohner and colleagues (1998) a minority source who was said to distinctively promote a minority view on the specific topic under consideration was more influential than a source who was said to non-distinctively promote minority positions on many other topics as well. However, the same distinctiveness effect was found for majority sources, although in general majority influence was stronger than minority influence. Obviously, a distinctive position gave rise to positive attributions, whereas non-distinctiveness was attributed either to the source's general deviance or to its general tendency to go along with the majority (Bohner, Erb, Reinhard, & Frank, 1996).

Technically speaking, distinctiveness, and presumably behavioural consistency, produce main effects over and above a main effect of consensus, but no interaction effects with consensus. Such main effects and the lack of interaction effects, however, demonstrate that these variables do not necessarily interact with minority and majority status. In fact, it is likely that any source of influence has more impact when consistency or distinctiveness produce positive attributions. Accordingly, a candidate variable to explain minority and majority influence has to impact the influence of minority sources differently from how it impacts the influence of majority sources. Examples of such demonstrations are the above presented factors of risk preference and deindividuation that produced interaction effects with consensus rather than main effects over and above a main effect of consensus.

## Final remarks

In this chapter we have discussed mere-consensus effects on information processing and judgement formation. As a starting point we chose the postulate that consensus is the only variable to necessarily covary with the status of an influence group as a minority or majority. In our empirical work, we demonstrated that mere consensus, detached from other variables that competing models accorded major explanatory relevance, can explain phenomena in minority and majority influence situations more parsimoniously, simply with the operation of consensus.

Our research into minority influence was also guided by consensus-based considerations. There exist variables that make minorities more influential than majorities even on the specific topic under consideration (direct influence). Low-consensus positions represent risky options, so that risk-inclined recipients yield to minority influence. Low-consensus positions also allow deindividuated individuals to regain a feeling of uniqueness and social distinction.

At the theoretical level, the mere-consensus approach enables researchers to re-examine the explanatory relevance of a number of variables previously studied in research on minority and majority influence. Variables that (a) offset the use of consensus information by calling to mind 'competing inferences' that seem to be more accessible or subjectively more relevant to recipients than consensus and (b) affect influence over and above a consensus main effect do not seem crucial to explaining minority and majority influence. Such variables likely promote the influence of any source. Thus, the mere-consensus approach sheds new light on mechanisms in minority and majority influence situations and will hopefully inspire and guide future research on this topic.

## References

Aronson, E., Ellsworth, P. C., Carlsmith, J. M., & Gonzales, M. H. (1990). *Methods of research in social psychology*. New York: McGraw-Hill.

Asch, S. E. (1956). Studies of independence and conformity: I. A minority of one against a unanimous majority. *Psychological Monographs, 70*(9), 1–70 (whole No. 416).

Axsom, D., Yates, S. M., & Chaiken, S. (1987). Audience response as a heuristic cue in persuasion. *Journal of Personality and Social Psychology, 53*, 30–40.

Baker, S. M., & Petty, R. E. (1994). Majority and minority influence: Source–position imbalance as a determinant of message scrutiny. *Journal of Personality and Social Psychology, 67*, 5–19.

Bohner, G., Dykema-Engblade, A., Tindale, R. S., & Meisenhelder, H. (2008). Framing of majority and minority source information in persuasion: When and how 'consensus implies correctness'. *Social Psychology, 39*, 108–116.

Bohner, G., Erb, H.-P., Reinhard, M.-A., & Frank, E. (1996). Distinctiveness across topics in minority and majority influence: An attributional analysis and preliminary data. *British Journal of Social Psychology, 35*, 27–46.

Bohner, G., Frank, E., & Erb, H.-P. (1998). Heuristic processing of distinctiveness information in minority and majority influence. *European Journal of Social Psychology, 28*, 855–860.

Bohner, G., Moskowitz, G. B., & Chaiken, S. (1995). The interplay of heuristic and systematic processing of social information. In W. Stroebe & M. Hewstone (Eds.), *European review of social psychology* (Vol. 6, pp. 33–68). Chichester, UK: Wiley.

Bohner, G., Ruder, M., & Erb, H.-P. (2002). When expertise backfires: Contrast and assimilation effects in persuasion. *British Journal of Social Psychology, 41*, 495–519.

Brewer, M. B. (1991). The social self: On being the same and different at the same time. *Personality and Social Psychology Bulletin, 17*, 475–482.

Brock, T. C., & Brannon, L. A. (1992). Liberalization of commodity theory. *Basic and Applied Social Psychology, 13*, 135–144.

Chaiken, S., Liberman, A., & Eagly, A. H. (1989). Heuristic and systematic processing within and beyond the persuasion context. In J. S. Uleman & J. A. Bargh (Eds.), *Unintended thought* (pp. 212–252). New York: Guilford Press.

Cialdini, R. B., & Trost, M. R. (1998). Social influence: Social norms, conformity, and compliance. In D. T. Gilbert, S. T. Fiske, & G. Lindzey (Eds.), *Handbook of social psychology* (4th ed., Vol. 2, pp. 151–192). Boston: McGraw-Hill.

Clark, R. D., III (1988). On predicting minority influence. *European Journal of Social Psychology, 18*, 515–526.

Crano, W. (2001). Social influence, social identity, and ingroup leniency. In N. K. De Vries & C. K. W. De Dreu (Eds.), *Group consensus and minority influence: Implications for innovation* (pp. 122–143). Oxford, UK: Blackwell.

Darke, P., Chaiken, S., Bohner, G., Einwiller, S., Erb, H.-P., & Hazlewood, D. (1998). Accuracy motivation, consensus information, and the law of large numbers: Effects on attitude judgment in the absence of argumentation. *Personality and Social Psychology Bulletin, 24*, 1205–1215.

David, D., & Turner, J. C. (2001). Majority and minority influence: A single process self-categorization analysis. In N. K. De Vries & C. K. W. De Dreu (Eds.), *Group consensus and minority influence: Implications for innovation* (pp. 91–121). Oxford, UK: Blackwell.

De Vries, N. K., De Dreu, C. K. W., Gordijn, E., & Schuurman, M. (1996). Majority and minority influence: A dual role interpretation. In W. Stroebe & M. Hewstone (Eds.), *European review of social psychology* (Vol. 7, pp. 145–172). Chichester, UK: Wiley.

Ditto, P. H., & Jemmott, J. B., III (1989). From rarity to evaluative extremity: Effects of prevalence information on evaluations of positive and negative characteristics. *Journal of Personality and Social Psychology, 57*, 16–26.

Erb, H.-P. (2006). *Inferred and explicit consensus: Moderating the impact of minorities and majorities on attitude judgments.* Unpublished manuscript, Chemnitz University of Technology.

Erb, H.-P., Bioy, A., & Hilton, D. J. (2002a). Choice preferences without inferences: Subconscious priming of risk attitudes. *Journal of Behavioral Decision Making, 15*, 251–262.

Erb, H.-P., & Bohner, G. (2001). Mere consensus effects in minority and majority influence. In N. K. De Vries & C. K. W. De Dreu (Eds.), *Group consensus and minority influence: Implications for innovation* (pp. 40–59). Oxford, UK: Blackwell.

Erb, H.-P., Hilton, D. J., Bohner, G., & Krings, L. (2009). *Conditions of minority influence: The risky option.* Unpublished manuscript, Helmut Schmidt University, Hamburg.

Erb, H.-P., Bohner, G., Rank, S., & Einwiller, S. (2002b). Processing minority and majority communications: The role of conflict with prior attitudes. *Personality and Social Psychology Bulletin, 28*, 1172–1182.

Erb, H.-P., Bohner, G., Schmälzle, K., & Rank, S. (1998). Beyond conflict and discrepancy: Cognitive bias in minority and majority influence. *Personality and Social Psychology Bulletin, 24*, 620–633.

Erb, H.-P., Bohner, G., Werth, L., Hewstone, M., & Reinhard, M.-A. (2006). Large minorities and small majorities: Interactive effects of inferred and explicit consensus on attitudes. *Basic and Applied Social Psychology, 28*, 221–231.

Erb, H.-P., & Thoben, D. F. (2009). *The social influence of consensus information in public opinion poll results.* Unpublished data, Helmut Schmidt University, Hamburg.

Festinger, L. (1954). A theory of social comparison processes. *Human Relations, 7*, 117–140.

Gardikiotis, A., Martin, R., & Hewstone, M. (2005). Group consensus in social influence: Types of consensus information as a moderator of majority and minority influence. *Personality and Social Psychology Bulletin, 31,* 1163–1174.

Grice, H. P. (1977). Logic and conversation. In P. Cole & J. L. Morgan (Eds.), *Syntax and semantics* (Vol. 3, pp. 41–58). New York: Academic Press.

Hastie, R., & Park, B. (1986). The relationship between memory and judgments depends on whether the judgment task is memory-based or on-line. *Psychological Review, 93,* 258–268.

Imhoff, R., & Erb, H.-P. (2009). What motivates non-conformity: Uniqueness seeking blocks majority influence. *Personality and Social Psychology Bulletin, 35,* 309–320.

Kahneman, D., & Tversky, A. (1979). Prospect theory: An analysis of decisions under risk. *Econometrica, 47,* 263–291.

Kelley, H. H. (1967). Attribution theory in social psychology. In D. Devine (Ed.), *Nebraska symposium on motivation.* Lincoln: University of Nebraska Press.

Kogan, N., & Wallach, M. (1964). *Risk taking: A study in cognition and personality.* New York: Holt, Rinehart, and Winston.

Kruglanski, A. W., & Mackie, D. M. (1990). Majority and minority influence: A judgmental process analysis. In W. Stroebe & M. Hewstone (Eds.), *European review of social psychology* (Vol. 1, pp. 229–261). Chichester, UK: Wiley.

Latané, B., & Wolf, S. (1981). The social impact of majorities and minorities. *Psychological Review, 88,* 438–453.

Levine, J. M. (1989). Reaction to opinion deviance in small groups. In P. Paulus (Ed.), *Psychology of group influence* (pp. 187–231). Hillsdale, NJ: Lawrence Erlbaum Associates, Inc.

Maass, A., & Clark, R. D., III (1984). Hidden impact of minorities: Fifteen years of minority influence research. *Psychological Bulletin, 95,* 428–450.

Maass, A., Clark, R. D., III, & Haberkorn, G. (1982). The effects of differential ascribed category membership and norms on minority influence. *European Journal of Social Psychology, 12,* 89–104.

Mackie, D. M. (1987). Systematic and nonsystematic processing of majority and minority persuasive communications. *Journal of Personality and Social Psychology, 53,* 41–52.

Maheswaran, D., & Chaiken, S. (1991). Promoting systematic processing in low-motivation settings: Effect of incongruent information on processing and judgment. *Journal of Personality and Social Psychology, 61,* 13–25.

Martin, R. (1998). Majority and minority influence using the afterimage paradigm: A series of attempted replications. *Journal of Experimental Social Psychology, 34,* 1–26.

Martin, R., Gardikiotis, A., & Hewstone, M. (2002). Levels of consensus and majority and minority influence. *European Journal of Social Psychology, 32,* 645–665.

Maslach, C. (1974). Social and personal bases of individuation. *Journal of Personality and Social Psychology, 29,* 411–425.

Moscovici, S. (1980). Toward a theory of conversion behavior. In L. Berkowitz (Ed.), *Advances in experimental social psychology* (Vol. 13, pp. 209–239). San Diego, CA: Academic Press.

Moscovici, S., & Lage, E. (1976). Studies in social influence III: Majority vs. minority influence in a group. *European Journal of Social Psychology, 6,* 149–174.

Moscovici, S., Lage, E., & Naffrechoux, M. (1969). Influence of a consistent minority on the responses of a majority in a color perception task. *Sociometry*, *32*, 365–379.

Moskowitz, G. B. (1996). The mediational effects of attributions and information processing in minority social influence. *British Journal of Social Psychology*, *35*, 47–66.

Mugny, G. (1982). *The power of minorities.* London: Academic Press.

Nemeth, C. (1986). Differential contributions of majority and minority influence. *Psychological Review*, *93*, 23–32.

Nowak, A., Szamrej, J., & Latané, B. (1990). From private attitude to public opinion: A dynamic theory of social impact. *Psychological Review*, *97*, 362–376.

Paicheler, G. (1977). Norms and attitude change: II. Polarization and styles of behavior. *European Journal of Social Psychology*, *6*, 405–427.

Simon, B., & Hamilton, D. L. (1994). Self-stereotyping and social context: The effects of relative in-group size and in-group status. *Journal of Personality and Social Psychology*, *66*, 699–711.

Snyder, C. R., & Fromkin, H. L. (1980). *Uniqueness, the human pursuit of difference.* New York: Plenum Press.

Tajfel, H., Billig, M. G., Bundy, R. P., & Flament, C. (1971). Social categorization and intergroup behaviour. *European Journal of Social Psychology*, *1*, 149–178.

Tanford, S., & Penrod, S. (1984). Social influence model: A formal integration of research on majority and minority influence processes. *Psychological Bulletin*, *95*, 189–225.

Tindale, R. S., Sheffey, S., & Scott, L. A. (1993). Framing and group decision making: Do cognitive changes parallel preference changes. *Organizational Behavior and Human Decision Processes*, *55*, 470–485.

Traugott, M. W., & Kang, M. E. (2000). Public attention to polls in an election year. In P. J. Lavrakas & M. W. Traugott (Eds.), *Election polls, the news media, and democracy* (pp. 185–205). London: Chatham House.

Turner, J. C. (1991). *Social influence.* Pacific Grove, CA: Brooks/Cole.

Wood, W., Lundgren, S., Ouellette, J. A., Busceme, S., & Blackstone, T. (1994). Minority influence: A meta-analytic review of social influence processes. *Psychological Bulletin*, *115*, 323–345.

Ziller, R. C. (1964). Individuation and socialization: A theory of assimilation in large organizations. *Human Relations*, *17*, 341–360.

Zimbardo, P. G. (1969). The human choice: Individuation, reason, and order vs. deindividuation, impulse, and chaos. In W. J. Arnold & D. Levine (Eds.), *Nebraska symposium on motivation* (Vol. 17, pp. 237–307). Lincoln: University of Nebraska Press.

# 5    Multiple roles for minority sources in persuasion and resistance

*Zakary L. Tormala*
Stanford University, USA

*Richard E. Petty*
Ohio State University, USA

*Victoria L. DeSensi*
Indiana University, USA

Research on minority influence over the years has revealed that although sources in the numerical majority tend to be very persuasive on an immediate, public, and direct level, sources in the numerical minority tend to be resisted on this level (e.g., Moscovici, 1980, 1985a; see Wood, Lundgren, Ouellette, Busceme, & Blackstone, 1994, for a review). Early theorizing by Moscovici (1980, 1985a, 1985b) and others (e.g., Mugny & Perez, 1991) suggested that people publicly agree with majority messages and reject minority messages out of hand to avoid aligning themselves with deviant groups. That is, public acceptance and rejection of majority and minority messages has been thought to occur with very little issue-relevant thought. Importantly, though, both majority persuasion and minority resistance have also been argued to involve more thoughtful processes. For example, Erb and Bohner (2001) have argued that the majority or minority status of the source of a persuasive message can bias message recipients' thinking about the attitude issue in one direction or another. Specifically, majority sources are postulated to produce more favourable thoughts (i.e., pro-arguments) in response to persuasive messages, whereas minority sources are posited to produce more unfavourable thoughts (i.e., counter-arguments). These thoughts, in turn, foster relative persuasion and resistance.

In addition to having a direct effect on attitudes or biasing the direction of thought, some researchers have argued that minority/majority source status can influence the *amount* of thinking that occurs. Moscovici's classic conversion theory (1980), for instance, proposed that minority sources can sometimes elicit true, lasting persuasion when they stimulate heightened levels of information-processing activity. Subsequent research has broadened this view, revealing that both minority and majority sources are capable of increasing the amount of issue-relevant thinking in which people engage (e.g., Baker & Petty, 1994; Martin, Hewstone, & Martin, 2003). Increased thinking can lead to either more persuasion or more resistance depending on the quality, or strength, of arguments included in the persuasive message (Petty & Cacioppo, 1986).

In short, multiple theories and processes have been put forth in an effort to explain differences in the effects of minority and majority sources on persuasion and resistance. With this in mind, the present chapter has two goals. First, we seek to apply a multiple-roles framework, based on the elaboration likelihood model of persuasion (ELM; Petty & Wegener, 1998), in an effort to integrate the numerous mechanisms for minority/majority-source effects in prior research. Second, we propose a new metacognitive effect for minority sources in persuasion settings that has not been identified previously. We focus on situations in which people resist immediate, focal persuasion because the source of a persuasive message is in the numerical minority. Based on our own recent research exploring metacognitive factors in resistance to persuasion (Tormala & Petty, 2002, 2004a, 2004b; Tormala, Clarkson, & Petty, 2006b), we propose that when people resist minority messages, they can perceive this resistance and form specifiable inferences about their attitudes that have implications for *attitude certainty* (Gross, Holtz, & Miller, 1995). These certainty effects, we argue, have the potential to account for the delayed and indirect attitude change that have often been associated with resisting immediate minority persuasion.

## Multiple roles for variables in persuasion settings

In order to understand the multiple roles minority and majority sources can play in persuasion and resistance, it is worthwhile considering multiprocess theories of persuasion such as the ELM (Petty & Cacioppo, 1986; Petty & Wegener, 1999; Petty, Wheeler, & Tormala, 2003) and the heuristic-systematic model (HSM; Chaiken, Liberman, & Eagly, 1989). According to these models, persuasion and resistance can occur through different mechanisms depending on message recipients' level of *elaboration*. In essence, elaboration refers to one's extent of thinking or information processing—that is, the degree of cognitive effort one is motivated and able to expend in processing a persuasive message. The ELM, in particular, holds that persuasion variables such as majority or minority source status can impact attitudes through different processes at different levels of elaboration. When elaboration is low, variables often affect attitudes through peripheral route mechanisms—that is, serving as quick heuristics or cues to persuasion or resistance. When elaboration is high, however, variables often play very different roles in persuasion settings. For example, under these conditions variables can influence persuasive outcomes by biasing the direction of thoughts people generate during persuasive messages, by serving as issue-relevant arguments (i.e., information relevant to the central merits of a persuasive message), or by affecting the amount of confidence people have in the thoughts they have generated (Petty, Briñol, & Tormala, 2002). Finally, when elaboration is moderate (i.e., neither high nor low) to begin with, variables sometimes determine the amount of elaboration in which people engage.

Consider research on divergent but classic variables such as source credibility and people's mood states. Research over the years has revealed a number of mechanisms through which credibility and mood produce effects on attitudes, and these mechanisms depend on message recipients' level of elaboration. The most common characterization of source credibility (e.g., Hovland & Weiss, 1951; Kiesler & Mathog, 1968; Petty, Cacioppo, & Goldman, 1981) and mood (e.g., Schwarz & Clore, 1983; Zanna, Kiesler, & Pilkonis, 1970) has been that they operate as peripheral cues (or heuristics) to persuasion when the likelihood of message elaboration is relatively low. For example, people who are unmotivated or unable to engage in extensive message processing might simply accept a message without scrutiny if its source is an expert, because experts are assumed to be correct. Similarly, people who are unmotivated or unable to think deeply might rely on their mood state to reject a message in a cue-based fashion, thinking 'I feel bad so I must not like this idea'.

Recent research guided by multiprocess theories of persuasion has enhanced our understanding of source credibility and mood effects, however, by showing that they can also play a role in persuasion when the likelihood of message elaboration is moderate as well as high. When elaboration is moderate to begin with and, thus, not constrained to be high or low, credibility (e.g., DeBono & Harnish, 1988; Eagly, Chaiken, & Wood 1981; Heesacker, Petty, & Cacioppo, 1983; Priester & Petty, 1995; see also Ziegler, Diehl, & Ruther, 2002) and mood (e.g., Bless, Bohner, Schwarz, & Strack, 1990; Wegener, Petty, & Smith, 1995; Worth & Mackie, 1987) have been shown to influence the amount of information processing that occurs. Receiving a message from a dishonest source, for instance, can boost elaboration for some individuals (Priester & Petty, 1995), thereby increasing persuasion when message arguments are strong but reducing persuasion when message arguments are weak.

Finally, when elaboration is high, a number of different roles for credibility and mood have been established. For example, these variables can bias the direction of thoughts people generate in response to persuasive messages. In the seminal study examining the multiple processes through which mood can affect persuasion, Petty, Schumann, Richman, and Strathman (1993) found that under high-elaboration conditions positive mood increased persuasion by boosting the production of message-favourable thoughts. Under low-elaboration conditions, positive mood also increased persuasion, but without influencing thoughts. Similarly, Chaiken and Maheswaran (1994) found that under high-elaboration conditions expert sources increased persuasion by increasing the favourability of message recipients' thoughts, at least when message arguments were ambiguous. Under low-elaboration conditions, the previously documented cue effect of credibility was obtained. Also under high-elaboration conditions, source credibility (e.g., Kruglanski & Thompson, 1999) and mood (e.g., Martin, Abend, Sedikides, & Green, 1997) can be evaluated as arguments, affecting attitudes when they provide compelling evidence for the advocacy. Finally, under high-elaboration conditions both source credibility (Briñol, Petty, & Tormala, 2004; Tormala, Briñol, & Petty, 2006a) and mood (Briñol, Petty, & Barden, 2006) have been shown to affect the amount of confidence people have in the thoughts they generate about a persuasive message. According to the self-validation hypothesis, thoughts have a greater impact on attitudes when thought confidence is high rather than low (Petty et al., 2002). The thought-confidence effect is especially likely to occur when source-credibility information or the mood induction follows the persuasive message (e.g., Tormala, Briñol, & Petty, 2007a).

## Multiple roles for minority-source information

Extending the multiple-roles idea to the current concerns, research on minority and majority influence is consistent with the notion that the numerical status of a source can influence attitudes through different mechanisms depending on message recipients' level of elaboration. In particular, recent research and theorizing (e.g., Erb & Bohner, 2001; Petty & Wegener, 1998) suggest that the minority/majority status of a source can influence persuasive outcomes by serving as a cue, by biasing thoughts, or by determining the amount of information processing in which message recipients engage. Although participants' initial level of elaboration has not typically been manipulated or measured in this research, the cue, message processing, and biased-thinking roles for minority sources appear to map onto low-, moderate-, and high-elaboration situations, respectively. After briefly reviewing these and other possible roles that minority/majority-source status might play in affecting persuasion, we will discuss an additional role we believe minority-source information can play in affecting attitude certainty following message exposure.

### *Low-elaboration conditions*

According to the multiple-roles framework of the ELM, majority- or minority-source status is most likely to operate as a simple cue to persuasion or resistance when conditions constrain the amount of thinking to be relatively low. That is, minority/majority status can provide an efficient means by which to assess the validity of a position when one has little personal interest in or knowledge about a message topic, or when one is under high cognitive load (e.g., there are many distractions present). High consensus, or majority support, would imply that a position is valid and should be adopted, whereas low consensus, or minority support, would imply that a position is invalid and should be rejected (e.g., Festinger, 1954). This notion is compatible with a host of studies in the broader persuasion literature indicating that under low-elaboration conditions people sometimes rely on numerosity heuristics as cues to message validity (e.g., Pelham, Sumarta, & Myaskovsky, 1994; Petty & Cacioppo, 1984; Tormala, Petty, & Briñol, 2002).

In the minority-influence domain, there is some evidence that source status can operate in a cue-based fashion. Moscovici (1980), for instance, argued that although minority persuasion tended to involve elevated levels of information processing, majority persuasion often occurred as a result of simple heuristic inferences. That is, even when people were not motivated to process message content very deeply, they were presumed to accept the majority position without question. Mackie (1987) further explored this notion, and found that even in the absence of any persuasive arguments, people were convinced by a majority position (see also Darke et al., 1998; Giner-Sorolla & Chaiken, 1997). Consistent with the idea that majority persuasion was heuristic in nature, it was less stable than persuasion stemming from more thoughtful processing of message arguments (see Petty, Haugtvedt, & Smith, 1995, for further discussion of elaboration and attitude stability). Importantly, although the evidence for this role for minority/majority-source status has focused on majority persuasion, the flipside is that these studies also point to low-elaboration processes leading to *minority resistance*. That is, just as people can thoughtlessly accept majority persuasion to align with the majority position, they can resist minority persuasion in cue-based fashion to avoid being in the minority and appearing deviant. As described later, however, it has not always been clear whether minority resistance involves genuine rejection of the position in a cue-based manner, or whether it stems from not wanting to be associated with the minority view despite careful processing.

### Moderate-elaboration conditions

When the level of elaboration is not constrained to be high or low to begin with, the multiple-roles notion of the ELM suggests that minority/majority-source status should determine the amount of message processing in which people engage. Indeed, this is probably the most common characterization of minority/majority-influence effects in prior studies. As noted earlier, Moscovici (1980, 1985a) was the first to advance the notion that minority influence often involves greater message processing than does majority influence. Moscovici argued that when people receive persuasive messages from minority sources they more carefully scrutinize the content of the message, which can lead to 'conversion,' or private and long-term acceptance of the minority position, even if people show no agreement on an initial public attitude assessment. Numerous researchers have followed up on this idea and produced evidence consistent with the contention that minority sources often engender greater information processing than do majority sources (e.g., Crano & Chen, 1998; Maass & Clark, 1983; Martin et al., 2003; Moskowitz, 1996). In one demonstration, Martin et al. (2003) presented participants with a persuasive message from a minority or majority source, and then presented another message in the opposite direction from the first. They found that although attitudes were equivalent following the initial message, these attitudes were more resistant to the second message in the minority relative to majority condition. Given the association between elaboration and attitude strength (Petty et al., 1995), this finding is consistent with the notion that the initial minority message was processed more deeply than the initial majority message. Further suggestive along these lines, participants' thoughts in response to the first message were more closely tied to message content in the minority rather than the majority condition.

Other research has painted a more complicated picture, however, suggesting that either minority or majority sources can lead to more processing than the other depending on various situational factors (e.g., Baker & Petty, 1994; Mackie, 1987; Martin & Hewstone, 2003). Baker and Petty (1994), for instance, found that processing of a minority- or majority-source's message depends on the extent to which that minority or majority endorses an expected position. When the position is unexpected—for example, a minority (majority) source endorses a pro-attitudinal (counter-attitudinal) position—message processing is high. When the position is expected—for example, a minority (majority) source endorses a counter-attitudinal (pro-attitudinal) position—message processing is low. Baker and Petty (1994) suggested that when a majority endorses a counter-attitudinal position, this could be more threatening than when a minority does so, thus increasing the need to process carefully.

Similarly, Martin and Hewstone (2003) examined the moderating role of message position, and found that when the message advocated a negative personal outcome for participants, majority sources led to increased levels of processing relative to minority sources. Martin and Hewstone attributed the effect to participants' defensive urge to protect self-interest upon learning that a majority of people were arguing for a negative personal outcome. Consistent with this reasoning, when the message did not promote a negative personal outcome, minority sources led to greater processing than did majority sources. In sum, then, it appears that both minority and majority sources can spark increased processing, depending on the position advocated (e.g., whether the message is threatening or not) or other moderating factors. It may be that in the absence of strong expectancies, minorities foster greater processing than do majorities because they generate more interest or curiosity, but variations in the specific issue addressed or position taken can attenuate or reverse the typical pattern.

*High-elaboration conditions*

Finally, according to the ELM, under high-elaboration conditions in which people are motivated and able to process, minority/majority-source status should play different roles in persuasion. For example, source status might bias the direction of ongoing issue-relevant thinking, especially if the source status is known prior to message processing. Consistent with this notion, one characterization of minority/majority-source effects under high elaboration has been that minority and majority sources engender a different pattern of thoughts in response to persuasive messages. Minority sources, for instance, have been shown to foster resistance by negatively biasing message recipients' thoughts about the persuasive message or attitude object (e.g., Erb, Bohner, Schmälzle, & Rank, 1998; Trost, Maass, & Kenrick, 1992). Majority sources, on the other hand, can prompt a positive bias in message recipients' thoughts, leading to greater persuasion (e.g., Mackie, 1987). In one test of the biased-thinking perspective, Erb et al. (1998) induced systematic processing and then presented participants with a minority or majority message and measured their attitudes toward the topic and the thoughts that they had while reading the message. They found that participants' thoughts were more negative following a minority message and more positive following a majority message. Moreover, this effect on thoughts mediated the effect of source status on attitudes. The more favourable participants' thoughts were during the message, the more favourable their attitudes were following the message. Providing further support for the hypothesis that the biased-processing effects are particularly likely under high-elaboration conditions, Trost et al. (1992) found greater evidence of biased processing of minority messages when participants found a message to be high rather than low in personal relevance.

Interestingly, biased thought processes have also been implicated in the minority-influence domain from a slightly different perspective. Wood, Pool, Leck, and Purvis (1996), for instance, examined people's interpretations of attitude issues in response to minority- versus majority-source information. Most germane to the present concerns, Wood et al. found that when people learned that a disliked minority group (e.g., the Ku Klux Klan) supposedly agreed with them on a personally relevant topic, they changed their attitudes in an effort to distance themselves from this group, and reinterpreted the attitude issue to justify the shift.

A biasing effect of source status on thoughts is possible when people are aware of the source before they start processing. However, if people do not become aware of the status of the source until after message processing, source status might have a different impact. Specifically, in accord with the self-validation hypothesis described earlier, minority/majority-source status might affect the confidence or doubt with which people hold their thoughts, as has been shown for source credibility (Briñol et al., 2004; Tormala et al., 2006a). Thus, if people were thinking mostly positive thoughts during a message only to find out that the position is endorsed by a minority, they might lose confidence in those thoughts (if they lose faith in the validity of the information presented), which would attenuate persuasion. But, if people were thinking mostly negative thoughts during a message and then find out that the position is endorsed by a minority, they might lose confidence in *those* thoughts, ultimately enhancing persuasion. Alternatively, people might gain confidence in their negative thoughts if the minority source reinforces the idea that the message is invalid. Although these possibilities have yet to be explored in the minority-influence domain, they provide an interesting direction for future inquiry.

One additional possibility for source status under high-elaboration conditions is that it could be scrutinized as an argument and affect persuasion accordingly. Imagine, for example, a product that is designed to appeal to a particular segment of society. The fact that it is liked by only a minority of people might serve as evidence for the exclusivity and uniqueness of the product, and thereby serve as a persuasive argument in favour of the product for some individuals. If the product is liked by a majority, however, this might not be perceived as providing good evidence for the fact that only the discerning favour the product. This possibility is speculative, of course, but future research examining minority and majority influence from a multiple-roles perspective would shed light on this and other intriguing possibilities.

## A new role for minority sources

Now that we have reviewed some of the previously articulated roles that minority/majority-source status has been thought to play in persuasion and resistance, the remainder of this chapter presents the possibility of a new role for minority sources in persuasion settings that has implications for attitude certainty (Gross et al., 1995). Our specific interest in this issue has been guided by our own metacognitive framework for resistance to persuasion, in which we have been exploring people's perceptions of their own resistance, and the implications these perceptions can have for the inferences people form about their attitudes (Tormala & Petty, 2004c). In a new line of research in the minority-influence domain, we have been extending our metacognitive perspective on resistance in general to examine the kinds of inferences people might form about their attitudes after they have resisted a persuasive message from a minority source. In the next section, we provide an overview of our general metacognitive framework for resistance to persuasion. Following this overview, we describe some recent studies relevant to the minority-influence domain, paying particular attention to the potential role of metacognitive factors in producing attitudes of differing certainty. Understanding attitude certainty is important because attitudes held with greater certainty are more resistant to change (e.g., Tormala & Petty, 2002), more stable over time (e.g., Bassili,

1996), and more predictive of behaviour (e.g., Fazio & Zanna, 1978) than are attitudes held with less certainty.

### A metacognitive framework for resistance to persuasion

Metacognition refers to people's thoughts about or perceptions of their own thoughts and thought processes. Although metacognition research has an extensive history in both social and cognitive psychology, it is only relatively recently that researchers have begun to explore the role of meta-cognitive factors in attitudes and persuasion (see Petty, Briñol, Tormala, & Wegener, 2007, for a review). Nevertheless, it is becoming increasingly clear within this domain that metacognitive perspectives have much to offer. Of particular relevance to this chapter, we have recently developed a metacog-nitive theory of resistance to persuasion (Tormala & Petty, 2004c; see also Petty, Tormala, & Rucker, 2004). We suggest that when people resist persuasive attacks, they can perceive this resistance and form attribution-like inferences about their own attitudes that have implications for attitude strength, or attitude certainty more specifically (see Gross et al., 1995). Depending on people's perceptions of their resistance and the situation in which it occurs, we have found that attitude certainty can either increase or decrease following resistance to persuasion. The direction of this effect is largely determined by the extent to which people are impressed or unim-pressed by their own resistance.

### Increasing attitude certainty

First, we have accumulated a great deal of evidence suggesting that when people perceive that they have successfully resisted a persuasive attack, they sometimes become more certain of their attitudes than they were to begin with. The logic behind this effect is that when people resist an attack on their attitude, they infer that the attitude was already correct (otherwise it would have changed), and this inference gets translated into a feeling of greater attitude certainty. In an initial experiment designed to test this possibility (Tormala & Petty, 2002, Experiment 1), we presented parti-cipants with a counter-attitudinal persuasive message and induced them to resist this message by generating counter-arguments. After reading the per-suasive message and listing their counter-arguments, participants reported their attitudes and attitude certainty with respect to the message topic. As predicted, people became more certain of their initial attitudes after they resisted the persuasive message.

In subsequent experiments, we (Tormala & Petty, 2002) extended this basic finding in several important ways. First, we found that it was confined to participants who perceived that their attitudes did, in fact, resist per-suasion. When participants perceived that they had shown some evidence of attitude change, even when they were actually just as resistant as the other participants, they became no more certain of their attitudes than they were to begin with. Second, we found that these effects had implications for a variety of important outcomes commonly associated with attitude certainty (see Gross et al., 1995, for a review). Specifically, when people resisted persuasion and became more certain of their attitudes, these attitudes also became more predictive of behavioural intentions and more resistant to subsequent attacks.

Consistent with the notion that these effects are particularly likely when people are impressed by their resistance, however, the increase in attitude certainty uncovered in each experiment was moderated by the perceived strength of the persuasive attack. People only became more certain of their attitudes, and only showed the effects of attitude certainty (on behaviour and future resistance), when they resisted a persuasive attack perceived to be strong. When participants resisted a persuasive attack perceived to be weak, attitude certainty was unchanged. This effect was particularly striking in that all participants actually received the exact same persuasive message. They were simply led to believe it was strong or weak. Our interpretation of this effect is that when people resist messages perceived as strong, this resistance is viewed as more successful, or more diagnostic with respect to the validity of the initial attitude. Resisting weak messages is presumably viewed as less successful or less diagnostic, because ambiguity remains about what would happen in the face of a stronger attack. In essence, perceived message strength can serve as an augmenting or discounting situational factor (see Kelley, 1972). Perceiving that one has resisted a strong message augments the effect of resistance on attitude certainty, whereas perceiving that one has resisted a weak message provides a discounting factor that eliminates this effect.

In follow-up research, the certainty result was both replicated and extended. In some studies, for instance, we manipulated the perceived expertise of the source of a message, rather than the perceived strength of the content of a message, and found that it had similar effects (Tormala & Petty, 2004a). That is, participants became more certain of their initial attitudes after resisting a counter-attitudinal message from an expert source (augmenting situational factor), but not after resisting the same message from an inexpert source (discounting situational factor). As in the earlier research, these differences in certainty had implications for the correspondence between attitudes and behavioural intentions. The more certain people became of their attitudes following resistance to persuasion, the better these attitudes predicted behavioural intentions. In addition, our follow-up work revealed that these processes were moderated by extent of elaboration (Tormala & Petty, 2004a, 2004b). Specifically, the effects of resistance on certainty were found to be confined to high-elaboration situations (e.g., low cognitive load; Tormala & Petty, 2004a) and individuals (e.g., high need for cognition; Tormala & Petty, 2004b). Such moderation makes sense given that metacognitive thought is higher order and, thus, requires greater motivation and ability (see also Petty et al., 2002).

*Decreasing attitude certainty*

Our framework also suggests that there are situations in which people resist persuasion but become *less* certain of their initial attitudes. As noted earlier, we have found that this effect is particularly likely when people are for some reason *un*impressed by their own resistance. In essence, when people are unimpressed by their resistance (e.g., they have doubts about the quality of their resistance or the manner in which they resisted) they begin to suspect that their attitude might be invalid, which can reduce attitude certainty. We have recently been exploring the factors that can lead people to be unimpressed by, or have doubts about, their resistance, and we have examined the impact of these perceptions on attitude certainty.

To begin with, an individual might be unimpressed by his or her resistance after perceiving that he or she struggled to resist persuasion. This struggle could stem from several sources such as the perception that it was difficult to generate counter-arguments or the perception that one's counter-arguments were specious. Under these conditions, we have found that attitude certainty is indeed undermined. In one study, for instance, Tormala et al. (2006b, Experiment 2) presented participants with a counter-attitudinal message that they were induced to resist using counter-arguments. Participants were then given false feedback about the quality, or strength, of their counter-arguments, after which they reported attitudes and attitude certainty. As expected, given that all participants were focused on generating counter-arguments, everyone (on average) resisted persuasion. Furthermore, when participants were led to believe they had resisted using strong counter-arguments, they maintained a relatively high degree of certainty in their initial attitudes and these attitudes predicted subsequent behavioural intentions. When participants were led to believe they had generated weak counter-arguments, however, they became significantly less certain of their initial attitudes, and these attitudes became poorer predictors of behavioural intentions. Consistent with the predictions of the Tormala and Petty (2004c) framework, then, attitude certainty was undermined when people had the perception that they had done a poor job resisting a persuasive message.

In a follow-up study (Tormala et al., 2006b, Experiment 3), we found that like the increase in certainty examined in Tormala and Petty (2004a), this *decrease* in certainty was also moderated by source credibility. That is, attitude certainty was particularly likely to decrease when people perceived that they had generated weak counter-arguments against an *in*expert source. When people perceived that they had generated weak counter-arguments against an expert source, they did not lose certainty. Thus, following the same attributional logic as before, source credibility served as an augmenting or discounting factor for the decrease in attitude certainty (see Kelley, 1972). In this case, low credibility augmented the decrease in certainty caused by struggling to resist persuasion. High credibility, on the other hand, served as a discounting factor that eliminated this effect.

In more recent research in this area, we have been exploring other factors that might lead people to be unimpressed by their resistance, thus reducing attitude certainty. Of particular relevance to the current concerns, individuals might be unimpressed by their resistance when they perceive that they have resisted by illegitimate means (e.g., by ignoring a message or derogating its source). In other words, people might sometimes resist persuasion but have the subjective assessment that their resistance *strategy* is invalid, which could cast doubt on their perceived ability to resist using more valid approaches. Past research is consistent with the notion that people can assess the validity of their processing mechanism, and that these assessments have implications for subsequent information processing (e.g., Mazursky & Schul, 2000) and feelings of confidence or doubt (e.g., Yzerbyt, Schadron, Leyens, & Rocher, 1994). Mazursky and Schul (2000), for example, found that when people perceive that relying on source information has produced an erroneous judgement following an initial message, they switch to more elaborative modes of processing on subsequent messages. Furthermore, Jacks and Cameron (2003) recently surveyed people's perceptions of their own resistance strategies, and found that people tend to view some strategies—particularly source derogation—as socially undesirable relative to others, such as counter-arguing. In short, people have been found to assess and reflect upon their processing strategies, and resistance strategies more specifically, in past research. We suspect that when people have the perception that they have resisted persuasion by illegitimate or invalid means, they will be unimpressed by their resistance, which should undermine attitude certainty.

### Applying metacognitive principles to the study of minority influence

Where does minority influence fit into this framework? We argue that when people resist minority messages, they can become less certain of the 'unchanged' focal attitude if they believe they have resisted by illegitimate means. In the classic minority-source situation, people have been thought to resist immediate focal persuasion to avoid being aligned with deviant minority sources (e.g., Moscovici, 1985a, 1985b; Mugny, 1982; see Wood et al., 1994, for a review). Moreover, it has been argued that when people dismiss minority sources in this fashion, they can perceive this action as a judgemental bias (Moscovici, 1980, 1985a, 1985b; Moskowitz, 1996; Moskowitz & Chaiken, 2001). In other words, past research suggests both that people do tend to be concerned with potential bias when they receive (and presumably resist) messages from minority or other stigmatized sources (e.g., Petty, Fleming, & White, 1999), and that this concern can have important implications for subsequent thought and judgement.

Following this logic, we postulate that when people perceive or acknowledge that they have resisted persuasion largely on the basis of a source's minority status, they may feel that this is a biased or invalid resistance strategy. Furthermore, we posit that when people perceive this bias, or acknowledge that their attitudes have been influenced by minority-source information, they might have doubts about the validity of their attitudes and their ability to defend those attitudes using a more reasoned strategy (e.g., counter-arguing). Such doubts should be particularly likely to emerge when people have the subjective assessment that relying on minority-source information as a basis for their attitudes is illegitimate, or invalid. Again, research from other domains suggests that 'writing off' or derogating the source of a message tends to be viewed as socially inappropriate (Jacks & Cameron, 2003; see Mazursky & Schul, 2000, for related findings). It follows naturally, we think, that perceiving that one has relied on this strategy would spark some attitudinal doubt. Moreover, by resisting persuasion using a mechanism that essentially ignores message content, people might be uncertain as to whether they could have resisted persuasion if they had more thoughtfully engaged the message.[1]

Importantly, we submit that this perspective on minority resistance could help explain the kind of hidden success that has been one of the hallmark findings of the minority-influence literature. For example, it is well documented in the minority-influence domain that after showing immediate public resistance to minority messages, people's attitudes often prove susceptible to delayed private change or even indirect change (e.g., Crano & Chen, 1998). As we will discuss later in the chapter, a drop in certainty with respect to the target attitude would be consonant with and have potential bearing on both of these findings.

In short, we propose that when people perceive that they have resisted a persuasive message largely because the position is endorsed by a minority source, they can under some conditions become less certain of their attitudes than they were to begin with. We predict that this effect will occur when people (1) perceive that they have used the minority status of the source as a basis for resisting persuasion, and (2) think this is an illegitimate thing to do. When people perceive that they have used minority status as a basis for their attitude and think this is a *legitimate* thing to do (e.g., they believe if very few people support a position it truly is not worthwhile), we would not expect them to lose certainty.

## Empirical evidence

In a recent line of studies we explored the tenability of the metacognitive perspective on minority influence (Tormala, DeSensi, & Petty, 2007b). In each study we exposed undergraduate participants to a counter-attitudinal persuasive message. We induced some of these participants to resist the message by attributing it to a minority source. Across studies we measured and manipulated various perceptions related to reliance on the minority status of the source as a basis for one's attitude, and then assessed attitude certainty. Our prediction was that participants' self-reported attitude certainty would decrease when they perceived that they resisted persuasion because of the minority status of the source. When participants perceived that they did not use the minority information to resist, or perceived that they did and that it was legitimate to do so, we expected no decrease in certainty.

As an initial assessment of this notion, we replicated some of the key conditions from past minority-influence studies (e.g., Baker & Petty, 1994; Crano & Chen, 1998). Specifically, we presented undergraduates with a persuasive message promoting the implementation of a new mandatory service programme at their university. This message argued in favour of requiring undergraduates to complete several hours per week of unpaid work as a graduation requirement. Participants were led to believe that either a minority (14%) or a majority (86%) of students on campus endorsed this policy, and that they would read a proposal in favour of it that had been prepared by a representative of this group (i.e., the minority or majority). We also randomly assigned a third group of participants to a control condition in which they learned about the service requirement, but did not receive a persuasive message or any information about the percentage of students who supported it. This condition was included to provide a baseline for determining whether persuasion or resistance occurred (resistance being indicated by attitudes that did not differ from the control condition) and whether attitude certainty actually decreased relative to baseline. Immediately following the persuasive message (or after learning of the policy in the control condition), participants reported both their attitudes toward the policy and the extent to which they felt certain of these attitudes.

To begin with, we replicated the classic effect of minority- versus majority-source status on focal attitudes. As illustrated in the top panel of Figure 5.1, attitudes toward the service requirement were more favourable in the majority condition than in the minority condition. In fact, including the control group in the analysis, majority-condition participants were persuaded to endorse the service requirement (i.e., their attitudes were more favourable than control attitudes), whereas minority-condition participants resisted persuasion (i.e., their attitudes were no more favourable than control attitudes). Interestingly, though, there was a different pattern with respect to attitude certainty. As illustrated in the bottom panel of Figure 5.1, participants were less certain about their attitudes in the minority condition than in the control or majority conditions, which did not differ from each other. In other words, after resisting persuasion due to a source's minority status, which was the only thing that differed between the minority and majority conditions, people held their attitudes with less certainty. This finding provided initial support for the predictions of the metacognitive framework for resistance in the minority-influence context.

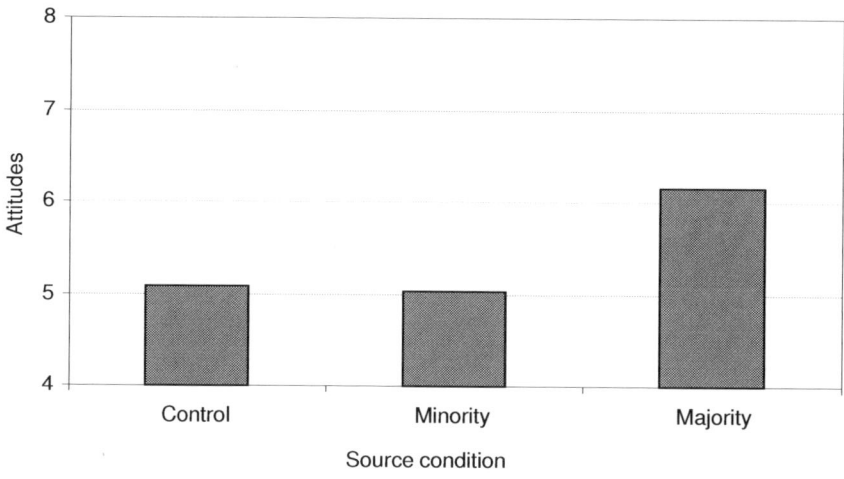

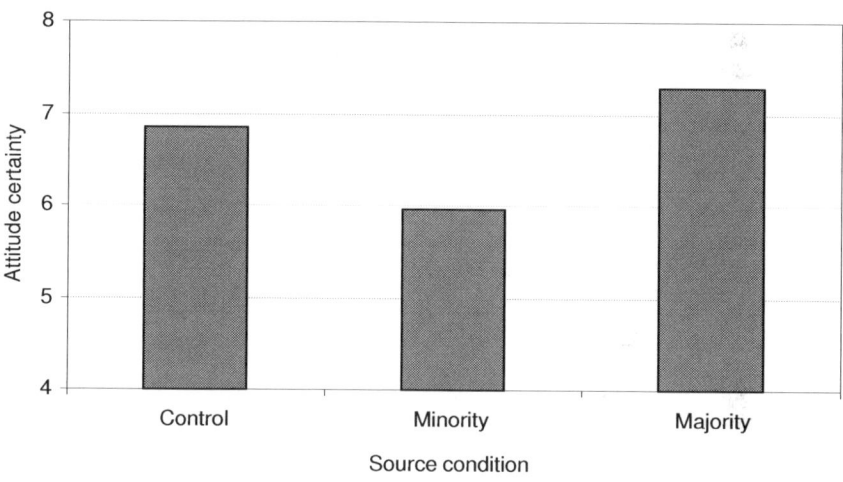

*Figure 5.1* Attitudes (top panel) and attitude certainty (bottom panel) as a function of source condition in Study 1 (Tormala et al., 2007b).

In subsequent studies, we sought to address the notion that these effects would be strongest when people perceived that they had relied on the percentage (i.e., minority source) information in determining their attitudes, and perceived that it was illegitimate to do so. In one study, we directly manipulated these perceptions. In this experiment, all participants received a persuasive message about the mandatory service programme from a minority source, after which they reported their attitudes. Immediately following the attitude responses, participants answered a series of questions designed to affect the extent to which they perceived that they relied on the minority status of the source as a basis for their attitudes (see Salancik & Conway, 1975). After completing these questions, participants were told that the computers running the experiment were programmed to analyse their responses and provide feedback regarding the extent to which people's attitudes were influenced by the minority-percentage information. Participants were then given false feedback that their attitudes did or did not show evidence of having been influenced by the percentage information. After the false-feedback procedure, we manipulated the perceived legitimacy of being influenced by the percentage information by telling participants that most other students in our studies did (legitimate condition) or did not (illegitimate condition) report being influenced by the percentage of students in favour of the service programme.

The results were consistent with our expectations. Although there was no difference in attitude ratings across conditions, participants had significantly lower attitude certainty when they had been led to believe they relied on the minority status of the source in forming their attitudes, but not many other students had done so. In other words, participants appeared to have reduced attitude certainty when they had the perception that they had illegitimately relied on the percentage information in forming their attitudes. When participants believed they had not used the percentage information, or believed they had but thought it was legitimate to do so because many other students did as well, they maintained a higher degree of attitude certainty.

Of course, our metacognitive perspective suggests that the decrease in attitude certainty that occurs in minority-resistance situations might have implications for delayed attitude change and other 'hidden' effects associated with resisted minority messages in past research. In a final study we tested these ideas by directly measuring perceived reliance on minority-source information and the perceived legitimacy of relying on minority-source information, and then assessing a consequence of attitude certainty. We presented all participants with the same counter-attitudinal persuasive message as in the earlier studies, and we led all participants to believe it was endorsed by a minority of students on campus. After they had read the message and reported their attitudes, we asked participants to report the extent to which they based their attitudes on the percentage of students who supported the university service programme. We then asked questions designed to tap the perceived legitimacy of this resistance strategy. Specifically, participants reported the extent to which they believed it was legitimate or illegitimate to base opinions on the kind of percentage information provided in this experiment, as well as the extent to which it was valid or invalid to disagree with an idea simply because a small number of people supported it. Following a brief delay and filler task, we then exposed participants to a second persuasive message about the service programme issue. This message argued in the same direction as the first, but it contained new arguments. We then measured attitudes a final time.

In accord with our metacognitive framework, and the findings of the aforementioned studies, we predicted that participants' attitudes would be most susceptible to later change when they reported both that they had used the percentage information and that it was illegitimate to do so. This is exactly what we found. In fact, participants who met these specifications were the only ones to evince significant attitude change in response to the second message. All other participants were essentially resistant to the later attack. Based on this pattern, we can infer that people had reduced feelings of attitude certainty when they perceived that they had illegitimately resisted the initial minority message. When participants either denied being affected by the minority-source information, or reported that it was legitimate to base attitudes on this kind of information, they appeared to maintain a relatively high degree of attitude certainty, and were more resistant to later persuasion.

### Summary

In summary, several recent studies (Tormala et al., 2007b) are compatible with the current metacognitive perspective on minority resistance. In general, the findings suggest that when people perceive that they have resisted persuasion because of the minority status of a message source, and perceive that it is illegitimate to do so, they become less certain of their attitudes. In other words, their attitudes are weakened under these conditions. This finding also appears to have consequences for other important evaluative outcomes such as susceptibility to later persuasive attacks. Under conditions in which we expect initial message recipients to experience attitudinal doubt, they show increased vulnerability to later persuasion. What remains to be determined is whether these findings can map onto the most intriguing effects from the minority-influence literature. We turn to this matter next.

## Implications for classic findings in minority influence

The metacognitive framework and findings discussed in this chapter highlight what we hope will be viewed as a new and useful direction in minority-influence research. We believe that much can be gained in the minority-influence domain by considering people's perceptions of their resistance against minority sources, and by exploring the impact such perceptions might have on attitude certainty, or attitude strength more generally (Petty & Krosnick, 1995). Consideration of these processes and outcomes has great potential to shed new light on the subtle yet dynamic effects of resistance in the minority-influence domain. Of course, particularly important for follow-up research will be the task of using the current metacognitive perspective to account for both the delayed and the indirect change effects that have been revealed in some past minority-influence studies. In this section of the chapter we offer some speculation along these lines.

### Delayed change

We think the present perspective speaks directly to the issue of delayed focal attitude change following initial resistance to a minority message. Past research on minority influence suggests that when people publicly resist focal attitude change from minority sources, they sometimes show evidence of delayed persuasion (i.e., 'conversion') when their attitudes are measured at a later point in time (e.g., Crano & Chen, 1998; Moscovici, 1980; see Wood et al., 1994, for a review). Importantly, attitude certainty has a well-established association with attitude stability, or attitudinal persistence over time (e.g., Bassili, 1996). The less certain someone is of an attitude, the more susceptible that attitude is to change as time passes. Given our finding that resisting a minority message can decrease feelings of attitude certainty, we see the current results as highly compatible with the delayed-change effect. Specifically, we argue that when people perceive that they have resisted a minority message solely on the basis of the message's minority support, they can lose attitude certainty, which destabilizes the attitude and opens it up to delayed change.

It is important to note that our perspective's emphasis on attitude certainty predicts not only the enhanced likelihood of delayed change in response to resisted minority messages, but also increased persuasion in response to subsequent messages (as illustrated in one of our studies) and *decreased* correspondence between initial attitudes and behaviour. Indeed, as noted earlier, attitude certainty has been linked with each of these outcomes in past research (e.g., Bassili, 1996; Fazio & Zanna, 1978; Tormala & Petty, 2002). The less certain people are of their attitudes, the more vulnerable those attitudes are to persuasive attack and the less predictive those attitudes are of future behaviour. Thus, the effects of resisted minority messages could ultimately prove much more expansive than anticipated by prior minority-influence work. The present framework takes a step in the direction of understanding these effects.

### Indirect change

We also see the present framework as having implications for indirect attitude change. Past research on minority influence (e.g., Alvaro & Crano, 1997; Crano & Chen, 1998) has revealed that when people resist minority messages on one issue (e.g., gays in the military), they sometimes show evidence of attitude change with respect to other issues (e.g., gun control). Various explanations for indirect change have been offered in prior work (see Crano, 2001), but we submit that the metacognitive processes suggested by our own studies might also speak to this effect. For example, it could be that when someone resists a message because its source is in the minority, and this person feels doubt about his or her attitude, this feeling of doubt might spread to other, related attitudes. Those attitudes, in turn, would be opened up to change, according to the same logic outlined above (i.e., reducing certainty destabilizes attitudes, increases their vulnerability, and so on). Interestingly, an effect of this nature would indicate that associative networks for attitudes contain not only attitude objects and their evaluations, but also confidence or doubt assessments (e.g., 'tags') for attitudes that can be altered through a kind of metacognitive spreading activation (see Petty, Tormala, Briñol, & Jarvis, 2006, for a related discussion of confidence and doubt tags).

One challenge for this explanation of indirect attitude change would be to accommodate Crano and colleagues' (e.g., Crano & Chen, 1998) finding that indirect change happens more quickly than, and can be at least partly responsible for, delayed focal attitude change. Our explanation for this effect would parallel the rationale offered by Crano (2001). That is, although people experience doubt with respect to the focal attitude after resisting a minority message, they still resist it in the immediate situation because they do not want to align themselves with the minority position (see also Moscovici, 1985a; Wood et al., 1994). They do not erect defences around attitudes toward other issues, however, so as the doubt spreads to those attitudes they change more readily. This puts pressure back on the focal attitude in order to maintain a coherent system of beliefs and opinions. This time around, the focal attitude is more feeble (i.e., it is held with less certainty), so it is more susceptible to change. The basic sequence of events in this scenario would be quite similar to what transpires according to Crano's leniency contract, but feelings of doubt are posited to be the driving force behind both indirect and delayed change. One interesting implication of this interpretation is that the doubt experienced with respect to the focal attitude following initial resistance must be sufficiently diffuse that it can spread to other attitudes. If true, this would suggest that any concept (e.g., the self-concept) can become doubted if it is activated during this feeling of attitudinal doubt. Obviously, this possibility awaits further empirical scrutiny. It is simply worth noting that the implications of the present perspective on minority resistance could prove far reaching in the long run.

## Final thoughts and questions

Past research suggests that minority sources can play multiple roles in persuasion settings. They can serve as simple cues, they can bias thoughts, and they can affect the amount of message processing that occurs. Furthermore, although it has not been investigated yet, we have suggested that under some conditions minority sources might serve as persuasive arguments or serve to cause doubt in people's minds in response to a persuasive message. Perhaps of greatest interest, we have also described how minority sources can affect the strength of people's attitudes. Based on our metacognitive framework for understanding resistance to persuasion, we propose that when people resist messages because those messages are endorsed by minority sources, they may perceive that they have based their attitudes on the minority-status information. To the extent that people do perceive this, and they believe that it is illegitimate to base their attitudes on such factors, they can become less certain of their initial attitudes. This lack of certainty, we argue, could be responsible for intriguing effects in the minority-influence domain such as delayed and indirect persuasion. Our position is not that this is the only mechanism for such minority-influence effects, but rather that it represents an additional means by which minority messages, though resisted in the immediate context, might have some hidden effects on persuasion.

From our initial findings, several questions remain. For instance, where does this metacognitive role for minority sources fit within the multiples-roles framework of the ELM? In general, our research points to high-elaboration (or thoughtful) conditions for these effects. In prior research exploring our metacognitive perspective on resistance, we have found that resistance affects attitude certainty primarily in high-elaboration situations (e.g., low cognitive load; Tormala & Petty, 2004a) and high-elaboration individuals (e.g., high need for cognition; Tormala & Petty, 2004b; see Petty et al., 2002, for related findings). The rationale for this moderation is that metacognitive reasoning demands not only thoughts, but also thoughts about thoughts, which is a higher-order level of processing requiring greater motivation and ability. The results summarized in this chapter are consistent with the notion that these are high-elaboration effects, as all participants were led to believe a new counter-attitudinal policy was being considered for implementation at their university. The clear personal relevance of this issue for our student sample likely created high-elaboration conditions across the board (Petty & Cacioppo, 1979a).

The interpretation of our effects as involving thoughtful processes is consistent with a great deal of past research in which minority influence has been described as involving extensive information-processing activity (e.g., Moscovici, 1980; Martin et al., 2003). Importantly, though, in the present research it is possible that even under less-thoughtful circumstances people could realize that they have resisted persuasion because of the minority status of a source. In fact, perhaps people who are not processing deeply would be more acutely aware of basing their attitudes on minority-source status as that is precisely the kind of information they would be seeking to facilitate quick decision making. In any case, it remains to be seen what impact resistance to minority sources would have under low-elaboration conditions. We see this as one useful direction for future research in this area.

Another question pertains to how we would reconcile the current perspective and findings with the Martin et al. (2003) research in which it was found that people had *stronger* attitudes after processing minority messages. Martin and colleagues found that because people processed minority messages extensively, their attitudes following such messages were quite strong and resistant to counter-persuasion. The key difference between the present perspective and the Martin et al. perspective is that in the Martin et al. work, participants were persuaded by the minority message, so their attitudes were equivalent to attitudes in the majority-source condition. In our own research, participants have been resisting the minority message, presumably because in addition to being supported by the minority these messages have been highly relevant and counter-attitudinal, conditions well-known to encourage resistance (Petty & Cacioppo, 1979b).

It could be that the direction of the attitude-strength effect depends on whether people initially resist or succumb to the minority message. Moreover, if true, this effect might not depend on processing differences. Rucker and Petty (2004) have taken a metacognitive perspective on these kinds of issues and found that when people try to resist persuasion but are nonetheless persuaded, they become highly certain of their newly changed attitudes. Extending this finding to the current concerns, perhaps when people are persuaded by minority messages despite presumably not wanting to be, they become highly convinced of the validity of the new attitude, making that attitude strong and resistant to counter-persuasion. In brief, our proposal is that when people *resist* minority messages (e.g., Tormala et al., 2007b), they might perceive that they have done so illegitimately, thereby undermining certainty in the unchanged attitude. When people are *persuaded* by minority messages (e.g., Martin et al., 2003), they might be more likely to assume they have been legitimately influenced (after all, they are not going along with the position on the basis of its source), thereby boosting attitude certainty. In fact, heightened processing (as in Martin et al., 2003) might contribute metacognitively to the effect if people feel more certain when they *perceive* that they have changed their attitudes through thoughtful processing, which is likely viewed as a legitimate way to be influenced (Barden & Petty, 2006). In any case, this metacognitive resolution is speculative, but it might prove useful to future work in this area.

## Conclusion

As reviewed in this chapter, minority/majority-source status can influence persuasive outcomes by serving as simple acceptance or rejection cues, by determining the amount of processing in which people engage, by biasing message recipients' issue-relevant thinking, or by influencing the certainty with which people hold their attitudes after being exposed to a persuasive message. It is our hope that the present chapter will spark an interest in the multiple roles through which minority sources influence both persuasion and resistance, and the attitude-strength consequences of each. Of particular emphasis in the present chapter are the metacognitive factors at play when people receive and defend their attitudes against minority-supported messages. We believe that metacognitive perspectives have much to offer in general, and that they have great potential to shed new light on issues of classic import in the minority-influence domain. In some ways, we see the metacognitive perspective as raising as many questions as it answers, but we hope new perspectives like the one we have presented can lend support to the effort to understand the hidden persuasive effects resisted minority sources have often been observed to have.

## Note

1 Although there is ample evidence suggesting that people do sometimes process minority messages rather thoroughly, there is also reason to believe that people often do so under the assumption that they will ultimately resist the minority point of view to avoid being aligned with a deviant group (e.g., Crano & Chen, 1998; see Crano, 2001).

## References

Alvaro, E. M., & Crano, W. D. (1997). Indirect minority influence: Evidence for leniency in source evaluation and counterargumentation. *Journal of Personality and Social Psychology, 72*, 949–964.

Baker, S. M., & Petty, R. E. (1994). Majority and minority influence: Source–position imbalance as a determinant of message scrutiny. *Journal of Personality and Social Psychology, 67*, 5–19.

Barden, J., & Petty, R. E. (2006). *A comprehensive process from antecedents of elaboration to attitude strength consequences: Mediation by the perception of elaboration.* Unpublished manuscript, Howard University, Washington, DC.

Bassili, J. N. (1996). Meta-judgmental versus operative indexes of psychological attributes: The case of measures of attitude strength. *Journal of Personality and Social Psychology, 71*, 637–653.

Bless, H., Bohner, G., Schwarz, N., & Strack, F. (1990). Mood and persuasion: A cognitive response analysis. *Personality and Social Psychology Bulletin, 16*, 331–345.

Briñol, P., Petty, R. E., & Barden, J. (2006). *Mood as a determinant of thought confidence in persuasion: A self-validation analysis.* Unpublished manuscript, Ohio State University, Columbus, OH.

Briñol, P., Petty, R. E., & Tormala, Z. L. (2004). The self-validation of cognitive responses to advertisements. *Journal of Consumer Research, 30*, 559–573.

Chaiken, S., Liberman, A., & Eagly, A. H. (1989). Heuristic and systematic information processing within and beyond the persuasion context. In J. S. Uleman & J. A. Bargh (Eds.), *Unintended thought* (pp. 212–252). New York: Guilford Press.

Chaiken, S., & Maheswaran, D. (1994). Heuristic processing can bias systematic processing: Effects of source credibility, argument ambiguity, and task importance on attitude judgment. *Journal of Personality and Social Psychology*, *66*, 460–473.

Crano, W. D. (2001). Social influence, social identity, and ingroup leniency. In C. K. W. De Dreu & N. K. De Vries (Eds.), *Group consensus and minority influence: Implications for innovation* (pp. 122–143). Oxford, UK: Blackwell.

Crano, W. D., & Chen, X. (1998). The leniency contract and persistence of majority and minority influence. *Journal of Personality and Social Psychology*, *74*, 1437–1450.

Darke, P. R., Chaiken, S., Bohner, G., Einwiller, S., Erb, H., & Hazlewood, J. D. (1998). Accuracy motivation, consensus information, and the law of large numbers: Effects on attitude judgment in the absence of argumentation. *Personality and Social Psychology Bulletin*, *24*, 1205–1215.

DeBono, K. G., & Harnish, R. J. (1988). Source expertise, source attractiveness, and the processing of persuasive information: A functional approach. *Journal of Personality and Social Psychology*, *55*, 541–546.

Eagly, A. H., Chaiken, S., & Wood, W. (1981). An attribution analysis of persuasion. In J. H. Harvey, W. J. Ickes, & R. F. Kidd (Eds.), *New directions in attribution research* (Vol. 3, pp. 37–62). Hillsdale, NJ: Lawrence Erlbaum Associates, Inc.

Erb, H., & Bohner, G. (2001). Mere consensus in minority and majority influence. In N. De Vries & C. De Dreu (Eds.), *Group consensus and minority influence: Implications for innovation* (pp. 40–59). Oxford, UK: Blackwell.

Erb, H., Bohner, G., Schmälzle, K., & Rank, S. (1998). Beyond conflict and discrepancy: Cognitive bias in minority and majority influence. *Personality and Social Psychology Bulletin*, *24*, 620–633.

Fazio, R. H., & Zanna, M. P. (1978). Attitudinal qualities relating to the strength of the attitude–behavior relationship. *Journal of Experimental Social Psychology*, *14*, 398–408.

Festinger, L. (1954). A theory of social comparison processes. *Human Relations*, *7*, 117–140.

Giner-Sorolla, R., & Chaiken, S. (1997). Selective use of heuristic and systematic processing under defense motivation. *Personality and Social Psychology Bulletin*, *23*, 84–97.

Gross, S., Holtz, R., & Miller, N. (1995). Attitude certainty. In R. E. Petty & J. A. Krosnick (Eds.), *Attitude strength: Antecedents and consequences* (pp. 215–245). Mahwah, NJ: Lawrence Erlbaum Associates, Inc.

Heesacker, M., Petty, R. E., & Cacioppo, J. T. (1983). Field dependence and attitude change: Source credibility can alter persuasion by affecting message-relevant thinking. *Journal of Personality*, *51*, 653–666.

Hovland, C. I., & Weiss, W. (1951). The influence of source credibility on communication effectiveness. *Public Opinion Quarterly*, *15*, 635–650.

Jacks, J. Z., & Cameron, K. A. (2003). Strategies for resisting persuasion. *Basic and Applied Social Psychology*, *25*, 145–161.

Kelley, H. H. (1972). Causal schemata and the attribution process. In E. E. Jones, D. E. Kanouse, H. H. Kelley, R. E. Nisbett, S. Valins, & B. Weiner (Eds.), *Attribution: Perceiving the causes of behavior* (pp. 151–174). Morristown, NJ: General Learning Press.

Kiesler, S. B., & Mathog, R. B. (1968). Distraction hypothesis in attitude change: Effects of effectiveness. *Psychological Reports, 23,* 1123–1133.

Kruglanski, A. W., & Thompson, E. P. (1999). Persuasion by a single route: A view from the unimodel. *Psychological Inquiry,* 10, 83–109.

Maass, A., & Clark, R. D., III (1983). Internalization versus compliance: Differential processes underlying minority influence and conformity. *European Journal of Social Psychology, 13,* 197–215.

Mackie, D. M. (1987). Systematic and nonsystematic processing of majority and minority persuasive communications. *Journal of Personality and Social Psychology, 53,* 41–52.

Martin, L. L., Abend, T., Sedikides, C., & Green, J. D. (1997). How would it feel if . . . ? Mood as input to a role fulfillment evaluation process. *Journal of Personality and Social Psychology, 73,* 242–253.

Martin, R., & Hewstone, M. (2003). Majority versus minority influence: When, not whether, source status instigates heuristic or systematic processing. *European Journal of Social Psychology, 33,* 313–330.

Martin, R., Hewstone, M., & Martin, P. Y. (2003). Resistance to persuasive messages as a function of majority and minority source status. *Journal of Experimental Social Psychology, 39,* 585–593.

Mazursky, D., & Schul, Y. (2000). In the aftermath of invalidation: Shaping judgment rules on learning that previous information was invalid. *Journal of Consumer Psychology, 9,* 213–222.

Moscovici, S. (1980). Toward a theory of conversion behavior. In L. Berkowitz (Ed.), *Advances in experimental social psychology* (Vol. 13, pp. 209–239). New York: Academic Press.

Moscovici, S. (1985a). Innovation and minority influence. In S. Moscovici, G. Mugny, & E. Van Avermaet (Eds.), *Perspectives on minority influence* (pp. 9–52). Cambridge, UK: Cambridge University Press.

Moscovici, S. (1985b). Social influence and conformity. In G. Lindsey & E. Aronson (Eds.), *The handbook of social psychology* (3rd ed., Vol. 2, pp. 347–412). New York: Random House.

Moskowitz, G. B. (1996). The mediational effects of attributions and information processing in minority social influence. *British Journal of Social Psychology, 35,* 47–66.

Moskowitz, G. B., & Chaiken, S. (2001). Mediators of minority social influence: Cognitive processing mechanisms revealed through a persuasion paradigm. In C. K. W. De Dreu & N. K. De Vries (Eds.), *Group consensus and minority influence* (pp. 60–90). Oxford, UK: Blackwell.

Mugny, G. (1982). *The power of minorities.* London: Academic Press.

Mugny, G., & Perez, J. A. (1991). *The social psychology of minority influence.* Cambridge, UK: Cambridge University Press.

Pelham, B. W., Sumarta, T. T., & Myaskovsky, L. (1994). The easy path from many to much: The numerosity heuristic. *Cognitive Psychology, 26,* 103–133.

Petty, R. E., Briñol, P., & Tormala, Z. L. (2002). Thought confidence as a determinant of persuasion: The self-validation hypothesis. *Journal of Personality and Social Psychology, 82,* 722–741.

Petty, R. E., Briñol, P., Tormala, Z. L., & Wegener, D. (2007). The role of metacognition in social judgment. In A. W. Kruglanski & E. T. Higgins (Eds.),

*Social psychology: Handbook of basic principles* (2nd ed., pp. 254–284). New York: Guilford Press.

Petty, R. E., & Cacioppo, J. T. (1979a). Effects of forewarning of persuasive intent and involvement on cognitive responses. *Personality and Social Psychology Bulletin, 5,* 173–176.

Petty, R. E., & Cacioppo, J. T. (1979b). Issue-involvement can increase or decrease persuasion by enhancing message-relevant cognitive responses. *Journal of Personality and Social Psychology, 37,* 1915–1926.

Petty, R. E., & Cacioppo, J. T. (1984). The effects of involvement on responses to argument quantity and quality: Central and peripheral routes to persuasion. *Journal of Personality and Social Psychology, 46,* 69–81.

Petty, R. E., & Cacioppo, J. T. (1986). The elaboration likelihood model of persuasion. In L. Berkowitz (Ed.), *Advances in experimental social psychology* (Vol. 19, pp. 123–205). New York: Academic Press.

Petty, R. E., Cacioppo, J. T., & Goldman, R. (1981). Personal involvement as a determinant of argument-based persuasion. *Journal of Personality and Social Psychology, 41,* 847–855.

Petty, R. E., Fleming, M. A., & White, P. H. (1999). Stigmatized sources and persuasion: Prejudice as a determinant of argument scrutiny. *Journal of Personality and Social Psychology, 76,* 19–34.

Petty, R. E., Haugtvedt, C. P., & Smith, S. M. (1995). Elaboration as a determinant of attitude strength. In R. E. Petty & J. A. Krosnick (Eds.), *Attitude strength: Antecedents and consequences* (pp. 93–130). Mahwah, NJ: Lawrence Erlbaum Associates, Inc.

Petty, R. E., & Krosnick, J. A. (Eds.). (1995). *Attitude strength: Antecedents and consequences.* Mahwah, NJ: Lawrence Erlbaum Associates, Inc.

Petty, R. E., Schumann, D. W., Richman, S. A., & Strathman, A. J. (1993). Positive mood and persuasion: Different roles for affect under high- and low-elaboration conditions. *Journal of Personality and Social Psychology, 64,* 5–20.

Petty, R. E., Tormala, Z. L., Briñol, P., & Jarvis, W. B. G. (2006). Implicit ambivalence from attitude change: An exploration of the PAST model. *Journal of Personality and Social Psychology, 90,* 21–41.

Petty, R. E., Tormala, Z. L., & Rucker, D. D. (2004). Resistance to persuasion: An attitude strength perspective. In J. T. Jost, M. R. Banaji, & D. A. Prentice (Eds.), *Perspectivism in social psychology: The yin and yang of scientific progress* (pp. 37–51). Washington, DC: American Psychological Association.

Petty, R. E., & Wegener, D. T. (1998). Attitude change: Multiple roles for persuasion variables. In D. T. Gilbert, S. T. Fiske, & G. Lindzey (Eds.), *The handbook of social psychology* (Vol. 1, pp. 323–390). New York: McGraw-Hill.

Petty, R. E., & Wegener, D. T. (1999). The elaboration likelihood model: Current status and controversies. In S. Chaiken & Y. Trope (Eds.), *Dual-process theories in social psychology* (pp. 37–72). New York: Guilford Press.

Petty, R. E., Wheeler, S. C., & Tormala, Z. L. (2003). Persuasion and attitude change. In T. Millon & M. J. Lerner (Eds.), *Handbook of psychology. Vol. 5: Personality and social psychology* (pp. 353–382). New York: Wiley.

Priester, J. R., & Petty, R. E. (1995). Source attributions and persuasion: Perceived honesty as a determinant of message scrutiny. *Personality and Social Psychology Bulletin, 21,* 637–654.

Rucker, D. D., & Petty, R. E. (2004). When resistance is futile: Consequences of failed counterarguing for attitude certainty. *Journal of Personality and Social Psychology, 86*, 219–235.

Salancik, G. R., & Conway, M. (1975). Attitude inferences from salient and relevant cognitive content about behavior. *Journal of Personality and Social Psychology, 32*, 829–840.

Schwarz, N., & Clore, G. (1983). Mood, misattribution, and judgments of well-being: Informative and directive functions of affective states. *Journal of Personality and Social Psychology, 45*, 513–523.

Tormala, Z. L., Briñol, P., & Petty, R. E. (2006a). When credibility attacks: The reverse impact of source credibility on persuasion. *Journal of Experimental Social Psychology, 42*, 684–691.

Tormala, Z. L., Briñol, P., & Petty, R. E. (2007a). Multiple roles for source credibility under high elaboration: It's all in the timing. *Social Cognition, 25*, 536–552.

Tormala, Z. L., Clarkson, J. J., & Petty, R. E. (2006b). Resisting persuasion by the skin of one's teeth: The hidden success of resisted persuasive messages. *Journal of Personality and Social Psychology, 91*, 423–435.

Tormala, Z. L., DeSensi, V. L., & Petty, R. E. (2007b). Resisting persuasion by illegitimate means: A metacognitive perspective on minority influence. *Personality and Social Psychology Bulletin, 33*, 354–367.

Tormala, Z. L., & Petty, R. E. (2002). What doesn't kill me makes me stronger: The effects of resisting persuasion on attitude certainty. *Journal of Personality and Social Psychology, 83*, 1298–1313.

Tormala, Z. L., & Petty, R. E. (2004a). Source credibility and attitude certainty: A metacognitive analysis of resistance to persuasion. *Journal of Consumer Psychology, 14*, 426–441.

Tormala, Z. L., & Petty, R. E. (2004b). Resistance to persuasion and attitude certainty: The moderating role of elaboration. *Personality and Social Psychology Bulletin, 30*, 1446–1457.

Tormala, Z. L., & Petty, R. E. (2004c). Resistance to persuasion and attitude certainty: A metacognitive analysis. In E. S. Knowles & J. A. Linn (Eds.), *Resistance and persuasion* (pp. 65–82). Mahwah, NJ: Lawrence Erlbaum Associates, Inc.

Tormala, Z. L., Petty, R. E., & Briñol, P. (2002). Ease of retrieval effects in persuasion: A self-validation analysis. *Personality and Social Psychology Bulletin, 28*, 1700–1712.

Trost, M. R., Maass, A., & Kenrick, D. T. (1992). Minority influence: Personal relevance biases cognitive responses and reverses private acceptance. *Journal of Experimental Social Psychology, 28*, 234–254.

Wegener, D. T., Petty, R. E., & Smith, S. M. (1995). Positive mood can increase or decrease message scrutiny: The hedonic contingency view of mood and message processing. *Journal of Personality and Social Psychology, 69*, 5–15.

Wood, W., Lundgren, S., Ouellette, J. A., Busceme, S., & Blackstone, T. (1994). Minority influence: A meta-analytic review of social influence processes. *Psychological Bulletin, 115*, 323–345.

Wood, W., Pool, G. J., Leck, K., & Purvis, D. (1996). Self-definition, defensive processing, and influence: The normative impact of majority and minority groups. *Journal of Personality and Social Psychology, 71*, 1181–1193.

Worth, L. T., & Mackie, D. M. (1987). Cognitive mediation of positive affect in persuasion. *Social Cognition, 5,* 76–94.

Yzerbyt, V. Y., Schadron, G., Leyens, J., & Rocher, S. (1994). Social judgeability: The impact of meta-informational cues on the use of stereotypes. *Journal of Personality and Social Psychology, 66,* 48–55.

Zanna, M. P., Kiesler, C. A., Pilkonis, P. A. (1970). Positive and negative attitudinal affect established by classical conditioning. *Journal of Personality and Social Psychology, 14,* 321–328.

Ziegler, R., Diehl, M., & Ruther, A. (2002). Multiple source characteristics and persuasion: Source inconsistency as a determinant of message scrutiny. *Personality and Social Psychology Bulletin, 28,* 496–508.

# Part III

# Factors affecting majority and minority influence

# 6 Ambivalence and social influence

*Angelica Mucchi-Faina*
University of Perugia, Italy

*Odi et amo. Quare id faciam, fortasse requiris.*
*Nescio, sed fieri sentio et excrucior.*

(I hate and I love: why I do so you may well ask.
I do not know, but I feel it happen and am in agony.)

(Catullo, *Carmina*, 85)

While the notion of ambivalence has been present in Western literature since ancient Roman times, it became the topic of scientific study, in psychiatry and psychoanalysis, only at the beginning of the twentieth century. In those early studies ambivalence was primarily considered a symptom of mental illness (e.g., schizophrenia, Bleuler, 1910; Freud, 1912, both cited in Laplanche & Pontalis, 1968). In the last few decades, ambivalence—namely, a reaction 'that contains both positive and negative elements' (Olson & Zanna, 1993, p. 123; see also Bell & Esses, 1997; Jonas, Diehl, & Broemer, 1997)—has been the object of much speculation and research in different areas of social psychology, including attitudes (see Jonas, Broemer, & Diehl, 2000; Thompson, Zanna, & Griffin, 1995, for reviews), stereotypes and prejudice (Fiske, Cuddy, Glick, & Xu, 2002; Gaertner & Dovidio, 1986; McConahay, 1986), persuasion (e.g., Broemer, 2002; Cavazza & Butera, 2008; Maio, Bell, & Esses, 1996; Petty, Fleming, & White, 1999), minority influence (e.g., Mucchi-Faina, 2000; Mucchi-Faina & Cicoletti, 2006; Mucchi-Faina & Pagliaro, 2008), interpersonal communication (Mongrain & Vettese, 2003), and inter-group evaluations (Mucchi-Faina, Costarelli, & Romoli, 2002; Mucchi-Faina, Pacilli, Pagliaro, & Alparone, 2009).

This chapter deals with ambivalence in social influence theory and research. Although some of the earliest researchers on minority influence noted contrasting reactions to the source (e.g., Moscovici, 1980; Mugny & Papastamou, 1984; Nemeth & Watchler, 1974), direct and empirical investigations of the relationship between ambivalence and influence are quite recent. My intention in this chapter is to shed light on the manifold roles that ambivalence can play in influencing processes and to indicate possible new extensions of this line of study. In the next two sections of this chapter, I briefly describe the different effects of majority and minority influence as presented in the classical literature on the topic and how ambivalence can be measured. I then examine research focusing on ambivalence as an independent variable. Subsequently, I propose that ambivalence may also be triggered by sources—especially minority sources—and I present the first empirical findings on ambivalence as a dependent variable and a mediator of influence. Finally, I discuss the implications and consequences of ambivalence in social influence processes.

## Which influence from which source?

Starting with the studies by Asch (1951), strong evidence has supported the idea that majorities—intended both as numerically prevailing groups and powerful dominant groups—may exert public and direct influence, i.e., *conformity*. According to conversion theory (Moscovici, 1980), since following the majority is socially encouraged and approved, the impact of majority sources is more public than private (*compliance effect*). Instead, minority sources typically exert a more covert, although deeper, impact (*conversion effect*). However, not all minorities are able to become sources of influence. Generally, in social sciences, a group that is perceived of as disadvantaged (compared with the majority) is considered a minority. This is the case of powerless autochthons or immigrant ethnic groups, the so-called weak categories (e.g., elderly people, disabled), or other groups that are stigmatized because of the peculiarity of their choices (e.g., sexual preferences, deviant beliefs or behaviours). In short, minorities are non-dominant groups versus a dominant majority. But being underprivileged is not enough to exert influence. The *anomic* minorities—those who accept being marginalized by the majority and are unable to build up a distinctive and coherent set of norms—are destined to be ineffective and to remain deviant (Moscovici, 1976).

In order to obtain social influence, minorities must be *nomic*; they must adopt a resolute style of behaviour, refuse a marginal status and propose themselves and their ideas as an alternative to the prevalent system. Successful minorities are *active* and able to affirm their opinions and rights with determination; their consistency and courage to open a conflict with the majority are the weapons that allow them to become sources of social influence (Moscovici, 1976). Minority groups that are taken into consideration in the social influence area are therefore only a restricted and special part of 'minorities' as generally intended.

Although people may be drawn to active and nomic minorities, they normally refuse to overtly follow these sources for self-protection reasons: indeed, normative pressures appear to encourage both alignment with majorities and differentiation from minorities (Wood, Pool, Leck, & Purvis, 1996). Showing dependence on a minority entails the attribution of its deviant features, thereby running the risk of being disapproved of by the majority and thus stigmatized. A covert change could represent a good compromise as it would permit the target to follow the source in some way without paying high social costs (Sanchez-Mazas & Falomir, 1995). Cumulative evidence shows that conversion to the minority position is often indirect (on issues related to but different from the one under discussion), delayed (not immediate) and private (unknown to the source; see Wood, Lundgren, Ouellette, Busceme, & Blackstone, 1994, for a review). Alternatively, a minority may constitute a model of dissent for the target, stimulating independent and original ideas (*divergence effect*; Nemeth, 1986). Conversion and divergence are thus different hidden effects of minority influence.

Researchers have hypothesized that the target's ambivalence could be related to the various effects of social influence in different ways. Thus, depending on the aim of each study, ambivalence has either been induced by using an experimental manipulation, e.g., increasing the accessibility of ambivalent versus univalent thoughts about the source—or measured.

## How to measure ambivalence

More than thirty years ago, Kaplan (1972) maintained that attitude is not a one-dimensional construct and that measuring attitudes with the usual bipolar scale (e.g., ranging from '*highly favourable*' to '*highly unfavourable*') is an oversimplified procedure. Kaplan stressed that people's reactions to an attitude target are often ambivalent, containing both positive and negative elements, and proposed considering the reactions of different valence separately and then calculating ambivalence by applying a statistical formula. Since then, how to measure ambivalence has remained the object of debate. The main methodological choice is between using a self-report measure and using, as Kaplan suggested, a statistical formula that takes into account the positive and negative aspects of the attitude. With the first approach, people are requested to state directly whether (or to what degree) their reactions towards an attitude object are mixed (versus one-sided; e.g., Tourangeau, Rasinski, Bradburn, & D'Andrade, 1989). With the second, participants are asked to indicate separately the extent of their negative and positive reactions to an object, and then their answers are combined. For example, using a well-known formula for close-ended measures proposed by Griffin and validated by Thompson et al. (1995), ambivalence is calculated by averaging positive and negative attitude scores and then subtracting the absolute value of the difference between the two scores from their average.[1] In this manner, both the similarity between the two reactions and their intensity are taken into account (see Bell, Esses, & Maio, 1996; Thompson et al. 1995, for further details).

It is also possible, of course, to use both self-report and formula-based methods. In this case, the two measures often appear to be correlated, although not very strongly, thus supporting the idea that they refer to two partly different phenomena (see Bassili, 1996; Jonas et al., 2000; Priester & Petty, 1996, for a comparison between formula-based and subjective measures of ambivalence). A possible explanation for this weak correlation is that people are not completely aware of their degree of ambivalence (Jonas et al., 2000). Therefore, the (less-direct) formula-based measures seem more suitable than the self-report measures for identifying the unintended part of an attitude (Bassili, 1996). Since the detection of non-explicit forms of change is a crucial point in social influence, researchers in this area have generally preferred formula-based measures.

## Ambivalence as an independent variable

Given that ambivalence may have different functions in social influence, it can be considered an independent variable, a dependent variable, or a possible mediator of social influence. As an independent variable, ambivalence has been investigated with reference to both majority and minority sources.

### *Majority influence*

Highly ambivalent people seem to be more inclined to conformity than less ambivalent people. In a study concerning the social welfare debate (Hodson, Maio, & Esses, 2001), participants high and low in ambivalence towards welfare were tested individually and asked to watch a videotaped debate between a pro-welfare person and an anti-welfare person. Then, depending on the experimental condition, they were informed that the majority of previous participants favoured either the pro-welfare or the anti-welfare debater. As expected, highly ambivalent participants shifted in the majority direction, becoming more favourable towards welfare after exposure to the majority pro-welfare debater than after exposure to the majority anti-welfare debater. Instead, less ambivalent participants showed a kind of boomerang effect, becoming particularly unfavourable towards welfare when exposed to the pro-welfare majority, thus reacting against the source. Hodson and colleagues (2001) interpreted these findings as suggesting that people high in ambivalence used consensus information as a source of social reality in order to reduce their ambivalence, while people low in ambivalence reacted against the majority position, given that they did not need to resolve an attitudinal conflict, and perceived consensus information as possibly biasing their judgement.

The idea that people high (vs. low) in ambivalence are more likely to conform to the majority's position was confirmed in another study (Cavazza & Butera, 2008). In two experiments, participants were divided into two groups according to the higher or lower ambivalence of their opinion on a topic. Participants were then informed that the (in-group) majority had expressed a counter-attitudinal opinion in a previous survey. Majority influence was measured at both the direct level (on the same topic) and the indirect level (on a topic different from, but related to, the persuasive message). Results consistently showed that highly ambivalent participants were more strongly influenced by the source at the direct level than at an indirect one, whereas less ambivalent participants were more strongly persuaded at the indirect level than at the direct one. The authors interpreted these findings on the basis of the conflict elaboration theory (Pérez & Mugny, 1996). According to this theory, indirect influence is not a peculiarity of minority sources: when people cannot comply with the opinion of the in-group majority because their personal position conflicts with the majority norm, an indirect (but not a direct) change would be observed, since indirect influence makes it possible to restore similarity to the majority while maintaining self-consistency. However, ambivalent people do not need to use this strategy because they can attain similarity by simply emphasizing the pro-majority component of their attitude. Therefore, ambivalence could be functional in the context of majority influence, permitting compliance without a deeper change. The idea that ambivalence entails greater overt submissiveness has also been confirmed by studies conducted outside the social-influence area (e.g., interpersonal communication; Mongrain & Vettese, 2003).

## Minority influence

The quantity and quality of cognitive activity that a source elicits is a crucial point in influence research because many studies have found that the impact of both majorities and minorities is largely related to the way people process their message (e.g., De Dreu & De Vries, 1993; Martin & Hewstone, 2001). In fact, as suggested by different theories on persuasion (e.g., elaboration likelihood model, Petty & Cacioppo, 1986; heuristic-systematic model, Chaiken, 1980), the persuasive effects of a message can be affected by the effort and the meticulousness that a target brings to processing the information. Specifically, people who are engaging in careful and systematic processing should be more likely to be persuaded by a strong message than by a weak message. On the contrary, people using heuristics and other less-effortful strategies to evaluate the message should be less differentially affected by strong versus weak messages.

Petty and colleagues (1999) conducted two studies in which participants, high or low in ambivalence towards a minority group, were exposed to a message that was attributed to a minority (Black in the first study and homosexual in the second study) or to a majority (White in the first study and heterosexual in the second study). Results showed that participants high or low in ambivalence towards the minority processed the message attributed to minority and majority sources in a similar way, thus suggesting that ambivalence towards minorities per se had no significant impact on information processing.

In Petty et al.'s (1999) studies, the topic of the message was unrelated to the minority group (i.e., the introduction of a senior comprehensive exam in the university). Actually, the fact that the topic is directly relevant or irrelevant to the group towards which one expresses ambivalence may affect the target's choice of information-processing strategy. For example, Maio et al. (1996) found that Canadian targets who were ambivalent towards Asian immigrants were more influenced by the quality (strong vs. weak) of the arguments in a message in favour of immigration from Hong Kong than were non-ambivalent targets. Therefore, ambivalent participants processed information more carefully than non-ambivalent participants. However, minority was the *topic*, but not the *source* of the message: thus the effects of ambivalence towards a minority source directly concerned with the topic of the communication remained unexplored.

In an experiment designed to address this subject (Mucchi-Faina & Pagliaro, 2006), a sample of university students was requested to evaluate a counter-attitudinal proposal regarding, once again, the introduction of a final exam in the university. The proposal was supported by a fictitious minority called 'Students for a Better University'. In this study, therefore, the source was directly concerned with the topic of the message. Ambivalence was manipulated by making either ambivalent or univalent thoughts accessible to the target (Maio, Greenland, Bernard, & Esses, 2001): participants were asked to imagine and write down both the positive *and* negative outcomes that might derive from meeting the minority source (ambivalence condition) or the possible positive *or* negative outcomes of this meeting (univalent positive and univalent negative conditions). Subsequently, direct influence (attitude change on the issue), indirect influence (attitude change on issues related to the one under discussion) and divergence (generation of proposals alternative to the one of the minority) were measured. Results showed no difference on direct influence according to condition, whereas indirect influence was higher and divergence lower in the ambivalence condition rather than in the univalent conditions. Consequently (induced) ambivalence seems to favour conversion but hinder divergence in minority-influence settings.

To interpret these findings, we suggested that, in the ambivalence condition, the accessibility of pro and con thoughts about the source could lead targets to an unsatisfying level of self-confidence that they try to compensate for by undertaking a careful and systematic processing of the minority *message*. This additional cognitive effort strengthens the minority impact, leading to (indirect) attitude change. On the contrary, in univalent conditions, self-confidence is less in question and, since the message is both personally relevant and counter-attitudinal, people are stimulated to think in a divergent manner about the *issue* in order to find possible alternative solutions. An ancillary self-confidence measure of the study supported this interpretation, since participants stated less self-confidence in ambivalence conditions than in univalent ones.

In sum, ambivalent targets appear more directly influenced by the majority and more indirectly influenced by the minority than non-ambivalent targets. Thus, as an independent variable, ambivalence seems to merely favour the usual effects: compliance to the majority and conversion to (but not divergence from) the minority. However, data concerning majority and minority sources have been collected in different studies using different measures: with reference to the majority, participants were divided on the basis of their pre-existent ambivalence toward the issue (Cavazza & Butera, 2008; Hodson et al., 2001) whereas, with reference to the minority, ambivalence towards the source was manipulated (Mucchi-Faina & Pagliaro, 2006). These preliminary findings now need to be confirmed in a single study that compares the effect of ambivalence towards majority and minority. In addition, ambivalence towards different foci (the source and the issue) should be considered separately. As we will see in the next section, these procedures have already been employed to examine ambivalence elicited during the influence process.

## Ambivalence as a dependent measure and mediator of social influence

In the studies presented above, participants high and low in ambivalence were compared in order to investigate the effects of pre-existing or induced ambivalence on information processing, attitude change and divergence. However, ambivalence may also be considered as a dependent variable and a possible mediator of social influence. Referring in particular to minorities, two conjectures have been formulated: (1) that people exposed to minority sources could become ambivalent *towards them*, and that this ambivalence could account for the hidden influence that minorities obtain, and (2) that minorities could increase the target's ambivalence *towards the issue* under debate and that, in certain conditions, this ambivalence could favour attitude change. Although both hypotheses have been the subject of many theoretical speculations, they have been supported by few empirical investigations.

### Ambivalence towards the source

The earliest studies and post-experiment enquiries revealed conflicting reactions in targets exposed to minority sources due to the fact that these sources were generally evaluated in terms of both negative and positive attributes (e.g., Nemeth & Watchler, 1974; see Mugny & Papastamou, 1984, on this topic). It was also found that the use of more than one dimension when evaluating a minority source could favour its impact (Ricateau, 1970). Moscovici (1994) proposed a theoretical interpretation of these findings. He argued that a nomic and active minority might arouse two opposing attitudes in a target, one of hostility or rejection, the other of attraction. 'In truth', Moscovici reasoned, 'one is inseparable from the other, for what attracts us most of the time, the novelty of ideas or actions, at the same time repels us by the conflict or break of consensus it provokes' (pp. 241–242). On the one hand, then, people reject and want to keep these minorities at a distance, since they do not like to be identified with a marginal and deviant source that may be threatening not only for self-presentation ('for fear of losing face'; Moscovici, 1980, p. 211), but also for self-definition and self-esteem (Pool, Wood, & Leck, 1998). On the other hand, people may be intrigued by a dissenting minority viewed as 'confident', 'courageous', 'independent', and 'worthy of respect' (Nemeth & Chiles, 1988). Consequently, active minorities would elicit ambivalence towards themselves and this ambivalence would favour their hidden impact.

Referring to Moscovici's interpretation (1994), we hypothesized in a study that ambivalence generated by a minority source would be mainly cross-dimensional (MacDonald & Zanna, 1998), resulting from positive judgement (respect) and negative feelings (aversion) (Pagliaro & Mucchi-Faina, 2006). Since previous research (e.g., Crano & Alvaro, 1998) had showed that minority influence was stronger when the personal relevance of the issue for the target was low (vs. high), in that study we advanced that the minority would induce more cross-dimensional ambivalence towards the source in a low-relevance condition than in a high-relevance condition. Moreover, we predicted higher ambivalence towards a minority than a majority source and a mediation of ambivalence on minority but not on majority influence. Using the classical paradigm adopted by Petty, Cacioppo, and Goldman (1981), a sample of students was exposed to a counter-attitudinal proposal (the introduction of a final comprehensive exam in the university curriculum) supported by a minority or a majority. Based on condition, the proposal was either personally relevant (taking effect the following academic year) or was not relevant (taking effect in eight to ten years) for the targets. Cross-dimensional ambivalence towards the source and private influence, i.e., attitude change expressed anonymously, were measured. Results showed that both influence and ambivalence were higher in the no-personal-relevance conditions but, contrary to expectations, the majority stimulated more ambivalence than the minority. Subsequent analyses showed that, as predicted, cross-dimensional ambivalence towards the source mediated minority influence whereas it did not mediate majority influence. Thus, ambivalence elicited by a source appears to facilitate social influence only when this source is a minority.

### Ambivalence towards the issue

Minority sources can foster ambivalence not only towards themselves but also towards the issue on which they express their standpoint. According to conversion theory (Moscovici, 1980), minorities stimulate *validation*, i.e., a careful examination of their message. In fact, research strongly supports the idea that when other variables (e.g., personal relevance) do not interfere, systematic processing of the minority message is the default (Martin &

Hewstone, 2001). Validation entails that people evaluate the pros and the cons of the source proposal thereby becoming less confident in their previous opinion on the issue. As a consequence, they generate both arguments and counter-arguments (Maass & Volpato, 1994), therefore becoming more ambivalent.

At present, we know that two contextual factors can facilitate ambivalence: (1) unbalanced settings, that is, conditions in which the target perceives an incongruity between the source and its position, and (2) low personal relevance of the issue for the target.

In the first experiment focusing on ambivalence toward the issue (Mucchi-Faina, 2000), participants were exposed to a message concerning chemical preservatives in food that was endorsed either by a minority perceived as reliable and close (World Wildlife Fund; WWF), or by a minority perceived as unreliable and distant (Jehovah's Witnesses; JW). The sources expressed either a counter-attitudinal position or a pro-attitudinal one. The main dependent measures were the number of positive and negative thoughts about the issue produced by participants, and indirect influence (evaluations on issues different from, but related to, preservatives in food). We predicted that participants exposed to the message endorsed by WWF would be more ambivalent (i.e., expressing more thoughts both in favour and against preservatives in food) when the source was con rather than pro and, vice versa, participants exposed to the message endorsed by JW would be more ambivalent when the source was pro rather than con. In other words, ambivalence would be higher when the setting was *unbalanced* (see Baker & Petty, 1994), because unusual or unexpected, rather than *balanced*, because in line with ordinary expectations. Moreover, we hypothesized that different strategies would underlie ambivalence in the two unbalanced conditions: assimilation (to WWF source) and differentiation (from JW source).

The results showed that, as predicted, ambivalence was higher in unbalanced conditions than in balanced conditions: the WWF message generated more ambivalence when it was con than when it was pro, whereas the JW message generated more ambivalence when it was pro than when it was con (see Figure 6.1).

A separate analysis of positive and negative thoughts also supported the prediction that different strategies fostered ambivalence in the two unbalanced conditions. In fact, participants in the WWF-con condition assimilated themselves to the source, generating more thoughts in favour of the minority message than participants in the WWF-pro condition. Vice versa, participants in the JW-pro condition differentiated themselves from the source, generating more thoughts against the minority message than participants in the JW-con condition. Moreover, WWF obtained more indirect influence than JW, and this effect was mediated by ambivalence. On the contrary, ambivalence of targets exposed to the JW message was not related to indirect influence; in this condition, ambivalence appeared similar to the boomerang reaction that minorities arouse when they are perceived

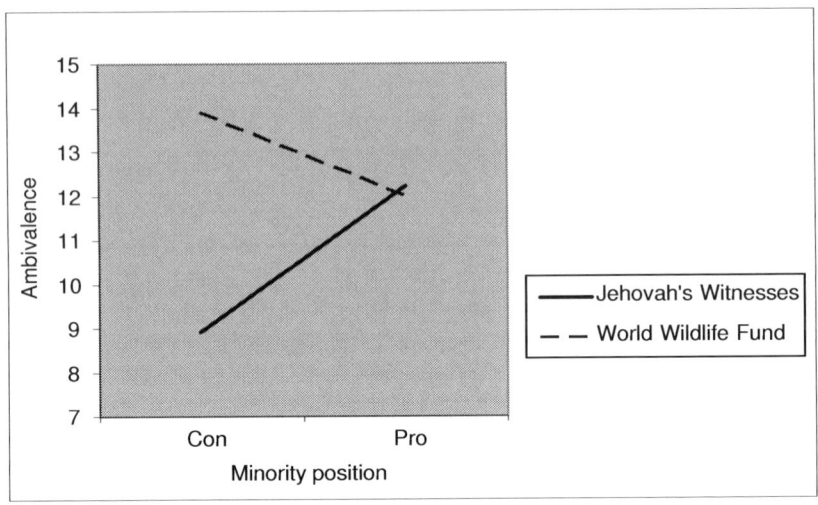

*Figure 6.1* Mean ambivalence as a function of minority source and minority position. Adapted from Mucchi-Faina (2000).

as too close or threatening (see Mucchi-Faina, 1994; Wood et al., 1996). Thus, this study showed that, based on the relationship between a source and its position, ambivalence toward the issue may hold different functions, facilitating or hindering minority influence.

In another study (Mucchi-Faina & Cicoletti, 2006), we measured both ambivalence (on thoughts about the issue) and divergence (alternative proposals) generated by the source in order to investigate whether the process stimulated by a minority would be different according to the personal relevance of the issue for participants. We speculated that, when the issue was personally relevant, people would perceive the counter-attitudinal proposal of the source as extremely threatening, and therefore they would promptly refuse—and would not carefully scrutinize—the minority's position. Moreover, being highly concerned about the issue, the target might prefer to find appropriate alternative solutions to the one proposed by the source (divergence effect), instead of simply reacting against the minority (boomerang effect). Instead, when personal relevance was low, the source's proposal would not appear threatening and thus people would be more willing to carefully scrutinize the minority's message. As a consequence, a *de-freezing* (Lewin, 1952; Moscovici, 1976) of prior opinion should come about: people would become less confident about their previous opinion, and then more ambivalent, by expressing both favourable and unfavourable thoughts at the same time. Therefore, we expected more ambivalent thoughts about the issue in the low-relevance condition than in the high-relevance condition and, vice versa, more divergence in the high-relevance condition than in the low-relevance condition. Two experiments in which a

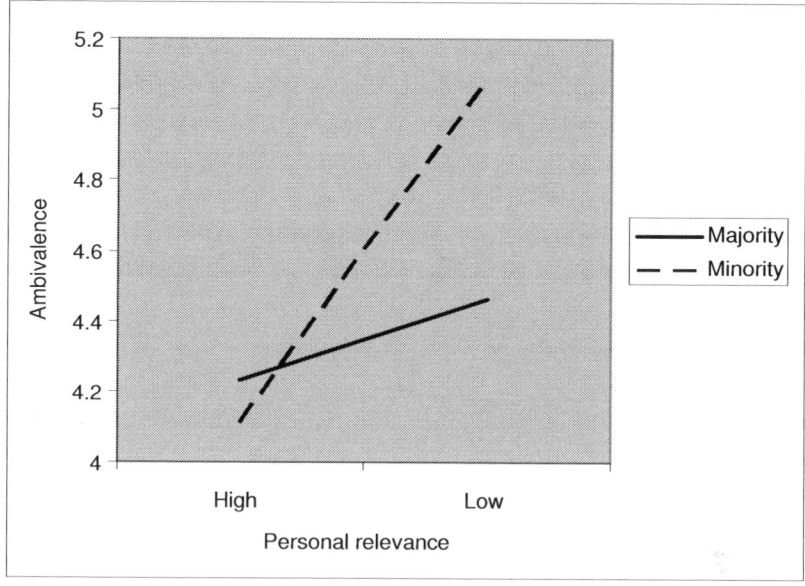

*Figure 6.2* Mean ambivalence as a function of influence source and personal relevance. Adapted from Mucchi-Faina and Cicoletti (2006), Study 1.

sample of undergraduate students was exposed to a counter-attitudinal proposal (the introduction of a final comprehensive exam in the university curriculum) by a minority or by a majority of university students supported these predictions. In Study 1, the number of alternative proposals produced by the targets was higher when the minority's proposal was personally relevant (taking effect the following academic year) than when the proposal was irrelevant to them (taking effect in eight to ten years). On the contrary, ambivalence was higher when the minority's proposal was irrelevant to the targets (see Figure 6.2). In fact, in this condition, participants carefully considered the position expressed by the source. As a consequence, they became less self-confident and more ambivalent, producing thoughts not only against, but also in favour of the minority proposal (see also Tormala et al., Chapter 5 in the present volume, for a discussion about the relationship between confidence and social influence). Results of Study 2 were consistent with the previous experiment. In addition, we found that ambivalence (rather than divergence) was correlated with, although not a significant mediator of, indirect influence. No effect of personal relevance was observed when the source was a majority.

Altogether, these findings showed that contextual factors moderate the ambivalence about an issue generated by exposure to minorities. In fact, unbalanced settings favour ambivalence, whereas personal relevance reduces it.[2]

## Summary and implications

Theoretical assumptions and empirical evidence concerning the role of ambivalence in social influence processes have been presented. Considering that research in the field is relatively recent, and findings at the moment are quite fragmentary, any conclusion is certainly premature. Nonetheless it is possible to advance some considerations in light of the above review.

First, when the source is a majority, targets that are highly ambivalent towards a topic appear to be more prone to classical compliance than less ambivalent targets. Furthermore, majorities may elicit ambivalence—even more than minorities—but without relevant consequences on their impact: targets become more or less ambivalent according to source position (pro or con their personal opinion), but the degree of ambivalence does not seem to exert an important role on majority influence.

Second, when the source is a minority, different results have been obtained in accordance with procedure and attitude focus. As predicted by Moscovici's theory (1980, 1994), ambivalence *towards the source*—either primed by the experimenter or elicited by the source itself—generally fosters conversion, namely indirect or private attitude change. However, ambivalence *towards the issue* seems related to conversion only in certain circumstances. In fact, research supports the idea that ambivalence towards the issue can result either from a negative reaction towards the source or from a de-freezing of previous opinions. The negative reaction (i.e., differentiation) has been observed when a source perceived as unreliable and distant expresses a pro-attitudinal position. Ambivalence based on a de-freezing process may instead favour and even mediate indirect influence but only when certain contextual factors contribute to produce this effect, for example, when the topic is not personally relevant for the target or a reliable and close minority supports a counter-attitudinal position. These results corroborate the idea that ambivalence alone is not a reliable predictor of subsequent behaviour (Bell & Esses, 1997). In fact, it is important to take into account not only the features of the source or the source's position but also the relationships between the source and its message and between the target and the topic, namely the *influence setting*.

Finally, whereas evidence supports the assumption that ambivalence and conversion could be related in some way, no relationship has been found between ambivalence and divergence, since they appear to be stimulated by different conditions. This finding suggests that dissimilar motivations could underlie the two processes. As ambivalence is generally correlated with low self-confidence whereas divergence is not, we may advance that ambivalence in non-threatening circumstances is an indicator of thorough information processing based on the accuracy motivation. By carefully considering a counter-attitudinal minority message, people become less sure about their previous position, more ambivalent about the issue and thus more open to attitude change. On the contrary, divergence is fostered when people are mainly focused on self, either because a competitive context stimulates the self-enhancement motivation (e.g., when individual performances in problem solving or creative tasks are assessed; Nemeth & Kwan, 1987; Nemeth & Watchler, 1983) or because a threatening context arouses the self-protection motivation (e.g., when the source's proposal is strongly counter-attitudinal and personally relevant for the targets; Mucchi-Faina & Cicoletti, 2006).

Future research should not only further verify the above preliminary contentions, but also examine aspects that have been disregarded thus far, for instance, the effects of ambivalence towards 'real' minorities should be investigated. We suspect that, when sources are social minorities (e.g., ethnic or religious groups, 'weak' categories), whether they are more or less protected by the social norms could affect the reactions towards them, and their impact as well. Indeed, minority sources that are highly protected by the social norm of fairness (e.g., blind people, see Crandall, Eshleman, & O'Brien, 2002) could arouse a positive univalent attitude towards themselves, and thus lower ambivalence, than could less protected minorities (e.g., drug users). As a consequence, protected minorities that express a counter-attitudinal message could foster direct—instead of indirect or private—attitude change. The effects of pre-experiment ambivalence towards social minorities and majorities also should be compared in order to observe whether, according to the status of the source, pre-existent ambivalence has a different weight on the influence process.

Additionally, the relationship between kind of ambivalence and kind of effects needs to be investigated. In fact, researchers on attitude have identified different forms of ambivalence. Some studies have treated ambivalence as a one-dimensional construct (e.g., Katz, 1981; Katz & Hass, 1988), while others have focused on the contemporary occurrence of negative judgements and positive feelings or, vice versa, of positive judgements and negative feelings (i.e., cross-dimensional ambivalence; MacDonald & Zanna, 1998). Others still have considered cognitive ambivalence (i.e., the coexistence of judgements and thoughts opposed in valence) and affective ambivalence (coexistence of feelings opposed in valence) separately (intra-dimensional ambivalence; Mucchi-Faina et al., 2002, 2009). At present, with only one exception (Pagliaro & Mucchi-Faina, 2006), ambivalence has been considered in social influence studies as a one-dimensional construct. It is now necessary to verify whether all kinds of ambivalence towards the source produce similar effects. Hodson and colleagues (2001) advanced that intra-dimensional ambivalence is more strongly tied to psychological tension and search of new information than is cross-dimensional ambivalence. Since there is evidence that minority influence is favoured when targets experience a state of tension (Pérez, Falomir, & Mugny, 1995), we might observe a stronger minority impact when people experience intra-dimensional rather than cross-dimensional ambivalence.

All in all, if future research unequivocally confirms the role of ambivalence as crucial in social (especially minority) influence processes, it will be possible to consider different indicators of ambivalence such as the level of physiological arousal (Maio et al., 2001), the quantity and quality of facial expressions (Heisel & Mongrain, 2004), or the inconsistency between verbal and non-verbal communication (Mongrain & Vettese, 2003) as additional indirect cues of social influence.

## Notes

1  The formula is: $(P + N)/2 - |P - N|$, where $P$ = positive attitude score, and $N$ = negative attitude score. A constant is generally added in order to avoid negative results.
2  The last finding is nicely in accordance with research conducted inside the attitude area (see Thompson et al., 1995).

## References

Asch, S. (1951). Effects of group pressure upon the modification and distortion of judgment. In H. Guetzkow (Ed.), *Groups, leadership and men* (pp. 177–190). Pittsburgh, PA: Carnegie Press.

Baker, S. M., & Petty, R. E. (1994). Majority and minority influence: Source–position imbalance as a determinant of message scrutiny. *Journal of Personality and Social Psychology, 67*, 5–19.

Bassili, J. N. (1996). Meta-judgmental versus operative indexes of psychological attributes: The case of measures of attitude strength. *Journal of Personality and Social Psychology, 71*, 637–653.

Bell, D. W., & Esses, V. M. (1997). Ambivalence and response amplification toward native people. *Journal of Applied Social Psychology, 27*, 1063–1084.

Bell, D. W., Esses, V. M., & Maio, G. R. (1996). The utility of open-ended measures to assess intergroup ambivalence. *Canadian Journal of Behavioural Science, 28*, 12–18.

Broemer, P. (2002). Relative effectiveness of differently framed health messages: The influence of ambivalence. *European Journal of Social Psychology, 32*, 685–703.

Cavazza, N., & Butera, F. (2008). Bending without breaking: Examining the role of attitudinal ambivalence in resisting persuasive communication. *European Journal of Social Psychology, 38*, 1–15.

Chaiken, S. (1980). Heuristic versus systematic information processing and the use of source versus message cues in persuasion. *Journal of Personality and Social Psychology, 39*, 605–614.

Crandall, C. S., Eshleman, A., & O'Brien, L. (2002). Social norms and the expression and suppression of prejudice: The struggle for internalization. *Journal of Personality and Social Psychology, 82*, 359–378.

Crano, W. D., & Alvaro, E. M. (1998). Indirect minority influence: The leniency contract revisited. *Group Processes and Intergroup Relations, 1*, 99–115.

De Dreu, C. K. W., & De Vries, N. K. (1993). Numerical support, information processing and attitude change. *European Journal of Social Psychology, 23*, 647–663.

Fiske, S. T., Cuddy, A. J., Glick, P., & Xu, J. (2002). A model of (often mixed) stereotype content: Competence and warmth respectively follow from perceived status and competition. *Journal of Personality and Social Psychology*, *82*, 878–902.

Gaertner, S. L., & Dovidio, J. F. (1986). The aversive form of racism. In J. Dovidio & S. Gaertner (Eds.), *Prejudice, discrimination, and racism* (pp. 61–89). San Diego, CA: Academic Press.

Heisel, M. J., & Mongrain, M. (2004). Facial expressions and ambivalence: Looking for *conflict* in all the right faces. *Journal of Nonverbal Behavior*, *28*, 35–52.

Hodson, G., Maio, G. R., & Esses, V. M. (2001). The role of attitudinal ambivalence in susceptibility to consensus information. *Basic and Applied Social Psychology*, *23*, 197–205.

Jonas, K., Broemer, P., & Diehl, M. (2000). Attitudinal ambivalence. In W. Stroebe & M. Hewstone (Eds.), *European review of social psychology* (Vol. 11, pp. 35–74). Chichester, UK: Wiley.

Jonas, K., Diehl, M., & Broemer, P. (1997). Effects of attitudinal ambivalence on information processing and attitude–intention consistency. *Journal of Experimental Social Psychology*, *33*, 190–210.

Kaplan, K. J. (1972). On the ambivalence–indifference problem in attitude theory and measurement: A suggested modification of the semantic differential technique. *Psychological Bulletin*, *77*, 361–372.

Katz, I. (1981). *Stigma: A social psychological analysis*. Hillsdale, NJ: Lawrence Erlbaum Associates, Inc.

Katz, I., & Hass, R. G. (1988). Racial ambivalence and American value conflict: Correlational and priming studies of dual cognitive structures. *Journal of Personality and Social Psychology*, *55*, 893–905.

Laplanche, J., & Pontalis, J.-B. (1968). *Vocabulaire de la psychanalyse*. Paris: Presses Universitaires de France.

Lewin, K. (1952). Group decision and social change. In G. E. Swanson, T. M. Newcomb, & E. L. Hartley (Eds.), *Readings in social psychology* (pp. 459–473). New York: Holt.

Maass, A., & Volpato, C. (1994). Theoretical perspectives on minority influence: Conversion versus divergence? In S. Moscovici, A. Mucchi-Faina, & A. Maass (Eds.), *Minority influence* (pp. 135–147). Chicago: Nelson-Hall.

MacDonald, T. K., & Zanna, M. P. (1998). Cross-dimension ambivalence toward social groups: Can ambivalence affect intentions to hire feminists? *Personality and Social Psychology Bulletin*, *24*, 427–441.

Maio, G. R., Bell, D. W., & Esses, V. M. (1996). Ambivalence and persuasion: The processing of messages about immigrant groups. *Journal of Experimental Social Psychology*, *32*, 513–536.

Maio, G. R., Greenland, K., Bernard, M., & Esses, V. M. (2001). Effects of intergroup ambivalence on information processing: The role of physiological arousal. *Group Processes and Intergroup Relations*, *4*, 355–372.

Martin, R., & Hewstone, M. (2001). Determinants and consequences of cognitive processes in majority and minority influence. In J. Forgas & K. Williams (Eds.), *Social influence: Direct and indirect processes* (pp. 315–330). Philadelphia: Psychology Press.

McConahay, J. B. (1986). Modern racism, ambivalence and the Modern Racism Scale. In J. F. Dovidio & S. L. Gaertner (Eds.), *Prejudice, discrimination and racism* (pp. 91–126). New York: Academic Press.

Mongrain, M., & Vettese, L. C. (2003). Conflict over emotional expression:

Implications for interpersonal communication. *Personality and Social Psychology Bulletin, 29*, 545–555.

Moscovici, S. (1976). *Social influence and social change.* London: Academic Press.

Moscovici, S. (1980). Toward a theory of conversion behavior. In L. Berkowitz (Ed.), *Advances in experimental social psychology* (Vol. 13, pp. 209–239). New York: Academic Press.

Moscovici, S. (1994). Three concepts: Minority, conflict, and behavioral style. In S. Moscovici, A. Mucchi-Faina, & A. Maass (Eds.), *Minority influence* (pp. 233–251). Chicago: Nelson-Hall.

Mucchi-Faina, A. (1994). Minority influence effects: Assimilation and differentiation. In S. Moscovici, A. Mucchi-Faina, & A. Maass (Eds.), *Minority influence* (pp. 115–133). Chicago: Nelson-Hall.

Mucchi-Faina, A. (2000). Minority influence and ambivalence. *Revue Internationale de Psychologie Sociale, 15*, 65–87.

Mucchi-Faina, A., & Cicoletti, G. (2006). Divergence vs. ambivalence: Effects of personal relevance on minority influence. *European Journal of Social Psychology, 36*, 91–104.

Mucchi-Faina, A., Costarelli, S., & Romoli, C. (2002). The effects of intergroup context of evaluation on ambivalence toward the ingroup and the outgroup. *European Journal of Social Psychology, 32*, 247–259.

Mucchi-Faina, A., Pacilli, G. R., Pagliaro, S., & Alparone, F. (2009). Ambivalence in intergroup evaluation: The role of fairness norm. *Social Justice Research, 22*, 117–133.

Mucchi-Faina, A., &. Pagliaro, S. (2006). *The effects of ambivalence towards the source on minority influence.* Unpublished manuscript, Università di Perugia.

Mucchi-Faina, A., &. Pagliaro, S. (2008). Minority influence: The role of ambivalence towards the source. *European Journal of Social Psychology, 38*, 612–623.

Mugny, G., & Papastamou, S. (1984). Les styles de comportement et leur representation sociale. In S. Moscovici (Ed.), *Psychologie sociale* (pp. 391–414). Paris: Presses Universitaires de France.

Nemeth, C. (1986). Differential contributions of majority and minority influence. *Psychological Review, 93*, 23–32.

Nemeth, C., & Chiles, C. (1988). Modeling courage: The role of dissent in fostering independence. *European Journal of Social Psychology, 18*, 275–280.

Nemeth, C., & Kwan, J. (1987). Minority influence, divergent thinking and detection of correct solutions. *Journal of Applied Social Psychology, 17*, 788–799.

Nemeth, C., & Watchler, J. (1974). Creating the perceptions of consistency and confidence: A necessary condition for minority influence. *Sociometry, 37*, 529–540.

Nemeth, C., & Watchler, J. (1983). Creative problem solving as a result of majority vs. minority influence. *European Journal of Social Psychology, 13*, 45–55.

Olson, J. M., & Zanna, M. P. (1993). Attitudes and attitude change. *Annual review of Psychology, 44*, 117–154.

Pagliaro, S., & Mucchi-Faina, A. (2006, September). *L'ambivalenza verso la fonte come mediatore dell'influenza minoritaria.* Paper presented at the VI Congresso Nazionale della Sezione di Psicologia Sociale AIP, Genoa.

Pérez, J. A., Falomir, J. M., & Mugny, G. (1995). Internalization of conflict and attitude change. *European Journal of Social Psychology, 25*, 117–124.

Pérez, J. A., & Mugny, G. (1996). The conflict elaboration theory of social influence.

In E. H. Witte & J. H. Davis (Eds.), *Understanding group behavior. Vol. 2: Small group processes and interpersonal relations* (pp. 191–210). Mahwah, NJ: Lawrence Erlbaum Associates, Inc.

Petty, R. E., & Cacioppo, J. T. (1986). The elaboration likelihood model of persuasion. In L. Berkowitz (Ed.), *Advances in experimental social psychology* (Vol. 19, pp. 123–205). New York: Academic Press.

Petty, R. E., Cacioppo, J. T., & Goldman, R. (1981). Personal involvement as a determinant of argument-based persuasion. *Journal of Personality and Social Psychology, 41*, 847–855.

Petty, R. E., Fleming, M. A., & White, P. H. (1999). Stigmatized sources and persuasion: Prejudice as a determinant of argument scrutiny. *Journal of Personality and Social Psychology, 76*, 19–34.

Pool, G. J., Wood, W., & Leck, K. (1998). The self-esteem motive in social influence: Agreement with valued majorities and disagreement with derogated minorities. *Journal of Personality and Social Psychology, 75*, 967–975.

Priester, J. R., & Petty, R. E. (1996). The gradual threshold model of ambivalence: Relating the positive and the negative bases of attitudes to subjective ambivalence. *Journal of Personality and Social Psychology, 71*(3), 431–449.

Ricateau, P. (1970). Processus de catégorization d'autrui et les mécanismes d'influence sociale. *Bulletin de Psychologie, 24*, 909–919.

Sanchez-Mazas, M., & Falomir, J. M. (1995). Dissociation et influence minoritaire. In G. Mugny, D. Oberlé, & J. L. Beauvois (Eds.), *Relations humaines, groupes et influence sociale* (pp. 301–318). Grenoble, France: Presses Universitaire de Grenoble.

Thompson, M. M., Zanna, M. P., & Griffin, D. W. (1995). Let's not be indifferent about (attitudinal) ambivalence. In R. E. Petty & J. A. Krosnick (Eds.), *Attitude strength: Antecedents and consequences* (pp. 361–386). Mahwah, NJ: Lawrence Erlbaum Associates, Inc.

Tourangeau, R., Rasinski, K. A., Bradburn, N., & D'Andrade, R. (1989). Carry-over effects in attitude surveys. *Public Opinion Quarterly, 53*, 495–524.

Wood, W., Lundgren, S., Ouellette, J. A., Busceme, S., & Blackstone, T. (1994). Minority influence: A meta-analytic review of social influence processes. *Psychological Bulletin, 115*, 323–345.

Wood, W., Pool, G. J., Leck, K., & Purvis, D. (1996). Self-definition, defensive processing, and influence: The normative impact of majority and minority groups. *Journal of Personality and Social Psychology, 71*, 1181–1193.

# 7 The impact of source consensus on majority and minority influence

*Antonis Gardikiotis*
Aristotle University of Thessaloniki, Greece

*Robin Martin*
Aston University, UK

*Miles Hewstone*
University of Oxford, UK

Consensus information is an integrative part of our social lives. Whether we intentionally seek, or unthoughtfully attend to, information conveyed by mass media, we learn about, for example, what other people believe on various issues, how other people intend to cast their vote in a forthcoming election, how many experts urge us to purchase a specific commodity, or how many fellow consumers are already satisfied with the use of a specific brand. Advertising and political communication frequently employ their persuasive campaigns on the basis of consensus information. From a social psychological perspective, to know what other people do or believe is an essential way to evaluate our own behaviour and attitudes. It has been long recognized that we turn to other people in order to verify or falsify our way of seeing the world (e.g., the *social testing* hypothesis of Festinger, 1950). The effect of consensus information on thinking and behaviour has been the focus of much social psychological research (see Hardin & Higgins, 1996). Since early research on conformity researchers have been interested in the degree to which people's attitudes and behaviour change under the influence of varying levels of group size (Asch, 1951).

Consensus information can be conveyed in three main ways. First, group consensus can be conveyed via the level of *numerical support* for a position (such as, percentages, actual numbers). The distinction between a majority and a minority is made on an objective dimension that allows their relative size, and also the difference between these groups, to be assessed. Second, consensus information can be inferred from the use of *consensus adjectives* that convey information about the relative size of the group (such as, 'many', 'few', 'large', 'small'). Third, consensus information can be conveyed using *social-status labels* (such as, 'majority' and 'minority'), which have commonly held connotations concerning group-consensus levels. Unlike numerical support, which is based on objective criteria, consensus adjectives and social-status labels do not convey information concerning the absolute size of the majority and minority, and therefore the difference between them cannot be judged. Indeed, a group needs to contain only one more individual than another group to be rightfully called 'larger' or the 'majority'.

An analysis of the relationship between group consensus and social influence, apart from the obvious interest in its effect on people's attitudes and behaviours, is useful for three reasons. First, it is evident from the examples above that this enquiry has social relevance; consensus information is an inescapable element of everyday social life. Second, source status in recent and contemporary social influence research is being operationalized in ways different from those investigated between the 1940s and 1970s. Since the 1980s majority and minority consensus is usually defined in terms of reported percentage information (e.g., 'a majority of 82%'). Therefore we still do not know exactly how reported consensus information affects social influence. Third, there is still no evidence on the effects of the different types of consensus information (e.g., percentages, consensus adjectives, source labels) on social influence.

The aim of this chapter is to evaluate the importance of group consensus to social influence. In doing so, it will: (a) provide a theoretical context for the relationship between group consensus and social influence; (b) examine the effect of group consensus as reported percentage information on majority and minority influence; (c) look in more detail at the qualities of consensus representation in mass media; (d) examine whether different types of consensus information affect this relationship; and (e) examine the psychological processes underlying the effects of group consensus.

## Prior research on group consensus and social influence

Early research on the effects of group size examined social influence in experimental settings where participants interacted face to face. Research examining the relationship between majority size and conformity conducted during the 1950s and 1960s showed mixed results. Asch (1951) was the first to study the impact of the *size* of a discrepant majority on a participant's conformity to a group norm. He studied conformity in groups of 1, 2, 3, 4, 6, 7, and 15 members. Yielding increased markedly from one to three majority members and then reached a plateau (see also Kishida, 1956; Rosenberg, 1961). However, other researchers found a linear relationship between group size and influence (e.g., Carlston, 1977; Gerard, Wilhelmy, & Conolley, 1968; Lascu, Bearden, & Rose, 1995; Nordholm, 1975), while some studies failed to report any relationship between group size and influence (e.g., Goldberg, 1954; Kidd, 1958; Reis, Earing, Kent, & Nezlek, 1976). The inconsistent findings in these studies have been attributed to the different tasks employed, the different manipulations of source, and the different perception of the majority by the participants (see Campbell & Fairey, 1989; Insko, Drenan, Soloman, Smith, & Wade, 1983; Wilder, 1977).

Subsequently, mathematical models (Latané & Wolf, 1981; Mullen, 1983; Tanford & Penrod, 1984; Wolf & Latané, 1983) developed to explain social influence suggested that the higher the number of influence agents the greater the amount of influence. Meta-analytic reviews of the literature on this topic have found that mathematical models explain a substantial amount of variance in social influence scores (see Bond & Smith, 1996; Wood, Lundgren, Ouellette, Busceme, & Blackstone, 1994; and Tindale, Davis, Vollrath, Nagao, & Hinsz, 1990, for a test of the three mathematical models). As noted in narrative reviews of this area (see Maass, West, & Cialdini, 1987; Martin & Hewstone, 2001) these models may reliably account for significant amounts of variance in conformity, but they provide little understanding of the *processes* underlying social influence, or why influence occurs.

This research on group size has, however, focused predominately on the size of the majority and this begs a second question, namely, is numerical size an important factor in minority influence? Relatively few studies have examined this question (see Erb, Bohner, Hewstone, Werth, & Reinhard, 2006, for an exception). Some studies have compared a minority composed of either one or two individuals and found the latter to have more influence than the former (e.g., Arbuthnot & Wayner, 1982; Mugny & Papastamou, 1980). Nemeth, Wachtler, and Endicott (1977) found that increasing the size of the minority can have positive and negative consequences for how it is perceived. In a colour-perception study members of different-size minorities (ranging from 1 to 4) gave erroneous judgements to a series of slides (group size varied from 7 to 14). Nemeth and colleagues found that a minority of one, two and four had more influence than a no-confederate control condition, but a minority of three had the most influence. Analysing participants' ratings of the characteristics of the minorities showed that as minority size increased so did its perceived competence, but its perceived confidence decreased. Increasing minority size can lead to perceptions that either augment or attenuate the minority's ability to influence others (see also Zdaniuk & Levine, 1996).

### Group consensus and psychological processes

Initial explanations of why group size is related to conformity argued that people conform to others because they wish to be accepted by the majority group (and, indeed, avoid being in the minority) and/or because they believe the majority is more likely to be correct or accurate than they are themselves (Deutsch & Gerard, 1955). The more a person is dependent upon others, either for social approval or validation of opinions, then the more likely that person will conform to the group. Many factors can increase dependency and one such factor is the numerical size of the majority. The greater the number of people the majority contains, the more desirable will be majority-group membership, and consequently the greater the ability of majority members to exercise social approval/rejection.

In contemporary research on social influence a central question concerns the types of processes linked with majority and minority influence (see Martin & Hewstone, 2001). While major theories in the area propose distinct processes for majority and minority influence (see conversion theory, Moscovici, 1980; convergence–divergence model, Nemeth, 1995; objective consensus approach, Mackie, 1987), there has recently been a shift in theoretical developments that recognizes that neither majorities nor minorities are linked exclusively with a particular process and that each kind of source can be associated with systematic or non-systematic processes under different conditions (the *source–position congruency model*, Baker & Petty, 1994; the *context/comparison model*, Crano & Alvaro, 1998; the *self-categorization theory*, David & Turner, 2001; and the *conflict elaboration theory*, Mugny, Butera, Sanchez-Mazas, & Pérez, 1995; see Martin & Hewstone, 2003a, for a review).

### Operationalization of group consensus in social influence research

Early research on the relationship between group size and social influence had mainly employed a face-to-face source status manipulation (see Asch, 1951; Carlston, 1977; Rosenberg, 1961). In the 1980s, however, a different manipulation of source status was introduced, that of fictional poll results. In this new paradigm participants are typically informed that, according to a survey, a sample of the population endorses either a majority or a minority position on a given issue (e.g., Baker & Petty, 1994; De Dreu & De Vries, 1993; Moscovici & Personnaz, 1980).[1]

In this context Mackie (1987) was the first to examine the effect of group consensus on social influence for different-sized majorities (82% vs. 64%), and found no difference in their ability to influence attitudes. Mackie (1987) suggested that the lack of difference between the majority of 82% and 64% was perhaps attributable to the fact that the majority in each case was clear cut (i.e., 31% and 13% above a simple majority of 51%). She also indicated that 'the gulf between 52% and 48% is wider than the numbers alone suggest' (p. 47).

The present chapter first examines whether group consensus as reported information affects social influence. Then it reports a content analysis of how consensus information concerning majorities and minorities is represented in the mass media. Finally, it examines how different ways of reporting consensus information affect social influence, and considers the psychological processes linked with these effects.

## Does group consensus affect social influence?

Our first two studies in this area examined the effect of group consensus on social influence when consensus is defined with percentages as in most research in this area. Martin, Gardikiotis, and Hewstone (2002, Experiment

1) examined two levels of consensus difference on majority and minority influence in a sample of students at a British university. The topic of the study concerned the legalization of voluntary euthanasia and we used a message that contained arguments that were against voluntary euthanasia as this was counter-attitudinal to the participants. The message followed the format of a newspaper article that was embedded into the university's student newspaper. We crossed source status (majority vs. minority) with group consensus difference, which had two levels—small (majority of 52% and minority of 48%) and large (majority of 82% and minority of 18%). We chose these two levels because the first represents a clear split between the source groups, while the second reports only a small difference, which would require a slight shift of opinion to change source-group membership.

We tested two hypotheses. First, we tested whether a majority would be more influential than a minority irrespective of consensus level (the *majority-source hypothesis*, i.e., 82% majority = 52% majority > 48% minority = 18% minority; Goldberg, 1954; Kidd, 1958; Mackie, 1987; Reis et al., 1976). It may be the case that the label 'majority' is sufficient to make members of the minority conform to the majority, with their relative size being unimportant. Thus majority status may act as a cue triggering heuristic acceptance of the majority position without processing the arguments that comprise its message (Erb, Bohner, Schmälzle, & Rank, 1998). Since this hypothesis states that numerical information is not important, other than defining the majority as (a) bigger than a minority and (b) equal to or greater than 50%, it is inconsistent with the mathematical models of social influence discussed above. We also tested a second hypothesis, that individuals respond more to the numerical size or consensus of the source than to its categorization as a 'majority' or 'minority' (the *linear-consensus hypothesis*, i.e., 82% majority > 52% majority > 48% minority > 18% minority; Carlston, 1977; Gerard et al., 1968; Latané & Wolf, 1981; Nordholm, 1975; Tanford & Penrod, 1984; Wolf & Latané, 1983). Thus individuals may ignore majority/minority status and simply be influenced by the consensus level of the group. Given that the difference between the 52% (majority) and 48% (minority) conditions is smaller than the difference between the other groups (e.g., 82% majority and 52% minority), we would expect a smaller difference in influence in the former condition.

The results (see Figure 7.1) supported the majority-source hypothesis and showed that, irrespective of consensus level, a majority had more influence than a minority, replicating Mackie's (1987) study that had also used reported percentages albeit only for a majority source. Further analyses offered no support for the linear-consensus hypothesis, and therefore this study did not support the mathematical models of social influence. It appears that majority status, irrespective of the level of consensus, was sufficient to influence the attitudes of the participants.

We cannot, however, draw precise conclusions yet, because the representation of the source in this study, and in most research in this area, involved

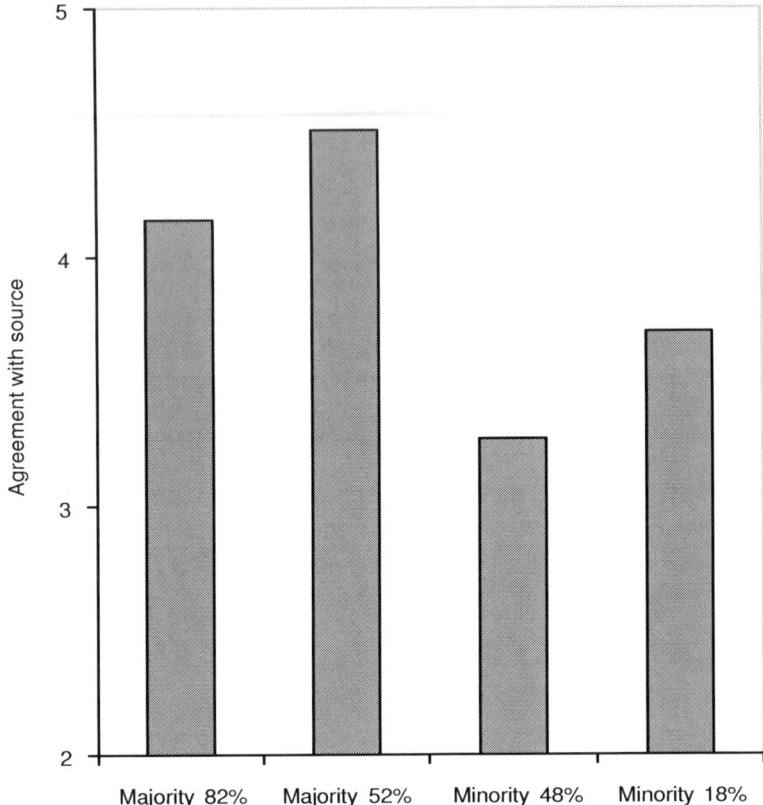

*Figure 7.1* Mean attitude scores as a function of source status and percentage consensus difference (Martin, Gardikiotis, & Hewstone, 2002, Experiment 1).

informing the participants of two things: the source-status label ('majority' or 'minority') *and* the numerical support (represented in a percentage). Because this information was combined, it is not possible to determine in the first experiment whether the majority effect was due to (a) the source label, (b) the consensus level, or (c) a combination of both.

In our next study (Martin et al., 2002, Experiment 2) we examined this issue by experimentally separating these two aspects of the source representation. We used the same anti-voluntary-euthanasia message that was employed in the previous experiment and again this took the format of an article contained in a student newspaper. To examine this the experiment manipulated five different message headings, of which the first two replicated those in Experiment 1: (a) label-plus-percentage, large consensus difference (i.e., Majority 82% vs. Minority 18%); (b) label-plus-percentage, small consensus difference (i.e., Majority 54% vs. Minority 48%); (c) percentage-only, large consensus difference (i.e., 82% vs. 18%); (d) percentage-only, small consensus difference (i.e., 52% vs. 48%); and (e) label-only (i.e., Majority vs. Minority).

The results showed that in the label-plus-percentage and the percentage-only conditions there was no effect of consensus difference for the majority (Majority 82% vs. Majority 52%) or the minority (Minority 18% vs. Minority 48%) source. Interestingly, the percentage-only majorities (i.e., 82% and 52%) led to significantly more influence than the label-plus-percentage majorities (i.e., Majority 82% and Majority 52%), while that was not the case for the minority condition.

A majority source had slightly more influence than a minority source in the label-plus-percentage conditions, replicating Experiment 1, and also in the percentage-only condition. However, there was no difference between the majority and minority in the label-only condition. Thus the superior influence of the majority source is not dependent on the label 'majority' but on consensus information, and the majority effect is due to the consensus information provided by the percentages of people supporting each position. Since there was no effect of level of consensus difference, this indicates that individuals were more influenced by positions supported by over 50% of the population than those supported by less than 50% of the population. The level of support beyond the 50% cut-off did not materially affect the level of influence. Further analyses showed that both the 82% and 52% conditions differed reliably from the 48% condition, but not from the 18% condition.

A series of planned contrasts were conducted to examine the relative importance of label and consensus information for each source condition (see Table 7.1). There was no difference between the label-plus-percentage and the other conditions for either the majority (contrast 1) or the minority (contrast 2). Percentage-only information had an impact when it represented a numerical majority (contrast 3) but not when it represented a numerical minority (contrast 4). In addition, influence was greatest when only the 'minority' label was presented (contrast 6) than when the 'majority' label was present (contrast 5). Put another way, the 'majority' label seems to impede consensus-driven majority influence, while consensus information impairs distinctiveness-driven minority influence. We also tested two further contrasts, comparing the percentage-only minority (contrast 4) and the label-only minority (contrast 5) against all other conditions; neither contrast was significant.

## Consensus information in a real-life mass-media context

> The newspaper carries home the voice of the many to every individual among them; by the newspaper each learns that others are feeling as he feels . . . The newspaper is the telegraph which carries the signal throughout the country.
> (John Stuart Mill, *Civilization, Collected Works*, Vol. XVIII, p. 125)

*Table 7.1* Planned contrasts testing key hypotheses

| Contrast | | Effect examined | E-Test | p < |
|---|---|---|---|---|
| 1 | Label-plus-percentage: Majority | Majority 82%, Majority 52% > 82%, 52%, Majority | < 1 | ns |
| 2 | Label-plus-percentage: Minority | Minority 48%, Minority 18% > 48%, 18%, Minority | 1.77 | ns |
| 3 | Percentage-only: Majority | 82%, 52% > Majority 82%, Majority 52%, Majority | 2.68 | .009 |
| 4 | Percentage-only: Minority | 48%, 18% > Minority 48%, Minority 18%, Minority | < 1 | ns |
| 5 | Label-only-Majority | Majority > Majority 82%, Majority 52%, 82%, 52% | 1.47 | ns |
| 6 | Label-only-Minority | Minority > Minority 48%, Minority 18%, 48%, 18% | 2.74 | .008 |

*Source:* Martin, Gardikiotis, and Hewstone (2002), Experiment 2.

It is interesting to note that the above two experiments presented the source's arguments in the format of a newspaper article that was contained within a student newspaper (the newspaper also contained other articles, unrelated to the topic of the study). We did this to provide a realistic medium in which to present the source's arguments.

The results from our first studies showed that group consensus did not affect influence but source status did. Yet these data only partially explain the relationship between consensus and influence. The representation of the source in these studies, and in most research in this area, involved informing the participants of the social-status label ('majority' or 'minority'), the level of numerical support (represented in a percentage), or the combination of both. Although the latter is the most common operationalization, there are other ways of providing consensus information. We followed up this idea by considering majority and minority representation in the real-life case of newspaper headlines.

Using archival data we conducted a content analysis of 1,500,000 articles drawn from five British newspapers in a five-year period (1994–1998; Gardikiotis, Martin, & Hewstone, 2004). The aim of this study was to explore one of the contexts in which people in real life are frequently exposed to majority- and minority-held opinions. Among other things the content analysis focused on the adjectives that accompany majorities and minorities in the newspaper headlines.

The adjectives that accompanied the majority titles were primarily identity and consensus adjectives (33% and 30%, respectively, of total majority adjectives). By contrast the adjectives that accompanied the minority referred primarily to ethnicity–race and evaluation (29% and 25%, respectively, of total minority adjectives). Regarding the adjectives pertaining to *source consensus*, eight adjectives were found in the minority headlines (9% of the total minority adjectives, e.g., 'A tiny minority with too much cultural clout', *The Sunday Times*, 23 January 1994) and 70 in the majority headlines (30.4% of the total majority adjectives, e.g., 'Big majority likely for British Gas split', *The Times*, 12 February 1997). Thus, the issue of the size of the source is more likely to be reported in the majority headlines (30% of total majority headlines) than in minority headlines (9% of total minority headlines). A closer look at these adjectives showed that all minority consensus adjectives (such as dwindling, small, tiny, etc., e.g., '. . . may be used only by a tiny minority—but it's a vociferous and sometimes scary one', *The Daily Telegraph*, 24 June 1997) report a 'small' minority (thus there are not any 'large' minorities). By contrast, the majority consensus adjectives were split into those reporting a 'large' majority (such as big, vast, absolute, huge, etc., e.g., 'Politics: We won't surrender: The vast majority of the Conservative Party opposes a single currency', *The Daily Telegraph*, 31 October 1997), those reporting a 'small' majority (such as slim, tiny, shrinking, narrow, etc., e.g., 'Kohl coalition heads for slim majority', *The Daily Telegraph*, 17 October 1994) and those reporting the exact size of a majority (such as 21-seat, 153, three-figure, etc., e.g., 'Shortlist quota for women fails to secure two-thirds majority', *The Times*, 24 September 1997).

Conclusively, while adjectives that preceded majority titles mainly identified political groups and referred to their consensus level, adjectives that preceded minority titles referred mainly to their ethnicity and evaluation. Moreover, the analysis of the adjectives included in this category showed that whereas majority adjectives referred to large and small majorities, minority adjectives referred only to small minorities. Therefore, majority consensus adjectives covered the whole range of the consensus continuum, whereas minority consensus adjectives covered only the lowest end of the continuum. This restricted representation (i.e., the non-existence of 'large' minorities) may account for the lack of influence of 'large' minorities in experimental studies (e.g., Martin et al., 2002), perhaps because participants do not consider them representative of minorities in general.

The content-analytic data reaffirmed in a different context the importance of consensus information to the majority source, and showed that provision of consensus adjectives is a frequent way of conveying information about group consensus in this context.

**Consensus via adjectives: Does it matter?**

Although the most common methodology used to represent majority and minority positions in experimental research has been through linking numerical support with source status (e.g., 'Majority of 82%', 'Minority of 18%') our content analysis showed that in a real-life context another way to provide consensus information is by consensus adjectives. The most common way of providing consensus information was with consensus adjectives such as, 'large', 'big', 'small', 'tiny', and often such adjectives were used to qualify majority and minority positions in the absence of objective numerical support (e.g., 'Huge majority want cannabis legalized' and 'A tiny minority with too much cultural clout'). The use of the consensus adjectives gives extra emphasis to the size of the majority and therefore, one might expect, how the majority is interpreted and its likely impact.

From a theoretical perspective we focused on two traditions for examining the effect of consensus adjectives on majority and minority influence. First, one might draw upon Moscovici's concept of *behavioural style* (1976, 1980; see also Moscovici & Nemeth, 1974), which refers to the way the source behaves and the corresponding inferences targets of influence make. If the source of influence behaves in a consistent way, then recipients of influence will infer that the source is committed, confident and sure of their position and this might lead them to question their own position. Consensus adjectives, like 'large', 'heavy' and 'huge' might lead people to assume that support for that position is strong compared to descriptive adjectives like 'small', 'narrow' and 'tiny'. Thus, one might predict that the use of consensus adjectives that emphasize relational qualities (e.g., large vs. small) might accentuate the effects of majority and minority influence.

Second, one can draw upon the way that consensus adjectives operate linguistically. Consensus adjectives can be understood in terms of both their general function as well as their specific content. According to the *linguistic category model* (Semin & Fiedler, 1988, 1991), adjectives convey 'highly abstract person dispositions, do not have situation or context reference, are highly interpretative and detached from specific behaviours' (Semin & Fiedler, 1996, p. 100). Adjectives generalize across specific events, describe only the source and therefore communicate enduring, person-specific characteristics. The description of a person's behaviour or characteristics by means of adjectives (as compared to other, less abstract and more context-specific linguistic devices, say descriptive action verbs) entails a representation that seems more reliable (i.e., it is likely that he or she will behave in the same way in the future; see Maass, Salvi, Arcuri, & Semin, 1989). Besides functioning as linguistic devices, however, adjectives also convey specific characteristics. The adjective 'large' connotes more positive qualities than the adjective 'small' (evident in the meaning given to these adjectives in dictionaries). The adjective 'large' is defined as above average, big, considerable, great, immense, substantial, etc., whereas, 'small' is defined as not large, not great in importance, not much, insignificant, on small scale, poor, humble, mean, and young (*The Oxford Dictionary and Thesaurus*, 1997). We propose that these characteristics (i.e., the heuristic-like function and the positive content), taken together, place 'large' sources as compared to 'small' ones in a relatively advantageous persuasive position.

In an experimental study (Gardikiotis, Martin, & Hewstone, 2005, Experiment 1) we investigated, for the first time, the effect of group consensus as expressed by the consensus adjectives 'large' vs. 'small' on majority and minority influence. The message was the same as employed in the above studies and concerned anti-voluntary euthanasia and took the form of a newspaper article. We tested two hypotheses (the same as in our previous experiments) concerning the effect of group consensus on social influence: (1) that influence is a linear function of increasing consensus size, the *linear-consensus* hypothesis, large majority > small majority > large minority > small minority (Carlston, 1977; Gerard et al., 1968; Nordholm, 1975; Tanford & Penrod, 1984; Wolf & Latané, 1983); (2) that consensus does not have an impact on influence, but majority status does, which we call the *majority-source* hypothesis, i.e., large majority = small majority > large minority = small minority (Goldberg, 1954; Kidd, 1958; Mackie, 1987; Reis et al., 1976).

In this study consensus adjectives had a reliable effect upon attitudes whereas source status did not (see Figure 7.2). Therefore, the majority-source hypothesis was not supported. However, group consensus was linearly related to attitudes and thus the *linear-consensus hypothesis* was supported. The results generally suggest that the characterization of a

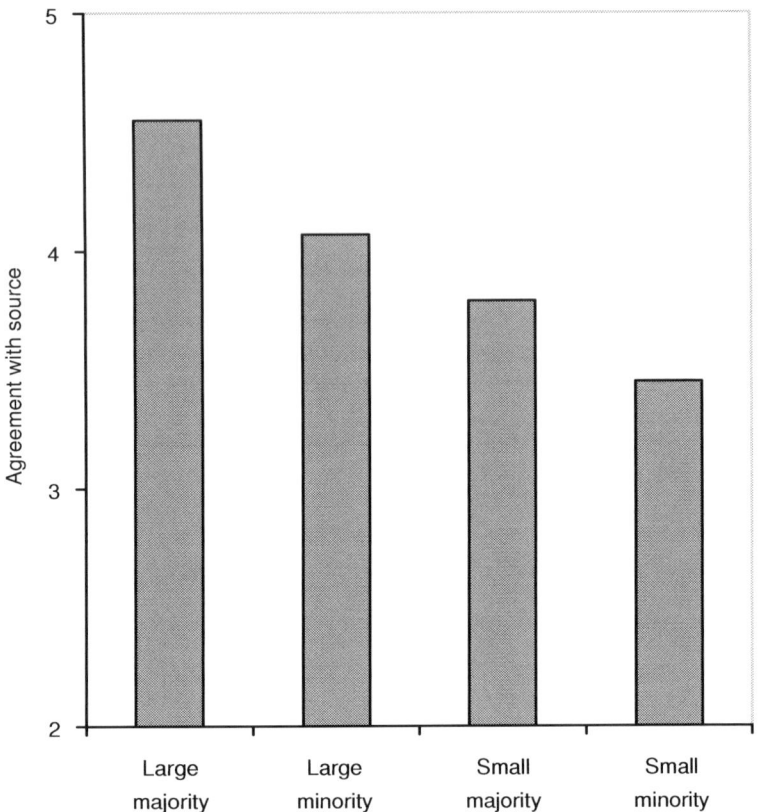

*Figure 7.2*  Mean attitude scores as a function of source status and adjective consensus (Gardikiotis, Martin, & Hewstone, 2005, Experiment 1).

group as 'large' or 'small' is more important than the source status of that group (either a majority or a minority) in determining influence. These data are in contrast to what was found in previous experiments (and Mackie, 1987) where consensus information was given in terms of percentages and it was source status that reliably affected attitudes irrespective of group consensus (majority source was more influential than minority source).

In our next study (Gardikiotis et al., 2005, Experiment 3) we tested the effect of both consensus adjectives and percentages on influence in the same experimental design. Consistent with the previous experiments the message contained anti-voluntary-euthanasia arguments. However, there were two differences in this study; first, the arguments were not presented as a newspaper article but listed on a page and second, the study took place at a university in Greece and the arguments were presented in Greek (unlike in English to British students in the previous studies).

Three hypotheses were tested: (1) when consensus information is expressed in terms of adjectives—'large' sources will be more influential than 'small' sources (irrespective of source status), the *adjective-consensus* hypothesis (as in the last experiment); (2) when consensus information is expressed in terms of numerical support (percentages), the majority will be more influential than the minority, the *majority-source* hypothesis (Mackie, 1987; Martin et al., 2002, Experiments 1 and 2); and (3) that the consensus effect will follow a linear trend, the *linear-consensus hypothesis* (Tanford & Penrod, 1984; Wolf & Latané, 1983).

In the consensus-adjective conditions, the 'large' source had more influence than the 'small' source while source status did not affect attitudes (replicating Gardikiotis et al., 2005, Experiment 1). In the numerical-support conditions, the majority had more influence than the minority, while consensus adjectives did not affect attitudes (replicating Mackie, 1987; Martin et al., 2002, Experiments 1 and 2). Taken together these results show that the type of consensus information moderates majority and minority influence (see Figure 7.3).

## Psychological processes and group consensus

What are the psychological processes responsible for the effects of percentage information and consensus adjectives on social influence? We tried to answer this question in the next two studies. First we focused on the percentage information. Is the superior influence of the majority in the first two studies (Martin et al., 2002, Experiments 1 and 2) due to systematic processing of the majority's arguments or simply to compliance with the majority's position, without evaluating its message? We examined the underlying psychological processes (systematic vs. non-systematic) by employing a methodology developed in cognitive research on persuasion, namely manipulating message quality (see Eagly & Chaiken, 1993; Petty & Cacioppo, 1986),

According to the elaboration likelihood model (ELM; Petty & Wegener, 1999) and the heuristic/systematic model (HSM; Chen & Chaiken, 1999) there are two basic routes to processing a message. The first concerns the systematic elaboration of the persuasive value of the argument contained in a message ('central-route persuasion', ELM, or 'systematic processing', HSM) whereas the second, non-systematic route, entails the use of other communication cues, such as the expertise or the status of the communication source ('peripheral-route persuasion', ELM, or 'heuristic processing', HSM). A common method employed to identify which information-processing route has been followed is to vary the quality of the arguments in the message (Petty & Cacioppo, 1986). If participants process the message systematically, then strong arguments should affect attitudes more than weak arguments. If, however, message quality does not influence

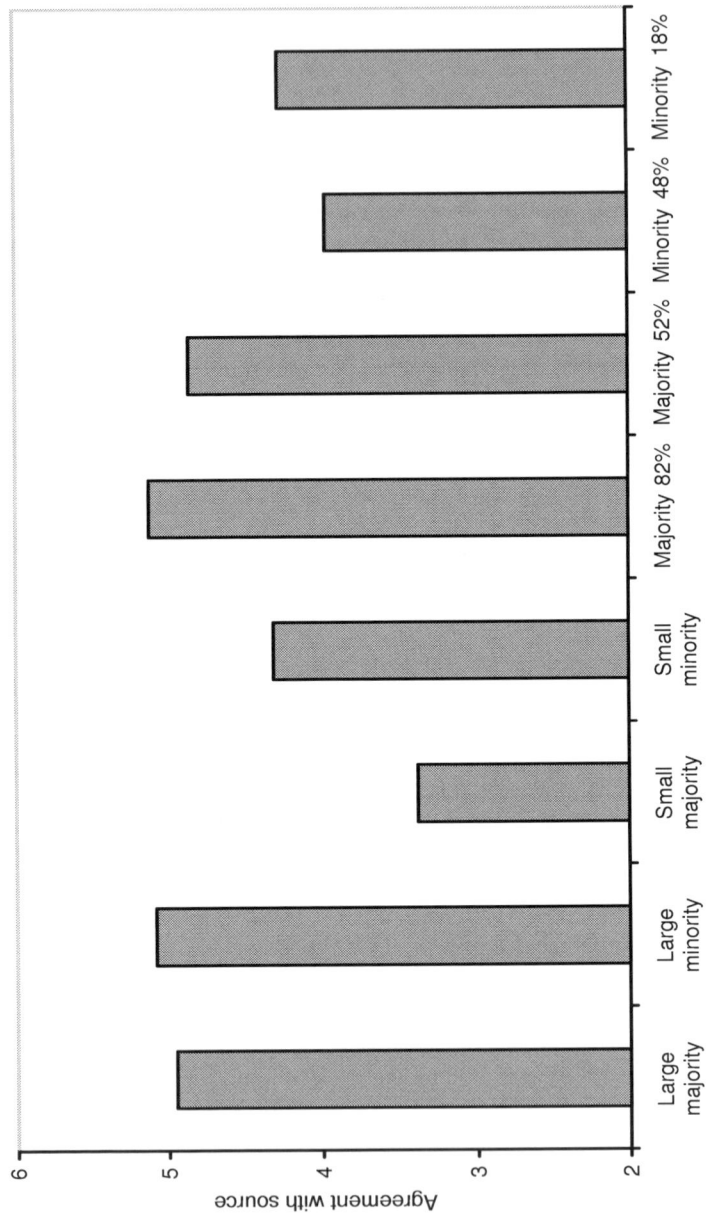

*Figure 7.3* Mean attitude scores as a function of source status, percentage consensus and adjective consensus (Gardikiotis, Martin, & Hewstone, 2005, Experiment 3).

attitudes this is taken as an indication of non-systematic processing (see Eagly & Chaiken, 1993; Petty & Cacioppo, 1986).

Contrasting theories propose that either majority or minority groups lead to systematic processing of the message (termed 'main effects theories'; Martin & Hewstone, 2003a). According to *conversion theory* (Moscovici, 1980) minorities instigate greater elaboration of the message compared to majorities that produce compliance without detailed scrutiny of the message. The *objective-consensus approach*, on the contrary, suggests that it is the majority that leads to greater message elaboration (Mackie, 1987; see also De Vries, De Dreu, Gordijn, & Schuurman, 1996). On the other hand, some models suggest that message scrutiny depends on the interaction between source status and situational factors (termed 'contingency theories'; e.g., the *source/position congruency* model; Baker & Petty, 1994). Social-influence studies that examined whether a majority or a minority instigates systematic processing have crossed source status with message quality (see Baker & Petty, 1994; Bohner, Frank, & Erb, 1998; Crano & Chen, 1998; De Dreu & De Vries, 1993; Martin & Hewstone, 2003b; see Chapter 8, this volume). These studies have yielded mixed findings concerning which source is associated with greater cognitive elaboration, with some suggesting that a majority instigates systematic processing (e.g., Mackie, 1987), others suggesting this for a minority (e.g., Moscovici, 1980), and still others suggesting that both sources can lead to systematic processing in different circumstances (e.g., Baker & Petty, 1994; De Dreu & De Vries, 1993; Martin & Hewstone, 2003b).

We conducted a series of studies to investigate these issues in more detail. Our first experiment (Martin et al., 2002, Experiment 3) crossed source status (majority vs. minority), with consensus difference (large 82%/18% vs. small 54%/48%) and message quality (strong vs. weak) and provided some evidence that majority and minority influence are determined by different processes. On the basis of extensive piloting, we employed two versions of the anti-voluntary-euthanasia message; one that contained strong and persuasive arguments and another that contained weak and unpersuasive arguments. In the majority condition, there was no effect of message quality, indicating that heuristic processing had occurred. The fact that this occurred irrespective of the absolute size of the majority (and that there was no difference between the 82% and 52% majorities) suggests that when a source is over 50% there is compliance to that position without detailed processing of its message. In contrast, in the 18% minority condition there was a reliable impact of message processing, indicating that participants had systematically processed the message (see also the results of Martin et al., 2002, Experiment 2, discussed earlier). Thus a minority needs to be small (numerically speaking) for it to lead to systematic processing as message quality had no effect on the 48% minority. The reason why the 48% minority did not lead to processing may be that its identity is blurred, as it is very close to 50%, and its status as a minority or majority could easily change with a swing of only 3%.

As predicted by the objective-consensus approach, the position endorsed by the counter-attitudinal majority was perceived as more surprising than the same position endorsed by a counter-attitudinal minority (Baker & Petty, 1994; Mackie, 1987). However, perceived surprise did not mediate the impact of source on attitude scores. Finally, there was some evidence consistent with Moscovici's (1976) prediction that a small minority would be perceived as having a more positive behavioural style than either a larger minority or a majority.

Next, we focused on the effect of consensus adjectives. Source status (majority vs. minority) was crossed with consensus adjective ('large' vs. 'small') and message quality (strong vs. weak). Results showed that when consensus information is in the form of consensus adjectives it affects attitudes, whereas source status does not (Gardikiotis et al., 2005, Experiment 1). In the majority condition 'large' sources had more influence than did 'small' sources and because this effect occurred irrespective of message quality, and there was no difference on message-congruent thinking, we can deduce this was due to non-systematic processing. On the other hand, it was only in the 'small' minority condition where message quality had an effect suggesting that participants systematically processed the source position. Both studies showed that a small minority (either in percentages or in adjectives) instigated systematic processing.

## Concluding remarks

The research programme reviewed in this chapter focused on the relationship between consensus and social influence. In doing so it posed three main questions. First, does group consensus affect majority and minority influence? Second, do different levels of consensus information affect majority and minority influence? And, third, what are the psychological processes responsible for the effect of group consensus on social influence?

### Group consensus and social influence

Our studies show that consensus information does impact on social-influence processes but in ways that current models have difficulty in fully explaining (see also Erb et al., 2006). Consensus information is important to majority influence, but primarily in showing that the majority group contains more than 50% of the population. By contrast, being numerically small is an advantage to a minority as it increases perceptions of being consistent, committed and confident, as Moscovici (1976) argued, and this can instigate a systematic evaluation of the minority's arguments.

All three experiments that used percentages to define group consensus supported the majority-source hypothesis, showing that a majority had more influence than a minority irrespective of the level of consensus. What is interesting is that the majority effect occurred even when the consensus difference between the groups was very small (52% vs. 48%). Thus a difference of only 4% was sufficient to lead to a reliable difference in influence.

### Consensus information and social influence

The content analysis of newspaper headlines revealed some interesting differences in majority and minority representation. Two points are relevant here: first, consensus adjectives are frequently used to convey consensus information about social groups. Second, a close inspection of consensus adjectives showed that whereas majority adjectives refer to large and small majorities (i.e., cover the whole range of the consensus continuum), minority adjectives refer only to small minorities (i.e., cover only the lowest end of the continuum).

Following the findings of content analysis, we experimentally investigated the effect of different types of consensus information on social influence and found that when group consensus is defined in terms of consensus adjectives (e.g., 'large' or 'small' majority or minority), then the 'large' sources had more influence than the 'small' sources irrespective of source status (i.e., majority or minority status). When group consensus is defined in terms of numerical support in percentages (Experiments 1, 2, and 4) majority source was more influential than the minority irrespective of level of group consensus. Percentage information about a group seems to focus attention on source status, a context that is beneficial to majority status. The majority was more influential: (a) when source label (i.e., 'majority') and consensus percentages were provided, and (b) when only consensus percentages were given. When only source labels were employed (i.e., 'majority' vs. 'minority') no difference was observed between majority and minority groups. These findings underlined the importance of expressing consensus in terms of percentages for majority influence.

In order to account for this difference between the two types of expressed consensus, one can examine the function and content of adjectives. Concerning the functional properties of adjectives the *linguistic-category model* (Semin & Fiedler, 1988, 1991) suggests that they occupy the more abstract pole in a lexical continuum used to describe human behaviour. Adjectives convey permanent and stable information about a person without any contextual references. On the other hand, concerning the specific content of the adjectives, definitions gleaned from the dictionary suggest a more positive connotation to the 'large' entities compared to the 'small' ones. This positive perception of 'large' entities was evident in both studies (Gardikiotis et al., 2005, Experiments 2 and 3) in which 'large' sources were perceived in a more positive way than the 'small' sources. Taken together, the functional and content properties of the adjectives 'large' and 'small' can explain the greater influence of 'large' sources.

### Consensus effects and psychological processes

In both experiments that examined whether a majority or minority source leads to systematic processing findings converged. The majority, whether conveyed as either percentages or adjectives, led to heuristic processing. There are two potential explanations why this might occur. First, people may wish to belong to the majority group to avoid aligning themselves (and being identified) with a minority group, and therefore they comply with the majority without the need to process its message (Moscovici, 1980). Second, people may employ a simple persuasion heuristic (such as 'the majority is more likely to be correct than the minority') and this guides their attitudes. Although we do not have data to determine which explanation is correct, we suspect that the first explanation cannot fully explain the results. If social comparison processes alone drive majority influence, as Moscovici suggests, then one would expect, in the percentage condition, a large majority (82%) to be more socially valued than a small majority (52%) and therefore lead to greater compliance. In fact, there was no difference between the majority conditions in any of the experiments.

The minority source, whether conveyed in percentages or adjectives, led to systematic processing. This is in accordance with the assumption of conversion theory (Moscovici, 1980) that a minority, through its distinctiveness, encourages a validation process in the target of influence. Supporting this assumption is the finding, in the percentage conditions, that the 18% minority was perceived as having a more positive behavioural style (in terms of consistency, commitment and confidence) than the 48% minority. Being perceived as having a consistent behavioural style is seen as an essential prerequisite for minority influence (Crano & Alvaro, 1998; Maass & Clark, 1984; Moscovici & Nemeth, 1974). The reason the 48% minority did not lead to systematic processing may be that it is near the 50% border defining source status and therefore was not perceived as being distinctive (note, there was no difference in the ratings of behavioural style between the 48% minority and the majority conditions). In order to instigate message elaboration a minority needs to be distinctive, either through being numerically small (Martin et al., 2002) or being labelled 'small' (Gardikiotis et al., 2004). It would be interesting for future research to determine where the numerical cut-off point is at which a minority source will lead to systematic message processing.

In summary, the experimental studies reported in this chapter show that it is important to consider the way in which consensus information is expressed in the context of social-influence processes. It is clear that consensus information has different effects if the source is a majority or a minority in terms of affecting the information-processing techniques employed to process the source's arguments and therefore the amount and type of attitude change. Further research should address how group consensus and majority and minority influence are operationalized in different social-influence settings to provide further insights into these processes.

## Note

1 Few researchers have manipulated majority and minority status as disagreeing people in a group discussion (e.g., Bohner, Erb, Reinhard, & Frank, 1996), or as 'real' groups (e.g., Alvaro & Crano, 1997).

## References

Alvaro, E. M., & Crano, W. D. (1997). Indirect minority influence: Evidence for leniency in source evaluation and counterargumentation. *Journal of Personality and Social Psychology, 72,* 949–964.

Arbuthnot, J., & Wayner, M. (1982). Minority influence: Effects of size, conversion, and sex. *Journal of Psychology, 111,* 285–295.

Asch, S. E. (1951). Effects of group pressure upon the modification and distortion of judgment. In H. Guetzkow (Ed.), *Groups, leadership and men* (pp. 177–190). Pittsburgh, PA: Carnegie Press.

Baker, S. M., & Petty, R. E. (1994). Majority and minority influence: Source–position imbalance as a determinant of message scrutiny. *Journal of Personality and Social Psychology, 67,* 5–19.

Bohner, G., Erb, H.-P., Reinhard, M.-A., & Frank, E. (1996). Distinctiveness across topics in minority and majority influence: An attributional analysis and preliminary data. *British Journal of Social Psychology, 35,* 27–46.

Bohner, G., Frank, S., & Erb, H. P. (1998). Heuristic processing of distinctiveness information in minority and majority influence. *European Journal of Social Psychology, 28,* 855–860.

Bond, R., & Smith, P. B. (1996). Culture and conformity: A meta-analysis of studies using Asch's (1952b, 1956) line judgment task. *Psychological Bulletin, 119,* 11–137.

Campbell, J. D., & Fairey, P. J. (1989). Informational and normative routes to conformity: The effect of faction size as a function of norm extremity and attention to the stimulus. *Journal of Personality and Social Psychology, 57,* 457–468.

Carlston, D. E. (1977). Effects of polling order on social influence in decision-making groups. *Social Psychology Quarterly, 40,* 115–123.

Chen, S., & Chaiken, S. (1999). The heuristic-systematic model in its broader context. In S. Chaiken & Y. Trope (Eds.), *Dual-process theories in social psychology* (pp. 73–96). New York: Guilford Press.

Crano, W. D., & Alvaro, E. M. (1998). The context/comparison model of social influence: Mechanisms, structure, and linkages that underlie indirect attitude change. In W. Stroebe & M. Hewstone (Eds.), *European review of social psychology* (Vol. 8, pp. 175–202). Chichester, UK: Wiley.

Crano, W. D., & Chen, X. (1998). The leniency contract and persistence of majority and minority influence. *Journal of Personality and Social Psychology, 74,* 1437–1450.

David, B., & Turner, J.C. (2001). Majority and minority influence: A single process self-categorization analysis. In C. K. W. De Dreu & N. K. De Vries (Eds.), *Group consensus and innovation* (pp. 91–121). Oxford, UK: Blackwell.

De Dreu, C. K. W., & De Vries, N. K. (1993). Numerical support, information processing and attitude change. *European Journal of Social Psychology, 23,* 647–663.

De Vries, N. K., De Dreu, C. K. W., Gordijn, E., & Schuurman, M. (1996). Majority and minority influence: A dual interpretation. In W. Stroebe & M. Hewstone (Eds.), *European review of social psychology* (Vol. 7, pp. 145–172). Chichester, UK: Wiley.

Deutsch, M., & Gerard, H. B. (1955). A study in normative and informational social influences upon individual judgment. *Journal of Abnormal and Social Psychology, 51,* 629–636.

Eagly, A. H., & Chaiken, S. (1993). *The psychology of attitudes.* Fort Worth, TX: Harcourt Brace Jovanovich.

Erb, H.-P., Bohner, G., Hewstone, M., Werth, L., & Reinhard, M.-A. (2006). Large minorities and small majorities: Interactive effects of inferred and explicit consensus on attitudes. *Basic and Applied Social Psychology, 28,* 221–231.

Erb, H.-P., Bohner, G., Schmälzle, K., & Rank, S. (1998). Beyond conflict and discrepancy: Cognitive bias in minority and majority influence. *Personality and Social Psychology Bulletin, 24,* 620–633.

Festinger, L. (1950). Informal social communication. *Psychological Review, 57,* 271–282.

Gardikiotis, A., Martin, R, & Hewstone, M. (2004). The representation of majorities and minorities in the British press: A content analytic approach. *European Journal of Social Psychology, 34,* 637–646.

Gardikiotis, A., Martin, R., & Hewstone, M. (2005). Group consensus in social influence: Type of consensus information as a moderator of majority and minority influence. *Personality and Social Psychology Bulletin, 31,* 1163–1174.

Gerard, H. B., Wilhelmy, R. A., & Conolley, E. S. (1968). Conformity and group size. *Journal of Personality and Social Psychology, 8,* 79–82.

Goldberg, S. C. (1954). Three situational determinants of conformity to social norms. *Journal of Abnormal and Social Psychology, 49,* 325–329.

Hardin, C. D., & Higgins, E. T. (1996). Shared reality: How social verification makes the subjective objective. In R. M. Sorrentino & E. T. Higgins (Eds.), *Handbook of motivation and cognition* (Vol. 3, pp. 28–84). New York: Guilford Press.

Insko, C. A., Drenan, S., Solomon, M. R., Smith, R., & Wade, T. J. (1983). Conformity as a function of the consistency of positive self-evaluation with being liked and being right. *Journal of Experimental Social Psychology, 19,* 341–358.

Kidd, J. S. (1958). Social influence phenomena in a task-oriented group situation. *Journal of Abnormal and Social Psychology, 56,* 13–17.

Kishida, M. (1956). A study of the effects of group norm upon the change of opinions [abstract]. *Japanese Journal of Psychology, 27,* 172–173.

Lascu, D. N., Bearden, W. O., & Rose, R. L. (1995). Norm extremity and inter-personal influences on consumer conformity. *Journal of Business Research, 32,* 201–212.

Latané, B., & Wolf, S. (1981). The social impact of majorities and minorities. *Psychological Review, 88*, 438–453.

Maass, A., & Clark, R. D. (1984). Hidden impact of minorities: Fifteen years of minority influence research. *Psychological Bulletin, 95*, 428–450.

Maass, A., Salvi, D., Arcuri, L., & Semin, G. (1989). Language use in intergroup contexts: The linguistic intergroup bias. *Journal of Personality and Social Psychology, 57*, 981–993.

Maass, A., West, S. G., & Cialdini, R. B. (1987). Minority influence and conversion. In C. Hendrick (Ed.), *Review of personality and social psychology* (Vol. 8, pp. 55–79). Newbury Park, CA: Sage.

Mackie, D. M. (1987). Systematic and nonsystematic processing of majority and minority persuasive communications. *Journal of Personality and Social Psychology, 53*, 41–52.

Martin, R., Gardikiotis, A., & Hewstone, M. (2002). Levels of consensus and majority and minority influence. *European Journal of Social Psychology, 32*, 645–665.

Martin, R., & Hewstone, M. (2001). Determinants and consequences of cognitive processes in majority and minority influence. In J. Forgas & K. Williams (Eds.), *Social influence: Direct and indirect processes* (pp. 315–330). Philadelphia: Psychology Press.

Martin, R., & Hewstone, M. (2003a). Social influence processes of control and change: Conformity, obedience to authority, and innovation. In M. A. Hogg & J. Cooper (Eds.), *Sage handbook of social psychology* (pp. 347–366). London: Sage.

Martin, R., & Hewstone, M. (2003b). Majority versus minority influence: When, not whether, source status instigates heuristic or systematic processing. *European Journal of Social Psychology, 33*, 313–330.

Moscovici, S. (1976). *Social influence and social change*. London: Academic Press.

Moscovici, S. (1980). Toward a theory of conversion behavior. In L. Berkowitz (Ed.), *Advances in experimental social psychology* (Vol. 13, pp. 209–239). New York: Academic Press.

Moscovici, S., & Nemeth, C. (1974). Social influence II: Minority influence. In C. Nemeth (Ed.), *Social psychology: Classic and contemporary integrations* (pp. 217–249). Chicago: Rand McNally.

Moscovici, S., & Personnaz, B. (1980). Studies in social influence V: Minority influence and conversion behavior in a perceptual task. *Journal of Experimental Social Psychology, 16*, 270–282.

Mugny, G., Butera, F., Sanchez-Mazas, M., & Pérez, J. A. (1995). Judgements in conflict: The conflict elaboration theory of social influence. In B. Boothe, R. Hirsig, A. Helminger, B. Meier, & R. Volkart (Eds.), *Perception–evaluation–interpretation* (pp. 160–168). Gottingen, Germany: Hogrefe & Huber.

Mugny, G., & Papastamou, S. (1980). When rigidity does not fail: Individualization and psychologization as resistances to the diffusion of minority innovations. *European Journal of Social Psychology, 10*, 43–61.

Mullen, B. (1983). Operationalizing the effect of the group on the individual: A self-attention perspective. *Journal of Experimental Social Psychology, 19*, 295–322.

Nemeth, C. J. (1995). Dissent as driving cognition, attitudes, and judgments. *Social Cognition, 13*(3), 273–291.

Nemeth, C. J., Wachtler, J., & Endicott, J. (1977). Increasing the size of the minority: Some gains and some losses. *European Journal of Social Psychology, 7,* 15–27.

Nordholm, L. A. (1975). Effects of group size and stimulus ambiguity on conformity. *Journal of Social Psychology, 97,* 123–130.

*Oxford Dictionary and Thesaurus, The.* (1997). Oxford, UK: Oxford University Press.

Petty, R. E., & Cacioppo, J. T. (1986). *Communication and persuasion: Central and peripheral routes to attitude change.* New York: Springer-Verlag.

Petty, R. E., & Wegener, D. T. (1999). The elaboration likelihood model: Current status and controversies. In S. Chaiken & Y. Trope (Eds.), *Dual-process theories in social psychology* (pp. 73–96). New York: Guilford Press.

Reis, H. T., Earing, B., Kent, A., & Nezlek, J. (1976). The tyranny of numbers: Does group size affect petition signing? *Journal of Applied Social Psychology, 6,* 228–234.

Rosenberg, L. (1961). Group size, prior experience, and conformity. *Journal of Abnormal and Social Psychology, 63,* 436–437.

Semin, G. R., & Fiedler, K. (1988). The cognitive functions of linguistic categories in describing persons: Social cognition and language. *Journal of Personality and Social Psychology, 54,* 558–568.

Semin, G. R., & Fiedler, K. (1991). The linguistic category model, its bases, applications and range. In W. Stroebe & M. Hewstone (Eds.), *European review of social psychology* (Vol. 2, pp. 1–30). Chichester, UK: Wiley.

Semin, G. R., & Fiedler, K. (Eds.). (1996). *Applied social psychology.* London: Sage.

Tanford, S., & Penrod, S. (1984). Social influence model: A formal integration of research on majority and minority influence. *Psychological Bulletin, 95,* 189–225.

Tindale, R. S., Davis, J. H., Vollrath, D. A., Nagao, D. H., & Hinsz, V. B. (1990). Asymmetrical social influence in freely interacting groups: A test of three models. *Journal of Personality and Social Psychology, 58,* 438–449.

Wilder, D. A. (1977). Perception of groups, size of opposition, and social influence. *Journal of Experimental Social Psychology, 13,* 253–268.

Wolf, S., & Latané, B. (1983). Majority and minority influences on restaurant preferences. *Journal of Personality and Social Psychology, 45,* 282–292.

Wood, W., Lundgren, S., Ouellette, J. A., Busceme, S., & Blackstone, T. (1994). Minority influence: A meta-analytic review of social influence processes. *Psychological Bulletin, 115,* 323–345.

Zdaniuk, B., & Levine, J. M. (1996). Anticipated interaction and thought generation: The role of faction size. *British Journal of Social Psychology, 35,* 201–218.

# 8 Consequences of attitudes changed by majority and minority influence

*Robin Martin*
Aston University, UK

*Miles Hewstone*
University of Oxford, UK

*Pearl Y. Martin*
Aston University, UK

But even in conclusions which can be known only by reasoning, I say that the testimony of many has little more value than that of a few, since the number of people who reason well in complicated matters is much smaller than that of those who reason badly. If reasoning were like hauling I should agree that several reasoners would be worth more than one, just as several horses can haul more sacks of grain than one can. But reasoning is like racing and not like hauling, and a single Barbary steed can outrun a hundred dray horses.

(*Le Opere di Galileo Galilei*, Vol. XI, Barbera, Firenze, 1969, p. 257; quoted in *Galileo Antichrist*, Michael White, 2007, p. 165)

## Preamble

In a previous publication, one of the authors recalled an occasion when he had been exposed to a minority position that argued in favour of smoking in his college: '. . . one of us, an aggressive non-smoker, found himself sitting in a college meeting at which the authorities were just about to ban smoking completely from all premises. He found himself, first, intrigued by the courage of the lone spokesman for the tiny rump of collegiate smokers; then listening to the eloquent, cogent arguments; then changing his mind about banning smoking from the college; and, finally, voting against it!' (Martin & Hewstone, 2008, p. 316). This story, which is typical of situations where minorities have influence, identifies some of the key stages in minority influence—initial reluctance to listen to the minority arguments, interest in the minority position because it is numerically distinctive and perhaps also novel, evaluation of the merits of the minority's arguments, agreement with the minority, and, finally, engaging in behaviours consistent with the minority-endorsed opinions (although happily the influence was limited to the voting behaviour as the author concerned has remained a non-smoker!). The above 'stages' mirror the aims of the vast bulk of research into majority and minority influence—understanding the underlying processes, when these occur and what effects they have on attitudes, opinions and behaviours.

The research described in this chapter takes a different perspective from that described above and the other chapters in this book. This chapter examines the *consequences* for attitudes that are formed via these different sources of influence. More specifically, we are concerned with the strength of attitudes that are formed following majority and minority influence. By 'strength' we mean the extent to which people feel their new position is one that is important to them, and that they are committed to it (see, e.g., Eaton, Majka, & Visser, 2008). In the example above, the person engaged in sufficient thinking about the issues to warrant a change from his original anti- to pro-smoking in college position, and in so doing he aligned himself with the minority group. Since his new position resulted from thinking about the issues in detail, it is likely that his new attitude was strong in nature (i.e., he was committed to the position). In some respects one might say that the strong attitude reflects a real change in the beliefs of the person. On the other hand, imagine that the lone spokesman had been a close and dear friend, in which case our message recipient may have simply complied with the pro-smoking in college position without thinking about the issues in detail. This would have led to a weak attitude that would probably only be expressed in the presence of the friend. By examining the nature of the attitudes that are formed following majority and minority influence—in this case the strength of the attitude—we gain an insight into the types of processes that occurred in their formation or change.

The remainder of this chapter is organized into four sections. In the first section we provide a brief outline of the concept of attitude strength and the types of underlying information-processing strategies that affect it. In the second section, we describe briefly a new theoretical framework (the source–context–elaboration model; SCEM) that explains the underlying processes involved in majority and minority influence, when they occur and how these affect the strength of attitudes following persuasion. In the third section, we review a range of studies from our own research programme that investigated the strength of attitudes formed following majority and minority influence using a number of different experimental paradigms. Finally, we draw conclusions from this research and raise some important theoretical implications.

## A brief outline of attitude strength

Most attitude theorists make a distinction between attitude direction (whether the attitude is positive or negative) and the extent to which the attitude is endorsed. The latter aspect is often referred to as the 'strength' of the attitude (see Eaton et al., 2008). Visser, Bizer, and Krosnick (2006) describe a distinction between strong and weak attitudes by noting that, '. . . although some attitudes exert a powerful impact on thinking and on behavior, others are largely inconsequential. Similarly, whereas some attitudes are tremendously durable, resisting change in the face of a persuasive appeal and remaining stable over long spans of time, others are highly malleable and fluctuate greatly over time' (p. 2).

Researchers have used many labels to represent the strength of attitudes. Raden (1985), for example, employed eleven attributes to reflect attitude strength: accessibility, affective–cognitive consistency, certainty, crystallization, direct experience, generalized attitude strength, importance, intensity, latitude of rejection, stability, and vested interest. Krosnick and Petty (1995) suggest that strength-related attributes of attitudes can be grouped into four categories. The first category includes aspects of the attitude itself, most notably extremity. The second category includes aspects of the attitude structure, such as accessibility, and quantity of knowledge. The third category includes aspects of the process by which attitudes are formed, and the degree of careful thinking engaged in. Finally, the fourth category includes people's subjective beliefs about their attitudes, such as personal importance and certainty. Research shows that aspects of the first two categories tend to be highly correlated with the latter two categories (Krosnick & Abelson, 1992).

High intercorrelations amongst measures of attitude strength led researchers to use them interchangeably when measuring attitude strength. A number of factor-analytic studies have tried to clarify what are the important characteristics of strong attitudes (e.g., Abelson, 1988; Verplanken, 1989). Pomerantz, Chaiken, and Tordesillas (1995) examined a variety of attributes of strong attitudes and found two underlying factors: one concerned *embeddedness* (the extent to which the attitude is central and important to the person), and the other factor was *commitment* (the extent to which the person thinks the attitude would not change, or their certainty concerning their position). In contrast, Prislin (1996) found three underlying factors (i.e., generalized attitude strength, extremity and ease of attitude expression). As Bassili (1996) noted, there may be many reasons for the inconsistency across studies that try to categorize the main dimensions of attitude strength and capture these with self-report measures, and these inconsistencies might be due to a number of methodological issues, such as each study measuring different subsets of elements of attitude strength (see Visser et al., 2006, for a review).

To overcome some of these problems Bassili (1996) distinguished between two types of measures of attitude strength, which he referred to as 'meta-attitudinal' and 'operative' measures. The meta-attitudinal measures are the ones described above, which ask the attitude holder to judge various aspects of their attitude relevant to its strength (such as, importance, conviction, commitment, etc.). The potential problem with these types of measures is that they rely on self-reports, and this raises the issue of whether people have direct access to the properties of their attitudes when, in fact, these judgements could be open to a number of contextual biases. Operative measures are directly linked to the cognitive processes that give rise to the strength of the attitude. These are indirect measures of the properties of the strength of an attitude that do not rely on direct self-report measures.

As we will see later in this chapter, the research that we report did not ask people to describe directly the strength of their attitudes; rather, we used a number of techniques to *infer* the strength of respondents' attitudes following majority and minority influence from the consequences of those attitudes. According to Bassili's categorization above, the techniques we employ are more operative than meta-attitudinal in nature. By employing these techniques we are able to examine attitude strength without relying on self-report measures of the properties of their attitude.

Dual-process models of persuasion (notably Chaiken, Liberman, & Eagly's, 1989, heuristic systematic model; HSM, and Petty & Cacioppo's, 1986, elaboration likelihood model; ELM) offer a theoretical account of the processes that lead to strong and weak attitudes. Although the ELM and the HSM make some different predictions (Visser & Cooper, 2003), they share some common assumptions. Both distinguish two strategies of information processing in persuasion settings. 'Central-route persuasion' (ELM) or 'systematic processing' (HSM) entails thinking carefully about persuasive arguments and other issue-related information. Systematic processing refers to a '. . . comprehensive, analytic orientation in which perceivers access and scrutinize all information input for its relevance and importance to their judgmental task' (Chaiken et al., 1989, p. 212); it can be biased or unbiased, depending on motivational factors (processing goals). In order to engage in systematic processing people have to be both motivated and able to process the source's message. In situations where people are unmotivated and/or unable to process the source's message, attitudes may be changed by 'peripheral-route persuasion' (ELM) or 'heuristic processing' (HSM), whereby systematic processing is minimal, and persuasion occurs due to some cue(s) in the persuasion environment (e.g., status of source) or use of simple heuristics (e.g., 'the majority is always right'). Heuristic processing refers to a '. . . more limited processing mode that demands much less cognitive effort and capacity than systematic processing . . . [it involves a] focus on that subset of available information that enables [respondents] to use simple, inferential rules, schemata, or cognitive heuristics to formulate their judgments and decisions' (Chaiken et al., 1989, p. 213).

According to the ELM, attitudes changed via systematic processing result from a detailed cognitive elaboration of the source's message, and these are referred to as 'strong' (Krosnick, Boninger, Chuang, Berent, & Carnot, 1993; Petty, 1995). In terms of identifying strong attitudes Krosnick and Petty (1995) suggested that strong attitudes are ones that are durable and should be more likely to resist counter-persuasion (Haugtvedt & Petty,

1992; Petty, Haugtvedt, & Smith, 1995), persist over time (Visser & Krosnick, 1998), and are predictive of behaviour (Holland, Verplanken, & van Knippenberg, 2002; Leippe & Elkin, 1987). By contrast, attitudes that are low in attitude strength, what are referred to as 'weak' attitudes, should yield to counter-persuasion, should not persist over time, and, finally, should not predict attitude-consistent behaviours.

Petty et al. (1995) described three reasons why message elaboration should result in these consequences. First, message elaboration can increase the structural consistency of an attitude because the process of elaboration might resolve pre-existing inconsistencies amongst attitude components. Second, message elaboration can increase the association between various aspects of people's attitudes and therefore increase their accessibility in memory (which is known to increase the attitude–behaviour link; Fazio, 1995). Third, message elaboration may increase people's belief that they have expended considerable cognitive effort, leading to increased confidence in their attitudes.

## Source–context–elaboration model

In this section we describe briefly the *source–context–elaboration model* (SCEM; Martin & Hewstone, 2008) with specific reference to its predictions concerning the strength of attitudes formed following majority and minority influence. SCEM is specifically, but not uniquely, related to the impact of majority and minority influence on attitudinal issues (like the issue of smoking at the college described above) and therefore takes a different approach from theoretical perspectives that focus on objective performance criteria and decision-making tasks (such as the conflict elaboration model; Mugny, Butera, Sanchez-Mazas, & Pérez, 1995; convergent–divergent theory; Nemeth, 1986).

SCEM proposes a contingency framework for understanding majority and minority influence where message elaboration depends on: (a) the status of the influence source (majority vs. minority); and (b) the 'context' in which influence occurs. The model describes the underlying processes, the contexts under which these processes occur, and the consequences for attitudes as a result of influence. Each of these aspects is briefly described below.

### *Processes*

SCEM is based on an integration of aspects of Moscovici's (1980) conversion theory and dual-process models of persuasion (Chaiken et al.'s, 1989, HSM, and Petty & Cacioppo's, 1986, ELM). Moscovici (1980) argued that all attempts to influence other people result in conflict and that individuals are motivated to reduce that conflict. The resolution of conflict varies depending on the nature of the source of influence. For majority influence, Moscovici proposed that individuals engage in a *comparison process* where they concentrate attention on '. . . what others say, so as to fit in with their opinions or judgments' (1980, p. 214). In this situation, people wish to belong to the majority group, as identification with a majority is desirable and, through social-comparison processes, they conform to the majority position. Because people wish to avoid being categorized as a minority, they accept the majority position without the need for a detailed appraisal of its arguments. For minority influence, favourable social comparison is unlikely as minority membership is typically associated with undesirable characteristics.

Moscovici (1976) argued that, to be persuasive, a minority would have to adopt a behavioural style of 'consistency'; by 'standing-up' to the majority, the minority would show that it was certain, confident and committed to its position, and would not be easily swayed. Through this behavioural style majority members begin to see that the minority has a valid alternative that deserves to be considered. Moscovici proposed that the minority could encourage a *validation process*, leading the recipient of minority influence to '. . . examine one's own responses, one's own judgments, in order to confirm and validate them . . . one's main preoccupation [is] to see what the minority saw, to understand what it understood' (1980, p. 215). Whereas minority influence may not lead to public agreement, due to fear of being categorized as a minority member (Mugny, 1982), the close examination of the minority's position may bring about attitude conversion on an indirect, latent or private level (i.e., a more unconscious level).

One can drawn a parallel between Moscovici's concepts of comparison and validation and those of non-systematic and systematic processing respectively (Maass & Clark, 1983; Martin & Hewstone, 2008). The SCEM framework combines many elements of these approaches and refers to elaborative and non-elaborative processing. Elaborative processing involves attending to the content of the source's arguments and trying to understand the underlying reasons why the source believes these arguments, generating pro- and counter-arguments, evaluating the merits of these arguments in the light of pre-existing attitudes, assimilating these new arguments into one's thinking about the attitude object, and finally being aware of the consequences of these 'new' attitudes to source-group membership (and, when necessary, redefining group identification). By contrast, non-elaborative processing involves few, if any, of the above stages and when it occurs pre-existing attitudes remain intact. Sometimes non-elaborative processing can guide attitudes by the application of a heuristic cue (e.g., 'several pairs of eyes are better than one', 'the majority position tends to prevail'). For example, source status can act as heuristic cue when source-group membership is psychologically important, as when majority-group membership is desirable (e.g., it forms part of the person's in-group) and/or minority membership is undesirable (e.g., it has deviant status).

## Contexts

An important aspect of SCEM it that it specifies the 'contexts' under which majority and minority influence will lead to either elaborative or non-elaborative processing. In common with dual-process models of persuasion, it proposes that whether a source will lead to elaborative versus non-elaborative processing will depend on where the context falls on an 'elaboration continuum' (Petty & Cacioppo, 1986). The elaboration continuum goes from '. . . no thought about the issue-relevant information presented, to complete elaboration of every argument, and complete integration of these elaborations into the person's attitude schema' (Petty & Cacioppo, 1986, p. 8). The position on the elaboration continuum is determined by a range of dispositional (e.g., need for cognition; Cacioppo & Petty, 1982) and situational (e.g., relevance of topic; Johnson & Eagly, 1989) factors that affect people's ability and/or motivation to engage in elaborative processing.

The ELM provides some insights into the potential effects of source status at different levels of the elaboration continuum (see Petty & Cacioppo, 1984). Petty and colleagues referred to the 'multiple roles' of majority/minority source status (Baker & Petty, 1994; Petty & Wegener, 1998). More specifically, they suggested that the effects of majority- versus minority-source status would vary along the elaboration continuum. For example, Petty and Wegener (1998) stated that '. . . when the elaboration likelihood is low, majority/minority source status is most likely to serve as a simple cue . . . when people are unsure whether they should carefully scrutinize the message or not, majority/minority status can determine the amount of message scrutiny . . . when motivation and ability to process an incoming message are high, majority/minority status should impact persuasion primarily by influencing the nature of the thoughts that come to mind' (pp. 347–348). Thus, majority/minority source could influence attitudes as a peripheral cue (at low levels of motivation and/or ability), as a factor that influences the amount of scrutiny of the message (at more intermediate levels of motivation and/or ability—although Petty and Wegener did not specify which source would have this effect), and as an argument, or through biased processing (at high levels of motivation and/or ability).

## Nature of attitudes following influence

The final part of SCEM considers the nature of attitudes that are formed following majority and minority influence. As outlined earlier, attitudes changed via elaborative processing result from a detailed consideration of the source's message and these are referred to as 'strong' (Krosnick et al., 1993). Strong attitudes are able to resist counter-persuasion, persist over time and predict behaviour. By contrast, attitudes formed via non-elaborative processing tend to be relatively 'weak', in that they have not been based upon message elaboration, and this means that they are unable to resist counter-persuasion, do not persist over time, and do not predict behaviour. Applying this reasoning to our framework leads to the prediction that attitudes changed via elaborative processing (whether from a majority or minority source) should lead to attitudes that resist counter-persuasion, persist over time and guide behaviours, compared to attitudes changed via non-elaborative or heuristic processing.

## Research programme

### Overview

In this section we review some of our experimental studies in relation to the nature and consequences of attitudes following majority and minority influence. According to SCEM, in most persuasion situations (what we refer to as 'intermediate' processing contexts), there will be heuristic acceptance of a majority position (without detailed consideration of the majority's arguments), whereas a minority should stimulate elaborative processing of the content of its arguments. If this is the case, then attitudes formed following minority influence should be relatively 'strong', compared to those formed following majority influence, and therefore message recipients' newly formed attitudes should be better able to resist counter-persuasion, should persist over time, and should predict behaviour. We first describe the methodology of these studies and then review some of our experiments on each of these issues.

### Research methodology

While there were some variations between the experiments reviewed in this chapter, they followed a similar methodology and procedure, which is briefly described below (full details are provided in the original articles).

The studies used a wide range of attitudinal issues, each of which had been pre-tested to be topical for participants. The messages employed in these studies were developed using procedures described by Eagly and Chaiken (1993, p. 311) and Petty and Cacioppo (1986, p. 133). Each message typically contained five or six persuasive arguments (see Martin & Hewstone, 2008, for details of message development and example arguments).

Most experiments consisted of three main stages, with a separate booklet for each: pre-test, message exposure, and post-test. In the pre-test, participants were asked to indicate their attitude to a range of social issues, one of which concerned the topic of influence. As well as providing a pre-test score, this measure also served as a screening item to ensure that only participants who met sample selection criteria were included in the study.

For example, in some experiments participants were only included if the source message was counter-attitudinal with respect to their initial attitude.

The second booklet reported the results of a survey of students at their college concerning the topic of influence. This (fictitious) survey formed the basis for the source-status manipulation and participants were informed about the proportion of the population that supported the message (which was stated as being 'in favour' of or 'against' the topic depending on which was counter-attitudinal to the population). Participants were informed that either 82% (majority) or 18% (minority) supported the arguments they were about to read. Participants were then informed that the main arguments given by this section of the population were printed on the following page. The third booklet contained the dependent measures which typically included: (1) checks on the manipulation of the independent variables (e.g., percentage of students believed to agree with the message); (2) a measure of attitude towards the topic; and (3) a thought-listing task in which participants wrote down their thoughts to the message (later rated by the participant as in favour of, against or neutral towards the topic).

### Experimental studies

In this section we review a small number of studies from our research programme to give the flavour of evidence we have accrued from studies on the effects of majority- versus minority-endorsed attitudes on resistance to counter-persuasion, attitude persistence over time, and prediction of behaviour.

### Resistance to counter-persuasion

The aim of this first set of studies was to see if the attitudes formed following majority and minority influence would resist or yield to a counter-persuasive communication. This was achieved by exposing participants, in turn, to two messages that argued different positions on the same topic, with attitude scores taken after each message (see, e.g., Haugtvedt & Petty, 1992; Haugtvedt & Wegener, 1994; Wu & Shaffer, 1987). If participants have engaged in elaborative processing of the first (initial) message this should provide them with arguments to resist the 'attack' from the second counter-message. If, however, attitudes to the initial message are formed via non-elaborative processing, they should be relatively weak and yield to the influence of the second counter-message. The prediction is that if minority influence leads to elaborative processing, then attitudes formed following exposure to a minority should be strong and therefore more resistant to counter-persuasion than attitudes formed following majority influence.

This hypothesis was tested in an experiment that measured participants' attitudes towards voluntary euthanasia at three time points (Martin,

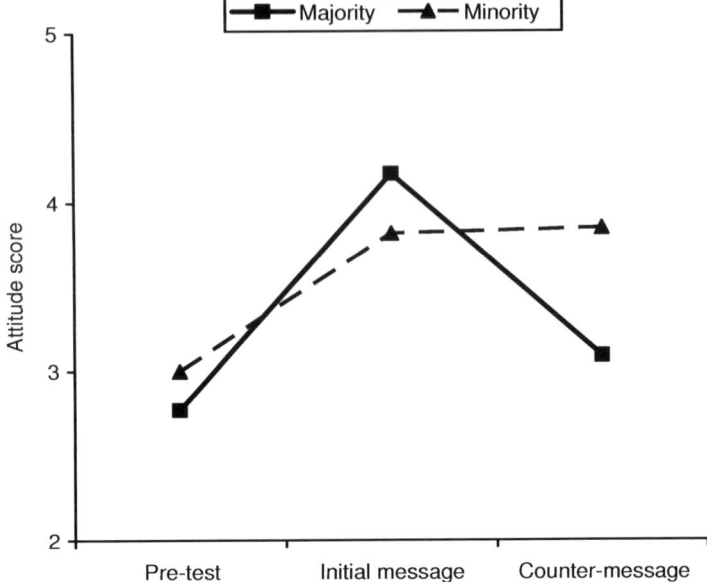

*Figure 8.1* Mean attitude scores as a function of measurement time and source status (Martin et al., 2003, Experiment 2). *Note*: Greater agreement with the source is reflected by *high* scores on the initial message and *low* scores on the counter-message.

Hewstone & Martin, 2003, Experiment 2). The time points were at the onset of the experiment (pre-test), after exposure to a counter-attitudinal message (anti-voluntary euthanasia, initial message, post-test I), and, finally, after exposure to a pro-attitudinal message (pro-voluntary euthanasia, counter-message, post-test II). It should be noted that the status of the source (majority or minority) was indicated only for the initial message and that there was a delay between the two messages (approximately fifteen minutes) to ensure that participants had sufficient time to engage in message elaboration, if they chose to, before exposure to the counter-message.

The results for the attitude data showed the expected two-way interaction between source status and measurement times (see Figure 8.1). The attitude data were reverse scored so that influence towards the source is shown by high scores on the initial message and by low scores on the counter-message. There was a reliable change across the measurement times for both the majority and minority conditions. When the source was a majority, participants were influenced by the initial message, as shown by a reliable increase between pre-test and initial message/post-test I; these attitudes were, however, vulnerable to the second counter-message, as shown by the reliable reduction between post-test I and post-test II. In fact, for the majority source, there was no difference between pre-test and post-

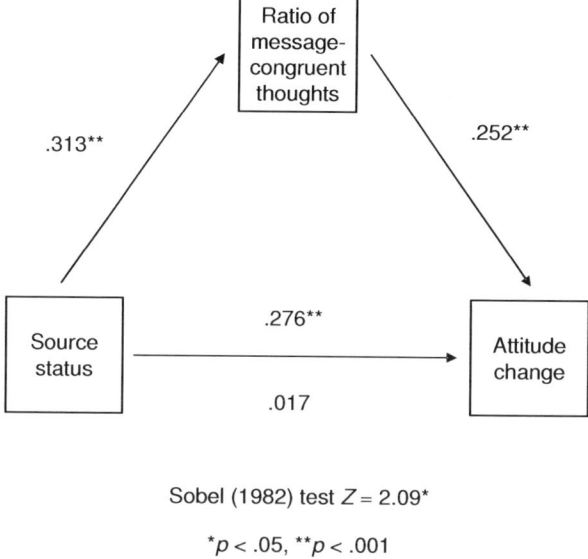

Sobel (1982) test $Z = 2.09*$

$*p < .05, **p < .001$

*Figure 8.2* Path model showing that the ratio of message-congruent thinking mediates the relationship between source status (majority vs. minority) and attitude change (change between initial and counter-message) controlling for pre-test and initial-message attitude (Martin et al., 2003, Experiment 2).

test II attitude scores, showing that attitudes following the counter-message returned to their pre-test levels. This pattern suggests that participants had heuristically accepted the majority's position to the initial message, without detailed processing of its arguments, and therefore the attitudes that resulted were weak and yielded to the counter-message. In the minority condition participants were also influenced by the initial message but, unlike in the majority condition, these attitudes did not change as a result of exposure to the counter-message. This pattern suggests that participants had processed the minority's arguments in the initial message and, as a result of doing this, these attitudes were relatively strong and they were able to resist the counter-message.

The data from the thought-listing task (completed after the initial message) supported the above conclusion. We computed a thought index by dividing the number of pro-message thoughts by the number of pro- and anti-message thoughts, so that the higher the index, the greater the message-congruent thinking. We found that participants in the minority condition engaged in more message-congruent thinking than did those in the majority condition, suggesting that minorities encouraged greater elaborative processing. Furthermore, the proportion of message-congruent thinking mediated the change in attitudes between the initial message and counter-message (see Figure 8.2). Therefore, those informed that the initial message was supported by a minority generated a higher proportion of message-congruent thoughts, compared to when the initial message was supported by a majority, and this led to less change in response to the counter-message (i.e., it led to greater resistance).

A particular feature of the experimental design of this study was the use of a series of two messages that took opposite attitudinal positions (anti- and pro-voluntary euthanasia respectively). Therefore, knowing the source status of the initial message would enable recipients to infer the source status of the counter-message (e.g., in the above experiment, recipients who were informed that the majority were anti-voluntary euthanasia could easily infer that the pro-voluntary euthanasia counter-message would be held by the minority). This situation might lead to an alternative interpretation of the findings. Changes in attitude between the messages in the majority-endorsed initial message condition could be due to either: (a) attitudes formed following majority endorsement being weak and yielding to counter-persuasion, as we predicted, or (b) a minority-endorsed counter-message leading to more influence than a majority-endorsed counter-message. We examined these alternatives in a subsequent experiment that replicated the majority and minority conditions but also added two conditions, one in which participants were exposed to *only* a majority-endorsed counter-message, and one in which they were exposed to *only* a minority-endorsed counter-message (Martin et al., 2003, Experiment 3). According to the alternative hypothesis, the change observed in the majority-endorsed initial message may have been due to the greater influence of a minority-endorsed counter-message. This could, however, not have been the case because the minority-endorsed counter-message alone did not lead to greater influence than receiving only the majority-endorsed counter-message. This result, together with others in the experiment, further supports the view that those in the majority- and minority-endorsed initial message conditions had yielded to and resisted the counter-message, respectively.

Our conjecture in the above experiments is that the resistance to the counter-message was due to recipients processing the minority arguments elaboratively. It is only when attitudes have been changed via elaborative processing that these attitudes will be strong and therefore able to resist counter-persuasion. This assumption was tested in an experiment that varied the quality of the arguments contained in the initial message—that is, participants read either a message that contained strong and persuasive arguments or one that contained weak and non-persuasive arguments (Martin, Hewstone, & Martin, 2008, Experiment 1). If attitude change following majority influence led to compliance (through non-elaborative processing), then the extent to which these 'new' attitudes yielded to counter-persuasion should not be affected by the quality of the arguments in the initial message. However, if attitude change following minority influence was due to elaborative processing, then there should be greater attitude change following the initial message when it contained strong compared to weak arguments, and these attitudes should be better able to resist the counter-message.

This experiment was similar in procedure to that described above, except that the initial message contained either strong or weak arguments (the counter-message always had strong arguments). To further examine attitude change, this experiment also included an indirect measure of attitude change that was not mentioned in the message; the indirect attitude concerned 'Genetic screening for medical disorders (e.g., cystic fibrosis, sickle cell anaemia)', whereas the direct attitude concerned voluntary euthanasia. Our pilot research had shown that there was a reliable, positive correlation between the direct and indirect attitudes at pre-test. There is evidence showing that the impact of minorities is greater on indirect attitudes than direct ones because people often do not want to align themselves publicly with a deviant group (Wood, Lundgren, Ouellette, Busceme, & Blackstone, 1994).

The results for the direct attitude showed the expected reliable three-way interaction between source status, argument quality and measurement time. For the majority source, the participants were influenced by the initial message but, as expected, these attitudes yielded to the second counter-message, with attitudes returning to the pre-test levels. This pattern of results was the same for both the strong and weak arguments in the initial message, showing that participants had heuristically accepted the majority position without considering its arguments in detail. For the minority source, participants were influenced by the initial message when it contained strong arguments and, as expected, these attitudes subsequently resisted the counter-message (supporting the findings of Martin et al., 2003). When the minority had weak arguments, however, a different pattern emerged in that the minority-endorsed initial message did not affect attitudes and these attitudes then yielded to the counter-message. This result was anticipated: if the minority encourages elaborative processing, then elaboration of weak arguments should not lead to influence (which it did not), and because no attitude change occurs, message recipients' attitudes are vulnerable to the counter-message. The proportion of message-congruent thinking mediated attitude change between the initial and counter-message, again supporting the idea that resistance to the counter-message was due to elaborative processing of the initial message.

The results for the indirect attitude revealed one important finding, in the condition where the minority source expressed strong arguments. In this condition participants were influenced by the initial message, as shown by the increase from pre- to post-test I, but these attitudes resisted counter-persuasion as there was no difference between post-test I and post-test II. These results indicate that in the minority condition with strong arguments the elaborative processing of these arguments led to conversion to the minority position that was detected on an issue related to, but not mentioned in, the initial- or counter-messages.

The above experiments show that majority and minority influence led to non-elaborative and elaborative processing, respectively, and they show that this differentially affected the tendency of people to yield to or resist counter-persuasion. However, SCEM specifies these relationships only when the elaboration context is at an intermediate level, and the above experiments were designed to employ messages at this level (Martin, Hewstone, & Martin, 2007a). Changing the elaboration context should have corresponding effects on the types of processes instigated by majority and minority sources and the nature of attitudes formed subsequently. In a further experiment (Martin et al., 2008, Experiment 2) we examined this prediction by increasing the amount of message elaboration; we did this by asking participants to remember the arguments contained in the message. We hypothesized that asking participants to remember the arguments should lead to elaborative processing of the message from both the majority and minority source and therefore increase resistance to a counter-message. This experiment employed the same procedures as the last experiment with two exceptions. First, it used only the strong arguments for the initial message and, second, in one condition participants were told that they would later be required to recall the arguments in the message (this procedure should lead participants to pay closer attention to the message, and process the arguments in greater depth).

When the participants were not told that they would have to recall the arguments in the initial message, the pattern of results was the same as in previous experiments—attitude change to the initial message yielded to or resisted the counter-message when the initial message was attributed to a majority or minority, respectively (see Figure 8.3). In the condition where participants were told that they would later have to recall the arguments in the initial message attitudes following the initial message resisted the counter-message for both the majority and the minority source. Thus, this experiment shows that in a high-elaboration context people will elaboratively process both majority- and minority-endorsed arguments, resulting in 'strong' attitudes that resist counter-persuasion.

To summarize, these studies on resistance to counter-persuasion show that attitudes formed following minority influence were relatively strong in that they were able to resist counter-persuasion. On the other hand, attitudes formed following majority influence were relatively weak and yielded to counter-persuasion, unless there was a secondary task that increased message elaboration of the arguments in the initial message.

*Persistence over time*

According to our approach, attitudes changed by minorities should be relatively strong and should persist over time compared to attitudes changed by majorities, which are relatively weak (see also Crano & Chen, 1998; Moscovici, Mugny, & Papastamou, 1981; Tafani, Souchet,

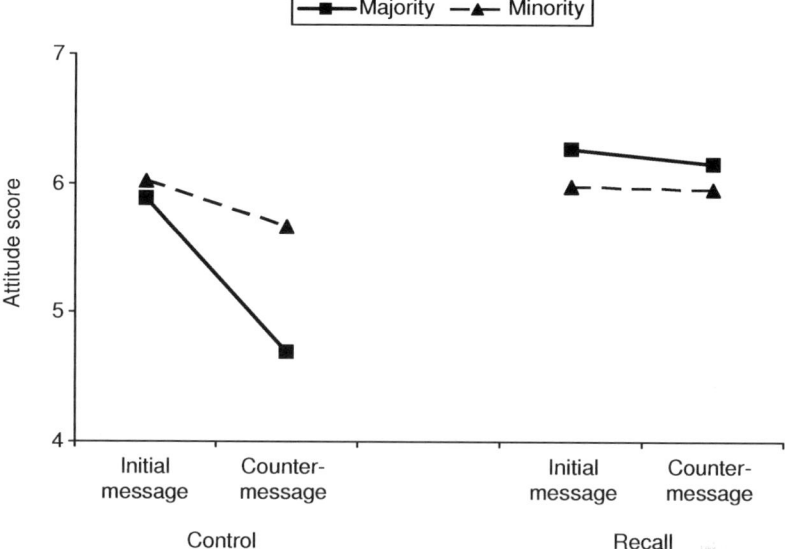

*Figure 8.3* Mean attitude scores as a function of measurement time, source status and recall condition (Martin et al., 2008, Experiment 2). *Note*: Greater agreement with the source is reflected by *high* scores on the initial message and *low* scores on the counter-message.

Codaccioni, & Mugny, 2003). We tested this hypothesis in an experiment in which participants were exposed to persuasive arguments against a voluntary euthanasia message (Martin & Hewstone, 2009a). Attitudes were assessed on three occasions: prior to reading the message (pre-test), immediately after reading the message (post-test: immediate), and two weeks after the experiment (post-test: delayed). On each occasion attitudes were measured to both voluntary euthanasia (direct attitude) and abortion (indirect attitude). It should, perhaps, be emphasized that the issue of abortion was not mentioned in the voluntary-euthanasia arguments and that piloting had shown a small, but reliable, correlation between the two attitudes.

There was a reliable two-way interaction between source status and measurement time for both the direct and indirect attitudes. For the direct attitude, the majority led to an immediate change in attitudes towards its position (pre-test vs. post-test: immediate) but attitudes returned to their pre-test level two weeks later. In the case of the minority, there was a small immediate effect on attitudes (between pre-test and post-test: immediate), but there was a larger shift to the minority position two weeks after message exposure. For the indirect attitude, there was no change over time for the majority source. In the case of the minority, however, there was a reliable change towards the indirect attitude after exposure to the message and this change persisted over time. Taken together, these results suggest that the majority induced compliance to its position, without detailed message processing, which resulted in an immediate change to the direct attitude that did not persist over time, and had no effect on the indirect attitude. The minority source led to elaborative processing that brought about a delayed change in direct attitudes, and an immediate change to the indirect attitude that persisted over time. This different pattern of effects suggests minorities lead to elaborative message processing that results in conversion (Moscovici, 1980) to the source's position that is most noticeable on indirect attitudes (i.e., ones related, but not specifically linked, to the minority's arguments).

*Predicting behaviours*

The final area of research concerns the impact of majority and minority influence on intentions to behave in line with one's attitudes (behavioural intentions) and on actual attitude-relevant behaviours. It should be noted that very few studies have investigated changes to people's behaviours as a result of majority and minority influence (see Falomir-Picastor, Butera, & Mugny, 2002; Joule, Mugny, & Pérez, 1988, but note that these studies did not explicitly manipulate both majority- and minority-source status). Applied to the context of majority–minority influence, the prediction is that if attitude change following majority influence is due to non-elaborative processing, whereas attitude change following minority influence is due to elaborative processing, then attitude-consistent behavioural intentions should be expressed more strongly following a minority- than a majority-endorsed message.

We tested this hypothesis in an experiment in which participants were exposed to a counter-attitudinal message (anti-voluntary euthanasia) attributed to either a numerical majority or minority (Martin, Martin, Smith, & Hewstone, 2007b, Experiment 1). After reading the message, participants indicated their intention to engage in an attitude-consistent behaviour (in this case their willingness to sign a 'living will', which is a form of advance directive that stipulates that, in specified circumstances, medical procedures should not be used to keep the signer alive). If participants are influenced by the anti-voluntary euthanasia message (i.e., their attitude becomes *less* in favour of voluntary euthanasia) then they should be *less* likely to engage in an attitude-consistent behaviour (i.e., *less* likely to sign a living will). In addition, the above relationship should occur only when participants had been influenced by the message. When participants were not influenced by the message, presumably because they had not elaborated on the source's arguments, we did not expect any effect of source status on behavioural intentions. We examined this hypothesis by dividing the sample into those who did, and did not, change their attitudes to the message.

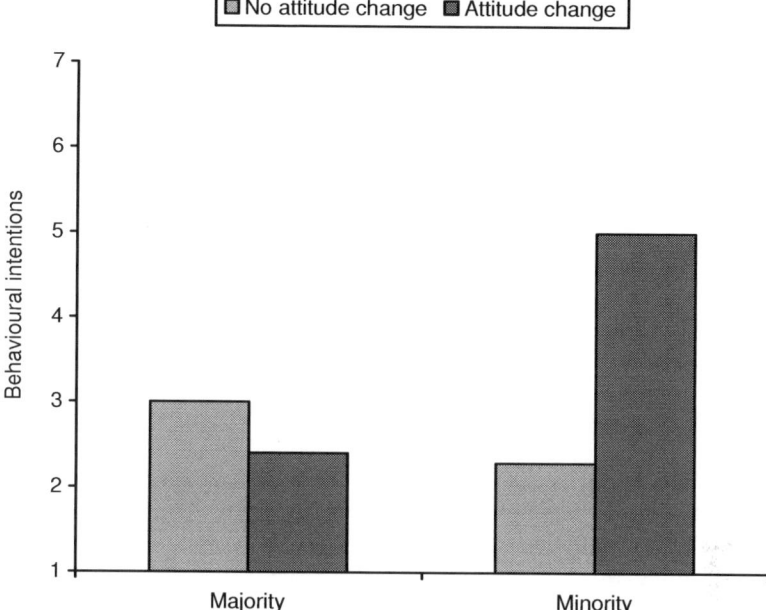

*Figure 8.4* Mean behavioural intention scores as a function of attitude change and source status (Martin et al., 2007b, Experiment 1).

As predicted there was a reliable two-way interaction between source status and whether attitudes had been changed or not (see Figure 8.4). When participants did not change their attitude there was no difference between the majority and minority conditions in their attitude-consistent intentions. This is probably because in these conditions non-elaborative processing occurred. However, when participants were influenced by the source (i.e., became less in favour of voluntary euthanasia), those in the minority condition reported higher attitude-consistent behavioural intentions (i.e., they were less likely to sign a living will) than did those in the majority condition. Although the majority source resulted in the same amount of attitude change as the minority source, the change in attitude was due to non-elaborative processing (heuristic acceptance of the majority without considering their arguments) and thus it was 'weak' in nature and therefore did not affect attitude-consistent behavioural intentions.

This last experiment used a self-report measure of behavioural intention and it is possible that this measure might be affected by participants' reported attitude scores (i.e., the behavioural intention is a generalization of the attitude measure). In our next experiment, therefore, we tried to overcome this potential weakness by having a measure of 'actual' behaviour that was taken outside the context of the experimental situation and under conditions of participant anonymity (Martin et al., 2007b, Experiment 2).

We believe that this is the first study of majority and minority influence to include a direct behavioural measure.

The study concerned the introduction of voluntary student unions (VSU) into an Australian university, a policy that we knew, through piloting, most students favoured. We therefore exposed participants to an anti-VSU message. At the end of the experiment participants were given a card, addressed to the Australian Minister for Education, Science and Training, that stated '. . . opposition at any moves to introduce voluntary student unionism at Australian universities'. Participants were told that if they wished they could sign the card and place it in a sealed box (which was located away from the experimental room and on a different floor of the building). Since the message was anti-VSU, and the card voiced opposition to VSU, the act of signing and posting the card constituted an attitude-consistent behaviour. Participants were under no obligation to sign the card, and they received their course credit before they could have posted the card. In addition, participants believed that the experimenter would not know if they had signed the card but, by the use of invisible ink, we were able to identify which participants had posted the card.

We predicted that when the message was of low/medium personal relevance, as in the last experiment, engaging in an attitude-consistent behaviour would be most likely for those in the minority condition who changed their attitude. This is indeed what was found (see Figure 8.5). When participants had not changed their attitude towards VSU, there was no effect of source status on the number of people engaging in the behaviour. However, when participants had changed their attitude, they were more likely to sign and return the card when exposed to a minority, compared to a majority, source. Once again the level of attitude change to the anti-VSU message was the same for those in the majority- and the minority-source conditions. However, whereas majority-induced non-elaborative processing led to compliance to the message (weak attitude) that did not affect attitude-relevant behaviours, the minority-induced elaborative processing led to conversion to the message (strong attitude) and change in attitude-related behaviours.

*Summary*

The studies reviewed in this section investigated the resistance and persistence of attitudes, and the prediction of behaviour induced by majority versus minority messages. The results showed that majority messages were vulnerable to a second counter-message, whereas minority messages resisted the counter-message, due to elaborative processing of the initial message (and also affected an indirect measure of attitude). However, when we experimentally increased elaboration of the message the resultant attitudes were strong and resisted counter-persuasion, for both the majority and minority source. Further evidence of stronger attitudes in the minority

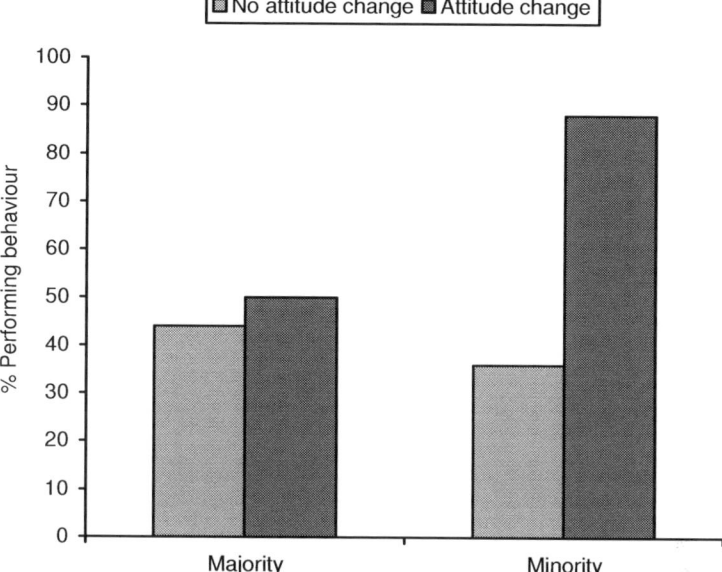

*Figure 8.5* Percentage of participants performing behaviour as a function of attitude change and source status (Martin et al., 2007b, Experiment 2).

condition was shown in the persistence paradigm. Whereas majority influence resulted only in immediate compliance, minority influence persisted in a two-week follow-up for both direct and indirect attitudes. Finally, we showed a greater impact of the minority than the majority source on attitude-consistent behavioural intentions and also behaving in a manner consistent with the position argued by the minority. In combination, these results, across a number of paradigms exploring various consequences of attitudes, support the view that minority sources engender stronger resultant attitudes than do majority sources.

## Conclusions and future directions

Our research perspective has asked the question: What is the nature of the attitudes that have been formed following majority and minority influence in terms of their attitude strength? There are two major reasons why we have examined the nature of attitudes that are formed following majority and minority influence. First, the nature of attitudes following persuasion gives a good clue as to how these attitudes were formed. Research from the persuasion literature shows that strong attitudes result from systematic processing of the source's arguments, while weak attitudes arise from non-systematic processing or from the adoption of a simple heuristic cue (Petty, 1995). Therefore, examining the nature of attitudes (strong vs. weak) following majority and minority influence can provide an insight into the processing strategies that led to them. Second, virtually all research in this area has examined the immediate impact of majority and minority influence and has not considered the consequences of changed attitudes in terms of the construct of attitude strength. By examining the strength of attitudes we are able to look ahead in time to see how people might deal with attempts to influence them back to their original position (counter-persuasion), how their attitudes might change over time (persistence), and how their attitudes might lead them to behave (predict behaviour).

To summarize, we have found, in situations we define as requiring intermediate elaboration (Martin & Hewstone, 2008), that majority sources lead to non-elaborative processing and compliance to the majority position, while minority sources lead to elaborative processing and conversion to the minority position. As a result of engaging in different processing strategies, majority and minority sources lead to weak and strong attitudes, respectively, and these attitudes differentially resist counter-persuasion,[1] persist over time, and predict behaviour.

The results of these studies, and many others not reviewed here for reasons of space (see Martin & Hewstone, 2008), are integrated in our theoretical model of majority and minority influence, which we outlined earlier with respect to situations of intermediate elaboration. In addition the model makes specific predictions concerning the effects of source status at both low and high levels of elaboration. To date we have not conducted research examining the consequences of attitudes at low levels of elaboration (where we would predict non-elaborative processing for both sources with heuristic acceptance of the majority position). However, we do have additional evidence when the elaboration context is high. When the elaboration context is high the results support the model by showing that both majority and minority sources lead to strong attitudes that resist counter-persuasion (e.g., by using a secondary task; Martin & Hewstone, 2009b), persist over time (by examining those high in need for cognition; Martin & Hewstone, 2009a), and predict behaviour (e.g., by examining those who report the topic as being high in personal relevance; Martin et al., 2007b, Experiment 2).

Another fruitful avenue for future research is to include key control conditions to further examine the nature of the underlying processes determining attitude strength. As Martin and Hewstone (2008) noted, there has been a '. . . curious absence of control conditions' (p. 302) in majority- and minority-influence research (see Erb, Bohner, Schmälzle, & Rank, 1998, for an exception). Part of the reason may be due to the methodological difficulties associated with control conditions that present participants with a persuasive message but no source information. In the absence of source information (i.e., the number of people who agree with the message), participants could use the 'false-consensus effect' (Ross, Greene, & House, 1977)—the assumption that the majority of people share the same opinions as oneself, and that the minority of people have different opinions from oneself. Since studies in majority and minority influence typically employ a counter-attitudinal message, in the absence of source information we would expect participants to *assume* that it is a minority position. Thus, it might not be an exaggeration to claim that the vast literature on persuasion and attitude-change research, which has deliberately employed counter-attitudinal messages, has, in fact, unwittingly been studying minority influence!

The benefits of including control conditions are outlined in detail by Stroebe (Chapter 9, this volume). One control condition in particular is of relevance to the current research and that concerns a *message-only* condition (in which participants receive the message arguments but no source information). Stroebe argues that without a message-only condition it is difficult to determine whether any biasing effects are due to the majority source inducing a positive bias (i.e., more positive than the control) or the minority source inducing a negative bias (i.e., less positive than the control), or both. In the context of the current research programme, we have argued that majority status leads to non-elaborative processing of the message, which results in weak attitudes that are unable to resist a counter-message. If this is the case then one would expect attitudes formed following majority influence to yield more to a counter-message compared to attitudes formed following a message-only control condition. If there is no difference between these conditions, in terms of yielding to a counter-message, then it would not support the idea that majority status itself promotes non-elaborative processing.

Although none of the studies described in this chapter employed a message-only control condition, we have additional data from a study that employed such a condition (Martin & Hewstone, 2009b). This study was a replication of one of the studies described above using the counter-persuasion paradigm. In addition to the majority and minority conditions we also included a message-only control condition in which participants read the same arguments as did those in the source conditions, but did not receive any information concerning the numerical support of those arguments. We were careful to include in the analysis only participants who believed that approximately 50% of the population agreed with the message, to avoid including those participants who might have succumbed to the false-consensus bias described above. The pattern of results for the majority and minority conditions was similar to our previous study (Martin et al., 2003, Experiment 2) namely, attitudes following majority and minority influence yielded to and resisted the counter-message, respectively. Crucially, attitudes formed in the message-only condition also yielded to the counter-message *but not to the same extent as those formed following majority influence.* In other words, majority status led to greater yielding to the counter-message than did a message-only condition, further strengthening our claim that majorities lead to non-elaborative processing, resulting in weak attitudes.

The research that we have described in this chapter assesses the strength of attitudes following majority and minority influence by the extent to which they can resist counter-persuasion, persist over time and predict behaviour. Krosnick and Petty (1995) have identified a fourth aspect of strong attitudes, in that strong attitudes can guide information processing, i.e., a strong attitude can bias the manner in which people think about the topic of the message. To some extent the other three aspects of attitude strength (resistance, persistence and predicting behaviour) are all dependent upon biasing people's thoughts, but this additional feature focuses on the interpretation of future attitude-relevant material. While there has not been a great deal of research examining this feature of attitude strength, some studies have shown that strong attitudes can bias information processing of attitude-relevant information (Houston & Fazio, 1989; Lord, Ross, & Lepper, 1979). We intend to conduct research on this final consequence of attitude strength in the future.

## Epilogue

A story of the 1952 US presidential campaign tells of a woman who rushed up to candidate Adlai Stevenson after one of his speeches and gushed, 'You have captured the vote of every thinking person in America!' Apparently Mr Stevenson was not encouraged by her enthusiasm, and he replied, 'Ma'am, we need a majority!'[2] This story neatly captures the idea, central to the research reviewed in this chapter, that minorities, in our case people exposed to minority rather than majority sources, are associated with relatively more *thinking* than is true for majorities.

The consequences of minority-led influence, which we have outlined in this chapter, have a number of implications for a wide variety of social-influence processes, including formation and change of attitudes and opinions in a range of settings from persuasion, through group processes, to the political arena. Across these settings, the broader achievement of minorities, and their social utility, is that they encourage a deeper processing, that has real consequences and is likely to result in better thought-out attitudinal positions. Francis Bacon (1625/1996) advised, 'Read not to contradict and confute, nor to believe and take for granted, nor to find talk and discourse, but to weigh and consider.' Minorities, rather than majorities, are more likely to encourage recipients of their messages to 'weigh and consider', and, as we have shown in this chapter, this deeper processing has several important consequences.

## Notes

1   We should also acknowledge that recent research by Tormala, DeSensi, and Petty (2007; see also Tormala, Petty, & DeSensi, Chapter 5, this volume) offers a potentially different interpretation based on their metacogntitive framework to

resistance to persuasion. They found that after initially resisting a minority message, attitudes became weaker and they were less resistant to the second message. However, a key difference between Tormala et al.'s (2007) studies and our own studies is that in their studies participants *resisted* the initial message whereas in our studies participants were *persuaded* by the initial message. In our approach we are specifically interested in the attitudes that are formed following majority and minority influence, but we also recognize that whether participants resist or are persuaded by the initial message might moderate the effects of the counter-message.

2 Story reported in *The New York Times*, 25 June 2000.

# References

Abelson, R. P. (1988). Conviction. *American Psychologist, 43,* 267–275.

Bacon, F. (1625). Of studies in: Essays or counsels, civil and moral. *The major works* (pp. 439–440). Oxford: Oxford University Press (1996 edn., Ed. B. Vickers).

Baker, S. M., & Petty, R. E. (1994). Majority and minority influence: Source–position imbalance as a determinant of message scrutiny. *Journal of Personality and Social Psychology, 67,* 5–19.

Bassili, J. N. (1996). Meta-judgmental versus operative indexes of psychological attributes: The case of measures of attitude strength. *Journal of Personality and Social Psychology, 71,* 637–653.

Cacioppo, J. T., & Petty, R. E. (1982). The need for cognition. *Journal of Personality and Social Psychology, 42,* 116–131.

Chaiken, S., Liberman, A., & Eagly, A. H. (1989). Heuristic and systematic information processing within and beyond the persuasion context. In J. S. Uleman & J. A. Bargh (Eds.), *Unintended thought: Limits of awareness, intention and thought* (pp. 212–252). New York: Guilford Press.

Crano, W. D., & Chen, X. (1998). The leniency contract and persistence of majority and minority influence. *Journal of Personality and Social Psychology, 74,* 1437–1450.

Eagly, A. H., & Chaiken, S. (1993). *The psychology of attitudes.* Fort Worth, TX: Harcourt Brace Jovanovich.

Eaton, A. A., Majka, E. A., & Visser, P. S. (2008). Emerging perspective on the structure and function of attitude strength. In W. Stroebe & M. Hewstone (Eds.), *European review of social psychology* (Vol. 19, pp. 165–201). Hove, UK: Psychology Press.

Erb, H.-P., Bohner, G., Schmälzle, K., & Rank, S. (1998). Beyond conflict and discrepancy: Cognitive bias in minority and majority influence. *Personality and Social Psychology Bulletin, 24,* 620–633.

Falomir-Picastor, J. M., Butera, F., & Mugny, G. (2002). Persuasive constraint and expert versus non-expert influence in intention to quit smoking. *European Journal of Social Psychology, 32,* 209–222.

Fazio, R. H. (1995). Attitudes as object-evaluation associations: Determinants, consequences, and correlates of attitude accessibility. In R. E. Petty & J. A. Krosnick (Eds.), *Attitude strength: Antecedents and consequences* (pp. 247–282). Hillsdale, NJ: Lawrence Erlbaum Associates, Inc.

Haugtvedt, C. P., & Petty, R. E. (1992). Personality and persuasion: Need for cognition moderates the persistence and resistance of attitude change. *Journal of Personality and Social Psychology, 63,* 308–319.

Haugtvedt, C. P., & Wegener, D. T. (1994). Message order effects in persuasion: An attitude strength perspective. *Journal of Consumer Research, 21,* 205–218.

Holland, R., Verplanken, B., & van Knippenberg, A. (2002). On the nature of attitude–behavior relations: The strong guide, the weak follow. *European Journal of Social Psychology, 32,* 869–876.

Houston, D. A., & Fazio, R. H. (1989). Biased processing as a function of attitude accessibility: Making objective judgments subjectively. *Social Cognition, 7,* 51–66.

Johnson, B. T., & Eagly, A. H. (1989). Effects of involvement on persuasion: A meta-analysis. *Psychological Bulletin, 106,* 290–314.

Joule, R. V., Mugny, G., & Pérez, J. A. (1988). When a compliance without pressure strategy fails due to a minority dissenter. A case of 'behavioral conversion'. *European Journal of Social Psychology, 18,* 531–535.

Krosnick, J. A., & Abelson, R. P. (1992). The case for measuring attitude strength in surveys. In J. Tanur (Ed.), *Questions about survey questions* (pp. 177–203). New York: Russell Sage.

Krosnick, J. A., Boninger, D. S., Chuang, Y. C., Berent, M. K., & Carnot, C. (1993). Attitude strength: One construct or many related constructs? *Journal of Personality and Social Psychology, 65,* 1132–1151.

Krosnick, J. A., & Petty, R. E. (1995). Attitude strength: An overview. In R. E. Petty & J. A. Krosnick (Eds.), *Attitude strength: Antecedents and consequences* (pp. 1–24). Hillsdale, NJ: Lawrence Erlbaum Associates, Inc.

Leippe, M. R., & Elkin, R. A. (1987). When motives clash: Issue involvement and response involvement as determinants of persuasion. *Journal of Personality and Social Psychology, 52,* 269–278.

Lord, C. G., Ross, L., & Lepper, M. R. (1979). Biased assimilation and attitude polarization: The effects of prior theories on subsequently considered evidence. *Journal of Personality and Social Psychology, 37,* 2098–2109.

Maass, A., & Clark, R. D., III (1983). Internalization versus compliance: Differential processes underlying minority influence and conformity. *European Journal of Social Psychology, 13,* 197–215.

Martin, R., & Hewstone, M. (2008). Majority versus minority influence, message processing and attitude change: The source–context–elaboration model. In M. Zanna (Ed.), *Advances in experimental social psychology* (Vol. 40, pp. 237–326). San Diego, CA: Academic Press.

Martin, R., & Hewstone, M. (2009a). *Attitude persistence to persuasive messages as a function of majority and minority source status.* Manuscript under review.

Martin, R., & Hewstone, M. (2009b). *The use of a secondary task to vary resistance to a counter-message following majority and minority influence.* Manuscript in preparation.

Martin, R., Hewstone, M., & Martin, P. Y. (2003). Resistance to persuasive messages as a function of majority and minority source status. *Journal of Experimental Social Psychology, 39,* 585–593.

Martin, R., Hewstone, M., & Martin, P. Y. (2007a). Systematic and heuristic processing of majority- and minority-endorsed messages: The effects of varying outcome relevance and levels of orientation on attitude and message processing. *Personality and Social Psychology Bulletin, 33,* 43–56.

Martin, R., Hewstone, M., & Martin, P. Y. (2008). Majority versus minority influence: The role of message processing in determining resistance to counter-persuasion. *European Journal of Social Psychology, 38,* 16–34.

Martin, R., Martin, P. Y., Smith, J., & Hewstone, M. (2007b). Majority and minority influence and prediction of behavioral intentions and behavior. *Journal of Experimental Social Psychology, 43,* 763–771.

Moscovici, S. (1976). *Social influence and social change.* London: Academic Press.

Moscovici, S. (1980). Toward a theory of conversion behavior. In L. Berkowitz (Ed.), *Advances in experimental social psychology* (Vol. 13, pp. 209–239). New York: Academic Press.

Moscovici, S., Mugny, G., & Papastamou, S. (1981). 'Sleeper effect' et/ou effet minoritaire? Etude théorique et expérimentale de l'influence sociale à retardement. *Cahiers de Psychologie Cognitive, 1,* 199–221.

Mugny, G. (1982). *The power of minorities.* London: Academic Press.

Mugny, G., Butera, F., Sanchez-Mazas, M., & Pérez, J. A. (1995). Judgements in conflict: The conflict elaboration theory of social influence. In B. Boothe, R. Hirsig, A. Helminger, B. Meier, & R. Volkart (Eds.), *Perception–evaluation–interpretation* (pp. 160–168). Göttingen, Germany: Hogrefe & Huber.

Nemeth, C. (1986). Differential contributions of majority and minority influence. *Psychological Review, 93,* 23–32.

Petty, R. E. (1995). Attitude change. In A. Tesser (Ed.), *Advanced social psychology* (pp. 195–255). New York: McGraw-Hill.

Petty, R. E., & Cacioppo, J. T. (1984). Source factors and the elaboration likelihood model of persuasion. In T. C. Kinnear (Ed.), *Advances in consumer research* (Vol. 11, pp. 668–672). Provo, UT: Association for Consumer Research.

Petty, R. E., & Cacioppo, J. T. (1986). *Communication and persuasion: Central and peripheral routes to attitude change.* New York: Springer-Verlag.

Petty, R. E., Haugtvedt, C., & Smith, S. M. (1995). Elaboration as a determinant of attitude strength: Creating attitudes that are persistent, resistant, and predictive of behavior. In R. E. Petty & J. A. Krosnick (Eds.), *Attitude strength: Antecedents and consequences* (pp. 93–130). Hillsdale, NJ: Lawrence Erlbaum Associates, Inc.

Petty, R. E., & Wegener, D. T. (1998). Attitude change: Multiple roles for persuasion variables In D. T. Gilbert, S. T. Fiske, & G. Lindzey (Eds.), *The handbook of social psychology* (4th ed., pp. 323–390). Boston: McGraw-Hill.

Pomerantz, E. M., Chaiken, S., & Tordesillas, R. S. (1995). Attitude strength and resistance processes. *Journal of Personality and Social Psychology, 69,* 408–419.

Prislin, R. (1996). Attitude stability and attitude strength: One is enough to make it stable. *European Journal of Social Psychology, 26,* 447–477.

Raden, D. (1985). Strength-related attitude dimensions. *Social Psychology Quarterly, 48,* 312–330.

Ross, L., Greene, D., & House, P. (1977). The 'false consensus effect': An egocentric bias in social perception and attribution processes. *Journal of Experimental Social Psychology, 13,* 279–301.

Sobel, M. E. (1982). Asymptotic intervals for indirect effects in structural equations models. In S. Leinhart (Ed.), *Sociological methodology* (pp. 290–312). San Francisco: Jossey-Bass.

Tafani, E., Souchet, L., Codaccioni, C., & Mugny, G. (2003). Influences majoritaire et minoritaire sur la représentation sociale de la drogue. *Nouvelle Revue de Psychologie Sociale, 2,* 343–354.

Tormala, Z. L., DeSensi, V. L., & Petty, R. E. (2007). Resisting persuasion by illegitimate means: A meta-cognitive perspective on minority influence. *Personality and Social Psychology Bulletin, 33,* 354–367.

Verplanken, B. (1989). Involvement and need for cognition as moderators of beliefs–attitude–intention consistency. *British Journal of Social Psychology, 28,* 115–122.

Visser, P. S., Bizer, G. Y., & Krosnick, J. A. (2006). Exploring the latent structure of strength-related attitude attributes. In M. Zanna (Ed.), *Advances in experimental social psychology* (Vol. 38, pp. 1–67). San Diego, CA: Academic Press.

Visser, P. S., & Cooper, J. (2003). Attitude change. In M. A. Hogg & J. Cooper (Eds.), *Sage handbook of social psychology* (pp. 211–231). London: Sage.

Visser, P. S., & Krosnick, J. A. (1998). Development of attitude strength over the life cycle: Surge and decline. *Journal of Personality and Social Psychology, 75,* 1389–1410.

Wood, W., Lundgren, S., Ouellette, J. A., Busceme, S., & Blackstone, T. (1994). Minority influence: A meta-analytic review of social influence processes. *Psychological Bulletin, 115,* 323–345.

Wu, C., & Shaffer, D. R. (1987). Susceptibility to persuasive appeals as a function of source credibility and prior experience with the attitude object. *Journal of Personality and Social Psychology, 52,* 677–688.

# 9 Majority and minority influence and information processing: A theoretical and methodological analysis

*Wolfgang Stroebe*
*Utrecht University, The Netherlands*

It is almost a truism that the groups we belong to play an important role in shaping our beliefs and attitudes. And yet, for most of their short history, the study of persuasion and attitude change developed almost independently from research on social or group influence. The two fields used different stimulus materials and developed different theoretical perspectives. Research on persuasion studied the impact of complex messages on individual attitudes. In contrast, studies of majority/minority influence focused mainly on the effect that knowledge of the judgements of other group members had on an individual member's judgement of simple physical stimuli (e.g., Asch, 1956; Moscovici, 1980; Moscovici & Faucheux, 1972; Sherif, 1936). Only during the last few decades has there been a convergence between the two research traditions, with students of group influence increasingly using complex messages in their research (e.g., Baker & Petty, 1994; Maass & Clark, 1983; Mackie, 1987).

Since there appeared to be clear parallels between the theories of conversion developed by Moscovici and colleagues (Moscovici, 1980; Moscovici & Faucheux, 1972) and dual-process theories of persuasion (Chaiken, 1980; Petty & Cacioppo, 1986), researchers had high hopes that the application of theories and methods of persuasion research to the study of majority and minority influence would clarify the relationship between majority and minority influence and patterns of information processing. These hopes remained largely unfulfilled. The application of dual-process theories to the study of minority and majority influence has resulted in an immensely complex set of findings that defies attempts at theoretical integration (e.g., de Vries, de Dreu, Gordijn, & Schuurman, 1996; Martin & Hewstone, 2001a). In this chapter, I will try to review this research, highlight the inconsistencies, and point at some methodological shortcomings that, in my view, greatly contributed to this confusion. Based on dual-process theories, I will finally discuss a number of theoretical principles, which might help to account for some of contradictions that emerged from this review.

## Early studies of minority influence

Stimulated by the classic studies of Sherif (1936) and Asch (1956), research on social influence focused exclusively on the ability of majorities to induce conformity in individual group members. It was one of the great contributions to social psychology that Moscovici argued that social influence is not a one-way street and that, under certain conditions, minorities can also influence majorities. In two influential chapters Moscovici (Moscovici, 1980; Moscovici & Faucheux, 1972) presented empirical evidence for minority influence and also developed two theories to account for these effects.

Mosocovici and Faucheux (1972) argued that the one-sided focus on majority influence prevalent in American research on social influence should be replaced by the acceptance that influence processes in groups are reciprocal. Thus, majorities influence minorities, but minorities can also influence majorities. They argued that the influence of the minority is caused by their *behavioural style*. The most important behavioural style is consistency, both intrapersonal consistency across time and situations and interpersonal consistency (i.e., consensus). Thus, to be effective, minority members have to stick to their position and agree with each other. By being consistent, the minority is not only visible and attracts attention, minority members also signal that they are confident in the validity of their position, committed to this position, and unlikely to move. This behavioural style creates a conflict in the majority and induces intensive cognitive activity in the members of the majority. These authors further speculated that it was this intensive cognitive work, induced by the disagreement with the minority, that was responsible for the fact that minority influence resulted in a modification of their own perception.

Moscovici (1980) developed these ideas further in what became known as his dual-process or conversion theory. The starting point of this theory is again the assumption that all influence attempts create a conflict between individuals' wish to be appear consistent and remain socially acceptable to others and their need to make sense of their physical and social environment. Although both majority and minority sources might induce an informational conflict, it is finally the motive to be accepted and liked by the majority members that determines conflict resolution in the case of the majority. This analysis of majority influence corresponds with the mode of normative social influence, as described by Deutsch and Gerard (1955). In contrast, consistent minorities induce a 'validation process, that is an examination of the relations between its response and the object or reality' (Moscovici, 1980, p. 215). Thus, the persistence of the minority on their deviant position induces an informational conflict in individuals. Although they want to be liked and accepted by the majority, they also would like to hold a correct perspective on reality, and the persistence of the minority on their deviant position induces a goal conflict between the goals to be liked and to be correct. The minority point of view will therefore be sub-jected to relentless criticism, it will attract many more counter-arguments than a position expressed by a majority, but in the course of this criticism, some members of the majority will be converted, and this 'conversion produced by a minority implies a real change of judgments or opinions, not just an individual's assuming in private a response he has given in public' (Moscovici, 1980, p. 217).

Empirical tests of conversion theory resulted in a rather mixed pattern (see Martin & Hewstone, 2001a; Wood, Lundgren, Ouellette, Busceme, & Blackstone, 1994, for reviews). One of the most provocative findings has been Moscovici and Personnaz's (1980) claim that a minority but not a majority can cause perceptual conversion. Using a colour-perception para-digm, Moscovici and Personnaz reported that individuals who had been exposed to a consistent minority judging blue colour slides as green, were not only more likely to judge the blue slides as green, but also tended to reveal a shift in their perceptual after-effects to the direction of the com-plementary colour of green (rather than blue). Since such changes in after-effects (i.e., after-images shifting to the complement of the slide advocated by a source) only occurred in response to minority but not majority influence, this study offered the strongest support of conversion theory.

Unfortunately, attempts to replicate these findings have resulted in conflicting patterns. Whereas Moscovici and colleagues have reported repli-cations of these findings (e.g., Moscovici & Personnaz, 1986; Personnaz, 1981) other researchers were less successful (e.g., Doms & van Avermaet, 1980; Martin, 1995, 1998; Sorrentino, King, & Leo, 1980). Furthermore, a recent review by Martin and Hewstone (2001b) has again highlighted many methodological problems with this paradigm and implied that the after-effect findings are the result of methodological artefacts.

## The impact of minority and majority influence on persuasion

With the rise of dual-process theories of persuasion (e.g., heuristic-systematic model: Chaiken, 1980; Chen & Chaiken, 1999; elaboration-likelihood model: Petty & Cacioppo, 1986; Petty & Wegener, 1999), the focus of attitude change research had broadened to include information processing as well as outcomes.[1] This was made possible by the fact that these theories also provided the methodology to assess information pro-cessing more directly (e.g., thought listing; manipulation of argument quality). According to these theories recipients of a persuasive message can base their evaluation of the validity of that message either on careful scrutiny of the arguments contained in that message (i.e., systematic processing) or on peripheral aspects of the message, such as relevant char-acteristics of the communicator (e.g., expertise, trustworthiness, attractive-ness), the number of arguments contained in a message or whether the position advocated in the message is supported by a majority or a minority.

Systematic processing based on thoughtful evaluation of the validity of the arguments contained in a message is effortful and requires ability and relevant knowledge. Dual-process theories therefore assume that people will engage in systematic processing of a message only if they are motivated to do so *and* possess the necessary ability/knowledge. The most frequently studied determinant of processing motivation has been personal relevance. People have been shown to be more willing to scrutinize message arguments, if the issue at stake was of personal importance (e.g., Petty, Cacioppo, & Goldman, 1981). However, there are also other motives, which could induce individuals to engage in message-relevant thinking, such as curiosity or simply the wish to know things (e.g., Cacioppo & Petty, 1982). When individuals use peripheral cues to evaluate the validity of a message, they are assumed to rely on simple heuristics or decision rules to assess the validity of an argument (e.g., consensus implies correctness, therefore the majority must be right; expert opinions must be valid). This type of processing has therefore been referred to as heuristic processing (e.g., Chaiken, 1980; Chen & Chaiken, 1999).

When recipients are highly motivated and able to systematically process a message, their acceptance or rejection of the position argued in the message will mainly be determined by the quality of the arguments contained in the message. The less they are motivated or able to process the message, the less they will be influenced by argument quality and the more they will be affected by heuristic cues. However, as discussed below, heuristic cues can affect attitudes (and add to the impact of arguments) even under conditions that facilitate systematic processing (e.g., if the arguments contained in a message do not allow recipients to draw clear-cut conclusions; see Chaiken & Maheswaran, 1994).

Information about whether a given attitude position is held by a majority or minority (i.e., source status) can be considered *consensus* information, which recipients of a message can use as a heuristic cue in their evaluation of the validity of the position advocated. Empirical tests of the predictions of dual-process theories combined the methods of research on minority/ majority effects with those of research on persuasion. Participants in these studies were exposed to persuasive communications, with argument quality manipulated in some of these studies. Although source status was sometimes defined through group membership, most studies manipulated majority/ minority influence numerically through information that a majority or a minority of a relevant reference group had agreed with the positions argued in the persuasive communication.

The early applications of dual-process theories of persuasion to the study of minority and majority influence were guided by main-effect models that assumed that one source leads to deeper message processing than the other (Martin & Hewstone, 2001a). Later, contingency models were proposed, which assumed that the impact of source status on information processing would be moderated by variables such as the personal relevance of the attitude issue, the source/position constellation, or the prior attitude of the recipients of a communication.

## Main-effect models

Maass and Clark (1983), who were the first to apply dual-process theories of attitude change to minority and majority influence, translated the language of Moscovici's conversion theory directly into that of dual-process theories, suggesting that minorities induce active thinking (i.e., systematic processing) leading to permanent attitude change, whereas majorities trigger heuristic information processing, leading only to public compliance. Respondents, who had been selected to hold relatively neutral attitudes towards gay rights, were provided with a transcript of a group discussion on gay rights. In this discussion a minority of one gave eight arguments in favour of gay rights while a majority of four presented eight statements opposing gay rights (or vice versa). Thus, participants were *simultaneously* exposed to minority and majority influence.[2] In order to highlight the uncompromising consistency of the minority, which Moscovici considered a key aspect of their influence, Maass and Clark added a one-sentence statement to the end of the summary, which explained that the minority individual did not change her opinion during the course of the discussion. According to Kelley's (1973) augmentation principle, this should trigger the perception of the minority individual as firmly committed to his/her position. Subsequently, participants were asked to indicate their own position on gay rights, expecting it either to be publicly disclosed or to remain private. In support of their theoretical predictions, Maass and Clark (1983) found that minority sources induced greater attitude change than majorities when the attitude measure was taken in private, whereas a greater majority effect was found when respondents believed that their attitudes would be disclosed in public. Although there was no source effect on the quantity of thoughts, there was a tendency for minorities to trigger thoughts that were supportive of their position. Furthermore, hierarchical regression analysis conducted to assess mediation resulted in a pattern that was consistent with the assumption that private acceptance but not public compliance was mediated by the message recipients' generation of arguments and counterarguments.

Although this pattern of results was supportive of the predictions offered by Maass and Clark (1983), it is actually quite puzzling, if one looks at it from the perspective of the goal conflict created by their experimental manipulations. Maass and Clark (1983) appeared to have induced a conflict in their research participants, between the goals to be correct and to be liked by the majority. Given that the attitude issue was not very involving to these research participants, they could have easily resolved this goal conflict by accepting the majority position. Instead, they were privately persuaded by the minority, but avoided the cost of dissent by paying lip service to the majority.

Why did they pay so much attention to the minority so as to engage in systematic thinking on a topic that was not really involving? I suspect that the effect is due to the way in which Maass and Clark (1983) manipulated source status by creating real numerical minorities in a group situation and to the uncompromising consistency of their minority source. It would seem plausible that the valiant minority person in the Maass and Clark (1983) study, who held her own against the onslaught of a majority of four, may have elicited sympathy and therefore private support. The results of a later study by Maass and Clark (1986) tend to support this assumption. In this replication of their earlier study, Maass and Clark (1986) added conditions where participants were only exposed to a majority that was either in favour of or opposed to gay rights. Whereas the dual-message conditions replicated their earlier findings, with greater minority effects in private and greater majority effects in public, participants who were *only* exposed to a majority changed in the direction advocated by the majority on public as well as private measures. Thus, in the absence of a consistent minority, participants accepted the majority position in private as well as in public.

Furthermore Mackie (1987), who like Maass and Clark (1983) exposed her participants simultaneously to *both* majority and minority influence but with a *different* source manipulation, found the majority to have more impact than the minority on both public and private measures. The attitude topics used were either the role of the USA in ensuring the military balance in the West or the disclosure of names of juveniles convicted of crimes as an effective deterrent, thus topics on which female undergraduates were unlikely to hold strong commitments. After having responded to a pre-test opinion measure embedded in a larger questionnaire, participants listened to a discussion between two individuals (confederates). Whereas one confederate presented four strong arguments in favour of the issue being discussed (e.g., military balance), the other presented four strong arguments opposed to it. Majority versus minority position was manipulated by informing participants that in a campus survey either a large majority or a small minority had opposed the issue (or vice versa).[3] Mackie (1987) assessed both attitudes and thoughts privately. In contrast to the findings of Maass and Clark (1983), majority positions in this study stimulated not only more cognitive responding, but responses to the majority were also more positive. Furthermore, respondents disagreeing with the majority position (majority-influence condition) showed greater change than respondents disagreeing with the minority position (minority-influence condition) both on immediate and delayed measures of private change. In fact, the minority appeared to have no significant impact on opinions. Finally, message-content thoughts were a better predictor of attitude change when participants disagreed with the majority than when they disagreed with the minority.

Mackie (1987) interpreted her findings in terms of what she called the 'objective-consensus' view. People accept evidence from consensus (i.e., the majority position) as reflecting objective reality. Although Mackie (1987, p. 42) accepted that the fact that the majority position is seen as reality could also operate as a consensus heuristic and result in superficial heuristic processing, she argued that individuals are more likely to systematically process a majority-endorsed message.

### Contingency theories

Whereas main-effect models posit a direct effect of minority- or majority-source status on depth of information processing, contingency theories assume that this effect is moderated by some other variable.[4] In the context of the present discussion, I will restrict myself to contingency theories that focus on the role of factors that moderate the association between source status and depth of information processing.

### Personal relevance as a moderator

An early contingency approach was introduced by Trost, Maass, and Kenrick (1992), who modified the Maass and Clark (1983) main-effect model by suggesting personal relevance of the attitude issue as a moderator. They used the classic comprehensive exam issue as attitude topic, a proposal that all undergraduate seniors must pass a mandatory comprehensive exam to be eligible for graduation (e.g., Petty & Cacioppo, 1986). Personal relevance was manipulated by recommending that this system would be instituted within a year (high personal relevance) or within nine years (low personal relevance). The persuasive message arguing for this change in exam system was presented as either the majority or the minority position of a focus group of students who had earlier discussed the proposal, but had failed to reach a consensus. Thus, defending a minority position might again be seen as an indication of a deep commitment to one's opinion.

In line with the findings of Maass and Clark (1983), Trost and her colleagues predicted that under low-relevance conditions the message, which contained mainly strong arguments, would be more persuasive when it was attributed to a minority rather than a majority. This prediction was based on the assumptions: (1) that due to its salience and its consistent advocacy of a counter-attitudinal position the minority position would stimulate more careful scrutiny and thus increase processing motivation, and (2) that increased (but unbiased) processing of compelling arguments should result in more persuasion.

Although this prediction is not implausible, strong theoretical arguments could also have been made for the opposite prediction of a more powerful majority influence. For example, one could have argued that since the attitude issue was of low relevance, participants would use type of source as a heuristic cue and therefore change more under majority rather than minority influence. Alternatively, anticipating the position of Baker and Petty (1994), which is discussed below, one could also have reasoned that any change in the exam system was so unpopular that participants might have been surprised to learn that a majority took such an unusual position. Since the fact that a minority was in favour of this unpopular measure would have been less puzzling, participants might have scrutinized arguments more in the majority than the minority condition.

Predictions for the high-relevance condition were less problematic. Under high relevance, Trost and her colleagues expected the majority to be more influential than the minority. 'The negatively biased scrutiny afforded a highly involving and personally costly minority position should lead to attitudinal responses that are more reminiscent of responses to deviates . . . and we expected a highly relevant advocacy to induce resistance to the minority position' (Trost et al., 1992, p. 237). In contrast, the majority advocacy should stimulate minimal processing regardless of the issue relevance. This prediction would also have been consistent with the assumption of dual-process theories that heuristic cues can add to argument-quality effects and influence attitude change even under conditions that favour systematic processing (e.g., Chaiken & Maheswaran, 1994; Petty & Wegener, 1999).

In support of their predictions, Trost and colleagues found the minority to be more persuasive than the majority under low-relevance conditions and the effect to reverse under high-relevance conditions. An analysis of cognitive responses revealed that, whereas relevance did not affect the valence of the cognitive responses to the majority message, the thoughts elicited by a message attributed to the minority were much more negative under high than low relevance.

Several conceptual replications of the study of Trost and her colleagues failed to replicate this pattern. Most importantly, all studies found majorities to have greater persuasive impact than minorities even under conditions of low relevance. In a study conducted in Britain, Martin and Hewstone (2001a, Experiment 5) exposed their student participants to either strong or weak arguments in favour of introducing oral exams. Personal relevance was manipulated by informing respondents that these oral exams would be introduced either in their own or a different college. Source status was manipulated through a fictitious student survey reporting either that a majority or a minority were in favour of introducing oral exams. Martin and Hewstone (2001a) found a source main effect, with the majority being more persuasive than the minority under low and high relevance. In addition, they found an argument-quality effect in the condition of high, but not low, personal relevance and this effect was mediated by the degree of message-congruent thinking.

Crano and Chen (1998) also manipulated source status, argument quality and relevance. They used a message containing strong or weak arguments in favour of the introduction of mandatory university service for which students would not be compensated. Majority versus minority status was manipulated through fictitious information about a student survey. The authors attempted to manipulate personal relevance by claiming that the proposal would either be introduced the following year or seven to eight years later. On the immediate post-test, there were two main effects, namely an effect of source, with the majority having more impact than the minority, and one of argument strength, with strong arguments having more impact than weak arguments. There was no source by argument strength interaction. Furthermore, the manipulation of issue involvement had no effect on attitude change, probably because the issue of introducing compulsory university service was highly threatening, even if planned for a period when the student participants expected to have left their university. Since it is reasonable to assume that Crano and Chen (1998) failed to create a condition of *low personal relevance*, their findings are consistent with those of the high-relevance condition of Martin and Hewstone (2001a).

Kerr (2002) also conducted a close replication of the Trost et al. (1992) study using the comprehensive-exam issue under high- and low-relevance conditions. However, he added two modifications: He manipulated argument quality and type of advocacy, in addition to relevance and source status. The advocacy manipulation was introduced to test the argument of Moscovici and Faucheux (1972) that minorities are most likely to be effective, if they actively oppose the majority at potentially high costs to themselves. In the condition with passive advocacy, the source of the persuasive message (allegedly an essay written by a university student) was never aware of how popular or unpopular his or her position was and did not expect to have to publicly defend that position. In the condition with active advocacy, the student who wrote the essay was aware of the unpopularity of his/her position and expected to have to defend that position in class.

In line with the findings of Martin and Hewstone (2001a) and Crano and Chen (1998), Kerr found a source main effect with the majority source having greater impact than the minority source. Under high relevance, this main effect was only marginally significant, accompanied by a highly significant main effect of argument quality. Under low relevance, the source main effect was qualified by a significant three-way interaction. In the passive-advocacy condition there was neither a source nor an argument-quality effect. In the active-advocacy condition, there was a source main effect (favouring the majority) and an argument-quality main effect.

For attitude issues that are *highly relevant* the pattern of findings obtained in the studies reviewed in this section is fairly consistent. All studies found source main effects (although the effect was only marginal in the study by Kerr, 2002): Majority sources were more persuasive than minority sources for highly relevant attitude issues. Furthermore, the three studies that also manipulated argument quality reported main effects of argument quality. Consistent with predictions based on dual-process theories of persuasion, messages were more persuasive if they communicated a majority rather than a minority position and if they contained high-quality rather than low-quality arguments.

The pattern that emerged under *low relevance* was less consistent, mainly due to the findings of Trost et al. (1992). In contrast to Trost et al. (1992), who found the minority source to be more persuasive than the majority source, Martin and Hewstone (2001a) and Kerr (2002, active-advocacy condition) reported the reverse effect.[5] Their majority sources were more effective than the minorities. In Kerr's (2002, active-advocacy condition) study, this source main effect was qualified by a source by argument-quality interaction, with the minority source being more effective with high- rather than low-quality arguments. It appears that the active advocacy of the minority induced systematic processing even when the issue was of low personal relevance. However, even under these favourable conditions, the minority failed to outperform the majority.[6]

All in all, these findings suggest that increasing relevance increases the influence of argument quality relative to source status. Under low relevance source status acts as a heuristic cue, with majority status being more influential than minority status. However, if the minority behaves in ways that somehow trigger curiosity in research participants, they might attend to the message. Under these conditions, argument quality could become more important than source status even under conditions of low relevance. If, in addition, participants feel pity or admiration for a valiant minority they might take their side on issues that are of little personal relevance to them. This could have happened in the study by Trost and colleagues (1992). As personal relevance increases, the effect of source status is likely to become attenuated, provided the arguments are compelling and leave little doubt in the minds of recipients, who feel competent to evaluate the issue. However, since arguments are often less than compelling, or since participants in experiments are often less than fully motivated, source-status effects might emerge even with attitude issues that are of great personal relevance.

*Source position as a moderator*

In a classic paper, Baker and Petty (1994) suggested the position of the source as another moderator of the impact of source status on information processing and attitude. They argued that it was not the fact that a position was supported by a majority per se that induced systematic processing but rather the combination of a majority endorsement *and* a strongly counter-attitudinal position. Phenomena such as the false-consensus effect (Ross, Greene, & House, 1977) suggest that people expect that their attitudes are shared with the majority of people. It would therefore be surprising if a majority supported a position that one would find somewhat aversive.

Thus, Baker and Petty (1994) predicted that the degree of message processing is determined by the status of the source (majority/minority) *and* by whether the position advocated breaks the consensus heuristic. When the source/position is balanced (i.e., pro-attitudinal majority/counter-attitudinal minority) this situation is not surprising. It is unlikely to result in systematic message processing and the source information will act as a heuristic cue. However, when the source/position is imbalanced (pro-attitudinal minority/counter-attitudinal majority), recipients are surprised and engage in systematic message processing. Baker and Petty (1994) further suggested that, in addition to the violation of expectancies, majority disagreement on an important issue may be perceived as threatening by the individual, stimulating message scrutiny.[7]

Baker and Petty conducted two studies to test these assumptions. In Study 1, students were exposed to a counter-attitudinal message arguing for the introduction of a compulsory community service programme in which students must carry out two years of community service in exchange for maintaining current tuition rates. The message contained either strong or weak arguments and was said to be supported by a majority or a minority of the students polled. There was a main effect of source status with the majority being more influential and a source status by argument quality interaction, with argument quality being more important when the position was endorsed by a majority.

In their second experiment, Baker and Petty (1994) exposed students to a pro-attitudinal message (tuition fee breaks for students who perform university services) or a counter-attitudinal message (dramatic increase in tuition fees for students who do not participate in university service programme), which was endorsed by a majority or a minority and supported by strong or weak arguments. There was again a source main effect (more change when the message was endorsed by a majority) and an argument-quality main effect (more change with strong arguments), but these main effects were moderated by the predicted source by position interaction. When the source–position pairing was imbalanced (majority counter; minority pro), attitude change was mainly due to argument quality. In contrast, when the source–position pairing was balanced (majority pro; minority counter), there was hardly any argument-quality effect and change was mainly due to source status. Under these conditions, attitudes 'following the message with strong arguments ($M = 5.68$) did not differ from attitudes following the message with weak arguments ($M = 5.5$, $F < 1$)' (Baker & Petty, 1994, p. 13). Finally, a mediational analysis indicated that the impact of source on attitude was mediated by thoughts in the imbalanced but not the balanced setting.

It appears that Baker and Petty (1994) assumed, at least implicitly, that the source/position effect would only occur for issues of high personal relevance because, with the issue of university service or tuition increase, Baker and Petty chose a topic that must have been highly involving to the student participants. However, if we accept this, we are confronted with a theoretical problem. Given that the issues addressed in both messages in the Baker and Petty (1994) study were highly involving, one would expect argument-quality effects independent of whether the source/position was balanced or imbalanced. The fact that argument quality had practically no impact on attitudes under balanced conditions, suggests that the information that a majority agrees with one's position (or a minority disagrees) substantially *reduces* respondents' need to scrutinize the arguments in the message. Since Baker and Petty (1994) did *not* include a control group in their design, which exposed respondents to the message without consensus information, it is *not possible* to check this hypothesis with their data.

Two conceptual replications of the Baker and Petty (1994) study have been published by Martin and Hewstone (2003).[8] Both experiments crossed source status (majority vs. minority) with message quality (strong vs. weak arguments). In the first study, high-school students who were either in favour or opposed to 'animal experimentation for scientific and medical research' were exposed to high- or low-quality messages that were either in favour or opposed to animal experimentation. There was a main effect of argument quality, but this effect was qualified by an interaction with source status. Message quality was only effective with a minority but not a majority source.

This pattern of findings is clearly inconsistent with the results reported by Baker and Petty (1994). One potential explanation for this discrepancy could be that the issue of animal experimentation was not really personally relevant for these student participants. A related explanation was suggested by Martin and Hewstone (2003), who argued that the topic used by Baker and Petty was not only personally highly relevant, it was also arguing against the participants' self-interest. In contrast, the animal experimentation issue had no implications for participants' self-interest.

To test this hypothesis, Martin and Hewstone (2003, Study 2) partially replicated the design of the Baker and Petty (1994) study, using either a message that implied no negative personal consequences (opposed to voluntary euthanasia) or one that did (favouring the introduction of the euro to Britain). In each case, students were exposed to strong or weak arguments either opposed to voluntary euthanasia or in favour of Britain adopting the euro. When negative personal outcome was low (voluntary euthanasia) the argument-quality effect occurred only with a minority but not a majority source. In contrast, when the negative personal outcome was high, the pattern of results was reversed: there was an argument-quality effect for the majority but not the minority source.

Unfortunately, the two topics not only differed in their implication for participants' self-interest but also in their personal relevance, with euthanasia being personally much less relevant than the euro. Furthermore, the findings for the euro as well as the comparable results of the two studies reported by Baker and Petty (1994) are inconsistent with the results of three of the studies on the moderating role of personal relevance reported earlier (Crano & Chen, 1998; Kerr, 2002; Martin & Hewstone, 2001a, Experiment 5). Whereas Baker and Petty (1994) and Martin and Hewstone (2003, Study 2) obtained an argument quality by source status interaction, with argument quality affecting attitudes only in the imbalanced condition (a counter-attitudinal position being presented as a majority position), Crano and Chen (1998), Kerr (2002) and Martin and Hewstone (2001a, Experiment 5) reported argument-quality main effects in their high-relevance conditions. Their findings indicate that under high relevance, participants processed the counter-attitudinal message systematically regardless of whether it was attributed to a majority (imbalanced) or a minority source (balanced). One possible explanation could be that personal relevance is higher (or more salient) in studies in which it is specifically manipulated (i.e., Crano & Chen, 1998; Kerr, 2002; Martin & Hewstone, 2001a, Experiment 5) than in research where determination of relevance is left to the perception of participants (i.e., Baker & Petty, 1994; Martin & Hewstone, 2003, Experiment 2). But, until this hypothesis is tested empirically, it is difficult to draw clear conclusions about the role of source position as a moderator of majority/minority influence.

*Prior attitude as a moderator*

A third moderator of the impact of source status on attitudes has been recently introduced by Erb, Bohner, Rank, and Einwiller (2002), who suggested that the impact of source status would be moderated by the prior attitude the recipient of a message held on the attitude issue. Erb and colleagues argued that the perception that 'consensus implies correctness' may only apply to individuals who hold a relatively moderate attitude towards the issue and are not strongly committed to a judgement formed prior to the influence attempt. Under these conditions, when individuals are relatively open-minded, they are likely to apply the consensus implies correctness heuristic and form the initial judgement that the majority is probably correct (or the minority incorrect). These predictions are consistent with assumptions about heuristic processing implied by dual-process theories. More problematic are the predictions Erb and his colleagues (2002) made about the effort individuals with moderate attitudes invest in processing a communication. Erb and colleagues suggested that these individuals would be uninterested in arguments reflecting a minority position, expecting these arguments to be incorrect anyway. Instead, the 'consensus implies correctness' heuristic will direct their attention to the majority position. They will scrutinize these arguments and, as a result, be more persuaded by strong rather than weak arguments.

Under conditions of high discrepancy, when individuals hold an opposing prior attitude, recipients of a majority message will not be very interested in the validity of these arguments and will not engage in much argument-relevant thought. Under these conditions, 'social concern with deviance from a majority position prevails, hindering the cognitive elaboration of issue-relevant information' (Erb et al., 2002, p. 1174). Since no such worries will arise with regard to a powerless minority, curiosity as to why these people hold such a discrepant position is likely to prevail, and minority arguments will be scrutinized. As a result, argument quality will affect attitudes in the minority, but not the majority condition.

Like Baker and Petty (1994), Erb and colleagues (2002) failed to specify the level of personal relevance at which they assumed prior attitude to operate as a moderator. This is particularly problematic, because attitude discrepancy is likely to be related to personal relevance or involvement: individuals who hold extreme attitudes are likely to be more involved in their positions than individuals who hold neutral positions (e.g., Abelson, 1995).

I also have doubts about theoretical reasoning of Erb and his colleagues. Why should individuals who hold relatively neutral attitudes process the majority position more extensively than the minority position? As I argued earlier in discussing Mackie's 'objective-consensus' position, why should people who accept the 'consensus implies correctness' heuristic invest effort in scrutinizing arguments that they believe to be correct anyway? Although the reasoning of Erb and colleagues (2002) is consistent with the findings of Mackie (1987), who observed more systematic processing with the majority position, it is inconsistent with the results of Maass and Clark (1983), who reported the opposite pattern.

I also have problems with the processes they expect to operate under high discrepancy. This prediction appears to be inconsistent with predictions of Baker and Petty (1994) that the fact that a majority takes a counter-attitudinal position is unexpected and therefore motivates individuals to scrutinize the majority message. As I argued earlier, I would not expect such a source/position imbalance to stimulate processing if the issue was one of very low relevance. However, if the issue is of low relevance, one wonders why message recipients should be concerned about the potential consequences of deviating from a majority position?

Erb and colleagues (2002) conducted two experiments, which both supported their hypotheses. Both experiments used issues that probably were of low to moderate personal relevance. Experiment 1 exposed participants to a message about a (fictitious) proposal to build a tunnel under the Rhine to connect the city of Mannheim (where these participants were studying) with the neighbouring city of Ludwigshafen, on the other side of the Rhine. Since there are also bridges connecting the two cities, the tunnel issue should not be of great personal relevance. On the other hand, huge construction projects always inconvenience people and, furthermore, could have environmental implications. Experiment 2 used the fluoridation of drinking water as an issue. German citizens have traditionally opposed fluoridation and therefore drinking water is not fluoridated. Thus, again, the issue is not terribly relevant, but not totally irrelevant either. Since both studies used different manipulations but led to the same findings, I will focus here on Experiment 2.

Participants in this experiment were either assigned to the group with clearly opposing or with moderate prior attitude, on the basis of their prior attitudes (measured in the same experimental session). They were then exposed to a persuasive message, which contained either strong or weak arguments in favour of fluoridation. Majority versus minority status was manipulated via (fictitious) information about the opinion distribution at a discussion meeting of elected participants of public health insurance plans. There was no main effect of source status. Thus, minorities were as effective as majorities in persuading participants. There was, however, a main effect of prior attitude that was qualified by a three-way interaction of prior attitude, source status, and argument quality. As would be expected, moderate participants agreed more with fluoridation than participants who had been extremely opposed. More surprising, but consistent with the authors' predictions, is the finding that for moderate respondents argument quality had a greater effect when the message was attributed to a majority than a minority. In contrast, for respondents who had been strongly opposed to fluoridation, argument quality had a stronger effect when the message was attributed to a minority rather than a majority.

Finally, Erb and colleagues (2002, Footnote 1) reported findings from an additional study, which demonstrated that participants were not surprised by their disagreement with a majority position. Because attitude discrepancy was not assessed in this additional study, we do not know whether this would also have been true for individuals in the high-discrepancy condition. Nevertheless, these findings tend to support my assumption that the issues used in the study by Erb and colleagues were of low personal relevance. If this was the case, however, one wonders why there was no evidence of a source main effect. All the studies we have reviewed so far, reported source main effects in their low-relevance conditions.

## Towards a generic dual-process model of majority/minority influence

The studies reviewed in the previous section exposed respondents to two types of information about the validity of the position argued in the persuasive message, namely consensus information and arguments supporting the position advocated. Although the authors of these studies have mostly relied on dual-process theories in deriving their predictions, they focused on the variables that they happened to have manipulated in their studies. As a result, their analyses provide only partial accounts. They fail to do justice to the full range of predictions about the impact of majority and minority influence on the processing of persuasive messages that could be derived from dual-process theories. In this section I will therefore try to develop a generic dual-process model of majority/minority influence.

According to dual-process theories of persuasion, the information about the distribution of opinions on the issue in question can affect attitudes in two ways: (1) it can be used directly by respondents as information about the validity of the position argued in the communication (i.e., social reality) and as an indicator for the pursuit of social identity goals; and (2) it can also affect attitudes indirectly through influencing the processing of the arguments contained in the persuasive communication.

### Direct effects

Dual-processing theories of persuasion assume that individuals need to have high processing motivation and ability to engage in systematic processing. When people are not motivated or able to scrutinize the arguments contained in a persuasive message, they base their decision on whether to accept or reject the position advocated in the persuasive communication on heuristic cues only. In contrast, when they are motivated to scrutinize message arguments and are able to do so, they base their decision on their evaluation of these arguments, but not exclusively so. However, this is not meant to imply that individuals necessarily disregard the informational value of heuristic cues, once they have begun to engage in systematic processing. Revised versions of the heuristic-systematic model of Chaiken and her colleagues (Bohner, Moskowitz & Chaiken, 1995; Chaiken & Maheswaran, 1994) assume that at high levels of motivation and ability, *both* processing modes are likely to affect persuasion. The heuristic-systematic model makes several theoretical assumptions specifying the conditions of such interplay of processing modes.

According to the *additivity hypothesis* both heuristic cues and content information exert independent main effects on persuasion. This is most likely to happen when heuristic and systematic processing lead to the same conclusion, for example, if an expert communicator also presents strong arguments. However, the greater the number of strong arguments presented by the expert communicator, the greater the probability that the independent effect of the heuristic cue will be submerged under this wealth of content information. As a result the effect of the heuristic cue on persuasion may no longer be detectable (*attenuation hypothesis*).

The relative impact of message arguments and source status is therefore likely to depend on both processing motivation or ability and the quantity and quality of the arguments contained in the communication. With high processing motivation and a message that contains many strong arguments, source status should have only a relatively minor impact. On the other hand, if processing motivation or ability is low, or if the message contains few strong arguments, the impact of the source-status information should be greater. However, as long as source status has any direct impact at all, it should always be the majority that has the greater effect. As long as recipients heuristically use the consensus information in their evaluation of the validity of the position advocated in a message, they should always be more swayed by a majority rather than a minority position.

This effect should be accentuated if processing is motivated by impression rather than accuracy motivation. Whereas accuracy motivation encourages objective and unbiased information processing, the impression motive is assumed to encourage the expression of attitudes that are socially accept-able. It is assumed to be aroused in influence settings in which the identities of significant audiences are salient or when people must communicate their attitudes to others who may have the power to reward or punish them. Since individuals will want to be liked by the majority impression-motivated processing should also favour majority over minority influence. It is even conceivable that message recipients will want to distance themselves from a disliked minority by moving away from the minority position. To assess this latter hypothesis a message-only control group is needed in which participants are exposed to a message without being given any consensus information. I know of only one study that included such a control group (Erb, Bohner, Schmälzle, & Rank, 1998). There was some evidence that a message that was attributed to a minority source had less impact than a control message with no source-status attribution. However, this effect appears to have been due to a biasing effect of source status on systematic processing to be discussed in the next section.

One can, however, conceive of special circumstances under which message recipients may want to align themselves with a minority. For example, if a minority is extremely prestigious and powerful (i.e., an elite), it may be quite appealing to agree, and to be seen agreeing, with the minority position. However, even if the minority is the underdog, but has fought a valiant fight against the majority, it may have gained so much sympathy and admiration that a fair-minded message recipient would be tempted to support the minority view, especially if the issue is of little personal relevance. On the basis of my review of the literature, one has to conclude, however, that this happens only in rare exceptions. In line with the meta-analysis of early studies (Wood et al., 1994), the overwhelming majority of more recent studies reviewed in this chapter found majority status to have greater impact than minority status. Furthermore, the results of the studies of the impact of majority/minority-source status that mani-pulated relevance appear to have been more in line with the additivity than the attenuation hypothesis. Under high relevance, all three studies reported both source main effects and argument-quality main effects (Crano & Chen, 1998; Kerr, 2002; Martin & Hewstone, 2001a). Thus, the consensus information affected persuasion even under conditions where message recipients engaged in systematic processing. However, it is unclear from these reports whether participants relied on heuristic as well as systematic processing (i.e., additivity), or whether the source main effect was mediated by the kind of biasing effect of source status on information processing to be discussed in the next section.

### Impact on processing

There are two ways in which consensus information can affect processing, namely: (1) by biasing processing of the persuasive information; or (2) by affecting processing motivation (i.e., elaboration likelihood). For example, Erb and colleagues (1998) demonstrated that on issues where individuals had no prior position, they not only use the consensus heuristic to establish a position, use of this heuristic is also likely to bias their processing of information presented in support of a position. In this study, German students were presented with arguments in favour of a tunnel project in Rotterdam (a town in the Netherlands), an issue totally irrelevant to these students. 'To induce some extent of systematic processing, they were asked to read the text attentively because later they would be asked some questions about it' (1998, p. 623). The authors found that arguments had greater impact when attributed to a majority rather than a minority, and that this effect was totally due to thought valence. When the message was attributed to a majority it elicited more argument-congruent thoughts than when it was attributed to the minority.

Although we would suspect that without the instruction aimed at inducing systematic processing, the source effect would have been mediated by heuristic processing in the present study, it does demonstrate the biasing effect of consensus information on the systematic processing of arguments. Furthermore, there is reason to believe that consensus information will bias information processing even of issues that are more involving, not only because respondents tend to believe that majorities are right, but also because arriving at the majority conclusion might serve social-identity goals. Consistent with these assumptions, the review of earlier studies indicated that messages attributed to majorities stimulated more argument-congruent thoughts and fewer counter-arguments than messages attributed to minority sources. Unfortunately, since none of these studies included a control group that exposed respondents to the persuasive message without providing consensus information, it is impossible to tell whether these biasing effects were due to majority information inducing a positive bias, minority information inducing a negative bias, or both.

Finally, the impact of consensus information on elaboration likelihood can result in either a *decrease* or an *increase* of processing motivation, probably depending on the degree of issue involvement of the respondents. On issues where individuals have no previous commitment or vested interest, consensus information is likely to act as substitute for argumentation. If respondents believe that majorities are right ('consensus implies correctness'), they can save themselves the effort of carefully scrutinizing the arguments. Consistent with this assumption, Erb and colleagues (1998), in the only study in this area that also included a condition in which no consensus information was given (argumentation only), reported that consensus information (minority as well as majority) reduced systematic processing.

For issues on which individuals are highly committed, it is not the consensus information per se, but the relation between source and position that is likely to determine depth of processing. For example, for student participants, communications that argue for compulsory community service, increase in tuition fees, increase in workload, or dramatic changes in the exam system are likely to be perceived to be against their best interest. Students will therefore be greatly surprised, if they hear that a majority of fellow students is in favour of these changes or only a minority opposed.[9] Thus, whereas the cue impact of source status decreases with increasing issue involvement, the impact of source status as a motivator is likely to increase. Finally, as I suggested in my discussion of the findings of Baker and Petty (1994), consensus information that is balanced (i.e., a disagreeing minority or an agreeing majority) is likely to reduce respondents' motivation to scrutinize arguments, even on issues that are highly involving. Although this effect has not yet been supported by direct evidence, the pattern reported by Baker and Petty (1994) is difficult to understand without such an assumption.

Whereas the biasing effect of consensus information is again likely to favour the majority (unless the minority is especially prestigious or powerful), the impact of source status on processing motivation could conceivably work to the advantage of minority groups. However, the conditions under which this is likely to occur are rather unusual: The minority has to advocate a position (on an issue of high personal relevance) with which the recipient is already in agreement.

This discussion of the impact of consensus information on information processing reveals a fundamental shortcoming of practically all the research that assessed the effectiveness of majority and minority influence in persuasion settings. To assess the effect of source status on information processing, a control group is essential, which is exposed to the message (or messages) without source-status information. Without such a comparison group, it is neither possible to test whether the information about the majority or minority status of a source increases or decreases the level of information processing, nor whether such information biases information processing in a positive or negative direction.

## Conclusions

The fusion of social influence and persuasion research has led to changes in research methodology as well as in research questions. Since research on social influence was traditionally part of the study of small groups, the methods used to study social influence were modelled after small-group research. Thus, in the studies by Asch (e.g., 1956) and in most studies by Moscovici and colleagues (Moscovici, 1980; Moscovici & Faucheux, 1972) majority and minority influence was exerted by 'real people' who interacted in small-group settings. Admittedly, these settings were rather impoverished, due to the constraints of laboratory research, and the 'real people' were usually confederates of the experimenter. But to the genuine research participants, they must have been more 'real' then the percentage information conveyed in the later studies.

With the fusion of social influence and persuasion research, the study of majority/minority effects began to adopt paradigms of persuasion research as a model. Thus, from being considered parts of reference groups, majorities and minorities became *sources* of persuasive communications or peripheral cues. Sometimes the persuasive communication was attributed to these minorities or majorities, but more often research participants were merely informed that a large or small proportion of members of relevant reference groups had indicated their agreement with the position advocated in the persuasive communication. One of the results of this change in paradigm has been the loss of interest in the impact of variables (e.g., behavioural style) reflecting the way in which minority members support their position.

Despite differences in procedures, the results of studies using opinions issues rather than perceptual tasks reveal a pattern of findings that is very similar to that of the earlier studies: The impact of majority sources is much greater than that of minorities, at least for public as well as direct private measures. With regard to indirect private measures, the pattern is somewhat less clear. Very few studies used such measures in the context of a persuasion paradigm, and those that did revealed conflicting results. For example, Mackie (1987) and de Dreu and de Vries (1996) found greater majority impact (at least descriptively), whereas Crano and Chen (1998) and Alvaro and Crano (1997) reported greater minority effect on their indirect private measures. It is interesting to note that in their meta-analysis of early studies, Wood and colleagues (1994) observed the superiority of minorities on indirect measures only for perceptual tasks, but not for subjective opinion judgements. For subjective opinion tasks, the impact of majorities was greater than that of minorities even for indirect measures. This does not always appear to be the case, but the conditions that determine when it is are not yet clear.

One of the great advantages of adopting the methodology of persuasion research for the study of majority and minority influence has been the dramatic advance in our knowledge of the impact of consensus information on processing of persuasive arguments. We now know that consensus information affects the processing of persuasive arguments both by influencing depth of processing and by biasing the processing of persuasive arguments. However, as I pointed out earlier, inferences from this research have been hampered by the failure of most of these studies to include important control groups. Whereas it has become standard for researchers in this area to manipulate argument quality and source status, studies fail to include three types of control groups, which would greatly help in interpreting findings. First, more recent studies rarely include a baseline or no-information control group, which would allow one to assess whether minority and majority influence results in significant change. Second, we know of only one study (Mackie, 1987, Experiment 4) that provided consensus information without including persuasive arguments. This type of control group would allow us to assess the impact of the consensus information as a purely peripheral cue. Third, and even more importantly, none of the studies reviewed earlier included a control group that exposed respondents to persuasive arguments without at the same time exposing them to consensus information. This last control group is essential for assessing the validity of our hypotheses about the impact of consensus information on the processing of the persuasive arguments.

Another point of concern in this area is that apparently minor changes in procedure appear to moderate the impact of the consensus information. One example is the differential effect of dual-message compared to single-message paradigms (e.g., Maass & Clark, 1983, 1986), which we reported earlier. However, whereas this inconsistency has been successfully explained by Maass and Clark (1986), there are still a number of studies with discrepant findings that we are as yet unable to reconcile. The most striking example is a study by Trost and colleagues (1992) that is very similar in design to the studies by Crano and Chen (1998) and Martin and Hewstone (2001a, Study 5). In contrast to these studies, Trost and her colleagues found a greater impact of the minority under low personal relevance and no significant difference under high personal relevance. Under low personal relevance, the minority also stimulated more positive thoughts than under high personal relevance. Relevance had no impact on the proportion of relevant thoughts for the majority. Since their pattern of findings under low relevance is quite similar to the result of the Maass and Clark (1983) study, which also employed an issue of low relevance, we suspect that the mention of a minority sticking to their guns against an overwhelming majority might have raised sympathy for the minority (underdog effect), and that this sympathy swayed opinions under low relevance, and even dampened the impact of the majority under high relevance.

This leads me to the last point of concern, namely the extent to which the findings of the research reported earlier can be used to predict majority or minority influence in interacting groups. The situation in interacting groups is likely to be much more similar to the paradigm used in the Maass and Clark (1983) than to that used in any of the other studies which I reviewed. The manipulation of consensus through information about the distribution of opinions among in-group members avoids variations on factors which may be important determinants of attitude change in real-life settings. For example, in interacting groups, variations in the behavioural style of minorities will emerge which might have a powerful impact on attitude change. The fact that respondents in the Maass and Clark (1983) study were informed that the individuals who were holding the minority opinion had not changed their position despite strong majority opposition may have made the minority appear confident, committed and consistent. This image could have contributed to their impact on measures of private attitudes. Thus, even though the numerical manipulations, which have become widely accepted as standard manipulations of consensus effect, produced findings that were readily interpretable in terms of dual-process theories, we may have to take account of other factors such as the behavioural style of minorities if we want to predict majority/minority influence in real groups.

## Notes

1 These theories use a slightly different terminology and, under certain conditions, make slightly different predictions. Since these differences are not relevant for the purpose of this chapter, I will not distinguish between the two theories and also use a generic terminology.

2 It should be noted that besides Maass and Clark (1983) only Mackie (1987) used this dual-message paradigm. In all other research reviewed in this chapter, participants were presented either with a majority or a minority position, never with both.

3 Thus, there was no indication that members of the minority were highly committed to their position.

4 All studies reviewed in this section assessed attitudes privately.

5 I do not discuss the Crano and Chen (1998) findings here, because it is doubtful whether they succeeded in creating a low-relevance condition.

6 In his passive advocacy condition, Kerr found neither a source nor an argument-quality effect. Although this condition appears to be similar to the standard conditions in majority/minority-influence studies, a student who claims that he/she is totally unaware whether his/her position on comprehensive exams is shared by fellow students may have seemed strange. Nevertheless, one would have expected a source main effect, with the majority having more influence than the minority.

7 Although Baker and Petty's (1994) theoretical reasoning is elegant and plausible, it is surprising that they fail to discuss the potential role of *personal relevance*. I would expect source/position effects to occur *only on issues that are involving* for research participants, and on which they hold a position to which they are strongly committed. There are at least two reasons for this assumption. First, individuals are more likely to expect their peers to agree with them, when the issue is of great importance for the group. On trivial issues, or issues which are not relevant to the group, individuals should not expect widespread opinion consensus among their peers. Second, the source/position effect is also based on the assumption that disagreement with a majority or agreement with a minority will be experienced as threatening. Obviously being in a minority on a trivial issue unrelated to group interests is unlikely to be threatening.

8 A study by Shuper and Sorrentino (2004), which is nearly an exact replication of Baker and Petty (1994, Study 2) failed to replicate their results. However, since this study did not find any effects of either source status or message on attitudes, I do not report it here.

9 Baker and Petty (1994, p. 17) reported evidence from an additional study in which student participants, who were exposed to alleged newspaper headlines (e.g., 'Majority favors tuition fee increase' or 'Minority favors tuition fee increase') along with the sentence giving the relevant information, had to rate their reactions to these articles. Results showed that students responded with significantly greater surprise to imbalanced than balanced headlines.

# References

Abelson, R. (1995). Attitude extremity. In R. E. Petty & J. A. Krosnick (Eds.), *Attitude strength* (pp. 25–42). Mahwah, NJ: Lawrence Erlbaum Associates, Inc.

Alvaro, E. M., & Crano, W. D. (1997). Indirect minority influence: Evidence for leniency in source evaluation and counter argumentation. *Journal of Personality and Social Psychology, 72*, 949–964.

Asch, S. E. (1956). Studies of independence and conformity: A minority of one against a unanimous majority. *Psychological Monographs, 70* (whole No. 416).

Baker, S. M., & Petty, R. E. (1994). Majority and minority influence: Source–position imbalance as a determinant of message scrutiny. *Journal of Personality and Social Psychology, 67*, 5–19.

Bohner, G., Moskowitz, G. B., & Chaiken, S. (1995). The interplay of heuristic and systematic processing of social information. In W. Stroebe & M. Hewstone (Eds.), *European review of social psychology* (Vol. 6, pp. 33–68). Chichester, UK: Wiley.

Cacioppo, J. T., & Petty, R. E. (1982). The need for cognition. *Journal of Personality and Social Psychology, 41*, 116–131.

Chaiken, S. (1980). Heuristic versus systematic information processing and the use of source versus message cues in persuasion. *Journal of Personality and Social Psychology, 39*, 752–766.

Chaiken, S., & Maheswaran, D. (1994). Heuristic processing can bias systematic processing: Effects of source credibility, argument ambiguity, and task importance on attitude judgment. *Journal of Personality and Social Psychology, 66*, 460–473.

Chen, S., & Chaiken, S. (1999). The heuristic-systematic model in its broader context. In S. Chaiken & Y. Trope (Eds.), *Dual process theories in social psychology* (pp. 73–96). New York: Guilford Press.

Crano, W. D., & Chen, X. (1998). The leniency contract and persistence of majority and minority influence. *Journal of Personality and Social Psychology, 74*, 1437–1450.

De Dreu, C., & De Vries, N. K. (1996). Differential processing and attitude change following majority and minority arguments. *British Journal of Social Psychology, 35*, 77–90.

De Vries, N. K., De Dreu, C., Gordijn, E., & Schuurman, M. (1996). Majority and minority influence: A dual role interpretation. In W. Stroebe & M. Hewstone (Eds.), *European review of social psychology* (Vol. 7, pp. 31–62). Chichester, UK: Wiley.

Deutsch, M., & Gerard, H. B. (1955). A study of normative and informational influence upon individual judgment. *Journal of Abnormal and Social Psychology, 51*, 629–636.

Doms, M., & van Avermaet, E. (1980). Majority influence, minority influence and conversion behavior: A replication. *Journal of Experimental Social Psychology, 16*, 283–292.

Erb, H.-P., Bohner, G., Rank, S., & Einwiller, S. (2002). Processing minority and majority communications: The role of conflict with prior attitudes. *Personality and Social Psychology Bulletin, 28*, 1172–1182.

Erb, H.-P., Bohner, G., Schmälzle, K., & Rank, S. (1998). Beyond conflict and discrepancy: Cognitive bias in minority and majority influence. *Personality and Social Psychology Bulletin, 24*, 620–633.

Kelley, H. (1973). The process of causal attribution. *American Psychologist, 28*, 107–128.

Kerr, N. L. (2002). When is a minority a minority? Active versus passive minority advocacy and social influence. *European Journal of Social Psychology, 32*, 471–483.

Maass, A., & Clark, R. D., III (1983). Internalization versus compliance: Differential processes underlying minority influence and conformity. *European Journal of Social Psychology, 13*, 197–216.

Maas, A., & Clark, R. D., III (1986). Conversion theory and simultaneous majority/minority influence: Can reactance offer an alternative explanation. *European Journal of Social Psychology, 16*, 305–309.

Mackie, D. (1987). Systematic and nonsystematic processing of majority and minority persuasive communications. *Journal of Personality and Social Psychology, 53*, 41–52.

Martin, R. (1995). Majority and minority influence using the afterimage paradigm: A replication with an unambiguous blue slide. *European Journal of Social Psychology, 25*, 373–381.

Martin, R. (1998). Majority and minority influence using the afterimage paradigm: A series of attempted replications. *Journal of Experimental Social Psychology, 34*, 1–26.

Martin, R., & Hewstone, M. (2001a). Determinants and consequences of cognitive processes in majority and minority influence. In J. P. Forgas & K. D. Williams (Eds.), *Social influence* (pp. 315–330). Hove, UK: Psychology Press.

Martin, R., & Hewstone, M. (2001b). Afterthoughts on afterimages: A review of the afterimage paradigm in majority and minority influence research. In C. De Dreu & N. De Vries (Eds.), *Group consensus and minority influence* (pp. 15–39). Oxford, UK: Blackwell.

Martin, R., & Hewstone, M. (2003). Majority versus minority influence: When, not whether source status instigates heuristic or systematic processing. *European Journal of Social Psychology, 33*, 313–330.

Moscovici, S. (1980). Toward a theory of conversion behavior. In L. Berkowitz (Ed.), *Advances in experimental social psychology* (Vol. 13, pp. 209–239). New York: Academic Press.

Moscovici, S., & Faucheux, C. (1972). Social influence, conformity bias, and the study of active minorities. In L. Berkowitz (Ed.), *Advances in experimental social psychology* (Vol. 6, pp. 150–202). New York: Academic Press.

Moscovici, S., & Personnaz, B. (1980). Studies on latent influence V: Minority influence and conversion behavior in a perceptual task. *Journal of Experimental Social Psychology, 16*, 270–282.

Moscovici, S., & Personnaz, B. (1986). Studies on the latent influence by the spectrometer method I: The impact of psychologization in the case of conversion by a minority or a majority. *European Journal of Social Psychology, 16*, 345–360.

Personnaz, B. (1981). Studies in social influence using the spectrometer method: Dynamics of the phenomena of conversion and covertness in perceptual responses. *European Journal of Social Psychology, 11*, 431–438.

Petty, R. E., & Cacioppo, J. T. (1986). *Communication and persuasion: Central and peripheral routes to attitude change.* New York: Springer.

Petty, R. E., Cacioppo, J. T., & Goldman, R. (1981). Personal involvement as a determinant of argument-based persuasion. *Journal of Personality and Social Psychology, 41*, 847–855.

Petty, R. E., & Wegener, D. T. (1999). The elaboration likelihood model: Current status and controversies. In S. Chaiken & Y. Trope (Eds.), *Dual process theories in social psychology* (pp. 37–72). New York: Guilford Press.

Ross, L., Greene, D., & House, P. (1977). The 'false consensus effect': An egocentric bias in social perception and attribution processes. *Journal of Experimental Social Psychology, 13*, 279–301.

Sherif, M. (1936). *The psychology of social norms.* New York: Harper & Row.

Shuper, P. A., & Sorrentino, R. M. (2004). Minority versus majority influence and uncertainty orientation. Processing persuasive messages on the basis of situational expectancies. *Journal of Social Psychology, 144*, 127–147.

Sorrentino, R. M., King, G., & Leo, G. (1980). The influence of minority on perception. A note on possible alternative explanations. *Journal of Experimental Social Psychology, 16*, 293–301.

Trost, M. R., Maass, A., & Kenrick, D. T. (1992). Minority influence: Personal relevance biases cognitive processes and reverses private acceptance. *Journal of Experimental Social Psychology, 28*, 234–254.

Wood, W., Lundgren, S., Ouelette, J. A., Busceme, S., & Blackstone, T. (1994). Minority influence: A meta-analytic review of social influence processes. *Psychological Bulletin, 115*, 323–345.

**Part IV**

# Dynamic interplay between majority and minority factions

# 10 Newcomers as change agents: Minority influence in task groups[1]

*John M. Levine*
University of Pittsburgh, USA

*Hoon-Seok Choi*
Sungkyunkwan University in Seoul, Korea

Because groups are not static entities, efforts to explain group processes and outcomes must take account of temporal aspects of group life (Arrow, McGrath, & Berdahl, 2000). In this chapter we focus on how groups respond to changes in membership occasioned by the entry of new members. In particular we are interested in the conditions under which newcomers influence the groups they enter.

Newcomers are typically numerical minorities, and, when this is the case, the influence they exert represents an important, though neglected, form of minority influence. Research on newcomer influence is interesting in part because it demonstrates that members of minority factions can produce innovation in groups performing complex tasks involving extensive interaction among members. Thus, in contrast to the vast bulk of the work on minority influence, which focuses on how minority dissent affects the cognitive dynamics of individual majority members, research on newcomer influence focuses on the social dynamics of groups containing majority and minority factions (Levine & Kaarbo, 2001; Prislin, Levine, & Chistensen, 2006).

A dramatic example of newcomer influence, albeit in an organizational rather than small-group context, involved the impact of Lyndon Johnson on the US Senate. According to Robert Caro's (2002) biography of Johnson:

> At the time he arrived in the Senate, seniority governed all its workings. New members were not supposed to speak much, or at all, on the floor during their first year or two . . . After *his* first two years in the Senate, Lyndon Johnson was Assistant Leader of his party. In another two years . . . he became the Democratic Leader of the Senate . . . two years later . . . he became the Majority Leader . . . the youngest Leader in history . . . Lyndon Johnson transformed the Senate, pulled a nineteenth-century—indeed . . . an eighteenth-century—body into the twentieth century. It was not only men he bent to his will but an entire institution, one that had seemed, during its previous century and three-quarters of existence, stubbornly unbendable.
>
> (Caro, 2002, p. xxii)

Before discussing newcomer innovation, it is useful to consider group composition and membership change more generally. The entry and exit of members is an important mechanism for altering group composition, which can be defined as the number and type of people who belong to the group (Levine & Moreland, 1998). Group composition has been studied as a *consequence* of certain social or psychological processes, as a *context* that moderates various social psychological phenomena, and as a *cause* that influences group dynamics and performance (Moreland & Levine, 1992a). The last perspective (composition as cause) is our primary concern here. A wide range of group-member attributes, including demographic charac- teristics (e.g., race, gender, ethnicity), abilities, opinions, personality traits, functional backgrounds, and tenure in the group, have been studied as possible determinants of members' interpersonal relations and collective performance (see Levine & Moreland, 1998; Moreland, Levine, & Wingert, 1996; Neale, Mannix, & Gruenfeld, 1998).[2]

In recent years, research on group composition as a causal factor has focused primarily on the effects of *differences* between members (i.e., diver- sity). Evidence indicates that the impact of diversity on members' inter- personal relations and collective performance is complex (Mannix & Neale, 2005; Milliken, Bartel, & Kurtzberg, 2003a; van Knippenberg & Schippers, 2007; Williams & O'Reilly, 1998). For example, in brainstorming groups, although knowledge diversity can enhance the group's ability to generate creative ideas, it can also inhibit effective communication, decrease social interaction, and elicit a focus on shared rather than unshared knowledge (Paulus, Larey, & Dzindolet, 2001). Given the absence of clear main effects of diversity, it is critical to understand the factors that moderate its impact (van Knippenberg & Schippers, 2007). These include the specific type and visibility of the diversity (e.g., demographic vs. opinion), the requirements of the group task (e.g., convergent vs. divergent thinking), the distribution of attributes across group members, the reason why the group is diverse (e.g., internal choice vs. external mandate), and the organizational context in which the group functions (e.g., Lau & Murnighan, 1998; Milliken et al., 2003a; Moreland et al., 1996; Owens, Mannix, & Neale, 1998; van Knippen- berg, De Dreu, & Homan, 2004).

Although substantial theoretical and empirical attention have been devoted to clarifying the consequences of group composition in general and group diversity in particular, much remains to be learned. In particular, more work is needed on temporal aspects of group composition. As McGrath (1998) noted, group composition can be altered by two types of membership change. In one case, current members change as the result of their experiences in the group (e.g., by acquiring new skills), which alters the role and status systems of the group (Levine, Moreland, & Hausmann, 2005). In the second case, which is our focus here, membership change occurs as the result of turnover, defined as the entry of new members and/or the exit of current ones (Arrow & McGrath, 1995; Thomas-Hunt &

Phillips, 2003).[3] Turnover is a ubiquitous feature of 'open' groups, which have permeable boundaries that allow newcomers to join (Ziller, 1965).

## Newcomers as recipients and sources of influence

Being a newcomer is a highly stressful experience for several reasons, including 'reality shock' associated with unrealistic expectations about group life, lack of familiarity with other members, low status and power, uncertainty regarding role demands, and performance anxiety (Levine & Moreland, 1999; Moreland & Levine, 1982, 1989). This stress is heightened by the fact that newcomers are often numerical minorities. It is not surprising, therefore, that newcomers often feel anxious about their level of acceptance in the group. And this anxiety is not groundless, as indicated by evidence that newcomers often receive negative treatment at the hands of old-timers (Levine et al., 2005). This treatment can range from embarrassing and mildly painful to psychologically degrading and physically dangerous. A striking example of the risks that newcomers sometimes face is revealed in the following quote:

> One day at Anzio [the Anglo-American landing in Italy in January 1944] we got eight new replacements into my platoon. We were supposed to make a little feeling attack that same day. Well, by next day, all eight of them replacements were dead . . . But none of us old guys were. We weren't going to send our own guys out on point in a damnfool situation like that . . . We sent the replacements out ahead.
> (Fussell, 2003, p. 98)

And it is not only human newcomers who have problems with old-timers— monkeys introduced into intact groups are frequently attacked and sometimes killed (Bernstein, Gordon, & Rose, 1974). Moreover, the stress of being a newcomer, even in a group where everyone else is also a newcomer, can have other deleterious effects on health. Compared to monkeys living in stable groups, those living in unstable groups (in which group composition changed repeatedly for many months) were more likely to develop coronary artery disease, especially if they were dominant animals (Manuck, Kaplan, & Clarkson, 1986).

The stress that (human) newcomers experience elicits two major motives. First, newcomers desire information that will allow them to adapt to, and succeed in, the group they are entering. This 'epistemic' goal has been discussed under several rubrics, including uncertainty reduction and sense making. Second, as suggested above, newcomers desire acceptance by the group they are entering. This 'social' goal has also been discussed under various rubrics, including social integration and inclusion (Levine & Kerr, 2007). These two motives, in turn, often make newcomers highly susceptible to influence from old-timers (Levine & Moreland, 1991, 1999).

It is not correct to assume, however, that newcomers are always passive recipients of influence. Newcomers can play an active role in their socialization and can serve as sources of influence. Although much of the work on this topic has dealt with newcomers in organizations (e.g., Bauer, Morrison, & Callister, 1998; Feldman, 1994; Sutton & Louis, 1987), we will focus primarily on small groups, which are an important context for organizational socialization (Moreland & Levine, 2001). We will discuss two types of newcomer influence. The first involves general adaptations that groups make to the presence of newcomers (Levine, Moreland, & Choi, 2001). The second involves specific changes that newcomers stimulate in how groups perform their tasks (Levine, Choi, & Moreland, 2003). Both kinds of influence can have consequences for the quality of group performance.

### General group adaptations to newcomers

Research on 'proactive socialization' in organizations indicates that newcomers often play an active role in their socialization by engaging in such activities as information and feedback seeking, relationship building, and behavioural self-management (Bauer et al., 1998; Griffin, Colella, & Goparaju, 2000; Moreland & Levine, 2001). Although these activities are typically conceptualized as resulting from newcomers' desire to 'fit in', proactive socialization sometimes produces adaptations in the organization or group. For example, newcomers' efforts to acquire information (e.g., by asking questions about sensitive issues) may violate group norms, which may cause old-timers to engage in actions, such as hiding information, that interfere with their other duties. Alternatively, newcomers' efforts to establish close relationships with old-timers may produce conflict between factions that are competing for newcomers' allegiance (cf. Sutton & Louis, 1987; Ziller, 1965), which may harm group performance.

In some cases, newcomers can produce adaptations in a group even before they enter it. For example, old-timers' expectation that they will have to transmit the group culture to newcomers may stimulate them to think carefully about it, which may cause them to discover inconsistencies that they never noticed before (cf. Feldman, 1994). This discovery, in turn, may cause them to change certain aspects of the culture or to alter the mechanisms traditionally used to transmit it. In addition, the expectation of transmitting cultural information may cause old-timers to develop more organized and polarized cognitive structures regarding this information (cf. Guerin & Innes, 1989).

Newcomers can also produce group adaptations as a result of old-timers' attempts to transmit cultural information. For example, research on the 'saying-is-believing' effect shows that communicating a message to an audience can influence a speaker's memory for message-relevant information, because speakers want to establish shared reality with their audience (Higgins, 1992). Therefore, old-timers' memories of cultural information they communicated to newcomers may be influenced by the messages they used to transmit this information. If these communication-induced changes are sufficiently great, over time they may alter the content of the group culture.

Group adaptations to newcomers may also occur as old-timers try to assess and maximize new members' contributions to the group. Newcomers who fall short of group expectations are likely to be carefully monitored and given reduced responsibilities, while newcomers who meet these expectations are likely to elicit the opposite reactions. Both sets of responses change the group by altering the time and energy old-timers expend on socialization. Moreover, the changes induced by such newcomers may generalize beyond the people who elicited them. 'Bad' newcomers, for example, may motivate old-timers to raise the entry criterion for new people joining the group.

Additional factors may also influence how old-timers behave toward newcomers. For example, the greater the number of newcomers relative to old-timers, the more effort old-timers must expend in socializing the newcomers, which may reduce the group's ability to achieve other goals. The size of the newcomer contingent may also affect the socialization tactics that old-timers use (e.g., common experiences for all newcomers vs. different experiences for different newcomers; Van Maanen & Schein, 1979). Finally, the similarity between old-timers and newcomers on such dimensions as demographic characteristics and opinions may be important (Arrow, 1998; Lau & Murnighan, 1998). Old-timers are typically more motivated to integrate similar than dissimilar newcomers into the group (Jackson, Stone, & Alvarez, 1992).

Group adaptations to newcomers' presence can also alter old-timers' relationships with one another. For example, when newcomers are viewed negatively, old-timers may become more cohesive (Merei, 1949). Moreover, as noted above, if newcomers' entry strengthens some factions and weakens others, their presence may produce conflicts within the group. And, in an effort to cope with newcomer entry, groups may alter their role and status systems, for example by giving greater weight to seniority (cf. Insko et al. 1980).

Finally, newcomers can change how the group they are entering relates to out-groups, and such change can be either harmful or beneficial. For example, if newcomers' entry into Group A weakens Group B because the two groups have a competitive relationship, Group A may be forced to devote more resources to inter-group conflict and fewer resources to meeting its other goals (Levine, Moreland, & Ryan, 1998). In contrast, if newcomers' entry into Group A strengthens Group B because the two groups have a cooperative relationship, Group A may be able to devote more resources to meeting its other goals (Levine et al., 1998).

## Newcomer-induced changes in group task strategies

In many cases, newcomers possess useful ideas that would improve group performance if only old-timers would recognize and utilize them. Often, however, old-timers are reluctant to consider, much less accept, newcomers' ideas. This might occur for several reasons, including old-timers' distrust of newcomers who have not proven themselves, comfort with familiar routines (Gersick & Hackman, 1990), or preference for discussing shared rather than unshared information (Stasser, 1999). In addition, as noted above, newcomers are often numerical minorities in the groups they join. This puts them at a disadvantage when it comes to exerting influence, as indicated by evidence that minority members have difficulty producing direct, or public, influence (Wood, Lundgren, Ouellette, Busceme, & Blackstone, 1994) and are often disliked and rejected (Levine & Thompson, 1996). But minority members are not always weak. They can produce indirect, or private, influence (Martin & Hewstone, 2001; Wood et al., 1994) and can stimulate majority members to engage in divergent thinking (Nemeth & Nemeth-Brown, 2003). Moreover, by using the right tactics, minorities can produce direct influence as well (Levine & Kaarbo, 2001). It is ironic, in light of Moscovici's (1976) interest in the dynamic properties of majority–minority relations, that little attention has been devoted to minority influence in interacting groups (Levine & Kaarbo, 2001). Research on newcomer innovation suggests a potentially important mechanism by which numerical minorities can exert influence in interacting groups, thereby contributing to the growing literature on group creativity (Janssen, van de Vliert, & West, 2004; Levine & Moreland, 2004; Nijstad & Levine, 2007; Paulus & Nijstad, 2003; Thompson & Choi, 2006).

Levine et al. (2003) recently analysed the conditions under which newcomers produce innovation in workgroups by introducing new ideas that have the potential to improve group performance (cf. West & Farr, 1990). Levine et al. viewed innovation as the outcome of an implicit or explicit negotiation between newcomers and old-timers. They suggested that innovation occurs if two conditions are satisfied: (1) newcomers generate and suggest ideas for improving group performance; and (2) old-timers accept and implement these ideas. These two necessary conditions, in turn, depend on characteristics and behaviours of the newcomers and characteristics of the groups they join.

## Newcomers' production of ideas

Levine et al. (2003) argued that, in order for innovation to occur, newcomers must have the motivation to produce change in the group they are entering and the ability to generate ideas that can enhance group performance.

*Newcomers' motivation to produce change*

Several analyses of individual creativity and innovation have emphasized the importance of motivation (e.g., Amabile, 1988; Ford, 1996). Three factors are assumed to influence newcomers' motivation to change the groups they are entering. One factor is newcomers' level of commitment to the group, which depends on its past, present, and anticipated future rewardingness (Moreland & Levine, 1982). In general, newcomers are probably more motivated to change groups that elicit low commitment (because they are not rewarding) than groups that elicit high commitment (because they are rewarding). Such motivation is likely to stimulate efforts by newcomers to identify problems in the group and develop ways of solving them (cf. Moreland & Levine, 1992b). This negative relationship between commitment to the group and motivation to change it may not be linear, however. Extremely low commitment may cause newcomers to withdraw, physically or psychologically, from the group rather than attempt to change it.

Newcomers' motivation to produce innovation may also be influenced by their perceived self-efficacy in developing good ideas for solving group problems (cf. Bandura, 1986; Tierney & Farmer, 2002). Several factors may affect newcomers' feelings of self-efficacy, including past success in producing good ideas and prior training on the group task. Self-efficacy may have consequences beyond motivating newcomers to generate an initial idea, most notably by increasing their efforts to see that their idea is adopted (Morrison & Phelps, 1999).

Finally, newcomers' motivation to produce innovation may be affected by their belief that efforts to produce change will yield benefits for themselves and/or the group. Given that people who deviate from group norms are often punished (Levine & Thompson, 1996) and newcomers are often anxious about how old-timers will treat them (Moreland & Levine, 1989), newcomers are typically reluctant to introduce innovations unless they believe their efforts will be rewarded. Evidence that innovation will be welcomed rather than rebuffed is likely to increase newcomers' feeling of 'psychological safety' (Edmondson & Mogelof, 2006) and thereby enhance their willingness to introduce new ideas (cf. Edmondson, 2003; Milliken, Morrison, & Hewlin, 2003b). In addition, the size of the newcomers' faction may be important (Levine & Kaarbo, 2001). Compared to newcomers in smaller factions, those in larger factions may be less fearful that they will be punished for challenging group orthodoxy and more confident that their ideas will be accepted (Zdaniuk & Levine, 1996).

*Newcomers' ability to generate ideas*

Several approaches to predicting individual creativity have been offered. The traditional approach focuses on personality traits that characterize

creative people, such as independence, self-confidence, tolerance of ambiguity, cognitive flexibility, and propensity for risk-taking (cf. Agrell &
Gustafson, 1996; Simonton, 2000). Newcomers who possess these traits
probably have an advantage in generating innovative ideas in workgroups.

Other individual-difference perspectives emphasize creativity styles and
cognitive skills. Regarding creativity styles, Kirton (1976) argued that
people vary on a continuum from adaptation to innovation, with the former
favouring refinement of current practices and the latter favouring radical
change in these practices (Mudd, 1996). Thus, newcomers who favour
adaptation versus innovation may generate rather different ideas about how
to improve group performance. In addition, general cognitive skills (e.g.,
divergent thinking, mental imagery) and specific task-relevant skills are
related to creativity (Amabile, 1988; Ford, 1996; Smith, Gerkens, Shah,
& Vargas-Hernandez, 2006). Both kinds of skills would be expected to
enhance newcomers' ability to generate useful ideas for improving group
performance. Specific skills might be acquired through individual training
or working in another group. The latter activity may be especially useful in
helping newcomers understand the factors underlying group performance
and facilitating their ability to diagnose and solve group problems. In fact,
because newcomers are not committed to their group's routines and do not
have strong personal ties to other members, they may even be better than
old-timers at diagnosing group problems and generating ideas for
improving group performance (Nijstad & Levine, 2007; Ziller, 1965).

### Old-timers' acceptance of newcomers' ideas

As noted above, having the motivation and ability to generate new ideas is
not sufficient for newcomers to produce innovation. They must also convince old-timers to accept and implement their ideas, which can be a
difficult task. In spite of this resistance, however, newcomers are sometimes
able to 'sell' their ideas. Their success in doing so is influenced by their
characteristics and behaviours, as well as the characteristics of the group
they are entering (Levine et al., 2003). Because systematic research has not
been conducted on newcomer innovation, our analysis of the factors that
influence this process was based on extrapolation from research on related
topics, such as minority influence and group productivity.

### Newcomer characteristics and behaviours

One potentially important determinant of newcomers' influence is their
perceived expertise on the group task. Newcomers who are seen as more
competent than old-timers are likely to exert greater influence than newcomers who are seen as less competent. This prediction is consistent with
evidence regarding the impact of source expertise on both conformity to
group pressure and attitude change (Allen, 1965; Eagly & Chaiken, 1993).

Newcomers' status may be important as well. This status may be influenced by several factors, including newcomers' reputation prior to entering the group, their contributions to the group after they join, and their personal characteristics (e.g., race, sex; Ridgeway, 2001). Compared to newcomers with low status, those with high status elicit more commitment from old-timers (Moreland & Levine, 1989) and higher performance expectations (cf. Milanovich, Driskell, Stout, & Salas, 1998). In addition, because they can often have attractive options outside the group, high-status newcomers can threaten to leave unless their ideas are accepted (cf. Ziller, 1965). For these reasons, high-status newcomers probably elicit less punishment for deviating from group norms (cf. Wiggins, Dill, & Schwartz, 1965) and gain more acceptance for new ideas (cf. Torrance, 1955). In fact, when they occupy leadership positions, high-status newcomers may be expected to challenge group norms and produce innovation (cf. Homans, 1974; Suchner & Jackson, 1976).

The size of the newcomers' faction is another potentially critical determinant of their ability to exert influence (Levine & Kaarbo, 2001). On the one hand, larger factions may be more effective than smaller ones (Tanford & Penrod, 1984), because they seem more correct (Nemeth, Wachtler, & Endicott, 1977) and more likely to retaliate if their views are rejected. On the other hand, smaller factions may be more effective, because they seem more confident and courageous (Nemeth et al., 1977), more distinct and salient (Maass, West, & Cialdini, 1987), and less threatening (cf. Crano, 2001).

Newcomers' similarity to old-timers may also play a significant role. As noted earlier, old-timers are more motivated to integrate similar than dissimilar newcomers into the group (Jackson et al., 1992), which no doubt facilitates the ability of similar newcomers to produce innovation (Levine & Moreland, 1985). There may be cases, however, in which dissimilar newcomers can introduce change. This may occur, for example, when they receive social support from other group members (Jackson et al., 1992) or their dissimilarity represents a form of superiority (e.g., because they possess unique skills that the group needs). A particularly important form of newcomer–old-timer similarity is in-group status, based on shared social identity. People view in-group members more positively than out-group members and show in-group favouritism on a variety of behavioural dimensions (Brewer & Brown, 1998). In addition, people are generally more susceptible to influence from in-group than from out-group members (Abrams, Wetherell, Cochrane, Hogg, & Turner, 1990; David & Turner, 1996; Mackie & Queller, 2000). Therefore, newcomers who share a social identity with old-timers are more likely to produce innovation than are newcomers who do not share such an identity (cf. Crano, 2001).

Newcomers' ability to exert influence may also be affected by their behavioural style—the organization, timing, and intensity of their responses (Moscovici, 1985). It is likely, for example, that consistent newcomers will be more influential than inconsistent ones (cf. Wood et al., 1994) and that assertive newcomers will be more effective than non-assertive ones (cf. Jentsch & Smith-Jentsch, 2001). In addition, newcomers who conform to group norms before trying to produce change may be more influential than those who offer the same suggestions immediately after entering the group (cf. Hollander, 1960).

Newcomers can use a variety of impression-management tactics to convince old-timers that they have expertise on the group task and are motivated to help the group (cf. Levine & Kaarbo, 2001). These include communicating that their views reflect careful analysis and are shared by knowledgeable outsiders and that they want to help the group rather than further their personal interests (cf. Ridgeway, 1982). Newcomers who can convince old-timers that they possess these characteristics are probably more likely to gain acceptance for their ideas.

Our analysis so far suggests that newcomers must convince old-timers of the validity of their ideas. In some cases, however, newcomers may use punishment and reward tactics to get their way (cf. Levine & Kaarbo, 2001). In the former case, newcomers might threaten to undermine group performance or to leave the group. In the latter case, newcomers might promise to work hard or to remain in the group in spite of attractive options outside. Newcomers may also use tactics designed to maximize the size of their faction (e.g., by convincing old-timers to recruit people sympathetic to their views) or to control how the group processes information and reaches consensus (e.g., by convincing old-timers to use the unanimity, rather than the majority, rule during discussion—cf. Miller, 1989).

*Group characteristics*

Because innovation is the result of an implicit or explicit negotiation between newcomers and old-timers, group characteristics that affect old-timers' receptivity to newcomers' ideas must be considered. These include the group's openness to membership change, size and staffing level, development, cohesion and climate, leadership, performance, and commitment to its current task strategy.

Groups vary in their openness to membership change (Ziller, 1965). 'Open' groups have high turnover and unstable memberships; 'closed' groups have low turnover and stable memberships. Evidence suggests that open groups have a shorter time perspective, implement decisions more quickly, work harder to minimize turnover-related problems, and are more receptive to new ideas (Ziller, Behringer, & Goodchilds, 1960). It is therefore not surprising that newcomers have an easier time producing innovation in open rather than in closed groups (cf. Ziller, Behringer, & Jansen, 1961).

Two competing predictions can be made about the relationship between group size and responsiveness to newcomer innovation. On the one hand, larger groups may be more open to innovation than smaller groups, because their memberships are more diverse (and hence they have more experience in dealing with new ideas) and they have more resources to implement new ideas. On the other hand, larger groups have more directive leadership than do smaller groups (Mullen, Symons, Hu, & Salas, 1989), which can discourage innovation, and they have a harder time reaching consensus (Moreland & Levine, 1992b), which may reduce their likelihood of accepting and implementing innovations. A related factor that may affect newcomer innovation is group staffing level, defined as the relationship between the number of current group members and the number needed to perform group tasks (Barker, 1968). Compared to adequately and overstaffed groups, understaffed groups are more eager to recruit and retain new members, which may increase their receptivity to newcomer innovation (cf. Cini, Moreland, & Levine, 1993; Petty & Wicker, 1974).

Group dynamics change as a function of group development, which is often defined in terms of how long group members have worked together (Moreland & Levine, 1988). Although scholars disagree about the exact nature of the group development process (e.g., Gersick, 1988; Tuckman, 1965), they generally agree that relationships between group members stabilize over time and that group structure and dynamics become more complex (e.g., Worchel, 1996). Therefore, it is likely that newcomer innovations will be more successful in earlier rather than in later stages of group development (Ford & Sullivan, 2004; Moreland & Levine, 1988; but see Worchel, Grossman, & Coutant, 1994).

One consequence of group development is increased cohesion. Compared to members of less-cohesive groups, members of more-cohesive groups are more likely to participate in group activities, remain on the group, and resist group disruptions (Levine & Moreland, 1998). Cohesion also increases conformity to group norms (Festinger, Schachter, & Back, 1950) and punishment of deviates (Schachter, 1951). It is therefore likely that members of highly cohesive groups will resist newcomers' innovation efforts (cf. Brawley, Carron, & Widmeyer, 1988; Schachter, 1951). It is important to note, however, that cohesion can be operationalized in different ways, for example as interpersonal attraction, group pride, or task commitment (Mullen & Copper, 1994). When cohesion is defined as task commitment, highly cohesive groups may be quite receptive to newcomers' innovation attempts.

Besides varying in cohesion, groups also vary in climate. According to West (1990), innovation is most likely in groups that have clear objectives, are non-judgemental and supportive of individual suggestions, are committed to excellence, and have norms favouring innovation (Anderson & West, 1998). Other work is consistent with the notion that group norms affect innovation. Some groups have norms discouraging dissent (Janis, 1982), whereas others have norms permitting or encouraging it (Coser, 1962). These norms affect the likelihood that people holding minority views will attempt to exert influence and succeed in doing so (Moscovici & Lage, 1978).

Moreover, group norms regarding innovation may affect how new members are socialized, with consequences for their later behaviour (Jones, 1986).

Research on group problem solving demonstrates that leadership can play an important role in fostering creativity. For example, Maier and Solem (1970) found that groups developed better solutions if leaders protected minority views from social pressure and encouraged consideration of opposing perspectives (see also Edmondson, 2003). In addition, research on workgroup innovation suggests that participative, or democratic, leadership can facilitate innovation (Nyström, 1979). This may occur because democratic leaders give subordinates a sense of empowerment (Burpitt & Bigoness, 1997) and provide them with emotional support (West & Wallace, 1991) and psychological safety (Edmondson, 2003), which in turn motivate them to attempt innovation. It is therefore likely that newcomers will introduce more new ideas and gain more acceptance for these ideas in groups with democratic as opposed to autocratic leaders. It is possible, however, that democratic leaders may be less effective than autocratic leaders in implementing innovations (cf. King & Anderson, 1995). Finally, groups may have prototypes stipulating that new leaders should be forceful (Kenney, Blascovich, & Shaver, 1994), which should increase group receptivity to innovation efforts by these leaders.

Another variable that may affect newcomer innovation is the group's performance history. Just as a newcomer in a failing group may perceive a need for innovation, so the group may believe that change is necessary. If so, failing groups should be more receptive to newcomer suggestions than succeeding groups (Ziller & Behringer, 1960). Group failure may not always increase the likelihood of newcomer innovation, however. Some unsuccessful groups are reluctant to change their task strategy (Gersick & Hackman, 1990) and instead execute this strategy with increased vigour. This behaviour, sometimes labelled entrapment, is especially common when groups have chosen (rather than been assigned) their strategy (Bazerman, Giuliano, & Appelman, 1984; Kameda & Sugimori, 1993).

These findings suggest that groups that choose their task strategy, whether it fails *or* succeeds, may be more resistant to innovation efforts than groups that are assigned their strategy. Research on individuals indicates that choice produces commitment, which in turn produces resistance to change (Kiesler, 1971). Among the consequences of choice-induced commitment to decisions are selective exposure to information, biased evaluation of decision outcomes, and resistance to counter-persuasion. Of greatest relevance to our present concerns, commitment also produces behavioural persistence (Staw, 1976).

## Experimental evidence

As noted above, little theoretical or empirical attention has been devoted to the conditions under which newcomers influence the groups they enter. In the previous sections, we discussed two forms of newcomer influence, namely: (1) general adaptations that groups make to the presence of newcomers; and (2) specific changes that newcomers stimulate in how groups perform their tasks. In so doing, we presented a number of hypotheses about when and how newcomers exert influence. In this section, we discuss five recent studies designed to investigate the conditions under which newcomers can influence the task strategies that workgroups use and/or the performance of these groups.

### *Study 1: Group strategy choice and performance prior to newcomer entry*

In this experiment, we investigated how a workgroup's receptivity to a newcomer's innovation attempt was influenced by two group characteristics—the group's degree of choice in determining its initial task strategy and its performance using this strategy prior to the newcomer's arrival (Choi & Levine, 2004). We predicted, based on reasoning presented earlier, that a newcomer's innovation attempt would be more successful (a) when the group was assigned its strategy than when it chose this strategy and (b) when the group failed than when it succeeded.

The hypothesis that failing groups are more susceptible to a newcomer's innovation attempt than are successful groups was supported in an early study by Ziller and Behringer (1960). This study did not provide a strong test of the hypothesis, however, because the group's task was much more difficult after the newcomer entered than before and because the newcomer provided objectively correct answers and the process for obtaining them. Under these conditions, the likelihood of the group accepting the newcomer's suggestion was very high. In the present study, the group's task remained the same after the newcomer entered, and the newcomer offered a plausible, but not necessarily correct, alternative to the group's current strategy.

In this study, male undergraduates were randomly assigned to three-person groups in a 2 (Strategy Choice: assignment/choice) × 2 (Group Performance: failure/success) between-subjects design. Groups worked on a team air-surveillance task that ran on networked personal computers. After being seated in cubicles containing personal computers, one participant was randomly designated as team leader (commander), and remaining members were designated as subordinates (specialists).

During training on the air-surveillance task, specialists were taught how to use their computers to monitor eight characteristics of planes flying through a simulated airspace (e.g., airspeed, altitude, weapons readiness), assign parameter values to these characteristics, and transmit these values to the commander using an e-mail system. After looking up characteristics, specialists identified their parameter values (low, medium, or high danger) using a table (e.g., for airspeed, < 435 mph = low danger; 435–570 mph =

medium danger; > 570 mph = high danger). The commander was taught how to use a formula to integrate the parameter values sent by specialists in calculating a threat value for each plane and how to enter these values into his computer. Because parameter values changed over time, the specialists had to monitor planes on a continuous basis, and the commander had to update threat values in a timely manner. After a practice period, participants were told that they would complete two work shifts during which they could earn 0–100 points, depending on the accuracy of the commander's threat assignments.

The two independent variables were then manipulated. In the strategy-choice condition, groups were asked to choose one of two equally plausible strategies for assigning specialists' monitoring responsibilities. Both strategies required each specialist to monitor four parameters of all planes that entered the airspace. In the strategy-assignment condition, each group was assigned a strategy selected by a group in the choice condition, using a yoking procedure. Participants then filled out a questionnaire assessing their commitment to the group's strategy. After completing a shift (Shift 1) on the air-surveillance task, group members were informed that their team score was either below (65) or above (85) the criterion for good performance (75). Next, participants filled out a questionnaire assessing their perception of their group's performance.

Participants were then told that they could win money if they scored 75 or higher on the next shift (Shift 2) and that specialist B would be replaced by a new member who had completed individual training but had not worked as part of a team before. After the newcomer (a confederate) entered, the team was given a get-acquainted e-mailing session, during which the newcomer suggested a major change in the group's monitoring strategy. This strategy was a plausible, but not demonstrably correct, way of dividing up the specialists' monitoring responsibilities. The newcomer wrote, 'I thought of something during training that we could try. Instead of dividing up the char how about each spec takes care of all 8 char of each plane. So spec A gets the first plane, I do the second, spec A gets the third, etc. This might be easier and work better. Since I am new I think you guys should decide whether we try my idea. I'll shut up and you can talk to each other. Let me know what you decide'. After the newcomer made this suggestion, the commander and specialist A used the e-mail system to decide whether to accept it or continue using their initial strategy. During Shift 2, the newcomer looked up plane information according to whatever strategy the other two group members had selected.

Data from 44 groups (11 per condition) were included in the analyses. Questionnaire responses indicated the experimental manipulations were successful. Before Shift 1, participants reported that they were significantly more committed to their initial strategy in the strategy-choice than in the strategy-assignment condition. After Shift 1, they reported that their performance was significantly higher in the success than in the failure condition. They also reported that their performance was significantly higher in the strategy-choice than in the assignment condition.

Group acceptance/rejection of the newcomer's proposed innovation was assessed by examining the messages between the commander and specialist A after the newcomer suggested his strategy. Results indicated, consistent with our hypotheses, that the newcomer's suggestion was accepted significantly more often (a) in the strategy-assignment than in the strategy-choice condition (73% vs. 36%) and (b) in the failure than in the success condition (77% vs. 32%). It is worth noting that over 90% of the strategy-assignment/failure groups accepted the newcomer's suggestion, whereas fewer than 10% of the strategy-choice/success groups did so. The overall amount of group acceptance we obtained is striking in light of three characteristics of the study. First, newcomers occupied low status in the groups they entered. Second, they did not offer demonstrably correct solutions to the group's task. And third, they were 'imposed' on the group by an outsider (the experimenter), rather than selected by group members themselves.

In order to clarify the factor(s) responsible for the impact of the strategy-choice manipulation, we examined the extent to which both commitment and perceived performance mediated the effect of this manipulation on receptivity to newcomer innovation. These analyses indicated that strategy choice influenced receptivity via two routes—through commitment to the team's strategy before Shift 1 and through perception of the team's performance after Shift 1. Other data (e.g., participants' expectations about working on their team before Shift 1 and reactions to working on their team after Shift 1) also suggested that strategy choice had a strong impact on participants' reactions.

Although results in Study 1 supported our hypotheses, it is possible that strategy choice and performance might yield different results in other circumstances. In the case of choice, an *assigned* strategy might elicit high commitment (and hence low acceptance of a newcomer's suggestion) if the group used that strategy for a long time prior to the newcomer's entry or if that strategy was presented as highly effective (e.g., because it worked well in the past). And low performance might *not* lead to acceptance of a newcomer's suggestion if failure was dramatic (e.g., 40, rather than 10, points below the success criterion) because of learned helplessness, or if a substantial amount of behavioural change was needed to implement the newcomer's suggestion.

### Study 2: Newcomer task expertise and social identity

In Study 1, we examined the impact of two group characteristics (strategy choice and performance) on newcomer innovation. In Study 2, we shifted our attention to newcomer characteristics—task expertise and shared social identity with other group members (Kane, Argote, & Levine, 2005). We predicted, based on reasoning presented earlier, that newcomers would be more influential (a) when they had more expertise than other group members than when they had less expertise and (b) when they shared a social identity with other group members than when they did not. In addition, we predicted an interaction between newcomer expertise and shared social identity, based on evidence that people (a) often analyse in-group messages more thoroughly than out-group messages, especially when the information contained in the message is important to the in-group, and (b) are more influenced by high-quality than by low-quality arguments from in-group members, but not from out-group members (see Mackie & Queller, 2000; van Knippenberg, 1999). We therefore expected that members of groups that shared a social identity with a newcomer would adopt his or her task strategy when it was superior, but not when it was inferior, to their own. In contrast, we expected that members of groups that did not share a social identity with a newcomer would pay little attention to the quality of his or her task strategy and instead would base their acceptance/rejection of this strategy on their evaluation of the newcomer (cf. Petty & Cacioppo, 1986). Because out-group members generally elicit negative evaluations (Brewer & Brown, 1998), we expected that the newcomer's task strategy would be rejected regardless of its quality (Mackie & Queller, 2000; van Knippenberg, 1999).

In this study, male and female undergraduates were randomly assigned to same-sex three-person groups in a 2 (Social Identity: shared/unshared) × 2 (Newcomer Expertise: superior/inferior) × 2 (Trials: Trial 1/Trial 2) mixed analysis of variance (ANOVA), with trials as a repeated measure. Participants were brought to the lab in groups of six and told they would work as three-person teams to make origami sailboats, using an assembly-line procedure. Shared (unshared) social identity was manipulated by assigning the two three-person groups the same name (different names), giving them the same colour (different colour) name tags and pens, seating them in an integrated (segregated) fashion around a table, and informing them the best six-person (three-person) group would win a monetary prize at the end of the semester.

Next, participants were divided into two three-person groups (randomly determined in the shared-social-identity condition) and trained on the origami task in separate rooms. Newcomer expertise was manipulated by training one group to use a superior routine and the other group to use an inferior routine. Both routines produced sailboats that met specified criteria (e.g., have precise folds, stand up on their own). The superior routine required 7 folds; the inferior routine required 12 folds. The superior routine was more efficient, but more difficult to learn. Following training, each group worked on the origami task for two trials.

Groups were then told that there would be a temporary change in membership, and each group received a replacement for the member occupying the second role in the assembly line. The newcomer, who had occupied this role in the other group during training, either did or did not share a social identity with the recipient group and either possessed a superior or an inferior routine. (Note that newcomers who possessed a superior routine entered groups trained to use an inferior routine and vice versa.) The reconstituted groups then worked on the origami task for two trials. During this period, either the newcomer influenced the group to use his or her task strategy, or the group influenced the newcomer to use its strategy. Following the second trial, participants completed a questionnaire assessing their identification with the six-person group.

Data from 48 groups (12 in each Social Identity × Newcomer Expertise condition) were included in the analyses. Questionnaire responses indicated that participants felt significantly more identification with the six-person group in the shared- than in the unshared-social-identity condition. Our major dependent variable was newcomer influence, defined as the proportion of recipient groups that adopted the newcomer's task strategy during the first trial after he or she entered. Results supported our three hypotheses. Regarding main effects, we found that the newcomer's strategy was adopted significantly more often (a) in the shared-social-identity than in the unshared-social-identity condition (38% vs. 13%) and (b) in the superior-expertise than in the inferior-expertise condition (46% vs. 4%). In addition, we found the expected interaction, namely that the newcomer's expertise had a much greater impact on group adoption in the shared-social-identity condition (67% vs. 8%) than in the unshared condition (25% vs. 0%). Thus, groups that shared a social identity with the newcomer were more likely to adopt a task routine that was superior, rather than inferior, to their own. In contrast, groups that did not share a social identity with the newcomer rarely adopted the newcomer's task routine, even when it was superior to their own and would have improved their performance.

Given the design of the study, there are two plausible explanations for these results. Groups that shared a social identity with the newcomer may have been especially receptive to his or her task-relevant knowledge, or newcomers who shared a social identity with the group may have been especially motivated to transmit their knowledge. We favour the former interpretation for two reasons. First, all newcomers but two used their task routine in the group they entered, suggesting that newcomers' motivation to share their knowledge was constant (and high) across conditions. Second, recipient group members' perceptions of shared social identity mediated the impact of manipulated identity on adoption of the newcomer's strategy, and this mediating effect was moderated by the newcomer's expertise. Similar mediational analyses using newcomers' perceptions of shared social identity did not yield these effects. Clearly, however, additional work is needed to clarify the mechanisms underlying the impact of shared social identity on group receptivity to newcomers' ideas. The possibility that, under certain conditions, shared social identity will inhibit, rather than enhance, newcomers' ability to exert influence should also be considered (Rink & Ellemers, 2005; see also Phillips, 2003).

The findings discussed so far have focused on newcomers' ability to influence the task strategies of the groups they are entering, with no attention to how this influence affects group performance. Because prior research indicates that newcomers can have an impact on the performance of the groups they enter (e.g., Rogelberg & O'Connor, 1998; Trow, 1960), we collected performance data in Study 2 and the studies reported below. In Study 2, we found that, when newcomers possessed a superior routine, the increase in the mean number of sailboats produced from Trial 1 to Trial 2 was much greater in the shared-social-identity condition than in the unshared condition ($Ms$ = 5.88 vs. 1.83, respectively). In contrast, when newcomers possessed an inferior routine, the increase was almost identical in the shared and unshared conditions ($Ms$ = 4.29 vs. 4.48, respectively). Our interpretation of these finding is based on our earlier observation that the group either learned to use the newcomer's strategy or taught the newcomer to use its strategy. The fact that groups with an inferior strategy learned more from a superior newcomer in the shared- than unshared-social-identity condition is not surprising, given the influence data reported above. But why did performance improve when an inferior newcomer entered the group? We would argue that in this condition the group influenced the newcomer to adopt its superior strategy during Trial 1, thereby producing an improvement in group performance from Trial 1 to Trial 2.

### Study 3: Newcomer task expertise and status

As Study 2 showed, newcomers can influence the performance of the groups they enter, and, at least under certain conditions, their level of task expertise can be an important determinant of this influence. In Study 3, we investigated the joint effects of newcomer expertise and status on group performance in an air-surveillance task (Levine & Choi, 2004). We predicted that (a) newcomers with higher task expertise would have more positive impact on group performance than would those with lower expertise (Naylor & Briggs, 1965; Trow, 1960) and (b) newcomers with higher status would have more impact, for better or worse, than newcomers with lower status (Ridgeway, 2001). We also predicted that communication among group members would increase following both the receipt of negative information about their performance and the entry of newcomers. These predictions were based on the assumption that both poor performance and personnel turnover are disruptive events in the life of the group and hence stimulate communication among members.

In this study, male undergraduates were randomly assigned to 30 three-person groups and trained on an earlier version of the air-surveillance task described in Study 1. During training, group members learned how to monitor nine characteristics of planes flying through a simulated airspace. As in Study 1, each specialist was responsible for monitoring four characteristics of each plane. In Study 3, however, the commander was responsible for monitoring a ninth plane characteristic (identity friend or foe; IFF), as well as calculating threat values for the planes. Following practice, the group performed four shifts (Shifts 1, 2, 3, and 4), which were followed by veridical feedback regarding the group's performance. In addition, team members were given the opportunity to communicate by e-mail between shifts. Approximately one week later, participants returned for a second work session (Shifts 5, 6, 7, and 8), in which they followed the same procedure as on Day 1, with one major exception. In 20 groups (10 commander change and 10 specialist change), the person who played the role of commander or specialist on Day 1 was replaced by someone who previously played the same role in another group. In the remaining 10 groups (no change), membership remained stable across Days 1 and 2.

Before assessing the impact of membership change on group performance on Day 2, we examined how performance changed across Shifts 1–4 on Day 1. We found that performance improved across shifts, indicating group learning. In addition, we examined the behaviours that group members emitted while monitoring planes and making threat assignments. This was possible because the air-surveillance program stored all the computer-based actions of the commander and specialists.

We first identified several behavioural indices that we thought might affect group performance and then assessed their utility in predicting performance, using multiple regression analyses. On the basis of these analyses, we derived an equation, using just four predictors, that accounted for approximately half the variance in overall group performance on Day 1 ($R^2 = .49$, $p < .01$). These predictors were: (1) commander's IFF latency (the amount of time that elapsed between a plane entering the airspace and the first IFF look-up by the commander, log transformed); (2) commander's threat latency (the amount of time that elapsed between a plane entering the airspace and the first threat assignment by the commander, log transformed); (3) specialists' critical look-ups (the ratio of look-ups involving the two most important characteristics of enemy planes, in terms of the commander's threat formula, to the total number of look-ups made by the two specialists, arcsine transformed); and (4) specialists' message latency (the latency in reading messages sent by team-mates, log transformed). (Predictors for specialists were created by combining the data from the two specialists in each group.) The regression equation indicated that teams performed better when commander's IFF latency (X1), commander's threat latency (X2), and specialists' message latency (X4) were low and when specialists' critical look-ups (X3) was high.

We did not expect personnel turnover per se to substantially affect group performance on Day 2, because the group's task was highly structured and members received a good deal of practice in performing their specialized roles on Day 1. To assess the impact of turnover, we conducted a 3

(Condition: commander change, specialist change, no change) × 4 (Shift: 5, 6, 7, 8) mixed ANOVA, with shift as a repeated measure, on Day 2 group performance scores. Neither the Condition main effect nor the Condition × Shift interaction attained significance, indicating that membership change did not influence group performance. As on Day 1, however, group performance increased over shifts on Day 2.

We predicted that newcomers' expertise and status would affect group performance. Specifically, we expected that (a) newcomers with higher task expertise would have a more positive effect on group performance than would those with lower expertise and (b) newcomers with higher status (commanders) would have more impact, for better or worse, than newcomers with lower status (specialists). To test these hypotheses, we developed an index of newcomers' ability based on their task-relevant behaviour on Day 1, namely their emission of the behaviours included in the regression equation described earlier (IFF latency and threat latency for commanders; critical look-ups and message latency for specialists). We reasoned that newcomers who were highly proficient in using these behaviours had more expertise than those who were less proficient. We then computed four partial correlations (two for the commander-change condition; two for the specialist-change condition) between the four indices of newcomers' ability and their receiving team's performance on Day 2, holding constant the receiving team's performance on Day 1. When membership change involved new specialists, neither correlation was significant (critical lookups: $r = .29$, $ns$; message latency: $r = .31$, $ns$). In contrast, when membership change involved new commanders, both correlations were significant (IFF latency: $r = -.65$, $p < .05$; threat latency: $r = -.67$, $p < .05$). These results indicate that, as expected, newcomers with high ability and high status were particularly useful to the teams they entered.

We also predicted that communication among group members would increase following both the receipt of negative information about their performance and the entry of newcomers, because these events are disruptive. Recall that, on both days of the experiment, team members had an opportunity to communicate by e-mail between shifts (i.e., after Shifts 1, 2, and 3 on Day 1; after Shifts 5, 6, and 7 on Day 2). Of the 895 messages sent during these periods, 62% were strategy messages, which included task queries, statements of problems with the team's strategy, and suggestions for improving this strategy. Another 16% were motivational messages, which included compliments and encouragements (e.g., 'good job, we'll hit 100 next time'). Remaining messages were either task-irrelevant (18%), such as 'we should be getting paid more, let's go on strike', or simple acknowledgements (4%), such as 'I got it'. We restricted our analysis to strategy-relevant and motivational messages.

To determine the impact of team performance on communication, we examined the relationship between performance in a given shift and the volume of messages sent immediately after the shift. We found a consistent *negative* relationship between team performance in a given shift and the number of strategy messages sent afterwards (*r*s ranging from – .37 to −.53, *p*s ranging from .05 to .01). These results suggest that, as predicted, lower performance stimulated team members to communicate about their task strategy. We also found a *positive* relationship between team performance in a given shift and the number of motivational messages sent afterwards in all shifts but one (*r*s ranging from .34 to .47, *p*s ranging from .07 to .01). These results suggest that higher performance stimulated team members to congratulate themselves for past performance and energize themselves for future performance. It is also possible, of course, that causality operated in the opposite direction, with message production influencing performance. To assess this possibility, we correlated the volume of strategy and motivational messages sent *before* a given shift with performance in that shift. These correlations did not yield any significant relationships between communication and performance on either Day 1 or Day 2.

Finally, we used simultaneous multiple regression analyses to examine how personnel turnover affected the number of strategy and motivational messages sent after Shifts 5, 6, and 7, holding constant team performance in those shifts. There was no association between personnel turnover and strategy messages after Shift 5. However, after Shift 6, significantly more strategy messages were sent in both the commander-change and specialist-change conditions than in the no-change condition. A similar, though somewhat weaker, trend was found after Shift 7. These results suggest that, as predicted, membership change stimulated team members to communicate about their task strategy. In contrast, there was little evidence that turnover influenced motivational messages.

Although newcomers do not always improve the performance of groups they enter (Gruenfeld, Martorana, & Fan, 2000), Studies 2 and 3 indicate that they can do so under certain conditions. More specifically, newcomers are most likely to have a positive effect on group performance when they have relatively high task expertise and either share social identity with the group they enter or have high status in that group (three factors that we identified earlier as likely to affect newcomers' ability to produce changes in a group's task strategy). In extending our work on how newcomers influence group performance, with a special focus on newcomer expertise, we shifted our attention to groups working on creativity tasks, because we believe that such groups provide a particularly interesting context for studying newcomer influence. In analysing group creativity, Nijstad and Levine (2007) argued that the creative process consists of three stages— problem finding (i.e., identifying and defining the problem), idea finding (i.e., generating solutions to the problem), and solution finding (i.e., choosing the best solution and then developing and implementing it). In addition, they suggested that newcomers can make unique contributions to group creativity in each of these stages.

### Studies 4 and 5: Newcomer influence on a creativity task

Two studies were conducted to investigate the impact of newcomers on group creativity (Choi & Thompson, 2005). In both studies, it was predicted that groups that underwent membership change (replacement of a current member by a new member with experience in another group) would perform better on an idea-generation task than would groups with stable membership. This might occur for at least two reasons. First, the entry of newcomers may increase the group's task focus, which has been found to enhance creativity (Anderson & West, 1998). Second, as noted earlier, newcomers may diversify a group's knowledge base by introducing new ideas and information, which can promote creativity (Milliken et al., 2003a; O'Reilly, Williams, & Barsade, 1998; see also Nemeth & Nemeth-Brown, 2003).

In Study 4, male and female business students and managers in an executive-education course were randomly assigned to three-person groups. During Part 1 of the study, groups initially worked on an idea-generation task in which they were asked to generate as many criteria as possible to classify 12 fruits (e.g., oranges, grapes) into subgroups (e.g., citrus vs. non-citrus). Next, half the groups experienced membership change (one member was replaced by someone from another group), and half did not. During Part 2 of the study, groups were asked to generate sorting criteria for 12 vegetables. During both tasks, one member recorded the group's ideas. Two measures of group creativity were used: (1) fluency (the number of non-redundant, or unique, ideas the group generated); and (2) flexibility (the number of idea categories the group used). Examples of ideas generated included big vs. small, canned vs. non-canned, and seeded vs. non-seeded. Examples of idea categories included physical characteristics, nutritional content, and longevity.

Data from 20 groups were included in the analyses (12 in the newcomer condition and 8 in the stable-membership condition). During Part 1, the two conditions did not differ significantly in either fluency or flexibility. Controlling for group fluency in Part 1, fluency in Part 2 was significantly higher in the newcomer condition than in the stable-membership condition ($M$s = 52.37 vs. 41.94). Similarly, controlling for group flexibility in Part 1, flexibility in Part 2 was significantly higher in the newcomer condition than in the stable-membership condition ($M$s = 16.60 vs. 13.10).

Additional data were collected to explore the possibility that the superiority of the newcomer condition was due simply to group members' exposure to new ideas. To test this notion, an additional condition was run in which participants remained in the same group during Parts 1 and 2 of the study but listened to an audiotape of another group working on Part 1 before beginning Part 2. In this condition, fluency in Part 2 was significantly lower than in the previous newcomer condition and not significantly different than in the previous stable-membership condition. Similar results were obtained for flexibility. These data suggest that the superiority of the newcomer condition to the stable membership condition was due to social interaction with the newcomer, not simply exposure to new ideas.

Study 5 was designed to provide additional information about factors underlying the effectiveness of the newcomer condition. Because newcomers in Study 4 generated ideas for two kinds of stimuli that shared the same category membership (fruits and vegetables), it was possible that they imported stimulus-specific knowledge into their new groups. To rule out this possibility, Study 5 employed different kinds of stimuli in Parts 1 and 2. In addition, whereas Study 4 did not measure the specific contributions that newcomers and old-timers made to creativity after the newcomer joined the group, Study 5 did obtain this information.

Participants in Study 5 were male and female undergraduates or managers enrolled in an executive-training course. Experimental procedures were the same as those in Study 4, with two exceptions. First, after working on the vegetable task from Study 4 in Part 1, groups switched to a new task in Part 2, namely generating possible uses for a cardboard box. Second, the ideas of each group member were recorded separately in colour-coded boxes.

Data from 33 groups were included in the analyses. As in Study 4, in Part 1 of Study 5 the newcomer and stable-membership conditions did not differ significantly in either fluency or flexibility. In addition, controlling for group fluency and flexibility in Part 1, both fluency and flexibility in Part 2 were significantly higher in the newcomer condition than in the stable-membership condition ($Ms$ = 59.71 vs. 48.75 and $Ms$ = 38.99 vs. 33.42, respectively). To assess newcomers' contributions to group creativity, partial correlations were calculated between newcomers' individual fluency and flexibility in Part 1 and their receiving group's creativity in Part 2, holding constant the receiving group's creativity in Part 1. Results indicated that the higher the newcomers' fluency and flexibility in Part 1, the higher the receiving group's fluency and flexibility in Part 2 ($r$ = .67, $p$ < .01, and $r$ = .49, $p$ < .07, respectively). These findings complement those obtained in Studies 2 and 3 by indicating once again that newcomers' task expertise was an important determinant of their impact on group performance.

But a second important question remains. Did newcomers stimulate old-timers to be more creative? To assess old-timers' contributions in Part 2, differences between their fluency and flexibility in Parts 1 and 2 of the study were compared (scores were based on data from two old-timers in the newcomer condition and three old-timers in the stable-membership condition). Results showed that old-timers in both conditions were more creative in Part 2 than in Part 1. Importantly, however, this increase was significantly greater in the newcomer condition than in the stable membership condition ($Ms$ = 9.72 vs. 5.04 for fluency; $Ms$ = 6.41 vs. 3.78 for flexibility), indicating that newcomers did indeed stimulate the creativity of old-timers.

## Conclusion

In this chapter, we initially argued that newcomer influence represents an interesting form of minority influence, because newcomers are typically numerical minorities in the groups they enter and because research designed to clarify their impact has focused on interpersonal, rather than simply intrapersonal, processes. We then discussed two forms of newcomer innovation in workgroups. The first involved general adaptations that groups make to the presence of newcomers (Levine et al., 2001); the second involved specific changes that newcomers stimulate in how groups perform their tasks (Levine et al., 2003). We also suggested that both kinds of influence can have consequences for the quality of group performance. We then presented studies dealing with newcomers' ability to change the task strategies of the groups they entered (Study 1), newcomers' impact on the performance of these groups (Studies 3, 4, and 5), or both (Study 2). Results revealed that three variables identified as potentially important determinants of newcomers' ability to change group strategies (newcomers' expertise, status, and shared social identity with old-timers) also affected group performance. These findings suggest the utility of developing an integrated account of newcomers' influence on both group strategies and performance.

Such an account might benefit from considering work on information distribution and recognition of expertise in groups. Although groups whose members possess task-relevant knowledge have a potential advantage over groups that do not possess such knowledge, there is no guarantee that the former groups will effectively use their knowledge. A basic precondition for such use is that group members communicate their knowledge to one another. Unfortunately, substantial evidence indicates that groups often fail to discuss, much less consider, all of the knowledge that their members possess. This occurs because group discussions tend to focus on common information that all members initially share, rather than on unique information that only certain members possess (Gigone & Hastie, 1993; Stasser & Titus, 1985). In cases where consideration of this unique information is necessary for effective group performance, failure to discuss it leads to suboptimal group decisions (see Stasser, 1999, for a review).

One reason why groups do not pay sufficient attention to unique information, even when it is offered, is that they have difficulty recognizing the expertise of the people who transmit this information (Littlepage, Schmidt, Whisler, & Frost, 1995). This tendency, which is especially true for groups operating in complex-task environments, can be overcome by certain types of group training (Littlepage, Robison, & Reddington, 1997; Moreland, 1999). In addition, explicitly informing group members about their own and others' expertise is effective in increasing the distribution of unshared information (Stasser, Stewart, & Wittenbaum, 1995).

Member status, which can be both a cause and consequence of perceived expertise, is also an important determinant of information sharing in groups. Evidence indicates, for example, that high-status members are less biased in communicating shared (as opposed to unshared) information than are low-status members and that unshared information communicated by high-status members is remembered better and repeated more often than is unshared information communicated by low-status members (Wittenbaum & Bowman, 2005).

Work on information distribution and recognition of expertise is potentially useful in analysing the effectiveness of newcomers as change agents for several reasons. First, it addresses the two functions of newcomers highlighted in this chapter—introducing new ideas into groups and influencing group performance. Second, it has identified as important certain variables (expertise and status) that also affected newcomer influence in our studies. And, third, it suggests a number of interesting research directions for investigators interested in newcomer influence. One such direction is more emphasis on information exchange between newcomers and old-timers. Although we obtained some data about this process in Study 3, much remains to be learned about the extent to which newcomers mention unique information and old-timers acknowledge and repeat this information. Another direction is more attention to factors that affect old-timers' perceptions of newcomers' task expertise. It may be, for example, that certain features of newcomers' behavioural style (e.g., assertiveness, consistency) influence such perceptions, which in turn affect old-timers' attention to and acceptance of newcomers' suggestions (cf. Jentsch & Smith-Jentsch, 2001; Moscovici, 1976). These and related questions deserve systematic attention from researchers interested in the role that newcomers play in group life.

## Notes

1 Preparation of this chapter was supported by NSF Grant SES-03–45840.
2 Though our focus here is on how a group's composition affects its internal dynamics, composition can also influence external (boundary) activities (Ancona & Caldwell, 1998; Thomas-Hunt & Gruenfeld, 1998).
3 We define entry as occurring when new members join an *existing* group in order to differentiate it from group formation, which occurs when people come together to create a new group. Moreover, we define exit as occurring when a *subset* of current members leaves a group in order to differentiate it from group dissolution, which occurs when all current members leave and thereby end the group's existence (Levine & Choi, 2004).

## References

Abrams, D., Wetherell, M., Cochrane, S., Hogg, M. A., & Turner, J. C. (1990). Knowing what to think by knowing who you are—Self-categorization and the nature of norm formation, conformity and group polarization. *British Journal of Social Psychology*, 29, 97–119.

Agrell, A., & Gustafson, R. (1996). Innovation and creativity in work groups. In M.

A. West (Ed.), *Handbook of work group psychology* (pp. 317–343). Chichester, UK: Wiley.

Allen, V. L. (1965). Situational factors in conformity. In L. Berkowitz (Ed.), *Advances in experimental social psychology* (Vol. 2, pp. 133–175). New York: Academic Press.

Amabile, T. M. (1988). A model of organizational innovation. In B. M. Staw & L. L. Cummings (Eds.), *Research in organizational behavior* (Vol. 10, pp. 123–167). Greenwich, CT: JAI Press.

Ancona, D. G., & Caldwell, D. F. (1998). Rethinking team composition from the outside in. In M. A. Neale, E. A. Mannix, & D. H. Gruenfeld (Eds.), *Research on managing groups and teams: Composition* (pp. 21–37). Greenwich, CT: JAI Press.

Anderson, N. R., & West, M. A. (1998). Measuring climate for work group innovation: Development and validation of the team climate inventory. *Journal of Organizational Behavior, 19*, 235–258.

Arrow, H. (1998). Standing out and fitting in: Composition effects on newcomer socialization. In M. A. Neale, E. Mannix, & D. H. Gruenfeld (Eds.), *Research on managing groups and teams: Composition* (pp. 59–80). Greenwich, CT: JAI Press.

Arrow, H., & McGrath, J. E. (1995). Membership dynamics in groups at work: A theoretical framework. In B. M. Staw & L. L. Cummings Eds.), *Research in organizational behavior* (Vol. 17, pp. 373–411). Greenwich, CT: JAI Press.

Arrow, H., McGrath, J. E., & Berdahl, J. L. (2000). *Small groups as complex systems: Formation, coordination, development, and adaptation.* Thousand Oaks, CA: Sage.

Bandura, A. (1986). *Social foundations of thought and action.* Englewood Cliffs, NJ: Prentice Hall.

Barker, R. G. (1968). *Ecological psychology.* Stanford, CA: Stanford University Press.

Bauer, T. N., Morrison, E. W., & Callister, R. R. (1998). Organizational socialization: A review and directions for future research. In G. R. Ferris (Ed.), *Research in personnel and human resources management* (Vol. 16, pp. 149–214). Greenwich, CT: JAI Press.

Bazerman, M. H., Giuliano, T., & Appelman, A. (1984). Escalation of commitment in individual and group decision making. *Organizational Behavior and Human Decision Processes, 33*, 141–152.

Bernstein, I. S., Gordon, T. P., & Rose, R. M. (1974). Factors influencing the expression of aggression during introductions to rhesus monkey groups. In R. L. Holloway (Ed.), *Primate aggression, territoriality, and xenophobia: A comparative perspective* (pp. 211–240). New York: Academic Press.

Brawley, L. R., Carron, A. V., & Widmeyer, W. N. (1988). Exploring the relationship between cohesion and group resistance to disruption. *Journal of Sport and Exercise Psychology, 10*, 199–213.

Brewer, M. B., & Brown, R. J. (1998). Intergroup relations. In D. T. Gilbert, S. T. Fiske, & G. Lindzey (Eds.), *The handbook of social psychology* (4th ed., Vol. 2, pp. 554–594). Boston: McGraw-Hill.

Burpitt, W. J., & Bigoness, W. J. (1997). Leadership and innovation among teams: The impact of empowerment. *Small Group Research, 28*, 414–423.

Caro, R. A. (2002). *The years of Lyndon Johnson: Master of the Senate.* New York: Knopf.

Choi, H.-S., & Levine, J. M. (2004). Minority influence in work teams: The impact of newcomers. *Journal of Experimental Social Psychology, 40*, 273–280.

Choi, H.-S., & Thompson, L. (2005). Old wine in a new bottle: Impact of membership change on group creativity. *Organizational Behavior and Human Decision Processes, 98*, 121–132.

Cini, M., Moreland, R. L., & Levine, J. M. (1993). Group staffing levels and responses to prospective and new members. *Journal of Personality and Social Psychology, 65*, 723–734.

Coser, L. A. (1962). Some functions of deviant behavior and normative flexibility. *American Journal of Sociology, 68*, 172–181.

Crano, W. D. (2001). Social influence, social identity, and ingroup leniency. In C. K. W. De Dreu & N. K. De Vries (Eds.), *Group consensus and minority influence: Implications for innovation* (pp. 122–143). Oxford, UK: Blackwell.

David, B., & Turner, J. C. (1996). Studies in self-categorization and minority conversion: Is being a member of the out-group an advantage? *British Journal of Social Psychology, 35*, 179–199.

Eagly, A. H., & Chaiken, S. (1993). *The psychology of attitudes.* Orlando, FL: Harcourt.

Edmondson, A. C. (2003). Speaking up in the operating room: How team leaders promote learning in interdisciplinary action teams. *Journal of Management Studies, 40*, 1419–1452.

Edmondson, A. C., & Mogelof, J. P. (2006). Explaining psychological safety in innovation teams: Organizational culture, team dynamics, or personality? In L. L. Thompson & H. S. Choi (Eds.), *Creativity and innovation in organizational teams* (pp. 109–136). Mahwah, NJ: Lawrence Erlbaum Associates, Inc.

Feldman, D. C. (1994). Who's socializing whom? The impact of socializing newcomers on insiders, work groups, and organizations. *Human Resource Management Review, 4*, 213–233.

Festinger, L., Schachter, S., & Back, K. (1950). *Social pressures in informal groups.* New York: Harper.

Ford, C. M. (1996). A theory of individual creative action in multiple social domains. *Academy of Management Review, 21*, 1112–1142.

Ford, C. M., & Sullivan, D. M. (2004). A time for everything: How the timing of novel contributions influences project team outcomes. *Journal of Organizational Behavior, 25*, 279–292.

Fussell, P. (2003). *The boys' crusade: The American infantry in northwestern Europe, 1944–1945.* New York: Modern Library/Random House.

Gersick, C. J. (1988). Time and transition in work teams: Toward a new model of group development. *Academy of Management Journal, 31*, 9–41.

Gersick, C. J., & Hackman, J. R. (1990). Habitual routines in task-performing groups. *Organizational Behavior and Human Decision Processes, 47*, 65–97.

Gigone, D., & Hastie, R. (1993). The common knowledge effect: Information sampling and group judgment. *Journal of Personality and Social Psychology, 65*, 959–974.

Griffin, A. E. C., Colella, A., & Goparaju, S. (2000). Newcomer and organizational socialization tactics: An interactionist perspective. *Human Resource Management Review, 10*, 453–474.

Gruenfeld, D., Martorana, P. V., & Fan, E. T. (2000). What do groups learn from their worldliest members? Direct and indirect influence in dynamic teams. *Organizational Behavior and Human Decision Processes, 82*, 45–59.

Guerin, B., & Innes, J. M. (1989). Cognitive tuning sets: Anticipating the consequences of communication. *Current Psychology: Research and Review, 8*, 234–249.

Higgins, E. T. (1992). Achieving 'shared reality' in the communication game: A social action that creates meaning. *Journal of Language and Social Psychology, 11*, 107–125.

Hollander, E. P. (1960). Competence and conformity in the acceptance of influence. *Journal of Abnormal and Social Psychology, 61*, 365–359.

Homans, G. C. (1974). *Social behavior: Its elementary forms*. New York: Harcourt.

Insko, C. A., Thibaut, J. W., Moehle, D., Wilson, M., Diamond, W. D., Gilmore, R., et al. (1980). Social evolution and the emergence of leadership. *Journal of Personality and Social Psychology, 39*, 431–448.

Jackson, S. E., Stone, V. K., & Alvarez, E. B. (1992). Socialization amidst diversity: The impact of demographics on work team oldtimers and newcomers. In L. L. Cummings & B. M. Staw (Eds.), *Research in organizational behavior* (Vol. 15, pp. 45–109). Greenwich, CT: JAI Press.

Janis, I. L. (1982). *Groupthink* (2nd ed.). Boston: Houghton Mifflin.

Janssen, O., van de Vliert, E., & West, M. (2004). The bright and dark side of individual and group innovation: A special issue introduction. *Journal of Organizational Behavior, 25*, 129–154.

Jentsch, F., & Smith-Jentsch, K. A. (2001). Assertiveness and team performance: More than 'just say no'. In E. Salas, C. A. Bowers, & E. Edens (Eds.), *Improving teamwork in organizations: Applications of resource management training* (pp. 73–94). Mahwah, NJ: Lawrence Erlbaum Associates, Inc.

Jones, G. (1986). Socialization tactics, self-efficacy, and newcomers' adjustments to organizations. *Academy of Management Journal, 29*, 262–279.

Kameda, T., & Sugimori, S. (1993). Psychological entrapment in group decision making: An assigned decision rule and a groupthink phenomenon. *Journal of Personality and Social Psychology, 65*, 282–292.

Kane, A. A., Argote, L., & Levine, J. M. (2005). Knowledge transfer between groups via personnel rotation: Effects of social identity and knowledge quality. *Organizational Behavior and Human Decision Processes, 96*, 56–71.

Kenney, R. A., Blascovich, J., & Shaver, P. (1994). Implicit leadership theories: Prototypes for new leaders. *Basic and Applied Social Psychology, 15*, 409–437.

Kiesler, C. A. (1971). *The psychology of commitment: Experiments linking behavior to belief*. New York: Academic Press.

King, N., & Anderson, N. (1995). *Innovation and change in organizations*. London: Routledge.

Kirton, M. J. (1976). Adaptors and innovators: A description and measure. *Journal of Applied Psychology, 61*, 622–629.

Lau, D. C., & Murnighan, J. K. (1998). Demographic diversity and faultlines: The compositional dynamics of organizational groups. *Academy of Management Review, 23*, 325–340.

Levine, J. M., & Choi, H.-S. (2004). Impact of personnel turnover on team performance and cognition. In E. Salas & S. M. Fiore (Eds.), *Team cognition: Understanding the factors that drive process and performance* (pp. 153–176). Washington, DC: American Psychological Association.

Levine, J. M., Choi, H.-S., & Moreland, R. L. (2003). Newcomer innovation in work teams. In P. B. Paulus & B. A. Nijstad (Eds.), *Group creativity: Innovation through collaboration* (pp. 202–224). Oxford, UK: Oxford University Press.

Levine, J. M., & Kaarbo, J. (2001). Minority influence in political decision-making groups. In C. K. W. De Dreu & N. K. De Vries (Eds.), *Group consensus and minority influence: Implications for innovation* (pp. 229–257). Oxford, UK: Blackwell.

Levine, J. M., & Kerr, N. L. (2007). Inclusion and exclusion: Implications for group processes. In A. E. Kruglanski & E. T. Higgins (Eds.), *Social psychology: Handbook of basic principles* (2nd ed., pp. 759–784). New York: Guilford Press.

Levine, J. M., & Moreland, R. L. (1985). Innovation and socialization in small groups. In S. Moscovici, G. Mugny, & E. Van Avermaet (Eds.), *Perspectives on minority influence* (pp. 143–169). Cambridge, UK: Cambridge University Press.

Levine, J. M., & Moreland, R. L. (1991). Culture and socialization in work groups. In L. Resnick, J. Levine, & S. Teasley (Eds.), *Perspectives on socially shared cognition* (pp. 257–279).Washington, DC: American Psychological Association.

Levine, J. M., & Moreland, R. L. (1998). Small groups. In D. T. Gilbert, S. T. Fiske, & G. Lindzey (Eds.), *The handbook of social psychology* (4th ed., Vol. 2, pp. 415–469). Boston: McGraw-Hill.

Levine, J. M., & Moreland, R. L. (1999). Knowledge transmission in work groups: Helping newcomers to succeed. In L. L. Thompson, J. M. Levine, & D. M. Messick (Eds.), *Shared cognition in organizations: The management of knowledge* (pp. 267–296). Mahwah, NJ: Lawrence Erlbaum Associates, Inc.

Levine, J. M., & Moreland, R. L. (2004). Collaboration: The social context of theory development. *Personality and Social Psychology Review, 8,* 164–172.

Levine, J. M., Moreland, R. L., & Choi, H.-S. (2001). Group socialization and newcomer innovation. In M. A. Hogg & R. S Tindale (Eds.), *Blackwell handbook of social psychology: Group processes* (pp. 86–106). Oxford, UK: Blackwell.

Levine, J. M., Moreland, R. L., & Hausmann, L. R. M. (2005). Managing group composition: Inclusive and exclusive role transitions. In D. Abrams, M. A. Hogg, & J. M. Marques (Eds.), *The social psychology of inclusion and exclusion* (pp. 139–160). New York: Psychology Press.

Levine, J. M., Moreland, R. L., & Ryan, C. S. (1998). Group socialization and intergroup relations. In C. Sedikides, J. Schopler, & C. A. Insko (Eds.), *Intergroup cognition and intergroup behavior* (pp. 283–308). Mahwah, NJ: Lawrence Erlbaum Associates, Inc.

Levine, J. M., & Thompson, L. (1996). Conflict in groups. In E. T. Higgins & A. W. Kruglanski (Eds.), *Social psychology: Handbook of basic principles* (pp. 745–776). New York: Guilford Press.

Littlepage, G., Robison, W., & Reddington, K. (1997). Effects of task experience and group experience on group performance, member ability, and recognition of expertise. *Organizational Behavior and Human Decision Processes, 69,* 133–147.

Littlepage, G. E., Schmidt, G. W., Whisler, E. W., & Frost, A. G. (1995). An input–process–output model of influence and performance in problem-solving groups. *Journal of Personality and Social Psychology, 69,* 877–889.

Maass, A., West, S. G., & Cialdini, R. B. (1987). Minority influence and conversion. In C. Hendrick (Ed.), *Review of personality and social psychology* (Vol. 8, pp. 55–79). Newbury Park, CA: Sage.

Mackie, D. M., & Queller, S. (2000). The impact of group membership on persuasion: Revisiting 'Who says what to whom with what effect?' In D. J. Terry & M. A. Hogg (Eds.), *Attitudes, behaviors, and social context: The role of norms and group membership* (pp. 135–155). Mahwah, NJ: Lawrence Erlbaum Associates, Inc.

Maier, N. R. F., & Solem, A. R. (1970). The contribution of a discussion leader to the quality of group thinking: The effective use of minority opinions. *Human Relations, 5,* 277–288.

Mannix, E., & Neale, M. A. (2005). What differences make a difference? The promise and reality of diverse teams in organizations. *Psychological Science in the Public Interest, 6,* 31–55.

Manuck, S. B., Kaplan, J. R., & Clarkson, T. B. (1986). Atherosclerosis, social dominance, and cardiovascular reactivity. In T. H. Schmidt, T. M. Dembroski, & G. Blumchen (Eds.), *Biological and psychological factors in cardiovascular disease.* Hamburg, Germany: Springer-Verlag.

Martin, R., & Hewstone, M. (2001). Conformity and independence in groups: Majorities and minorities. In M. A. Hogg & R. S Tindale (Eds.), *Blackwell handbook of social psychology: Group processes* (pp. 209–234). Oxford, UK: Blackwell.

McGrath, J. E. (1998). A view of group composition through a group-theoretic lens. In M. A. Neale, E. A. Mannix, & D. H. Gruenfeld (Eds.), *Research on managing groups and teams: Composition* (pp. 255–272). Greenwich, CT: JAI Press.

Merei, F. (1949). Group leadership and institutionalization. *Human Relations, 2,* 23–39.

Milanovich, D. M., Driskell, J. E., Stout, R. J., & Salas, E. (1998). Status and cockpit dynamics: A review and empirical study. *Group Dynamics: Theory, Research, and Practice, 2,* 155–167.

Miller, C. E. (1989). The social psychological effects of group decision rules. In P. B. Paulus (Ed.), *Psychology of group influence* (2nd ed., pp. 327–355). Hillsdale, NJ: Lawrence Erlbaum Associates, Inc.

Milliken, F. J., Bartel, C. A., & Kurtzberg, T. R. (2003a). Diversity and creativity in work groups: A dynamic perspective on the affective and cognitive processes that link diversity and performance. In P. B. Paulus & B. A. Nijstad (Eds.), *Group creativity: Innovation through collaboration* (pp. 32–62). Oxford, UK: Oxford University Press.

Milliken, F. J., Morrison, E. W., & Hewlin, P. F. (2003b). An exploratory study of employee silence: Issues that employees don't communication upward and why. *Journal of Management Studies, 40,* 1453–1476.

Moreland, R. L. (1999). Transactive memory: Learning who knows what in work groups and organizations. In L. L. Thompson, J. M. Levine, & D. M. Messick (Eds.), *Shared cognition in organizations: The management of knowledge* (pp. 3–31). Mahwah, NJ: Lawrence Erlbaum Associates, Inc.

Moreland, R. L., & Levine, J. M. (1982). Socialization in small groups: Temporal changes in individual-group relations. In L. Berkowitz (Ed.), *Advances in experimental social psychology* (Vol. 15, pp. 137–192). New York: Academic Press.

Moreland, R. L., & Levine, J. M. (1988). Group dynamics over time: Development and socialization in small groups. In J. E. McGrath (Ed.), *The social psychology of time: New perspectives* (pp. 151–181). Newbury Park, CA: Sage.

Moreland, R. L., & Levine, J. M. (1989). Newcomers and oldtimers in small groups.

In P. Paulus (Ed.), *Psychology of group influence* (2nd ed., pp. 143–186). Hillsdale, NJ: Lawrence Erlbaum Associates, Inc.

Moreland, R. L., & Levine, J. M. (1992a). The composition of small groups. In E. Lawler, B. Markovsky, C. Ridgeway, & H. Walker (Eds.), *Advances in group processes* (Vol. 9, pp. 237–280). Greenwich, CT: JAI Press.

Moreland, R. L., & Levine, J. M. (1992b). Problem identification by groups. In S. Worchel, W. Wood, & J. Simpson (Eds.), *Group process and productivity* (pp. 17–47). Newbury Park, CA: Sage.

Moreland, R. L., & Levine, J. M. (2001). Socialization in organizations and work groups. In M. Turner (Ed.), *Groups at work: Theory and research* (pp. 69–112). Mahwah, NJ: Lawrence Erlbaum Associates, Inc.

Moreland, R. L., Levine, J. M., & Wingert, M. L. (1996). Creating the ideal group: Composition effects at work. In E. Witte & J. Davis (Eds.), *Understanding group behavior. Vol. 2: Small group processes and interpersonal relations* (pp. 11–35). Hillsdale, NJ: Lawrence Erlbaum Associates, Inc.

Morrison, E. W., & Phelps, C. C. (1999). Taking charge at work: Extrarole efforts to initiate workplace change. *Academy of Management Journal, 42*, 403–419.

Moscovici, S. (1976). *Social influence and social change.* New York: Academic Press.

Moscovici, S. (1985). Social influence and conformity. In G. Lindzey & E. Aronson (Eds.), *Handbook of social psychology* (3rd ed., pp. 347–412). Reading, MA: Addison-Wesley.

Moscovici, S., & Lage, E. (1978). Studies in social influence IV: Minority influence in a context of original judgments. *European Journal of Social Psychology, 8*, 349–365.

Mudd, S. (1996). Kirton's A-I theory: Evidence bearing on the style/level and factor composition issues. *British Journal of Psychology, 87*, 241–254.

Mullen, B., & Copper, C. (1994). The relation between group cohesiveness and performance: An integration. *Psychological Bulletin, 115*, 210–227.

Mullen, B., Symons, C., Hu, L., & Salas, E. (1989). Group size, leadership behavior, and subordinate satisfaction. *Journal of General Psychology, 116*, 155–170.

Naylor, J. C., & Briggs, G. E. (1965). Team-training effectiveness under various conditions. *Journal of Applied Psychology, 49*, 223–229.

Neale, M. A., Mannix, E. A., & Gruenfeld, D. H. (Eds.). (1998). *Research on managing groups and teams: Composition.* Greenwich, CT: JAI Press.

Nemeth, C. J., & Nemeth-Brown, B. (2003). Better than individuals? The potential benefits of dissent and diversity for group creativity. In P. B. Paulus & B. A. Nijstad (Eds.), *Group creativity: Innovation through collaboration* (pp. 63–84). Oxford, UK: Oxford University Press.

Nemeth, C. J., Wachtler, J., & Endicott, J. (1977). Increasing the size of the minority: Some gains and some losses. *European Journal of Social Psychology, 7*, 15–27.

Nijstad, B. A., & Levine, J. M. (2007). Group creativity and the stages of creative group problem solving. In M. Hewstone, H. A. W. Schut, J. B. F. de Wit, K. van den Bos, & M. S. Stroebe (Eds.), *The scope of social psychology: Theory and applications. Essays in honour of Wolfgang Stroebe* (pp. 159–171). Hove, UK: Psychology Press.

Nyström, H. (1979). *Creativity and innovation.* New York: Wiley.

O'Reilly, C. A., Williams, K. Y., & Barsade, S. (1998). Group demography and innovation: Does diversity help? In M. A. Neale, E. A. Mannix, & D. H.

Gruenfeld (Eds.), *Research on managing groups and teams: Composition* (pp. 183–207). Greenwich, CT: JAI Press.

Owens, D. A., Mannix, E. A., & Neale, M. A. (1998). Strategic formation of groups: Issues in task performance and team member selection. In M. A. Neale, E. A. Mannix, & D. H. Gruenfeld (Eds.), *Research on managing groups and teams: Composition* (pp. 149–166). Greenwich, CT: JAI Press.

Paulus, P. B., Larey, T. S., & Dzindolet, M. T. (2001). Creativity in groups and teams. In M. E. Turner (Ed.), *Groups at work: Theory and research* (pp. 319–338). Mahwah, NJ: Lawrence Erlbaum Associates, Inc.

Paulus, P. B., & Nijstad, B. A. (Eds.). (2003). *Group creativity: Innovation through collaboration.* Oxford, UK: Oxford University Press.

Petty, R. E., & Cacioppo, J. T. (1986). *Communication and persuasion: Central and peripheral routes to attitude change.* New York: Springer-Verlag.

Petty, R. M., & Wicker, A. W. (1974). Degree of manning and degree of success of a group as determinants of members' subjective experiences and their acceptance of a new group member. *Catalog of Selected Documents in Psychology, 4,* 1–22.

Phillips, K. W. (2003). The effects of categorically based expectations on minority influence: The importance of congruence. *Personality and Social Psychology Bulletin, 29,* 3–13.

Prislin, R., Levine, J. M., & Christensen, P. N. (2006). When reasons matter: Quality of support affects reactions to increasing and consistent agreement. *Journal of Experimental Social Psychology, 42,* 593–601.

Ridgeway, C. L. (1982). Status in groups: The importance of motivation. *American Sociological Review, 47,* 76–88.

Ridgeway, C. L. (2001). Social status and group structure. In M. A. Hogg & R. S Tindale (Eds.), *Blackwell handbook of social psychology: Group processes* (pp. 352–375). Oxford, UK: Blackwell.

Rink, F., & Ellemers, N. (2005, July). When group composition changes: The acceptance of informational diverse newcomers in work groups. In A. O'Brien & R. Swaab (Chairs), *The many facets of diversity: Ways to manage difference.* Symposium conducted at the meeting of the European Association of Experimental Social Psychology, Wurzburg, Germany.

Rogelberg, S. G., & O'Connor, M. S. (1998). Extending the stepladder technique: An examination of self-paced stepladder groups. *Group Dynamics: Theory, Research, and Practice, 2,* 82–19.

Schachter, S. (1951). Deviation, rejection, and communication. *Journal of Abnormal and Social Psychology, 46,* 190–207.

Simonton, D. K. (2000). Creativity: Cognitive, personal, developmental, and social aspects. *American Psychologist, 55,* 151–158.

Smith, S. M., Gerkens, D. R., Shah, J. J., & Vargas-Hernandez, N. (2006). Empirical studies of creative cognition in idea generation. In L. L. Thompson & H. S. Choi (Eds.), *Creativity and innovation in organizational teams* (pp. 3–20). Mahwah, NJ: Lawrence Erlbaum Associates, Inc.

Stasser, G. (1999). The uncertain role of unshared information in collective choice. In L. L. Thompson, J. M. Levine, & D. M. Messick (Eds.), *Shared cognition in organizations: The management of knowledge* (pp. 49–69). Mahwah, NJ: Lawrence Erlbaum Associates, Inc.

Stasser, G., Stewart, D. D., & Wittenbaum, G. M. (1995). Expert roles and information exchange during discussion: The importance of knowing who knows what. *Journal of Experimental Social Psychology, 31*, 244–265.

Stasser, G., & Titus, W. (1985). Polling of unshared information in group decision making: Biased information sampling during discussion. *Journal of Personality and Social Psychology, 48*, 1467–1478.

Staw, B. M. (1976). Knee-deep in the big muddy: A study of escalating commitment to a chosen course of action. *Organizational Behavior and Human Decision Processes, 16*, 27–44.

Suchner, R. W., & Jackson, D. (1976). Responsibility and status: A causal or only a spurious relationship? *Sociometry, 39*, 243–256.

Sutton, R. L., & Louis, M. R. (1987). How selecting and socializing newcomers influences insiders. *Human Resource Management, 26*, 347–361.

Tanford, S., & Penrod, S. (1984). Social influence model: A formal integration of research on majority and minority influence processes. *Psychological Bulletin, 95*, 189–225.

Thomas-Hunt, M. C., & Gruenfeld, D. H. (1998). A foot in two worlds: The participation of demographic boundary spanners in work groups. In M. A. Neale, E. A. Mannix, & D. H. Gruenfeld (Eds.), *Research on managing groups and teams: Composition* (pp. 39–57). Greenwich, CT: JAI Press.

Thomas-Hunt, M. C., & Phillips, K. W. (2003). Managing teams in the dynamic organization: The effects of revolving membership and changing task demands on expertise and status in groups. In R. S. Peterson & E. A. Mannix (Eds.), *Leading and managing people in the dynamic organization* (pp. 115–133). Mahwah, NJ: Lawrence Erlbaum Associates, Inc.

Thompson, L. L., & Choi, H. S. (Eds.). (2006). *Creativity and innovation in organizational teams*. Mahwah, NJ: Lawrence Erlbaum Associates, Inc.

Tierney, P., & Farmer, S. M. (2002). Creative self-efficacy: Its potential antecedents and relationship to creative potential. *Academy of Management Journal, 45*, 1137–1148.

Torrance, E. P. (1955). Some consequences of power differences on decision making in permanent and temporary three-man groups. In A. P. Hare, E. F. Borgatta, & R. F. Bales (Eds.), *Small groups* (pp. 482–492). New York: Knopf.

Trow, D. B. (1960). Membership succession and team performance. *Human Relations, 13*, 259–269.

Tuckman, B. W. (1965). Developmental sequence in small groups. *Psychological Bulletin, 63*, 384–399.

van Knippenberg, D. (1999). Social identity and persuasion: Reconsidering the role of group membership. In D. Abrams & M. A. Hogg (Eds.), *Social identity and social cognition* (pp. 315–331). Malden, MA: Blackwell.

van Knippenberg, D., De Dreu, C. K. W., & Homan, A. C. (2004). Work group diversity and group performance: An integrative model and research agenda. *Journal of Applied Psychology, 89*, 1008–1022.

van Knippenberg, D., & Schippers, M. C. (2007). Work group diversity. *Annual Review of Psychology, 58*, 515–541.

Van Maanen, J., & Schein, E. (1979). Toward a theory of organizational socialization. In B. M. Staw (Ed.), *Research in organizational behavior* (Vol. 1, pp. 209–264). Greenwich, CT: JAI Press.

West, M. A. (1990). The social psychology of innovation in groups. In M. A. West

& J. L. Farr (Eds.), *Innovation and creativity at work: Psychological and organizational strategies* (pp. 309–333). Chichester, UK: Wiley.

West, M. A., & Farr, J. L. (1990). Innovation at work. In M. A. West & J. L. Farr (Eds.), *Innovation and creativity at work: Psychological and organizational strategies* (pp. 3–13). Chichester, UK: Wiley.

West, M. A., & Wallace, M. (1991). Innovation in health care teams. *European Journal of Social Psychology, 21*, 303–315.

Wiggins, J. A., Dill, F., & Schwartz, R. D. (1965). On 'status-liability'. *Sociometry, 28*, 197–209.

Williams, K. Y., & O'Reilly, C. A. (1998). Demography and diversity in organizations: A review of 40 years of research. In B. M. Staw & R. I. Sutton (Eds.), *Research in organizational behavior* (Vol. 20, pp. 77–140). Greenwich, CT: JAI Press.

Wittenbaum, G. M., & Bowman, J. M. (2005). Member status and information exchange in decision-making groups. In E. A. Mannix, M. A. Neale, & M. C. Thomas-Hunt (Eds.), *Research on managing groups and teams: Status and groups* (pp. 143–168). London: Elsevier.

Wood, W., Lundgren, S., Ouellette, J. A., Busceme, S., & Blackstone, T. (1994). Processes of minority influence: Influence effectiveness and source perception. *Psychological Bulletin, 115*, 323–345.

Worchel, S. (1996). Emphasizing the social nature of groups in a developmental framework. In J. L. Nye & A. M. Brower (Eds.), *What's social about social cognition? Research on socially shared cognition in small groups* (pp. 261–282). Thousand Oaks, CA: Sage.

Worchel, S., Grossman, M., & Coutant, D. (1994). Minority influence in the group context: How group factors affect when the minority will be influential. In S. Moscovici, A. Mucchi-Faina, & A. Maass (Eds.), *Minority influence* (pp. 97–114). Chicago: Nelson-Hall.

Zdaniuk, B., & Levine, J. M. (1996). Anticipated interaction and thought generation: The role of faction size. *British Journal of Social Psychology, 35*, 201–218.

Ziller, R. C. (1965). Toward a theory of open and closed groups. *Psychological Bulletin, 64*, 164–182.

Ziller, R. C., & Behringer, R. D. (1960). Assimilation of the knowledgeable newcomer under conditions of group success and failure. *Journal of Abnormal and Social Psychology, 60*, 288–292.

Ziller, R. C., Behringer, R. D., & Goodchilds, J. D. (1960). The minority newcomer in open and closed groups. *Journal of Psychology, 50*, 75–84.

Ziller, R. C., Behringer, R. D., & Jansen, M. J. (1961). The newcomer in open and closed groups. *Journal of Applied Psychology, 45*, 55–58.

# 11 Direct and indirect minority influence in groups

*Christine M. Smith*
Grand Valley State University, USA

*R. Scott Tindale*
Loyola University, USA

Thirty-five years ago the study of social influence could be equated with the study of the processes by which individuals conformed to majority opinion (i.e., Festinger, 1950, 1954). The work of Moscovici (Moscovici, Lage, & Naffrechoux, 1969) challenged this definition by demonstrating that minority factions were also powerful sources of social influence. While Moscovici's (1976) early theoretical work regarding minority impact conceived of social influence as an interactive phenomenon whereby reciprocal influence occurred between minority and majority factions, his early empirical work highlighted a much narrower and less dynamic aspect of the influence process. This work de-emphasized social interaction in that it focused on individual cognitive processes in response to minority-influence exposure. Clearly, these classic experiments played a large role in defining the research paradigm adopted by later minority-influence researchers. Although this is slowly changing, the most typical research paradigm used by minority-influence researchers to date focuses upon majority members' cognitive responses (e.g., attitude change, problem-solving ability, thought listing) to an often faceless individual who ostensibly holds a minority opinion regarding the topic at hand and with whom the majority member never interacts (Clark, 1988; Martin & Hewstone, 1999; Mucchi-Faina, Maass, & Volpato, 1991; Paicheler, 1976).

Without a doubt, the non-interaction paradigm has been utilized successfully in the generation of a rich body of empirical findings describing several conditions under which minority sources have an impact upon the majority (see Martin & Hewstone, 2001, for an excellent review of this work). However, it is our contention that the most consistent findings that (a) minority influence is much more likely to be indirect rather than direct, (b) is more frequently found in private rather than public contexts, and (c) tends to be delayed rather than immediate (see Wood, Lundgren, Ouellette, Busceme, & Blackstone, 1994) might well be paradigm-specific conclusions. That is, when influence processes are studied within contexts that allow for reciprocal exchange between minority and majority factions (e.g., freely interacting groups), especially when consensus must be reached, minority influence is often direct, immediate, and public (Smith, Tindale, &

Anderson, 2001). Stated somewhat differently, the interdependence that exists between minority and majority factions is likely to be much more salient in interacting groups relative to other contexts (e.g., a single majority member reading a persuasive message authored by a minority source). The norms that govern decision-making groups usually empower minority factions to insist that their viewpoint be heard and that the final group product reflect their position in some way (Miller & Anderson, 1979; Miller, Jackson, Mueller, & Schersching, 1987; Nemeth, 1977; Smith, Tindale, & Dugoni, 1996). Furthermore, an additional advantage of studying the interaction between minority and majority factions is that it allows the changes in group processes attributable to the presence of minority factions to be identified. Research using freely interacting groups has shown that the presence of a minority source of influence systematically changes the manner in which the groups consider and treat the evidence before them, and, generally speaking, this change in process serves to improve the group's products/decisions (Brodbeck, Kerschreiter, Mojzisch, Frey, & Schulz-Hardt, 2002; Smith, 2003).

In the present chapter we review the literature on minority impact within the context of freely interacting groups. We make the distinction between direct and indirect minority influence and organize the work around this particular classification. We consider direct minority influence to be minority impact regarding the group's focal issue/task at hand (i.e., the group adopts the minority point of view as its own or shifts its position in the direction of the minority source of influence). Indirect minority influence, on the other hand, is any change in the group process associated with exposure to minority dissent. That is, the minority's point of view is not adopted as the group's own, but the minority's presence changes the manner in which the information exchanged amongst members is treated and acted upon. Of course, as mentioned above, these process changes often lead to the consideration of perspectives or ideas that would have otherwise remained unexplored in the absence of minority influence. This, in turn, results in a group decision/product that is superior to the one that would have been generated in the absence of minority dissent.

## Direct minority influence

### *When minorities prevail*

The small group-decision-making and problem-solving literature is replete with examples of direct minority influence. Unfortunately, this literature is rarely construed as being relevant to minority influence research (but see Kerr, 2001; Smith et al., 2001). Interestingly, social psychological evidence of direct minority influence in groups predated Moscovici's (1976) seminal work by more than four decades. Shaw's (1932) classic study comparing individual and group problem-solving accuracy showed that groups were quite good at solving problems that very few individuals could solve alone. Shaw believed that groups outperformed individuals because groups engaged in error checking more effectively, thereby reducing the chances that an incorrect response alternative would be chosen. Although there is empirical evidence supporting the notion that group members engage in error checking (e.g., Hinsz, 1990; Tindale & Sheffey, 1988), several combinatorial models of group performance (e.g., Davis, 1973; Lorge & Solomon, 1955; Smoke & Zajonc, 1962) predict that groups outperform individuals without making an error-checking assumption. One such example, Lorge and Solomon's (1955) 'Model A', an early mathematical model of group performance, states that the probability of a group solving a particular problem correctly is equal to the probability that the group contains at least one member who is capable of solving the problem correctly. In other words whenever a group contains a correct minority faction (either single or supported), Model A predicts strong direct minority influence. However, the fifty years of research following the publication of Lorge and Solomon's classic paper suggest that Model A, in many instances, over predicts group performance. In other words, groups with the resources necessary to solve a problem successfully (i.e., they contain at least one 'solver') frequently fail to do so. Clearly, the ability to predict group problem-solving performance accurately requires the consideration of more than whether or not the group contains one or more 'solvers'.

*When minority position is an easily demonstrated 'truth'*

Laughlin's intellective–judgemental task dimension is an extremely useful tool in predicting when minority factions will prevail in group-decision-making contexts (Laughlin, 1980; Laughlin & Ellis, 1986). Intellective tasks are those for which a 'demonstrably correct' solution exists. For example, naming the 27 members of the European Union, stating the number of times an American president has been impeached, and calculating the area of a circle are all intellective tasks. In contrast, judgemental tasks are those for which no objectively correct solution exists. Examples of judgemental tasks include deciding whether or not Turkey should be allowed into the European Union, naming the best deterrent against global terrorism, and deciding whether or not the 40 million dollars spent on George W. Bush's presidential inauguration was extravagant. In other words, judgemental tasks are those that require the group members to state their collective opinion regarding a particular topic. According to Laughlin and Ellis (1986), a problem has a demonstrably correct solution when it meets the following four criteria: (1) the group members share a symbolic system that may be utilized in solving the problem; (2) the group members collectively possess enough information to solve the problem within the symbolic system; (3) every group member possesses enough knowledge about the system to recognize the correct response when proposed; and (4) individuals who correctly solve the problem must be able and motivated to explain and demonstrate why the response is correct. Conversely, according to Laughlin, none of the response alternatives for a judgemental task can be demonstrated as correct. In such cases, the 'correctness' of a particular alternative depends, in part, on the degree to which most people feel it is the best alternative.

According to Laughlin and Ellis (1986), group consensus processes will vary as a function of the position of the task along the intellective–judgemental continuum. 'Eureka' tasks are extremely high in demonstrability (therefore well to the intellective end of the continuum), and once a single individual within the group generates the correct response she or he has little difficulty convincing the group of the solution's correctness. For example, when a group is presented with the words 'ship', 'suit', and 'parking', and asked for a fourth word that is related to all three as is done with the Remote Associates Test (Mednick & Mednick, 1967), the individual who suggests 'space' will have little difficulty convincing her/his fellow group members that the solution is correct (Laughlin, 1980). A 'truth-wins' group-decision process (which is identical to Lorge and Solomon's, 1955, 'Model A') appears to be the best-fitting model for most problems with extremely high demonstrability. Laughlin found that single minority members arguing in favour of 'truth' prevailed in five-person groups working on highly demonstrable mathematics problems (Laughlin & Ellis, 1986) and the Remote Associates Test (Laughlin, Kerr, Munch, & Haggarty, 1976).

When decision-making groups work on tasks that are lower in demonstrability than Eureka tasks, the consensus process is best described as 'truth-supported wins'. That is, there must be at least two group members who advocate the correct alternative before the group accepts the solution as the correct one. Some examples of intellective tasks that are lower in demonstrability include vocabulary problems (Laughlin, Kerr, Davis, Halff, & Marciniak, 1975) and verbal analogies (Laughlin et al., 1976). Laughlin and Adamopoulos (1980) found that six-person groups working on verbal analogy problems operated under a 'truth-supported wins' consensus process. In this particular study, the probability of the group adopting the correct minority position increased substantially when at least two group members (as opposed to one) were arguing in favour of the correct alternative. It should be noted that in the minority-influence literature parallel effects have been found. That is, minority impact typically increases as minority faction size changes from one to two sources of influence (Arbuthnot & Wayner, 1982; Gordijn, De Vries, & De Dreu, 2002; Tindale, Davis, Vollrath, Nagao, & Hinsz, 1990).

When groups work on tasks where no demonstrably correct solution exists (i.e., closer to the judgemental end of the intellective–judgemental continuum), most groups operate under a majority/plurality process (Davis, 1982; Stasser, Kerr, & Davis, 1989). In such contexts minority factions are at a distinct disadvantage because, in the absence of a shared symbolic system or framework that could be used to demonstrate the correctness of a solution, social support is instead used to determine which alternative is correct or optimal. Therefore a group's decision regarding which grant proposal to fund, which job candidate to hire, or whether to convict or acquit a defendant will most often be determined by the size of the factions favouring each alternative.

In summary, position verifiability is a key determinant of direct minority impact in decision-making and problem-solving groups. A consistent finding within the group-decision-making/problem-solving literature is that minority factions are more influential, and quite frequently prevail, when they can easily demonstrate the veracity of their position to fellow group members. It necessarily follows, then, that direct minority impact will be observed more frequently in contexts where the minority faction can appeal to a shared symbolic system that can be used to demonstrate the validity of its position or when it can frame the problem in such a way that dependence upon the principle of social proof (Cialdini, 2001; Festinger, 1950, 1954) is minimized. Of course, we do not wish to imply that the principle of social proof is never employed to validate minority points of view successfully. For example, in the United States those who are opposed to reproductive rights (i.e., against a woman's right to decide to terminate a pregnancy) have gained political power by stating repeatedly that their position is held by a majority of Americans (Snow, Rochford, Worden, & Benford, 1986), whereas, in reality those who uniformly oppose a woman's right to an abortion are in the minority. Experimental evidence for this can also be found in the *Zeitgeist* literature regarding minority influence. This research suggests that messages attributed to a minority source are more influential when the content is consistent with the position that is most prevalent within the general population as compared to when the message runs counter to the *Zeitgeist* (Clark & Maass, 1990; Paicheler, 1976, 1977). Clark (1990) proposed that minority arguments in line with the *Zeitgeist* are perceived as valid because of the implied social support for the position being argued.

### When minority position is consistent with a shared representation

As mentioned above, within the group-performance literature, minority factions are not frequently predicted to prevail when the group's task involves reaching consensus regarding an issue that is well toward the judgemental end of the intellective–judgemental continuum. In such instances the use of social support to demonstrate the validity of a particular alternative favours majority rather than minority factions within groups. Not surprisingly, Wood et al.'s (1994) meta-analytic review of the minority-influence literature draws the same conclusion. They found that, relative to majority influence, minority influence was weak when subjective opinion judgements were studied. However, Tindale's work on shared representations suggests that it might not always be the objective or subjective nature of the task per se that determines who will be influential. Often the position being argued can be implied correct by a shared task representation and when this is the case the faction whose position is consistent with the shared representation is most powerful (Kameda, Tindale, & Davis, 2003; Tindale & Kameda, 2000; Tindale, Smith, Thomas, Filkins, & Sheffey, 1996).

A shared representation is 'any task/situation relevant concept, norm, perspective, or cognitive process that is shared by most or all of the group members' (Tindale et al., 1996, p. 84). Examples of shared representations include learned rules or axioms, cognitive heuristics, cultural or societal norms, and ways of framing the problem. In a series of group-decision-making studies, Tindale and his colleagues have shown that when group members, regardless of their minority or majority status, argue in favour of the position consistent with the shared representation, their influence potential is greatly enhanced (Smith, Dykema-Engblade, Walker, Niven, & McGough, 2000; Smith, Tindale, & Steiner, 1998; Tindale, Anderson, Smith, Steiner, & Filkins, 1998; Tindale, Sheffey, & Scott, 1993). The influence advantage results from the shared representation creating a context within which arguments favouring a particular alternative are seen as valid or plausible. Stated somewhat differently, shared representations often allow for 'truth' to be defined in a way other than social consensus.

Asymmetries in the social-influence patterns consistently found in the jury-decision-making literature illustrate this point nicely. The jury's task is one that falls somewhere between the intellective and judgemental anchors of Laughlin's task dimension. In criminal cases there is always a correct alternative (i.e., the defendant either did or did not commit the crime) but it is often low in demonstrability. Not surprisingly, a 2/3 majority model tends to provide a good description of the jury decision process (Davis, 1980; Tindale & Davis, 1983). Overall, however, jurors who support acquittal tend to be more influential than those who support conviction (Davis, Kerr, Stasser, Meek, & Holt, 1977; Kerr & MacCoun, 1985; Tindale et al., 1990). Therefore, even if seven members of a twelve-person jury favour guilty at the beginning of their deliberation, the final verdict is more likely than not to be defined by the five-person minority favouring not guilty. This 'defendant-protection norm' (Tindale & Davis, 1983) is likely due to the processing goal shared by the jurors. The reasonable-doubt criterion requires that jurors vote for conviction only in the event that they cannot generate any reasonable doubts concerning the defendant's guilt. Therefore, arguing in favour of acquittal is often much easier than is arguing in favour of conviction because only one reasonable doubt needs to be generated in order to validate the acquittal position. Consistent with this notion, Kerr and MacCoun (1985) found that minority factions favouring acquittal were not influential (i.e., the leniency bias disappeared) when the reasonable-doubt criterion was replaced by a preponderance-of-the-evidence criterion. Under the preponderance-of-evidence criterion (i.e., the verdict rendered favours the side with the most evidence supporting it) there is no inherently easier verdict to validate, and, therefore, majority factions tend to prevail.

Smith et al. (2000) compared numerical minorities arguing in favour of and against the death penalty in the context of five-person freely interacting groups who were asked to either hold a discussion or to reach a group decision regarding the issue (consensus-seeking groups). As mentioned earlier, the *Zeitgeist* literature has consistently shown that minorities arguing against the spirit of the times are less influential than those arguing in favour of the *Zeitgeist*. In contrast, Smith et al. (2000) found the exact opposite pattern of results in the attitude change among majority members who were members of consensus-seeking groups. Minorities who argued against the death penalty, which in the United States is a position held by a minority of the population, were more influential than those who argued in favour of the death penalty (see Figure 11.1). Smith et al. argued that the shared religious beliefs of their participants affected the ease with which anti-capital-punishment minorities demonstrated the correctness of the position they were arguing. Majority attitude change was significantly related to whether or not the anti-death-penalty minority member presented arguments that were grounded in religious principles (e.g., thou shalt not kill, criminals will pay for their crimes in the afterworld, only God can be just). Therefore, in this particular study, an issue quite judgemental in nature was validated by a shared representation (religious beliefs). These results are also consistent with our earlier argument that the heightened interdependence between minority and majority factions that results from the need to reach consensus on an issue empowers the minority faction. Figure 11.1 reveals that minorities arguing against the *Zeitgeist* were only influential when they were members of groups whose task was to reach a collective decision regarding the death penalty.

Within the early group-polarization research (i.e., research showing the 'risky shift'), risk was posited as a value that was shared by group members (Myers & Lamm, 1976). Although there is ample evidence suggesting that the context determines whether risk or caution is valued, a number of studies have shown that decisions involving risk produce direct minority influence. For example, in a study employing the 'Asian Disease' problem, Tindale et al. (1993) found strong asymmetries in the social-influence patterns favouring the risky alternative when problems were framed in terms of losses. Consistent with Kahneman and Tversky's (1979) prospect theory, minorities favouring the risky alternative were more powerful when most group members were presented with the loss version of the problem. Similarly, Laughlin and Early (1982) found that the group-consensus process for choice dilemmas that typically result in large shifts in favour of risk or in favour of caution were best described as 'risk-supported wins' and 'caution-supported wins', respectively. For items that showed less

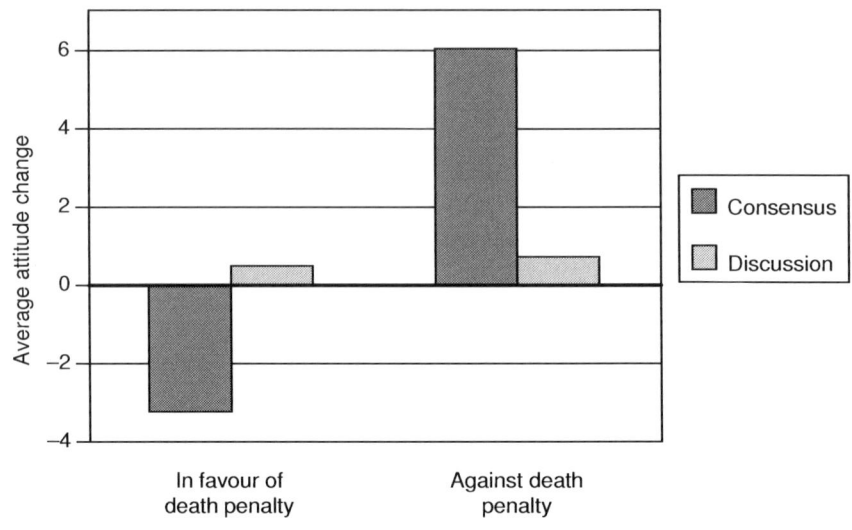

Position argued by minority

*Figure 11.1* Majority members' mean attitude change as a function of position argued by minority and group's goal. Negative change indicates movement away from the minority position whereas positive change indicates movement towards the minority position.

polarization, majority models tended to produce the best fits to the data. Therefore, for items where the respective values of risk or caution are strong, minorities favouring the value-consistent positions were much more influential. Clark (1988) also found that for risky-choice dilemmas, minority factions arguing in favour of risk were extremely influential.

In summary, the research reviewed above suggests that minority factions become much more powerful when they can frame their counter-normative position within the context of a widely shared belief, value, or normative principle. Interestingly, Lakoff (2004) has attributed the recent electoral failures of the American Democratic Party to the party's inability to properly frame their issues. He argued that American progressive politicians will continue to fail unless they learn to frame their values in such a way that they appeal to a wider audience. For example, gay rights, affirmative action, reproductive rights, and breaking up media monopolies are issues that should be framed in terms of the personal freedom they imply. Given that most Americans consider personal freedom a moral imperative, the opposition of the above-mentioned issues becomes more difficult when presented within the freedom frame. An additional example of a minority faction attempting to frame an issue to gain the support of the majority can be found in the words of Michel Barnier, France's minister of foreign affairs. When urging French citizens to vote in favour of the

European Union's constitution in the May 2005 referendum, he claimed, 'The choice is between a European Europe and a Europe under American influence' (Barnier, 2005). Framing the issue as a choice between Europe and America capitalizes on the French citizens' discomfort with perceived American dominance and their desire to be regarded as a world power of equal status to the United States.

### *Minorities who block change, reduce polarization and prevent decisions*

As mentioned earlier, a focus on overt attitude change as the single indicator of minority impact results in the consistent underestimation of the power held by minority factions (Levine & Kaarbo, 2001; Smith & Diven, 2002). For example, Levine and Kaarbo (2001) argued that in addition to promoting change, minority factions can be influential by blocking changes advocated by majority factions. That is, influential minority factions can prevent groups from adopting new policies (i.e., Spain and Poland's initial rejection of the European Union's constitution on the grounds that it affords them fewer votes than they have under the 2000 Nice Treaty). Levine calls the blocking of a change to a new position 'conservative influence'. In contrast, 'modernist influence' occurs when a minority faction successfully blocks the majority's attempt to return to an older policy or decision (e.g., the blocking of George W. Bush's 'Clear Skies' legislation in the US Senate because it relaxes the regulation of carbon dioxide emissions to levels higher than those allowed by the Clean Air Act, or US senators blocking elements of the Patriot Act because it removes too many individual freedoms).

Several studies that have explored minority and majority influence simultaneously within the context of freely interacting discussion groups have shown that minority factions are quite influential in that they prevent the majority from adopting an even more extreme version of their original position. For example, in a study where group members discussed but did not reach a collective decision regarding establishing English as the official language of the United States, Smith et al. (1996) found that members of unanimous groups favouring the issue (the majority point of view) became polarized following group discussion. Majority members in groups with a single minority member arguing against establishing English as the official language shifted their attitudes to a less extreme position as did majority members of groups with two minority members (see Figure 11.2). Similarly, Smith and Hirchert (1996) found that group decisions regarding acceptance/ rejection of the death penalty were significantly affected by the presence of a minority faction (against the death penalty). That is, unanimous groups' collective decisions were more extreme (in favour of the death penalty) than the decisions made by groups with minority members present. Thus, in each of these studies the minority faction's influence is analogous to a rein or weight, reducing the degree of attitude polarization within the group.

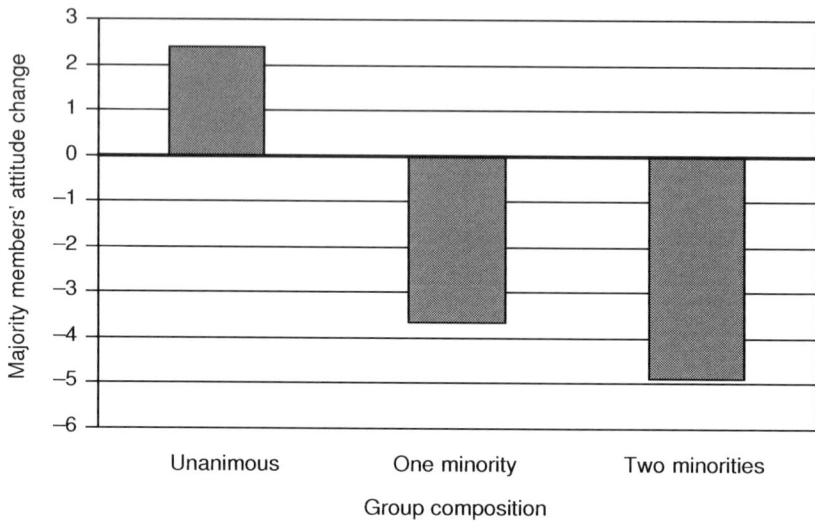

*Figure 11.2* Majority members' attitude change as a function of group composition. Negative attitude change indicates movement towards the minority position, whereas positive attitude change reflects polarization of majority position.

The decision rule under which a group operates plays a large role in determining the extent to which the minority factions are likely to be influential. That is, minority factions within groups where unanimous decisions are required wield far more power than those within groups where decisions are rendered once a majority faction is formed (Miller, 1989; Miller et al., 1987). Under the unanimity rule, minority factions cannot be ignored and their commitment to their position necessarily impedes the group's goal attainment (i.e., reaching a decision) thereby making minority and majority factions interdependent in a way that they are not under majority rule. Therefore, compromise positions that reflect both the majority and minority point of view are much more likely in contexts where unanimous decisions are required or the norm (Miller, 1989).

The degree to which a group accepts impasse is most likely determined by a variety of contextual variables. Within the context of the American jury, however, the failure to reach a unanimous decision (resulting in a hung jury) is a viable and acceptable outcome. Both mock jury research (Kerr & MacCoun, 1985) and real jurors' accounts of their pre- and post-deliberation verdicts (Zeisel & Diamond, 1987) suggest that hung juries are a relatively commonplace occurrence when minority factions are present (with the rate being somewhat more pronounced when the minority faction favours acquittal). Therefore, the viability of the 'no decision' alternative affords the minority faction within a jury a considerable amount of power in that 'hold out' jurors can prevent the majority faction from prevailing.

Finally, a group's procedural rules regarding discussion might serve to enhance the direct impact of minority factions. For example, within the United States Senate, there are no rules regarding the length of time any given issue can be discussed. A senator may take and keep the floor for as long as desired provided the senator continues to stand and remains in the senate chamber. Therefore, minority factions who have too few votes to prevail can prevent a vote by refusing to end the discussion. The filibuster has been used in the US Senate with varying degrees of success. For example, Senator Strom Thurmond was unsuccessful in preventing a vote on a civil rights bill in 1957 although he spoke for 24 hours and 18 minutes against it. More recently, Senator Robert Byrd successfully prevented a vote on George W. Bush's nomination of Miguel Estrada to the Federal Court of Appeals by using the filibuster tactic.

Our understanding of the impact of minority factions is certainly made richer by the consideration of task-oriented groups with goals requiring that a collective decision is made. Our review of this literature suggests that evidence of minority influence is easily found when the notion of influence is broadened (e.g., reducing polarization, preventing a decision). Furthermore, in situations where consensus must be reached, the task has a correct or optimal solution, and the members share an appropriate task representation for solving the problem, minorities favouring the correct solution are quite influential, in a direct, immediate, and public way.

## Indirect minority influence

Nemeth and Nemeth-Brown (2003) have argued that dissent is a great liberator of thought and a considerable amount of empirical work supports the notion that exposure to minority influence leads to divergent thinking (De Dreu & De Vries, 1993; Nemeth, 1995; Nemeth & Kwan, 1985, 1987; Smith & Fountaine, 1995; Smith et al., 1996; Van Dyne & Saavedra, 1996). That is, minority sources of influence prompt majority members to explore the issue under debate from multiple perspectives as well as to consider novel, previously overlooked aspects of the problem. This, almost invariably, leads to more effective problem solving. For example, exposure to minority dissent was found to be associated with enhanced analogous thinking (Martin & Hewstone, 1999), detection of useful problem-solving strategies (Nemeth, 1995), and recall of information (Nemeth, Mayseless, Sherman, & Brown, 1990). At the individual level, minority dissent has been associated with responses/solutions that are higher in creativity than the responses of those exposed to majority influence (De Dreu & De Vries, 1993; Nemeth, 1995). For example, during a colour-perception task Nemeth and Kwan (1985) exposed individuals to a disagreeing minority source of influence or to no influence at all (control condition). Later these individuals were asked to generate word associations to the colours blue and green (the colours used in the colour-perception task). Those exposed to minority influence generated more original/creative associations to the colour words than did members of the control condition.

Despite the large literature suggesting a relationship between exposure to minority influence and divergent thinking, until recently, the notion that group products would be affected and thus improved by each individual's divergent thinking was largely conjectural. That is, well-known group-level phenomena (i.e., motivation loss, coordination loss) might serve to 'cancel out' the beneficial effects of individual-level divergent thinking. In the following sections we turn our attention to a diverse collection of studies, all using freely interacting groups that demonstrate the benefits of minority dissent.

### The search for information

Effective group decision making and problem solving requires that group members thoroughly explore and consider information that is available and relevant to the task at hand (Hinsz, Tindale, & Vollrath, 1997). One of the reasons that groups outperform individuals working alone is that groups tend to have many more resources available to them than do single individuals, both in terms of knowledge (collectively held) and information-processing capacity. The simple existence of these additional resources does not ensure that they will be utilized fully, however. An extremely robust finding in the group-decision-making literature is that groups often fail to effectively share and combine the information that is available to them, with the end result being a suboptimal group decision. The work most illustrative of this phenomenon has used the hidden-profile paradigm (Stasser, Stewart, & Wittenbaum, 1995; Stasser & Titus, 1985, 1987).

A hidden profile exists within a group when the optimal decision is supported by information uniquely held by individual group members. In order for the hidden profile to be revealed, all group members must share their uniquely held information regarding the decision at hand. Imagine a three-person group attempting to decide between two job candidates named Jeanne and Robert. Each group member holds one unshared piece of information favouring Jeanne. Each group member also holds two shared (by all group members) pieces of information favouring Robert. Assuming that all information is weighted equally in terms of importance, before group discussion, each individual member of the group ought to prefer Robert, even though Jeanne is the superior candidate (she has one more piece of evidence favouring her hire than does Robert). Jeanne's superior qualifications will be revealed only if each group member, during discussion, shares her/his uniquely held information. There are several reasons why this may fail to happen. First, group members might begin their group discussion of the candidates by stating their initial preferences. Such an approach typically results in only the information consistent with each member's preference being discussed (Gigone & Hastie, 1993, 1997), and increases the likelihood of discussing shared rather than unique information, especially when a hidden profile exists. If all group members are in agreement at the outset of their discussion the members may see little reason for discussing any of Jeanne's characteristics (Stasser & Stewart, 1992) thereby reducing the likelihood that the hidden profile will be revealed.

Minority dissent stimulates the consideration of multiple perspectives in a decision-making task (Nemeth & Kwan, 1987; Nemeth & Rogers, 1996). Several studies utilizing the hidden-profile paradigm have revealed that exposure to minority dissent can increase the likelihood that group members will share information unique to them, thereby improving the quality of the group's decision (McLeod, Baron, Marti, & Yoon, 1997; Stewart & Stasser, 1998). Brodbeck et al. (2002) found that minority dissent was associated with significant gains in the amount of information discussed by groups making a hiring decision. Even when the information was distributed within the group in such a way that the minority individuals preferred the less desirable of the candidates (i.e., a candidate inconsistent with the hidden profile), their influence was positively associated with both the quantity and the quality of information processing that occurred within groups. In other words, regardless of the veracity of their position, the presence of minority sources of influence improved the sharing and consideration of evidence within the decision-making groups.

Interestingly, individual group members seem to be aware of their enhanced information processing/group performance when exposed to minority dissent. In the Smith and Hirchert (1996) study mentioned earlier, individuals who were members of groups with minority factions reported that their discussions regarding the death penalty were considerably more robust, thorough, and careful than did members of unanimous groups. Discussion lengths of groups with minority factions were more than double the length of unanimous groups.

### Minority influence and creativity/innovation

Creativity is defined as the process by which novel, acceptable, and useful ideas are developed (Amabile, 1996; Stein, 1953). Until recently, most researchers have assumed that the creative process was solely an individual one. As a matter of fact, social interaction was often assumed to hinder the creative process. Advertising executive Charles Brower captured this sentiment in his well-known quote: 'The good ideas are all hammered out in agony by individuals, not spewed out by groups' (Simpson, 1964). Yet, creativity is an inherently social process. After all, innovations are not judged in a social vacuum. Ideas and innovations are judged as acceptable and useful by large groups of people, not single individuals. Furthermore, these groups of individuals have culturally and historically determined beliefs and values that most certainly affect the degree to which any idea is considered creative (Csikszentmihalyi, 1988; Simonton, 1984). Recent research suggests that the role that groups play in the creative process most certainly extends beyond that of determining the creative value of products (Paulus & Nijstad, 2003).

Several studies using a variety of research paradigms have demonstrated that group creativity is enhanced as a function of minority-influence exposure. In a recent study using freely interacting laboratory dyads, Smith (2008) found that dyad performance, evaluated along a variety of dimensions, was enhanced as a function of minority influence. She used three different types of dyads in an attempt to disentangle exposure to disagreement/conflict and exposure to minority influence. Agreement dyads were composed of two individuals who were in agreement regarding the ranking of three candidates ostensibly running for student senate. Conflict dyads contained members who disagreed regarding their top choice for student senate. Finally, minority dyads were the same as conflict dyads but members were also told that one of the members' top choice had been endorsed by a small minority of individuals at the same university (there-fore, one member of the dyad represented the 'minority' point of view). All dyads were asked to reach a collective decision regarding which candidate to endorse, to list all of the reasons they preferred their candidate of choice, to brainstorm in an attempt to solve an important campus problem (lack of parking spaces for students and faculty), and, finally, to choose their best idea from the brainstorming session and develop it further into a formal proposal to solve the parking problem.

Dyads that contained a minority source of influence discussed the candi-dates for a longer amount of time than did agreement and conflict groups. Although minority dyads did not list more reasons for choosing their preferred candidate, their reasons represented significantly more distinct categories (i.e., they evaluated the candidate from multiple perspectives). Similarly, the minority dyads did not generate more solutions to the park-ing problem but their solutions represented many more distinct categories of solutions relative to either of the other two types (a pattern associated with higher creativity in brainstorming groups). Both the breadth of reasons for candidate choice and parking solutions are presented in Figures 11.3 and 11.4. Finally, the proposals developed by minority dyads were evaluated by independent coders to have a significantly higher 'action orientation' to them than did the proposals of either other dyad type. That is, the proposals developed by minority dyads contained more constructive and effective solutions to the parking problem. In addition to stimulating divergent and creative thought, the sources of minority influence in Smith's study were very positively perceived by their partner relative to the sources of conflict. This finding was surprising because the minority-influence literature consistently shows that being in the minority, especially under conditions where group consensus is required, reduces liking and accept-ance of the minority source of influence (Levine, 1980). It seems, then, at

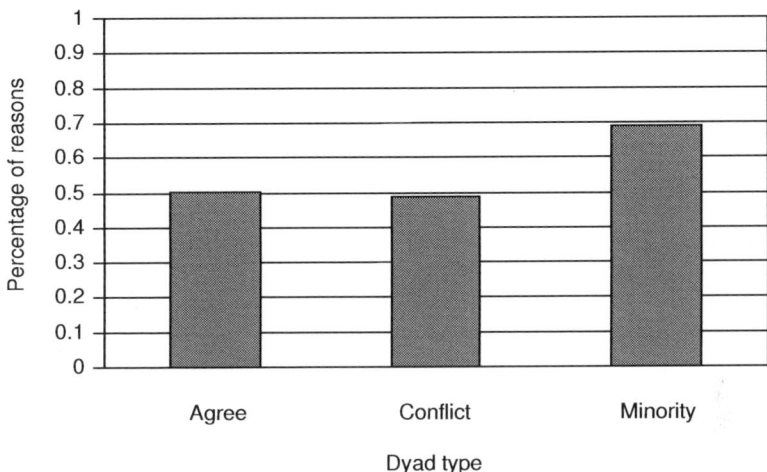

*Figure 11.3* The breadth of reasons generated for supporting a political candidate as a function of dyad type.

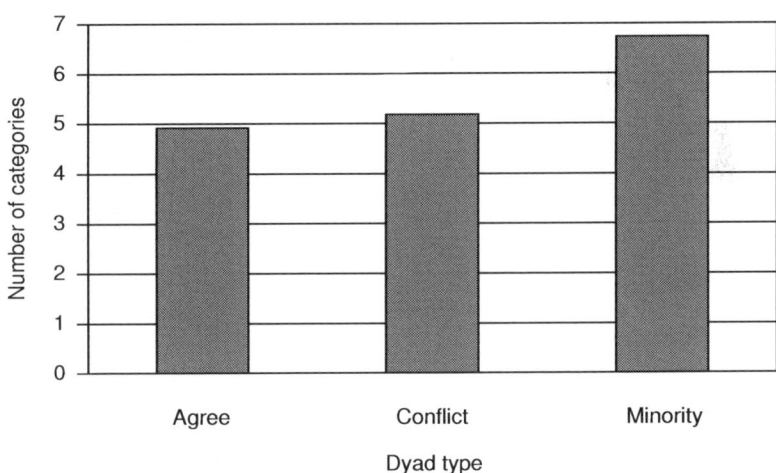

*Figure 11.4* Breadth of brainstorming categories as a function of dyad type.

least in this context, that the relative benefits associated with the expression of a minority point of view were without cost to the minority source of influence.

It might be expected that the cost associated with being in the minority would increase in groups with a history longer than that of the typical laboratory group. Van Dyne and Saavedra (1996) had ongoing university classroom groups work on a variety of tasks in either the presence or absence of a minority influence confederate. They found that the groups exposed to minority influence generated higher quality, more original products than did those groups who were not exposed to minority influence. They did find, however, that a considerable amount of stress was felt by the individual in the minority position.

Further evidence linking exposure to dissent with enhanced group creativity has been generated by De Dreu and his colleagues (e.g., De Dreu, 2002; De Dreu & West, 2001). In one set of studies, diverse work teams were surveyed regarding both the amount of minority dissent present within their work groups and the degree to which work-group/team members perceived themselves to play a role in work-group/team decision making. Supervisors' ratings of work-group/team innovations (i.e., creative ideas actually put into action) were positively associated with the presence of minority dissent, but only under conditions where there was a high level of team participation in the decision-making process (De Dreu & West, 2001). Similarly, De Dreu (2002) found a positive relationship between minority dissent and team innovations in a heterogeneous sample of semi-autonomous management teams. However, this relationship was found only when the teams reflected upon the processes by which they could best achieve team goals and objectives. De Dreu (2002) argued that minority dissent was linked to innovation under conditions of high participation and when group members reflected upon the decision-making process because each of these conditions serves to increase the likelihood that the minority dissent present in the environment will be processed thoroughly. In other words, in each of these conditions the overall attentiveness to divergent points of view was likely enhanced.

These three studies taken together suggest that the relationship between exposure to minority dissent and group creativity is quite robust. Evidence converging on this notion was found in a wide variety of groups (ranging from ad hoc laboratory dyads to intact work teams) using a wide variety of research methodologies (e.g., experimental, surveys).

## Summary and implications

We have attempted to broaden the context in which the beneficial effects of minority dissent are considered by focusing on the findings generated from a paradigm quite different from that typically used in minority influence research. The study of minority influence within the context of freely interacting groups allows for the detection of a wider variety of ways in which minority sources are influential. Examples drawn from the small group-decision-making/problem-solving literature demonstrate the importance of minority dissent, both in terms of enhancing the overall quality of the group's products as well as improving the group's information processing. We also demonstrated that the group-decision-making context is one where direct minority impact is frequently observed. We argued that in this context, compromise positions are more likely, due in part to the interdependence that exists between minority and majority factions within the group.

An obvious lacuna in the literature reviewed is research that systematically studies simultaneously direct and indirect minority influence within freely interacting groups. Although all of the examples we have presented involved tasks where divergent thinking was beneficial, this is not likely to be the case in all instances. It seems likely that when groups are working on tasks where divergent thinking is likely to hinder performance, the presence of minority dissent might be associated with poorer, rather than better, group performance. The careful study of issues regarding the timing of minority dissent within the overall decision-making process would also be extremely beneficial. Many studies have shown that the effects of minority dissent generalize to subsequent tasks (Nemeth & Kwan, 1985; Smith et al., 1996). The longevity of these effects has not been tested, however. It is not clear whether the divergent thinking associated with minority dissent generalizes beyond one additional task. Finally, more research ought to be carried out with groups who have a history working on tasks of importance to their members. The effects of minority dissent in such groups, as well as the fate that they experience, is quite likely different from that of minority sources of influence in ad hoc laboratory groups.

## References

Amabile, T. (1996). *Creativity in context*. Boulder, CO: Westview Press.

Arbuthnot, J., & Wayner, M. (1982). Minority influence: Effects of size, conversion, and sex. *Journal of Psychology: Interdisciplinary and Applied, 11*, 285–295.

Barnier, M. (2005, April 27). 'You must choose a . . . European Europe'. *Ta Nea*, p. N41.

Brodbeck, F. C., Kerschreiter, R., Mojzisch, A., Frey, D., & Schulz-Hardt, S. (2002). The dissemination of critical, unshared information in decision-making groups: The effects of pre-discussion dissent. *European Journal of Social Psychology, 32*, 35–56.

Cialdini, R. B. (2001). *Influence: Science and practice*. Needham Heights, MA: Allyn & Bacon.

Clark, R. D., III (1988). On predicting minority influence. *European Journal of Social Psychology, 18*, 515–526.

Clark, R. D., III (1990). Minority influence: The role of argument refutation of the majority position and social support for the minority position. *European Journal of Social Psychology, 20*, 489–497.

Clark, R. D., III, & Maass, A. (1990). The effects of majority size on minority influence. *European Journal of Social Psychology, 20*, 119–132.

Csikszentmihalyi, M. (1988). Society, culture, and person: A systems view of creativity. In R. J. Sternberg (Ed.), *The nature of creativity* (pp. 15–35). Cambridge, UK: Cambridge University Press.

Davis, J. H. (1973). Group decision and social interaction: A theory of social decision schemes. *Psychological Review, 80*, 97–125.

Davis, J. H. (1980). Group decision and procedural justice. In M. Fishbein (Ed.),

*Progress in social psychology* (Vol. 1, pp. 157–229). Hillsdale, NJ: Lawrence Erlbaum Associates, Inc.

Davis, J. H. (1982). Social interaction as a combinatorial process in group decision making. In H. Brandstatter, J. H. Davis, & G. Stocker-Kreichgauer (Eds.), *Group decision making* (pp. 27–58). London: Academic Press.

Davis, J. H., Kerr, N. L., Stasser, G., Meek, D., & Holt, R. (1977). Victim consequences, sentence severity, and decision processes in mock juries. *Organizational Behavior and Human Performance, 18,* 346–365.

De Dreu, C. K. W. (2002). Team innovation and team effectiveness: The importance of minority dissent and reflexivity. *European Journal of Work and Organizational Psychology, 3,* 285–298.

De Dreu, C. K. W., & De Vries, N. K. (1993). Numerical support, information processing, and attitude change. *European Journal of Social Psychology, 23,* 647–663.

De Dreu, C. K. W., & West., M. A. (2001). Minority dissent and team innovation: The importance of participation in decision making. *Journal of Applied Psychology, 86*(6), 1191–1201.

Festinger, L. (1950). Informal social communication. *Psychological Review, 57,* 217–282.

Festinger, L. (1954). A theory of social comparison processes. *Human Relations, 7,* 117–140.

Gigone, D., & Hastie, R. (1993). The common knowledge effect: Information sharing and group judgment. *Journal of Personality and Social Psychology, 65,* 959–974.

Gigone, D., & Hastie, R. (1997). The impact of information on small group choice. *Journal of Personality and Social Psychology, 72,* 132–140.

Gordijn, E., De Vries, N. K., & De Dreu, C. K. W. (2002). Minority influence on focal and related attitudes: Change in size, attributions and information processing. *Personality and Social Psychology Bulletin, 28,* 1315–1326.

Hinsz, V. B. (1990). Cognitive and consensus processes in group recognition memory performance. *Journal of Personality and Social Psychology, 59,* 705–718.

Hinsz, V. B., Tindale, R. S., & Vollrath, D. A. (1997). The emerging conceptualization of groups as information processors. *Psychological Bulletin, 121,* 43–64.

Kahneman, D., & Tversky, A. (1979). Prospect theory: An analysis of decision under risk. *Econometrica, XLVII,* 263–291.

Kameda, T., Tindale, R. S., & Davis, J. H. (2003). Cognitions, preferences, and social sharedness: Past, present and future directions in group decision making. In S. L. Schneider & J Shanteau (Eds.), *Emerging perspectives on judgment and decision research* (pp. 215–240). Cambridge, UK: Cambridge University Press.

Kerr, N. L. (2001). Is it what one says or how one says it? Style vs. substance from an SDS perspective. In C. K. W. De Dreu & N. De Vries (Eds.), *Group consensus and minority influence: Implications for innovation* (pp. 201–228). Oxford, UK: Blackwell.

Kerr, N. L., & MacCoun, R. J. (1985). The effects of jury size and polling method on the process and product of jury deliberation. *Journal of Personality and Social Psychology, 48,* 349–363.

Lakoff, G. (2004). *Don't think of an elephant! Know your values and frame the debate: The essential guide for progressives.* White River Junction, VT: Chelsea Green Publishing.

Laughlin, P. R. (1980). Social combination processes of cooperative, problem-solving groups on verbal intellective tasks. In M. Fishbein (Ed.), *Progress in social psychology* (Vol. 1, pp. 127–155). Hillsdale, NJ: Lawrence Erlbaum Associates, Inc.

Laughlin, P. R., & Adamopoulos, J. (1980). Social combination processes and individual learning for six-person cooperative groups on an intellective task. *Journal of Personality and Social Psychology, 38,* 941–947.

Laughlin, P. R., & Early, P. C. (1982). Social combination models, persuasive arguments theory, social comparison theory, and choice shift. *Journal of Personality and Social Psychology, 42,* 273–280.

Laughlin, P. R., & Ellis, A. L. (1986). Demonstrability and social combination processes on mathematical intellective tasks. *Journal of Experimental Social Psychology, 22,* 177–189.

Laughlin, P. R., Kerr, N. L., Davis, J. H., Halff, H. M., & Marciniak, K. A. (1975). Group size, member ability, and social decision schemes on an intellective task. *Journal of Personality and Social Psychology, 31,* 522–535.

Laughlin, P. R., Kerr, N. L., Munch, M. M., & Haggarty, C. A. (1976). Social decision schemes of the same four-person groups on two different intellective tasks. *Journal of Personality and Social Psychology, 33,* 80–88.

Levine, J. M. (1980). Reaction to opinion deviance in small groups. In P. Paulus (Ed.), *Psychology of group influence* (pp. 187–231). Hillsdale, NJ: Lawrence Erlbaum Associates, Inc.

Levine, J. M., & Kaarbo, J. (2001). Minority influence in political decision making groups. In C. K. W. De Dreu & N. K. De Vries (Eds.), *Group consensus and innovation: Fundamental and applied perspectives* (pp. 229–257). Oxford, UK: Blackwell.

Lorge, I., & Solomon, H. (1955). Two models of group behavior in the solution of Eureka-type problems. *Psychometrika, 20,* 139–148.

Martin, R., & Hewstone, M. (1999). Minority influence and optimal problem solving. *European Journal of Social Psychology, 29,* 825–832.

Martin, R., & Hewstone, M. (2001). Conformity and independence in groups: Majorities and minorities. In M. Hogg & R. S. Tindale (Eds.), *Blackwell handbook of social psychology: Group processes* (pp. 209–234). Oxford, UK: Blackwell Publishing.

McLeod, P. L., Baron, R. S., Marti, M.W., & Yoon, K. (1997).The eyes have it: Minority influence in face-to-face and computer mediated group discussion. *Journal of Applied Psychology, 82,* 706–718.

Mednick, S. A., & Mednick, M. T. (1967). *Examiners manual: Remote Associates Test.* Boston: Houghton-Mifflin.

Miller, C. E. (1989). The social psychological effects of group decision rules. In P. Paulus (Ed.), *Psychology of group influence* (2nd ed., pp. 327–355). Hillsdale, NJ: Lawrence Erlbaum Associates, Inc.

Miller, C. E., & Anderson, P. D. (1979). Group decision rules and the rejection of deviates. *Social Psychology Quarterly, 42,* 354–363.

Miller, C. E., Jackson, P., Mueller, J., & Scherching, C. (1987). Some social psychological effects of group decision rules. *Journal of Personality and Social Psychology, 52,* 325–332.

Moscovici, S. (1976). *Social influence and social change.* London: Academic Press.

Moscovici, S., Lage, E., & Naffrechoux, M. (1969). Influence of a consistent minority on the responses of a majority in a color perception task. *Sociometry*, *32*, 365–380.

Mucchi-Faina, A., Maass, A., & Volpato, C. (1991). Social influence: The role of originality. *European Journal of Social Psychology*, *21*, 183–197.

Myers, D. G., & Lamm, H. (1976). The group polarization phenomenon. *Psychological Bulletin*, *83*, 602–627.

Nemeth, C. (1977). Interactions between jurors as a function of majority vs. unanimity decision rules. *Journal of Applied Social Psychology*, *7*, 38–66.

Nemeth, C. J. (1995). Dissent as driving cognition, attitudes and judgments. *Social Cognition*, *13*, 273–291.

Nemeth, C. J., & Kwan, J. (1985). Originality of word associations as a function of majority and minority influence. *Social Psychology Quarterly*, *48*, 277–282.

Nemeth, C. J., & Kwan, J. (1987). Minority influence, divergent thinking, and detection of correct solutions. *Journal of Applied Social Psychology*, *17*, 788–799.

Nemeth, C. J., Mayseless, O., Sherman, J., & Brown, Y. (1990). Exposure to dissent and recall of information. *Journal of Personality and Social Psychology*, *58*, 429–437.

Nemeth, C. J., & Nemeth-Brown, B. (2003). The potential benefits of dissent and diversity for group creativity. In P. B. Paulus & B. A. Nijstad (Eds.), *Group creativity: Innovation through collaboration* (pp. 63–84). London: Oxford University Press.

Nemeth, C. J., & Rogers, J. (1996). Dissent and the search for information. *British Journal of Social Psychology*, *35*, 67–76.

Paicheler, G. (1976). Norms and attitude change: I. Polarization and styles of behavior. *European Journal of Social Psychology*, *6*, 405–427.

Paicheler, G. (1977). Polarization of attitudes in homogeneous and heterogeneous groups. *European Journal of Social Psychology*, *9*, 85–96.

Paulus, P. B., & Nijstad, B. A. (2003). *Group creativity: Innovation through collaboration*. London: Oxford University Press.

Shaw, M. E. (1932). Comparison of individuals and small groups in the rational solution of complex problems. *American Journal of Psychology*, *44*, 491–504.

Simonton, D. K. (1984). *Genius, creativity, and leadership*. Cambridge, MA: Harvard University Press.

Simpson, J. B. (1964). *Contemporary quotations*. New York: Crowell.

Smith, C. M. (2003). *Disentangling the effects of exposure to minority influence and exposure to conflict*. Paper presented at the Small Group Meeting on Minority Influence Processes, Oxford University, UK.

Smith, C. M. (2008). Disentangling the effects of minority influence and exposure to conflict: Influence processes and product quality in dyads. *European Journal of Social Psychology*, *38*(1), 75–83.

Smith, C. M., & Diven, P. (2002). Minority influence and political interest groups. In V. Ottati et al. (Eds.), *The social psychology of politics* (pp. 175–192). New York: Plenum Press.

Smith, C. M., Dykema-Engblade, A., Walker, A., Niven, T., & McGough, T. (2000). Asymmetrical social influence in freely interacting groups discussing the death penalty: A shared representations interpretation. *Group Processes and Intergroup Relations*, *3*(4), 387–401.

Smith, C. M., & Fountaine, K. A. (1995). *Minority influence and divergent thinking:*

*The effects of group composition and expected group interaction.* Paper presented at the IV European Congress of Psychology, Athens, Greece.

Smith, C. M., & Hirchert, J. M. (1996). *Minority influence: Its impact upon attitude change and perceptions of group discussion in consensus seeking groups.* Paper presented at the annual meeting of the Midwestern Psychological Association, Chicago, IL.

Smith, C. M., Tindale, R. S., & Anderson, E. (2001). The impact of shared representations on minority influence in freely interacting groups. In N. K. De Vries & C. K. W. De Dreu (Eds.), *Group consensus and innovation* (pp. 183–200). Oxford, UK: Blackwell.

Smith, C. M., Tindale, R. S., & Dugoni, B. L. (1996). Minority and majority influence in freely interacting groups: Qualitative vs. quantitative differences. *British Journal of Social Psychology: Special Issue on Minority Influence, 35,* 137–149.

Smith, C. M., Tindale, R. S., & Steiner, L. (1998). Investment decisions by individuals and groups in 'sunk cost' situations: The potential impact of shared representations. *Group Processes and Intergroup Relations, 1,* 175–189.

Smoke, W. H., & Zajonc, R. B. (1962). *On the reliability of group judgments and decisions.* Stanford, CA: Stanford University Press.

Snow, D. A., Rochford, E. B., Worden, S. K., & Benford, R. D. (1986). Frame alignment processes, micromobilization, and movement participation. *American Sociological Review, 51,* 464–481.

Stasser, G., Kerr, N. L., & Davis, J. H. (1989). Influence processes and consensus models in decision making groups. In P. Paulus (Ed.), *Psychology of group influence* (2nd ed., pp. 279–326). Hillsdale, NJ: Lawrence Erlbaum Associates, Inc.

Stasser, G., & Stewart, D. D. (1992). Discovery of hidden profiles by decision-making groups: Solving a problem versus making a judgment. *Journal of Personality and Social Psychology, 63,* 426–434.

Stasser, G., Stewart, D. D., & Wittenbaum, G. (1995). Expert roles and information exchange during discussion: The importance of knowing who knows what. *Journal of Experimental Social Psychology, 31,* 244–265.

Stasser, G., & Titus, W. (1985). Pooling of unshared information in group decision making: Biased information sampling during discussion. *Journal of Personality and Social Psychology, 48,* 1467–1478.

Stasser, G., & Titus, W. (1987). Effects of information load and percentage of common information on the dissemination of unique information during group discussion. *Journal of Personality and Social Psychology, 53,* 81–93.

Stein, M. I. (1953). Creativity and culture. *Journal of Psychology, 36,* 311–322.

Stewart, D. D., & Stasser, G. (1998). The sampling of critical, unshared information in decision-making groups: The role of an informed minority. *European Journal of Social Psychology, 28,* 95–113.

Tindale, R. S., Anderson, E. M., Smith, C. M., Steiner, L., & Filkins, J. (1998). *Further explorations of conjunction errors by individuals and groups.* Paper presented at the British Psychological Society Social Psychology Section Conference, Canterbury, UK.

Tindale, R. S., & Davis, J. H. (1983). Group decision making and jury verdicts. In H. H. Blumberg, A. P. Hare, V. Kent, & M. F. Davies (Eds.), *Small groups and social interaction* (Vol. 2, pp. 9–38). Chichester, UK: Wiley.

Tindale, R. S., Davis, J. H., Vollrath, D. A., Nagao, D. H., & Hinsz, V. B. (1990). Asymmetrical social influence in freely interacting groups: A test of three models. *Journal of Personality and Social Psychology, 58,* 438–449.

Tindale, R. S., & Kameda, T. (2000). Social sharedness as a unifying theme for information processing in groups. *Group Processes and Intergroup Relations, 3,* 123–140.

Tindale, R. S., & Sheffey, S. (1988). *Task assignment redundancy and group memory.* Paper presented at the American Psychological Association Annual Convention, Atlanta, GA.

Tindale, R. S., Sheffey, S., & Scott, L. A. (1993). Framing and group decision making: Do cognitive changes parallel preference changes? *Organizational Behavior and Human Decision Processes, 55,* 470–485.

Tindale, R. S., Smith, C. M., Thomas, L. S., Filkins, J., & Sheffey, S. (1996). Shared representations and symmetric social influence processes in small groups. In E. Witte & J. H. Davis (Eds.), *Understanding group behavior: Consensual action by small groups* (Vol. 1, pp. 81–103). Hillsdale, NJ: Lawrence Erlbaum Associates, Inc.

Van Dyne, L., & Saavedra, R. (1996). A naturalistic minority influence experiment: Effects of divergent thinking, conflict and originality in work-groups. *British Journal of Social Psychology, 35,* 151–167.

Wood, W., Lundgren, S., Ouellette, A., Busceme, S., & Blackstone, T. (1994). Minority influence: A meta-analytic review of social influence processes. *Psychological Bulletin, 115,* 323–345.

Zeisel, H., & Diamond, S. (1987). 'Convincing empirical evidence' on the six-member jury. In L. S. Wrightsman, S. M. Kassin, & C. E. Willis (Eds.), *In the jury box: Controversies in the courtroom* (pp. 193–208). Thousand Oaks, CA: Sage.

# 12 Dynamics of change: Minority influence makes the world go around

*Radmila Prislin*
San Diego State University, USA

In an open challenge to public opinion and law of the state of California, San Francisco city authorities marked the beginning of 2004 by issuing marriage licences to same-sex partners. Waving his licence, one of the first recipients commented jubilantly: 'At long last . . . all the humiliation and ignorance and hate . . . could not change our love for each other. Our love has changed the world'.

The backlash that followed these developments proved that jubilation was premature. Though the world (of California, at least) may not have changed enough to accept same-sex marriages, the comment about its change is telling. It encapsulates a goal for many minorities. Their attempts at influence are intended to alter the status quo into a new social structure that will favour the minority worldview. Even minorities that do not seek to become majorities must require that the system accommodates them. Whether seeking to prevail or be tolerated, active minorities are in pursuit of changing the world. They exert influence, seeking to convert members of the majority to their own position in order to redefine positions within a social system. The engine of minority influence keeps the system in motion. Of course, this does not imply that change and innovation are the exclusive domains of minorities. Majorities, too, may promote change while minorities may work to prevent it (e.g., conservative minorities; see Levine & Kaarbo, 2001). Yet, even a majority-promoted change likely originated as a minority idea. Advocates for change may be many, but the original momentum almost invariably comes from minority influence.

However energizing, minorities do not effectively change the system until their ideas are embraced by a sufficient number of members currently in the majority. Changing individuals, therefore, is a key to changing the system. As if subscribing to the rule that the world is changed one individual at a time, the social psychology of minority influence has aimed primarily at explaining an individual's conversion to the minority position. This approach, exemplified by research on attitude change in response to minority advocacy, has documented that in-group minorities (Alvaro & Crano, 1996; David & Turner, 1996), that consistently advocate their positions (Wood, Lundgren,

Ouellette, Busceme, & Blackstone, 1994), are likely to attract recipients' attention, especially if they unexpectedly corroborate rather than contradict the target's position (Baker & Petty, 1994). When their message reflects the *Zeitgeist* (e.g., Erb, Bohner, & Hilton, 2003), as indicated by initial conversion of a few majority members (Clark, 1998; Gordijn, De Vries, & De Dreu, 2002), and when it contains cogent arguments (Kerr, 2002; Martin, Gardikiotis, & Hewstone, 2002), including appeals to higher-order values shared by the recipients (Smith, Dykema-Engblade, Walker, Niven, & McGough, 2000), such a message is likely to induce change in recipients' attitudes. Although change may occur on focal issues, it is especially likely on issues indirectly related to the object of advocacy (Crano & Chen, 1998; Gordijn et al., 2002). Attitudes that change in response to minority advocacy are resistant to subsequent persuasive attempts (Martin, Hewstone, & Martin, 2003), stable over time, and directive in regulating a rebalance of the attitudinal system (Crano & Chen, 1998). In short, attitude change in response to minority influence, though likely only under a highly circumscribed set of conditions, is important in that such a change produces potent attitudes. The strength of these attitudes is evidenced by their resistance, stability, and directive influence on the dynamics of the attitudinal system (Petty & Krosnick, 1995).

To the extent that the strength of attitudes changed in response to minority advocacy represents an entrenchment into a newly accepted position, it could be argued that in the persuasive context, successful minority influence fosters close-mindedness. This, however, need not be an unavoidable outcome of minority advocacy. Cognitive responses to minority influence need not necessarily include conversion to the minority position. When exerted in the problem-solving context, minority influence may not produce any convert to the minority-advocated solution. Yet, its effect is evident in a broader scope and improved quality of thought about the problem at hand, and, ultimately, in superior solutions (Doise & Mugny, 1984; Gruenfeld, 1995; Nemeth, 1986; Smith, Tindale, & Dugoni, 1996; Van Dyne & Saavendra, 1996). In the problem-solving context, therefore, minority influence fosters open-mindedness.

As impressive as these findings are, it is not clear what they imply for the presumed ultimate goal of minorities, namely systemic change. How is a system changed once a sufficient number of individuals respond favourably to minority advocacy to make it normative? Judgements about the desirability of change are mostly ideological and can hardly inform discussion about the effects of successful minorities on the system as a whole. Moreover, reducing discussion about change to judgemental issues and away from functional and structural issues has little heuristic value. It carries a strong notion that change represents nothing but a mechanical reversal of positions: When one normative position replaces another, change is profound for advocates of these positions, however, it is inconsequential for the overall system that presumably remains intact. According to this view, therefore, successful minorities do not change the world. All they change is which party holds a (non)normative and numerically superior (inferior) position in the world.

Conceptualization of change as a mechanical reversal of positions, however, neglects the social nature of attitudes targeted by minority influence (Prislin & Wood, 2005). More than being mere evaluative reactions to objects and issues, attitudes are social commitments. Arising from interdependence with others, attitudes also reflect and regulate relationships with others. As Asch (1952) argued eloquently, 'There are . . . no private opinions on social issues', because attitudes '. . . are either an endorsement of a group and therefore a bond of social unit or an expression of conflict with it' (pp. 576–577).[1] Thus, attitudes changed in response to minority influence represent not only altered evaluations of particular issues under consideration but, equally importantly, they redefine social relationships within a group. In the text that follows, this idea is elaborated in a model that explains consequences of successful minority influence for group dynamics. Next, a series of studies testing the model is summarized in a meta-analytical procedure. Finally, results are discussed within a motivational framework that addresses a largely neglected issue of motives that may drive minority attempts at social influence. Casting minority influence in motivational terms may prove helpful not only for understanding group dynamics in the aftermath of social change, but for understanding the dynamics of influence in general.

## The group in the aftermath of successful minority influence: The gain–loss asymmetry model of change in minority and majority positions

Does the world change in the aftermath of successful minority influence? To begin answering this question, my collaborators and I have proposed the gain–loss asymmetry model of change in minority and majority positions (Prislin & Christensen, 2005a; Prislin, Limbert, & Bauer, 2000). The model focuses on the dynamics of a group in which a minority faction gains a sufficient following among its initial opponents to transform itself into a new majority. The remaining opponents, initially in the majority, *ipso facto*, are transformed into a new minority.

Consequences of this structural change for the social dynamics of the group are rooted in the differential valuation of the two positions. The presumed preferential valuation of the majority position is derived from the empirically well-documented superiority of the position for the satisfaction of important needs (see Prislin & Christensen, 2005a, for a review). The minority position, elites notwithstanding, does not only make need satisfaction more challenging, it also carries numerous disadvantages. This imbalance in outcomes, both tangible and intangible, between the two positions is the very reason for the minority to exert influence in an attempt to become a majority (Moscovici, 1976).

When influence attempts are successful, the minority moves away from a disadvantaged position to an advantageous position; thus, it should experience the change as a gain. In contrast, the majority that moves in the opposite direction should experience the change as a loss. Although the two changes appear to be mirror images of each other, they should not be experienced equally intensely. The presumed differential experience of change stems from different initial contexts for members of a majority and a minority. Consistent with the postulates of social-identity and self-categorization theories (Tajfel, 1981; Turner, Hogg, Oakes, Reicher, & Wetherell, 1987), members of a majority should find the basis for their in-group category in perceived similarity with others. Because their opinions, attitudes, or other salient and comparison-relevant characteristics are shared by others, they should assimilate with and positively value the in-group category. This, in turn, should create expectations for further agreement and support from the in-group members and dislike for disagreements (Turner & Oakes, 1989). By the same token (minority) members whose opinions are initially rejected should be less likely to self-categorize and adopt the group as a social identity. As a result, they should consider others' reactions less consequential than if they had originally identified with them.

When, in response to minority influence, disagreements with the initial majority accrue to an extent that they transform the initial majority into a new minority, the result should be a decrease in valuation and, ultimately, decategorization from the group. For the initial minority, however, opponents' reactions, including their subsequent conversion to supporters, should have less of an impact. Thus, reactions of former minorities (new majorities) in response to their gain should be less intense than reactions of former majorities (new minorities) in response to their loss. This line of reasoning conforms to the general gain–loss asymmetry postulate of prospect theory: Because losses loom larger than the corresponding gains (Kahneman & Tversky, 1979), negative reactions to losing the majority position should be stronger than positive reactions to gaining the majority position.

The presumed asymmetrical reactions to the loss and gain of the majority position should reflect negatively on the overall level of identification with the group. The former minority's anticipated modest increase in positive reactions toward the group cannot compensate for the former majority's anticipated dramatic decrease in positive reactions toward the group; consequently, changes in minority and majority positions should be associated with an overall decrease in attachment to the group. Thus, belying the apparent simplicity of change as a cyclical recurrence in the perpetual battle for advantaged positions, the gain–loss asymmetry model postulates that change *within* the group is also change *of* the group.

**Identification in groups with stable and changed minorities and majorities: Empirical evidence**

All tests of the gain–loss asymmetry model have been conducted in experimentally created interacting groups that exchanged opinions on important social issues (e.g., death penalty, immigration). The basic procedure involves one participant and three to seven confederates who were extensively trained to provide scripted responses during the course of the group's interaction. Their responses placed the participant in an opinion-based minority or majority faction, which either remained stable or was reversed during the course of the interaction. That is, the participant's opinion was initially shared by either few members of the group (minority) or most members of the group (majority). The initially established pattern of (dis)-agreement either remained stable throughout the group interaction, or was changed when some of the confederates switched from opposing (supporting) to supporting (opposing) the participant half-way through the interaction. An important aspect of this procedure is that participants actively experienced their social positions within the interacting group. This stands in contrast to the prevailing methodological approach in the social-influence research that treats social relations, including minority and majority positions, as merely information to be processed (Levine & Kaarbo, 2001; Prislin & Wood, 2005).

To illustrate, in a procedure used in several studies, one naïve participant (the candidate) and five voters (confederates), engaged in a mock political campaign in which they exchanged opinions on ten aspects of an important social issue. The candidate's task was to attain majority support for her or his position on the issue. Initial position for the candidate was established by either four of the five voters disagreeing with the candidate during the first half of the campaign (initial minority) or three of the five voters agreeing with the candidate (initial majority). This established a 4 : 2 (dis)agreement ratio. In stable conditions, this ratio remained constant keeping the candidates in their initially established majority or minority positions. In change (reverse) conditions, this ratio was modified in the second half of the campaign when two voters converted from opposing to supporting the candidate (minority-to-majority change) or from supporting to opposing the candidate (majority-to-minority change). Following the campaign the voters and the candidate cast their ballots to decide whether to 'elect' the candidate by a simple majority vote. Ballots were cast in accordance with the final ratio of (dis)agreements.

The five studies to be reviewed here (Prislin & Christensen, 2002; 2005b, Study 1; Prislin, Brewer, & Wilson, 2002; Prislin et al., 2000, Studies 1 and 2), assessed identification with a group as a function of initial position (minority vs. majority) and change in the initially established position (no change vs. complete change). The review is limited to change occurring within the group context as a result of opinion conversion (the group condition in the Prislin et al., 2000 study; the conversion condition in Prislin & Christensen, 2002). Consistent with Tajfel's (1982) multidimensional conceptualization of social identification, two dimensions of identification were assessed: Self-categorization, as indicated by group–self similarity (e.g., Brewer & Weber, 1994; Ellemers, Kortekaas, & Ouwerkerk, 1999), and positive evaluation of the group, as indicated by group attraction (e.g., Granberg, Jefferson, Brent, & King, 1981; Simon, Pantaleo, & Mummendey, 1995). Confirmatory factor analyses on each of the five data sets indicated that perceived group–self similarity and group attraction were better represented as two correlated but distinct constructs rather than as a unitary construct (see Prislin & Christensen, 2005b, for analytical details). Thus, in all analyses, perceived group–self similarity and group attraction were treated as distinct indicators of group identification.

To summarize how these indicators were affected by changes in the initially established minority and majority positions, results across the five studies were combined in a meta-analytical procedure (Rosenthal, 1991). First, Pearson's $r$ was computed for each indicator as the effect size of losing the majority position (majority-to-minority change) and gaining the majority position (minority-to-majority change). Next, Pearson $r$ coefficients were converted to Fisher $Z$ scores and mean weighted effect sizes were computed as $\Sigma[(n_j - 3)Z]/\Sigma(n_j - 3)$, where $n_j - 3$ is the inverse of the standard error of the correlation coefficient. The weighted means were then converted back to correlation coefficients.

As is evident in Table 12.1, effect sizes for perceived group–self similarity for the majority-to-minority change (weighted average $Z = 0.64$, $r = .57$) were uniformly higher than effect sizes for the minority-to-majority change (weighted average $Z = 0.11$, $r = .11$). Indeed, the contrast between the two sets of conditions proved significant, $Z = 7.75$, $p \leq .001$ (Figure 12.1). Mirroring these findings, the corresponding analysis on the group-attraction variable revealed a stronger effect of losing the majority position (weighted average $Z = 0.55$, $r = .50$) than gaining the majority position (weighted average $Z = 0.18$, $r = .18$); contrast $Z = 4.18$, $p \leq .001$.

These findings provide strong support for the hypothesis that change away from the majority position affects identification with the group more profoundly than change toward the majority position. Whereas loss dramatically decreases identification with the group, gain of the majority position increases it only slightly. Similar asymmetry was evident in expectations about positive interactions with the group in the future. The average effect size of losing the majority position across three studies that assessed such expectations (Prislin & Christensen, 2002; Prislin et al., 2000, Study 1, 2002) was $Z = 0.63$, $r = .56$, whereas the corresponding effect of gaining the majority position was $Z = 0.12$, $r = .12$. Two types of change produced significantly different effect sizes, contrast $Z = 4.11$, $p \leq .001$. Moreover, the gain of the majority position not only failed to increase expectations for positive interactions, it also failed to decrease expectations for negative

Table 12.1 Effect sizes of loss (MA→MI) and gain (MI→MA) of the majority position on perception of group–self similarity, group attraction, and positive expectations

| Study | Group–self similarity | | | | Group attraction | | | | Positive expectations | | | |
|---|---|---|---|---|---|---|---|---|---|---|---|---|
| | Loss (MA→MI) | | Gain (MI→MA) | | Loss (MA→MI) | | Gain (MI→MA) | | Loss (MA→MI) | | Gain (MI→MA) | |
| | r | $Z_r$ | r | $Z_r$ | R | $Z_r$ | R | $Z_r$ | r | $Z_r$ | r | $Z_r$ |
| Prislin, Limbert, & Bauer, 2000, Study 1 (n = 181) | .55 | 0.61 | .18 | 0.18 | .33 | 0.34 | .24 | 0.24 | — | — | — | — |
| Prislin, Limbert, & Bauer, 2000, Study 2 (n = 253) | .50 | 0.54 | .00 | 0.00 | .54 | 0.60 | .18 | 0.18 | .46 | 0.50 | .06 | 0.06 |
| Prislin, Brewer, & Wilson, 2002, Group condition (n = 72) | — | — | — | — | .65 | 0.78 | .06 | 0.06 | .57 | 0.66 | .04 | 0.04 |
| Prislin & Christensen, 2002, Conversion condition (n = 62) | .77 | 1.03 | .30 | 0.31 | — | — | — | — | .75 | 0.97 | .33 | 0.35 |
| Prislin & Christensen, 2005b, Study 1 (n = 220) | .55 | 0.61 | .10 | 0.10 | .50 | 0.56 | .17 | 0.17 | — | — | — | — |

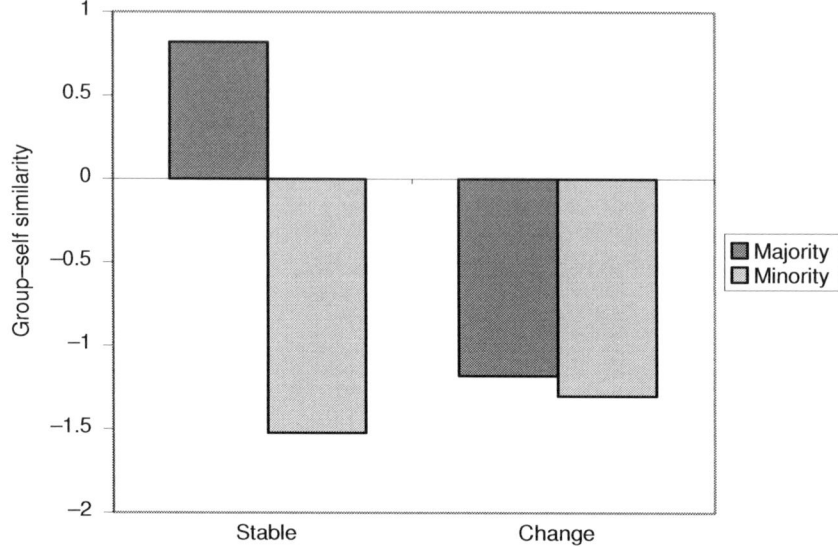

*Figure 12.1* Group–self similarity as a function of initial position and stability of initial position (aggregate results across five studies). Rating expressed on a scale ranging from –4 = *not at all similar* to 4 = *very much similar.*

interactions in the future (Prislin et al., 2000, Study 2). Thus, upon success-fully converting a sufficient number of initial opponents to become a majority, former minority members appear reluctant to identify with the group, continuing to be cautious regarding their future in the group.

The established asymmetry between cautiously positive reactions to becoming a majority and strong negative reactions to becoming a minority leaves a group weak in the immediate aftermath of social change. Indeed, further analyses comparing overall identification with the group with stable and changed minorities and majorities across the five studies included in the meta-analysis revealed lower identification with the group with changed factions. This was evident in both perceived group–self similarity (weighted average $Z = 0.25$, $r = .25$) and group attraction (weighted average $Z = 0.21$, $r = .21$). This overall lower level of identification is likely to impair group functioning. For example, a recent study has demonstrated that changes in group identification in response to the reversal of minority and majority positions are likely to translate into a preference to exit the group. That is, members of both factions (the former majority and the former minority), showed little preference to remain with their current group and were likely to seek alternative group membership, at least when there were no apparent costs associated with such a move (Prislin & Christensen, 2005b).

The apparent fragility of a group in the aftermath of social change is consistent with the hypothesis that a change in minority and majority posi-tions *within* the group is a change *of* the group. Yet, does the underlying process involve the experience of loss and gain among former majorities and former minorities? It could be argued that any experience of loss and gain may be alleviated by cognitive reinterpretation of the situation. For example, final (post-change) positions could be reinterpreted as more similar to initial (pre-change) positions than they actually were. The misperceived similarity between initial and final numerical positions should necessarily diminish the overall experience of change and its valuation as loss or gain. In none of the reviewed studies, however, was there any evidence of such a reinterpretation. Manipulation checks consistently indicated that participants accurately perceived their initial and final numerical positions within the group. Moreover, there was no evidence that loss of the majority position was rationalized by decreasing its importance. To the contrary, a recent study found that group members who lost their majority position considered being in the majority just as important as their stable majority counterparts (Christensen, Prislin, & Jacobs, 2009).

Whereas the importance of being in the majority appears constant irrespective of change, the importance of a group in which one loses the majority position sharply declines. Such a group ceases to be a source of social identity. This appears to be the case under conditions that afford ample opportunities to influence others just as in those with limited opportunities to influence others (Prislin & Christensen, 2005b). In both cases, negative reactions to loss of the majority position are more intense than the corresponding positive reactions to gain of the majority position. Gaining majority position, although accurately detected as soon as it occurs, does not immediately translate into identification with the group. Apparently, numerical dominance in the group is not sufficient for (identity) merging with the group.

Is there any evidence for these processes outside the social psychological laboratory? Though the complexity of real-world phenomena dictates caution when drawing parallels to laboratory findings, some similarities are too apparent to be ignored. For example, in 1994 the Republican party, a long-time minority in the United States Congress, won the majority position. With the majority in both chambers of Congress, Republicans in effect controlled the legislative branch of the government. Yet, when some of their proposals met strong Democratic opposition, Republicans virtually shut down the government—the very same group that they now dominated. Apparently, winning numerical dominance does not immediately translate in the phenomenological experience of majority.

This reluctance of new majorities to identify with the group may have important implications for their interactions with new minorities. Group identification facilitates positive interactions within the group in that it promotes favourable treatment of all its members (e.g., Dovidio, Gaertner, Isen, & Lowrance, 1995; Gaertner, Rust, Dovidio, Bachman, & Anastasio, 1994). If so, then new majorities' lack of identification with the group may foster intolerant if not hostile treatment of new minorities. This may occur even in groups that normatively protect minorities. This possibility was explained eloquently by the former Chief Justice of the United States Supreme Court William Rehnquist (1952) in a memo that he wrote as a young court clerk: 'To the argument . . . that a majority may not deprive a minority of its constitutional right, the answer must be made that while this is sound in theory, in the long run it is the majority who will determine what the constitutional rights of the minority are'. In an illustration of how this principle may work in the aftermath of social change, the new Republican majority in the United States Congress threatened to eliminate filibustering—a time-honoured procedure that has enabled a minority party to delay or block legislation or nomination. Of course, this, just like any other political decision was complexly determined. Nevertheless, it is telling that the proposal to do away with the procedure that has traditionally protected a party in a minority came from a new political majority.

### Seeking conversion but distancing from converts: A motivational approach to understanding the minority influence paradox

The well-documented lack of enthusiasm that former minorities exhibit for the group in which they become a majority seemingly contradicts an almost axiomatic preference for the majority position (Ellemers, Doosje, van Knippenberg, & Wilke, 1992; Erb & Bohner, 2001; Krueger, 1998; Simon & Hamilton, 1994). Excluding elites, almost all other minorities strive to become majorities (Moscovici, 1993). Yet, when successful, they are reluctant to embrace the group in which they achieved their goal. In what seems to be a paradox of minority influence, minorities seek conversion but appear to reject converts.

How then can the minorities' preference for the majority position be reconciled with the (former) minorities' continual detachment from the group that elevates them to the preferred position? The paradox may be best understood in light of the possible motives minorities have for becoming a majority. The many advantages of the majority position (Prislin & Christensen, 2005a) suggest a variety of motives for becoming a majority. For example, being in the majority by virtue of sharing consensus within a group provides a sense of correctness (Festinger, 1954) and self-enhancement (Festinger, 1950; Moscovici & Faucheux, 1972). Additionally, the attractiveness of the majority position stems from the feeling of acceptance and belonging to a group (Baumeister & Leary, 1995; Sachdev & Bourhis, 1984), whereas much of the unattractiveness of the minority position comes from the feeling of peripherality, marginalization, or even exclusion from the group (e.g., Brewer & Pickett, 1999; Frable, Blackstone, & Scherbaum, 1990; Moscovici, 1994).

These advantages of the majority position and disadvantages associated with the minority position suggest that social validation and social acceptance (belonging) may be among the motives that drive minorities' struggle to become a majority. Of course, minorities must initially believe in their position in order to exert influence. Minorities' initial belief in the correctness of their position may be grounded in non-social or remotely social factors, as it is often the case among innovators in science and art. For example, Galileo's once-minority position that the Earth revolves around the Sun rather than the reverse was based on his accurate measurements of objects in the solar system. His measurements could be considered remotely social criteria in that their principles had been agreed upon long before Galileo applied them to his discovery. Additionally, minorities' initial sense of correctness may stem from an innovative association of a (minority) position and a broader (consensual) value as it is often a case in politics and policy. For example, abolitionists' once-minority position on slavery was grounded in the argument that it reflected the consensually accepted value of equality.

Whatever the source of minorities' initial conviction about the correctness of their position, they are unlikely to sustain that position without additional social support. After all, the initial sense of correctness that Galileo must have had was not enough. He, just like many innovators after him, sought to convert others to his position even when it meant paying a stiff price. Why are minorities willing to pay such a price? Apparently, their initial sense of correctness may inspire innovation in the way lightning sparks fire. Yet, for the fire to burn, the kindling wood of social support is needed. Hence, minorities often seek broader social validation for their position. Because socially validated opinions have the power to define reality, such opinions may well be an elementary social variable to which all, including minorities, may be especially tuned (Erb & Bohner, 2001). Once socially validated, idiosyncratic minority positions become transformed into 'objective' reality (Hardin & Higgins, 1996). Social validation is the magic that transforms the subjective into the objective, minority fiction into consensual fact, and the proposition for action into the prescription for action. Indeed, once socially validated, Galileo's eccentric idea became scientific fact, and the abolitionists' activist position became normative.

Along with redefining reality, minorities may seek others' support for their position in order to satisfy their need for acceptance and belonging (Baumeister & Leary, 1995). The motive for social acceptance and belonging is thought to reflect the survival value of alignment with others that presumably has developed through evolution (Barchas, 1986; Caporael & Baron, 1997; Moreland, 1987). Because belonging is experienced as a state of (cognitive) merging of the included parties, minorities cannot satisfy this motive by simply giving up their position or their identity (Baumeister & Leary, 1995). This strategy may satisfy their need for affiliation, but it cannot satisfy their need for integration. Similarly, hiding one's minority position from others may protect against rejection but absence of rejection is not identical to acceptance. However genuinely they may strive to belong, yielding minorities are often suspected (e.g., Snow &

Machalek, 1984), whereas closet minorities are often fearful that their cover may be unveiled (Quinn, 2006). Neither can fully satisfy their need to belong. In order to integrate themselves and others into a category that will satisfy their need for belonging, minorities must exert social influence to attract others to their side. Alternatively, they may seek others' tolerance for their position. In either case, minorities act as agents of influence rather than pose as targets of influence. An important implication of this proposition is that the motive to belong may drive (minorities') attempts at social influence and not only their yielding to social influence as it has been traditionally assumed (Deutsch & Gerard, 1955).[2]

When either the social validation motive or the belonging motive is activated, minorities are likely to seek converts to their position. Both motives likely operate under the rule that strength (of truth, of belonging) is in the numbers. Yet, solely increasing the number of converts to the minority position cannot fully satisfy either of the two motives. Increasing the number of converts is a necessary but not sufficient condition for satisfaction of the social validation and belonging motives. In addition, both motives require conversion to be authentic. The quality of support for the minority position matters just as much as size of support. After all, neither Galileo's presumed need for social validation nor his possible need for belonging would have been satisfied by supporters pitying him, patronizing him, or agreeing with him for any reason other than the value of their position. The authenticity of conversion, therefore, should be evident in the acceptance of the minority position due to its merit.

How would minorities go about assessing the authenticity of conversion to their position? Attribution theory (Kelley, 1973) suggests that the two elements needed to attribute conversion to the merits of the minority position include consensus (in support for a position) and consistency (of support for the position). Thus, the minority position could be validated only through consensual support that is consistently demonstrated over a period of time. Similarly, the sense of belonging should originate from consensual acceptance that must be (relatively) consistent. Indeed, two main features of the motive to belong are positive interactions '. . . marked by stability and . . . continuation into the foreseeable future' (Baumeister & Leary, 1995, p. 500). Clearly, neither Galileo nor abolitionists would have been satisfied with a one-time pat on the shoulder as a show of support. Rather, they would have preferred continual evidence of support over a period of time and across different situations.

If, indeed, consistency of support, as an indicator of authenticity of conversion, is important to validation-motivated and belonging-motivated minorities, it follows that these minorities face two seemingly incompatible challenges. To increase the following for their position, they must convert their opponents. Yet, conversion negates consistency. The crux of the problem is in the conflicting implications of conversion for the presumed need for consensual and consistent support. Conversion carries an inherent

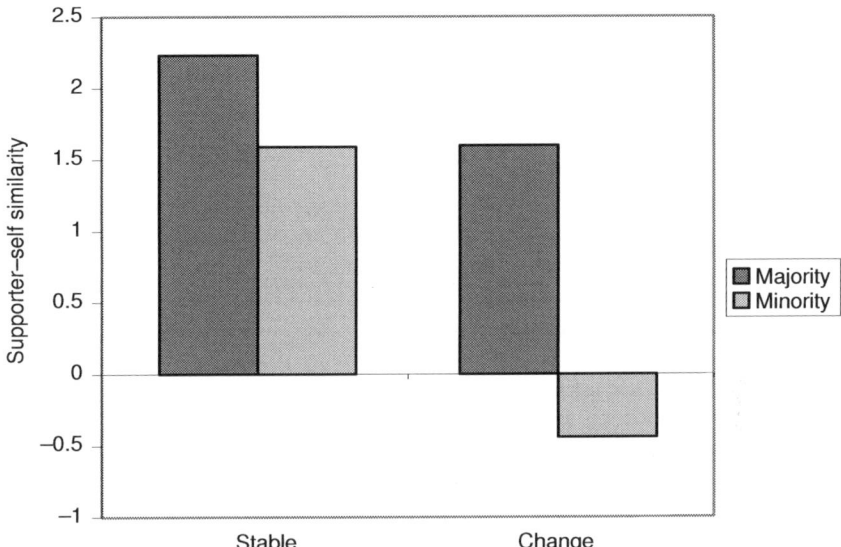

*Figure 12.2* Supporter–self similarity as a function of initial position and stability of initial position (Prislin & Christensen, 2002). Contrast between the minority change condition and the remaining three conditions was significant, $t(58) = 4.90$, $p < .001$; ratings expressed on a scale ranging from $-4 = $ *not at all similar* to $4 = $ *very much similar*.

contradiction: By definition, it denotes instability. The instability inherent in conversion is a condition *sine qua non* for attaining support: It renders minorities into new majorities thus satisfying one aspect of the goal, namely, achieving consensual support. Satisfaction of this aspect of the goal, however, comes at the expense of the other, namely, obtaining consistent or reliable support. Thus, converts may be sought, but their very act of conversion may cast doubt on their value as authentic supporters.[3]

The hypothesized ambivalence toward converts received initial empirical support in a study in which reactions toward both supporters and the group as a whole were assessed among members of stable and changed minorities (new majorities) and stable and changed majorities (new minorities; Prislin & Christensen, 2002). Changed minorities (new majorities) perceived their supporters (former opponents who converted to their position) as substantially less similar to the self than the remaining three factions that did not differ among themselves (Figure 12.2). Importantly, supporters in the three remaining groups were not converts but rather reliable advocates of the group positions. Moreover, this differential perception of supporters partially mediated reactions toward the group as a whole. Most important for this discussion was the finding that former minorities (new majorities), who perceived little similarity between their converted supporters and themselves, also perceived little similarity between the group as a whole and themselves. In fact, their perception of group–self similarity ($M = -1.81$) did not differ from stable minorities' perception of group–self similarity ($M = -2.88$); $t(119) = 1.75$, *ns.*

These findings suggest that the generally high threshold for support needed to consider others members of one's own category (Leyens & Yzerbyt, 1992) may be even higher in successful minorities whose advocacy attracts converts to their position. Because of the contradictory role converts play in satisfying motives that presumably drive minority influence, successful minorities may be especially reluctant to identify with the group in which they attained the majority position. Converts build consensual support for the minority position, while simultaneously violating the requirement for reliable support. Partially satisfied conditions necessarily leave the presumed social validation and belonging motives only partially fulfilled. As a result, successful minorities may seek additional ways of satisfying their motives that go beyond mere recruitment of converts to their position.

If, indeed, reliability of support remains critical for fulfilment of the motives, it can be satisfied only over a period of time. Only by consistently advocating the minority position over a period of time can converts demonstrate that they have adopted the minority position because of its merit rather than factors unrelated to the minority advocacy (e.g., condescending gesture, converts' inherent instability, jumping on the *Zeitgeist* bandwagon). Evidence of converts' continual support accumulated over a period of time should satisfy the presumed motives for minority advocacy because both criteria, consensus and consistency, are met. Full satisfaction of the motives should ultimately improve successful minorities' reactions toward the group in which they become a new majority. That is, over time, former minorities should gradually increase self-categorization and positive evaluation of the group in which they attained the majority position.

These hypotheses were examined in a study that was presented to the participants as a longitudinal examination of debate groups (Prislin & Christensen, 2005b, Study 2). Across five conditions, participants were initially placed in the minority position (i.e., all other debaters opposed participants' views on the issues under discussion). In one of these conditions, the participant was placed in the minority position for one session. In the four additional conditions, the participant who was initially placed in the minority position returned for either one, two, three, or four additional sessions over the period of one to four additional weeks. Beginning with the second session, the participants' positions were changed from minorities to majorities when most of the initial opponents converted to supporters. Participants who returned for their third, fourth, and fifth session continued to enjoy the majority position. In total, there were five experimental conditions in which participants initially were placed in the minority position: a one-week stable minority, and two-, three-, four-, and five-week minorities that changed to majorities during the second sessions.

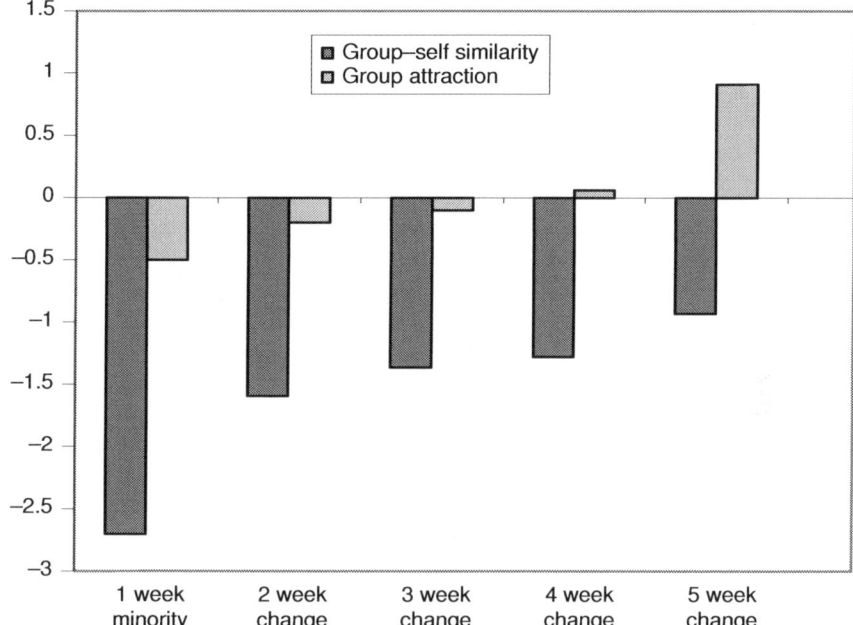

*Figure 12.3* Increase in perception of group–self similarity and group attraction over time (Prislin & Christensen, 2005b, Study2). Ratings expressed on a scale ranging from –4 to 4 with higher numbers indicating stronger similarity and attraction.

Supporting the hypothesis about former minorities' gradual increase in group identification, significant linear trends were found in both perception of group–self similarity and positive evaluation (attraction) of the group (Figure 12.3). Moreover, the gradual increase in perceived group–self similarity and positive evaluation of the group mediated the effect of the time spent in the acquired majority position on the conceptual representation of the interaction during debates. Specifically, increased perceptions of similarity and positive evaluation shaped participants' conceptualization of their interaction with others as occurring at a single-group level (Figure 12.4). This inclusive level of conceptualization is important because of its well-documented association with favourable treatment of the included members (e.g., Dovidio et al., 1995; Gaertner et al., 1994).

The presented series of studies suggests that minorities presumably motivated to be socially validated or socially accepted may be more 'ambitious' than typically assumed: Not only do they strive to increase support for their position but also they appear to care about the quality of their newly won support. As a result, their goals are not fully satisfied until newly generated support is proven reliable over time. Merely winning over sufficient numbers of new supporters to achieve numerical supremacy in a

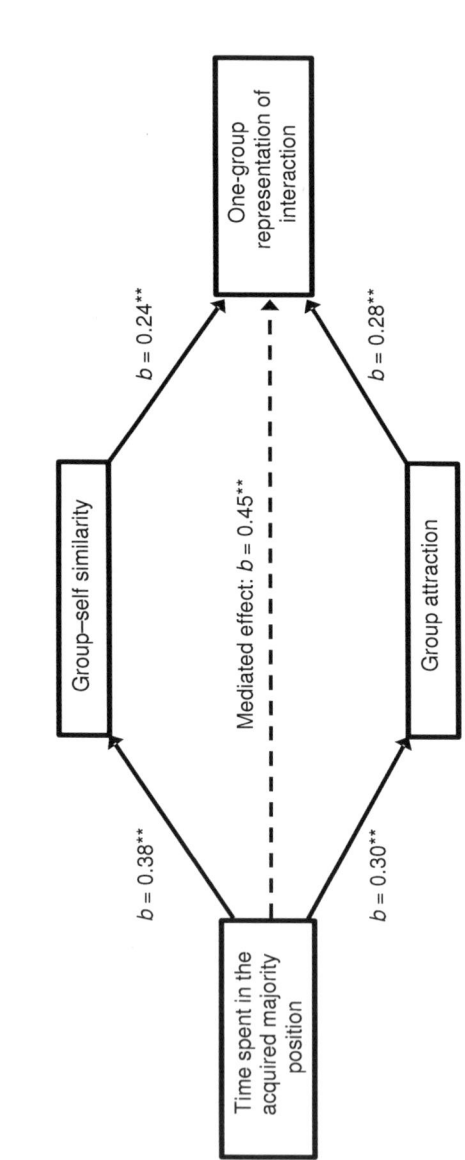

*Figure 12.4* Perceptions of group–self similarity and group attraction mediate the effect of time spent in the acquired majority position on the one-group representation of interaction (Prislin & Christensen, 2005b, Study 2). The *b*s represent unstandardized regression coefficients for the final model; **$p < .01$. The statistically significant reduction in the effect of the experimental conditions (from $b = 0.62$ to $0.45$) was a function of both mediators (both *Z*s > 2.11).

group does not immediately translate into an increased identification with the group. Rather, identification with the group increases gradually as former minorities (new majorities) become reassured about reliability of their newly won support. The gradual nature of this process implies that immediately after social change and for some time afterwards, the group remains fragile as neither of its factions seems to use the group as a source of social identity. Apparently, the complexity of goals that minorities strive to achieve and time needed to achieve those goals has its price paid in the currency of group strength.

These findings also emphasize the importance of a time-oriented perspective in understanding minority influence. Motives for minority influence likely develop over time, growing out of the experience of being a minority. These motives likely have their own dynamics that could be captured only by examining them longitudinally. As the presented findings suggest, initial conversion to the minority position—an outcome that represents an endpoint in typical minority influence research—does not appear to fully satisfy the social validation and belonging motives that presumably drive at least some of the attempts minorities make to influence others. Rather, initial conversion appears to activate (implied) expectations on converts to prove that their support is enduring and genuine. In freely interacting groups, these expectations may manifest themselves in influence tactics that former minorities use in their interactions with converts to their position. For example, former minorities (new majorities) may demand that converts denounce their original positions, elaborate their support for their newly adopted position, recruit new supporters, or curtail their ties with those who refuse to convert to the (former) minority position. In short, minority influence strategies may evolve over time in service of full satisfaction of their motives for attaining the majority position.

## Beyond validation and belonging: Reactions of successful minorities motivated by the instrumentality of the majority position

The many advantages associated with the majority position include not only intangible benefits such as a sense of correctness and a sense of belonging but also many tangible benefits. The latter include both preferential treatment in the distribution of positive outcomes, e.g., easier access to jobs and better salaries (Sidanius & Veniegas, 2000), better mortgage rates (Yinger, 1996), and lenient treatment in the allocation of negative outcomes, e.g., sentencing in the penal system (Sweeney & Haney, 1992). Being in the majority, therefore, often means an easier access to a larger slice of the social advantage pie and a shield against a bitter pill of social burdens. The worth of these tangible benefits may be a potent motivator in social influence. Hence, minorities may be motivated to become majorities not only because of the value of the majority position in and of itself but also because of the instrumentality of the majority position in achieving tangible benefits.

The instrumental value of the majority position in achieving tangible benefits and the presumed motivation that it may create have been largely neglected in social-influence research. This is unfortunate given that instrumentality motivates influence exchanges among many groups outside social psychological research laboratories. Politically and economically disadvantaged minorities strive to become majorities not so much to be socially validated and accepted (though these motives may be present too), as to enjoy the tangible benefits associated with the majority position. Neglecting the existence and motivation of these kinds of minorities may come at a serious epistemological price. Social influence exerted by instrumentally motivated minorities may differ from social influence exerted by their validation-motivated and belonging-motivated counterparts. For example, in their analysis of minority influence in political decision-making groups, Levine and Kaarbo (2001) argued that influence strategies employed by political minorities go beyond informational influence to include the reinforcement and procedural strategies (see also Smith & Diven, 2002). This is not to say that any single influence strategy is reflective of any particular single motive; however, the same strategy may be employed differently in the service of different motives. For example, the exhaustively studied informational influence strategy has been limited to message-based persuasion whose goal is to change understanding of an issue through evaluation of message content. Yet, the informational strategy could be used differently to emphasize common group identity (belonging) or quid pro quo (instrumentality) by belonging- and instrumentally motivated minorities, respectively. Moreover, the informational influence strategy may be combined differently with other strategies in service of a particular motive. In short, acknowledging that minority influence originates from a variety of motives necessarily expands the scope of influence strategies under consideration.

More important to the topic of this chapter is the role of instrumental motivation in successful minorities' reactions to social change. The crucial distinction between previously discussed social validation and belonging motives, on the one hand, and the instrumental motivation, on the other, is the psychological function of the majority position. For validation- and belonging-motivated minorities, the majority position is a goal in and of itself. Thus, for these motives to be satisfied, the goal must be fully achieved in that the acquired majority position must reflect consensual and genuine support. In contrast, for the instrumentally motivated minorities, the majority position is a means toward some other, ultimate ends. For them, achieving the majority position is an intermediary goal toward realization of another goal. Thus, for this motive to be satisfied, the intermediary goal must be sufficiently achieved to generate the ultimately desired goal. This just-sufficient threshold is lower than the threshold postulated for the previous two motives. Consequently, if a newly acquired level of consensual support is sufficient enough to lead former minority members to the ultimately desired goal, their instrumental motivation should be satisfied.

If this reasoning about instrumental motivation is correct, then instrumentally motivated minorities that become majorities should react more positively toward the group in which they effected social change. Their presumed more positive reactions toward the group should be evident in comparison to: (a) stable minorities whose position blocks their goal; and (b) minorities that achieve the majority position as a goal in itself (non-instrumentally motivated minorities). As for losing majorities (majorities that become minorities), loss should be equally intense regardless of whether it frustrates instrumental motivation or non-instrumental motivation. As a result, their reactions toward the group should be comparably negative. Comparably negative reactions of new minorities irrespective of their motivation, coupled with more positive reactions of instrumentally motivated than non-instrumentally motivated new majorities, should result in overall (a) symmetrical reactions to social change under instrumental motivation but (b) asymmetrical reactions to social change under non-instrumental motivation.

These hypotheses were tested in a study in which 143 participants were randomly assigned to one of the conditions of a 2 (Initial Position: majority vs. minority) × 2 (Change in the Initial Position: change vs. no change) × 2 (Motivation for Attainment of the Majority Position: instrumental vs. non-instrumental) between-subjects design. Initial position and its change (stability) were operationalized in a similar manner to the previously described studies. This operationalization created a minority faction of 2 members and a majority faction of 4 members that either remained stable throughout the entire group interaction, or was reversed half-way through the interaction. Instrumental motivation was manipulated by informing participants that either a larger faction (majority) would evaluate and financially reward an essay to be written by a smaller faction (minority), or that it would be randomly assigned which faction would write and which one would evaluate the writing (see Christensen et al., 2009, for details). This manipulation was intended to create an asymmetrical interdependence between the factions in the instrumental motivation conditions such that the size of a faction was associated with the power to control outcomes and resources (Fiske, 2004).

As predicted, instrumentally motivated minorities that became majorities found the group significantly more attractive than (a) minorities whose position remained stable, and (b) non-instrumentally motivated minorities that became majorities, both $ts(135) > 3.80$, $ps < .001$ (Table 12.2). Group attraction in the latter condition did not differ significantly from group attraction in the stable minority condition under non-instrumental motivation, $t(135) = 0.87$, $p = .39$. Also as predicted, majorities that became minorities found the group significantly less attractive than

*Table 12.2* Group attraction and perception of group–self similarity as a function of motive, initial position, and change in the initial position

| | Instrumental motive | | | | Non-instrumental motive | | | |
|---|---|---|---|---|---|---|---|---|
| | Initial majority | | Initial minority | | Initial majority | | Initial minority | |
| | No change (n = 18) | Change (n = 17) | No change (n = 17) | Change (n = 18) | No change (n = 17) | Change (n = 17) | No change (n = 18) | Change (n = 21) |
| *Group attraction* | | | | | | | | |
| M | 2.03 | −1.68 | −1.43 | 1.54 | 1.76 | −0.48 | −0.88 | −0.43 |
| SD | 1.79 | 1.51 | 1.77 | 1.16 | 1.10 | 2.60 | 1.50 | 1.38 |
| *Group–self similarity* | | | | | | | | |
| M | 1.00 | −0.94 | −2.74 | −1.56 | 1.47 | −1.85 | −1.86 | −1.48 |
| SD | 1.73 | 2.56 | 1.27 | 1.11 | 1.01 | 1.60 | 1.53 | 1.04 |

*Note*: Measures were taken on a 9-point scale (−4 to 4) with higher numbers indicating stronger attraction and perception of group–self similarity.

majorities whose positions remained stable irrespective of motivation, both $t$s(135) > 4.05, $p$s < .001. This pattern of results produced symmetrical valuation of group attraction in response to social change under instrumental motivation but asymmetrical valuation of group attraction in response to social change under non-instrumental motivation. Interestingly, the type of motivation did not moderate perceptions of group–self similarity. Across motivation conditions, loss of the majority position significantly decreased perceptions of group–self similarity, $t(135) = 7.07$, $p <$ .001, whereas gain of the majority position significantly increased such perceptions, $t(135) = 2.10$, $p < .05$. However, the effect size of loss ($r = .58$, $Z = 0.66$) was greater than the effect size of gain ($r = -.30$, $Z = -0.31$), $Z = 5.57$.

In contrast to previous studies where motivation was inferred from the experimental context and reactions toward the group, in this study, motivation was assessed separately and independently from reactions toward the group.[4] On a 9-point scale (1 = *not at all*, 9 = *very much*), participants estimated the extent to which being in the majority was important because of the resultant power, control, authority, influence, and goal achievement ($\alpha = .86$). As anticipated, estimates of importance were significantly higher in the instrumental-motive conditions ($M = 6.04$) than in the non-instrumental-motive conditions ($M = 4.82$). However, within the instrumental-motive conditions, initial position and change interacted to indicate that an already elevated instrumental motivation was further increased with gain of the majority position. Specifically, gaining the majority position significantly increased instrumentality motivation ($M = 5.20$ and $M = 7.10$ for the stable minority and minority changed to majority conditions, respectively), $t(135) = 3.83$, $p < .01$, whereas loss of the majority position did not affect the motive significantly ($M = 5.73$ and $M = 6.07$ for the stable minority and minority changed to majority conditions, respectively), $t(135) = 0.69$, *ns*; see Christensen et al. (2009) for details.

This pattern of results indicates that the type of motivation to achieve the majority position moderates reactions toward the group in the aftermath of social change effected by successful minority influence. Whereas non-instrumental-motivation conditions that likely activated the belonging motive, the social validation motive, or both, replicated previous asymmetrical reactions to change, instrumental motivation produced more complex, multifaceted reactions. Under instrumental motivation, gain of the majority position increased group attraction significantly more than under non-instrumental motivation. Yet, perception of group–self similarity among new majorities was comparable across the motivation conditions. If attraction is taken as an indicator of group valuation and similarity is taken as an indicator of self-categorization (Tajfel, 1982), the obtained pattern of results suggests that the two facets of group identification may develop differently under different motivations. Positive valuation appears to develop more rapidly and proportionally to tangible benefits of a newly acquired majority position. Acceptance of the group as one's own social category, however, appears to be a more cautious, slowly emerging process, not affected by tangible benefits.

New majorities in a position to capitalize on their acquired numerical superiority appear to be more calculating in developing social attraction than self-categorization. Their liking for the group increases as soon as they have enough supporters in the group to obtain tangible benefits that go with numerical supremacy. Liking, however, is not accompanied by acceptance of the group as one's own, at least not immediately. Former minorities (new majorities) seem to appreciate the group for the benefits delivered; however, they stop short of perceiving others in the group and themselves as interchangeable members of the same social category. This somewhat Machiavellian pattern of reactions may be temporary in that self-categorization to the group may be delayed but, eventually, it may follow readily exhibited increase in group attraction. Alternatively, this liking without accepting reaction may persist in groups whose new majorities are solely instrumentally oriented. It may be that instrumental orientation need to be supplemented by other, non-instrumental motives whose satisfaction provides a foundation for self-categorization. Indeed, political parties, paragons of instrumental orientation, define themselves mostly in non-instrumental, value-based terms, while courting (new) supporters in pursuit of very tangible benefits.

## Conclusion

The answer to the opening question about change of a group whose minority and majority factions switch their positions is clearly affirmative. Change within a group is change of the group. As successful minorities attract new followers to become majorities, they redefine not only their own position within the group, but also the dynamics of the group as a whole. In support of the proposed gain–loss asymmetry model, the reviewed series of studies documented that in the immediate aftermath of social change, the group is substantially weakened. This weakening of the group is due to the profound disidentification from the group among new minorities in response to their loss of the majority position, coupled with the only modest increases in identification with the group among new majorities in response to their gain of the majority position. Restoration of identification with the group is a gradual process because former minorities need time to be assured about their newly acquired majority position through proofs of genuine acceptance of their position.

The seeming paradox between former minorities' less than enthusiastic responses to becoming majorities and the widely accepted notion that almost all minorities are motivated to become majorities could be resolved within a motivational approach to minority influence. The proposed motivational framework postulates that minorities strive to become majorities in the service of a variety of motives. Among them, motivation to be socially validated, to belong and to be accepted for who they are, and to enjoy tangible benefits of the majority position (instrumentality) stand most prominently. Satisfaction of the validation and belonging motives presumably requires more than mere conversion of initial opponents to the minority position. Attracting a sufficient number of converts is a necessary, but not sufficient, condition for former minorities to feel validated and accepted for who they are. In addition, they appear to seek evidence that converts' support for their position is authentic. Such evidence can be provided over a period of time—hence, the slow, gradual increase in identification with the group among new majorities. The instrumentality motive, in contrast, requires only consensual support in order for the former minority (new majority) to enjoy the tangible benefits associated with their newly acquired position. As a result, instrumentally motivated former minorities develop an attraction to the group that is strong enough to balance the decrease in attraction among former majorities. Yet, instrumentally motivated former minorities appear to be just as cautious in self-categorizing with the group as are validation- and belonging-motivated former minorities.

The proposed motivational framework for understanding former minorities' reactions stems from the general need to cast social influence in motivational terms (Prislin & Wood, 2005). Different motives that may underlie minority influence are likely to produce differently crafted influence strategies. By the same token, different motives that may underlie targets' responses are likely to produce different cognitive, but also (currently largely neglected) affective and behavioural responses. (In)compatibility of motives that guide minorities and majorities could additionally aid in understanding social influence. Admittedly, opening a Pandora's box of motives may release many theoretical and methodological pains. Yet, it should not be forgotten that the last to leave Pandora's box was hope. Adopting a motivation approach brings hope for better understanding of social influence. Minorities among us, curious enough to open the box, may well be socially validated, gain enough of a following to satisfy the belonging motive, and even bear some tangible fruits.

## Notes

1 Interestingly, in his pioneering work on minority influence, Moscovici (1976) also postulated the critical role of interpersonal relations and social conflicts; however, the postulate never received the attention accorded to the resolution of intra-individual conflict presumably instigated by minority advocacy. Contemporary approaches to minority influence acknowledge the importance of social relations in a postulate about influence potential of in-group, but not out-group, minorities (Crano, 2001; David & Turner, 2001). Yet, with notable exceptions such as Levine and his collaborators' work on newcomers (Levine, Choi, & Moreland, 2003), these approaches, too, cast minority influence as an intrapersonal rather than interpersonal process.
2 The suggested motives for exerting social influence fit the classical dual-motive scheme for responding to social influence (Deutsch & Gerard, 1955). Indeed, early theorizing about minority influence postulated that positive (yielding) responses are motivated by informational needs (Moscovici, 1976). Later models, however, constrained such responses to influence attempts coming from in-group minorities whose in-group status serves as a buffer against normative dismissal (e.g., Crano, 2001; David & Turner, 1996).
3 This ambivalence about converts may be functional in that it may provide more coping efficacy in dealing with a changing social environment than the opposite, uncritical acceptance (Kanouse & Hanson, 1971; McGuire & McGuire, 1992). Potential costs of unconditional acceptance of converts are likely to be higher than potential costs of ambivalence, thus rendering the latter less hazardous.
4 Although lack of an independent assessment of motivation is an obvious weakness of previous studies, it is reasonable to assume that instrumental motivation was not activated. It is less clear, however, to what extent the social validation motivation, the belonging motivation, or both were present in previous studies.

## References

Alvaro, E. M., & Crano, W. D. (1996). Cognitive responses to minority- or majority-based communications: Factors that underlie minority influence. *British Journal of Social Psychology*, *35*, 105–121.

Asch, S. E. (1952). *Social psychology*. Englewood Cliffs, NJ: Prentice Hall.

Baker, S. M., & Petty, R. E. (1994). Majority and minority influence: Source–position imbalance as a determinant of message scrutiny. *Journal of Personality and Social Psychology*, *67*, 5–19.

Barchas, P. (1986). A sociophysiological orientation to small groups. In E. Lawler (Ed.), *Advances in group processes* (Vol. 3, pp. 209–246). Greenwich, CT: JAI Press.

Baumeister, R. F., & Leary, M. R. (1995). The need to belong: Desire for interpersonal attachments as a fundamental human motivation. *Psychological Bulletin, 117*, 497–529.

Brewer, M. B., & Pickett, C. L. (1999). Distinctiveness motives as a source of the social self. In T. R. Tyler, R. M. Kramer, & O. P. John (Eds.), *The psychology of the social self* (pp. 71–87). Mahwah, NJ: Lawrence Erlbaum Associates, Inc.

Brewer, M. B., & Weber, J. G. (1994). Self-evaluation effects of interpersonal versus intergroup social comparison. *Journal of Personality and Social Psychology, 66*, 268–275.

Caporael, L. R., & Baron, R. M. (1997). Groups as the mind's natural environment. In J. A. Simpson & D. T. Kendrick (Eds.), *Evolutionary social psychology* (pp. 317–343). Mahwah, NJ: Lawrence Erlbaum Associates, Inc.

Christensen, P. N., Prislin, R., & Jacobs, E. (2009). Motives for seeking the majority: Effects of power, faction size, and change. *Social Influence, 4*, 200–215.

Clark, R. D., III (1998). Minority influence: The role of the rate of majority defection and persuasive arguments. *European Journal of Social Psychology, 28*, 787–796.

Crano, W. D. (2001). Social influence, social identity, and ingroup leniency. In C. K. W. De Dreu, & N. K. De Vries (Eds.), *Group consensus and minority influence: Implications for innovation* (pp. 122–159). Oxford, UK: Blackwell.

Crano, W. D., & Chen, X. (1998). The leniency contract and persistence of majority and minority influence. *Journal of Personality and Social Psychology, 74*, 1437–1450.

David, B., & Turner, J. C. (1996). Studies in self-categorization and minority conversion: Is being a member of the out-group an advantage? *British Journal of Social Psychology, 35*, 179–199.

David, B., & Turner, J. C. (2001). Majority and minority influence: A single process. In C. K. W. De Dreu, & N. K. De Vries (Eds.), *Group consensus and minority influence: Implications for innovation* (pp. 91–121). Oxford, UK: Blackwell.

Deutsch, M., & Gerard, H. B. (1955). A study of normative and informational influences upon individual judgment. *Journal of Abnormal and Social Psychology, 51*, 629–636.

Doise, W., & Mugny, G. (1984). *The social development of the intellect*. Oxford, UK: Pergamon Press.

Dovidio, J. F., Gaertner, S. L., Isen, A. M., & Lowrance, R. (1995). Group representations and intergroup bias: Positive affect, similarity, and group size. *Personality and Social Psychology Bulletin, 21*, 856–865.

Ellemers, N., Doosje, B. J., van Knippenberg, A., & Wilke, H. (1992). Status protection in high status minority groups. *European Journal of Social Psychology, 22*, 123–140.

Ellemers, N., Kortekaas, P., & Ouwerkerk, J. W. (1999). Self-categorization, commitment to the group and group self-esteem as related but distinct aspects of social identity. *European Journal of Social Psychology, 29*, 371–389.

Erb, H.-P., & Bohner, G. (2001). Mere consensus effects in minority and majority influence. In C. K. W. De Dreu & N. K. De Vries (Eds.), *Group consensus and minority influence: Implications for innovation* (pp. 40–59). Oxford, UK: Blackwell.

Erb, H.-P., Bohner, G., & Hilton, D. J. (2003, September). *Conditions of minority influence: The risky option*. Paper presented at the small group meeting of the European Association of Social Psychologists on Minority Influence Processes, Oxford, UK.

Festinger, L. (1950). Informal social communication. *Psychological Review, 57,* 271–282.

Festinger, L. (1954). A theory of social comparison processes. *Human Relations, 7,* 117–140.

Fiske, S. T. (2004). *Social beings: A core motivational approach to social psychology.* Hoboken, NJ: Wiley.

Frable, D. E. S., Blackstone, T., & Scherbaum, C. (1990). Marginal and mindful: Deviants in social interactions. *Journal of Personality and Social Psychology, 59,* 140–149.

Gaertner, S. L., Rust, M. C., Dovidio, J. F., Bachman, B. A., & Anastasio, P. A. (1994). The contact hypothesis: The role of a common ingroup identity in reducing intergroup bias. *Small Group Research, 25,* 224–249.

Gordijn, E. H., De Vries, N. K., & De Dreu, C. K. W. (2002). Minority influence on focal and related attitudes: Change in size, attributions, and information processing. *Personality and Social Psychology Bulletin, 28,* 1315–1326.

Granberg, D., Jefferson, N. L., Brent, E. E., & King, M. (1981). Membership group, reference group, and the attribution of attitudes to groups. *Journal of Personality and Social Psychology, 40,* 833–842.

Gruenfeld, D. H. (1995). Status, ideology, and integrative complexity on the US Supreme Court: Rethinking the politics of decision making. *Journal of Personality and Social Psychology, 68,* 5–20.

Hardin, C. D., & Higgins, E. T. (1996). Shared reality: How social verification makes the subjective objective. In R. M. Sorentino & E. T. Higgins (Eds.), *Handbook of motivation and cognition* (Vol. 3, pp. 28–84). New York: Guilford Press.

Kahneman, D., & Tversky, A. (1979). Prospect theory: An analysis of decision under risk. *Econometrica, 47,* 263–291.

Kanouse, D. E., & Hanson, L. R., Jr. (1971). Negativity in evaluations. In E. E. Jones, D. E. Kanouse, H. H. Kelley, R. E. Nisbett, & B. Weiner (Eds.), *Attributions: Perceiving the causes of behavior* (pp. 47–62). Morristown, NJ: General Learning Press.

Kelley, H. H. (1973). The process of causal attribution. *American Psychologist, 28,* 107–128.

Kerr, N. L. (2002). When is a minority a minority? Active versus passive minority advocacy and social influence. *European Journal of Social Psychology, 32,* 471–483.

Krueger, J. (1998). On the perception of social consensus. In M. Zanna (Ed.), *Advances in experimental social psychology* (Vol. 30, pp. 164–240). San Diego, CA: Academic Press.

Levine, J. M., Choi, H.-S., & Moreland, R. L. (2003). Newcomer innovation in work teams. In P. B. Paulus (Ed.), *Group creativity: Innovation through collaboration* (pp. 202–224). London: Oxford University Press.

Levine, J. M., & Kaarbo, J. (2001). Minority influence in political decision-making. In C. K. W. De Dreu & N. K. De Vries (Eds.), *Group consensus and minority influence: Implications for innovation* (pp. 229–257). Oxford, UK: Blackwell.

Leyens, J.-P., & Yzerbyt, V. Y. (1992). The ingroup overexclusion effect: Impact of valence and confirmation on stereotypical information search. *European Journal of Social Psychology, 22,* 549–569.

Martin, R., Gardikiotis, A., & Hewstone, M. (2002). Levels of consensus and majority and minority influence. *European Journal of Social Psychology, 32,* 645–665.

Martin, R., Hewstone, M., & Martin, P. Y. (2003). Resistance to persuasive messages as a function of majority and minority influence. *Journal of Experimental Social Psychology, 39,* 585–593.

McGuire, W. J., & McGuire, C. V. (1992). Cognitive-versus-affective positivity asymmetries in thought systems. *European Journal of Social Psychology, 22,* 549–569.

Moreland, R. L. (1987). The formation of small groups. In C. Hendrick (Ed.), *Group processes. Review of personality and social psychology* (Vol. 8, pp. 80–110). Newbury Park, CA: Sage.

Moscovici, S. (1976). *Social influence and social change.* New York: Academic Press.

Moscovici, S. (1993). *The invention of society: Psychological explanations for social phenomena.* Cambridge, UK: Polity Press.

Moscovici, S. (1994). Three concepts: Minority, conflict, and behavioral style. In S. Moscovici, A. Mucchi-Faina, & A. Maas (Eds.), *Minority influence* (pp. 233–251). Chicago: Nelson-Hall.

Moscovici, S., & Faucheux, C. (1972). Social influence, conformity bias, and the study of active minorities. In L Berkowitz (Ed.), *Advances in experimental social psychology* (Vol. 6, pp. 149–202). New York: Academic Press.

Nemeth, C. J. (1986). Differential contributions of majority and minority influence. *Psychological Review, 93,* 23–32.

Petty, R. E., & Krosnick, J. A. (Eds.). (1995). *Attitude strength: Antecedents and consequences.* Mahwah, NJ: Lawrence Erlbaum Associates, Inc.

Prislin, R., Brewer, M., & Wilson, D. J. (2002). Changing majority and minority positions within a group vs. an aggregate. *Personality and Social Psychology Bulletin, 28,* 640–647.

Prislin, R., & Christensen, P. N. (2002). Group conversion versus group expansion as modes of change in majority and minority positions: All losses hurt but only some gains gratify. *Journal of Personality and Social Psychology, 83,* 1095–1102.

Prislin, R., & Christensen, P. N. (2005a). Social change in the aftermath of successful minority influence. *European Review of Social Psychology, 16,* 43–73.

Prislin, R., & Christensen, P. N. (2005b). The effects of social change within a group on membership preferences: To leave or not to leave. *Personality and Social Psychology Bulletin, 31,* 595–609.

Prislin, R., Limbert, W. M., & Bauer, E. (2000). From majority to minority and vice versa: The asymmetrical effects of losing and gaining majority position within a group. *Journal of Personality and Social Psychology, 79,* 385–397.

Prislin, R., & Wood, W. (2005). Social influence: The role of social consensus in attitude and attitude change. In D. Albarracín, B. T. Johnson, & M. P. Zanna (Eds.), *Handbook on attitudes and attitude change* (pp. 671–706). Newbury Park, CA: Sage.

Quinn, D. M. (2006). Concealable versus conspicuous stigmatized identities. In S.

Levine & C. van Laar (Eds.), *Stigma and group identity: Social psychological perspectives* (pp. 83–103). Mahwah, NJ: Lawrence Erlbaum Associates, Inc.

Rehnquist, W. H. (1952). *A random thought on the segregation cases.* (Available at: http://a255.g.akamaitech.net/7/255/2422/26sep20051215/www.gpoaccess.gov/congress/senate/judiciary/sh99–1067/324–325.pdf)

Rosenthal, R. (1991). *Meta-analytic procedures for social research.* Newbury Park, CA: Sage.

Sachdev, I., & Bourhis, R. Y. (1984). Minimal majorities and minorities. *European Journal of Social Psychology, 14*, 35–52.

Sidanius, J., & Veniegas, R. C. (2000). Gender and race discrimination: The interactive nature of disadvantage. In S. Oskamp (Ed.), *Reducing prejudice and discrimination. The Claremont symposium on applied social psychology* (pp. 47–69). Mahwah, NJ: Lawrence Erlbaum Associates, Inc.

Simon, B., & Hamilton, D. L. (1994). Self-stereotyping and social context: The effects of relative in-group size and in-group status. *Journal of Personality and Social Psychology, 66*, 699–711.

Simon, B., Pantaleo, G., & Mummendey, A. (1995). Unique individual or interchangeable group member? The accentuation of intragroup differences versus similarities as an indicator of individual self versus collective self. *Journal of Personality and Social Psychology, 69*, 106–119.

Smith, C. M., & Diven, P. J. (2002). Minority influence and political interest groups. In V. C. Ottati et al. (Eds.), *The social psychology of politics* (pp. 175–192). New York: Kluwer Academic/Plenum Press.

Smith, C. M., Dykema-Engblade, A., Walker, A., Niven, T. S., & McGough, T. (2000). Asymmetrical social influence in freely interacting groups discussing death penalty: A shared representation interpretation. *Group Processes and Intergroup Relations, 3*, 387–401.

Smith, C. M., Tindale, R. S., & Dugoni, B. L. (1996). Minority and majority influence in freely interacting groups: Qualitative versus quantitative differences. *British Journal of Social Psychology, 35*, 137–149.

Snow, D. A., & Machalek, R. (1984). The sociology of conversion. *Annual Review of Sociology, 10*, 167–190.

Sweeney, L. T., & Haney, C. (1992). The influence of race in sentencing: A meta-analytic review of experimental studies. *Behavioral Science and Law, 10*, 179–195.

Tajfel, H. (1981). *Human groups and social categories: Studies in social psychology.* Cambridge, UK: Cambridge University Press.

Tajfel, H. (1982). *Social identity and intergroup relations.* Cambridge, UK: Cambridge University Press.

Turner, J. C., Hogg, M. A., Oakes, P. J., Reicher, S. D., & Wetherell, M. S. (1987). *Rediscovering the social group: A self-categorization theory.* Oxford, UK: Basil Blackwell.

Turner, J. C., & Oakes, P. J. (1989). Self-categorization theory and social influence. In P. B. Paulus (Ed.), *The psychology of group influence* (2nd ed., pp. 233–275). Hillsdale, NJ: Lawrence Erlbaum Associates, Inc.

Van Dyne, L., & Saavendra, R. (1996). A naturalistic minority influence experiment: Effects on divergent thinking, conflict, and originality in work groups. *British Journal of Social Psychology, 35*, 151–167.

Wood, W., Lundgren, S., Ouellette, J. A., Busceme, S., & Blackstone, T. (1994).

Minority influence: A meta-analytical review of social influence processes. *Psychological Bulletin, 115,* 323–345.

Yinger, J. (1996). Discrimination in mortgage lending: A literature review. In J. Goering & R. Wienk (Eds.), *Mortgage lending, racial discrimination and federal policy* (pp. 29–73). Washington, DC: The Urban Institute Press.

# 13 Bringing social structure to both sides of an issue: How proximal and distal ties interact with minority and majority positions to affect influence in workgroups

*Federico Aime*
Oklahoma State University, USA

*Linn Van Dyne*
Michigan State University, USA

At a meeting not long ago, we overheard a conversation between two managers in which one asked the other: 'How come we are taking this approach to our project? I thought that we had all agreed on the alternative approach?' The answer: 'Well, you know that Nils and two other group members were certain this was the best option. And of course, you know that he has to be on board for the project to fly.' Interestingly, Nils was neither the manager of the team, nor the expert in that particular area. This raises the question: What made Nils a key determining factor in the decision making? Studies of social influence have often looked at Darwin, Galileo, Churchill, and Picasso as examples of the success of scientific, political, and artistic minorities. Scholars have advanced various explanations for these examples of minority influence success. At the same time, few have stopped to analyse the question: Why these specific people? Why Galileo? Why Darwin? Why Nils?

Social influence can be defined as a process by which an individual's cognitions, attitudes and/or behaviours are affected by the real or imagined presence of one or more others (Allport, 1985). In the prototypic representation of social influence, agent A's influence over target T's cognitions, attitudes and behaviours differs based on A's situation as a minority position (publicly advocating beliefs, attitudes, and ideas that challenge the perspective of the majority) or as a majority position (Moscovici, 1980; Nemeth, 1986). This work has provided increasingly comprehensive models of the mechanisms through which the minority or majority position of an agent (or a target) on a specific issue creates pressures towards non-conformity or conformity, with subsequent effects on intra- and inter-group conflict, decision making, and performance.

To date, however, these efforts have focused almost exclusively on the agent's or the target's situation (i.e., assuming either minority or majority position) and have acknowledged individual personal bases of power for influence (French & Raven, 1959), but prior theorizing has overlooked individual social capital (embedded in an individual's social network) as a source of potential to exercise influence within specific situations. Responding to these gaps, we develop a framework of social capital mechanisms (based on the agent's position in the social network) that enable situated agents to influence others.

The objective of this chapter is to present a theoretical model that explicates ways in which characteristics of employee social networks (i.e., the strength of their proximal and distal ties) interact with their situated perspectives (i.e., being in a minority or majority position on an issue) to influence employee involvement and effectiveness in exercising influence through five specific influence mechanisms: (1) ease of access and frequency of interaction with others in the workgroup; (2) trust, liking, and status; (3) visibility and salience to co-workers; (4) access to non-redundant information; and (5) third-party support. We argue that the characteristics of an employee's social networks provide many of the raw inputs and motivations to exercise influence in more or less effective ways for employees situated in both minority and majority positions. More specifically, we emphasize the effects of social network characteristics (proximal and distal ties) on minority and majority influence.

This is an important gap in the literature because work and employee roles are almost always situated in a specific social context (Burt, 1997; Salancik & Pfeffer, 1978; Sparrowe, Liden, Wayne, & Kraimer, 2001; Wrzesniewski, Dutton, & Debebe, 2003). Few, if any, employees function with total independence. Instead, work is increasingly interdependent because organizations increasingly use teams as the building blocks of organizational structure (Ilgen, 1999; Wageman, 1995). As a result of this interdependence, structural characteristics of employee ties are an important (but to date overlooked and under-researched) aspect of work that has potentially profound impact on employee influence.

This structural contribution to minority-influence approaches may also help disentangle the major discrepancy between the very small impact of minorities on group decision making in laboratory results and field evidence regarding much greater success of minorities in imposing their views (Clark, 1994). Those in minority positions are often successful in imposing their views in workgroups and society in general, and developments in minority-influence studies may benefit from cross-mapping social structure with minority and majority positions held by actors to be able to better understand where there is more chance of prevailing and what alternative strategies are available to influence others to adopt their positions. Organizations recognize the value of diversity to projects through an ever-growing reliance on cross-functional and diverse workgroups in core organizational projects. Each member is situated in a social network that may enable or constrain influence in group decision making. To introduce structure into minority-influence theoretical and empirical work should help guide these applied initiatives.

In sum, we aim to describe how social-network characteristics (strength of proximal and distal ties) provide employees with access to differential causal influence mechanisms that have relevance to majority and minority influence. More specifically, we explicate ways in which these structural resources interact with employee perspectives (i.e., minority or majority positions) to provide them with particular mechanisms for exercising minority or majority influence (Deutsch & Gerard, 1955; Moscovici, 1980; Nemeth, 1986). Access to these causal-influence mechanisms (which we theorize is a function of employee distal and proximal ties) leads to differences in involvement (amount of influence attempts) and effectiveness (changes in target attitudes, behaviours, and cognitions).

Our chapter is organized as follows. First, we describe characteristics of employee social networks: diversity of ties (proximal and distal ties) and strength of ties (weak vs. strong). Based on these ties, we then delineate the mechanisms (ease and frequency of interaction with others in the work-group; trust, liking, and status; visibility and salience to co-workers; access to non-redundant information; and third-party support) that employees can use to induce changes in the attitudes, cognitions, and behaviours of their targets. Second, we combine the effects of distal and proximal ties to propose a workgroup social influence network typology. Third, we apply this typology and propose that specific influence mechanisms have differential effects on employee influence involvement (number of influence attempts) and employee influence effectiveness (success in changing targets).

Traditional work on majority/minority influence has typically addressed personal characteristics (e.g., consistency and certainty) and situational characteristics (e.g., sitting at the head of the table). Moving beyond past research and theorizing, we consider the interaction between social-network mechanisms and situational (i.e., minority, majority) characteristics as having critical (but to date under-researched) effects on influence outcomes.

## Minority and majority influence

Numerous phenomena have shaped research on social influence. In this chapter we draw primarily on two of these (i.e., conformity or majority influence and minority influence) in predicting employee motivation and effectiveness in persuading others to adopt their perspective on issues important to work functioning. The conformity or majority-influence literature advocates the idea that numbers convey social influence. Several mechanisms have been advanced and received support in explaining major-ity support. First, classical work focused on the need to develop uniformity to accomplish group goals (Festinger, 1954; Festinger, Schachter, & Back,

1950) and on comparison as a means to validate personal views with the purpose of being correct (Deutsch & Gerard, 1955; Festinger et al., 1950). Second, normative processes that create tension between advocating (or accepting) a unique point of view and conforming to the prevailing majority perspective are important in explaining conforming behaviours (i.e., public alignment with majority positions regardless of private beliefs; Deutsch & Gerard, 1955; Nord, 1969).

Two additional theoretical perspectives are relevant to these issues. Self-categorization and social-identity processes view alignment with majorities as efforts to establish or maintain self-views or social identity (Cialdini & Trost, 1998; Clark & Maass, 1988; David & Turner, 1992; Turner, 1991). This argument has also been used to explain the development of reference or membership groups for social minorities. Finally, social impact theory (Latané, 1981; Latané & Nida, 1980; Latané & Wolf, 1981; Tanford & Penrod, 1984) emphasizes number of group members, strength (e.g., power, knowledge), and immediacy (proximity in space and time) as antecedents to social influence. In this approach, relative size is critically important, such that majorities have more impact than minorities due to their greater number (Maass & Clark, 1984).

Majority influence produces either conversion or compliance. Conversion (Berger & Luckman, 1967; Nail, 1986; Nail, MacDonald, & Levy, 2000) is a change in position at both the private and the public levels similar to Kelman's (1958) idea of internalization. In contrast, compliance represents public agreement and private disagreement (Kelman, 1958; Moscovici, 1980; Nail, 1986).

The minority-influence approach emphasizes different influence processes. Compared to majorities, minorities, by definition, have limited power (Latané & Wolf, 1981). Therefore, their influence is based on something other than their situational position. Prevalent explanations of minority influence can be viewed as extensions of Kelley's (1967, 1973) attribution theory (e.g., Moscovici, 1980, 1985; Moscovici & Nemeth, 1974; Nemeth, Mayseless, Sherman, & Brown, 1990). This research considers behavioural style of minorities as an antecedent of minority-influence effectiveness.

Consensus (i.e., agreement across minority actors), consistency (i.e., stability of agent response or position over time), and distinctiveness (i.e., clearly articulated social reality or perspective that differs from that of the majority group) were originally identified as key to positive attributions about the minority, and therefore key sources of potential minority influence (Moscovici & Faucheux, 1972; Moscovici & Nemeth, 1974). Of these, consistency has received the most attention in the literature. Consistency over time: (a) accentuates conflict and triggers a review of positions in order to progress toward group goals (i.e., similar to Festinger's, 1950, locomotion concept); (b) increases exposure to minority arguments (i.e., repetition) and expands information about minority positions and salience of information that is available to majority targets (Maass & Clark, 1984;

Wood, Lundgren, Ouellettte, Busceme, & Blackstone, 1994); and, finally, (c) is viewed as more objective (Moscovici, 1985).

Social-impact approaches (Latané, 1981; Latané & Nida, 1980; Latané & Wolf, 1981; Tanford & Penrod, 1984) have also been applied to minority influence. For example, the larger the minority membership (with respect to a majority), the larger the potential influence of that minority. In a meta-analysis of minority influence, Wood and colleagues (1994) demonstrated consistent support for a positive relationship between size of the minority (relative to the majority target) and both public and private direct influence (i.e., specific to the issue). This study also demonstrated a negative relationship between the relative size of the minority and private indirect influence (i.e., similar in content but not identical to the specific issue under discussion). Minority influence is also affected by prestige and status of the influence agent within the group (Ridgeway & Berger, 1986). For example, high-status minority-influence agents have more credibility and influence potential than lower status agents (lower discounts; Kelley, 1971). Likewise, minority-influence agents can increase their influence by being seen as flexible and/or sincere (Maass & Clark, 1984; Wood et al., 1994).

In the next section, we develop the constructs and typology for our workgroup social influence network and then describe specific mechanisms that enhance or limit the potential of agents to exercise majority and minority influence. Later, we build on this to develop our propositions.

## The workgroup social influence network

We define a workgroup social influence network (WSIN) as the relational structure (or pattern of relationships) in an individual's formal and informal work-related social interactions. In WSINs, individuals exchange information, advice, and support (Higgins & Kram, 2001; Krackhardt, 1990; Lincoln & Miller, 1979) that have relevance to their involvement and effectiveness in influencing others. WSINs include relationships that are within the organization and relationships that go beyond organizational boundaries. Given the hierarchical nature of most organizational structures and organizational relationships, WSINs include multi-level and cross-level relationships. In sum, a WSIN is the work-related subset of an individual's entire social network (Wasserman & Faust, 1994).

Our chapter starts with the core premise that an employee's influence potential is affected by the mutual coordination that occurs between organizational members at different levels in the hierarchy and at different degrees of proximity. For example, an employee may interact with superiors, subordinates, and peers who are internal to the organization as well as with clients, suppliers, and consultants who are external to the organization. Thus, we highlight the importance of the broader social system and an employee's social network of relationships as an essential source of influence on attitudes, cognitions, and behaviours.

In the next section, we describe the structural diversity of ties and the strength of ties. We then further delineate structural diversity of ties by differentiating proximal and distal ties. This is an important point because the existing literature does not conceptualize proximal ties and distal ties as different constructs. Differentiating these ties conceptually allows us to consider their separate and interactive (joint) effects in ways that can enrich our understanding of social influence. Thus, our approach should have theoretical implications not yet addressed by existing research on social networks.

## Types of ties

Two structural characteristics of an employee's network are especially relevant to our theory building: structural diversity of the social network and strength of the ties in that network. This is because diversity and strength of ties in a work-related social network enable five key interaction mechanisms that affect an individual's influence at the workgroup level: (1) ease of access and frequency of interaction with others in the workgroup; (2) trust, liking, and status; (3) visibility and salience to co-workers; (4) access to non-redundant information; and (5) third-party support.

*Structural diversity of ties*   This is the degree to which those in a network are similar or dissimilar (Burt, 1992; Granovetter, 1973; Higgins & Kram, 2001). When employees have diverse ties, they have access to non-redundant information and the opportunity to transfer information and referrals among otherwise unrelated individuals. Diverse ties enable employees to use/control information and contacts that are not generally available to others.

*Strength of ties*   This is the level of emotional affect, reciprocity, and frequency of communication within a relationship (Granovetter, 1973; Higgins & Kram, 2001; Krackhardt, 1992). When employees have strong ties in their workgroup network, they have enhanced access to resources that provide them with more influence mechanisms within that network. Strong ties enable employees to gain information and support from others.

## Proximal and distal ties

The structural diversity of ties can be further specified by differentiating proximal ties and distal ties. In organizations, social ties between individuals reflect the interdependencies among formal positions (i.e., as defined by workflow diagrams and organizational charts), the interdependencies among informal positions (i.e., personal relationships between individuals), or both. Thus, individuals may interact with others because of their particular work interdependencies, because of informal ties (e.g., advice), or because of the development of informal ties within a formal work relationship (e.g., friendship that develops from a formal mentoring programme and extends beyond it).

We define proximal ties as ties that are totally or partially characterized by the requirements of workflow interaction (Brass, 1984), such as those that reflect task interdependence. Proximal ties may have low or high range. For example, proximal ties could include all the analysts working in the loan department (low range) or they could include all analysts in the department and their work-task-interdependence contacts (high range: e.g., the sales-force members and the supervisor of the loan department). Since our theorizing addresses new issues related to social networks and social influence, we focus in this chapter on the relative constraints and reinforcements faced by individuals in similar organizational positions (i.e., with shared or similar proximal network configurations) for exercising influence (either majority or minority).

In organizational contexts, distal ties represent work-related informal ties beyond the workflow (Brass, 1984; Podolny & Baron, 1997). These ties arise independent of work-task interdependencies but include work-related content. For example, an employee might have cross-functional ties horizontally across departments (e.g., a loan analyst's personal relationship with an employee in the bond department), vertically across hierarchical levels (e.g., a loan analyst's personal relationship with the vice president of the loan division), or across organizational boundaries (e.g., a loan analyst's personal relationship with loan analysts in other organizations).

*Weak and strong ties*

Ties can also be characterized as weak or strong. Strong ties involve ongoing relationships, including obligations and dependencies. Strong ties have been alternatively characterized as involving regular contact and interaction (Granovetter, 1973, 1982), commitment and investment in close personal relationships (Lund, 1985), empathy and unconditionality of regard (Cramer, 1986), and intimacy (Wegener, 1991). Through intense, repeated, or durable interaction, strong ties lead to particularistic relationships and particularistic knowledge of each other (Marsden, 1990). In organizations, however, frequency and duration may be a result of formal interdependencies, as was found by Marsden and Campbell (1984) in their study of best-friend ties and by Mitchell's (1987) work on ties among homeless women. For example, some information is exchanged in the workplace based purely on formal positions, while other information (more political in nature) is exchanged based on informal conditions like attraction, trust, or friendship (Podolny & Baron, 1997). Therefore, for the purpose of our theorizing, we define strong ties in organizations as ties between employees that reflect high levels of closeness or intensity. Weak ties, on the other hand, involve occasional interaction, impersonal relationships, and high substitutability (Granovetter, 1973, 1982; Lin, Ensel, & Vaughn, 1981). When employees have weak ties, their relationships are less personal, contain less affective content, and are less likely to be reciprocal.

To summarize, an employee's network contains proximal ties (those who are in the work-task interdependence network of the focal employee) that may be weak or strong. Also, an employee's network may or may not contain distal ties. When distal ties exist, they can be internal or external to the organization and they can also be weak or strong.

### Influence mechanisms as a function of an employee's WSIN

Integrating these concepts, we propose that an individual's types of ties (proximal and distal, weak and strong) help determine the causal influence mechanisms he/she has available for exercising influence. An individual's network structure provides access and control of valued resources to exercise influence. These resources are independent of minority and majority perspectives and influence mechanisms. Thus, considering each separately and then jointly should expand our thinking about influence mechanisms.

In other words, the nature of an employee's ties (distal and proximal, weak and strong) provides facilitating and inhibiting factors that affect influence behaviours. In addition, individuals hold majority or minority positions within the group on various topics. Thus, employees have access to specific influence mechanisms associated with their position as minority or majority members. Finally, our model also explicates the joint effects of ties and situated perspectives. The first two columns in Table 13.1 list specific types of ties and the corresponding causal mechanisms. The next four columns in the table describe specific influence implications within an individual's workgroup.

### Proximal ties and causal influence mechanisms

Social interaction between people is promoted by proximity (Festinger et al., 1950; Shaw, 1981), similar tasks (Carley, 1991), formal structure, and workflow design (Brass & Burkhardt, 1992). When employees have proximal ties, they share workflow and communication content. In some situations, these interdependencies expand to include advice and friendship (Bridge & Baxter, 1992), which increases the amount and breadth of shared information (Brass, Galaskiewicz, Greve, & Tsai, 2004; Sias & Cahill, 1998) as well as the level of trust in the relationship (Gibbons, 2004). Strong proximal work ties are characterized by interpersonal attraction, trust, support, and information sharing. Strong ties enhance the employee's social position in the workgroup and make it easier to influence others to support their ideas for change (Gibbons, 2004). Finally, trusting relationships that are characteristic of those with strong ties allow people to take the risk of speaking up and

Table 13.1 Network ties, causal mechanisms, and influence

| Types of ties | Causal mechanisms | Minority influence (MI) | | Majority influence (MAJ) | |
|---|---|---|---|---|---|
| | | Increases effectiveness of (MI) because of: | Increases involvement in (MI) because of: | Increases effectiveness of (MAJ) because of: | Decreases involvement of in (MAJ) because of: |
| Strong proximal | (a) Ease of access and frequency of interaction with others in the workgroup | Perceived certainty, consistency, and commitment | | | |
| | (b) Trust, liking, and status | Less discounting and role stress | Reduced threat to the agents' relationships | Increased social impact | Increased threat to the agents' relationships |
| | (c) Visibility and salience to co-workers | | | Reduced effort needed to communicate agents' position (influence economy) | Reduced need to communicate position |
| Strong distal | (a) Access to non-redundant information | Higher quantity and quality of arguments | | Higher quantity and quality of counter-arguments | |
| | (b) Third party support | Less discounting of agent's position | | Augmentation of majority position | |

proposing changes in work practices (LePine & Van Dyne, 2001) because generalized trust allows employees to experience change as not threatening to the relationships. In sum, employees with strong proximal ties have more influence within their workgroup.

Strong ties provide employees with several resources that have direct relevance to influence that are independent of situated position (minority or majority position with respect to a particular issue). First, strong proximal ties provide easy access to others. Strong proximal ties also increase the frequency of interaction with others in the workgroup. Thus, strong proximal ties provide more, and better, opportunities to obtain and share information—as well as opportunities to discuss alternative views. Second, strong proximal ties indicate trust, liking, and status that allow the employee to attract more attention and gain more consideration for their views, regardless of whether they are in the minority or the majority on a particular issue (Ridgeway, 1982, 1984). Third, employees with strong proximal ties (friendship) are especially visible and salient to co-workers in workgroups. This, in turn, further enhances their interpersonal influence during the process of establishing uniform cognitions and opinions (Festinger et al., 1950).

Additional support for the general proposition about the influence level embedded in strong proximal ties can also be inferred from the leadership literature, which demonstrates that those who are liked and respected in their groups (i.e., strong proximal ties) are more likely to emerge as leaders and will have greater influence in the group (Hollander & Julian, 1969). For example, Friedkin's (1993) longitudinal study of the structural bases of interpersonal influence in groups demonstrated that stronger ties increased influence within the group, even after controlling for the elementary basis of interpersonal power (e.g., reward, coercive, legitimate, expert, and referent; French & Raven, 1959). In conclusion, employees with strong proximal ties have more influence in the workgroup, and those with weak proximal ties have little or no structural sources of influence.

We note that the above description of the causal mechanisms associated with strong proximal ties differs from some traditional approaches. This is intentional and represents one of the potential contributions of our approach. In the past, scholars have typically assumed that dense networks of strong ties constrain independent action by providing sanctions for behaviours that deviate from group norms (Coleman, 1988, p. 103). For example, Coleman demonstrated a negative relation between cohesion in parent–teacher networks (strength of proximal ties) and dropping out of school (deviant behaviour; Coleman, 1990, pp. 306–307).

Our approach differs from Coleman's in two ways. First, we focus on an individual's own network and the personal benefits to that individual (in our model: influence effectiveness and influence involvement). We argue that strong proximal ties within the workgroup allow employees to influence others (based on liking and trust). In contrast, the strong cohesive network in Coleman's example belonged to the parents and the outcome focused on benefits to the students. Second, we emphasize the broader social system and the possibility that actors also have additional ties (e.g., weak to strong distal ties). In contrast, Coleman's study adopted Simmel's (1955) group-affiliation perspective and focused on the development of trust and norms in a singular affiliation group. Thus, our approach considers additional group affiliations, both proximal and distal ties, as well as the situated perspective of the employee (minority or majority on the issue at hand).

In sum, differentiating proximal and distal ties and the influence mechanisms associated with each is another potential contribution of our theorizing. We expand upon each of these processes later in the chapter when we develop our specific propositions for majority and minority influence.

### Distal ties and causal influence mechanisms

In addition to proximal ties, some employees also have distal ties outside the immediate workgroup. When employees have distal ties, they have access to non-redundant information and external support. Strong distal ties provide easy access to unique information (different from that shared within the proximal workgroup) and thus are a potential source of important influence in the proximal group (Ancona & Caldwell, 1992). For example, an employee can share (or not share) information from distal ties as a technique for influencing others in the group. Strong distal ties also provide employees with easy access to external support (Druskat & Wheeler, 2003). For example, an employee can obtain outside 'objective' support that can be useful for influencing others in the workgroup. In sum, strong distal ties allow employees to expand their social capital and increase their influence based on access to non-redundant information and third-party support.

Even weak distal ties can provide employees with influence mechanisms that are not available to those with only proximal ties. For example, even though weak distal ties are not as easily accessed as strong distal ties, weak distal ties still provide access to non-redundant information and external support. In both cases, this creates influence opportunities because the information and support are generally not available to others in the workgroup. Note, therefore, that distal ties can be shared (redundant) or not-shared (non-redundant) ties outside of the proximal workgroup. While shared ties are less likely to provide non-redundant information and support, the differential strength of ties may result in different information and levels of support being transferred through the tie. Distal ties that are not shared by all group members will provide more non-redundant information. Distal ties that are partially shared within the group will still provide differential amounts and quality of information based on their strength. Thus, we acknowledge the number and the strength of the distal ties held by an employee. We define strength of distal ties as the number of distal ties held by an employee weighted by the strength of those distal ties.

We note that the above description of the causal mechanisms associated with distal ties diverges from some traditional approaches. Initial social-network research typically implied that strong ties represent shared access to social resources (redundancy). In contrast, weak ties were viewed as non-redundant, more likely to bridge structural holes, and more likely to provide access to broader social resources (Granovetter, 1973). More recent approaches, however, acknowledge that non-redundant ties are not necessarily weak ties (Gabbay, 1997; Higgins & Kram, 2001). When people are members of parallel social systems, they hold a combination of strong and weak ties (without redundancy) across social systems. At the same time, however, each partner usually has strong, unshared relationships with other people in other areas of life. For example, McEvily and Zaheer (1999) demonstrated that new ideas, information, and opportunities can be sourced through contacts that are simultaneously strong and non-redundant. Thus, our theorizing moves beyond prior research that has viewed strong ties as redundant (focused on only one social system). Instead, we consider proximal and distal relationships in the broader social context.

To summarize, differentiating proximal and distal ties allows us to enrich the conceptualization of ties by specifying causal-influence mechanisms as a function of the characteristics of both proximal and distal ties. We specify strength of proximal ties and strength of distal ties, which allows us to consider their separate and joint effects (e.g., main effects and the interactions between proximal and distal ties). In the next section, we present a typology of WSINs and contrasting causal-influence mechanisms that become the basis for our predictions about influence involvement and influence effectiveness.

## A typology of workgroup social influence networks (WSIN typology)

As noted above, employees can have various combinations of weak proximal ties, strong proximal ties, weak distal ties, and strong distal ties. Combining these types of ties produces the four cells in our typology and creates four distinct types of WSIN: Entrepreneurial; Developmental; Coordinating; and Adaptive (see Figure 13.1). In the following paragraphs, we explicate the typology and each of the four network types in more detail. Later, we build on these differences as the basis for our propositions.

### Entrepreneurial workgroup social influence network

An *entrepreneurial WSIN* (cell 1) exists when an employee has strong proximal and strong distal ties. These individuals have the most social network resources for exercising influence and will be most successful in

|  | Weak distal ties | Strong distal ties |
|---|---|---|
| Weak proximal ties | ADAPTIVE [a]<br><br>4 | DEVELOPMENTAL<br><br>2 |
| Strong proximal ties | 3<br><br>COORDINATING | 1<br><br>ENTREPRENEURIAL |

*Figure 13.1* A typology of workgroup social influence networks (WSINs). *Note*: [a]Cell name = type of workgroup social influence network.

effecting change (compared to the other three networks). This is because they have access to all five of the influence mechanisms we describe in this paper based on their social capital (social network ties). Consistent with Burt (1997) and Higgins and Kram (2001), we refer to this type of network that spans multiple groups and exhibits brokerage capabilities as entrepreneurial. Prototypical holders of an entrepreneurial WSIN are high potential middle managers with extensive strong networks.

### Developmental workgroup social influence network

A *developmental WSIN* (cell 2) is based on weak proximal ties and strong distal ties. Like those with an entrepreneurial WSIN, employees with a developmental WSIN have access to the influence mechanisms based on strong distal ties: (a) access to non-redundant information; and (b) third-party support. Unlike entrepreneurial-WSIN employees, however, they do not have access to the other three influence mechanisms. We refer to this configuration of social network ties as developmental because these employees are newcomers to their immediate work unit and thus have weak proximal ties. Since they also have strong, trusting relationships in other parts of the organization, however, they are well positioned to develop proximal ties. Examples include employees recently promoted across functions or divisions and those who have long tenure with the organization.

### Coordinating workgroup social influence network

A *coordinating WSIN* (cell 3) is defined by strong proximal ties and weak distal ties. Individuals with this kind of network can use the influence mechanisms that derive from having strong proximal ties: (a) ease of access and frequency of interaction with others in the workgroup; (b) trust, liking, and status; and (c) visibility and salience to co-workers. We refer to this type of network as coordinating because those with strong ties within the group are ideally positioned to facilitate exchanges within the group. Prototypical examples include informal workgroup leaders with weak links to other parts of the organization.

### Adaptive workgroup social influence network

An *adaptive WSIN* (cell 4) is based on weak proximal ties and weak distal ties. These employees have generally weak ties. As a result, their ties provide them with minimal network resources for exercising influence within the workgroup. We refer to this type of WSIN as adaptive because these employees most likely must adapt to the influence efforts of others who have strong ties (proximal and distal). Examples include employees who have recently finished cross-functional rotation in management development programmes and have just started regular positions in the firm.

## WSINs and influence effectiveness and involvement

In this section of the chapter, we consider the effects of WSINs on two key behavioural outcomes with direct relevance to minority influence. First, we focus on influence effectiveness. Second, we shift our attention to influence involvement.

### WSINs and minority influence: Influence effectiveness

Our first outcome of interest is influence effectiveness. This is the most commonly researched outcome of agent minority influence: the extent to which a minority-influence agent can persuade others to change their attitudes, cognitions, and/or behaviours. Prior research has identified at least four factors that enhance effectiveness of minority-influence agents. These are: (1) consistency of position; (2) quality (persuasiveness) of arguments; (3) positive attributions regarding status, prestige, and trust of the minority-influence agent; and (4) the level of discounting applied to those in the minority position (Alvaro & Crano, 1997; Clark, 1999; Moscovici, 1980, 1985).

In developing our propositions, we start in the lower right corner of the matrix (Figure 13.1, cell 1) and contrast the entrepreneurial cell with the other three cells. Strong proximal and strong distal ties give employees with entrepreneurial WSINs four important advantages based on the structure of their WSIN.

As illustrated in Table 13.1 and Figure 13.1, strong proximal ties provide several key resources that facilitate exercise of minority influence (speaking up and expressing an opinion that differs from the majority position). First, ease of access and frequent informal interaction with others in the workgroup provide more and better opportunities to share information and discuss alternative views. Thus, employees with an entrepreneurial WSIN have repeated opportunities to present their positions. Repetition of the minority position increases their potential to influence majority targets because it increases perceptions of certainty, consistency, and perceived commitment (Maass & Clark, 1984). Second, strong proximal ties indicate trust, liking, and status, which, in turn, allow the employee to attract more attention and consideration to their ideas, regardless of their position (minority or majority) on a specific topic (Ridgeway, 1982, 1984). Having strong proximal ties reduces the possibility that others will discount their opinions and arguments based on alternative and/or negative causal attributions (Mugny & Papastamou, 1980; Shackelford, Wood, & Worchel, 1996). In addition, strong proximal ties also have psychological implications for the agent that undoubtedly enhance his/her effectiveness as a minority-influence agent. For example, minority-influence agents who have higher trust and status in the group experience less role stress because they anticipate positive responsiveness of their influence targets (Ng & Van Dyne, 2001).

Strong distal ties also provide key resources that facilitate use of minority influence. More specifically, these ties facilitate more and easier access to unique information. Since distal ties are not redundant with proximal ties (they are different from), they are a critical source of new or unique information, which is different from that shared within the proximal workgroup. This non-redundant information can be shared or withheld (Salancik & Pfeffer, 1978) and can be an important source of influence in the proximal group (Ancona & Caldwell, 1992). More important, non-redundant information allows those with an entrepreneurial WSIN to improve the quality and persuasiveness of their arguments (Anderson & Graesser, 1976; Clark, 1994). Finally, strong distal ties provide employees with access to external support (Druskat & Wheeler, 2003), which can reduce the amount of discounting that targets apply to opinions and arguments because external (e.g., cross-functional or organizational level) support causes the targets to perceive minority positions as less idiosyncratic and more representative of a larger social reference group. In addition, external support and validation can have second-level normative effects on other group members, further enhancing the influence of employees with an entrepreneurial WSIN. For example, a high-tenured employee that worked on an international rotation and is back in her or his former division with strong proximal ties from her or his former tenure in that area and with strong distal ties developed in her or his business rotation. She or he may now be in an excellent position to be effective in proposing and implementing minority position initiatives because she or he has access to non-redundant information to propose and defend her or his positions, access to informal opportunities to discuss it, trust based on her or his strong relationships in the group and external support to provide background influence to her or his claims. Overall, the strong social position provided by the entrepreneurial WSIN provides employees with the most resources and causal influence mechanisms to succeed at exercising minority influence (compared to other WSIN types). Thus, we propose that minority members with entrepreneurial networks will have the highest influence effectiveness.

> *Proposition 1a*: Minority-influence agents with an entrepreneurial WSIN are more likely to be effective in persuading majority targets to adopt their alternative perspectives than minority-influence agents with other types of WSIN.

We now further refine our comparisons by contrasting the resources and mechanisms available to those with developmental and coordinating WSINs (cells 2 and 3) compared to those with an adaptive WSIN (cell 4). Those in developmental and coordinating networks are similar in that they both have strong and weak ties. Developmental-WSIN holders (strong distal ties) have access to non-redundant information and third-party support. In contrast, coordinating-WSIN holders (strong proximal ties) have ease of access and frequent interaction, positive relationships and status, as well as visibility and salience to co-workers. Although these differences in influence mechanisms most likely cause differences in the specific influence efforts of those in these two WSINs, they do not suggest differences in effectiveness. Thus, we propose that developmental and coordinating WSINs have relatively equal influence effectiveness. In contrast, those in adaptive networks have only weak ties. Since weak ties provide few resources and influence mechanisms, we posit that minority member employees in developmental and coordinating networks will have higher influence effectiveness than those in an adaptive WSIN.

> *Proposition 1b*: Minority-influence agents with developmental or coordinating WSINs are more likely to be effective in persuading majority targets to adopt their alternative perspectives than minority-influence agents with an adaptive WSIN.

*WSINs and minority influence: Influence involvement*

We now focus on our second outcome: influence involvement. Although influence effectiveness is important and commonly considered in the minority-influence literature, we suggest that influence involvement is also important. Overall, research has paid less attention to involvement than to effectiveness. Thus, it represents a potentially useful area for extending work on minority influence. We define influence involvement as the level or amount of minority-influence behaviour. Influence involvement represents the quantity of influence. It is a behaviour. Thus, it is different from motivation to influence and quality of influence.

Overall, we propose that, when in minority positions, employees with strong proximal ties will have higher influence involvement (they will exhibit a higher quantity of influence behaviour than those with weak proximal ties). In other words, those with strong proximal ties are more likely to voice their minority positions. Those with strong proximal ties have the benefits of friendship and liking that provide a comfortable context for discussing uncertainties and concerns. In addition, these relationships are more stable and enduring (Shah, 2000) and thus less likely to be threatened by professional divergence (Gibbons, 2004) or functional conflict (Jehn, 1995).

Strong proximal ties allow employees to be more active in expressing their views (especially when these views represent minority positions) because speaking up will not threaten their relationships and social structure. In contrast, employees who do not have strong proximal ties do not have local support or a comfortable context that facilitates speaking up with divergent or controversial ideas. In this sense, new members of a team who typically have no strong relationships in the group are known to be less likely to voice their minority opinions and positions until they develop a safety net of strong relationships within the group. Returning to Figure 13.1 and the WSINs allows us to summarize this prediction based on cells in the typology. Thus, we propose that minority members with strong proximal ties (entrepreneurial and coordinating networks) will have higher levels of influence involvement than those who have weak proximal ties (developmental and adaptive networks).

> *Proposition 1c*: Minority-influence agents with entrepreneurial or coordinating WSINs are more likely to be involved in persuading majority targets to adopt their alternative perspectives than minority-influence agents with developmental or adaptive WSINs.

*WSINs and majority influence: Influence effectiveness*

We now take a different perspective and consider these same relationships for majority-influence agents. Thus, we make predictions for the effects of the network ties of majority-influence agents on their influence effectiveness and their influence involvement. Prior research has identified four key factors that enhance the effectiveness of majority-influence agents. These, as we discussed in our brief review of majority influence earlier in the chapter, are: (1) group continuity; (2) validation of personal views; (3) normative processes; and (4) positive attributions for status, trust, and prestige of majority-influence agents.

Once again, we start in the lower-right corner of the matrix and contrast the entrepreneurial WSIN (cell 1) with the other three cells in the typology. When majority employees have strong proximal ties and strong distal ties, they have access to all four facilitating factors that enhance effectiveness for exercising majority influence. As illustrated in Table 13.1 and Figure 13.1, strong proximal ties provide specific resources that enhance the individual's position. First, strong proximal ties indicate trust, liking, and status that attract more attention and consideration toward their positions, regardless of situated status on an issue (being in the minority or the majority; Ridgeway, 1982, 1984). When a majority opinion is held by a highly regarded other, this creates an additional need for minority member to validate their personal views. Thus, it represents a higher threat to group continuity (i.e., locomotion or achievement of group goals). Consistent with social-impact theory, status and personal relationships provide benefits, even to majority members (Latané, 1981; Latané & Nida, 1980; Latané & Wolf, 1981; Tanford & Penrod, 1984).

Second, employees who have majority views and also have strong proximal ties (friendship) in the workgroup are especially visible and salient to their peers, further enhancing their interpersonal influence in the group during the process of establishing uniform cognitions and opinions (Festinger et al., 1950). This salience and visibility allows economy in expressing views. It also causes their views (majority perspective) to be the reference point used by others who propose counter positions. Strong proximal ties reduce the effort the agent must use to communicate. They also cause targets to consider the majority position more carefully. These processes make majority-influence agents with strong proximal ties more effective in influencing others towards their majority position.

Third, strong distal ties provide majority members with more access and easier access to unique information (different from that shared within the proximal workgroup). As with minority members, this non-redundant information can be an important source of influence in the proximal group (Ancona & Caldwell, 1992). Non-redundant information increases the quantity and quality of counter-arguments available to majority agents. In addition, strong distal ties provide majority employees with easier access to external support (Druskat & Wheeler, 2003). External support further augments the weight of opinions and arguments used by those in the majority position. By gaining external support, majority members become a 'double majority' in that they are in the majority within the group and they also have external validation and support. This augmentation of arguments requires minority targets to search further for validation of their minority views. This augmentation is the opposite of traditional conceptualizations of 'double minorities' (Maass, Clark, & Haberkorn, 1982; Tajfel, 1978), where holding a minority position is harder if the individual is also perceived as member of an additional idiosyncratic (minority) group (Van Dyne & Saavedra, 1996).

Linking these four sources of influence back to our network typology allows us to summarize these points. Since majority members with an entrepreneurial WSIN have strong proximal ties and strong distal ties, they are in a better structural position than majority members in other types of WSIN. This is because their strong ties provide them with more resources that facilitate influence effectiveness in persuading others to change their attitudes, cognitions, and behaviours (Anderson & Graesser, 1976; Clark, 1994). Consequently, their strong social position (strong proximal ties and strong distal ties) provides them with more opportunities and causal mechanisms to succeed at exercising majority influence (compared to other WSIN types). Thus, we propose that majority members in an entrepreneurial WSIN will have the highest influence effectiveness.

> *Proposition 2a*: Majority-influence agents with an entrepreneurial WSIN are more likely to be effective in persuading minority targets to adopt their prevalent perspective than majority-influence agents with other types of WSIN.

We now further refine our comparisons by contrasting the resources and mechanisms available to those with developmental and coordinating WSINs (cells 2 and 3) compared to those with an adaptive WSIN (cell 4). We noted in earlier sections that those in developmental and coordinating networks are similar because they both have strong and weak ties. Holders of a developmental WSIN (strong distal ties) have access to non-redundant information and third-party support. Holders of a coordinating WSIN (strong proximal ties) have ease of access and frequent interaction, positive relationships and status, as well as visibility and salience to co-workers. Although these differences in influence mechanisms most likely cause differences in the specific influence efforts of majority members in development compared to coordinating WSINs, they do not suggest differences in majority-influence effectiveness. Thus, we propose that developmental and coordinating WSINs have relatively equal influence effectiveness. In contrast, majority members in adaptive networks have only weak ties. Since weak ties provide few resources and influence mechanisms, we posit that majority member employees in developmental and coordinating networks will have higher influence effectiveness than those in adaptive WSINs.

> Proposition 2b: *Majority-influence agents with developmental or coordinating WSINs are more likely to be effective in persuading*

*minority targets to adopt their prevalent perspective than majority-influence agents with an adaptive WSIN.*

### WSINs and majority influence: Influence involvement

We now focus on our second outcome for majority members: influence involvement. In contrast to our influence involvement prediction for minority influence where we proposed that minority members with strong proximal ties would have higher influence involvement (they will exhibit a higher quantity of influence behaviour than those with weak proximal ties), we here predict that majority members with strong proximal ties will have lower influence involvement (they will exhibit less influence behaviour than those with weak proximal ties). In other words, we argue that employees with strong proximal ties are less likely to speak up and voice their majority positions than employees with weak proximal ties.

When majority members have strong proximal ties, their views are salient in the group. Others try to anticipate and support their positions. Their views are the referent point – the foundation. As a consequence, they have less need for high involvement in influencing others, less need to communicate their position actively, and less need to take on the threat to their personal relations that can result from exercising power from a majority position. In contrast, majority members with weak proximal ties can use speaking up as an opportunity to develop their local social capital with minimal social cost.

Returning to Figure 13.1 and the WSINs allows us to summarize this prediction based on cells in the typology. Thus, we propose that majority members with strong proximal ties (entrepreneurial and coordinating networks) will have lower levels of influence involvement than those who have weak proximal ties (developmental and adaptive networks).

*Proposition 2c*: Majority-influence agents with developmental or adaptive WSINs are more likely to be involved in persuading minority targets to adopt their prevalent perspective than majority-influence agents with entrepreneurial or coordinating WSINs.

### Discussion

In this chapter, our goal was to develop and explicate a theoretically based model of social network factors that combine with employee-situated perspectives (minority or majority member status on a particular topic) to provide employees with five differential influence mechanisms. Extending the model, we also predicted differential effects on two key outcomes: influence involvement and influence effectiveness. In doing this, we emphasized the social context of work and the nature of employee social capital (distal and proximal ties). In the process, we developed a WSIN typology that characterizes the basic influence mechanisms available to those in four generic social networks. Finally, we used this typology as the basis for making theoretical predictions for differences in influence involvement and influence effectiveness.

This is important because considering similarities and differences in the social networks of minority and majority members allows us to enhance our understanding of why some minorities succeed in persuading others to adopt their views and why some majorities fail to persuade others to adopt their views. Additionally, this theorizing provides complementary arguments for influence effectiveness and influence involvement beyond the traditional focus on numerical comparisons.

In the next section, we expand upon these ideas and address the question of why we think it is important to theorize about the social structures of actors in minority and majority positions. To answer this question, we move beyond the initial arguments in this chapter to explicate further possible implications for this socially embedded view of minority and majority influence. Our goal here is to stimulate further research and theorizing.

Scholars have previously noted a large discrepancy between laboratory results and historical evidence regarding the success of minorities in imposing their views (Clark, 1994). For example, empirical studies show that minorities rarely have the direct effect of changing the views of others (compared to majority influence). In contrast, managerial accounts and history provide a more balanced narrative of the impact of minorities and majorities on issues that are important to group functioning. These narratives indicate that successful minority influence is not as rare as indicated in laboratory experiments (Clark, 1994), that the majority can be dependent on the social positions of minority actors and, interestingly, that different outcomes result, depending on the specific actors involved in the influence process. While there are alternative versions of the evolutionary model (e.g., Wallace's evolutionary model), Darwin exercised minority influence. Darwin was able to diffuse and impose his model. Perhaps Darwin succeeded because of his social network; perhaps Wallace could not impose his views because he was less established and academically embedded than Darwin. Interestingly, if Wallace had been able to impose his model, which was based on a cybernetic metaphor, cybernetics may have emerged 60 years earlier. Similarly, our example of Nils at the beginning of the chapter could represent an individual with strong social capital that allowed him to impose his preference for a particular technology platform (from a minority position and without any other source of power). Perhaps his social embeddedness in the organization had implications not only for the decision that was adopted, but also for the manner in which the project was implemented.

As described in this chapter, minority and majority influence operate through different mechanisms and produce different reactions in influence targets. The leniency contract holds that minority messages are elaborated without derogation and counter-argument (Crano & Chen, 1998). Minorities are not seen as threatening and therefore do not incite defensive derogation and/or aggressive counter-arguments (Alvaro & Crano, 1997). It is therefore expected that minorities will be active and their success is usually associated with involvement, insistence, repetition, and consistency. Majority members typically do not engage in negative or defensive reactions when exposed to minority influence. Instead, they elaborate the inputs of minority messages in an attempt to evaluate whether the minority position corresponds with reality (Moscovici, 1980, 1985; Nemeth, 1986). More minority input triggers more elaboration by targets. This leads to more involvement and more effectiveness in getting minority positions heard. Contrarily, majority activity may be viewed as overly intrusive or as illegitimate pressure (Alvaro & Crano, 1997).

Moving to the group level of analysis suggests a number of interesting implications with relevance to both majority and minority influence. When minority member factions of a group are more involved and more effective, the potential composite influence of the minority faction is higher. They have a better chance of successfully persuading the majority to adopt their position. Based on our model, involvement and effectiveness reflect stronger ties. Thus, minority factions who have strong ties in the overall group and also have distal ties are more likely to be successful in promoting their views. Group-level implications of our model, however, differ for majorities.

In most situations, people assume that majority positions are true. Thus, the majority conveys influence by serving as a reference point that validates personal views, norms, group locomotion needs, and prestige. As described in our model, majority influence does not rely on argumentation and activity (i.e., involvement). Instead, majority influence is based on the simple connotation (labelling) of being a majority-held view, which promotes conformity to the majority position in group members. Therefore, activity or involvement is not necessary for majority members and may, in fact, trigger conflictive, defensive, or counter-arguments from minority members—who then may instigate minority activity. Since majority involvement may be seen as pressure tactics, it may create reactions within the majority in defence of minority in-group members, since criticizing or putting pressure on a fellow in-group member may threaten the self-identity of in-group majority members (Alvaro & Crano, 1997).

By being active, those in the majority increase the opportunities for the minority faction to present their views. This, thus, can have debilitating consequences on the majority position and goal of achieving conformity. Furthermore, consistent with proposition 2c, majority members with weak proximal ties to others in the group are more likely to be active in trying to impose their views on others in the group. This activity by weakly embedded members may produce conversions to the minority position and should promote maintenance of group structure (e.g., the set of close relationships within the group). In sum, extending our model to the group level suggests that group majority involvement has the potential to decrease overall group majority influence effectiveness based on conformity to the majority.

This suggests an important new avenue for research on minority influence. While much prior research has emphasized specific minority behaviours and size of minority in explaining minority-influence success, our socially embedded view of minority and majority influence suggests the possibility of social structural factors as a source of advantage for minority influence. It also identifies potential weaknesses in majority-influence positions based on majority member structural positions and behaviours. In our view, this opens a wide range of research opportunities that may identify alternative explanations for reconciling the differences between previous laboratory findings and historical evidence.

For example, minority-influence research may find the opportunity to reconcile field and laboratory findings by adding social structure through longitudinal laboratory studies in which network structure is allowed to emerge. Similarly, taking into account social structure in field settings may explain away the differences in previous research. Another interesting line of questioning beyond testing our model would come from the implications of debilitating factors to majority positions that emerge from our theorizing. When socially disconnected actors jump start the discussions on majority positions this may create opportunities for the minority arguments to be heard and succeed.

In practice, this opens several avenues for both majority- and minority-position defenders to strengthen their positions and a series of institutional avenues to promote or silence minority views. Minority positions should benefit from developing strong in-group ties or attracting actors with strong ties in the group since those actors can be more vocal and also more effective in their arguments. Also, actors supporting a minority position should be aware of the value to their position of extending and strengthening their distal ties in ways that allow for access to new information and relevant external support. Majority-position supporters will benefit by normatively silencing their membership to avoid promoting group reactions, especially when structural ties in the group are divided between positions. Also, they may want to strengthen the relationships with disconnected co-majority position holders to avoid intra-group defence of in-group minority position holders that might otherwise debilitate their majority-position claims.

Although our theorizing has a number of strengths, our approach is under-specified and incomplete. Since we have presented an initial conceptual model of the effects of social network ties on minority and majority influence, additional theorizing could consider key boundary conditions to the relationships we have proposed. Thus, we recommend that future research expand and refine the ideas we have presented here. We also encourage future research that moves beyond our focus on social-network influence. This could include organizational-level influences (e.g., organizational culture, norms, and climate), individual-level influences (e.g., interpersonal basis of power), task influences (e.g., task complexity and criticality), and supervisory influences (e.g., personality and management style).

To conclude, we have theorized that proximal and distal ties in employee social networks can be differentiated and that they can range from weak to strong. We also have proposed that specifying these network-tie characteristics enhances our conceptualizations of influence processes. This is because they combine to provide differential causal influence mechanisms for exercising minority and majority influence. Based on these ties, we have developed a typology of workgroup social influence networks (WSINs) and used these conceptual differences as the basis of our propositions that predict differential influence effectiveness and influence involvement for minority and majority members. We hope our theorizing stimulates empirical research and additional theory building.

## References

Allport, G. W. (1985). The historical background of social psychology. In G. Lindzey & E. Aronson (Eds.), *Handbook of social psychology* (Vol. 1, pp. 1–46). New York: Random House.

Alvaro, E. M., & Crano, W. D. (1997). Indirect minority influence: Evidence for leniency in source evaluation and counterargumentation. *Journal of Personality and Social Psychology, 72*, 949–964.

Ancona, D. G., & Caldwell, D. F. (1992). Bridging the boundary: External activity and performance in organizational teams. *Administrative Science Quarterly, 37*, 634–665.

Anderson, N. H., & Graesser, C. C. (1976). An information analysis of attitude change in social discussion. *Journal of Personality and Social Psychology, 33*, 210–222.

Berger, P. L., & Luckman, T. (1967). *The social construction of knowledge: A treatise on the sociology of knowledge.* Garden City, NY: Anchor Press.

Brass, D. J. (1984). Being in the right place: A structural analysis of individual influence in an organization. *Administrative Science Quarterly, 29*, 518–539.

Brass, D. J., & Burkhardt, M. E. (1992). Centrality and power in organizations. In N. Nohria & R. Eccles (Eds.), *Networks and organizations: Structure, form, and action* (pp. 191–215). Boston: Harvard Business School Press.

Brass, D. J., Galaskiewicz, J., Greve, H. R., & Tsai, W. (2004). Taking stock of networks and organizations: A multilevel perspective. *Academy of Management Journal, 47*, 795–818.

Bridge, K., & Baxter, L. A. (1992). Structural holes: The social structure of competition. *Western Journal of Communication, 56*, 200–225.

Burt, R. S. (1992). *Structural holes: The social structure of competition.* Cambridge, MA: Harvard University Press.

Burt, R. S. (1997). The contingent value of social capital. *Administrative Science Quarterly, 42,* 339–365.

Carley, K. (1991). A theory of group stability. *American Sociological Review, 56,* 331–354.

Cialdini, R. B., & Trost, M. R. (1998). Social influence: Social norms, conformity, and compliance. In D. Gilbert, S. Fiske, & G. Lindzey (Eds.), *Handbook of social psychology* (4th ed., Vol. 2, pp. 151–192). New York: McGraw-Hill.

Clark, R. D., III (1994). A few parallels between group polarization and minority influence. In S. Moscovici, A. Mucchi-Faina, & A. Maass (Eds.), *Minority influence* (pp. 47–66). Chicago: Nelson-Hall.

Clark, R. D., III (1999). The effect of majority defectors and number of persuasive minority arguments on minority influence. *Representative Research in Social Psychology, 23,* 15–21.

Clark, R. D., III, & Maass, A. (1988). Social categorization in minority influence: The case of homosexuality. *European Journal of Social Psychology, 18,* 347–364.

Coleman, J. S. (1988). Social capital in the creation of human capital. *American Journal of Sociology, 94,* 95–120.

Coleman, J. S. (1990). *Foundations of social theory.* Cambridge, MA: Harvard University Press.

Cramer, D. (1986). An item factor analysis of the original relationship inventory. *Journal of Sociology and Personal Relations, 3,* 121–127.

Crano, W. D., & Chen, X. (1998). The leniency contract and persistence of majority and minority influence. *Journal of Personality and Social Psychology, 74,* 1437–1450.

David, B., & Turner, J. C. (1992, July). *Studies in self-categorization and minority conversion.* Paper presented at the joint meeting of the European Association of Experimental Social Psychology and the Society for Experimental Social Psychology, Leuven, Belgium.

Deutsch, M., & Gerard, H. G. (1955). A study of normative and informational social influence upon individual judgment. *Journal of Abnormal and Social Psychology, 51,* 629–636.

Druskat, V. U., & Wheeler, J. V. (2003). Managing from the boundary: The effective leadership of self-managing work teams. *Academy of Management Journal, 46,* 435–457.

Festinger, L. (1950). Informal social communication. *Psychological Review, 57,* 271–282.

Festinger, L. (1954). A theory of social comparison processes. *Human Relations, 7,* 117–140.

Festinger, L., Schachter, S., & Back, K. (1950). *Social pressures in informal groups: A study of human factors in housing.* New York: Harper.

French, J. R. P., & Raven, B. (1959). The bases of social power. In D. Cartwright (Ed.), *Studies of social power* (pp. 118–149). Ann Arbor, MI: Institute for Social Research.

Friedkin, N. E. (1993). Structural bases of interpersonal influence in groups: A longitudinal study. *American Sociological Review, 58,* 861–872.

Gabbay, S. M. (1997). *Social capital in the creation of financial capital: The case of network marketing.* Champaign, IL: Stipes.

Gibbons, D. E. (2004). Friendship and advice networks in the context of changing professional values. *Administrative Science Quarterly, 49,* 238–262.

Granovetter, M. S. (1973). The strength of weak ties. *American Journal of Sociology*, *78*, 1360–1380.

Granovetter, M. S. (1982). The strength of weak ties: A network theory revisited. In P. V. Marsden & N. Lin (Eds.), *Social structure and network analysis* (pp. 105–130). Beverly Hills, CA: Sage.

Higgins, M. C., & Kram, K. E. (2001). Reconceptualizing mentoring at work: A developmental network perspective. *Academy of Management Review*, *26*, 264–288.

Hollander, E. P., & Julian, J. W. (1969). Contemporary trends in the analysis of leadership processes. *Psychological Bulletin*, *71*, 387–397.

Ilgen, D. R. (1999). Teams in organizations: Some implications. *American Psychologist*, *54*, 129–139.

Jehn, K. A. (1995). A multimethod examination of the benefits and detriments of intragroup conflict. *Administrative Science Quarterly*, *40*, 256–282.

Kelley, H. H. (1967). Attribution theory in social psychology. In D. Levine (Ed.), *Nebraska symposium on motivation* (Vol. 15, pp. 192–238). Lincoln: University of Nebraska Press.

Kelley, H. H. (1971). *Attribution in social interaction*. New York: General Learning Press.

Kelley, H. H. (1973). The processes of causal attribution. *American Psychologist*, *28*, 107–128.

Kelman, H. C. (1958). Compliance, identification and internalization: Three processes of attitude change. *Journal of Conflict Resolution*, *2*, 51–60.

Krackhardt, D. (1990). Assessing the political landscape: Structure, cognition, and power in organizations. *Administrative Science Quarterly*, *35*, 342–369.

Krackhardt, D. (1992). The strength of strong ties: The importance of philos in organizations. In R. E. N. Nohria (Ed.), *Networks and organizations: Structure, form and action* (pp. 216–239). Cambridge, MA: Harvard Business School Press.

Latané, B. (1981). The psychology of social impact. *American Psychologist*, *36*, 343–356.

Latané, B., & Nida, S. (1980). Social impact theory and group influence: A social engineering perspective. In P. B. Paulus (Ed.), *Psychology of group influence* (pp. 3–34). Hillsdale, NJ: Lawrence Erlbaum Associates, Inc.

Latané, B., & Wolf, S. (1981). The social impact of minorities and majorities. *Psychological Review*, *88*, 438–453.

LePine, J. A., & Van Dyne, L. (2001). Voice and cooperative behavior as contrasting forms of contextual performance: Evidence of differential relationships with Big Five personality characteristics and cognitive ability. *Journal of Applied Psychology*, *86*, 326–336.

Lin, N., Ensel, W. M., & Vaughn, J. C. (1981). Social resources and strength of ties. *American Sociological Review*, *46*, 393–405.

Lincoln, J. R., & Miller, J. (1979). Work and friendship ties in organizations: A comparative analysis of relational networks. *Administrative Science Quarterly*, *24*, 181–199.

Lund, M. (1985). The development of investment and commitment scales for predicting continuity of personal relationships. *Journal of Sociology of Personal Relations*, *2*, 3–23.

Maass, A., & Clark, R. D., III (1984). Hidden impact of minorities: Fifteen years of minority influence research. *Psychological Bulletin*, *95*, 428–450.

Maass, A., Clark, R. D., III, & Haberkorn, G. (1982). The effects of differential ascribed category membership and norms on minority influence. *European Journal of Social Psychology, 12,* 89–104.

Marsden, P. V. (1990). Network measurement and data. *Annual Review of Sociology, 16,* 435–463.

Marsden, P. V., & Campbell, K. E. (1984). Measuring tie strength. *Sociological Forces, 63,* 482–501.

McEvily, B., & Zaheer, A. (1999). Bridging ties: A source of firm heterogeneity in competitive capabilities. *Strategic Management Journal, 20,* 1133–1156.

Mitchell, J. C. (1987). The components of strong ties among homeless women. *Sociological Networks, 9,* 37–47.

Moscovici, S. (1980). Toward a theory of conversion behavior. In L. Berkowitz (Ed.), *Advances in experimental social psychology* (Vol. 13, pp. 209–239). New York: Academic Press.

Moscovici, S. (1985). Social influence and conformity. In G. Lindzey & E. Aronson (Eds.), *Handbook of social psychology* (Vol. 2, pp. 347–412). New York: Random House.

Moscovici, S., & Faucheux, C. (1972). Social influence, conformity bias, and the study of active minorities. *Advances in Experimental Social Psychology, 6,* 149–202.

Moscovici, S., & Nemeth, C. (1974). Social influence: II. Minority influence. In C. Nemeth (Ed.), *Social psychology: Classic and contemporary integrations* (pp. 217–249). Chicago: Rand McNally.

Mugny, G., & Papastamou, S. (1980). When rigidity does not fail: Individualization and psychologization as resistances to the diffusion of minority innovations. *European Journal of Social Psychology, 10,* 43–61.

Nail, P. R. (1986). Toward an integration of some models and theories of social response. *Psychological Bulletin, 100,* 190–206.

Nail, P. R., MacDonald, G., & Levy, D. A. (2000). Proposal of a four-dimensional model of social response. *Psychological Bulletin, 126,* 454–470.

Nemeth, C. (1986). Differential contributions of majority and minority influence. *Psychological Review, 93,* 23–42.

Nemeth, C. J., Mayseless, O., Sherman, J., & Brown, Y. (1990). Exposure to dissent and recall of information. *Journal of Personality and Social Psychology, 58,* 429–437.

Ng, K. Y., & Van Dyne, L. (2001). Individualism–collectivism as a boundary condition for effectiveness of minority influence in decision making. *Organizational Behavior and Human Decision Processes, 84,* 198–225.

Nord, W. R. (1969). Social exchange theory: An integrative approach to social conformity. *Psychological Bulletin, 71,* 174–208.

Podolny, J. M., & Baron, J. N. (1997). Resources and relationships: Social networks and mobility in the workplace. *American Sociological Review, 62,* 673–693.

Ridgeway, C. (1982). Status in groups: The importance of motivation. *American Sociological Review, 47,* 76–88.

Ridgeway, C. (1984). Dominance, performance, and status in groups: A theoretical analysis. In E. J. Lawler (Ed.), *Advances in group processes* (Vol. 1, pp. 59–93). Greenwich, CT: JAI Press.

Ridgeway, C. L., & Berger, J. (1986). Expectations, legitimation, and dominance behavior in task groups. *American Sociological Review, 51,* 603.

Salancik, G. R., & Pfeffer, J. (1978). A social information processing approach to job attitudes and task design. *Administrative Science Quarterly, 23*, 224–253.

Shackelford, S., Wood, W., & Worchel, S. (1996). Behavioral styles and the influence of women in mixed-sex groups. *Social Psychology Quarterly, 59*, 284–294.

Shah, P. P. (2000). Network destruction: The structural implications of downsizing. *Academy of Management Journal, 43*, 101–112.

Shaw, M. E. (1981). *Group dynamics: The psychology of group behavior.* New York: McGraw-Hill.

Sias, P. M., & Cahill, D. J. (1998). From coworkers to friends: The development of peer friendship in the workplace. *Western Journal of Communication, 62*, 273–299.

Simmel, G. (1955). *Conflict and the web of group affiliations* (K. H. Wolff & R. Bendix, Trans.). New York: Free Press.

Sparrowe, R. T., Liden, R. C., Wayne, S. J., & Kraimer, M. L. (2001). Social networks and the performance of individuals and groups. *Academy of Management Journal, 44*, 316–325.

Tajfel, H. (1978). *Differentiation between social groups: Studies in the social psychology of intergroup relations.* London: Academic Press.

Tanford, S. E., & Penrod, S. (1984). Social influence model: A formal integration of research on majority and minority influence processes. *Psychological Bulletin, 95*, 189–225.

Turner, J. C. (1991). *Social influence.* Pacific Grove, CA: Brooks/Cole.

Van Dyne, L., & Saavedra, R. (1996). A naturalistic minority influence experiment: Effects on divergent thinking, conflict, and originality in work groups. *British Journal of Social Psychology, 35*, 151–167.

Wageman, R. (1995). Interdependence and group effectiveness. *Administrative Science Quarterly, 40*, 145–180.

Wasserman, S., & Faust, K. (1994). *Social network analysis: Methods and applications.* Cambridge, UK: Cambridge University Press.

Wegener, B. (1991). Job mobility and social ties: Social resources, prior job, and status attainment. *American Sociological Review, 56*, 60–71.

Wood, W., Lundgren, S., Ouellette, J. A., Busceme, S., & Blackstone, T. (1994). Minority influence: A meta-analytic review of social influence processes. *Psychological Bulletin, 115*, 323–345.

Wrzesniewski, A., Dutton, J. E., & Debebe, G. (2003). Interpersonal sensemaking and the meaning of work. In R. M. Kramer & B. M. Staw (Eds.), *Research in organizational behavior* (Vol. 25, pp. 93–135). Oxford, UK: Elsevier.

# 14 Dissent within and among groups in organizations: Lessons for group empowerment and organizational innovation

*Andreas W. Richter*
Instituto de Empressa Business School, Madrid, Spain

*Claudia A. Sacramento and Michael A. West*
Aston University, UK

The world is full of minorities. These minorities are of many different types, for example, religious, racial, ethnic or linguistic. Minorities are often associated with negative events such as society instability or even war. This is a consequence of the negative image that history offers of the relationship between majorities and minorities. Majorities are stained by the abuse of power and minorities by radical actions.

This is only half the story. Social development over the centuries has been driven partly by confident and consistent minorities. Women's right to vote, something irrevocable in current Western society, was not possible in the United States until 1920. In England, women were only given an equal right to vote in 1928 due to the suffragette minority, a group of people in the beginning of the nineteenth century who fought and protested against the inequality inherent in the democratic system. They had a vision of what their society should be like and pressed their message through all the means they could, including hunger strikes, demonstrations, disrupting sporting events and chaining themselves to railings. The suffragettes' confidence, persistence and coherence led the majority to accept reforming the electoral system. Another example is the Civil Rights Movement in the USA. As victims of injustice by the segregation politics in the USA since the end of slavery, African Americans had to undertake a long political, legal and social struggle to gain full citizenship rights. Inspired by Martin Luther King, a strong leader who was able not only to align his followers around a shared vision but also to manage the fragile boundaries of racial groups in American society, their persistence was rewarded with the Voting Rights Act of 1965. This victory illustrates how a minority can create and sustain fundamental change in society.

In this chapter we argue that in the same way as social minorities contribute to the shaping of society by bending powerful majorities, less-powerful groups in organizations can also contribute to an organizational shift through their interaction with majority groups. When tested in the complex and fiery settings of work organizations, theoretical predictions of social psychology may well prove too fragile to survive the heat. Alternatively, they may suggest to practitioners and organizational psychologists simplistic solutions to organizational problems that undermine rather than support efforts to enable organizational effectiveness. We apply research findings and theory about minority influence to two domains of organizational psychology: how minority dissent *within* groups can lead to group innovation; and how minority dissent *across* groups can bring about organizational innovation. We first review the findings from the minority-influence literature and consider the implications for our understanding of innovation in workgroups. We then build upon this body of literature in order to extend theory by developing a model of how minority dissent across groups can help relatively powerless groups in organizations to bring about organizational change and innovation.

## Minority dissent and innovation in groups

### Group innovation

Whether it is finding new ways of diagnosing and treating breast cancer in hospitals, developing new forms of protection from the sun's rays, marketing bicycles or finding ways of developing more destructive land mines, innovation is central to the success of organizations in achieving their aims. And it is groups that are largely responsible for developing and implementing new ideas in work organizations (West, 2002). The challenge for researchers and practitioners is to identify the factors that predict group innovation. What do we know so far from our research endeavours?

The factors identified in research as likely to influence levels of innovation in workgroups include 'inputs' of groups such as the task the group is required to perform, the composition of the group (such as its diversity), and the organizational context (e.g., manufacturing, health service, organizational size). Research suggests that the overriding influence, however, is group processes, which mediate the relationships between inputs and innovation (West, 2002; West & Anderson, 1996). How can social psychological research help to advance knowledge of these processes? One promising area of research, hitherto ignored by organizational psychologists, is the influence of dissenting minorities in groups—those who go against the prevailing view and persistently argue for what is a minority position.

### Minority dissent and group innovation

Conformity and compliance within a group may enhance group performance by minimizing process loss (Steiner, 1972). Alignment of opinions in groups fulfils the useful function of bundling energy and resources while reducing coordination loss and conflict, in the service of accomplishing shared goals. However, several disadvantages of concurrence seeking have been reported in the literature. Janis's (1972) analysis of groupthink revealed that strong conformity pressures in groups may lead to erroneous group decision making, which may have disastrous consequences. Indeed, individuals' tendencies to yield to conformity pressures even when a decision is at odds with objective criteria have been documented in numerous social psychological experiments (e.g., Asch, 1951). Similarly, Hackman and Morris (1975) argued that a premature movement to consensus with oppression of dissenting opinions hampers group performance. Moreover, research on group polarization (Bem, Wallach, & Kogan, 1965) shows how dominant initial positions within groups may result in more extreme group decisions. Finally, research on the 'group discontinuity effect' (Insko & Schopler, 1998; Schopler et al., 2001) reveals that groups behave more competitively than individuals. All these findings illustrate the drawbacks of conformity and compliance, as well as their potentially detrimental effects on group effectiveness. One process that may counteract these problems is minority dissent.

Minority dissent occurs when a minority in a group publicly opposes beliefs, attitudes, ideas, procedures, or policies supported by the majority of the group (McLeod, Baron, Marti, & Yoon, 1997). Social psychological research has shown that minority consistency of arguments over time (against the position of the majority in a group) is likely to lead to change in majority views in groups and to innovation (Moscovici, Mugny, & van Avermaet, 1985; Nemeth & Nemeth-Brown, 2003). People exposed to a confident and consistent minority change their private views prior to expressing public agreement. Minority-influence researchers have labelled this process as 'conversion'. Research on minority influence suggests that conversion is most likely to occur where a minority is consistent and confident in the presentation of its arguments. Moreover, it is a behavioural style of persistence that is most likely to lead to attitude change and innovation (Nemeth & Owens, 1996). Nemeth and others suggest that we explore the view expressed by a minority more thoroughly than we do the view of a majority with which we disagree. In the latter case, we look for information that supports the majority's position since we feel uncomfortable disagreeing with the majority. But, it is proposed, when we hear a persistently expressed minority position we think more creatively around the issue because there is no imperative to find reasons to agree. In addition, the impact of minority dissent on creativity and improved decision making can be explained from a cognitive perspective. Nemeth (1995) suggested that the focus of disagreement has an effect on the type of cognition. Whereas a majority disagreement stimulates cognitive processes that are convergent in form, a minority disagreement stimulates divergent thought. When the majority disagrees, people tend to think about the issue from the perspective of the majority excluding all other possibilities. On the other hand, when a minority disagrees, people tend to think about the issue from multiple perspectives, one of those being the perspective supported by the minority. The minority disagreement stimulates the consideration of alternatives that have not been suggested by the majority, and that but for the minority would not have been considered. This stronger divergent thinking enhanced by minority dissent is at the heart of creativity and innovation. De Dreu and De Vries (1997) suggested that a homogeneous workgroup in which minority dissent is suppressed will have low levels of creativity, innovation, individuality, and interdependence (De Dreu & De Vries, 1993). In contrast, task-related debate may lead group members to re-evaluate the status quo and adapt their objectives, strategies, or processes more appropriately to their situation, thereby innovating. Moscovici details the underlying processes and posits the existence of dual mechanisms for the influence of majorities and minorities. Majorities are associated with compliance mechanisms. When exposed to majorities, individuals agree due to normative pressures rather than due to the elaboration of their arguments. The effects of majority exposure are consequently immediate, temporary and direct. On the other hand, minorities are associated with conversion mechanisms. Individuals facing minorities agree with them not because of social pressure but due to informational processing. Hence, the effects of conversion are not immediate but delayed, long lasting, and private rather than public (Moscovici, 1980). It seems that although minority-dissent effects are not as evident as the majority-dissent effects at the beginning, minority-influence processes are more powerful in terms of the type and durability of the change they promote. When transported to the organizational context, these findings may be very useful in terms of understanding and promoting long-lasting changes.

Numerous studies in the laboratory suggest the value of minority dissent on a variety of outcome measures. This may be best demonstrated in a seminal experimental study by Moscovici, Lage, and Naffrechoux (1969), showing that a minority, even when wrong, can influence decision making. The researchers requested their participants to name the colour of a series of slides presented. In a group of six participants, two confederates consistently called blue slides 'green'. This minority influence led to an increase of 8% green responses from the other naive participants. This effect only persisted as long as the confederates were consistent in their answers. A later study suggested that minority dissent stimulates divergent thinking and enhances creativity. Nemeth and Wachtler (1983) compared the effects of facing a majority disagreement or facing a minority disagreement. Individuals in groups of six were shown a series of eight slides with a standard figure on the left and six comparison figures on the right. They were then asked to name all of the comparison figures that contained the standard. One of the comparisons was very obvious but the others were less evident. Depending on the condition, two or four of the six group members were confederates and identified both the easy and another less-obvious figure, that could be right or wrong. Majorities had a stronger influence: individuals faced with a majority of confederates were more likely to follow their answers. However, individuals in the minority-dissent condition were more likely to find novel correct solutions than those in the majority condition and they also identified other figures rather than those suggested by the minority. Minority dissent also positively affects the recall of information. In a recall task, participants who had been exposed to consistent minority dissent exhibited a better recall of information than those in a control condition and those in a majority-dissent condition (Nemeth, Mayseless, Sherman, & Brown, 1990). The effect of minority dissent is not restricted to the timeframe minorities and majorities are physically in contact. Another experimental study showed that individuals exposed to minority dissent in a word-association task were more original in their associations, and this effect remained even after the interaction with the minority group had ceased (Nemeth & Kwan, 1985).

Replication studies in field settings, however, are scant. In two longitudinal studies of workgroups in the Netherlands, De Dreu and West (2001) found that minority dissent did, indeed, predict group innovation (as rated by the groups' supervisors), but only in groups with high levels of participation. They suggested that one of the main threats to effective group work is the group's tendency to move to premature consensus and hypothesized that minority dissent in organizational groups would increase creativity and divergent thought. They further argued that creativity induced by minority dissent would lead to innovation only when group members participated in decision making. Through participation (frequent group member interaction and regular meetings; group members influencing key group decisions about the group's work; and group members keeping each other informed fully about the task and their contribution to it) creative ideas and solutions induced by minority dissent may be critically examined.

Accordingly, the authors tested the hypothesis that participation and minority dissent interact to predict innovation in teams, such that higher levels of minority dissent lead to more divergent thought. However, they proposed that it was only under conditions of high levels of participation that novel ideas would be turned into innovative procedures, services, and products.

The hypothesis was tested with two samples: teams of an international postal service in the Netherlands and semi-autonomous teams from a database of a private company involved in recruitment, selection, and assessment. While self-completion questionnaires were used to measure team members' perceptions of minority dissent, team innovation was assessed either based on team-supervisor interviews (Study 1) or by team-supervisor ratings (Study 2).

The results of the two studies supported the predictions. Moderated multiple regression analysis revealed that the interaction term of minority

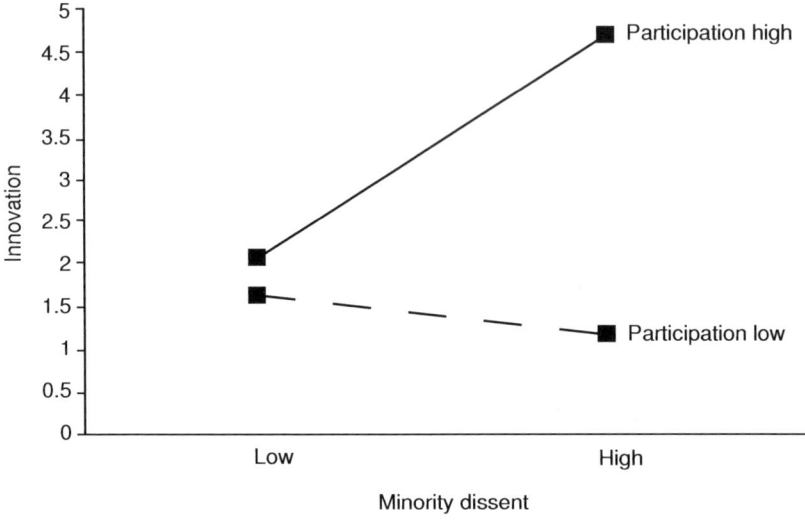

*Figure 14.1* Team innovation as a function of minority dissent and participation in decision making.

dissent and participation indeed predicted additional significant variance in both samples: sample 1: $\Delta R^2 = .11$, $F(1, 14) = 5.13$, $p < .05$; sample 2: $\Delta R^2 = .16$, $F(1, 21) = 4.15$, $p < .05$. As illustrated in Figure 14.1, minority dissent was associated with group innovation under high (but not low) levels of participation in decision making.

This is an example of how applying social psychological research to organizational contexts leads us to discover more about the process predictors of group innovation and suggests ways that theory could be developed—levels of interaction, information exchange and influence over decision making may be additional important moderators that future research may examine. Hostile interactions might have the opposite effect. Group members might avoid processing arguments by hostile minorities since the arguments and the processes engender anxiety rather than curiosity. These issues could be explored in laboratory settings prior to testing them in field settings.

## Minority dissent among groups and organizational innovation

Now we turn to examine the potential value of minority-dissent theory, if it is applied to dissent between and among groups in relation to new perspectives on organizational change. Most academic and practitioner models of organizational change take a 'top down' perspective, neglecting to consider how minorities and those at the lower echelons in organizations— say a group of hospital nurses wanting to have more responsibility for diagnosis and treatment decisions—can bring about change. In order to illustrate this, three steps are necessary: First, we need to explain the concept of organizational innovation. Second, we need to clarify what the concept of minority dissent in organizations means at the group level—i.e., when a group as a whole dissents from a position taken by other groups in an organization, and demarcate it from other forms of dissent between groups, such as inter-group conflict. And third, we need to build a theory that links minority dissent among groups to organizational change and innovation.

### Organizational innovation

In this chapter, organizational innovation is viewed as a result of inter-action between strategy and structure, with organizational culture and climate as important intervening variables (Nystrom, 1990, p. 143). Innovation in organizations is often prompted by environmental factors but it is mainly the result of the combined efforts of individuals and groups within the organization to adapt to the environment. The innovativeness of an organization depends, therefore, to a great extent on the support given to their groups to take initiative to create something new. Several streams of research have reported the influence of variables such as leadership style, organizational structure or organizational climate on organizational innovation (e.g., Damanpour, 1991). For instance, aspects of culture such as support for ideas and willingness to tolerate if they fail, climates of freedom and constructive controversy, egalitarianism and norms for innovation are usually accepted to be engines of innovation (Anderson & King, 1993). We suggest that organizational characteristics such as climate impact on organizational innovation partly due to their role in fostering dissent among minorities and in enabling their success. This issue will be further explored later.

### Minority dissent among groups

In order to transfer the concept of minority dissent from interpersonal dissent to dissent among organizational groups, it is important to understand what a group is. Alderfer (1987) differentiated two types of groups in organizations: *Identity groups*, to which individuals belong to by virtue of birth and biology, such as gender, age, and ethnicity; and *organizational groups*, to which individuals belong to by virtue of organizational groupings. We consider both groups—identity and organizational groups—to be relevant for the purpose of this chapter. Social psychology researchers have treated minorities as just that—numerical minorities. It may well be that those in positions of relative powerlessness, *regardless of their numerical superiority or inferiority*, could also be considered a minority that, by dissenting, provoke creative processing of issues by those they seek to influence. Indeed, Nemeth and Nemeth-Brown (2003) suggested that it is the courage of the dissenting group that leads others to process the issues under discussion more creatively than they otherwise would. Although majority members do not share the same perspectives as the minority, they acknowledge the difficulty of endorsing a minority view, often associated with doubts, risk of rejection and exposure to ridicule. Thus, when majority members are faced with a minority that consistently argues for its position, they inevitably accord the minority members admiration and attribute courage to them (Nemeth & Chiles, 1988). This recognition of the positive features of the opposition prompts majorities to further reassess the controversial issues that were under discussion.

We suggest that majorities who are relatively powerless (e.g., nurses in healthcare organizations) will have the same impact as minorities on the relatively powerful (e.g., doctors) through dissent. The courage of the relatively powerless (not all minorities are powerless) rather than the numerical ratio between opposing groups may be the important element in 'minority' influence processes. With that in mind we now suggest a strategy for those in minorities or relatively powerless positions in organizations to bring about change in the face of resistance from a majority or from a relatively powerful minority.

It is important at this stage to make a conceptual distinction between classical inter-group conflicts, such as labour/union–management conflicts over wages, and dissent between a minority group and other groups. We argue that these concepts differ in the nature of the disagreement (i.e., the issue which is at stake), and the motivation for the conflict. First, we argue inter-group conflict of the first category is rooted in *conflicts of interest*, such as a limited pool of common resources. Resulting tensions may then be multiplied by the dysfunctional dynamics of social categorization (cf. Kramer, 1991; van Knippenberg, 2003). These conflicts may be characterized by win–lose conflicts, which aim to enhance the resources, status, or power, of one's own group relative to others. Both groups perceive their goals to be negatively interlinked, such that one group's gain is another group's loss (Tjosvold, 1988). In contrast to classical inter-group conflicts, we argue that minority groups who dissent with other groups can be understood as addressing a common organizational need, innovation, or justified claim, which—in the long run—aims to benefit the organization as a whole, and therefore all groups within it. Thus, the dissent is not rooted in negative interdependence characterized by win–lose conflicts, but is cognitive in nature and based on constructive disagreement that is cooperative inasmuch as it aims to benefit all groups. Negative interdependence and social-categorization processes may still be operating as hampering factors that may lead to misinterpretation of intentions; but they are essentially unrelated to the dissent issue, rather than at the heart of the conflict. Second, the *motivation* is likely to be different. While the motivation in classical inter-group conflict is competitive towards out-groups in order to

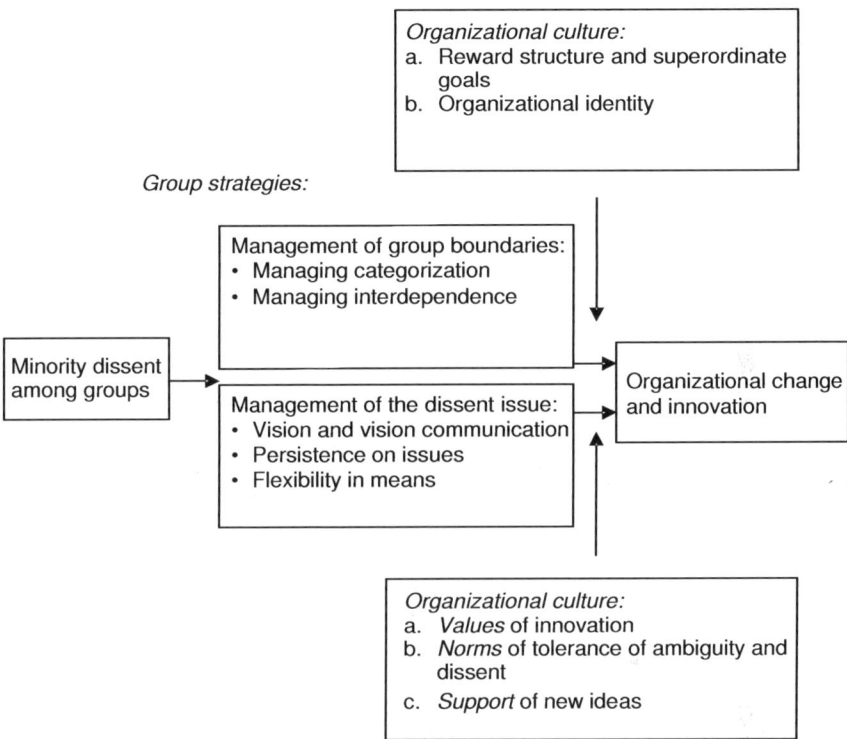

*Figure 14.2* Minority dissent among groups and organizational change and innovation.

enhance the in-group's status, power, or resources, motivation in the case of minority dissent is prosocial, as the dissent aims to benefit the organization as a whole.

### The relationship between minority dissent among groups and organizational change and innovation

How and when does minority dissent among groups lead to organizational change and innovation? We argue for the relevance of two broad categories (Figure 14.2), one being a group's strategies in representing their issues toward other groups; the other being aspects of the organizational culture.

### Group strategies

We argue that minority groups will only affect organizational outcomes if they choose the right strategies to represent the issues across group boundaries. This may include both the management of group boundaries and the management of the dissent issue by itself. Thus, in order to influence organizational-level change and innovation, groups need to manage their boundaries with other groups, *and* communicate their dissent issues effectively.

First, and in contrast to minority dissent within a group, minority dissent between groups has to overcome qualitatively different odds, as the imperative to disagree is stronger. Obstacles to effective cross-group working, i.e., the dynamics of social categorization and negative interdependence, need to be managed effectively (Kramer, 1991; van Knippenberg, 2003). Social-identity and self-categorization theories (Tajfel, 1978; Tajfel & Turner, 1979) suggest that the potential for conflict and competition between groups is immanent for a number of reasons. Brewer and Gaertner (2001) summarized motivational factors at the heart of these processes, including the enhancement and maintenance of group members' self-esteem and positive distinctiveness (Tajfel, 1978; Turner, 1975), uncertainty reduction (Hogg & Abrams, 1993), and the needs for belonging and differentiation (Brewer, 1991). Additionally, while group members to a large extent share common goals, inter-group relations are frequently set up in win–lose interdependencies by management (cf. Kramer, 1991; Walton & Dutton, 1969). So the marketing department may get rewarded for quick, flexible service to good customers, while manufacturing gets rewarded for having cost-efficient, long-term production lines. Furthermore, cognitive biases germane to inter-group relations, such as the inter-group distrust schema (Insko & Schopler, 1998), which suggests that groups are by default perceived not to be trustworthy and collaborative, need to be managed successfully. These processes are of primary importance for between-group relations, but to a lesser extent and in different ways for within-group processes. Even though they are not directly related to the dissent issue, they may hamper effective inter-group relations in general and thereby hamper the effect minority dissent can have on organizational innovation and change. What can groups do to manage these general barriers between groups successfully? Many strategies are beyond the control of the group itself (see Brewer & Brown, 1998; Hogg & Terry, 2000, for overviews), however research on inter-group conflict and inter-group contact may represent fruitful avenues. Group managers who approach interface conflicts between groups with an active, problem-solving approach, appear to be more effective than those who use alternative strategies such as smoothing conflicts over (e.g., Blake, Shepard, & Mouton, 1964; Lawrence & Lorsch, 1967). In a similar vein, research concerned with the so-called 'contact hypothesis' (Allport, 1954; Pettigrew, 1998) posits that contact between members of different groups is a means by which to overcome inter-group hostilities subject to the presence of common goals, inter-group cooperation, and equal group status in the inter-group contact situation. Although researchers have often claimed that the potential of inter-group contact to reduce inter-group bias would depend on whether the contact situation is characterized by those essential conditions, research has shown that these conditions facilitate the bias-reducing effect of inter-group contact. In a meta-analysis embracing over 700 samples across contact settings, 94% of the samples showed positive effects of inter-group contact on inter-group attitudes, with 81% of these samples having contact situations without the presence of the suggested essential conditions (Pettigrew & Tropp, 2006). Pettigrew and Tropp (2006) described those mediating mechanisms by which contact reduces prejudice, and which have received some empirical support, namely the reduction of uncertainty, feelings of threat, and inter-group anxiety. Others have pointed to additional mechanisms to explain how inter-group contact may reduce inter-group hostility, including suggestions that inter-group contact provides information that disconfirms stereotypes; leads people to perceive more similarities between themselves and the out-group; serves as a conduit for information contradicting group biases, group polarization and inter-group conflict; and provides channels for dispute resolution when conflicts arise (e.g., Labianca, Brass, & Gray, 1998; Stangor, 2004). Therefore group managers need to actively engage with out-groups in order to create harmonious relationships that allow the constructive discussion of dissent.

Second, we argue that groups need to actively manage the dissent issue itself. The group must have a clear vision of what it wishes to achieve. In order to be effective and to sustain minority influence, the vision must be one that motivates and inspires group members—a future they really feel is worth fighting for. The nurses who are convinced that their role in preventative healthcare in their organization should be significantly broadened because this will lead to better patient care and saving of healthcare resources have a clear vision. This vision must be clearly articulated and coherently expressed. In order to be effective, minorities must put across a clear, consistent message backed up by convincing underlying arguments. The nurses might develop three clear basic arguments in relation to: (i) the value of preventative healthcare to patients; (ii) the efficacy of preventative healthcare in reducing costs; and (iii) their expertise to deliver this care without placing extra demands on doctors.

The dissenting group must be flexible in responding to the views of others. Minorities that are perceived to be inflexible are rejected by the majority as too extreme to bargain with. Evidence for this claim stems from the studies conducted by Mugny involving negotiation styles. The author distinguished between two negotiation styles. The first, referred to as rigid style, is characterized by a complete refusal from the minority to compromise on any issue or abandon any claim. The opposite second style is characterized by a more flexible approach in which the minority is willing to negotiate with the majority and accept certain compromises. Results showed that when the two minority groups were perceived as equally consistent, the minority with a flexible style of negotiation had more influence on the majority than the more rigid minority (Mugny, 1975).

Minorities must therefore appear willing to listen to others' views and modify their proposals, while not fundamentally distorting their vision. The nurses must listen to doctors' concerns about their authority being diminished and explore how their concerns can be managed. This means working collaboratively with doctors to find creative solutions that meet or exceed both groups' needs.

Furthermore, persistence and consistency are essential. Minorities cause majorities to think through issues from more perspectives and the majority's views are thereby altered (not necessarily in the direction of the minority). This results partly from the repeated presentation of the same coherent arguments. In a meta-analysis comprising 97 studies on minority dissent, consistency emerged as the most powerful predictor of minority-dissent influence (Wood, Lundgren, Ouellette, Busceme, & Blackstone, 1994). The strategy implied by research is for the group to prepare, rehearse, present, and present again. So, the nurses must not accept failure when after three or four group meetings with the doctors they keep being denied the opportunities they seek. They must raise the issue in other arenas, with senior health administrators, with patients, via e-mails, newsletters and water-cooler conversations. This is how revolutionary movements succeed—through persistence. The value of a minority dissent relies not only in the correctness of the decision it stands for, but on the processes it stimulates. Even if the minority is wrong, the organization can benefit from the attention and the thought processes the minority groups led the majority groups to engage in.

Would these strategies alone suffice to yield organizational change and innovation? We argue that the organizational context plays a decisive role in whether or not groups' endeavours will be successful. As can be seen in Figure 14.2, the organization may have a complementary influence on both the nature of inter-group relations per se, as well as on the successful management of dissent for organizational change and innovation.

## Organizational culture and inter-group relations

### Organizational culture and the management of group boundaries

#### Reward structure and superordinate goals

Managers frequently reward group performance exclusively for the achievement of group goals and targets. These goals, however, may be at odds with the goals of other groups, as the above example between manufacturing and sales illustrates. Thus, rewarding the maintenance and development of harmonious and functional inter-group relations in addition to group performance may be an important means by which to reduce inter-group conflict (Walton & Dutton, 1969). Since the seminal Robbers' Cave experiments (Sherif & Sherif, 1966), the introduction of cooperative over competitive goals is widely recognized to be a powerful way to reduce prejudice, hostilities and competition between groups. In organizations, the goals between groups may be competitive rather than cooperative. Groups often differ in their agendas, goals, and work practices. On top of this, some managers deliberately stimulate competition and rivalry between groups in order to enhance group performance. While inter-group competition may enhance group performance and motivation subject to whether or not groups are able to affect each other's task performance (Richter, West, Sacramento, & Hirst, 2005; Tauer & Harackiewicz, 2004), its effect on inter-group relations may be detrimental rather than beneficial. Groups in competition restrain each other not only by hoarding valuable resources, but also from the benefits of critical exchange of information, which is at the heart of innovation. Thus, in order to enable minority dissent among groups to result in organizational innovation, management needs to set up groups in cooperative rather than competitive interdependence.

*Organizational identity*

As we consider the inter-group level of minority dissent, it is important to analyse to what extent a group allows itself to be influenced by an out-group. On one hand, self-categorization theorists argue that the basis for social influence is social identification (Turner, 1982), and therefore the existence of a perceived similarity between source and recipient of influence is necessary for the process to take place. According to this perspective, the out-group is not expected to have a significant effect on the in-group because the latter does not identify with the former and therefore perceives no reason to consider their views. This assumption found some support in experimental settings (David & Turner, 1996). In a scenario study, the authors exposed students to in-group and out-group minority and majority conditions. Each participant's in-group was accessed using an attitude test that was filled in previously. Participants were then given an audio message from an alleged majority or a minority source that belonged to their in-group or out-group. It was observed that only the in-group conditions led to the classic pattern of majority—compliance and minority—conversion. The out-group minority and majority failed to yield the same effects. This finding suggests that only in-group minorities are able to promote change. On the other hand, Moscovici's studies (e.g., Moscovici, 1980) suggest that when facing minority dissent from an out-group, one is free from inhibitive social-comparison pressures that would lead to compliance, and is quicker to engage in validation processes. This enables active consideration of the minority's position in terms of their information content. Opposite to the position outlined above, it is suggested here that a dissenting out-group has more power to promote change. It is our stance that each proposal is partially correct. In fact, we agree with the social-categorization perspective to the extent that if the out-group is perceived as threatening for a group's identity, their views will not be given any consideration, resulting in no impact. However, if the out-group is seen as a member of the same organizational group with which an organizational identity is shared, for example a different team working within the same hospital, the out-group is less likely to be perceived as threatening, and common ground may enable the occurrence of influence processes. In this case, we agree with Moscovici's perspective and argue that a situation when a traditionally less-powerful group, for example nurses, assumes a dissent position from the doctors' group, then this is more conducive to significant and long-lasting organizational changes than when a minority of doctors dissents from a majority of doctors. We advocate that the larger amplitude and perspective brought by the intervention of two professional classes as described in the second situation can offer a larger framework of possibilities for organizational change. This reinforces our argument that minority dissent between groups can bring about innovation, and organizational identity may be an important moderator. Organizational theory suggests organizations may provide employees with two forms of identity, either ideographic or holographic (Albert & Whetten, 1985). While in the former type, organizations exhibit subgroups with differentiated identities, the latter organizations exhibit a common identity across subgroup boundaries. In ideographic organizations, strong group identification in combination with low organizational identification may stimulate inter-group rivalry and competition (cf. Hogg & Terry, 2000). One way to overcome this is for managers to foster and enhance individuals' identification with the organization as a whole (Gaertner et al., 1999; Hogg & Terry, 2000). The nurturing of a 'dual identity' may in fact help to integrate the interests of members of other groups into a group's agenda, and facilitate inter-group relations. Experimental research strongly supports the idea that inter-subgroup relations are more harmonious when subgroups are salient *within* the context of a salient superordinate group, than when either the subgroup or the superordinate group alone is salient (González & Brown, 2003; Hornsey & Hogg, 1999, 2000). Similarly, Gaertner and colleagues found in an experimental study that the primary set of mediators between conditions of inter-group contact and bias reduction involved participants' representations of membership as two subgroups within a superordinate category (Gaertner et al., 1999). Similarly, organizational research recently found support for the dual-identity effect: In a study with 53 workgroups of five British healthcare organizations, Richter, West, van Dick and Dawson (2006) found that if group-boundary spanners (those group members involved in work-related contacts with other groups) identified with both the workgroup and the organization, this was related to both harmonious inter-group relations, and line managers' ratings of inter-group productivity. Thus, providing and rewarding an organizational identity, we argue, would be an organizational factor that facilitates groups' boundary management, which in turn increases the likelihood of organizational innovation and change.

*Organizational culture and the management of dissent*

Whether or not dissenting ideas result in organizational change and inno-vation will also depend on how dissent is managed within the organization, i.e., whether the organization: (a) has values of innovativeness; (b) has developed norms to tolerate ambiguity and dissent; and (c) actively supports new ideas.

*Values of innovativeness*

Management needs to develop a culture that values innovation to harvest the benefits of group dissent within organizations. In cultures low on innovativeness, dissent is considered an unnecessary hassle. If top manage-ment within a hospital does not value innovative ideas and procedures, a nursing team bringing up suggestions of how to improve patient care may encounter little support in its endeavours to change common practice.

*Norms*

Values of innovativeness may not suffice for minority dissent to result in organizational change, if organizations do not have behavioural norms of tolerance for ambiguity and dissent. Such norms will allow for the tensions that minority dissent involves, without blocking dissent processes in their early stages. So, a nursing team suggesting alternative, perhaps revolu-tionary work practices, may be labelled as 'rebellious' if norms of tolerance and ambiguity are not in place but 'constructively controversial' where they are cultural norms.

*Support for new ideas*

Management needs to practise reflexivity in relation to their strategies and ideas in order to be open to new ways of thinking and acting. Furthermore, management needs to provide active support for innovation, for instance in the form of resources needed to implement the changes, or encouragement for groups to engage in dissent if they feel the majority is following the wrong path. A potent way of reducing resistance to change is by involving people in the change process (Heller, Pusic, Strauss, & Wilpert, 1998). By seeking the views of people throughout the organization and encouraging others to be involved in contributing ideas to the proposals, the group can reduce the resistance of people in the organization to the proposed change. Thus, nurses can invite the views of patients; set up meetings for general discussions about the issues with other healthcare professionals; invite external speakers with expertise in the area; send out newsletters; and add the issue to the agendas of any meetings that they attend.

Groups that adopt such strategies may seem a threat to organizations but without them organizations are likely to be less innovative and adaptable. Conformity processes damp down the fiery forces for change; minority dissent fans them.

## Conclusions

In the course of this chapter we highlighted the few studies that illustrate the effect of minority dissent within experimental and organizational groups for workgroup innovation and effectiveness. We then considered minority dissent at the organizational level in order to develop a theoretical model of how minority dissent between and among groups may result in organizational change and innovation. In the remainder of this chapter we discussed implications for theory, management, and directions for future research.

### *Implications for theory*

The primary contribution to theory intended by this chapter was the development and application of the concept of minority dissent from the group level to the inter-group level, i.e., dissent between and among groups. Although they have received little attention in experimental research, we believe power minorities in organizations and the wider society—characterized as groups of individuals who might be numerically superior but have inferior power—can bring about change and innovation. Minority-dissent research may provide the scientific basis that helps us to understand these processes. For organizational contexts, the theoretical model we developed illustrates that application of minority dissent to the inter-group level is not that straightforward. Research and theory on inter-group relations suggest that groups dissenting on important issues with other groups may additionally have to overcome obstacles of social categorization and interdependence between groups. Similarly, aspects of the organizational culture are unique across organizational settings, and need to be taken into consideration in theorizing. Comparative tests of predictions derived from conversion theory and self-categorization theory, such as the study by David and Turner (1996), would be desirable to test the usefulness of the model presented.

### *Implications for managers*

Our model may also have implications for practitioners. Managers who want to build effective team-based organizations in order to achieve organizational change and innovation may start by considering those aspects of the organizational culture we have outlined in our model. They may actively foster and reward constructive dissent across, for example, functional groups, in order to utilize the diverse expertise and knowledge these groups have. Managers may also create groups with the aim and legitimization to produce dissent in a safe environment, by setting up quality-improvement teams, or ensure they give power minorities an equal voice in forums such as cross-functional groups.

### Directions for future research

Organizational research offers social psychologists the opportunity to understand how minority-influence processes play out in workgroups with contexts and histories (in comparison to student samples in laboratory settings); and in the face of task imperatives—a breast cancer care group has to save lives and dissent may be valued rather than puzzled over in such circumstances. They can study other elements such as task identity (the extent to which the group task is a whole piece of work), task variety (variety of task elements), level of group autonomy and level of feedback about task performance. Variations in processes may be studied in highly cohesive versus low-cohesive groups and in groups with a history of success versus a history of failure.

Minority-influence studies conducted in the laboratory will allow organizational psychologists to discover the influence on innovation of key variables such as majority perceptions of the minority (self-interested vs. altruistic); the level of trust in the group; and perceptions of psychological safety. In this way they can come to develop effective prescriptions for encouraging innovation amongst workgroups—and groups such as breast cancer care groups need help in discovering how to promote innovation in patient care (e.g., West et al., 2003). Minority-influence research suggests a radical model of organizational change. Organizational psychologists have studied change primarily from the perspective of those in positions of power in organizations. Minority-influence research offers a model of change for the relatively powerless and a strategy for creating change by encouraging creative and independent exploration of change issues throughout an organization. For social psychologists, applying minority-influence research to the study of organizational change dramatically extends the boundaries of the applicability of this research. We can explore how inter-group relations are affected when groups use such influence processes for organizational change; the hostility or otherwise they engender; if and how these processes produce organizational change and innovation; how long minorities must persist for change to occur and how long these changes continue. Organizationally based studies will also indicate what are effective strategies for minority-influence groups in bringing about change and thereby what may be key variables to study in laboratory settings.

## References

Albert, S., & Whetten, D. A. (1985). Organizational identity. In L. Cummings & B. M. Staw (Eds.), *Research in organizational behavior* (Vol. 7, pp. 263–295). Greenwich, CT: JAI Press.

Alderfer, C. P. (1987). An intergroup perspective on group dynamics. In J. Lorsch (Ed.), *Handbook of organizational behavior* (pp. 190–222). Englewood Cliffs, NJ: Prentice Hall.

Allport, G. W. (1954). *The nature of prejudice.* Reading, MA: Addison-Wesley.

Anderson, N., & King, N. (1993). Innovation in organizations. In C. L. Cooper & I. T. Robertson (Eds.), *International review of industrial and organizational psychology* (Vol. 8, pp. 1–34). Chichester, UK: Wiley.

Asch, S. W. (1951). Effects of group pressure upon the modification and distortion of judgements. In H. Guetzkow (Ed.), *Groups, leadership, and men.* Pittsburgh, PA: Carnegie Press.

Bem, D. J., Wallach, M. A., & Kogan, N. (1965). Group decision-making under risk of aversive consequences. *Journal of Personality and Social Psychology, 95,* 453–460.

Blake, R. R., Shepard, H. A., & Mouton, J. S. (1964). *Managing intergroup conflict in industry.* Houston, TX: Gulf Publishing Company.

Brewer, M. B. (1991). The social self: On being the same and different at the same time. *Personality and Social Psychology Bulletin, 17,* 475–482.

Brewer, M. B., & Brown, R. J. (1998). Intergroup relations. In D. T. Gilbert, S. K. Fiske, & G. Lindzey (Eds.), *The handbook of social psychology* (4th ed., pp. 554–594). Boston: McGraw-Hill.

Brewer, M. B., & Gaertner, S. L. (2001). Toward reduction of prejudice: Intergroup contact and social categorization. In R. Brown & S. L. Gaertner (Eds.), *Blackwell handbook of social psychology: Intergroup processes* (pp. 451–472). Malden, MA: Blackwell.

Damanpour, F. (1991). Organizational innovation: A meta-analysis of effects of determinants and moderators. *Academy of Management Journal, 34*(3), 555–590.

David, B., & Turner, J. C. (1996). Studies in self-categorization and minority conversion: Is being a member of the out-group an advantage? *British Journal of Social Psychology, 35,* 179–199.

De Dreu, C. K. W., & De Vries, N. K. (1993). Numerical support, information processing, and attitude change. *European Journal of Social Psychology, 23,* 647–662.

De Dreu, C. K. W., & De Vries, N. K. (1997). Minority dissent in organizations. In C. K. W. De Dreu & E. Van der Vliert (Eds.), *Using conflict in organizations* (pp. 72–86). London: Sage.

De Dreu, C. K. W., & West, M. A. (2001). Minority dissent and team innovation: The importance of participation in decision making. *Journal of Applied Psychology, 86*(6), 1191–1201.

Gaertner, S. L., Dovidio, J. F., Rust, M. C., Nier, J. A., Bankers, B. S., Ward, C. M., et al. (1999). Reducing intergroup bias: Elements of intergroup cooperation. *Journal of Personality and Social Psychology, 76,* 388–402.

González, R., & Brown, R. J. (2003). Generalization of positive attitude as a function of subgroup and superordinate group identifications in intergroup contact. *European Journal of Social Psychology, 33,* 195–214.

Hackman, J. R., & Morris, C. G. (1975). Group tasks, group interaction process and group performance effectiveness: A review and proposed integration. In L. Berkowitz (Ed.), *Advances in experimental social psychology* (Vol. 8, pp. 45–99). New York: Academic Press.

Heller, F., Pusic, E., Strauss, G., & Wilpert, B. (1998). *Organizational participation: Myth and reality*. Oxford, UK: Oxford University Press.

Hogg, M. A., & Abrams, D. (1993). Toward a single-process uncertainty-reduction model of social motivation in groups. In M. A. Hogg & D. Abrams (Eds.), *Group motivation: Social psychological perspectives* (pp. 173–190). London, UK: Harvester Wheatsheaf.

Hogg, M. A., & Terry, D. J. (2000). Social identity and self-categorization processes in organizational contexts. *Academy of Management Review, 25*(1), 121–140.

Hornsey, M. J., & Hogg, M. A. (1999). Subgroup differentiation as a response to an overly-inclusive group: A test of optimal distinctiveness theory. *European Journal of Social Psychology, 29*(4), 543–550.

Hornsey, M. J., & Hogg, M. A. (2000). Intergroup similarity and subgroup relations: Some implications for assimilation. *Personality and Social Psychology Bulletin, 26*(8), 948–958.

Insko, C. A., & Schopler, J. (1998). Differential distrust of groups and individuals. In C. Sedikides, J. Schopler, & C. A. Insko (Eds.), *Intergroup cognition and intergroup behavior: Applied social research* (pp. 75–107). Hillsdale, NJ: Lawrence Erlbaum Associates, Inc.

Janis, I. L. (1972). *Victims of groupthink: A psychological study of foreign-policy decisions and fiascos*. Boston: Houghton Mifflin.

Kramer, R. (1991). Intergroup relations and organizational dilemmas. *Research in Organizational Behavior, 13*, 191–228.

Labianca, G., Brass, D. J., & Gray, B. (1998). Social networks and perceptions of inter-group conflict: The role of negative relationships and third parties. *Academy of Management Journal, 41*(1), 55–67.

Lawrence, P. R., & Lorsch, J. W. (1967). *Organization and environment: Managing differentiation and integration*. Boston: Harvard Graduate School of Business Administration.

McLeod, P. L., Baron, R. S., Marti, M. W., & Yoon, K. (1997). The eyes have it: Minority influence in face-to-face and computer-mediated group discussion. *Journal of Applied Psychology, 82*(5), 706–718.

Moscovici, S. (1980). Toward a theory of conversion behavior. In L. Berkowitz (Ed.), *Advances in experimental social psychology* (Vol. 13, pp. 209–242). San Diego, CA: Academic Press.

Moscovici, S., Lage, E., & Naffrechoux, M. (1969). Influence of a consistent minority on the responses of a majority in a color perception task. *Sociometry, 32*, 365–380.

Moscovici, S., Mugny, G., & van Avermaet, E. (1985). *Perspectives on minority influence*. Cambridge, UK: Cambridge University Press.

Mugny, G. (1975). Negotiations, image of the other and the process of minority influence. *European Journal of Social Psychology, 5*(2), 209–238.

Nemeth, C., & Chiles, C. (1988). Modelling courage—The role of dissent in fostering independence. *European Journal of Social Psychology, 18*(3), 275–280.

Nemeth, C., Mayseless, O., Sherman, J., & Brown, Y. (1990). Exposure to dissent and recall of information. *Journal of Personality and Social Psychology*, 58(3), 429–437.

Nemeth, C., & Owens, P. (1996). Making work groups more effective: The value of minority dissent. In M. A. West (Ed.), *Handbook of work group psychology* (pp. 125–141). Chichester, UK: Wiley.

Nemeth, C. J. (1995). Dissent as driving cognition, attitudes, and judgments. *Social Cognition*, 13(3), 273–291.

Nemeth, C. J., & Kwan, J. L. (1985). Originality of word-associations as a function of majority vs. minority influence. *Social Psychology Quarterly*, 48(3), 277–282.

Nemeth, C. J., & Nemeth-Brown, B. (2003). Better than individuals? The potential benefits of dissent and diversity for group creativity. In P. Paulus & B. Nijstad (Eds.), *Group creativity* (pp. 63–84). Oxford, UK: Oxford University Press.

Nemeth, C. J., & Wachtler, J. (1983). Creative problem-solving as a result of majority vs. minority influence. *European Journal of Social Psychology*, 13(1), 45–55.

Nystrom, H. (1990). Organizational innovation. In M. A. West (Ed.), *Innovation and creativity at work* (pp. 143–161). New York: Wiley.

Pettigrew, T. F. (1998). Intergroup contact theory. *Annual Review of Psychology*, 49(1), 65–85.

Pettigrew, T. F., & Tropp, L. R. (2006). A meta-analytic test of intergroup contact theory. *Journal of Personality and Social Psychology*, 90(5), 751–783.

Richter, A. W., West, M. A., Sacramento, C. A., & Hirst, G. (2005). *The relationship between intergroup competition and longitudinal change in group effectiveness*. Paper presented at the Academy of Management Conference, Honolulu.

Richter, A. W., West, M. A., Van Dick, R., & Dawson, J. F. (2006). Boundary spanners' identification, intergroup contact, and effective intergroup relations. *Academy of Management Journal*, 49, 1252–1269.

Schopler, J., Insko, C. A., Wieselquist, J., Pemberton, M., Witcher, B., Kozar, R., et al. (2001). When groups are more competitive than individuals: The domain of the discontinuity effect. *Journal of Personality and Social Psychology*, 80(4), 632–644.

Sherif, M., & Sherif, C. W. (1966). *Groups in harmony and tension*. New York: Octagon Books.

Stangor, C. (2004). *Social groups in action and interaction*. New York: Psychology Press.

Steiner, I. D. (1972). *Group process and productivity*. New York: Academic Press.

Tajfel, H. (1978). *Differentiation between social groups: Studies in the social psychology of intergroup relations*. Oxford, UK: Academic Press.

Tajfel, H., & Turner, J. C. (1979). An integrative theory of intergroup conflict. In W. G. Austin & S. Worche (Eds.), *The social psychology of intergroup relations* (pp. 33–47). Monterey, CA: Brooks/Cole.

Tauer, J. M., & Harackiewicz, J. M. (2004). The effects of cooperation and competition on intrinsic motivation and performance. *Journal of Personality and Social Psychology*, 86, 849–861.

Tjosvold, D. (1988). Cooperative and competitive interdependence: Collaboration between departments to serve customers. *Group and Organization Studies*, 13(3), 274–289.

Turner, J. C. (1975). Social comparison and social identity: Some prospects for intergroup behavior. *European Journal of Social Psychology*, 5, 5–34.

Turner, J. C. (1982). Toward a cognitive redefinition of the social group. In H. Tajfel (Ed.), *Social identity and intergroup behavior* (pp. 15–40). Cambridge, UK: Cambridge University Press.

van Knippenberg, A. (2003). Intergroup relations in organizations. In M. A. West, D. Tjosvold, & K. G. Smith (Eds.), *International handbook of organizational teamwork and cooperative working* (pp. 381–400). Chichester, UK: Wiley.

Walton, R. E., & Dutton, J. M. (1969). The management of interdepartmental conflict: A model and review. *Administrative Science Quarterly, 14*, 73–84.

West, M. A. (2002). Sparkling fountains or stagnant ponds: An integrative model of creativity and innovation implementation in work groups. *Applied Psychology: An International Review—Psychologie Appliquee: Revue Internationale, 51*(3), 355–387.

West, M. A., & Anderson, N. R. (1996). Innovation in top management teams. *Journal of Applied Psychology, 81*(6), 680–693.

West, M. A., Borrill, C. S., Dawson, J., Brodbeck, F., Shapiro, D., & Haward, B. (2003). Leadership clarity and team innovation in health care. *Leadership Quarterly, 14*(4–5), 393–410.

Wood, W., Lundgren, S., Ouellette, J. A., Busceme, S., & Blackstone, T. (1994). Minority influence: A meta-analytic review of social-influence processes. *Psychological Bulletin, 115*(3), 323–345.

# Part V
# Epilogue

# 15 Minority influence: From groups to attitudes and back again

*Miles Hewstone*
University of Oxford, UK

*Robin Martin*
Aston University, UK

The strongest man in the world is he who stands most alone.
(Heinrik Ibsen, *An Enemy of the People*, 1882)

One person with a belief, is a social power equal to ninety-nine who have only interests.
(John Stuart Mill, 1861/1924)

## Prologue

We have recently celebrated two highly significant anniversaries for any student of minority influence who adopts a historical perspective. First, 2006 saw the two-hundredth anniversary of the birth of John Stuart Mill, who was born on 20 May 1806. Mill, particularly in his volumes *Considerations on Representative Government* (1861/1924) and *On Liberty* (1859/1986), championed the cause of minorities, warned of the dangers of the 'despotism of custom' (Reeves, 2007), opposed the 'tyranny of the majority' and enshrined the value of liberty. As Mill famously put it, in his essay *On Liberty*, 'If all mankind minus one, were of one opinion, and only one person were of the contrary opinion, mankind would be no more justified in silencing that one person than he, if he had the power, would be justified in silencing mankind' (p. 23). Isaiah Berlin captured Mill's passionate defence of heterodoxy in his essay 'John Stuart Mill and the Ends of Life', 'What he hated and feared was narrowness, uniformity, the crippling effect of persecution, the crushing of individuals by the weight of authority or of custom or of public opinion' (1969, p. 177).

The second bicentenary commemorated the signing into law, by King George III on 25 March 1807, of a bill to abolish the entire British slave trade, an occasion that served as a timely reminder of the influence of minorities. Many individuals were crucial to the slave-trade abolition movement, all of them courageous, tireless and committed, albeit in different ways. Thomas Clarkson, founder of the *Society for Effecting the Abolition of Slavery* in 1787, rode on horseback round England to spread his message and collect signatures, and published 700 iconic posters showing a diagram of the slave-ship *Brookes*. Granville Sharpe was the writer of countless polemics of protest. Former slave Olaudo Equiano spoke out for those still in bondage and had huge influence through his autobiography. And, of course, William Wilberforce's persistent efforts to introduce a Bill into parliament to abolish the slave trade is a classic example of the consistency and commitment of minorities.

Yet the anti-slavery *movement* owed much to the activities of small social *groups*, and not just individuals, as well as networking skills and social organization of the Quakers. They were crucial in organizing the boycott of slave-grown sugar, joined at one time by more than 300,000 people. It is fitting, in the present context, that Quakers are referred to as religious 'nonconformists'. Determined, persistent and persuasive as they may be, individual minorities often fail to have an impact unless they start a social movement.

Minorities are everywhere, and they come in many shapes and forms. Historically, we are used to thinking of figures such as Copernicus, and Galileo. More recent minorities include Dame Cicely Saunders, pioneer of the hospice movement; Noam Chomsky, peace activist and scourge of capitalism; Nobel Peace Prize laureate Aung San Suu Kyi, described by the chairman of the Nobel Peace Prize committee, Francis Sejested, as 'An outstanding example of the power of the powerless' (cited in *The Guardian*, 30 September 2008); and Richard Dawkins, Emeritus Simonyi Professor of the Public Understanding of Science at Oxford University, and fervent critic of religion. Galileo Galilei is, perhaps, the prototypical instance of a minority: a lone dissenter, dragged before a Vatican committee of eleven 'qualifiers', or experts, in 1616, whose task was to come to a judgement on Galileo's heliocentric view of the world. He was later subjected to a full trial in 1633 and almost certainly tortured for his views; he eventually recanted and lived out his days under house arrest in Florence. As a recent biographer wrote about him, 'he has become a symbol of the struggle for freedom of thought, the epitome of the enlightened individual facing down institutionalized ignorance, and winning . . . eventually'. (White, 2007, p. xv). Also tellingly, Galileo is described as 'loud, forceful, argumentative and combative. He loved vigorous debate, and the cleverer his opponent, the more he enjoyed arguing' (White, 2007, p. 133).

If any reader of this volume, having got this far, still doubts in the phenomenon of minority influence, consider the success of the organization 'People for the Ethical Treatment of Animals' (PETA; see Glass, 2008). Started by an individual, Ingrid Newkirk, supported by a small, committed group of supporters, it now has nearly two million members. In their own terms, their influence has been extraordinary, both direct and indirect. It led to Burger King introducing the 'veggie burger', McDonald's tightening controls in their slaughterhouses, Calvin Klein dropping fur cuffs and collars from its clothing range, and even Mercedes-Benz offering a non-leather option for seats in its vehicles. As the title of Newkirk's (with Ratcliffe, 2008) book says, *One Can Make a Difference*.

In this final chapter we will do three things. First, although we are primarily concerned with minority influence, we will consider closely what defines the field of social influence generally, and seek to differentiate it from the field of attitude change, but to show how both areas can complement one another. Second, we will spell out a 'romantic' view of minority influence, and try to convey why we as editors of this volume, and scholars in this field, believe that minority influence *matters*. Third, and finally, we will try to integrate the foregoing contributions by drawing out a small number of key themes, and pointing to the kind of future research that would take the field forward once again, and help to retain its position at the heart of our discipline.

## Social influence and attitude change: The same or different?

One of us is co-editor of a textbook in social psychology that recently appeared in its fourth edition. As we made plans for that edition a fellow editor suggested that we could perhaps dispense with a chapter on 'social influence' and, instead, accommodate the relevant material in the chapter on 'attitude change'. Since the authors of the proposed chapter on social influence were the editors of this book (and the authors of this chapter) he might as well have questioned the Virgin Birth to the Pope. We were forced to defend ourselves, however, and to do so vigorously and convincingly.

An excellent chapter on the topic of social influence in the previous edition of our textbook (van Avermaet, 1996) had resolved this issue by acknowledging that, broadly speaking, the study of social influence coincides with social psychology itself, because the entire field deals with the influence of social factors on thought and behaviour. As he went on to show, however, the concept of social influence is typically given a more restricted meaning: social influence refers to a change in the judgements, opinions and attitudes of an individual as a result of being exposed to the judgements, opinions and attitudes of other individuals (de Montmollin, 1977).

So, at one level, the study of social influence is broader than the study of attitude change, because it is concerned not merely with opinions and attitudes, but also with judgements. Indeed, some of the classic studies of social influence, whether of majorities (Asch, 1955) or minorities (e.g., Moscovici, Lage, & Naffrechoux, 1969; Moscovici & Personnaz, 1980; Nemeth & Wachtler, 1983), have not studied opinions or attitudes at all, but have investigated the ability of different numerical sources to bring about change in judgements of the colours of stimuli, or the number of embedded figures than can be found in a target figure. Social influence also differs from attitude change in that it typically concerns the influence of a group, or representatives of a group, on an individual, or of a subgroup (e.g., the majority) on another subgroup (e.g., the minority), whereas attitude change typically concerns the impact of a persuasive communication from a *source* (not necessarily another person) on a *target* (typically an individual). Arguably, the definition of social influence should also include impact on behaviour although, as we note below, studies of social influence have very rarely included behavioural outcomes.

We believe that the richness and variety of the contributions to this volume justify keeping social influence separate from attitude change. They overlap somewhat, they have much to offer each other, but they each have their own distinctive theories, measures, phenomena, and applications.

## The study of social influence in social psychology: A romantic view

The study of social influence has a long and illustrious history in social psychology; it lies close to the heart of the discipline. Gordon Allport (1954), in his classic chapter on the history of social psychology, published in the second edition of the *Handbook of Social Psychology*, defined the discipline as follows: 'Social psychology is the attempt to understand and explain how the thoughts, feelings, and behaviours of individuals are influenced by the actual, imagined, or implied presence of other human beings' (p. 5). Apart from being a useful definition of the whole discipline, Allport's use of the key term *influenced* underlines why the phenomena, theories, and classic experimental demonstrations of social influence are seen as so central to discipline of social psychology. Quintessentially social-psychological topics—from conformity to obedience, from leadership to group processes, from altruism to aggression—all have some element of social influence.

We believe that there is also a certain romance to minority influence, and we admit that we have succumbed to it. This romance has, generally for the area of social influence, something to do with the frequently surprising results of social-influence studies. After all, social psychology is especially interesting when it generates counter-intuitive results, which either grow out of or stimulate creative theorizing in order to explain them. The paradigmatic case is, of course, Festinger's (1957) theory of cognitive dissonance.

Within the field of social influence Solomon Asch (1951, 1956) began his famous studies using the line-judging task expecting to show that people were *not* as suggestible as was generally believed at that time. Indeed, Blass (2004) wrote that Asch vigorously disagreed with a prevailing view of human beings that had 'almost exclusively stressed the slavish submission of individuals to group forces' (Asch, 1958, quoted in Blass, 2004, p. 27). Asch also believed that the norm-following behaviour shown in Sherif's (1936) classic studies could be attributed to the ambiguous nature of the autokinetic stimulus. Asch contended that when unambiguous stimuli were used, and where there was a clearly correct answer, people would remain independent of the group's inaccurate judgements. As we know now, of course, the results turned out rather differently. Incidentally, Stanley

Milgram's (1974) infamous experimental studies of obedience to authority started from the same expectation of a null result. Prior to his research Milgram doubted that most people would show destructive obedience, and indeed his first study was intended to be the 'baseline', a situation in which few people would obey. Later research was then to manipulate key variables and investigate their impact on rates of obedience (see Milgram, 1974; see also Blass, 1999).[1]

But the romance, perhaps, also has something to do with Serge Moscovici himself, and the manner in which he wrote about the issues and came to embody his own beliefs about how minorities succeed in effecting influence and bringing about a change in how majority members perceive the world—through their consistent behavioural style, indirectly, and through the originality of their arguments. Erin Brockovich, environmental advocate immortalized in the Hollywood film of the same name, described herself as having this same attribute, which she named '*stick-to-it-ive-ness*', 'It's a noun. It means dogged persistence. Stubbornness' (*The Guardian*, 27 September 2008).

We were both inspired many years ago, as undergraduate students, by Moscovici's compelling use of examples to illustrate the phenomena of minority influence. He wanted to explain paradigm shifts in science (e.g., Galileo, Freud), changes of fashion and contemporary music, the emergence of 'Green Party' politics in Europe. He even added a case study on Alexander Solzhenitsyn as an appendix to a later French edition of his monograph *Social Influence and Social Change*, a salient example of a dissenting minority described in a leading obituary as possessing 'self-scrutiny, [and] adamantine moral and physical courage' (*The Economist*, 9 August 2008).

In reading and re-reading the original and exciting message of Moscovici's (1976, 1980; Moscovici et al., 1969) writings on the topic over the years, we are both struck by the obstacles he must have had to overcome in drawing attention to his new *phenomena*, gaining appreciation and respect for his work, but overcoming precedent and prejudice. We have not always been convinced by every paradigm or been confident about every result (see Martin, 1998; Martin & Hewstone, 2001a), but over more than 30 years we have both been not merely influenced, but persuaded. As our own experiments have shown (see Martin & Hewstone, 2008, for an overview), minority messages seem to have an advantage when it comes to perlustration, inviting attention and exerting an influence that can be direct, but is often indirect, latent, and removed in time (Wood, Lundgren, Ouellette, Busceme, & Blackstone, 1994). Minorities can, moreover, help us to see the world differently, adopt new, more critical perspectives and ideas, and be agents of social change (Moscovici, 1976; Nemeth, 1986, 1995).

In his characteristic style, Moscovici began his 1985 chapter with the subheading 'The parable of the lonely minority'. He has, in fact, for 40 years himself been 'the lonely influence theorist (and researcher)', the very prototype of minority influence. Going back to the era of Asch's (1956) studies of majority influence, and the subsequent 'dependency' perspective on group influence, we are struck by the parallels between Serge Moscovici's own minority position arguing for the influence of minorities against the dominant perspective of majority influence, and the very phenomenon whose study he initiated. Crano (Chapter 3, this volume) refers to 'Moscovici's dogged persistence in the face, initially, of disregard or outright rejection, his contention that an asymmetrical understanding of social influence that focused on majority but not minority influence was myopic if not illogical, and his consequent insistence on the necessity to focus on minority *as well as* majority influence'.[2]

Moscovici's pioneering role yielded impressive influence. As Crano (Chapter 3, this volume) writes: 'The pace of experimentation, theory building, and application of insights into minority influence has quickened over the years'. There has been considerable theoretical development over the years, and the sheer volume of published work is daunting for any reviewer. Impressive reviews were published, first, by Maass and Clark (1984) and, ten years later, by Wood and colleagues (1994), the latter being a meta-analysis of 97 studies.

Yet our sense is that progress has faltered somewhat more recently. After the initial impact of Moscovici's ideas in the 1970s, taken up by several European (notably Gabriel Mugny; see Mugny, 1982; Mugny & Pérez, 1991) and North American (notably Charlan Nemeth; e.g., Nemeth, Swedlund, & Kanki, 1974) researchers, the area of majority–minority influence seemed to have slipped into a period of acedia or torpor, as if the initial period of theoretical and empirical activity had run out of steam. A telling indication that perhaps the topic, its theories, and its leading figures have been forgotten is that a recent volume on the topic of social influence (Pratkanis, 2007)—which lists the key phenomena/theories of the field, and its pioneers—astonishingly neglected to list either minority influence as a topic or Serge Moscovici as a pioneer. We believe that the marriage of European and North American ideas reflected in our international array of outstanding authors has the potential to reinvigorate the area, and guide much further research too.

## Themes of the present volume

In Table 15.1, we show schematically the emergence of key themes across the 13 core chapters of this volume. We have not by any means attempted to list all the themes, but instead have chosen to highlight a small number of themes identified across a number of chapters. We have chosen to limit our selection to seven such themes; we draw out each one in turn, and speculate about opportunities and necessities of future research:

Table 15.1 Key themes across the chapters of this volume

| Chapter | Authors | More sophisticated conception of attitudes | Dual process models of persuasion | Indirect vs. direct influence | Task type | Intra-group dynamics | Organizational context | The diversity of minority sources of social influence |
|---|---|---|---|---|---|---|---|---|
| 2 | Quiamzade, Mugny, Falomir-Pichastor, & Butera | | | | | | | |
| 3 | Crano | ✓ | | ✓ | | | | |
| 4 | Erb & Bohner | | ✓ | ✓ | ✓ | | | |
| 5 | Tormala, Petty, & DeSensi | ✓ | ✓ | | | | | |
| 6 | Mucchi-Faina | ✓ | | ✓ | | | | ✓ |
| 7 | Gardikiotis, Martin, & Hewstone | | ✓ | | | | | |
| 8 | Martin, Hewstone, & Martin | ✓ | ✓ | ✓ | | | | ✓ |
| 9 | Stroebe | | ✓ | ✓ | | | | ✓ |
| 10 | Levine & Choi | | | | ✓ | ✓ | ✓ | |
| 11 | Smith & Tindale | | ✓ | ✓ | ✓ | ✓ | ✓ | |
| 12 | Prislin | | | | ✓ | ✓ | ✓ | |
| 13 | Aime & Van Dyne | | | | | ✓ | ✓ | |
| 14 | Richter, Sacramento, & West | | | | | | ✓ | ✓ |

1 Closer links with the broader social-psychological literature on attitudes.
2 The interplay between minority influence and dual-process models of persuasion.
3 The importance of indirect, as well as direct, influence.
4 The variety of tasks used in minority-influence studies.
5 Minority influence in dynamic, intra-group contexts.
6 Minority influence in organizational contexts.
7 The diversity of minority sources of social influence.

### Theme 1: Closer links with the broader social-psychological literature on attitudes

Although we have argued that social influence should not simply be equated with attitude change, much has been gained from a closer acquaintance with this literature, and indeed with the literature on attitudes more generally. This is evident in several chapters of this volume.

Crano (Chapter 3, this volume) confronts the 'rather glaring complication' between conversion theory's (Moscovici, 1980) prediction that the minority will have only a delayed influence and the finding in many studies of immediate minority influence (e.g., Crano & Hannula-Bral, 1994; Martin, Gardikiotis, & Hewstone, 2002; Martin, Hewstone, & Martin, 2003). Crano draws on the distinction between attitude formation and attitude change (Chaiken, Wood, & Eagly, 1996), to try to explain this inconsistency, highlighting the importance of attitude strength in attitude-change contexts. He suggests that the likelihood of minority influence will be greater in attitude-formation contexts, when prior attitudes do not exist and counter-argumentation will be lower, and his chapter is replete with ideas for future research.

Attitude strength is also fundamental to Martin, Hewstone, and Martin's (Chapter 8, this volume) research programme, which develops the 'source–context–elaboration model' (SCEM) to predict when majorities and/or minorities will tend to be associated with stronger attitudes. The value of this model is that it can explain a wide variety of results, in a range of paradigms. Across variations of orienting tasks, there is consistent evidence of mediation of influence, especially minority influence, by thought listing under predicted conditions. Moreover, this model demonstrates the consequences of minority-instigated attitudes for attitude resistance, persistence, prediction of behaviour, and guiding information processing. For example, in terms of resistance to counter-persuasion, Martin et al. report research showing that minorities trigger greater resistance than majorities. Jane Austen wrote (in *Pride and Prejudice*, 1813) that 'It is particularly incumbent on those who never change their opinion, to be secure of judging properly at first'. Recipients of a minority message seem more inclined to 'judge properly first' by elaborating upon the minority's message, whereas recipients of a majority message are more inclined to change their opinions later, precisely because they failed to do this.

Martin et al.'s chapter, consistent with Crano's, challenges the classic, dual-process model of conversion theory (Moscovici, 1980), to emphasize that both majority and minority sources can instigate attitude change via issue-relevant thinking, depending on cognitive and motivational factors present in the influence setting. However, it is consistent with Moscovici's conversion model insofar as minorities tend to be strongly associated with a default of systematic processing.

Tormala, Petty, and DeSensi (Chapter 5, this volume) apply the elaboration likelihood model's (ELM; e.g., Petty & Cacioppo's, 1986; Petty & Wegener, 1998) 'multiple-role' framework to social influence. Thus majority/minority source could influence attitudes as a peripheral cue (at low levels of motivation and/or ability), as a factor that influences the amount of scrutiny of the message (at more intermediate levels of motivation and/or ability—although Petty and Wegener do not specify which source would have this affect), and as an argument, or through biased processing (at high levels of motivation and/or ability). Tormala et al. propose a new metacognitive effect for minority sources in persuasion settings. They argue that when people resist minority messages they are aware of this resistance, and draw specific inferences about their attitudes that have implications for attitude strength. Specifically, successfully resisting a persuasive attack can increase message recipients' certainty about their attitudes but, intriguingly, certainty is influenced by whether the means of resistance are perceived by the recipient as legitimate or not. Tormala et al. also specify different outcomes and different impacts on confidence in thoughts generated in cases where the perceiver learns source information before, or only after, message processing.

Finally, Mucchi-Faina (Chapter 6, this volume) draws from the literature on attitude ambivalence (instances where an individual both likes and dislikes an attitude object) to suggest a new dependent variable for minority-influence research. While ambivalence is often considered as a moderator of persuasion, Mucchi-Faina presents initial data showing that minority sources can trigger ambivalence towards both themselves and the issue in question. She reports that recipients of a minority message that was not personally relevant not only became less confident (cf. Tormala et al., Chapter 5, this volume), but also became more ambivalent. One of the reasons for the emergence of attitudinal ambivalence as an important construct is its potential to explain why people sometimes react in very polarized ways to controversial groups or issues (see, e.g., MacDonald & Zanna, 1998). We believe that there is a rich vein of research to be tapped, exploring ambivalence towards both minorities and the issues they endorse.

*Theme 2: The interplay between minority influence and dual-process models of persuasion*

Staying with a focus on attitudes, the link between minority influence and attitude change has been strong since the first research that systematically investigated majority–minority influence using cognitive-persuasion paradigms. This honour belongs to Maass and Clark (1983), who drew a parallel between Moscovici's (1980, 1985) concepts of comparison/validation and non-systematic/systematic processing strategies proposed in models of persuasion (Petty & Wegner's, 1998, ELM, and Chen & Chaiken's, 1999, 'heuristic/systematic model', HSM). Both these cognitive models of attitude change distinguished two strategies of information processing in persuasion settings—'non-systematic' and 'systematic' (called 'peripheral' vs. 'central', and 'heuristic' vs. 'systematic' in the ELM and HSM, respectively). This integration simultaneously offered a novel methodology and opened up intriguing new theoretical avenues.

The methodology was the measurement of cognitive responses ('thought listing') in response to persuasive messages, now widely used in the majority/minority-influence literature (see chapters by Crano; Erb & Bohner; Gardikiotis, Martin, & Hewstone; Martin, Hewstone, & Martin; Stroebe; Smith & Tindale; and Tormala et al., this volume). Several other research techniques have also been applied, for example, research manipulating message quality (i.e., 'strong' vs. 'weak' messages) to identify which source condition is associated with systematic processing (see Martin & Hewstone, 2003), the use of orientating tasks to manipulate processing demands (De Dreu, De Vries, Gordijn, & Schuurman, 1999; Martin & Hewstone, 2001b), and the use of attitude-resistance paradigms to examine strength of attitude change (Martin et al., 2003).

Theoretically, the ELM and the HSM provided the potential for a more detailed cognitive analysis of attitude change than the available theories of majority and minority influence. Both the ELM and the HSM distinguish two strategies of information processing in persuasion settings. 'Central-route persuasion' (ELM) or 'systematic processing' (HSM) entails thinking carefully about persuasive arguments and other issue-related information. Alternatively, attitudes may be changed by 'peripheral-route persuasion' (ELM) or 'heuristic processing' (HSM), whereby systematic processing is minimal, and persuasion occurs due to some cue(s) in the persuasion environment (e.g., status of source) or use of simple heuristics (e.g., 'the majority is always right'). These different routes to persuasion lead to different outcomes.

Attitudes formed through systematic processing are 'strong' (Eaton, Majka, & Visser, 2008; Krosnick, Boninger, Chuang, Berent, & Carnot, 1993; Krosnick & Petty, 1995) in terms of being more resistant to counter-persuasion, persistent over time, predictive of behaviour, and likely to guide information processing, compared to attitudes formed via non-systematic processing (Petty, 1995). If this analogy is valid, then one would expect majority and minority influence to lead to attitudes varying in attitude 'strength', a claim for which Martin and Hewstone (2008) have recently provided extensive evidence (see Martin et al., Chapter 8, this volume).

The continuing popularity of dual-process models in the area of minority influence is evident in many other contributions to this volume (see chapters by Crano; Erb & Bohner; Tormala et al.; Gardikiotis et al.; Smith & Tindale). We would argue that the benefits of the marriage between minority–majority influence and persuasion have been both fruitful and reciprocal. The use of the cognitive response approach has provided a more convincing analysis of information processing in minority influence than had prior techniques, such as the now-disputed 'blue–green slide/afterimage paradigm' (Moscovici & Personnaz, 1980; see Martin, 1998; Martin & Hewstone, 2001a, for a critical review). Studies on majority–minority influence have also contributed towards the development of both the HSM (e.g., Bohner, Moskowitz, & Chaiken's, 1995, conception of source as a factor influencing heuristic processing) and the ELM (see Baker & Petty's, 1994, recognition of the multiple roles that source status can play). And Crano (Chapter 3, this volume) makes a persuasive case that Moscovici's (1980) insistence on the need to focus on minority *as well as* majority influence 'revitalized a critical facet of social psychology—attitude change and social influence—that had lost intellectual direction and velocity' (see Crano, 2000).

All is not quite perfect, however. As Stroebe (Chapter 9, this volume) argues, we have still not yet made use of the full potential of dual-process models of persuasion for the study of minority and majority influence, and research has overlooked critical control conditions. A further limitation is that research continues to neglect the impact of social influence on *behaviour*.

Both the ELM (Petty & Wegener, 1998) and the HSM (Bohner et al., 1995) are complex, sophisticated models that include a wide range of variables not yet fully exploited by research on majority–minority influence. Stroebe (Chapter 9, this volume) has outlined a range of predictions that could be derived from dual-process theories concerning the impact of majority and minority influence on the processing of persuasive messages. These include, notably, tests of the HSM's 'additivity' and 'attenuation' hypotheses, and investigation of the different types of motivation conceived by the HSM to underpin attitude change—accuracy, impression, and defence. We know of no work that has explicitly manipulated these types of motivation and investigated their impact in this area.

Stroebe (Chapter 9, this volume) also provides a compelling analysis of which additional control conditions would be needed to assess further hypotheses derived from the ELM and the HSM, and why. For example, to test the hypothesis that message recipients might (in some circumstances) wish to distance themselves from a negatively viewed minority, one would need a *message-only* control condition, in which participants were exposed to the same message as other participants, but without being told that the source was either majority or minority. Stroebe explains that without this particular control condition it is not possible to ascertain whether any biasing effects are due to the majority source inducing a positive bias (i.e., more positive than the control) or the minority source inducing a negative bias (i.e., less positive than the control), or both. Stroebe notes that only one study appears to have run this control condition (Erb, Bohner, Schmälzle, & Rank, 1998).

Notwithstanding its utility for testing such hypotheses, the adoption of such a control condition is not without difficulty; the problem is that participants may *infer* the source of the message when none is given, and, given the false-consensus effect (Ross, Greene, & House, 1977) they are likely to infer a pro-attitudinal majority and a counter-attitudinal minority. This problem may explain, in part, the almost complete absence of this control condition. Stroebe argues, however, that this condition is essential for testing hypotheses about the impact of consensus information on the processing of persuasive arguments.

Moreover, Stroebe proposes two further control conditions. The first, *consensus-information only*, would specify a majority or minority source, but present them without any persuasive arguments, allowing the researcher to assess the impact of the consensus information as a peripheral cue (only one study appears to have included this control condition; Mackie, 1987, Experiment 4). The third and final control condition is a *no-information* condition (where neither consensus information nor message is given) as a baseline for assessing the amount of majority and minority influence.

Of course, the addition of all these control conditions would add considerably to the size and complexity of the minority-influence researchers' task. Most of the experiments reported in the chapters in this volume are already complex, multi-factorial studies. For example, the basic building blocks of our own research programme (reviewed in Chapters 7 and 8, this volume) require between-subjects manipulations of source (majority vs. minority), and argument quality (strong vs. weak), onto which must be grafted some additional factor that adds value to the literature (e.g., low vs. high relevance; positive vs. negative personal outcome; low vs. intermediate vs. high elaboration). We believe that a sensible compromise, for now, would be for future research to begin systematically to include *some* of the control conditions.

The third limitation of current research, and one that we think is associated with the popularity of dual-process models of *attitude*, is that almost all research focuses on attitude change, and almost never on behaviour change. Exceptions are a study in which minority influence effected change of behaviour (Martin et al., Chapter 8, this volume), and those studies of minorities in freely interacting groups, which sometimes include outcomes such as group productivity and other behavioural indices, and sometimes study the *interaction* between minority and majority factions *as* behaviour (see Levine & Choi, Chapter 10; Smith & Tindale, Chapter 11; Prislim, Chapter 12, all this volume).

We are not, unfairly, excoriating minority-influence researchers here; their counterparts in other areas of social psychology have also been reluctant to include measures of 'real behaviour' in their research studies. Two recent articles (Baumeister, Vohs, & Funder, 2007; Patterson, 2008) have called for more psychological research featuring real behaviour. Unfortunately for researchers, Baumeister et al. note, '. . . the sad fact is that many studies [including real behaviour] fail to show meaningful significant differences' (p. 399). Thus Friese, Hofmann, and Schmitt (2008) argue that, 'As a consequence, many researchers may be discouraged from conducting laborious studies with real behaviour because non-significant results are difficult to publish'. In the light of this trend, it is heartening to report that Martin, Martin, Smith, and Hewstone (2007, Experiment 2) did successfully show the impact of minority influence on behaviour. They reported that a minority had greater impact than a majority in persuading message recipients to sign a protest card about a target issue, and moreover to send the card to the relevant government department.

### Theme 3: The importance of indirect, as well as direct, influence

A key element of Moscovici's (1980) dual-process model of majority–minority social influence is the prediction that whereas minority influence may not lead to public agreement, due to fear of being categorized as a minority member (Mugny, 1982), the close examination of the minority's position may bring about attitude conversion on an indirect, latent or private level (i.e., a more unconscious level). This is a prediction that is not found in more general dual-process models of persuasion, and should therefore be of special interest and research focus for scholars of social influence. Predictions concerning indirect influence are central not only to conversion theory, but also to conflict elaboration theory (see Quiamzade, Mugny, Falomir-Pichastor, & Butera, Chapter 2, this volume), the context/categorization theory developed by Crano and colleagues (e.g., Alvaro & Crano, 1997; Crano, 2001), and the dual role model proposed by De Dreu, De Vries and colleagues (De Dreu, 2007; De Vries, De Dreu, Gordijn, & Shuurman, 1996).

Numerous chapters in this volume attest to the continued research attention paid to indirect influence. Crano (Chapter 3, this volume) provides a thoughtful theoretical analysis in terms of attitude structure, and explores how indirect change may pave the way for direct influence. Mucchi-Faina (Chapter 6, this volume) proposes that a covert change could represent 'a good compromise', permitting the recipient to move towards the source without paying a high social cost; this touches on a possible link between ambivalence and indirect influence. Stroebe (Chapter 9, this volume), however, reports that very few studies used indirect measures in the context of a *persuasion paradigm*, and those that did revealed conflicting results. Moreover, as both he and Smith and Tindale (Chapter 11, this volume) note, Wood et al.'s (1994) meta-analysis only detected the superiority of minorities, compared with majorities, on indirect measures in conjunction with perceptual tasks (e.g., Moscovici & Personnaz's, 1980, 'blue–green afterimage' paradigm), but not for subjective opinion judgements. For subjective opinion tasks, majorities exerted greater influence than minorities, even for indirect measures. Here, again, there is a need for future research.

Finally, Smith and Tindale (Chapter 11, this volume) adopt a broader conception of indirect minority influence in their studies within freely interacting groups, considering it to be any change in the group process associated with exposure to minority dissent. That is, the minority's point of view is not adopted as the group's own, but the minority's presence changes the manner in which the information exchanged amongst members is treated and acted upon. They note, however, that the research literature lacks studies that have systematically investigated direct and indirect minority influence simultaneously within freely interacting groups.

### Theme 4: The variety of tasks used in minority-influence studies

At first glance social influence may seem like a straightforward process: source (e.g., majority or minority) attempts to influence target (e.g., minority or majority). But as several of the chapters in this volume illustrate, it is considerably more complicated than that. Specifically, a wide variety of tasks has been used, mediating variables are frequently assessed and tested, and research programmes have compared the impact of different sources under a wide range of conditions.

In Quiamzade et al.'s conflict elaboration theory (Chapter 2, this volume) *conflict elaboration* occurs when people give meaning to the difference between themselves and a source of influence. These authors argue that sense can be made of the mixed pattern of results in this literature as a whole by sorting results according to the different types of task that they have used. They distinguish, in particular, objective non-ambiguous tasks (where there is clearly a correct judgement) and aptitude tasks (where there may be several correct judgements). Through the use of a variety of paradigms they show that majority and minority influence can be affected by whether people believe that there is only one possible answer to a task, or whether many positions are possible.

Crano (Chapter 3, this volume) also considers the type of task. He argues that a minority source, through its salience, enjoys an advantage in contexts involving attitude or norm formation, where no strong initial position exists. This advantage is intensified when the judgement task is cast as involving an objective, rather than a subjective, choice.

In a quite different context Levine and Choi (Chapter 10, this volume) report that the openness, or resistance, of task groups to innovation efforts varies as a function of whether groups choose, or are assigned, their task strategy. It appears that groups that choose their task strategy, whether it fails or succeeds, may be more committed to their way of doing things and more resistant to innovation efforts than groups that are assigned their strategy.

Smith and Tindale (Chapter 11, this volume) acknowledge that their chapter focuses on tasks for which divergent thinking is beneficial, and that this will not be the case in all instances. They conjecture that minority dissent might be associated with poorer performance when groups work on tasks in which divergent thinking is likely to hinder performance, and that minorities face distinct disadvantages in certain tasks. For example, when groups work on tasks where no demonstrably correct solution exists, minority factions within the groups are at a disadvantage; in the absence of a shared symbolic system or framework that could be used to demonstrate the correctness of a solution, social support is instead used to determine which alternative is correct or optimal. Thus, in tasks such as deciding which job candidate to hire, or whether to convict or acquit a defendant, the outcome will most often be determined by the size of the factions favouring each alternative. Finally, Smith and Tindale propose that future research should investigate the timing of minority dissent within the overall decision-making process, a suggestion that recalls Hollander's (1958) idea of 'idiosyncrasy credits', whereby earlier conformity would increase allowance for later dissent and innovation.

### Theme 5: Minority influence in dynamic, intra-group contexts

As we argued above, many chapters in this volume have constructively adopted dual-process persuasion paradigms, and we are convinced that these offer great insights into the processes of majority and minority influence. However, we must raise one potential concern, that this approach reinforces an information-processing approach to understanding social influence. Such an approach, by virtue of its methodologies, places much emphasis upon cognitive processes to the neglect of normative issues.

Smith and Tindale (Chapter 11, this volume) note that this narrowing of focus dates, in fact, from Moscovici's own writings. Whereas his original theoretical work (Moscovici, 1976) conceived of social influence as an interactive phenomenon involving reciprocal influence between minority and majority factions, his later and paradigmatic empirical work (e.g., Moscovici & Personnaz, 1980) adopted a narrower and less dynamic vision of the influence process, concentrating on the cognitive process of 'validation' as the main vehicle of minority influence.

As Stroebe (Chapter 9, this volume) notes, research on social influence was traditionally part of the study of small groups, or group dynamics. This was typified by Asch's (1956) famous line-judging task, which had participants performing the task publicly and in small groups of 6–9, answering aloud. But subsequent studies on conformity tended to move away from Asch's group-based paradigm to the Crutchfield (1955) paradigm, in which participants sit in separate cubicles and the numerical majority is implied through feedback on a console about other people's supposed responses. Not surprisingly, comparison between different paradigms shows reliable differences, with conformity rates being highest in face-to-face situations (e.g., Levy, 1960), where normative pressure to conform to the majority is greater.

A virtue of a subset of other chapters in this volume is that they help to reorient minority-influence literature, away from attitude paradigms and back to groups (hence our choice of subtitle for this commentary). These chapters are the last five contributions in this volume. Beginning with Levine and Choi (Chapter 10, this volume), these chapters focus more on intra-group dynamics between majority and minority members, and less on message-based information processing.

Levine and Choi draw a clever parallel between 'newcomers' to and 'old-timers' in a group and, respectively, minorities and majorities, which of course they typically are within the group. Drawing out research on group productivity, they consider how minorities can best avoid the pitfalls of being disliked and rejected (e.g., Levine & Thompson, 1996) and be more effective agents of change. Expertise, status and shared social identity with old-timers are key factors in this influence process, but there are also many other relevant group characteristics that determine openness to innovation, including group size, cohesion, and leadership. Levine and Choi refer to an 'implicit or explicit negotiation' between newcomers and old-timers, and this work could usefully be integrated with Crano's notion of a leniency contract (see Crano, Chapter 3, this volume), whereby in-group, compared with out-group, minorities receive relatively open-minded elaboration of their message, by virtue of shared group membership, and they will not typically be derogated (what one might call 'elaboration without derogation'; see Aime & Van Dyne, Chapter 13, this volume). Levine and Choi's chapter highlights two forms of newcomer innovation in workgroups, both of which are kinds of influence that can have consequences for the quality of group performance. The first involves general adaptations that groups make to the presence of newcomers; and the second involves specific changes that newcomers stimulate in how groups perform their tasks.

Smith and Tindale (Chapter 11, this volume) pose the intriguing question of whether some of the accepted 'truths' of minority influence may, in fact, be paradigm specific. As they write, Wood et al.'s (1994) meta-analysis enshrined the ideas that minority influence is more likely to be indirect rather than direct, is more frequently found in private rather than public contexts, and tends to be delayed rather than immediate. They conjecture, however, that when influence processes are studied in freely interacting groups, which allow for reciprocal exchange between minority and majority members, and especially when consensus must be reached, minority influence may often be direct, immediate, and public. As they also contend, when researchers study the *interaction* between minority and majority factions then, and only then, can they identify which changes in group processes the presence of minority factions brings about. Research conducted already using freely interacting groups has shown that the presence of a minority source of influence brings about a change in how the group considers and treats the evidence before it (see Schulz-Hardt, Frey, Lüthgens, & Moscovici, 2000), and, generally, this is associated with an improvement in the group's products or decisions (e.g., Brodbeck, Kerschreiter, Majzisch, Frey, & Schulz-Hardt, 2002; Smith, 2003).

Stroebe (Chapter 9, this volume) makes a related point about the differences between minority influence in information-processing paradigms and freely interacting groups. It is only in interacting groups that true variations in the behavioural style of minorities can emerge that might have a powerful impact on attitude change. He refers to the study by Maass and Clark (1983) in which participants were informed that the individuals holding the minority opinion had not changed their position *despite strong majority opposition*. Stroebe points out that this information may have made the minority appear confident, committed and consistent, promoting their impact on measures of private attitudes. This seems to align with historical instances of minority influence, such as William Wilberforce's 20-year struggle, pursued by means of persuasive oratory and the introduction of multiple parliamentary motions, to end the slave trade in Britain.[3]

Aime and Van Dyne (Chapter 13, this volume) pick up this theme, referring to the large discrepancy between laboratory results and historical evidence regarding the success of minorities in imposing their views (Clark, 1994). Whereas empirical studies in our laboratories show that minorities, compared with majorities, are rarely able to exert direct influence in changing the views of others, Aime and Van Dyne contend that 'managerial accounts and history provide a more balanced narrative of the impact of minorities and majorities on issues that are important to group functioning'. From this perspective, successful minority influence is not as rare as laboratory experiments would indicate; majorities can be dependent on, and be frustrated by, minorities, and not just *vice versa*.

Arguably, there are some aspects of minority influence, notably those concerning behavioural style, that can only be studied in freely interacting groups, as in the well-known example of Henry Fonda's lone juror in the film, *Twelve Angry Men*. We must be alert, then, to the possibility of paradigm-specific effects, and of the emergence of different mediators and moderators in different paradigms. We are not arguing that one paradigm is right, and the other wrong; or even that one is better than the other. We can be influenced in everyday life by reading a newspaper headline that conveys consensus information (see Gardikiotis et al., Chapter 7, this volume), which is typically not even an intended influence attempt, or by sitting in a committee and observing how two dissenting members prevent a majority steamrollering their views.

Prislin (Chapter 12, this volume) confronts the issue of how minorities can produce systemic change, yet how they cannot even aspire to do so until and unless they persuade a sufficient number of majority members to go along with their view. She identifies social validation and social acceptance as key motives that propel minorities' struggles to become majorities, along with instrumentality, because of the inherent advantages of the majority position in achieving desired goals and obtaining tangible benefits. Prislin introduces an important theoretical distinction between minorities that have different motivations, 'instrumentally motivated' and 'validation-motivated' minorities, proposing that they may exert different types of influence, produced via different strategies. She also makes a unique contribution in considering more broadly the changing dynamics within and between factions when minorities succeed in becoming majorities, and thereby transform majorities into minorities. Her rather surprising finding is that former minorities are 'less than enthusiastic' at becoming majorities.

'Never underestimate a minority', said Winston Churchill; yet this is exactly what we may have done with our over-zealous focus on the narrower information-processing approach to minority influence (Levine & Kaarbo, 2001; Smith & Diven, 2002). A narrow interpretation of what is constituted by 'influence' has, according to Smith and Tindale (Chapter 11, this volume), also contributed to this under-underestimation of the power of minorities. They argue that when the notion of influence is broadened, to include the reduction of attitude polarization within the group and preventing a group from taking a specific decision, then minority influence looks more impressive. It is increased further—and moreover it is direct, immediate, and public—when various other conditions are met, including the requirement to reach consensus, and presence of a task that has a correct or optimal solution.

### *Theme 6: Minority influence in organizational contexts*

Several chapters in this volume draw useful links between the minority-influence literature and that on group productivity. The potential applications of this work beyond social psychology are huge, and a number of chapters spell out some of these implications with reference to minority influence in 'the complex and fiery settings of work organizations' (Richter, Sacramento, & West, Chapter 14, this volume). But minorities can have an impact in organizational contexts above and beyond mere *productivity*. The contributors to this volume provide many examples, some more obvious, others quite subtle, of how minority factions within groups, especially face-to-face groups whose members and factions freely interact, can improve the quality of what groups achieve, and how they achieve it; this work has important implications for organizational psychology.

Perhaps the most obvious relevance of research on minority influence for organizations is the impressive evidence that minority dissent impacts on decision making. Nemeth's ground-breaking work (e.g., Nemeth, 1986, 1995, 2003; Nemeth & Kwan, 1987; Nemeth & Rogers, 1996; Nemeth & Wachtler, 1983) demonstrated that minority dissent stimulates the consideration of multiple perspectives in a decision-making task, and enhances group creativity. Research by De Dreu and colleagues (e.g., De Dreu & West, 2001) confirmed this relationship in real workgroups, specifically diverse work teams. Interestingly, part of this research found that dissent was only associated with teams' innovation (as assessed by supervisors' assessments of teams' innovation) when there was a high level of team participation in the decision-making process.

This theme is developed by Richter et al. (Chapter 14, this volume), who conceive 'participation' in terms of frequent group-member interaction, regular meetings, group members influencing key group decisions about the group's work, and group members keeping each other informed about the task and their contribution to it. In addition to participation, research on group problem solving demonstrates that leadership also plays an important role in fostering creativity. As Levine and Choi (Chapter 10, this volume) note, research has found that groups develop better solutions if leaders protect minority views from social pressure and encourage consideration of opposing perspectives (Edmondson, 2003; Maier & Solem, 1970). Thus, minorities are instrumental in resisting what William Blake (1789–1794/1977) called the 'mind-forg'd manacles' of cultural conformity.[4]

Science offers many examples, of which two from medicine have become classic cases of such innovation. The first is Ignaz Semmelweis' discovery of the importance of disinfectant in fighting the horrendous death rate among nursing mothers. Characteristically he was ridiculed, criticized and ultimately ostracized (see Waller, 2004). The second is the discovery of the role of helicobacter as the cause of peptic ulcer, by Australian physician Dr Barry Marshall, described as being 'able to think the "unthinkable" that peptic ulcer might be an infectious disease' (Le Fanu, 1999, p. 186). The value of minority influence, with its ability to shift not just what we think but how we think, reminds us of the advice of Francis Bacon (1625/1996, Book I. i. 3), 'If a man will begin with certainties, he shall end in doubts; but if he will be content to begin with doubts, he shall end in certainties'.

Later work has shown that exposure to minority dissent can increase the likelihood that group members will share information unique to them, engage in more discussion of available information, and make better-quality decisions (see Smith & Tindale, Chapter 11, this volume). Minorities sometimes pay a price for this, especially under conditions where group consensus is required, in terms of reduced liking and acceptance by the majority targets (Levine, 1980), and the stress that they experience as a minority member (Van Dyne & Saavedra, 1996). However, research by Smith (2003) shows that, at least in dyads, endorsing and defending a view held by the minority in a wider group does not always have these negative pay-offs.

Minority factions also exert influence in the way they can prevent the majority from adopting even more extreme versions of their original position. While unanimous groups typically become more polarized following discussion (the classic 'group-polarization' phenomenon; Moscovici & Zavalloni, 1969), the presence of a single minority member prevented polarization, and two minority members actually made the group less extreme in their post-discussion attitudes (see Smith & Tindale, Chapter 11, this volume). This effect was also found in group decisions concerning acceptance/rejection of the death penalty, and led Smith and Tindale to characterize the influence of a minority faction as 'a rein or weight, reducing the degree of attitude polarization within the group'.

Just how much influence the minority exerts, or is able to exert, depends on the decision rule under which a group operates. Minority factions exert more power within groups where unanimous decisions are required than minorities within groups where decisions are taken once a majority faction is formed. As Smith and Tindale explain, minority factions cannot be ignored under the unanimity rule, and the need to reach a consensual decision increases the interdependence of minority and majority factions, which in turn makes it more likely that both factions will adopt compromise positions.

Aime and Van Dyne (Chapter 13, this volume) consider how being in a minority or a majority interacts with structural characteristics of employee social networks to affect employee involvement and effectiveness in exercising influence. They operationalize characteristics of employee social networks in terms of the strength of their proximal or distal ties, and are concerned primarily with influence in terms of persuading others to adopt one's perspective on issues that are important for the functioning of the workgroup. Arguing from classic perspectives on social influence (e.g., Deutsch & Gerard, 1955; Moscovici, 1980; Nemeth, 1986), they propose that social-network characteristics interact with employees' minority or majority perspectives to impact both involvement (amount of influence attempts) and effectiveness (changes in target attitudes, behaviours, and cognitions) of influence. For example, they predict that employees with strong proximal ties are more likely to voice their minority positions, because they can benefit from their friendships and consensual liking, which makes the raising of potentially divisive issues less uncomfortable. In contrast, they predict that employees with strong proximal ties are less likely to voice their majority positions than employees with weak proximal ties, in part because they have less need to risk the threat to their personal relations that could result from an attempt at exercising influence from this position.

According to Richter et al. (Chapter 14, this volume), the impact of minority dissent goes even further, because while the presence of a minority within groups can lead to group innovation, minority dissent across groups can engender organizational innovation. The number of published studies on these issues is, however, still relatively small, but this work has implications for both practitioners and theorists. Managers might, for example, be encouraged to foster and reward constructive dissent to exploit the range and diversity of expertise and knowledge in different groups within an organization (e.g., functions), to create superordinate groups in which the safe expression of dissent was promoted and valued, and to empower minorities in equal-voice, cross-function forums. Theorists, on the other hand, can test their theories in groups with past histories, present-focused demands, and future-task imperatives, thereby extending the boundaries of their models.

Having admitted, above, to romanticism about minority influence, we should caution here about romanticizing too much. We have all had experience of workgroups, committees, and other small groups in which the expression of a minority position can frustrate the group from reaching its (or at least the majority's) goals, prolong (seemingly endlessly) discussion, and stymie progress. Less parochially, minorities include not just our favoured pantheon of individuals who have changed the world for the better, but also those including Stalin, Hitler and Pol Pot, who all changed the world for the worst. A contemporary illustration of the dangers of minority influence concerns the role of the maverick British physician Dr Andrew Wakefield, who published a paper claiming a connection between the MMR (measles, mumps, and rubella) vaccine, bowel disorders and autism (the section of the paper setting out its conclusions was subsequently retracted by ten of the paper's thirteen authors). Writing about the case in a national newspaper, journalist and physician Dr Ben Goldacre, a critic of Wakefield, attributed his success, in part, to his being 'a charismatic maverick fighting against the system, a Galileo-like figure' (*The Guardian*, 30 August 2008). Thanks to widespread media coverage of Wakefield's claims, there has been a rise in measles cases for the first time in decades, which is directly attributable to a fall in vaccination rates.

Smith and Tindale (Chapter 11, this volume) discuss Levine and Kaarbo's (2001) work, which argues that minority factions, in addition to promoting change, can be influential by blocking changes advocated by majority factions. That is, influential minority factions can prevent groups from adopting new policies. Levine and Kaarbo call the blocking of a change to a new position 'conservative influence', in contrast to 'modernist influence', which occurs when a minority faction successfully blocks the majority's attempt to return to an older policy or decision. We should, then, not lose sight of the fact that minorities are capable of both conservative and modernist influence. Nonetheless, we now know that minorities are a mainspring of the creative process in groups, organizations, and even societies. Sociologist and political theorist Seymour Martin Lipset emphasized in his book *Political Man: The Social Bases of Politics* (1960) that healthy democracy required institutions that support conflict and disagreement, and not just those that promote consensus.

### Theme 7: The diversity of minority sources of social influence

As Mucchi-Faina (Chapter 6, this volume) states, 'Not all social minorities are alike'; they evoke different values and, consequently, different judgements and feelings. Even if we consider just group consensus (which Erb & Bohner, Chapter 4, this volume, note is the only variable that defines majorities and minorities in *any* context; cf. Kruglanski & Mackie, 1990), this consensus information can be conveyed in many ways, with varying implications. Gardikiotis et al. (Chapter 7, this volume) contrast the implications of conveying consensus by means of numerical support (e.g., 60%), consensus adjectives (e.g., 'many', 'few'), and social-status labels (e.g., 'majority', 'minority'). Their studies show that consensus information is important to majority influence, but primarily in conveying that the majority group contains more than 50% of the population. By contrast, being numerically small is advantageous to being a minority, conveying as it does attributes of consistency, commitment and confidence (as Moscovici, 1976, argued), which can instigate a systematic evaluation of the minority's arguments. As Erb and Bohner (Chapter 4, this volume) state, 'it does not seem to hold that minorities are generally and without exception valued more negatively than majorities'. In other words, there are many different experimental operationalizations and real-life examples of minorities.

The sheer diversity of types of minority (apart from the multiple operationalizations of majority and minority influence, which we have noted earlier; see also Maass, West, & Cialdini, 1987) also presents a considerable challenge to the area, which constitutes a literature of often apparently inconsistent findings. In short, one should not expect studies using *different* minorities to show *similar* results, and there is a need for a critical review of the literature based on a theoretically coherent taxonomy of manipulations or operationalizations of minorities. Such complexity will not make for an easy task, especially in conjunction with the array of tasks we have already highlighted above under Theme 4, but it is essential for bringing further clarity to this area.

The idea that minorities can surmount the disadvantage of being small in number by means of other attributes (e.g., physical closeness and strength) is central to earlier work on social impact theory (e.g., Latané & Wolf, 1981). Comparisons of minorities that are powerful, as opposed to powerless, are especially interesting. As Stroebe (Chapter 9, this volume) states, there are circumstances in which message recipients may want to align themselves with a minority, such as when a minority is extremely prestigious and powerful (i.e., an elite; see Simmel's, 1908/1950, classic work on the sociology of elites). Future research could usefully explore priming paradigms (e.g., Bargh & Pietromonaco, 1982), using both supra- and subliminal manipulations, to investigate the influence of 'powerful' and 'powerless' majorities and minorities. Eaton et al. (2008) have also explored the idea that individuals occupy many varied social roles, including high- and low-power roles, at different times, not only over the course of a lifetime, but also over the course of a single day. They suggest the intriguing idea that attitude strength, and thus susceptibility to influence, may be quite fluid.

However, it is not just their social or hierarchical attributes that define when and how minorities effect influence. An elegant study by Kerr (2001) showed that a minority source may be more effective when adopting an 'active', as opposed to a 'passive', advocacy. An active advocacy would be a case such as when the minority is aware of the unpopularity of its position, and expects to have to defend it vigorously. This finding is consistent with the view proposed by Moscovici and Faucheux (1972), that minorities are most likely to be effective if they actively oppose the majority at potentially high costs to themselves (cf. Kelley's, 1972, 'augmentation principle' in attribution theory). In a parallel effect, Kenworthy, Hewstone, Levine, Martin, and Willis (2008) found that participants told they were in a numerical minority condition and would later have to present arguments to other group members generated more original and convincing arguments (as rated by judges blind to experimental condition and hypotheses of the experiment) than participants in the numerical majority condition. This result seems entirely consistent with the fact that minorities are often deeply committed, and indeed this is arguably their greatest attribute. Thus Thurgood Marshall, the first African American to be elected to the United States Supreme Court and a member of a tiny liberal minority on the Court (with Justice Brennan), was described by colleague Justice White as 'not averse to writing strong dissents and speaking out that way in conference' (quoted by Williams, 1998, p. 381).

We should not lose sight of the fact that there are many types of minorities. Some propose original ideas (e.g., ways to cut energy use), others oppose the status quo (e.g., protesters against the use of animals in laboratory experiments). And we need to review the literature with these dimensions in mind, in order better to understand when and how minorities are successful or unsuccessful in their influence attempts.

## Conclusion: Minority influence—'Sparkling fountain' or 'stagnant pond'?[5]

Where does the field of minority influence stand after the contributions to this volume? In concluding his chapter in the 1985 *Handbook of Social Psychology* Serge Moscovici wrote that, '. . . what amounts to a para-digmatic reversal has taken place. We now look at social relations not exclusively from the vantage point of majorities but from the minority perspective as well' (p. 403). This is most certainly true. The value of the minority perspective and the richness of theoretical and methodological contributions seen in the preceding chapters are testimony to an enduring ferment in this field.

We end by answering the question posed in the subtitle of this final section with a response that prolongs the aquatic metaphor. Minorities play a fundamental role in the renewal of our culture and thinking by, in Matthew Arnold's words, 'turning a stream of fresh and free thought upon our stock notions and habits, which we now follow staunchly but mechanically, vainly imagining that there is a virtue in following them staunchly which makes up for the mischief of following them mechanically' (*Culture and Anarchy*, 1869/1993). Minority influence is crucial to this questioning, challenging and creating, and we hope that this volume will contribute to the continuation of this tradition.

## Notes

1 Another notable example is Tajfel's (Tajfel, Billig, Bundy, & Flament, 1971) 'minimal-groups' paradigm. Tajfel and his co-authors did not expect that simple allocation of experimental participants to different groups, in the absence of any other manipulations, would be sufficient to induce behaviour in which the in-group was favoured over the out-group (see Tajfel, 1978). Their first experiment was similarly intended as a baseline, from which to strengthen manipulations. Given this lineage, perhaps more of us should run studies in which we expect *not* to find significant results . . . .

2 Occupying the position of a minority, challenging the majority, can, however, sometimes lead to the view that one is being singled out unfairly. Alone as a social psychologist from France submitting to the leading North American peer-reviewed journals, Moscovici was infuriated at an editorial comment that he should 'use ANOVA', to which he replied 'what's wrong with French computers?!' (story told to the first author by the late Jos Jaspars).

3 In an interesting example of Hollander's (1958) 'idiosyncrasy credit' theory, Wilberforce's recent biographer Hague (2008) reveals that Wilberforce was an establishment figure whose conservative economic and domestic-political credentials contributed to his views on the slave trade being listened to.

4 Blake (1789–1794/1977) used this phrase in his poem 'London' (in the collection, *Songs of Innocence and Experience*).

5 We have borrowed this phrase from an article by West (2002).

## References

Allport, G. W. (1954). The historical background of modern social psychology. In G. Lindzey (Ed.), *Handbook of social psychology* (2nd ed., Vol. 1, pp. 3–56). Reading, MA: Addison-Wesley.

Alvaro, E. M., & Crano, W. D. (1997). Indirect minority influence: Evidence for leniency in source evaluation and counterargumentation. *Journal of Personality and Social Psychology, 72*, 949–964.

Arnold, M. (1993). *Culture and anarchy and other writings* (S. Collini Ed.). Cambridge, UK: Cambridge University Press. (Originally published 1869)

Asch, S. E. (1951). Effects of group pressure upon the modification and distortion of judgments. In H. Guetzkow (Ed.), *Groups, leadership, and men* (pp. 177–190). Pittsburgh, PA: Carnegie Press.

Asch, S. E. (1955). Studies of independence and conformity: A minority against a unanimous majority. *Psychological Monographs, 70*, 1–70.

Asch, S. E. (1956). Studies of independence and conformity. A minority of one against a unanimous majority. *Psychological Monographs: General and Applied* (Whole No. 416).

Asch, S. E. (1958). Effects of group pressure on the modification and distortion of judgments. In E. E. Maccoby, T. M. Newcomb, & E. L. Hartley (Eds.), *Readings in social psychology* (3rd ed., pp. 174–182). New York: Holt, Rinehart, & Winston.

Austen, J. (1813). *Pride and prejudice*. London: T. Egerton.

Bacon, F. (1625). Of studies in: Essays or counsels, civil and moral. *The major works* (pp. 439–440). Oxford, UK: Oxford University Press (1996 edn., Ed. B. Vickers).

Baker, S. M., & Petty, R. E. (1994). Majority and minority influence: Source–position imbalance as a determinant of message scrutiny. *Journal of Personality and Social Psychology, 67*, 5–19.

Bargh, J. A., & Pietromonaco, P. (1982). Automatic information processing and social perception: The influence of trait information presented outside of conscious awareness on impression formation. *Journal of Personality and Social Psychology, 43*, 437–449.

Baumeister, R. F., Vohs, K. D., & Funder, D. C. (2007). Psychology as the science of self-reports and finger movements: Whatever happened to actual behavior? *Perspectives on Psychological Science, 2*, 396–403.

Berlin, I. (1969). *Four essays on liberty*. Oxford, UK: Oxford University Press.

Blake, W. (1977). *Songs of innocence and experience: Shewing the two contrary states of the human soul, 1789–1794*. Oxford, UK: Oxford University Press. (Originally published 1789–1794)

Blass, T. (1999). The Milgram paradigm after 35 years: Some things we now know about obedience to authority. *Journal of Applied Social Psychology, 29*, 955–978.

Blass, T. (2004). *The man who shocked the world: The life and legacy of Stanley Milgram*. New York: Basic Books.

Bohner, G., Moskowitz, G., & Chaiken, S. (1995). The interplay of heuristic and systematic processing of social information. In W. Stroebe & M. Hewstone (Eds.), *European review of social psychology* (Vol. 6, pp. 33–68). Chichester, UK: Wiley.

Brodbeck, F. C., Kerschreiter, R., Majzisch, A., Frey, D., & Schulz-Hardt, S. (2002). The dissemination of critical, unshared information in decision-making groups: The effects of pre-discussion dissent. *European Journal of Social Psychology, 32*, 35–56.

Chaiken, S., Wood, W., & Eagly, A. H. (1996). Principles of persuasion. In E. T. Higgins & A. W. Kruglanski (Eds.), *Social psychology: Handbook of basic principles* (pp. 702–742). New York: Guilford Press.

Chen, S., & Chaiken, S. (1999). The heuristic-systematic model in its broader context. In S. Chaiken & Y. Trope (Eds.), *Dual-process theories in social psychology* (pp. 73–96). New York: Guilford Press.

Clark, R. D., III (1994). A few parallels between group polarization and minority influence. In S. Moscovici, A. Mucchi-Faina, & A. Maass (Eds.), *Minority influence* (pp. 47–66). Chicago: Nelson-Hall.

Crano, W. D. (2000). Milestones in the psychological analysis of social influence. *Group Dynamics: Theory, Research, and Practice, 4*, 68–80.

Crano, W. D. (2001). Social influence, social identity, and ingroup leniency. In C. K. W. De Dreu & N. K. De Vries (Eds.), *Group consensus and innovation* (pp. 122–143). Oxford, UK: Blackwell.

Crano, W. D., & Hannula-Bral, K. A. (1994). Context/categorization model of social influence: Minority and majority influence in the formation of a novel response norm. *Journal of Experimental Social Psychology, 30*, 247–276.

Crutchfield, R. S. (1955). Conformity and character. *American Psychologist, 10*, 191–198.

De Dreu, C. K. W. (2007). Minority dissent, attitude change, and group perform- ance. In A. R. Pratkanis (Ed.), *The science of social influence: Advances and future progress* (pp. 247–270). New York: Psychology Press.

De Dreu, C. K. W, De Vries, N. K., Gordijn, E., & Schuurman, M. (1999). Convergent and divergent processing of majority and minority arguments: Effects on focal and related attitudes. *European Journal of Social Psychology, 29*, 329–348.

De Dreu, C. K. W., & West, M. A. (2001). Minority dissent and team innovation: The importance of participation in decision making. *Journal of Applied Psy- chology, 86*, 1191–1201.

de Montmollin, G. (1977). *L'influence sociale. Phénomènes, facteurs et théories.* Paris: Presses Universitaires de France.

De Vries, N. K., De Dreu, C. K. W., Gordijn, E., & Schuurman, M. (1996). Majority and minority influence: A dual interpretation. In W. Stroebe & M. Hewstone (Eds.), *European review of social psychology* (Vol. 7, pp. 145–172). Chichester, UK: Wiley.

Deutsch, M., & Gerard, H. G. (1955). A study of normative and informational social influence upon individual judgment. *Journal of Abnormal and Social Psychology, 51*, 629–636.

Eaton, A. A., Majka, E. A., & Visser, P. S. (2008). Emerging perspectives on the structure and function of attitude strength. In W. Stroebe & M. Hewstone (Eds.), *European review of social psychology* (Vol. 19, pp. 165–201). Hove, UK: Psychology Press.

Edmondson, A. C. (2003). Speaking up in the operating room: How team leaders promote learning in interdisciplinary action teams. *Journal of Management Studies, 40*, 1419–1452.

Erb, H.-P., Bohner, G., Schmälzle, K., & Rank, S. (1998). Beyond conflict and discrepancy: Cognitive bias in minority and majority influence. *Personality and Social Psychology Bulletin, 24*, 620–633.

Festinger, L. (1957). *A theory of cognitive dissonance.* Stanford, CA: Stanford University Press.

Friese, M., Hofmann, W., & Schmitt, M. (2008). When and why do implicit measures predict behavior? Empirical evidence for the moderating role of opportunity, motivation, and process reliance. In W. Stroebe & M. Hewstone (Eds.), *European review of social psychology* (Vol. 19, pp. 285–338). Hove, UK: Psychology Press.

Glass, S. (2008, November 8–9). The Peta principle. *FT Weekend* (magazine supplement of *The Financial Times*), pp. 32–37.

Hague, W. (2008). *William Wilberforce: The life of the great anti-slave trade campaigner.* London: Harper Perennial.

Hollander, E. P. (1958). Conformity, status, and idiosyncrasy credit. *Psychological Review, 65*, 117–127.

Ibsen, H. (1907, published 1882). *An enemy of the people.* London: Heinemann.

Kelley, H. H. (1972). Causal schemata and the attribution process. In E. E. Jones et al. (Eds.), *Attribution: Perceiving the causes of behavior* (pp. 151–174). Morristown, NJ: General Learning Press.

Kenworthy, J., Hewstone, M., Levine, J., Martin, R., & Willis, H. (2008). The phenomenology of minority–majority status: Effects on innovation in argument generation. *European Journal of Social Psychology, 38*, 624–636.

Kerr, N. L. (2001). Is it what one says or how one says it? Style vs. substance from an SDS perspective. In C. K. W. De Dreu & N. K. De Vries (Eds.), *Group consensus and minority influence: Implications for innovation* (pp. 201–228). Oxford, UK: Blackwell.

Krosnick, J. A., Boninger, D. S., Chuang, Y. C., Berent, M. K., & Carnot, C. (1993). Attitude strength: One construct or many related constructs? *Journal of Personality and Social Psychology, 65*, 1132–1151.

Krosnick, J. A., & Petty, R. E. (1995). Attitude strength: An overview. In R. E. Petty & J. A. Krosnick (Eds.), *Attitude strength: Antecedents and consequences* (pp. 1–24). Hillsdale, NJ: Lawrence Erlbaum Associates, Inc.

Kruglanski, A. W., & Mackie, D. M. (1990). Majority and minority influence: A judgmental process analysis. In W. Stroebe & M. Hewstone (Eds.), *European review of social psychology* (Vol. 1, pp. 229–261). Chichester, UK: Wiley.

Latané, B., & Wolf, S. (1981). The social impact of majorities and minorities. *Psychological Review, 88*, 438–453.

Le Fanu, J. (1999). *The rise and fall of modern medicine.* London: Abacus.

Levine, J. M. (1980). Reaction to opinion deviance in small groups. In P. B. Paulus (Ed.), *Psychology of group influence* (pp. 375–429). Hillsdale, NJ: Lawrence Erlbaum Associates, Inc.

Levine, J. M., & Kaarbo, J. (2001). Minority influence in political decision-making groups. In C. K. W. De Dreu & N. K. De Vries (Eds.), *Group consensus and innovation: Fundamental and applied perspectives* (pp. 229–257). Oxford, UK: Blackwell.

Levine, J. M., & Thompson, L. (1996). Conflict in groups. In E. T. Higgins & A. W. Kruglanski (Eds.), *Social psychology: Handbook of basic principles* (pp. 745–776). New York: Guilford Press.

Levy, L. (1960). Studies in conformity behaviour: A methodological note. *Journal of Psychology, 50*, 39–41.

Lipset, S. M. (1960). *Political man: The social bases of politics.* Garden City, NY: Doubleday.

Maass, A., & Clark, R. D., III (1983). Internalization versus compliance: Differential processes underlying minority influence and conformity. *European Journal of Social Psychology, 13*, 197–215.

Maass, A., & Clark, R. D., III (1984). Hidden impact of minorities: Fifteen years of minority influence research. *Psychological Bulletin, 95*, 428–450.

Maass, A., West, S., & Cialdini, R. B. (1987). Minority influence and conversion. In

C. Hendrick (Ed.), *Group processes: Review of personality and social psychology* (Vol. 8, pp. 55–79). Newbury Park, CA: Sage.

MacDonald, T. K., & Zanna, M. P. (1998). Cross-dimension ambivalence toward social groups: Can ambivalence affect intentions to hire feminists? *Personality and Social Psychology Bulletin, 24*, 427–441.

Mackie, D. M. (1987). Systematic and nonsystematic processing of majority and minority persuasive communications. *Journal of Personality and Social Psychology, 53*, 41–52.

Maier, N. R. F., & Solem, A. R. (1970). The contribution of a discussion leader to the quality of group thinking: The effective use of minority opinions. *Human Relations, 5*, 277–288.

Martin, R. (1998). Majority and minority influence using the afterimage paradigm: A series of attempted replications. *Journal of Experimental Social Psychology, 34*, 1–26.

Martin, R., Gardikiotis, A., & Hewstone, M. (2002). Levels of consensus and majority and minority influence. *European Journal of Social Psychology, 32*, 645–665.

Martin, R., & Hewstone, M. (2001a). Afterthoughts on afterimages: A review of the afterimage paradigm in majority and minority influence research. In C. K. W. De Dreu & N. K. De Vries (Eds.), *Group consensus and minority influence: Implications for innovation* (pp. 15–39). Oxford, UK: Blackwell.

Martin, R., & Hewstone, M. (2001b). Determinants and consequences of cognitive processes in majority and minority influence. In J. Forgas & K. Williams (Eds.), *Social influence: Direct and indirect processes* (pp. 315–330). Philadelphia: Psychology Press.

Martin, R., & Hewstone, M. (2003). Majority versus minority influence: When, not whether, source status instigates heuristic or systematic processing. *European Journal of Social Psychology, 33*, 313–330.

Martin, R., & Hewstone, M. (2008). Majority versus minority influence, message processing and attitude change: The source–context–elaboration model. In M. Zanna (Ed.), *Advances in experimental social psychology* (Vol. 40, pp. 237–326). San Diego, CA: Academic Press.

Martin, R., Hewstone, M., & Martin, P. Y. (2003). Resistance to persuasive messages as a function of majority and minority source status. *Journal of Experimental Social Psychology, 39*, 585–593.

Martin, R., Martin, P. Y., Smith, J. R., & Hewstone, M. (2007). Majority versus minority influence and prediction of behavioral intentions and behavior. *Journal of Experimental Social Psychology, 43*, 763–771.

Milgram, S. (1974). *Obedience to authority.* New York: Harper & Row.

Mill, J. S. (1924). *Considerations on representative government.* London: Oxford University Press. (Originally published 1861)

Mill, J. S. (1986). *On liberty.* New York: Prometheus Books. (Originally published 1859)

Moscovici, S. (1976). *Social influence and social change.* London: Academic Press.

Moscovici, S. (1980). Toward a theory of conversion behavior. In L. Berkowitz (Ed.), *Advances in experimental social psychology* (Vol. 13, pp. 209–239). New York: Academic Press.

Moscovici, S. (1985). Social influence and conformity. In G. Lindsey & E. Aronson

(Eds.), *The handbook of social psychology* (3rd ed., Vol. 2, pp. 347–412). New York: Random House.

Moscovici, S., & Faucheux, C. (1972). Social influence, conformity bias and the study of active minorities. In L. Berkowitz (Ed.), *Advances in experimental social psychology* (Vol. 6, pp. 149–202). New York: Academic Press.

Moscovici, S., Lage, E., & Naffrechoux, M. (1969). Influence of a consistent minority on the responses of a majority in a color perception task. *Sociometry*, *32*, 365–380.

Moscovici, S., & Personnaz, B. (1980). Studies in social influence: V. Minority influence and conversion behavior in a perceptual task. *Journal of Experimental Social Psychology*, *16*, 270–282.

Moscovici, S., & Zavalloni, M. (1969). The group as a polarizer of attitudes. *Journal of Personality and Social Psychology*, *12*, 125–135.

Mugny, G. (1982). *The power of minorities*. London: Academic Press.

Mugny, G., & Pérez, J. (1991). *The social psychology of minority influence*. Cambridge, UK: Cambridge University Press.

Nemeth, C. (1986). Differential contributions of majority and minority influence. *Psychological Review*, *93*, 23–32.

Nemeth, C. (1995). Dissent as driving cognition, attitudes and judgements. *Social Cognition*, *13*, 273–291.

Nemeth, C. (2003). Minority dissent and its 'hidden' benefits. *New Review of Social Psychology*, *2*, 21–28.

Nemeth, C. J., & Kwan, J. (1987). Minority influence, divergent thinking and detection of correct solutions. *Journal of Applied Social Psychology*, *17*, 788–799.

Nemeth, C., & Rogers, J. (1996). Dissent and the search for information. *British Journal of Social Psychology*, *35*, 67–76.

Nemeth, C., Swedlund, M., & Kanki, B. (1974). Patterning of the minority's response and their influence on the majority. *European Journal of Social Psychology*, *4*, 53–64.

Nemeth, C., & Wachtler, J. (1983). Creative problem solving as a result of majority versus minority influence. *European Journal of Social Psychology*, *13*, 45–55.

Newkirk, I. E. (with Ratcliffe, J.) (2008). *One can make a difference: How simple actions can change the world*. Avon, Massachusetts: Adams Media Corporation.

Patterson, M. L. (2008). Back to social behavior: Mining the mundane. *Basic and Applied Social Psychology*, *30*, 93–101.

Petty, R. E. (1995). Attitude change. In A. Tesser (Ed.), *Advanced social psychology* (pp. 195–255). New York: McGraw-Hill.

Petty, R. E., & Cacioppo, J. T. (1986). *Communication and persuasion: Central and peripheral routes to attitude change*. New York: Springer-Verlag.

Petty, R. E., & Wegener, D. T. (1998). Attitude change: Multiple roles for persuasion variables. In D. T. Gilbert, S. T. Fiske, & G. Lindzey (Eds.), *The handbook of social psychology* (4th ed., pp. 323–390). Boston: McGraw-Hill.

Pratkanis, A. R. (2007). An invitation to social influence research. In A. R. Pratkanis (Ed.), *The science of social influence: Advances and future progress* (pp. 1–15). New York: Psychology Press.

Reeves, R. (2007). *John Stuart Mill: Victorian firebrand*. London: Atlantic Books.

Ross, L., Greene, D., & House, P. (1977). The 'false consensus effect': An egocentric bias in social perception and attribution processes. *Journal of Experimental Social Psychology*, *13*, 279–301.

Schulz-Hardt, S., Frey, D., Lüthgens, C., & Moscovici, S. (2000). Biased information search in group decision making. *Journal of Personality and Social Psychology*, *78*, 655–669.

Sherif, M. (1936). *The psychology of social norms*. New York: Harper.

Simmel, G. (1950). *The sociology of Georg Simmel* (Kurt Wolff, Trans.). New York: Free Press. (Originally published 1908)

Smith, C. M. (2003). *Disentangling the effects of exposure to minority influence and exposure to conflict*. Paper Presented at the Small Group Meeting on Minority Influence Processes, Oxford University, UK.

Smith, C. M., & Diven, P. (2002). Minority influence and political interest groups. In V. Ottati et al. (Eds.), *The social psychology of politics* (pp. 175–192). New York: Kluwer Academic/Plenum Press.

Tajfel, H. (Ed.). (1978). *Differentiation between social groups: Studies in the social psychology of intergroup relations*. London: Academic Press.

Tajfel, H., Billig, M. B., Bundy, R. P., & Flament, C. (1971). Social categorization and intergroup behaviour. *European Journal of Social Psychology*, *1*, 149–178.

van Avermaet, E. (1996). Social influence in small groups. In M. Hewstone, W. Stroebe, & G. M. Stephenson (Eds.), *Introduction to social psychology: A European approach* (2nd ed., pp. 487–529). Oxford, UK: Blackwell.

Van Dyne, L., & Saavedra, R. (1996). A naturalistic minority influence experiment: Effects on divergent thinking, conflict, and originality in work groups. *British Journal of Social Psychology*, *35*, 151–167.

Waller, J. (2004). *Leaps in the dark: The making of scientific reputations*. Oxford, UK: Oxford University Press.

West, M. A. (2002). Sparkling fountains or stagnant ponds: An integrative model of creativity and innovation implementation in work groups. *Applied Psychology— An International Review/Psychologie Appliquee—Revue Internationale*, *51*, 355–387.

White, M. (2007). *Galileo Antichrist: A biography*. London: Weidenfeld & Nicolson.

Williams, J. (1998). *Thurgood Marshall: American revolutionary*. New York: Random House.

Wood, W., Lundgren, S., Ouellette, J. A., Busceme, S., & Blackstone, T. (1994). Minority influence: A meta-analytic review of social influence processes. *Psychological Bulletin*, *115*, 323–345.

# Author index

# Subject index

Printed in Great Britain
by Amazon